# Engaging Young Children in Mathematics:

## Standards for Early Childhood Mathematics Education

*Edited by:*

**Douglas H. Clements**
**Julie Sarama**
*University of Buffalo, State University of New York*

*Associate Editor:*
**Ann-Marie DiBiase**
*Brock University*

# STUDIES IN MATHEMATICAL THINKING AND LEARNING
## Alan H. Schoenfeld, Series Editor

# Engaging Young Children in Mathematics:

## Standards for Early Childhood Mathematics Education

*Edited by:*
### Douglas H. Clements
### Julie Sarama
*University at Buffalo, State University of New York*

*Associate Editor:*
### Ann-Marie DiBiase
*Brock University*

LAWRENCE ERLBAUM ASSOCIATES, PUBLISHERS
2004    Mahwah, New Jersey                    London

This book is based upon work supported in part by the National Science Foundation under Grant No. ESI-98-17540: "Conference on Standards for Preschool and Kindergarten Mathematics Education" and by a grant from ExxonMobil Foundation by the same name. Any opinions, findings, and conclusions or recommendations expressed in this material are those of the author(s) and do not necessarily reflect the views of the foundations.

Lawrence Erlbaum Associates, Inc., Publishers
10 Industrial Avenue
Mahwah, NJ 07430

Cover design by Kathryn Houghtaling Lacey

**Library of Congress Cataloging-in-Publication Data**

Engaging young children in mathematics : standards for pre-school
    and kindergarten mathematics education / edited by Douglas
    H. Clements, Julie Sarama, Ann-Marie DiBiase
        p.   cm.
Includes bibliographical references and index.
ISBN 0-8058-4210-1 (alk. paper)
ISBN 0-8058-4534-8 (pbk. : alk. paper)
    1. Mathematics—Study and teaching (Pre-school)—Standards.
    2. Mathematics—Study and teaching (Early childhood)—Standards   I. Clements, Douglas H.   II. Sarama, Julie   III. DiBiase, Ann-Marie.

QA135.6.E57 2003
372.7—dc21
                                                    2002192834
                                                    CIP

Books published by Lawrence Erlbaum Associates are printed on acid-free paper, and their bindings are chosen for strength and durability.

Printed in the United States of America
10   9   8   7   6   5   4   3   2

# Table of Contents

# Preface

The turn of the century has seen a dramatic increase in attention to the mathematics education of young children. This book is the result of a unique gathering of a diverse group of professionals involved with early childhood mathematics. In this preface, we describe this recent focus of attention, the conference that brought the professionals together to discuss critical issues in early mathematics education, and the result of their collaborative work—this book. Thus, this book includes the combined wisdom of experts, including mathematicians, mathematics educators, researchers, curriculum developers, teachers, and policymakers regarding the mathematics education of our nation's youngest learners.

## MATHEMATICS IN EARLY CHILDHOOD

Why is there such a surge of attention to mathematics in early childhood? First, increasing numbers of children attend early care and education programs. In 1999, 70% of 4-year-olds and 93% of 5-year-olds were enrolled in preprimary education, up from 62% and 90%, respectively, in 1991 (U.S. Department of Education, 2000, p. 7). Several states are instituting universal prekindergarten education, with about 1 million students enrolled in 1999, and that number is increasing (Hinkle, 2000). Various government agencies, federal and state, provide financial support for prekindergarten programs designed to facilitate academic achievement, particularly in low-income children.

Second, there is an increased recognition of the importance of mathematics (Kilpatrick, Swafford, & Findell, 2001). In a global economy with the vast majority of jobs requiring more sophisticated skills than in the past, American educators and business leaders have expressed strong concern about students' mathematics achievement (these concerns are echoed in international comparisons of mathematics achievement; see Mullis et al., 1997). Furthermore, the mathematics achievement of American students compares unfavorably with the achievement of students from several other nations, even as early as kindergarten. Some cross-national differences in informal mathematics knowledge appear as early as 4 to 5 years of age (see Klein & Starkey, chap. 14, this volume).

Third, differences are not just between nations. Cross-cultural differences within the United States raise troubling equity concerns: "Children from different sociocultural backgrounds enter elementary school at different levels of readiness for a standards-based mathematics curriculum" (Klein &

Starkey, chap. 14, this volume). This raises serious concerns of equity regarding children's prekindergarten experiences and elementary schools' readiness to adapt instruction to children at different levels of mathematical development. As mentioned, many government-funded programs serve low-income children, who often experience difficulties in mathematics and are at increased risk of school failure. Many of these children later experience difficulty in mathematics (Bowman, Donovan, & Burns, 2001; Natriello, McDill, & Pallas, 1990). For these children especially, the long-term success of their learning and development requires quality experience during their early "years of promise" (Carnegie Corporation, 1998). These children need to build the informal knowledge that provides the basis for later learning of mathematics. Thus, equity demands that we establish guidelines for quality early mathematics education for *all* children.

Fourth and finally, research indicates that better mathematics education can and should begin early. Research shows that higher quality programs result in learning benefits into elementary school, including in mathematics. Unfortunately, most children are not in high-quality programs (Hinkle, 2000). This is critical. Even prekindergartners show a spontaneous interest in mathematics. Caring for them well, in any setting, involves nurturing and meeting their intellectual needs, which includes needs for mathematical activity (Bowman et al., 2001; Kilpatrick et al., 2001). Early interventions in mathematics can prevent later learning difficulties in school for all children (Fuson, Smith, & Lo Cicero, 1997; see also Griffin, chap. 13, this volume).

For all these reasons, there has been much recent interest in, and attention to, the learning of mathematics before elementary school at both the prekindergarten and kindergarten levels. According to the Glenn Commission report (2000), "at the daybreak of this new century and millennium ... the future well-being of our nation and people depends not just on how well we educate our children generally, but on how well we educate them in mathematics and science specifically" (p. 6).

In 2000, the National Council of Teachers of Mathematics (NCTM) revised its standards to include prekindergartners for the first time. States are creating or modifying their own mathematics standards and curriculum guidelines for prekindergarten and kindergarten children. Nevertheless, at present, most teachers and caregivers do not know what to do about mathematics for the young children with whom they work.

## THE CONFERENCE ON STANDARDS FOR PREKINDERGARTEN AND KINDERGARTEN MATHEMATICS EDUCATION

As federal, state, and professional organizations begin this new enterprise, there are many opportunities to create developmentally appropriate mathematics education for prekindergarten and kindergarten children. At the same time, there is the danger of a veritable Babel of standards, some of which may be developmentally inappropriate for young children. A lack of consistency across various standards and guidelines will continue to produce "mile wide and inch deep" (National Center for Education Statistics, 1996) curricula as publishers struggle to meet a variety of different content standards and guidelines. At the early years, such lack of consistency has a special danger of producing incoherent and developmentally inappropriate curricula.

Therefore, early communication between, and coordination of efforts by, the relevant educational leaders and agencies is critical. A group of educators[1] decided to begin with a conference on standards for prekindergarten and kindergarten mathematics education. This work was funded by grants from the National Science Foundation and the ExxonMobil Foundation to the State University of New York at Buffalo.

The *Conference on Standards for Prekindergarten and Kindergarten Mathematics Education* was held on May 15–17, 2000, in Arlington, Virginia. This was a historic event: To our knowledge, it was the first conference to have ever brought together such a comprehensive range of experts in the diverse fields relevant to the creation of educational standards. Participants included representatives from almost every state developing standards for young children's mathematics; federal government officials; mathematicians; mathematics educators; researchers from mathematics education, early childhood education, and psychology; curriculum developers; teachers; policymakers; and representatives from national organizations such as the NCTM and the National Association for the Education of Young Children (NAEYC).

The purpose of the Conference was to facilitate early communication between, and ultimately coordination of efforts by, the educational leaders and agencies that are developing mathematics standards, curricula, and teaching methods for young children. We also wished to facilitate communication between those developing standards and experts in related fields, with an emphasis on the latest research findings concerning early mathematical thinking and education. Using resources such as research from a variety of disciplines, a compilation of standards and goals from various U.S. states (see the Appendix), and the recent NCTM *Principles and Standards for School Mathematics (PSSM)*, the main goal was to work collectively, to help those responsible for framing and implementing early childhood mathematics standards.

All audiotapes of the presentations and discussions, especially those of the working groups, were transcribed and studied along with the papers presented at the conference. Based on these sources, the senior editor (Clements), with advice from the other editors (Sarama and DiBiase), produced an initial draft of the main points and recommendations that

[1]The initial idea for the conference was generated by Douglas H. Clements, Julie Sarama, Herb Ginsburg, Carole Greenes, and Robert Balfanz. Clements wrote the proposals and obtained the funds for the grant. Clements and Sarama, along with the Conference Coordinator, Ann-Marie DiBiase, ran the conferences and coordinated the work.

emerged from the conference. An 18-person working group was selected with the goal of representing the same groups participating in the original conference (i.e., U.S. state departments of education, teachers, researchers, etc., as previously described). This working group met at the ExxonMobil Foundation site in Irving, Texas, in October 2000 to critique and complete this draft.[2] This draft was then disseminated to a representative sample of the main conference's participants for their reactions. The editors then incorporated advice from these participants into a final report, which is Part I of this book. Their advice guided the working group in developing this book, which will be disseminated to all participants, as well as other pertinent federal and state agencies, other organizations, and all ExxonMobil teacher leaders.

The reader will note that this book has its roots in the initial conference, which emphasized mathematics education in the prekindergarten and kindergarten years. However, because many of the speakers and participants discussed NCTM's full range of prekindergarten to Grade 2, the standards and recommendations we provide cover all these ages.

## WHAT DIFFERENT READERS WILL FIND IN THE BOOK

One main group of readers are those who create standards, scope and sequences, and curricula for young children, as well as professional development materials and activities for their teachers. This includes school district administrators and curriculum coordinators, curriculum writers, publishers of mathematics education material, and teacher leaders. You will find comprehensive summaries of research that provides specific guidelines for your work in each of these fields. Part I includes research-based recommendations that frame the important ideas in the field, detailed developmental guidelines for the mathematics development of children from 2 to 8 years of age, and suggestions for standards, curriculum, teaching, assessment, professional development, and policy. The chapters in Part II elaborate on each of these themes.

The book should also be of interest to undergraduate or graduate students, early childhood trainers or teacher educators, and faculty in mathematics education. It contains summaries of research in early childhood mathematics, as well as thoughtful articles on essential issues, that are not available elsewhere. These are connected to practical implications that provide valuable integration among theory, research, and practice.

---

[2]The Conference Working Group included the following: Mary Ellen Bardsley, Arthur J. Baroody, Douglas Clements, Chris Confer, Juanita Copley, Carol Copple, Ann-Marie DiBiase, Karen Fuson, Herbert Ginsburg, Joe Gonzales, Amy Kari, Alice Klein, Mary Lindquist, Jean Moon, Maggie Myers, Julie Sarama, Carolyn Trammell, and Jennifer Ware. In addition, Edward Chittenden, Richard Lehrer, Leslie Steffe, and Chuck Thompson reacted to and helped revise portions of the report.

For all readers, the contributions from a wide variety of disciplines and perspectives should be both illuminating and thought provoking. The next section describes the organization and content of the book.

## ORGANIZATION OF THE BOOK

The book is organized into two main parts and an online appendix (http://www.gse.buffalo.edu/org/conference/). Part I, *Major Themes and Recommendations*, consists of conclusions drawn from the expertise shared at the Conference and specific recommendations for mathematics education for young children. These recommendations provide specific guidelines for policy, curriculum, and teaching, and thus are intended to facilitate the creation of standards and curriculum materials for early childhood mathematics that are consistent and inclusive, and are developmentally appropriate—attainable yet challenging—for young children. Part II includes a compilation of papers written by the invited presenters, organized into coherent sections and introductory notes by the editors introducing and connecting these papers.

Thus, this book offers a framework for thinking about mathematics education in Pre-K to Grade 2 (Part I) and substantive detail regarding young students' understandings of mathematical ideas (Part II). Curriculum developers, mathematics supervisors, personnel in departments of education, and teachers may find their attention first drawn by Part I. There we lay out a coherent approach to curriculum, grounded in the best current understandings of the literature. To make that framework come alive for children there needs to be greater depth—more substance behind the coherent outline. That substance can be found in Part II. Research students and faculty may find their attention first drawn by the richness of detail regarding student thinking that appears in Part II. It is worth noting, however, that Part I offers an important way of seeing the forest for the trees—of seeing how the detail fits within the big picture.

Both Part I and Part II are organized into five sections. *Standards in Early Childhood Education* deals with general policy and pedagogical issues related to the creation and use of standards for young children, including different types of standards and the advantages and disadvantages of standards for the early childhood years. *Mathematics Standards and Guidelines* includes research summaries about young children's development and learning of specific mathematical topics and builds on this knowledge base to describe the "big ideas" of important mathematical topics at several, progressive, levels of detail, designed for different readers. *Curriculum, Learning, Teaching, and Assessment* includes descriptions of approaches to curriculum, instruction, and assessment that have been supported by research and expert practice. *Professional Development* describes research and expert practice that addresses the dire need for better preparation of teachers and child-care workers. Finally, *Toward the Future: Implementation and Policy* presents issues and recommendations that we believe must be considered when putting all these recommendations into practice.

The Appendix is available online only, at http://www.gse.buffalo. edu/org/conference/ (see "Writings on Project"). This includes several valuable additions. The first two articles are reactions to the conference from two participants taking different perspectives, Debra Borkovitz and Jennifer Ware. The third and fourth items are the agendas that were followed for the main and follow-up conferences. The fifth item is a useful document on state standards (compiled by Ann-Marie DiBiase), which includes links to each U.S. state's Web site for educational standards, as well as personal contact information for a representative from each of the states. Note that another helpful resource on the Web site are the biographical sketches of authors and conference panelists (see the link directly above "Writings on Project").

## ACKNOWLEDGMENTS

We would like to thank Alan Schoenfeld, Series Editor, and LEA editors, including Naomi Silverman and Lori Hawver, for their guidance and support in the creation of this book. We would also like to acknowledge the reviewers commissioned by LEA: Alfinio Flores, Arizona State University, and W. Gary Martin, Auburn University.

*—Douglas H. Clements, for the Editors*

## REFERENCES

Bowman, B. T., Donovan, M. S., & Burns, M. S. (Eds.). (2001). *Eager to learn: Educating our preschoolers.* Washington, DC: National Academy Press.

Carnegie Corporation. (1998). *Years of promise: A comprehensive learning strategy for America's children.* Retrieved June 1, 1999, from http://www.carnegie.org/execsum.html

Fuson, K. C., Smith, S. T., & Lo Cicero, A. (1997). Supporting Latino first graders' ten-structured thinking in urban classrooms. *Journal for Research in Mathematics Education, 28,* 738–760.

Glenn Commission. (2000). *Before it's too late: A report to the nation from the National Commission on Mathematics and Science Teaching for the 21st Century.* Washington, DC: U.S. Department of Education.

Hinkle, D. (2000). *School involvement in early childhood.* Washington, DC: National Institute on Early Childhood Development and Education, U.S. Department of Education, Office of Educational Research and Improvement.

Kilpatrick, J., Swafford, J., & Findell, B. (2001). *Adding it up: Helping children learn mathematics.* Washington, DC: National Academy Press.

Mullis, I. V. S., Martin, M. O., Beaton, A. E., Gonzalez, E. J., Kelly, D. L., & Smith, T. A. (1997). *Mathematics achievement in the primary school years: IEA's third international mathematics and science study (TIMSS).* Chestnut Hill, MA: Center for the Study of Testing, Evaluation, and Educational Policy, Boston College.

National Center for Education Statistics. (1996). *Pursuing excellence* (NCES Report No. 97-198, initial findings from the Third International Mathematics and Science Study; http://www.ed.gov/NCES/timss). Washington, DC: U.S. Government Printing Office.

National Council of Teachers of Mathematics. (2000). *Principles and standards for school mathematics.* Reston, VA: Author.

Natriello, G., McDill, E. L., & Pallas, A. M. (1990). *Schooling disadvantaged children: Racing against catastrophe.* New York: Teachers College Press.

U.S. Department of Education, National Center for Education Statistics. (2000). *The condition of education 2000.* Washington, DC: U.S. Government Printing Office.

# I

# Major Themes and Recommendations

# Summary of Part I: Assumptions and Recommendations

This section summarizes the two assumptions and the 16 recommendations that are described in detail in chapter 1, which comprises Part I.

*Assumption 1:* Knowledge of what young children can do and learn, as well as specific learning goals, are necessary for teachers to realize any vision of high-quality early childhood education. (p. 26)

*Assumption 2:* Prekindergarten children have the interest and ability to engage in significant mathematical thinking and learning. (p. 28)

*Recommendation 1:* Equity is a major concern in mathematics education at all levels. There is an early developmental basis for later achievement differences in mathematics: Children from different sociocultural backgrounds may have different foundational experiences. Programs need to recognize sociocultural and individual differences in what children know and in what they bring to the educational situation. Knowledge of what children bring should inform planning for programs and instruction. (p. 29)

*Recommendation 2:* The most important standards for early childhood are standards for programs, for teaching, and for assessment. These should be built on flexible, developmental guidelines for young children's mathematical learning. Guidelines should be based on available research and expert practice, focus on and elaborate the big ideas of mathematics, and represent a range of expectations for child outcomes that are developmentally appropriate. (p. 31)

*Recommendation 3:* Mathematics for young children should be an integrated whole. Connections—between topics, between mathematics and other subjects, and between mathematics and everyday life—should permeate children's mathematical experiences. (p. 73)

*Recommendation 4:* As important as mathematical content are general mathematical processes such as problem solving, reasoning and proof, communication, connections, and representation; specific mathematical processes such as organizing information, patterning, and composing; and habits of mind such as curiosity, imagination, inventiveness, persistence, willingness to experiment, and sensitivity to patterns. All should be involved in a high-quality early childhood mathematics program. (p. 73)

*Recommendation 5:* Curriculum development and teaching should be informed by research on teaching and learning and by the wisdom of expert practice. Educators and policymakers should support and insist on approaches to teaching, learning, curriculum, and assessment that are developed and tested extensively with children. (p. 74)

*Recommendation 6:* Mathematical experiences for very young children should build largely upon their play and the natural relationships between learning and life in their daily activities, interests, and questions. (p. 75)

*Recommendation 7:* Teachers' most important role with respect to mathematics should be finding frequent opportunities to help children reflect on and extend the mathematics that arises in their everyday activities, conversations, and play, as well as structuring environments that support such activities. Teachers should be proactive as well in introducing mathematical concepts, methods, and vocabulary. (p. 75)

*Recommendation 8:* Teachers should purposefully use a variety of teaching strategies to promote children's learning. Children benefit from a thoughtful combination of carefully planned sequences of activities and of integrated approaches that occur throughout the day. Successful early childhood teachers build on children's informal knowledge and everyday activities, considering children's cultural background, language, and mathematical ideas and strategies. (p. 76)

*Recommendation 9:* Children should benefit from the thoughtful, appropriate, ongoing use of various types of technology. Especially useful are computer tools that enrich and extend mathematical experiences. (p. 76)

*Recommendation 10:* Teachers should endeavor to understand each child's own mathematical ideas and strategies. Teachers should use those understandings to plan and adapt instruction and curriculum. (p. 77)

*Recommendation 11:* Teachers should help children develop strong relationships between concepts and skills. Skill development is promoted by a strong conceptual foundation. (p. 77)

*Recommendation 12:* Interview and performance tasks and ongoing, observational forms of assessment are useful and informative ways of assessing young children's mathematical learning and should be integrated as appropriate into the early childhood mathematics curriculum. The primary goal of assessing young children should be to understand children's thinking and to inform ongoing teaching efforts. (p. 79)

*Recommendation 13:* Professional development should be based on research and expert practice. It requires multiple strategies and an understanding of the variety of professional development models, with special emphasis on the importance of teacher leaders and collegial support groups. It needs to be sustained and coherent. (p. 82)

*Recommendation 14:* Deep knowledge of the mathematics to be taught, together with knowledge of how children think and develop those skills and understandings, is critical for improving teaching and should be learned in preservice and professional development programs. (p. 83)

*Recommendation 15:* One effective way to promote professional development is through the use of high-quality curriculum materials and programs. These should be included in professional development programs. (p. 83)

*Recommendation 16:* A coordinated effort should be created to translate the information in this book into a variety of forms for different audiences. (p. 85)

*Recommendation 17:* State agencies should collaborate across all states to form more coherent and related state mandates and guidelines for mathematics for young learners. Governments should provide adequate funding and structures so as to provide high-quality early childhood education for all children, including high-quality professional development for the adults who care for them. (p. 85)

# 1

# Major Themes and Recommendations

Douglas H. Clements
*University at Buffalo, State University of New York*

The Conference on Standards for Prekindergarten and Kindergarten Mathematics Education was held to facilitate early communication between, and coordination of efforts by, the educational leaders and agencies who are developing mathematics standards and curricula for young children. An 18-person working group, representative of conference participants, met in a follow-up meeting to summarize the main points raised, and research presented, at the conference, as well as the recommendations for action.[1] This group synthesized the various resources compiled by the conference participants (including transcriptions from each of the working groups and plenary sessions of the conference). The first draft was circulated widely among representatives of the more than 100 participants of the initial Conference and several additional experts; their advice was considered in producing the final revision of this chapter. Thus, these Major Themes and Recommendations represent, to the best of our ability, the contributions of existing research theory and the collaborative thinking of representatives from the diverse fields concerned with early mathematics education.

---

[1]Chapter 1 (which comprises Part 1) was written by Douglas H. Clements, with assistance and advice from the 18-person Conference Working Group (see pp. xii and Footnote 2 in the Preface for more details). Participants of both the main Conference and the working group included representatives from most of the U.S. states; federal government officials; mathematicians; mathematics educators; researchers from mathematics education, early childhood education, and psychology; curriculum developers; teachers; policymakers; and representatives from national organizations such as the National Council of Teachers of Mathematics and National Association of Educators of Young Children.

The five major themes are as follows:

- Standards in Early Childhood Education
- Mathematics Standards and Guidelines
- Curriculum, Learning, Teaching, and Assessment
- Professional Development
- Toward the Future: Implementation and Policy

## STANDARDS IN EARLY EDUCATION

Should there be standards for early childhood mathematics education? Should the nature of these standards change for children of different ages? This section summarizes themes on general policy and pedagogical issues related to the creation and use of standards for young children.

All individuals concerned with educational standards must conscientiously distinguish two types of standards. One type prescribes standards as requirements for mastery. The second type promotes standards as a vision of excellence.[2] An example of the former is the use of standards in making high-stakes decisions such as retaining students in a grade or determining teachers' salaries. An example of the latter is the vision of mathematics education in the Principles and Standards for School Mathematics (PSSM; National Council of Teachers of Mathematics [NCTM], 2000). Few specific mastery requirements are provided in that document. That is the basis for criticism by some. However, the NCTM has always taken the position that its mission was to establish a vision, not to dictate details. We agree with that position for the NCTM *Standards,* but also believe that certain specifics must be provided as the next step. Indeed, one rationale for the collaborative work of the Conference was to provide additional specific information, for example, what to look for in a program, in children's learning, and in teacher and caregiver[3] preparation.

*There is a substantial and critical difference between standards as a vision of excellence and standards as narrow and rigid requirements for mastery. Only the former, including flexible guidelines and ways to achieve learning goals, is appropriate for early childhood mathematics education at the national level.*

One aim of this book is to provide such specific yet flexible guidelines and ways to achieve goals for early childhood mathematics education. This book defines standards as guidelines that help realize visions of high-quality mathematics education. Standards can be for program and teachers, for

---

[2]More than a year after this was written, we discovered a similar distinction in Thompson (2001).

[3]As we describe in a succeeding section, adults who care for and teach young children are a particularly diverse population. For ease of expression, we use the term *teacher* for adults working not only in organized settings, but also in all settings in which mathematical learning of children is supported, from schools to day care to the child's home.

children, or for both. At the Conference, there was broad consensus that standards for programs and teachers were essential. Such standards protect children from harm and contribute to their development and learning.

In contrast, early childhood educators historically have been resistant to specifying learning goals for very young children (Bredekamp, chap. 2, this volume). A major concern—from both a philosophical and pedagogical perspective—is that, because children develop and learn at individually different rates, no one set of age-related goals can be applied to all children. A specific learning time line may create inaccurate judgments and categorizations of individual children, limit the curriculum to those outcomes and lead to inappropriate teaching of narrowly defined skills, and limit the development of the "whole child" (Bredekamp, chap. 2, this volume).

In defining and implementing standards, we seek to avoid these abuses and realizing the advantages of specifying goals. First, such standards can demystify what children are able to do, by describing their mathematical thinking and capabilities at various age levels. Second, they can provide teachers of young children with needed guidance about appropriate expectations for children's learning and can focus that learning on important knowledge and skills, including critical-thinking skills. Third, standards can help parents better understand their children's development and learning and provide appropriate experiences for them.

Fourth, in the classroom and home, such goals can help "level the playing field," achieving equity by ensuring that the mathematical potential of all young children is developed throughout their lives. Teachers have welcomed more specific guidance on learning goals linked to age/grade levels, as those published a recent joint position statement on developmentally appropriate practices in early literacy (Bredekamp, chap. 2, this volume; National Association for the Education of Young Children and the International Reading Association, 1998). Providing guidance is even more crucial for mathematics, where teachers' own knowledge of the discipline is typically insufficient to make these judgments (Bredekamp, chap. 2, this volume).

Fundamental questions for teachers are what to teach, when to teach it, and how to teach it meaningfully. For goals to truly be useful guides, they need to be more closely connected to age/grade levels than are those in NCTM's visionary *PSSM*. This assertion, voiced by Bredekamp and others, was echoed by most participants throughout the Conference. In summary, high-quality standards can provide a foundation upon which to build a program that is coherent with the K–12 system students will enter. We can assume the following:

*Assumption 1: Knowledge of what young children can do and learn, as well as specific learning goals, are necessary for teachers to realize any vision of high-quality early childhood education.*

Admittedly, pressure to create standards also comes from the concern that if experts do not do so, someone with far less experience will (Lindquist

& Joyner, chap. 20, this volume). However, we are not merely trying to fore-stall the disaster of inappropriate standards; we are convinced that articulat-ing standards is a useful and important act. We want to do this in a way that balances higher expectations with the goal of fostering a love for learning, a feeling of success, and the joy of being a child. Specific suggestions about how to develop standards that minimize disadvantages and realize the ad-vantages are discussed in a later section.

## MATHEMATICS STANDARDS AND GUIDELINES

We need standards for mathematics in the early years. These standards should lead to developmentally appropriate mathematics experiences for young children. *Developmentally appropriate means challenging but at-tainable for most children of a given age range, flexible enough to respond to inevitable individual variation, and, most important, consistent with children's ways of thinking and learning.* This definition of developmen-tally appropriate also implies providing experiences that are consistent with children's ways of thinking and learning.

### Criteria for Curriculum Standards for Early Childhood Mathematics

*In developing standards for early childhood, emphasis should be placed on standards for programs and for teaching.* However, high-quality curric-ula and teaching must be built on extensive knowledge of young chil-dren's mathematical acting, thinking, and learning. This knowledge can be structured as *curriculum standards*—descriptions of what programs should enable children to know and to do. We believe that mathematics curriculum standards for early childhood education should be flexible guidelines along learning paths for young children's mathematical learn-ing. These guidelines should meet the following criteria:

1. Guidelines should be based on available research and expert practice (e.g., Baroody, chap. 6, this volume; Bredekamp, chap. 2, this volume; Brown, Blondel, Simon, & Black, 1995; Clements & Sarama, 1999; Fuson, Carroll, & Drueck, 2000; Kilpatrick, Swafford, & Findell, 2001; Steffe, chap.8, this volume).
2. Guidelines should focus on the big ideas of the mathematics of children (e.g., Bowman, Donovan, & Burns, 2001; Clements, chap.10, this volume; Fuson, chap. 5, this volume; Griffin, Case, & Capodilupo, 1995; Heck, Weiss, Boyd, & Howard, 2002; Steffe, chap. 8, this volume; Tibbals, 2000; Weiss, 2002).
3. Guidelines should represent a range of expectations for child out-comes that are developmentally appropriate.

Before we turn to specific curriculum standards, we elaborate on these three criteria. The first addresses the importance of a foundation of research and expert practice for guidelines. One topic of research is children's knowledge of mathematics. Young children possess an informal knowledge of mathematics that is surprisingly broad, complex, and sophisticated (e.g., Baroody, chap. 7, this volume; Clements, Swaminathan, Hannibal, & Sarama, 1999; Fuson, chap. 5, this volume; Geary, 1994; Ginsburg & Seo, chap. 4, this volume; Kilpatrick et al., 2001; Piaget & Inhelder, 1967; Piaget, Inhelder, & Szeminska, 1960; Steffe, chap. 8, this volume). Whether in play or instructional situations, children engage in a significant level of mathematical activity. Prekindergartners engage in substantial amounts of foundational free play.[4] They explore patterns and shapes, compare magnitudes, and count objects. Less frequently, they explore dynamic changes, classify, and explore spatial relations. Important to note, this is true for children regardless of income level and gender (Ginsburg & Kyoung-Hye, chap. 4, this volume). Preschoolers engage in significant mathematical thinking and reasoning, especially if they have sufficient knowledge about the materials they are using (e.g., toys), if the task is understandable and motivating, and if the context is familiar and comfortable (Alexander, White, & Daugherty, 1997). Most entering kindergartners show a surprising high entry level of mathematical skills (Lindquist & Joyner, chap. 20, this volume). Mathematical knowledge begins during infancy and undergoes extensive development over the first 5 years of life. It is just as natural for young children to think mathematically as it is for them to use language, because "humans are born with a fundamental sense of quantity" (Geary, 1994, p. 1), as well as spatial sense, a propensity to search for patterns, and so forth.

Young children can learn more interesting and substantial mathematics than is introduced in most programs (Aubrey, 1997; Clements, 1984; Geary, 1994; Griffin & Case, 1997; Klein & Starkey, chap. 14, this volume; this is discussed more in subsequent sections). This leads to the following assumption:

*Assumption 2: Prekindergarten children have the interest and ability to engage in significant mathematical thinking and learning.*

Although young children possess rich experiential knowledge, they do not have equal opportunities to bring this knowledge to an explicit level of awareness. Without such "mathematization," there are fewer chances for children to connect their informal experiences to later

---

[4]Such everyday foundational experiences form the intuitive, implicit conceptual foundation for later mathematics. Later, children represent and elaborate these ideas—creating models of an everyday activity with mathematical objects, such as numbers and shapes; mathematical actions, such as counting or transforming shapes; and their structural relationships. We call this process "mathematization." A distinction between foundational and mathematics experiences is necessary to avoid confusion about the type of activity in which children are engaged (cf. Kronholz, 2000).

school experiences in mathematics. Mathematizing involves reinventing, redescribing, reorganizing, quantifying, structuring, abstracting, generalizing, and refining that which is first understood on an intuitive and informal level in the context of everyday activity. For example, in one prekindergarten, children were arguing, each saying, "*My* block building is bigger!" The teacher—and not the children—saw that one child was talking about height and the other talking about width, area, or even volume. She asked each, "How is your building big?" The resulting discussion clarified for the children that they were discussing different attributes. The children then discussed how they could represent the height and width of their buildings. Some used their bodies to compare, others stacked up unit blocks and counted. Two children decided to count the blocks each used to determine which "really was biggest" (the teacher planned to observe and see what they did about blocks of different sizes). In this episode, the teacher helped children start to mathematize and reflect on what had been an everyday, foundational experience.[5] Children need repeated experiences such as these to understand mathematical concepts. Such experiences are aided by rich environments and interactions with adults and peers.

Differences in specific aspects of young children's mathematical knowledge have been reported in two types of comparisons. First, there are cross-national differences. Some mathematical knowledge is more developed in East Asian children than in American children (Geary, Bow-Thomas, Fan, Siegler, 1993; Ginsburg, Choi, Lopez, Netley, & Chi, 1997; Miller, C. M. Smith, Zhu, & Zhang, 1995; Starkey et al., 1999). Second, there are differences related to socioeconomic status. Some mathematical knowledge is more developed in children from middle-income, compared to lower-income, families (Griffin & Case, 1997; Jordan, Huttenlocher, & Levine, 1992; Kilpatrick et al., 2001; Saxe, Guberman, & Gearhart, 1987; Starkey & Klein, 1992). We must meet the special needs of all children, especially groups disproportionately underrepresented in mathematics, such as children of color and children whose home language is different from that of school. All these children also bring diverse experiences on which to build meaningful mathematical learning (Moll, Amanti, Neff, & Gonzalez, 1992).

Too often, children are not provided with equivalent resources and support. They have different and inequitable access to foundational experiences, mathematically structured materials such as unit blocks, technology, and so forth. The settings in which children from different sociocultural backgrounds are served too often have fewer resources and lower levels of high-quality interaction. The needs of children with

---

[5]Certain everyday activities, such as matching cups to dolls, pouring water, or moving around a room, provide essential experiences that build the intuitive, implicit conceptual foundation for all later mathematics. We call these "foundational experiences."

physical difficulties (e.g., hearing impaired) and learning difficulties (e.g., the mentally retarded) must also be considered. There is a critical need for everyone involved with education to address this problem, so that children at risk receive equitable resources and additional time and support for learning mathematics. This does not mean we should treat children as if they were the same; it means equivalent resources should be available to meet the needs of children who differ in myriad ways, including socioculturally and individually (e.g., developmentally delayed and gifted children).

*Recommendation 1: Equity is a major concern in mathematics education at all levels. There is an early developmental basis for later achievement differences in mathematics: Children from different sociocultural backgrounds may have different foundational experiences. Programs need to recognize sociocultural and individual differences in what children know and in what they bring to the educational situation. Knowledge of what children bring should inform planning for programs and instruction.*

For all these reasons, we conclude that appropriate guidelines for mathematics curriculum must be based on available research and expert practice. One central implication is that knowledge of children's informal mathematical knowledge, across educational settings and socioeconomic contexts, should play a major role in determining appropriate mathematical standards. This is one major area in which research and expert practice inform guidelines for young children's mathematical learning; other relevant areas, including curriculum, learning, teaching, and educational reform, are described throughout the remainder of this chapter.

The second criterion for curriculum standards is that guidelines for early childhood mathematics should focus on the big ideas of mathematics (Bowman et al., 2001; Clements, chap. 10, this volume; Fuson, chap. 5, this volume; Griffin et al., 1995; Tibbals, 2000; Weiss, 2002). For our purposes, *we define the big ideas of mathematics as those that are mathematically central and coherent, consistent with children's thinking, and generative of future learning.* Research and expert practice identify what is challenging but accessible to children, *especially* at the Pre-K to Grade 2 levels, and thus allow us to describe these big ideas.

The third criterion is that guidelines should represent a range of expectations for child outcomes. This is consistent with the notion of developmentally appropriate as challenging but attainable for most children of a given age range *and* flexible enough to respond to inevitable individual variation. That is, expectations may have to be adjusted for children with different experiential backgrounds.

To meet all three criteria, the mathematical big ideas have to be elaborated in ways that fully support teaching and learning. A "more useful strategy is to articulate goals/standards for young children as a developmental or learning continuum"(Bredekamp, chap. 2, this volume).[6] Research strongly supports this approach. The few teachers in one study that actually had in-depth discussions in reform mathematics classrooms, saw themselves not as moving through a curriculum, but as helping students move through a learning trajectory (Fuson et al., 2000). Furthermore, research on systemic reform initiatives supports the focus on both "big ideas" and the "conceptual storylines" of curricula (Heck et al., 2002). Learning trajectories should facilitate developmentally appropriate teaching and learning for all children (cf. Brown et al., 1995). That is, continua, or learning trajectories, should illuminate potential developmental paths, and also encourage teachers to provide their children with activities appropriate to their abilities—attainable, but challenging for each child.

Deep knowledge of children's mathematics is critical to improved teaching (Ball & Bass, 2000; Ma, 1999). Furthermore, teachers should maintain a developmental perspective. "Even the best-motivated set of instructional objectives can be counterproductive if the emphasis shifts from engendering particular kinds of understanding to eliciting correct performance on particular tasks" (Sophian, chap. 9, this volume). A developmental perspective keeps the development of the whole mathematical idea and the whole child in mind, including how that idea and child will develop through the years. For example, children should count not only objects but also a variety of other mathematical units (cf. Shipley & Shepperson, 1990). They may count the number of colors in a group of objects, or determine the number of whole eggs, when some eggs are broken into sections. Such counting is developmentally productive. It helps children classify and think flexibly about *what it is they are counting*. Such thinking prepares them for measurement and fraction tasks, where they have to know *what the unit is*. Furthermore, children should be supported to learn along a deep trajectory, which leads to a variety of strategies, such as counting the counting numbers themselves (e.g., to answer 8 + 3, counting, "8 ... 9 is one, ten is two, 11 is three ... 11!").

There is another way we need to focus on core competencies, but avoid tunnel vision. A potential disadvantage of any such focus is in limiting children's mathematical experiences. We believe, with the late mathematics educator Bob Davis, that curriculum developers and teachers should maintain two complementary types of objects: basic competencies and "things that go beyond." Most of what we discuss here are basic competencies. Investigations that follow children's interests, that

---

[6]Several Conference participants presented variations on this theme. Sarama (chap. 15, this volume), calls these "learning trajectories" (consistent with Clements & Sarama, 1999; Fuson et al., 2000; Gravemeijer, 1999; Simon, 1995) and provides specific illustrations. Joyner said, "While individual children do not learn in a linear, lock-step fashion, there is a general trajectory that can be described to assist adults who are caring for and working with young children. Unless we give adults some insight into children's potential, we are likely to continue to see a huge gap in what children know and are able to do as they enter formal schooling."

spontaneously occur, that accompany or emerge from a non-mathematical project—these are "things that go beyond," which should also be cherished and supported.

Learning trajectories make additional contributions. For example, they can indicate when most children might learn certain topics. This would avoid the time spent relearning concepts and skills in later grades—a wasteful pattern of too many U.S. classrooms that is not present in countries more successful in mathematics education (Fuson, chap. 5, this volume). Finally, guidelines based on big ideas and learning trajectories could bring coherence and consistency to mathematics goals and curricula across the United States. If state representatives agree on core goals, then a variety of high-quality curricula can be developed to meet these goals. In addition, programs at different locations can provide more consistent experiences for children who move. These are especially important if we are to achieve equitable mathematics education, especially given the high rates of moving in the United States (Fuson, chap. 5, this volume; Klein & Starkey, chap. 14, this volume). Reviewing what has been argued to this point, we conclude the following:

*Recommendation 2: The most important standards for early childhood are standards for programs, for teaching, and for assessment. These should be built on flexible, developmental guidelines for young children's mathematical learning. Guidelines should be based on available research and expert practice, focus on and elaborate the big ideas of mathematics, and represent a range of expectations for child outcomes that are developmentally appropriate.*

If these recommendations are ignored, or implemented ineffectively—for example, if teachers are not provided adequate professional development—children may experience frustration and learn little. We elaborate on these issues in the following two sections.

## The Important Mathematical Ideas for Pre-K to Grade 2

In the remainder of this section (and before moving to Recommendations 3–17), we describe specific guidelines for mathematical content. NCTM's *Principles and Standards for School Mathematics* organizes content into five areas: number and operations, algebra, geometry, measurement, and data analysis and probability. In the early years, algebra is manifested through work with classification, patterns and relations, operations with whole numbers, explorations of function, and step-by-step processes (NCTM, 2000, p. 91).

In the opinion of the Conference Working Group, the *PSSM* lists "expectations," but does not specify the big ideas for each of these five areas. The big ideas of mathematics for Pre-K to Grade 2, as well as the relations between the content areas, are diagrammed in Fig. 1.1. The content standards are surrounded by a connected ring of *process standards,* which relate to all that they enclose.

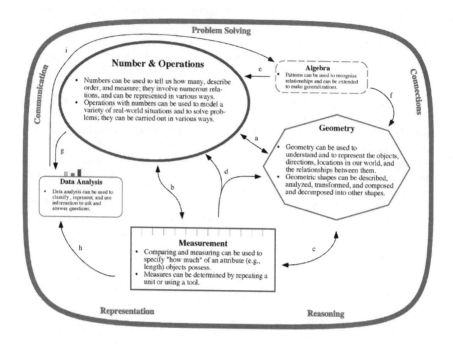

FIG. 1.1.  The five main content areas and the big ideas of mathematics for PreK-grade 2, as well as the relations between the content areas, surrounded by the five main processes. Links: a = Number can be used to quantify properties of geometric objects (e.g., number of sides or angles). Geometric objects provide models for number and operations (e.g., number line or arrays for multiplication. b = Number and operations are essential elements of measurement. The measurement process subdivides continuous quantities such as length to make them countable. Measurement provides a model and an application for both number and arithmetic operations. c = Geometry provides the major context for learning and teaching measurement. Measurement quantifies the attributes of geometic figures, such as side length or angle measure. d = In geometic measurment, the measurement process usually synthesizes the domain of number & operations, on the one hand, and geometry on the other. e = Algebra can be used to identify, describe, and extend number patterns. f = Algebra can be used to identify, describe, and extend geometric patterns g = Number concepts are essential in analyzing data. h = Measures are often used and analyzed as data. i = Data analyses can be used to organize information to uncover patterns.

Next we elaborate on the five content areas, emphasizing the three major areas for Pre-K to Grade 2 mathematics education: Number and Operations, Geometry, and Measurement. The process standards are discussed in Recommendation 3.

## Number and Operations

Number and Operations is arguably the most important of the areas. The learning of number and operations in the early childhood years may be the best-developed area in mathematics education research (e.g., Baroody, chap. 7, this volume; Fuson, chap. 5, this volume; Kilpatrick et al., 2001; Steffe, chap. 8, this volume). The domain of children's numerical concepts and operations can be thought of as consisting of two foundational ideas, one for number and one for operation—although these are highly interrelated. Operations are not limited to the four operations of adding, subtracting, multiplying, and dividing. By "operations" we include counting, comparing, grouping, uniting, partitioning, and composing. These ideas can be broken down into six topical big ideas, as shown in Fig. 1.2.

The big topical ideas span prekindergarten through Grade 2. They rest on early quantitative reasoning that begins to develop as early as the first year of life. It is crucial that this early knowledge be supported by experiences in homes, day-care settings, and prekindergartens so that all children build this rich base of numerical experiences and cultural knowledge.

*Counting.*    Number knowledge emerges surprisingly early in life and develops considerably during the first three years. Infants can discriminate among and match very small configurations (one to three) of objects. For example, when 6-month-old infants are shown a series of pictures that always depict three objects, albeit different types of objects from picture to picture, they gradually lose interest in the pictures. If the configuration of objects depicted in the pictures is then changed from three to two or four, infants notice the change and become interested again (Starkey, Spelke, & Gelman, 1990). So, they can "see" small configurations of objects nonverbally (called *subitizing*). By 18 months of age, infants can notice which of two collections contains more objects (Cooper, 1984). This provides an early perceptual basis for number, but it is not yet "number knowledge."

This illustrates a critical point: *Mathematical knowledge initially develops qualitatively.* In this instance, children's ability to "see small collections" grows from perceptual, to imagined, to numerical patterns (Steffe, 1992). Perceptual patterns are those the child can, and must, immediately see or hear, such as domino patterns, finger patterns, or auditory patterns (e.g., three beats). Later, children develop the ability to visualize, or imagine, such patterns. Finally, children develop numerical patterns, which they can operate on, as when they can mentally decompose a five pattern into two and three and then put them back together to make five again. These types of patterns may "look the same" on the surface, but are qualitatively different. All can support mathematical growth and thinking, but numerical patterns are the most powerful. As another illustration, see Richardson's (chap. 12, this volume) story on how for years she thought her children understood dice patterns. However, when she finally asked them to reproduce the patterns, she was amazed that they did not use the same number of counters, matching a dice nine with a "square" arrangement that did not have nine dots. Thus, without appropriate tasks and close observation, she did not see that her children

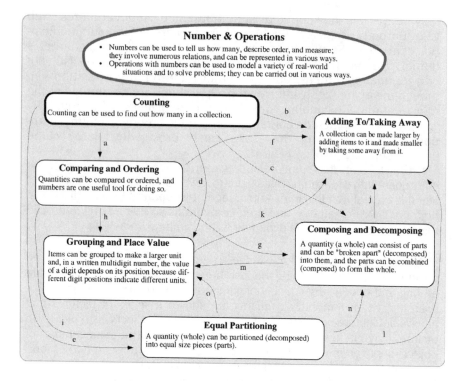

FIG. 1.2. The six main topical areas and their corresponding big ideas for the area of number and operations.

Links: a = Counting, or knowledge of the counting sequence, can be used to compare or order collections. b = Children use counting to compute sums and differences; for example, to solve 4 + 2, saying "foooour...five six!" c = A (cardinal) number such as 5 can be decomposed and recomposed in various ways (e.g., 4 + 1, 3 + 2...) d = Counting larger collections can be facilitated by creating larger groups and representing such collections can be economically represented by place-value notation. e = Counting can be used to ensure equal share and label their size. f = Understanding "same number as," "more," and "less" underlies recognizing whether a change makes a collection. g = Understanding "same number as," "more," and "less" underlies recognizing what a whole is larger then a part and that the sum of the parts equal a whole. h = Understanding "same number as," "more," and "less" underlies recognizing that 42 ones = 4 tens + 2 ones = 3 tens + 12 ones or that 47 is larger than 46. i = Understanding "same number as," "more," and "less" underlies decomposing a whole into equal-size parts or vice versa. j = Understanding part–whole relations can deepen understanding of additon and subtraction in a variety of ways, including additive commutativity (Part 1 + Part 2 = the same whole as Part 2 + Part 1) and the addition–subtraction complement principle (Whole - Part 1 = ?, Part 1 + ? = Whole). k = An understanding of grouping and place value can provide the basis for more effieient procedures for adding or subtracting larger number than counting single objects. l = The addition doubles such as 4 + 4 = 8 are a basic example of equal partitioning. m = Part–whole relations underlie an understanding that the total value of the digits of a multidigit number must equal the whole (e.g., 4 tens + 2 ones = 42). n = Equal partitioning is just a special case of decomposing/recomposing in that they parts are all equal. o = Understanding equal partitioning underlies understanding that one hundred can be decomposed into 10 tens.

18

did not even accurately imagine patterns, and their patterns were certainly not numerical. Such insights are not well reflected in brief descriptions, figures, and tables but are critical in understanding and promoting children's mathematical thinking.

By 24 months of age, many toddlers have learned their first number word (typically "two"). Words for larger collections do not appear until children have begun to use verbal counting. Depending on the early environment, children begin to try to count using verbal number names at age 2 or 3 years. Important developments in counting continue during the prekindergarten years. Children from ages 2 to 5 learn more of the system of number words ("one, two, three, …") due to a desire to count larger collections and a curiosity about the number word system itself (Fuson, 1988).[7] Learning the list of number words to ten requires learning an arbitrary list with no patterns. Children learn it as they do general language or the ABCs (thus, rhythms and songs can help). To count objects, children learn to coordinate this list of words with pointing or moving objects that ties each word said in time to an object to be counted (Fuson, 1988). This takes considerable practice to coordinate and can be facilitated by having children touch objects as they count and by counting objects organized into a row. However, children are also well prepared for such coordination, especially if rhythm is introduced, though they must concentrate and try hard to achieve continuous coordination throughout the whole counting effort. The easiest type of collection for 3-year-olds to count has only a few objects that are arranged in a straight line and can be touched as children proceed with their counting. Between 3 and 5 years of age, children acquire more skill as they practice counting, and they become able to cope with numerically larger collections in different arrangements, without needing to touch or move objects during the act of counting.

Recognizing how many items are in small configurations of items requires experiences in which the configurations are labeled with a number word by adults or older children ("Here are two blocks."). Such experiences enable children to build meaning for number words as telling how many items in a configuration or collection of items. The capstone of early numerical knowledge, and the necessary building block for all further work with number and operations, is connecting the counting of objects in a collection to the number objects in that collection. Initially, children may not know how many objects there are in a collection after counting them. If asked how many are there, they typically count again, as if the "how many?" question is a directive to count rather than a request for how many items are in the collection. Children must learn that the last number word they say when counting refers to how many items have been counted.

_____

[7]In this and other sections of chapter 1 (which comprises Part I), we cite some particularly appropriate references, but we have not repeatedly cited the many instances in which we have drawn from the researchers whose chapters are in Part II (e.g., for this section, Baroody, Fuson, Griffin, Klein, & Starkey, and Steffe).

Many 3-year-olds do learn this result of counting: "One, two, three, four. There are four olives."

In summary, early numerical knowledge has four interrelated aspects: instantly recognizing and naming how many items of a small configuration (subitizing; e.g., "That's two crackers."), learning the list of number words to at least ten, enumerating objects (i.e., saying number word in correspondence with objects), and understanding that the last number word said when counting refers to how many items have been counted. These four aspects are learned initially by different kinds of experiences, but they gradually become more connected. Indeed, having children represent their quantitative concepts in different ways, such as with objects, spoken words, and numerals, and connecting those representations, are important aspects of all six topic areas (see Fig. 1.2). Each of the four aspects begins with the smallest numbers and gradually includes larger numbers. Seeing how many, or subitizing, ends at three to five items and moves into decomposing/composing where small numbers are put together to see larger numbers as patterns. We conclude by repeating that mathematical knowledge develops qualitatively. As children's ability to subitize grows from perceptual, to imagined, to numerical patterns, so too does their ability to count and operate on collections grow from perceptual (counting concrete objects), to imagined (with six hidden objects and two shown, saying, "Siiiix ... seven, eight! Eight in all!"), to numerical (counting number words, as in "8 + 3? 9 is 1, 10 is 2, 11 is 3 ... 11!").

*Comparing and Ordering.*        Human beings naturally make perceptual judgments of relative quantities. But children need to learn the cultural methods of matching and counting to find out more dependably which quantity is more. Prekindergartners can learn to use matching to compare collections or to create equivalent collections. Many 3-year-olds judge that two collections are equal when the objects in one collection are placed in spatial proximity to (e.g., next to) the objects in another collection in a one-to-one fashion. By age 4, many children use such matching to create a collection equal to one that has already been constructed (Piaget & Szeminska, 1952). For many 4-year-olds, the number-word sequence develops into a kind of "mental number list." Consequently, children determine which of a pair of collections has more items by counting each collection and then using this mental number list to determine which number comes later and thus which collection is larger.

Finding out *how many more* (or less/fewer) there are in one collection than another is more demanding than simply comparing two collections to find which has more. Children have to understand that the number of elements in the collection with fewer items is contained in the number of items in the collection with more items. That is, they have to mentally construct a "part" of the larger collection (equivalent to the smaller collection) that is not visually present. They then have to determine the "other part" or the larger collection and find out how many elements are in this "leftover amount." The situational language in comparing situations is complex and children need considerable experience solving comparing problems and hearing and telling comparing stories.

***Adding To/Taking Away.*** Even toddlers notice the effects of increasing or decreasing small collections by one item. For example, 24-month-olds expect that when two objects (e.g., balls) are put into a covered box and then one ball is removed from the box, that one ball remains in the box. Likewise, when two balls are put into a box and then another ball is put into the box, most expect that the box then contains three balls. Prekindergarten children become more proficient in reasoning about the effects of increasing or decreasing the items of two collections of objects. When two collections are created simultaneously by placing items one-for-one in separate locations, many pre-kindergartners correctly judge that the items in the two collections are equal even though they do not know exactly how many objects are in the collections. If items of one collection are then increased or decreased, children as young as age 3 correctly judge that the collection added to contains more or the collection subtracted from contains fewer than the collection that was not changed. However, problems involving two collections that are initially unequal present a difficulty for 3-year-olds. For example, if two collections initially differ by two objects, and one object is added to the smaller collection, many 3-year-olds will incorrectly say that the collection to which the object was added has more. In contrast, some 5-year-olds know that this collection still has fewer. They know that both the addition and the initial inequality must be taken into account in reasoning about the effect of the addition on the collections (Cooper, 1984).

Problems such as six and two more can be solved by children as soon as they can accurately count. Children who cannot yet count on often follow three steps: counting objects for the initial collection of six items, counting two more items, and then counting the items of the two collections together. These children naturally use such counting methods to solve story situations as long as they understand the language in the story. Research and expert practice indicate that children develop, and eventually abbreviate, these solution methods. For example, when items are hidden from view, children may put up fingers sequentially while saying, "1, 2, 3, 4, 5, 6" and then continue on, putting up two more fingers, "7, 8. Eight." Children continue developing, and abbreviate their counting methods even further. Rather than putting up fingers sequentially to count the six hidden items, children who can count on simply say, "S-i-x—7, 8. Eight." Such counting on is a landmark in children's numerical development. It is not a rote step. It requires conceptually embedding the 6 inside the total.

Counting on when increasing collections and the corresponding counting-back-from when decreasing collections are powerful numerical strategies for children. However, they are only beginning strategies. In the case where the amount of increase is unknown, children count-up-to to find the unknown amount. If six items are increased so that there are now nine items, children may find the amount of increase by counting, "S-i-x; 7, 8, 9. Three." And if nine items are decreased so that six remain, children may count from nine down to six as follows: "Nine; 8, 7, 6. Three." However, counting backward, especially more than three counts, is difficult for children (Fuson, S. T. Smith, & Lo Cicero, 1997). When children realize that they can find the amount of decrease by putting the items back with the six and counting from six up to nine, they establish that subtraction is the inversion of addition and from that time on, addition can be used instead of subtraction. Children in many parts of the world learn to count up to the total to solve a subtraction situation because they realize that it is much easier. For example, the story "8 apples on the table. The children ate 5. How many now?" could be solved by thinking, "I took away 5 from those 8, so 6, 7, 8 (raising a finger with each count), that's 3 more left in the 8." This is another landmark in children's numerical development, and it is at this point that children can be encouraged to use strategic reasoning. For example, some children go on to invent recomposing and decomposing methods using doubles (6 + 7 is 6 + 6 = 12. 12 + 1 more = 13).

### Composing and Decomposing.

Composing and decomposing are combining and separating operations that allow children to build concepts of "parts" and "wholes." For example, children can develop the ability to recognize that the numbers two and three are "hiding inside" five, as are the numbers four and one. Such thinking develops significantly. Most prekindergartners can "see" that two items and one item make three items; even 3-year-olds can solve problems such as one and one more, nonverbally (i.e., by creating a matching collection), although this ability is limited to very small numbers. Later, children learn to separate a group into parts in various ways and then to count to produce all of the number "partners" of a given number; for example, 8 as 7 + 1, 6 + 2, 5 + 3, and so on. Eventually, children can generate an image of eight, and mentally operate on the elements of this image, combining them flexibly to produce any of the family of addition situations. They can use such combinations in solving problems.

Children can develop sophisticated composing and decomposing operations by bringing together two aspects of their early numerical knowledge: "seeing numbers" (visualizing little numbers inside bigger numbers, including seeing three as one and one and one) and counting. Children can come to see all of the different number "partners" for a given number by working with objects (e.g., six objects). Within a story context (e.g., animals in two different pens), children can separate the six objects into different partners that make six (five and one; four and two; three and three are all six-partners). Two kinds of special patterns are especially powerful and easy for children to see: doubles (3 + 3, 7 + 7), which allow access to combinations such as 7 + 8, and fives (6 made as 5 + 1, 7 as 5 + 2, etc.), which allow for decomposition into fives and tens. These number patterns and the number 10 can later in Grade 1 or 2 become the basis for adding and subtracting numbers by recomposing. Recomposing around 10 is a powerful and general method taught in many parts of the world (e.g., 8 + 6 = 8 + 2 + 4 = 10 + 4 = 14. These methods are especially useful in multidigit addition and subtraction, which work with tens in each position. These recomposing methods use the embedded numbers children learned earlier. In addition, the arithmetic principles of commutativity (5 + 2 = 2 + 5) and associativity ((5 + 2) + 8 = 5 + (2 + 8)) can be developed and discussed in such problem-solving sessions.

Such strategies develop number sense but also meet another major goal in early childhood mathematics—strategic reasoning. If children interpret 15 – 8 as finding how many numbers from 8 up to and including 15, they can reason strategically: 8 and 2 more are 10, and 10 and 5 more are 15, so adding 5 and 2 gives the difference. Strategic reasoning empowers children and adds enormously to their sense of numerical competence.

Children are fascinated with "big numbers," and elaborating their counting strategies to find sums and differences of two-digit numbers enhances this fascination. For example, to find the sum of 28 and 16, children might to count, "Twenty-eight; thirty-eight, 39, 40, 41, 42, 43, 44." And, to find the difference of eighty-one and thirty-five, children might count, "81; 71, 61, 51; 50, 49, 48, 47, 46." Some children also count from thirty-five up to eighty-one by tens and ones; others find many other strategies. Counting by tens and ones to find sums and differences of two-digit numbers is not meant to replace computational algorithms. Instead, these counting strategies are meant to enhance the children's sense of numerical competence.

Strategies involving counting by tens and ones can be altered along with children's developing understanding of numeration and place value. In fact, altering these sophisticated counting strategies is a natural site for developing children's understanding of numeration and place value. Rather than count by tens and ones to find the sum of 38 and 47, children could decompose 38 into its tens and ones and 47 into its tens and ones. This encourages the children to reason with ten as a unit like the unit of one and compose the tens together into 7 tens, or 70. After composing the ones together into 15 ones, they have transformed the sum into the sum of 70 and 15. To find this sum, the children take a 10 from the 15 and give it to the 70, so the sum is 80 and 5 more, or 85. Strategies like this are modifications of counting strategies involving ten and one just like strategies for finding the sum of 8 and 7 (children who know that 8 and 2 are 10 take 2 from 7 and give it to 8. So, 10 and 5. 15) are modifications of counting strategies involving only one. This brings us to our next topic.

*Grouping and Place Value.* Grouping is the operation (process) of combining objects into sets each having the same number of objects. For example, we can group by threes and describe, say a set of 18, as 6 groups of three. The big idea of grouping involves making larger units (in ʾe case of the example, the new unit is made of three objects). Grouping ιds to skip counting and multiplication and to later understanding of ,easuring with different units.

A special grouping organizes collections into groups of 10. That is, a numerical collection can be measured using units of 1, 10, 100, or 1,000, and, in a written multidigit numeral, the value of a digit depends on its position in the numeral because different digit positions indicate different units. To build understanding of numbers greater than ten, children must build on their early numerical knowledge and decomposing/composing to understand even the teen numbers as one 10 and some extras and later to understand numbers above 19 as some number of groups of 10 and some extras. Beginning with the teen numbers, the written numerals and the number words both refer to groups of 10 (e.g., 11 is one group of 10 and one 1). The patterns in the number words are complex and do not help children focus on 10 (e.g., *eleven* rather than "ten and one," *thirteen* rather than "threeteen" or "ten and three," *twenty* rather than twoty or "two tens," *fifty* rather than fivety; note that other languages, such as Chinese, in which 13 is read as "ten and three," are much more helpful). Rather, they mask the overall pattern. Also, neither "teen" nor "ty" say *ten*, although they mean ten. The written numbers are clearer in their pattern, but the written numerals are so succinct that they mislead children: A 52 looks like a 5 and a 2 side-by-side, without suggesting 50 or 5 tens to the beginner. Children can be helped to understand the 10-structured groupings named by our number words and written numbers if they see and work with quantities grouped into tens linked to number words and to written numbers. They may count 52 blocks into their own units of tens and ones, but counting and stacking blocks cannot take the place of working with the ideas and the symbols. That is, children might also pretend to make stacks of blocks, while counting, "11 is one ten and one, 12 is two, …, 20 is two tens" and so forth. They have to engage in many experiences to establish 10 as a benchmark and, more important, as a new unit (1 ten that contains 10 ones). Regular tens and ones words (52 is "five tens two ones") used along with the ordinary words can help establish a language that symbolizes decomposing and composing.

*Equal Partitioning.* Partitioning is the operation of decomposing a set of objects into sets of equal sizes. The simplest form of this big idea is readily understandable by children. It emerges around 3 years of age, when prekindergartners become able to share a small collection of objects equally between two toy animals. Three-year-olds can divide a collection into equal subsets (quotients) if the subsets are very small. Many 4- and 5-year-olds can work with larger numbers by inventing a one-to-one correspondence strategy to divide the initial collection into equal subsets. The idea is foundational for all kinds of multiplication situations and of measurement division (where you know the number in a group) and of partition division (where you know the number of groups). But the complexities of finding exact solutions with larger numbers except by trial and error and of reflecting on a series of repeated actions make this a big idea best pursued in detail at older grades.

*Notes on Multidigit Computation.* The ideas and skills involved in multidigit computation are supported by most of the big ideas of number and operations. Unfortunately, given present-day instruction, many children think of multidigit numbers only as single-digit numbers sitting side by side, ignoring their place value, which invites different kinds of errors. To develop computational methods that they understand, children require strong experiences in kindergarten (or earlier) hearing the pattern of repeating tens in the number words and relating them to quantities grouped in tens and seeing teen numbers and two-digit numbers as embedded numbers (52 is 50 and 2). First graders can use quantities grouped in tens or make drawings of tens and ones to do two-digit addition with regrouping and discuss how recording numerically their new ten: e.g., 48 + 26 makes 6 tens (from 40 and 20) and 1 ten and 4 (from 8 + 6), so there is a total of 7 tens and 4 for 74. Children invent and learn from each other many effective methods for adding such numbers and many ways to record their methods. Second graders can go on to add 3-digit numbers by thinking of the groups of hundreds, tens, and ones involved. And they can subtract (e.g., 82 –59) by thinking of breaking apart 82 into 59 and another number.

*Developmental Guidelines.* Central aspects of each of these big ideas and guidelines for children's development of those ideas are outlined in Table 1.1. This is the first of three tables in Part I that synthesize research (described in Parts I and II) on young children's development of mathematical ideas. Tables such as this help summarize ideas; however, they must leave information out, which can lead to misinterpretations. The tables in this document should be read with four major caveats in mind. *First, tables tend to inadequately reflect the qualitatively different ways of thinking and learning that young children develop through the early years.* For example, Table 1.1 includes "seeing" small collections (subitizing) and counting small and, later, larger collections. However, it does not capture well the many ways children develop number sense. As just one instance, recall how subitizing and counting grow from being perceptual, to being imagined, and, finally, numerical (Steffe, 1992).

*The second caveat is that curriculum developers, educators conducting professional development, and teachers need different levels of detail for each mathematical topic, from the biggest ideas of Fig. 1.1 to detailed learning trajectories.* The next level of detail for number and operations is presented in the Table 1.1. It is important to note that complete learning trajectories are more detailed, and different in nature from, the simple

Table 1.1

## Developmental Guidelines for Number and Operations

| Topic | Pre-K[a] | | Kindergarten | 1 | 2 |
|---|---|---|---|---|---|
| | 2–3 years | 4 years | 5 years | 6 years | 7 years |
| **Counting** Counting can be used to find out *how many* in a collection. | | | | | |
| a. A key element of object-counting readiness is nonverbally representing and gauging the equivalence of small collections. | Make and imagine small collections of 1 to 4 items nonverbally, such as seeing which is covered, and then putting out . Find a match equal to a collection of 1 to 4 items, such as matching :: or 4 drum beats to collections of 4 with different arrangements, dissimilar items, or mixed items (e.g., ). | | | | |

*b. Another key element of object-counting readiness is learning standard sequences of number words, learning that is facilitated by discovering patterns.*

— Verbally count by ones from … →

| 1 to 10 | 1 to 30 (and more) with emphasis on counting patterns; e.g., knowing that "twenty-one, twenty-two …" is parallel to "one, two …" | 1 to 100, with emphasis on patterns (e.g., the decades "sixty, seventy" parallel "six, seven"; also, the teens such as "fourteen" to "nineteen" parallel "four" through "nine") | 1 to 1,000, with emphasis on patterns (e.g., the hundreds, "one hundred, two hundred" parallel "one, two") |

Flexibly start verbal county-by-one sequence from any point—that is, start a count from a number other than the "one" (ends early in first grade for some)

— Flexibly state the next number word … →

| … after 2 to 9 with a running start | … after 2 to 9 without a running start to 9; also, the word before from 2 to 9 |

— Verbally count backward … →

| from 5 | from 10 | from 20 |

— Skip count … →

| by 10s | by 5s, 2s | by 3s, 4s |

Table 1.1 (continued)

| Topic | Pre-K[a] | | Kindergarten | 1 | 2 |
|---|---|---|---|---|---|
| | 2–3 years | 4 years | 5 years | 6 years | 7 years |
| c. Object counting involves creating a one-to-one correspondence between a number word in a verbal counting sequence and each item of a collection, using some action indicating each action as you say a number word. | Count the items in a collection and know the last counting word tells "how many" → | | | | |
| | 1 to 4 items | 1 to 10 items | 1 to 20 items | 1 to 100 items | |
| | Count out (produce) a collection of a specified size (lags a bit behind counting items in a collection) → | | | | |
| | 1 to 4 items | 1 to 10 items | 1 to 20 items | 1 to 100 items, using groups of 10 | |
| | | | | Use skip counting to determine how many ↔ | |
| | | | | 2, 5, or 10 at a time | Switch among counts (e.g., "100, 200, 300, 310, 320, 321, 322, 323") |
| d. Number patterns can facilitate determining the number of items in a collection or representing it | ← Verbally subitize (quickly "see") and label with a number ... → | | | | |
| | collections of 1 to 3 | collections of 1 to 5 | | collections of 1 to 6; patterns up to 10 | |
| | ← Represent collections with a finger pattern ... → | | | | |

| 1 and 2 | up to 5 | up to 10 | teens as 10 and more; used flexibly to count on, etc. |
|---|---|---|---|

*e. Estimating the number of a collection builds number sense.*

⟵———— Estimate the number in a collection ...————→

to 10 (some to 30), guessing "small" or "large" numbers

to 100, using mental number line, benchmarks, and, later, composition strategies

*f. Representing collections and numerical relations with written symbols is a key step toward abstract mathematical thinking.*

⟵——— Draw pictures or other informal symbols to represent a spoken number ———→

⟵— Draw pictures or other informal symbols to represent how many in a collection —→

⟵——— Use numeral skills ———→

Recognize one-digit numerals

Write one-digit numerals; later, teens

Write two-digit numerals

Write three-digit numerals

Read number words *one, two, three, ... ten*

Read two- and three-digit number words

Informally represent the equivalence or inequivalence of two collections.

Use symbols =, ≠, >, < (w/ single-digits)

29

Table 1.1 (*continued*)

| Topic | Pre-K[a] | | Kindergarten | 1 | 2 |
|---|---|---|---|---|---|
| | 2–3 years | 4 years | 5 years | 6 years | 7 years |
| **Comparing and Ordering** | | | | | |
| Collections can be compared or ordered, and numbers are one useful tool for doing so. | | | | | |
| a. Comparing and ordering build on nonverbal knowledge and experience with real collections | Identify whether collections are the "same" number or which is "more" visually | ⟶ Use counting or matching (one-to-one correspondence) to determine the equivalence or order (smaller or larger) of two collections, despite distracting appearances, and use words *equal, more, less, fewer* ⟶ | | | |
| | | to 5 | to 10 | to 18 | |
| b. Children compare, first visually, then using the verbal counting sequence. | | | ⟵ Determine how many more/less? ⟶ | | |
| | | | Matching, counting, 1–10 | Counting, counting on, 1–20 | Adding, subtracting, 1–100 |
| c. Learning language for ordinal numbers can build on children's concrete comparing and knowledge of counting words | ⟵ Understand and use verbal ordinal terms ⟶ | | | | |
| | "first" and "last" | "first" to "fifth" | "first" to "tenth" | "first" to "thirtieth" | |
| | | | | Read written ordinal terms *first, second, third, … ninth* and use them to represent ordinal relations. | |

## Adding To/Taking Away

A collection can be made larger by adding items to it and made smaller by taking some away from it.

Nonverbal addition and subtraction ... →

| one item + one item or two items – one item | sums up to 4 and subtraction involving 1 to 4 items |

*a. Nonverbal problem solving supports later adding and subtracting.*

Solve and make verbal word problems; add and subtract using →

| concrete modeling (objects or fingers), totals to 5 | counting-based strategies such as counting on, totals to 10 | advanced counting strategies, e.g., counting on or up (for subtraction and unknown addends) to 18; adding 3 #'s ≤ 10 |

*b. Solving problems using informal counting strategies is a critical step in learning adding and subtracting.*

Solve verbal word problems of the following types: →

| Join result unknown | Join result unknown; part-part-whole, whole unknown; separate, result unknown; some can do simple compare and join change unknown | [all previous types and] part-part-whole, part unknown; compare problems | [all previous types and] start unknown |

*c. Solving problems of different "types" or structures extends ability to succeed in varied situations and helps them build connec-tions.*

31

Table 1.1 (continued)

| Topic | Pre-K[a] | | Kindergarten | | |
|---|---|---|---|---|---|
| | 2–3 years | 4 years | 5 years | 6 years | 7 years |
| d. Linking symbolic addition and subtraction to concrete situations and solutions is necessary for meaningfully using formal symbolic. | | | Translate word problems (and their solutions) into number sentences and vice versa; determine sums and differences of number sentences by various means. ←→ | | |
| e. Facility with basic number combinations is achieved by making a variety of strategies, particularly reasoning strategies, rapid. | | | Find and use patterns and relations to devise reasoning strategies | | Facility with basic addition and subtraction combinations |
| | | | e.g., number-after (or before), i.e., + 1 is next counting word | e.g., doubles +/−1 (6 + 7 is 6 + 6 + 1 is 12 + 1 = 13), 3 + 5 = 5 + 3 (commutativity), addition complements, 5 − 3 = ? as 3 + ? = 5 | |

## Composing and Decomposing

A quantity (whole) can be "broken apart" (decomposed) into parts, and the parts can be combined (composed) to form the whole.

| | Understand and reason qualitatively and intuitively about part–whole relations | | |
|---|---|---|---|
| a. *Reasoning qualitatively about part–whole relations provides basis for more advanced composing and decomposing.* | increasing (decreasing) size of an uncounted part increases (decreases) the whole (visual only) | changing a part changes a counted whole; (e.g., adding to a collection creates a sum greater than the starting amount) | in a missing-addend word problem, a part (e.g., starting amount) is less than the whole |
| b. *Number sense include knowledge of number partners (other names for a number).* | Construct partners with objects up to 10; knowing partners to 5 (e.g., $5 = 1 + 4$, $2 + 3$, $3 + 2$, $4 + 1$); doubles to 10 (e.g., $3 + 3 = 6$) | Know partners up to 10 (e.g., $1 + 9$), especially with 5 as a partner (e.g., $6 = 5 + 1$); doubles to 20 (e.g., $12 = 6 + 6$) | Know partner involving decades up to 100 (e.g., $50 = 10 + 40$, $20 + 30$ … $40 + 10$, $100 = 10 + 90$, … $90 + 10$) |
| c. *Part–whole knowledge extends addition, subtraction.* | Informally solving part-part-whole, or "combine," word problems, sums to 10. | Recognition of additive commutativity (e.g., $3 + 6 = 6 + 3$); addition-subtraction complement (e.g., $5 - 3 = ?$, think of $3 + ? = 5$), and inverse principle (e.g. $5 + 3 - 3 = 5$). | |

Table 1.1 (continued)

| Topic | Pre-K[a] — 2–3 years | Pre-K[a] — 4 years | Kindergarten — 5 years | 1 — 6 years | 2 — 7 years |
|---|---|---|---|---|---|
| **Grouping and Place Value** | | | | | |
| Items can be grouped to make a larger unit and, in a written multidigit number, the value of a digit depends on its position because different digit positions indicate different units. | | | | | |
| *a. Concrete activities provides a conceptual basis for these grouping and place-value concepts.* | | Trade several small items for a larger one | Trade, involving … grouping into 5s or 10s; recognizing place value, e.g., 23, 32 are different | Trade, involving … decomposing a larger unit (esp. 10 and100) into smaller units; composing larger units. | |
| *b. Connecting multidigit numerals to concrete/pictorial models provides a meaningful basis for multidigit numeral skills.* | | | ← Translate between grouping/place-value models, count words, and numerals, and read/write multidigit numerals meaningfully to … → | 100 | 1,000 |
| | | | ← Recognize base-ten equivalents → | | |
| | | | 1 ten = 10 ones | 1 hundred = 10 tens or 100 ones | 1 thousand = 10 hundreds, etc. |

View concretely determined sums to 18 as a composite of ten and ones.

⎯ Invent concrete and mental procedures for adding and subtracting multidigit numbers, including shortcuts involves 10s, to …

100        1,000

Use and explain renaming algorithm, up to 1,000.

⎯ Use a front-end strategy with …→

two-digit numbers (e.g., 51 + 36 + 7 is at least 5 tens + 3 tens or 80)

3- and 4-digit numbers (e.g., 563 + 222 + 87 is at least 5 hundreds + 2 hundreds or 700)

*c. Relating written multidigit addition and subtraction to concrete or pictorial grouping and place-value model promotes understanding.*

*d. Grouping/place-value knowledge helps estimate sums and differences.*

35

Table 1.1 (*continued*)

| Topic | Pre-K^a | | Kindergarten | 1 | 2 |
|---|---|---|---|---|---|
| | *2–3 years* | *4 years* | *5 years* | *6 years* | *7 years* |
| **Equal Partitioning** | | | | | |
| A quantity (whole) can be partitioned (decomposed) into equal size pieces (parts). | | | | | |
| *a. Concrete equal-partitioning experiences with collections and then continuous quantities lay the groundwork for understanding division and fractions.* | | Use informal strategies to solve divvy-up fair-sharing problems with collections of … → | | | |
| | | up to 10 items between two people | up to 20 items among 3–5 people; knows fairs shares have same number | up to 100 items (grouped by tens and ones) among up to 10 people | up to 1,000 (grouped by hundreds, tens, and ones) among up to 20 people |
| | | | ——Use informal strategies to solve measuring-out fair-sharing problems with … → | | |
| | | | up to 20 items and shares of two to five items | up to 100 items (groups of tens and ones) and shares up to 10 items | up to 1,000 (grouped by hundreds, tens, and ones) and shares of up to 20 items |
| | | | | ——Use informal strategies to solve divvy-up fair-sharing problems with continuous quantities → | |

36

| | 1 to 10 wholes and two to five people | 1 to 20 wholes and two to ten people |
|---|---|---|

b. Connecting fraction names to equal-partitioning experiences builds knowledge that fractions involve a whole divided into equal size parts.

⎯⎯ Verbally label a fair-share of ⎯⎯⎯⎯⎯⎯⎯⎯⎯⎯⎯⎯⎯⎯⎯⎯ non-unit fractions, →

one of two as "half" or "one-half"        $\dfrac{1}{2}, \dfrac{1}{3}, \dfrac{1}{4}, \dfrac{1}{5}$        e.g., $\dfrac{2}{2}, \dfrac{2}{4}, \dfrac{2}{8}$

⎯⎯⎯⎯ Compare verbal divvy-up ⎯⎯⎯⎯⎯⎯→
or part-of-whole meaning of fractions involving ...

unit fractions $\dfrac{1}{2}, \dfrac{1}{3}$        nonunit fractions

Note.   This is the first of several tables of developmental guidelines. *It is essential to note that these are developmental guidelines. All such tables should be interpreted or used after reading the description and caveats in the section "Developmental guidelines" on p. 25; 38.* Table 1.1 was developed by an initial structure developed by a subset of the Conference Working Group led by Karen Fuson, and was then greatly elaborated in collaboration with Arthur Baroody (see his chapters in this volume—most of the table's content originally was written by Baroody in a draft of those chapters), to whom we owe a great deal of appreciation.

[a]Ages reflect those typically found in classes or groups of children; for example, the first category, a typical classroom of "3-year-olds" may begin the year with some 2-year-olds and end the year with some children just turning 4 years of age.

lists ing of capabilities even in its most detailed form. Several chapters provide better examples of learning trajectories in their more complete form (e.g., Baroody, chap. 3, this volume; Clements, chap. 10, this volume; Sarama, chap. 15, this volume).

*The next two caveats emphasize that these developmental guidelines do not constitute a curriculum. The third caveat is that children may work beyond those competencies, as they are able, both in the breadth and the depth of their learning.* These competencies are basic; mathematics should also include "things that go beyond." *The fourth and perhaps most important caveat is that the competencies in these tables are not directions for curriculum, teaching, or assessment.* The activities in which children engage to learn these competencies should provide rich, integrated experiences from whichildren develop several competencies simultaneously. *All aspects of mathematical thinking* (e.g., see Recommendation 3) *should be emphasized in the teaching and learning of such competencies.*

## Geometry

Geometry, measurement, and spatial reasoning are important, inherently, because they involve "grasping ... that space in which the child lives, breathes and moves ... that space that the child must learn to know, explore, conquer, in order to live, breathe and move better in it" (Freudenthal, in NCTM, 1989, p. 48). In addition, geometry learning in the early years can be particularly meaningful because it can be consistent with young children's way of moving their bodies (Papert, 1980). Especially for early childhood, geometry and spatial reasoning form the foundation of much learning of mathematics and other subjects (Clements, chap. 10, this volume). Although our knowledge of young children's geometric and spatial thinking is not as extensive as their numerical thinking, it has grown substantially and can be used as one basis for curriculum development and teaching. Figure 1.3 represents the big topical ideas within the major areas of geometry.

The big topical ideas of geometry discussed here, like number, span birth through Grade 2. This early knowledge can be supported by experiences in homes, day-care settings, and prekindergartens so that all children build a strong foundation of geometric and spatial thinking.

*Shape.* Through their everyday activity, children build both intuitive and explicit knowledge of geometric figures. Indeed, children often know as much about shapes entering school as their geometry curriculum "teaches" them in the early grades (Clements, chap. 10, this volume; Lehrer, Osana, Jacobson, & Jenkins, 1993). For example, most children can recognize and name basic two-dimensional (2-D) shapes at 4 years of age, and they do increase their knowledge significantly throughout elementary school (Clements, chap. 10, this volume). However, young children can learn richer concepts about shape if their educational

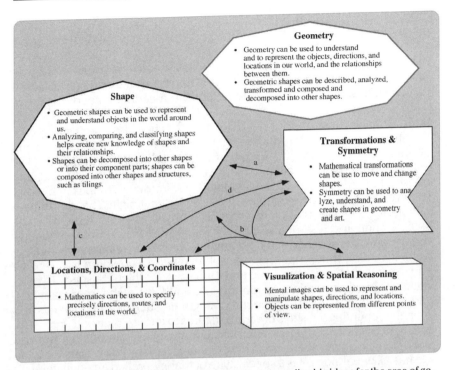

**Geometry**
- Geometry can be used to understand and to represent the objects, directions, and locations in our world, and the relationships between them.
- Geometric shapes can be described, analyzed, transformed and composed and decomposed into other shapes.

**Shape**
- Geometric shapes can be used to represent and understand objects in the world around us.
- Analyzing, comparing, and classifying shapes helps create new knowledge of shapes and their relationships.
- Shapes can be decomposed into other shapes or into their component parts; shapes can be composed into other shapes and structures, such as tilings.

**Transformations & Symmetry**
- Mathematical transformations can be use to move and change shapes.
- Symmetry can be used to analyze, understand, and create shapes in geometry and art.

**Locations, Directions, & Coordinates**
- Mathematics can be used to specify precisely directions, routes, and locations in the world.

**Visualization & Spatial Reasoning**
- Mental images can be used to represent and manipulate shapes, directions, and locations.
- Objects can be represented from different points of view.

FIG. 1.3. The five main topical areas and their corresponding big ideas for the area of geometry and spatial sense.
Note: The shape is the main emphasis at the PreK-Grade 2 band, although all four subtopics play some role, especially as they are connected with Shape.
Links: a =Transformations such as slides and turns are used to move and change geometric shapes in a way that is mathematically precise. This is of practical use (e.g., in computer programming or graphics) and also perhaps analysis of shapes (e.g., to ascertain congruence, similarity, or symmetry). b = Visualization and spatial reasoning mutually support the growth of all other areas of geometry. c = The domain of shape provides the structures for analyzing locations, directions, and coordinates (e.g., grids composed of arrayss of squares are used in maps). Ideas from the latter area can, in turn, provide alternate representations of shapes (e.g., directions such as those in Logo's turtle geometry, repeat 4 [fd 100 rt 90], can precisely represent shapes; coordinates can be similarly used to draw and represent shapes). d = Transformations such as turning and sliding are consistent with directions for following a path in a map (or those in Logo's "turtle geometry").

environment includes four features: varied examples and nonexamples, discussions about shapes and their characteristics, a wider variety of shape classes, and interesting tasks. First, curricula and teaching should ensure that children experience many different examples of a type of shape, so that they do not form narrow ideas about any class of shapes. Showing nonexamples and comparing them to similar examples help focus children's attention on the critical attributes of shapes and prompts

discussion. For example, they might compare a chevron ( ⟨◺⟩ ) or kite ( ◁ )
to a triangle ( △ ). Second, these discussions should encourage children's
descriptions while encouraging the development of language. Children
can learn to explain why a shape belongs to a certain category—"It has
three straight sides" or does not belong ( ⟨⟩ "The sides aren't straight!").
Eventually, they can internalize such arguments; for example, saying
about,⎯⎯⎯"It is a weird, long triangle, but it has three straight sides!"

Third, curricula and teachers should include a wide variety of shape
classes. Early childhood curricula traditionally introduce shapes in four basic-level categories: circle, square, triangle, and rectangle. The unfortunate
notion that a square is not a rectangle is rooted by age 5 (Clements et al.,
1999; Hannibal & Clements, 2000). Instead, children should encounter
many examples of squares and rectangles, varying orientation, size, and so
forth, including squares as examples of rectangles. If children say "that's a
square," teachers might respond that it is a square, which is a special type of
rectangle, and they might try double-naming ("it's a square-rectangle").
Older children can discuss "general" categories, such as quadrilaterals and
triangles, counting the sides of various figures to choose their category. Also,
teachers might encourage them to describe why a figure belongs or does
not belong to a shape category. Then, teachers can say that because a triangle has all equal sides, it is a special type of triangle, called an equilateral triangle. Further, children should experiment with and describe a wider
variety of shapes, including but not limited to semicircles, quadrilaterals,
trapezoids ( ◿▱◺ ), rhombi ( ▱ ), and hexagons.

In summary, children can and should discuss shapes and the parts and attributes of shapes. This brings us again to our fourth feature of a high-quality
early childhood geometry environment—interesting tasks. Activities that
promote reflection and discussion include building models of shapes from
components. For example, children might build representations of squares
and other polygons with toothpicks and marshmallows. They might also
form shapes with their bodies, either singly or with their friends.

To understand angles, they must discriminate angles as critical parts of
geometric figures, and construct and mentally represent the idea of turns.
Children possess intuitive knowledge of turns and angles and 5-year-olds
can match angles in correspondence tasks (Beilin, Klein, & Whitehurst,
1982). The long developmental process of learning about turns and angles
is best begun in the early and elementary classrooms, as children deal
with corners of figures, comparing angle size, and turns. Computer-based
shape manipulation and navigation environments can help mathematize
these experiences. Especially important is understanding how turning
one's body relates to turning shapes and turning along paths in navigation
and learning to use numbers to quantify these turn and angle situations

(see the "Measurement" section). For example, even 4-year-olds learn to click on a shape to turn it and say, "I need to turn it three times!" (see Sarama, chap.15, this volume).

Concepts of 2-D shapes begin forming in the prekindergarten years and stabilize as early as age 6 (Gagatsis & Patronis, 1990; Hannibal & Clements, 2000). It is therefore critical that children be provided better opportunities to learn about geometric figures between 3 and 6 years of age. Curricula should develop early ideas aggressively, so that by the end of Grade 2 children can identify a wide range of examples and nonexamples of a wide range of geometric figures; classify, describe, draw, and visualize shapes; and describe and compare shapes based on their attributes.

Young children move through levels in the composition and decomposition of 2-D figures. From lack of competence in composing geometric shapes, they gain abilities to combine shapes into pictures, then synthesize combinations of shapes into new shapes (composite shapes), eventually operating on and iterating those composite shapes (see Fig. 1.4).

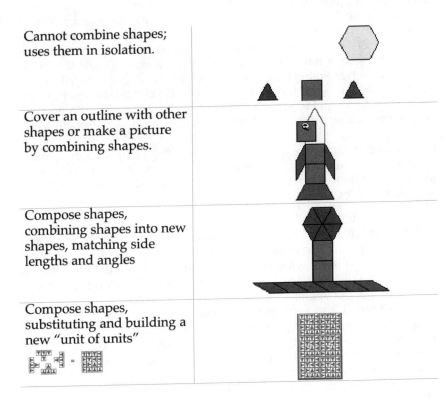

Cannot combine shapes; uses them in isolation.

Cover an outline with other shapes or make a picture by combining shapes.

Compose shapes, combining shapes into new shapes, matching side lengths and angles

Compose shapes, substituting and building a new "unit of units"

FIG. 1.4.  A learning trajectory for young children's composition of geometric figures.

As with 2-D figures, children need more and richer experiences with three-dimensional (3-D) figures. Manipulation and play with solids should lead to discussions of their overall shape ("it's like an ice-cream cone") and attributes ("all these are round and roll"). Construction activities involving nets (foldout shapes of solids) may help students learn to discriminate between 2-D and 3-D figures.

***Transformations and Symmetry.*** Pre-K–K, and even Grade 1–2 children, may be limited in their ability to mentally transform shapes, but there is evidence that they can do so in solving simple problems. Furthermore, they can learn to perform rotations on objects (physical or virtual), and a rich curriculum or set of experiences, enhanced by such manipulatives and computer tools, may reveal that such knowledge and mental processes are valid educational goals for most young children.

Beginning as early as 4 years of age, children can create and use strategies, such as moving shapes to compare their parts or to place one on top of the other, for judging whether two figures are "the same shape." In the Pre-K to Grade 2 range, they can develop sophisticated and accurate mathematical procedures for determining congruence. Older prekindergartners can learn to compare common geometric shapes that have undergone a transformation such as rotation or flip (Beilin et al., 1982). Children as young as 5–6 years can identify similar (scaled) shapes in certain situations and use computers to create similar shapes. First and second graders can identify similar shapes and use scaling transformations to check their predictions. Symmetry is also an area of strength. Very young children create designs with both line ( ) and rotational ( ) symmetry with manipulatives and in art. Children in Grades K–2 can learn to draw the other half of a geometric figure to create a symmetric figure and identify lines of symmetry.

***Visualization and Spatial Reasoning.*** One aspect of spatial reasoning, spatial orientation, involves knowing the shape of one's environment. This knowledge is intrinsically connected to knowledge of locations and directions and so is discussed in the following subsection. Another aspect of spatial reasoning is spatial visualization: the ability to create a mental image of geometric objects, "examine" it mentally to answer questions about it, and transform it. Prekindergarten children can generate and inspect images, especially if they are provided opportunities to develop this ability ("Think of a square. What do you see?). They can also learn to transform them in certain ways ("Think of a square cut down the middle. What do you have?"). Even prekindergarten and kindergarten children show initial abilities to slide, turn, and flip shapes mentally in certain settings, as previously discussed. All children should work on developing their ability to create, maintain, and represent mental images of geometric shapes and of the environments in which they live.

*Locations, Directions, and Coordinates.*  Infants and toddlers spend a great deal of time exploring space and learning about the properties and relations of objects in space. In the first year of life, infants can perceive the shape and size of objects and can represent the location of objects in a 3-D space (Haith & Benson, 1998; Kellman & Banks, 1998). Infants can use landmarks to keep track of locations in their environment (Acredolo & Evans, 1980) and associate objects as being near a person such as a parent (Presson & Somerville, 1985). Toddlers and 3-year-olds can place objects in specified locations near distant landmarks, but "lose" locations that are not specified ahead of time once they move. They may be able to form simple frameworks, such as the shape of the arrangement of several objects, which has to include their own location (Huttenlocher & Newcombe, 1984). Thus, very young children know and use the shape of their environment in navigation activities. With guidance, they can learn to mathematize this knowledge. They can learn about direction, perspective, distance, symbolization, location, and coordinates. Some studies have identified first grade as a good time to introduce learning of simple maps, such as maps of objects in the classroom or routes around the school or playground, but informal experiences in prekindergarten and kindergarten are also beneficial, especially those that emphasize building imagery from physical movement.

As stated previously, curriculum developers, educators conducting professional development, and teachers need different levels of detail for each mathematical topic, from the biggest ideas of Fig. 1.1 to detailed learning trajectories. The next level of detail for geometry and measurement is presented in Table 1.2. The four caveats described previously are critical—*tables inadequately reflect qualitatively different ways of thinking, details about learning are not included, children may work beyond those goals, and competencies in these tables are not directions for curriculum or teaching.* To emphasize the second caveat, tables and figures do not adequately describe the qualitatively different ways of thinking and learning about geometry and space that young children develop through the early years. See the chapters in Part II, and the references they contain, for further information.

## Measurement

Measurement is one of the main real-world applications of mathematics. As previously stated, counting is a type of measurement—it measures how many items in a collection (i.e., discrete quantity). Measurement of continuous quantities involves assigning a number to attributes such as length, area, and weight. Together, number and measurement are components of quanti-

Table 1.2

## *Developmental Guidelines for Geometry*

| Topic | 2-3 years | Pre-K 4 years | Kindergarten 5 years | 1 6 years | 2 7 years |
|---|---|---|---|---|---|
| **Shape** Geometric shapes can be used to represent and understand objects in the world around us. | Match shapes, first with same size and orientation, then with different sizes and orientation | Recognize and name some variations of the circle, square, triangle, rectangle | ← Identify and name 2-D shapes → | | |
| | | | Recognize and name circle, square, triangle, rectangle, in *any size or orientation* (varying shapes for triangles and rectangles) → | | |
| | | | | Recognize and name a variety of shapes (e.g., semicircles, quadrilaterals, trapezoids, rhombi, hexagons, in any orientation) → | |
| | | ← Visualize, describe, draw and represent 2-D shapes → | | | |
| | | Build, dramatize, and describe 2-D shapes informally | Build, dramatize, draw, and describe 2-D shapes informally | Accurately build, draw, describe, and visualize 2-D shapes, including geometric paths representing "route maps" → | |
| | | ← Identify congruent and noncongruent 2-D shapes → | | | |
| Analyzing, comparing, and classifying shapes helps create new knowledge of shapes and their relationships. | | Match shapes | Match shapes and parts of shapes to justify congruency | Use slides, flips, and turns and superposition to show congruency | |

Classify 2-D shapes by category →

Use shape class names informally

Use shape class names to classify and sort

Use class membership for shapes, based on properties

Name, describe, compare, and sort 3-D concrete objects →

Informal play with solids (e.g., building blocks)

Informally build with, name, describe solids

Name, describe, compare, and sort solids

Identify component parts of shapes →

Identify and count sides

Identify and count sides and angles

Independently identify shape in terms of their components and properties (defining attributes; e.g., "It has 1, 2, 3 sides … it's a triangle.)"

← Identify and describe faces of 3-D shapes as 2-D shapes →

Informally identify faces of solids

Identify and describe faces of 3-D shapes as specific 2-D shapes

Table 1.2 (continued)

| Topic | 2-3 years | 4 years | 5 years | 6 years | 7 years |
|---|---|---|---|---|---|
| | | Pre-K | Kindergarten | 1 | 2 |
| Shapes can be decomposed into other shapes or into their component parts; shapes can be composed into other shapes and structures, such as tilings. | Use shapes in isolation to make a picture. | Cover an outline with shapes without leaving gaps, first with trial-and-error, then with foresight.  Makes a picture by combining shapes. | Compose (put together) 2-D shapes to make new shapes →  Decompose simple shapes that have obvious clues for breaking them apart | Compose, combining shapes into new shapes  ← Decompose (break apart) 2-D shapes to make new shapes →  Decompose shapes using imagery that is suggested by the task or teacher | Compose, combining shapes into new shapes, *substituting* a combination of smaller shapes for a larger shape  Decompose shapes flexibly using independently generated imagery |
| | | | ← Compose (put together) and decompose (break apart) 3-D shapes to make real-world objects and other 3-D shapes, informally → | | |
| | | | | ← Understand and predict the effects of different sequences of transformations and compositions/decompositions → | |

46

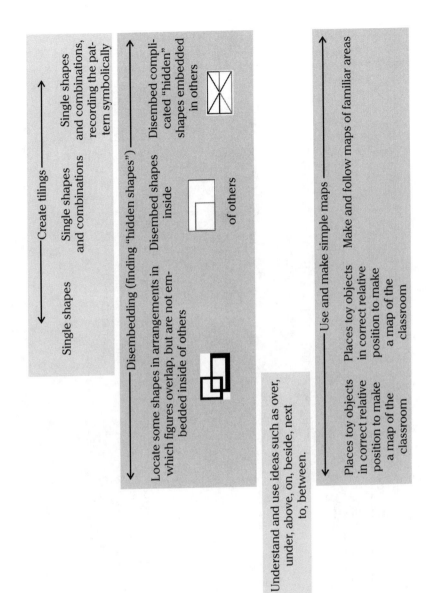

— Create tilings —

Single shapes

Single shapes and combinations

Single shapes and combinations, recording the pattern symbolically

— Disembedding (finding "hidden shapes") —

Locate some shapes in arrangements in which figures overlap, but are not embedded inside of others

Disembed shapes inside of others

Disembed complicated "hidden" shapes embedded in others

Understand and use ideas such as over, under, above, on, beside, next to, between.

— Use and make simple maps —

Places toy objects in correct relative position to make a map of the classroom

Places toy objects in correct relative position to make a map of the classroom

Make and follow maps of familiar areas

**Locations, Directions, and Coordinates**

Mathematics can be used to precisely specify directions, routes, and locations in the world.

Table 1.2 (continued)

| Topic | Pre-K | | Kindergarten | 1 | 2 |
|---|---|---|---|---|---|
| | 2-3 years | 4 years | 5 years | 6 years | 7 years |
| | ←————————— Uses coordinates to find and name locations —————————→ | | | | |
| | | Orient objects vertically or horizontally | Use coordinate labels to locate objects or pictures in simple situations | | Use coordinates to locate positions |
| **Transformations and Symmetry** Mathematical transformations can be use to precisely move and change shapes. | ←————— Perform slides, flips, and turns of 2-D shapes —————→ | | | | |
| | | Identify and use motions informally | | Visualize slides, flips, and turns of 2-D shapes | Predict the outcome of slide, flip, and turn motions on 2-D shapes |
| Symmetry can be used to analyze, understand, and create shapes in geometry and art. | | Informally create 2-D shapes and 3-D buildings that have line or rotational symmetry | Identify and create shapes that have line or rotational symmetry | Identify symmetry in 2-D shapes | Identify the mirror lines of shapes with line symmetry |

48

**Visualization and Spatial Reasoning**

Mental images can be used to represent and manipulate shapes, directions, and locations.

Create mental images of geometric shapes →

Copy a shape or small collection of shapes from memory after seeing a model for several seconds

Draw shapes from memory

Draw a collection of shapes or complex drawing from memory

Create a shape from verbal directions

Relate ideas in geometry to ideas in number and measurement

Recognize geometric shapes and structures in the environment and specify their location

Give and follow directions for moving in physical space and on a map, including understanding geometric paths as representations of movement

Understand that maps answer questions about direction, distance and location

Objects can be represented from different points of view.

Recognize and represent shapes from different perspectives

tative reasoning. In this vein, measurement helps connect the two realms of number and geometry, each providing conceptual support to the other. Figure 1.4 represents the big topical ideas within Measurement. The first box emphasizes concepts, the second skills.

As with number and geometry, children's understanding of measurement develops during the prekindergarten years. Prekindergarten children know that properties such as mass (amount), length, and weight exist, but they do not initially know how to reason about these attributes or to measure them accurately. If 3-year-olds have some amount of quantity (e.g., clay) and then are given an additional amount of quantity (more clay), they know that they have more than they did before. Three- and 4-year-olds encounter difficulty, however, when asked to judge which of two amounts of quantity that they currently have (e.g., which of two mounds of clay) is more. They tend to use perceptual cues to make this judgment. For example, when one of two identical balls of clay is rolled into a long sausagelike shape, children do not "conserve" the initial equivalence of the clay balls, and instead judge that the sausage has more clay than the ball because it is longer. Before kindergarten, many children lack measurement rules such as lining up an end when comparing the lengths of two objects (Piaget & Inhelder, 1967; Piaget et al., 1960), although they can learn about such ideas. At age 4–5 years, however, many children can,

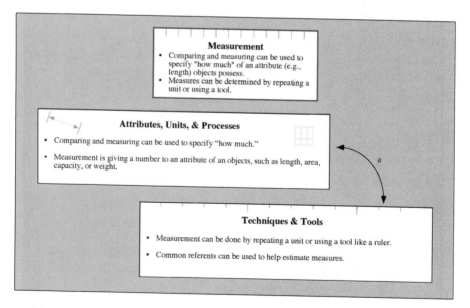

FIG. 1.4. The two main topical areas and their corresponding big ideas for the area of measurement.

with opportunities to learn, become less dependent on perceptual cues and thus make progress in reasoning about or measuring quantities.

*Attributes, Units, and Processes.* Young children naturally encounter and discuss quantities in their play (Ginsburg, Inoue, & Seo, 1999). They first learn to use words that represent quantity or magnitude of a certain attribute. Then they compare two objects directly and recognize equality or inequality, for example, of the length of two objects (Boulton-Lewis, Wilss, & Mutch, 1996). Next, children should learn to measure, connecting number to length. These involve learning many ideas, including the following: the need for equal-size units; that a line segment made by joining two line segments has a length equal to the sum of the lengths of the joined segments; that a number can be assigned to a length; and that you may need to repeat, or iterate, a unit, and subdivide that unit, to find that number (to a given precision).

Understanding of area measure also involves learning and coordinating many ideas. Children must understand that decomposing and rearranging shapes does not affect their area. Important is the ability to coordinate two linear dimensions to build the idea of a 2-D space. This explains why understanding of area is often not fully developed until 12–13 years of age. Young children should have experiences covering areas, and should develop the ability to cover using arrays (arrangements in rows and columns) by Grade 2. Such structuring is not a simple task. Elementary school children often confuse perimeter and area. For example, they believe that counting the units around a figure gives its area. Teachers help when they offer many experiences comparing areas, encouraging children to use their own strategies (even one-by-one counting) rather than teaching rote rules.

*Techniques and Tools.* Measurement involves critical skills, including techniques for comparing and measuring, either by iterating copies of a unit or using tools such as rulers. Children's development of these skills is a slow process. However, traditional opinion, based on Piaget, was that young children should not engage in measurement until they conserve quantity and that they should follow a rigid instructional sequence: gross comparisons of length, measurement with nonstandard units such as paper clips, measurement with manipulative standard units, and finally measurement with standard instruments such as rulers. Recent research suggests that children benefit from using objects and rulers to measure at any age. Not only do children prefer using rulers, but they can use them meaningfully and in combination with manipulable units to develop understanding of length measurement. Even if they do not understand rulers fully or use them accurately, they can use rulers *along with* manipulable units such as centimeter cubes and arbitrary units to develop their measurement skills.

Accurate measuring procedures such as placing manipulative units without leaving spaces between them can be developed through many experiences. Similarly, with rulers, teachers can help children develop concepts and procedures such as accurate alignment (e.g., ignoring the gap at the beginning of many rulers), starting at zero, and focusing on the lengths of the units rather than only the numbers on the ruler. Counting points rather than line segments is more likely in ruler activities and partitioning tasks. That is, accepting earlier use of rulers is *not* the same as believing that such use implies mastery either of the tool or of measurement concepts (Lehrer, Jenkins, & Osana, 1998). Rather, it is an additional way to present experiences and problems that will help children develop understanding. Using manipulable units to make their own rulers helps children connect their experiences and ideas.

Later, in second or third grade, teachers can introduce students explicitly to the ideas of the relationship between units and the need for standard units. The relationship between the size and number of units, the need for standardization of units, and additional measuring devices can be explored. The next level of detail for measurement is presented in Table 1.3.

## Algebra, Patterns, and Data Analysis

Though number, geometry, and measurement are the main emphases at the Pre-K to Grade 2 age, algebra and data analysis play supporting roles. Algebraic thinking can permeate much of the instruction of these main areas (and the smaller amount of research done on such thinking should not diminish its importance to the curriculum). Algebra begins with a search for patterns. Identifying patterns helps bring order, cohesion, and predictability to seemingly unorganized situations and allows one to make generalizations beyond the information directly available. The recognition and analysis of patterns are important components of the young child's intellectual development because they provide a foundation for the development of algebraic thinking. Although prekindergarten children engage in pattern-related activities and recognize patterns in their everyday environment, research has revealed that an abstract understanding of patterns develops gradually during the early childhood years (Klein & Starkey, chap. 14, this volume). It appears that this ability undergoes considerable development. In the prekindergarten years, children can learn to duplicate simple concrete patterns. In kindergarten, they can learn to extend and create patterns. Furthermore, children learn to recognize the relationship between patterns with nonidentical objects or between different representations of the same pattern (e.g., between visual and motoric, or movement, patterns). This is a crucial step in using patterns to make generalizations and to reveal common underlying structures. Through kindergarten and the primary grades, children must learn to identify the core unit (e.g., AB) that either repeats (ABABAB) or "grows" (ABAABAAAB), and then use it to generate both these types of patterns.

Table 1.3

***Developmental Guidelines for Measurement***

| Topic | Pre-K | | Kindergarten | 1 | 2 |
|---|---|---|---|---|---|
| | *2-3 years* | *4 years* | *5 years* | *6 years* | *7 years* |
| **Concepts** | ← Recognize, compare, and order attributes such as length, volume, weight, area, and time → | | | | |
| Measuring can be used to specify and compare "how much." | | Discuss and compare attributes informally, including comparing gross differences. Develop language such as "bigger," "longer," and "taller." | Name, discuss, and compare objects according to attributes in solving problems | | Name, discuss, distinguish, compare, and order objects according to the attributes of length, volume, weight, area, and time |
| | | | ← Understand how to measure length → | | |
| Measurement is giving a number to an attribute of an objects, such as length, area, capacity, or weight. | | Compare length directly | Compare length transitively; length of two objects can be compared by representing each using string or paper strip | Use centimeters or meters to measure | Compare the effects of measuring length using units of different size; determine the need for using a standard unit of measurement<br>Measure perimeter |

Table 1.3 (continued)

| Topic | 2-3 years | Pre-K<br>4 years | Kindergarten<br>5 years | 1<br>6 years | 2<br>7 years |
|---|---|---|---|---|---|
| | | | Measure by laying length units end-to-end | | Measure by iterating single unit and using ruler |
| | | ←——————— Understand how to measure area ———————→ | | | |
| | | Gross comparison of areas by placing one object on another ("more space") | Cover area with units and counts individual squares (not necessarily in an organized way) | Partial row or column structuring (e.g., "3 in this rows and 3 in this one makes 6, umm, 7, 8 ..." [continues counting by ones]) | Understands area as array with row and columns (e.g., "3 in each row ... 3, 6, 9, 12!" |
| | | | ←——— Understand how to measure turn and angle ———→ | | |
| | | | Use angle and turn measure intuitively in play | Understand that turns can be quantified (e.g., "I turned the shape on the computer three times") | Assign numbers to turns in certain situations |
| | | ←——— Recognize attributes of volume, weight, area, and time ———→ | | | |

54

## Skills and Tools

Measurement can be done by iterating a unit or using a tool such as a ruler.

Common referents can be used to help estimate measures.

⟵ Measure by laying length units end-to-end ⟶

| | |
|---|---|
| Measure with multiple copies of unit of the same size, such as paper clips laid end-to-end | Use repetition of a single unit to measure something larger than the unit, for instance, measuring the length of a room with a single meter stick |

⟵ Measure with tools ⟶

| | |
|---|---|
| Informal, exploratory use of simple ruler (single units) | Use simple ruler to measure units |

| | |
|---|---|
| Informal comparisons and estimation | Use common referents for measures to make comparisons and estimates |
| | Develop and use referents to estimate length measure (e.g., the top of door knobs are about a meter from the floor) |

Moving into the primary grades, children can learn to find and extend numerical patterns—extending their knowledge of patterns to thinking algebraically about arithmetic (Baroody, 1993). Two central themes are making generalizations and using symbols to represent mathematical ideas and to represent and solve problems (Carpenter & Levi, 1999). For example, children might generalize that when you add zero to a number the sum is always that number or when you add three numbers it does not matter which two you add first (Carpenter & Levi, 1999). In summary, students in the primary grades can learn to formulate, represent, and reason about generalizations and conjectures, although their justifications do not always adequately validate the conjectures they create. This body of research on young children's understanding of patterns can be used, in turn, to establish developmentally appropriate learning trajectories for pattern instruction in early mathematics education.

Data analysis contains one big idea: classifying, organizing, representing, and using information to ask and answer questions. The developmental continuum for data analysis includes growth in classifying and counting and in data representations. Regarding the former, children initially learn to sort objects and quantify their groups. For example, they might sort a collection of buttons into those with one to four holes and count to find out how many they have in each of the four groups. To do this, they focus on and describe the attributes of objects, classifying according to those attributes, and quantify the resulting categories. Children eventually became capable of simultaneously classifying and counting, for example, counting the number of colors in a group of objects, as described previously.

After gathering data to answer questions, children's initial representations often do not use categories. Their interest in data is on the particulars (Russell, 1991). For example, they might simply list each child in their class and each child's response to a question. They then learn to classify these responses and represent data according to category. Thus, children should use physical objects to make graphs (objects such as shoes or sneakers, then manipulatives such as connecting cubes), then picture graphs, then line plots, and, finally, bar graphs that include grid lines to facilitate reading frequencies (Friel, Curcio, & Bright, 2001). By second grade, most children should be able to organize and display data through both simple numerical summaries such as counts, tables, and tallies, and graphical displays, including picture graphs, line plots, and bar graphs (Russell, 1991). They can compare parts of the data, make statements about the data as a whole, and generally determine whether the graphs answer the questions posed initially.

## Themes

Several themes emerge across the mathematical topics. These are described only briefly here, as they are developed within the chapters in Part II. One theme is that, especially for younger students, it is more important not to treat mathematical topics as isolated topics; rather, they should be connected to each other, often in the context of solving a significant problem or engaging in an interesting project (Clements, 2001; Fuson, chap. 5, this volume).

*Recommendation 3: Mathematics for young children should be an integrated whole. Connections—between topics, between mathematics and other subjects, and between mathematics and everyday life—should permeate children's mathematical experiences.*

In a similar vein, our focus on mathematical content is not a de-emphasis on other aspects of mathematical power, which includes not just conceptual understanding, but also the flexible and thoughtful use of skills, the ability to conduct mathematical inquiry, and a positive disposition toward learning and using mathematics (Baroody with Coslick, 1998). Such aspects are essential for meaningful and substantive mathematics learning and teaching and involve the incorporation of two groups of processes. The first group includes the general processes of problem solving, representing, reasoning, communicating, and connecting, which should be interwoven throughout the teaching and learning of content—the NCTM *process standards* in Fig. 1.1. The second group includes mathematical processes used across mathematical domains, such as organizing information, patterning, decomposing/composing, and unitizing. Along with such habits of mind as being curious, creative, and willing to take risks, these processes might be the most long-lasting and important goals of mathematics education.

*Recommendation 4: As important as mathematical content are general mathematical processes such as problem solving, reasoning and proof, communication, connections, and representation; specific mathematical processes such as organizing information, patterning, and composing; and habits of mind such as curiosity, imagination, inventiveness, persistence, willingness to experiment, and sensitivity to patterns. All should be involved in a high-quality early childhood mathematics program.*

This section describes our recommendations for flexible guidelines for young children's mathematics. The following two sections address standards for programs and for teaching.

## CURRICULUM, LEARNING, TEACHING, AND ASSESSMENT

What is the nature of a high-quality prekindergarten mathematics curriculum? The trend to push the present kindergarten mathematics to preschool is not the answer (Lindquist & Joyner, chap. 20, this volume). Too often, that curriculum is not even appropriate for kindergarten. Too many U.S. curricula teach skills, but do not build on children's sense-making ability. Teaching and learning are most effective if they build on children's existing concepts (Bowman et al., 2001). Present textbooks predominate mathematics curriculum materials in U.S. classrooms and to a great extent determine teaching practices (Fuson, chap. 5, this volume; Goodlad, 1984), even in the context of reform efforts (Grant, Peterson, & Shojgreen-Downer, 1996). Publishers attempt to meet the criteria of a multitude of national, state, and local curriculum frameworks, and thus the educational vision of any one is, at best, diluted (Clements, 2002). Moreover, teachers' reliance on textbooks minimizes any effect of such visions.

## The Need for Curriculum to Be Informed by Research and the Wisdom of Expert Practice

Why does curriculum development in the United States not improve? One reason is that the vast majority of curriculum development efforts do not follow scientific research procedures (Battista & Clements, 2000; Clements & Battista, 2000). Only a minority follows even a minimal research-to-practice model, in which general research theories or findings are considered before designing a curriculum. "Based on the notion of a one-way translation of research results to principles to instructional designs, it [the minimal research-to-practice model] is flawed in its presumptions, insensitive to changing goals in the subject matter field, unable to contribute to a revision of the theory and knowledge on which it is built, and thus limited in its contribution to either theory or practice" (Clements, 2002, p. 605). More comprehensive models use empirically based learning models of children's thinking and learning, maintain close connections between activities and children's mathematical thinking, and employ design phases and cycles of revisions.[8] Thus they incorporate research on teaching and learning, action research, and the wisdom of expert practice, as well as the full creative processes from developers, teachers, and children in cyclic manner. Research and curriculum development must be closely connected, integrated, and interactive processes that include the big ideas of mathematics, learning trajectories, multiple strategies for assessment, and cycles of testing and revision.

*Recommendation 5: Curriculum development and teaching should be informed by research on teaching and learning and by the wisdom of expert practice. Educators and policymakers should support and insist on approaches to teaching, learning, curriculum, and assessment that are developed and tested extensively with children.*

## Learning and Teaching

As stated previously, mathematics education for the young child should be integrated. Young children do not perceive or act on their world as if it were divided into separate cubbyholes. Successful prekindergarten

---

[8]These efforts can lead to published curricula; however, similar processes and strengths are found in emergent curricula that carefully document goals, processes, decisions, and learning.

teachers help children develop experiential and mathematical knowledge throughout the day (Clements, 2001). Such teaching capitalizes on prekindergartners' high level of motivation to learn and practice competencies in a self-directed manner. It promotes a view of mathematics as positive, self-motivated, self-directed, problem-solving activity at the time children first develop their mathematical beliefs, habits, and feelings. A core principle is that teaching should relate the ideas and skills to what children know. Children's everyday activity, such as play, building, or stories can be used to begin number work for each big idea. Continual interweaving of such meaningful situations is necessary for building meanings within each big idea. Such interweaving is required to enable all children to learn the mathematical and situational language necessary to understand mathematical situations and to solve problems.

*Recommendation 6: Mathematical experiences for very young children should build largely upon their play and the natural relationships between learning and life in their daily activities, interests, and questions.*

The teacher's role in mathematizing young children's play and everyday activity is crucial. Early childhood teachers must design the environment so that children engage in interesting mathematics throughout the classroom and throughout the day. Teachers then must help children describe, quantify, and generalize these experiences.

*Recommendation 7: Teachers' most important role with respect to mathematics should be finding frequent opportunities to help children reflect on and extend the mathematics that arises in their everyday activities, conversations, and play, as well as structuring environments that support such activities. Teachers should be proactive as well in introducing mathematical concepts, methods, and vocabulary.*

In any of these roles, teachers must draw on the knowledge base on what young children know and are able to learn and understanding of the ways in which various concepts and skills build on others. To perform all these roles well, teachers draw on their own specific knowledge about what will be meaningful and engaging to the particular children in the group, individually and collectively.

Teachers need to consistently integrate real-world situations, problem solving, and mathematical content (Fuson, chap. 5, this volume). This integration is more than a pedagogical nicety; it is necessary to achieve both sense making and the development of skills such as computational fluency. It supports transfer to future learning and out-of-school contexts. Finally, mathematics itself involves a vast web of connections among concepts and topics (NCTM, 2000). *Programs for prekindergarten to Grade 2 should interweave real-world, meaningful contexts; problem solving; and mathematical concepts and skills.*

Young children benefit from a range of mathematical experiences, from the incidental and informal to the systematic and planned. Mathematics should be gleaned from myriad everyday situations (G. Fein, personal communication, Sept. 20, 2000). For example, a group of young children investigated many measurement ideas as they attempted to draw plans for a carpenter, so that he could build them a new table (Malaguzzi, 1997). Informal games can be introduced, and modified, to create opportunities to learn concepts and practice skills (Griffin, chap. 13, this volume; Kamii & Housman, 1999). Stories can similarly be a source of mathematical explorations (Casey, chap. 16, this volume; Sarama, chap. 15, this volume). Teaching techniques are tools, and as such, must be used carefully, thoughtfully, and appropriately. This leads to the following recommendation:

> *Recommendation 8: Teachers should purposefully use a variety of teaching strategies to promote children's learning. Children benefit from a thoughtful combination of carefully planned sequences of activities and of integrated approaches that occur throughout the day. Successful early childhood teachers build on children's informal knowledge and everyday activities, considering children's cultural background, language, and mathematical ideas and strategies.*

An instructional approach that can make a unique contribution is the use of technology. There have been waves of enthusiasm and criticism of technology in the media (most of which ignore or misinterpret empirical findings). In contrast, research and expert practice have consistently supported *intelligent* and *appropriate* use of technology for learning mathematics in early childhood (Clements, 1999). Computer technology is especially appropriate when it provides research-based computer tools that complement and expands what can be done with other media (Sarama, chap. 15, this volume). For example, children might use mathematical tools to decompose computer-based manipulatives, or make them larger or smaller, which is difficult or impossible with physical manipulatives. Software might also make a unique contribution by guiding children through research-based learning trajectories (Sarama, chap. 15, this volume). These and other technologies should be integrated into everyday classroom experiences. This leads to the following recommendation:

> *Recommendation 9: Children should benefit from the thoughtful, appropriate, ongoing use of various types of technology. Especially useful are computer tools that enrich and extend mathematical experiences.*

Regardless of instructional approach or strategy, educators must remember that the ideas young children construct can be uniquely different from those of adults (e.g., Piaget & Inhelder, 1967; Steffe & Cobb, 1988). Early childhood teachers must be particularly careful not to assume that children "see" situations, problems, or solutions as adults do. Successful teachers interpret what the child is doing and thinking and attempt to see the situation from the child's point of view. Based on their interpretations, they conjecture what the child might be able to learn or abstract from his or her experiences. Similarly, when they interact with the child, they also consider their own actions from the child's point of view. This makes early childhood teaching both demanding and rewarding.

*Recommendation 10: Teachers should endeavor to understand each child's own mathematical ideas and strategies. Teachers should use those understandings to plan and adapt instruction and curriculum.*

Not only are children's conceptions uniquely different from those of adults, they are the best foundation on which to build subsequent learning. Research and expert practice agree that children should learn skills in conjunction with learning the corresponding concepts—indeed, learning skills before developing understanding can lead to learning difficulties (Baroody, chap. 6 & 7, this volume; Clements, chap. 10, this volume; Fuson, chap. 5, this volume; Kilpatrick et al., 2001; Sarama, chap. 15, this volume; Sophian, chap. 9, this volume; Steffe, chap. 8, this volume). Successful innovative curricula and teaching build directly on students' thinking (the understandings and skills they possess), provide opportunities for both invention and practice, and ask children to explain their various strategies (Hiebert, 1999). Such programs facilitate conceptual growth and higher order thinking without sacrificing the learning of skills. This leads to the following recommendation:

*Recommendation 11: Teachers should help children develop strong relationships between concepts and skills. Skill development is promoted by a strong conceptual foundation.*

Teachers should encourage children to create and describe their own solution methods and should encourage methods found to be effective, introducing them when appropriate. Teachers should encourage children to describe and compare different solution methods.

Instruction that views children as active learners with relevant initial knowledge and that provides substantial support during learning, is superior to traditional instruction that lacks these characteristics (Fuson, chap. 5, this volume).

## Assessment

Educational assessments serve a variety of purposes (Chittenden, 1999). Sometimes "assessments" are equated with "high-stakes" standards, as discussed previously. Sometimes the term suggests a more diagnostic function, as in the identification of children with special needs. Finally, within the classroom, "assessment" serves to guide instruction and learning.

The purposes of assessment should determine the content of the assessment, the methods of collecting evidence, and the nature of the possible consequences for individual students, teachers, schools, or programs. In the past, misuse of tests and other instruments in early childhood have stemmed from confusion of purpose. Instruments designed for one purpose, such as identification, may be totally inappropriate as instruments to measure the success of a program. Here we emphasize assessment to support learning.

Assessment that supports early childhood learning should enhance teachers' powers of observation and understanding of children's mathematical thinking and learning. It should draw upon a range of sources of evidence of student learning, such as the following table (adapted from Chittenden, 1991, 1999).

At appropriate ages, all of these sources can be useful. However, in early childhood, group-administered, multiple-choice tests often are not adequate assessment tools (Fuson, chap. 5, this volume; Lindquist & Joyner, chap. 20, this volume). The younger the child, the more likely they can actually do harm. For individual assessment, observations, documentation of children's talk, interviews, samples of student work, and performance assessments that illuminate children's thinking constitute a positive approach to assessing children's strengths and needs (Lindquist & Joyner, chap. 20, this volume). These strategies are more likely to illuminate children's background knowledge and emerging ideas and skills and thus provide insight that teachers need to achieve the vision of early childhood mathematics education promoted here. The richer the instructional environment, the broader the range of evidence for assessing learning. Careful assessment is especially important for instruction of children with special needs or disabilities.

| General Observation and Records of Activities | Class Discussions and Conversations | Work Samples | Performance Tasks | Tests and Testlike Procedures |
|---|---|---|---|---|
| • anecdotal records <br> • checklists or logs of projects <br> • inventories of student activities | • group meetings <br> • student comments and questions about their work <br> • conferences and conversations | • drawings <br> • writing and journal entries <br> • constructions | • conducting investigations <br> • solving a problem, with explanation <br> • telling or writing a story problem | • teacher-made <br> • text-book/unit questions <br> • standardized, norm-referenced |

Another useful way to think about the purposes of assessment in the classroom is to consider three different functions it serves for teachers: keeping track, checking up, and finding out (Chittenden, 1991). Keeping track may involve knowing what activities and accomplishments each child has finished, perhaps recorded with informal folders and inventories. Checking up involves seeing if a child or class has learned something fairly specific. For example, before beginning a series of planned activities, a teacher may observe children working in an open-ended fashion with a set of materials such as shapes, and ask general questions to ascertain their level of interest, knowledge, thinking, and vocabulary related to shapes. In the middle of the series of activities, the teacher may introduce a task and observe and discuss the tasks with some of her children to develop a better sense of the children's understanding and to determine if the group needs more experience or is ready to move on to new, more challenging, tasks.

Emphasized here is the last of the three functions, finding out, which is the teacher's attempt to figure out what's going on. What does the child mean? How is she thinking? How did a child arrive at a particular solution/answer? What are they getting from the activities? Teachers again ask questions, but without determining what the answer is ahead of time. Rather, they inquire so as to understand the child's thinking. This may be the most critical purpose for expert teaching. Such teachers ask children to communicate their experiences in increasingly varied and abstract representations, from dramatizations to verbal descriptions to drawings, both for learning and for assessment.

*Recommendation 12: Interview and performance tasks and ongoing, observational forms of assessment are useful and informative ways of assessing young children's mathematical learning and should be integrated as appropriate into the early childhood mathematics curriculum. The primary goal of assessing young children should be to understand children's thinking and to inform ongoing teaching efforts.*

## Final Words on Curriculum, Learning, Teaching, and Assessment

Curriculum designers and teachers must not forget issues of equity, especially as research indicates that well-developed programs have significant benefits for at-risk children (Griffin, chap. 13, this volume; Klein & Starkey, chap. 14, this volume). These children need additional support for mathematics learning, such as opportunities to engage in foundational mathematical experiences (e.g., counting experiences and building with blocks) and to develop mathematical language about situations, as well as support for broader aspects of their environments. Summarizing points made in previous sections, we conclude the following:

*Curriculum designers and teachers can assume that all children have an informal mathematics on which they can build. Not only should all chil-*

*dren be exposed to challenging mathematics, but children at risk for low performance in school mathematics and those from groups underrepresented in mathematics should be provided more support, as necessary, to be on par with other children by first grade. Children should have high-quality mathematical experiences in the years before school in order to improve their chance of learning and performing successfully in school mathematics.*

To return to the theme with which we began this section, administrators and policymakers should accept and promote research-based curricula and instructional approaches. These do not include curricula with only spurious claims of being "based on research" (e.g., merely considering research results when designing the curriculum, or, worse, citing research results that are ostensibly consistent with the curriculum post hoc). Instead, curricula developers should consider research throughout development, design and sequence activities in accord with research-based big ideas and learning trajectories, field-test the curriculum in cycles of assessment and revision, and conduct summative evaluations (Clements, 2002). Educators at all levels should reject curricula or instructional approaches that are not developed to be consistent with research on students' learning of mathematics and that do not have the support of empirical evaluation. This is a strong position, but one that will ultimately benefit children. This is why we recommend that educators and policymakers should insist on curricula and assessments that are developed and field-tested extensively with children.

## PROFESSIONAL DEVELOPMENT

Research and expert practice from several fields suggests that the most critical feature of a high-quality educational environment is a knowledgeable and responsive adult (Bowman et al., 2001). So, ongoing, high-quality professional development is essential to reform (Sarama & DiBiase, chap. 19, this volume). Professional development demands considerable attention, especially given the diversity of the teacher/caregiver population. "Dramatic differences exist in the training and skills of those who care for young children, even if only those caring for children in group settings are considered" (Copple, chap. 3, this volume). Teacher/caregiver backgrounds range from a bachelors degree or beyond (31%) to a high school diploma or less (24%). "As we work to improve the quality of math curriculum and instruction in the early years, we need to remember that this is the reality: There are hundreds of thousands of virtually untrained early childhood workers, along with hosts of teachers with basic early childhood training but little if any preparation relating to math teaching and learning" (Copple, chap. 3, this volume).

Thus, a major deterrent to the implementation of a strong mathematics program for children in prekindergarten to third grade is the inadequate preparation of teachers. Early childhood teachers are often uncomfortable about mathematics (Copley, 1999), view necessary mathematics as only "counting, adding, subtracting, and knowing shapes," and have little or no knowledge about the mathematics standards" (Copple, chap. 3, this volume). Even trained teachers often have limited knowledge of the mathematics they are to teach, as well as children's thinking about that mathematics (Clements, chap. 10, this volume). Teachers need three kinds of knowledge: knowledge of mathematics, knowledge of children, and knowledge of instructional practices (Kilpatrick et al., 2001), including knowledge of how mathematics can be representing and presented pedagogically.

Effective professional development programs are those that actively involved the teacher and provide high-quality supervision (Bowman et al., 2001). Teachers are the ones chiefly responsible for implementing curriculum and, more specifically, any changes in that curriculum. Therefore any professional development must be relevant to teachers and must directly address their specific needs and concerns. In addition, professional development should incorporate findings on how teachers learn best. Research has identified many specific findings and recommendations, but the following five emerge as consistent themes across many works (Sarama & DiBiase, chap. 19, this volume):

1. Professional development should be standards based, ongoing, and job embedded (i.e., practical, concrete, immediate, gradually connecting to research and theory).

2. Teachers must have time to learn and work with colleagues, especially a consistent group.

3. Teachers should be provided with stable, high-quality sources of professional development that includes observation, experimentation, and mentoring, with plenty of time for reflection.

4. Professional development experiences should be grounded in a sound theoretical and philosophical base and structured as a coherent and systematic programs.

5. Professional development experiences should respond to each individual's background, experiences, and current context or role.

6. Professional development experiences should address mathematics knowledge as well as mathematics education. It should be grounded in particular curriculum materials that focus on children's mathematical thinking and learning, including learning trajectories.

Professional development should follow "multiple pathways" to success. The teaching and learning process is a complex endeavor that is embedded in contexts that are highly diverse, a description especially true in early childhood settings. Professional development must be integrated in ways that best suit the local values, norms, policies, structures, resources, and processes (McLaughlin, 1990). Thus, professional development demands multiple strategies and a variety of models (Guskey & Huberman, 1995; Sparks & Loucks-Horsley, 1989), including university courses, on-site assistance, action research (Holly, 1991), study groups (Murphy, 1995), coaching and mentoring (Showers & Joyce, 1996), examining student work and thinking (Fennema, Carpenter, & Franke, 1997), professional networks, satellite downlinks, and distance education. Innovative approaches should attempt to ameliorate present limitations. In-service teachers frequently expressed their frustration with typical professional development experiences. Workshops presented on Saturdays or after school, conference opportunities that necessitate a large amount of preparation for substitutes, and presentations that are geared to the intermediate grades all contributed to this frustration (Copley, 1999). Professional development for early childhood educators in mathematics should be viewed as a systematic, ongoing commitment of time and resources. This leads to the following recommendation:

> *Recommendation 13: Professional development should be based on research and expert practice. It requires multiple strategies and an understanding of the variety of professional development models, with special emphasis on the importance of teacher leaders and collegial support groups. It needs to be sustained and coherent.*

Professional development educators will need to learn new mathematics, new ideas about children's thinking and learning, new curricula, and new forms of teaching. All these are important. As mentioned previously, deep knowledge of the mathematics to be taught is critical for improving teaching (Ball & Bass, 2000; Ma, 1999). This will not be achieved by simply taking more mathematics courses (Kilpatrick et al., 2001); instead, courses must examine the nature of the mathematics that teachers use in the practice of teaching in the early years. Mathematical knowledge includes knowledge of mathematical facts, concepts, and procedures, as well as the relationships among these; knowledge of the ways that mathematical ideas can be represented; and knowledge of mathematics as a discipline, such as the nature of discourse in mathematics and the standards of evidence, argumentation, and proof (Kilpatrick et al., 2001). Furthermore, teachers must have a clear vision of the wider goals of instruction (e.g., including the "habits of mind" described previously) and what proficiency means for each specific mathematical topic they teach (Kilpatrick et al., 2001). Also, an understanding of how children's mathematical thinking and knowledge develop is often a neglected component of reform and professional development efforts (Baroody, chap. 6, this volume).

Practically all teachers need to know more about mathematics, children's mathematical thinking, and how to work with children in mathematics. They need to know much more about what mathematics young children are interested in and capable of doing; many vastly underestimate the range of young children's interests and the extent of their capabilities. Motivating and enhancing such knowledge will be a challenge, especially as most teachers believe they already have adequate mathematics preparation (Sarama & DiBiase, chap. 19, this volume). Professional development demands considerable attention, especially given the diversity of the teacher/caregiver population. This leads to the following recommendation:

> *Recommendation 14: Deep knowledge of the mathematics to be taught, together with knowledge of how children think and develop those skills and understandings, is critical for improving teaching and should be learned in preservice and professional development programs.*

Professional development educators need to consider the context of the learning situation, the unique and diverse characteristics of early childhood teachers, and research on how teachers learn. They should continue expanding their knowledge about mathematics, about children's thinking and learning, about curricula, and about forms of teaching.

Curriculum developers must consider the United States' diverse early childhood contexts and ask themselves many interrelated questions. "Is this curriculum or resource accessible for caregivers or teachers with relatively little background in child development, early childhood education, and math? Can they understand and make effective use of it? If not, what experiences and resources will they need to do so? What can be done to bring aspects of this curriculum into the home and other informal settings? How can the value of mathematics in general—and this curriculum approach specifically—be communicated to parents and other lay persons? Are there some simple things families can do with their children to enhance the impact of the curriculum (Copple, chap. 3, this volume)? Every curriculum should support and enhance the teacher's understanding of children's mathematical thinking. Research on systemic changes indicates that this is a particularly effective strategy (Heck et al., 2002).

> *Recommendation 15: One effective way to promote professional development is through the use of high-quality curriculum materials and programs. These should be included in professional development programs.*

For our part, we should not underestimate early childhood teachers. When they have this awareness and knowledge about math and the rich potentials for early math learning, a great many will think of wonderful ways to "mathematize" their classroom and curriculum.

## TOWARDS THE FUTURE: IMPLEMENTATION AND POLICY

Are children making expected progress? Are we accelerating learning progress for those children who come to prekindergarten far behind the typical expectation for their peer group? To answer these questions, we must know what the appropriate expectation is, we must know what to do to help children achieve it, and we must know how to assess what children have learned. "Setting standards is only the first step. Connecting standards to curriculum, teaching, and assessment is essential if the standards are to be implemented" (Bredekamp, chap. 2, this volume). Documents such as NCTM's *PSSM* recognize these connections, but do not address them fully, especially in the area of prekindergarten. Making the vision expressed here a reality is a daunting task that must involve all interested parties. In this final section, we summarize suggestions for implementation and professional development that emerged from the Conference.

Those responsible for policies and for implementation must consider the diverse audiences and diverse settings of early childhood mathematics education. *There is one other critical type of standard: standards for policymakers and governments. These parties should combine their expertise with the knowledge represented in this book in creating consistent guidelines for mathematics for young children. Moreover, they should provide adequate funding and structures so as to provide high-quality early childhood education for all children.*

An important issue, one that motivated the Conference, is producing or revising state-level standards for early childhood mathematics. Lindquist and Joyner (chap. 20, this volume) state that the importance and complexity of this enterprise suggests that states adapt and use the work of others in their own efforts to of producing or revising such guidelines. The guidelines provided in Part I constitute our effort to provide such a foundation.

A wide range of implementation strategies were suggested at the initial Conference, including licensing, legislation/administrative policies, and increased professional development and parent education (from suggestions on seeing mathematics in everyday activities to providing guidelines for selecting a prekindergarten). Finally, we return to our theme that all concerned parties must work together to achieve these goals. Lindquist and Joyner (chap. 20, this volume) suggest the following questions for all concerned parties to ask themselves: How can the environment be influenced to prepare the constituents for recommendations such as those given here? What public relations issues need to be addressed? Who should be involved; in particular, what professional organizations should be brought in from the beginning? Who should take the lead? Who has the responsibility for decisions? Lindquist and Joyner (chap. 20, this volume) propose several strategies in this vein. They echo recommendations that organizations and governmental bodies actively promote public understanding of early childhood education (Bowman et al., 2001), emphasizing that special efforts need to be made to promote appropriate mathematical teaching and learning in the early years. These might include (a) simple, direct pamphlets that parents might get through libraries or doctors' offices or stores, (b) booklets for prekindergarten directors and teachers, (c) public service announcements (15- to 30-second spots that might be organized around themes, like math in the kitchen, math at bedtime, etc.), (d) information for policymakers that can help them make appropriate decisions, and (e) professional development for caregivers in day-care/prekindergarten settings that relates to observations of and conversations with their children about mathematical ideas. These ideas lead to the following recommendation:

> *Recommendation 16: A coordinated effort should be created to translate the information in this book into a variety of forms for different audiences.*

Mathematics and early childhood educators should bring high-quality exemplars, appropriate language, and realistic goals to these efforts, giving guidance to the documents related to the "what" and "how."

> *Recommendation 17: State agencies should collaborate across all states to form more coherent and related state mandates and guidelines for mathematics for young learners. Governments should provide adequate funding and structures so as to provide high-quality early childhood education for all children, including high-quality professional development for the adults who care for them.*

## REFERENCES

Acredolo, L. P., & Evans, D. (1980). Developmental changes in the effects of landmarks on infant spatial behavior. *Developmental Psychology, 16,* 312–318.

Alexander, P. A., White, C. S., & Daugherty, M. (1997). Analogical reasoning and early mathematics learning. In L. D. English (Ed.), *Mathematical reasoning: Analogies, metaphors, and images* (pp. 117–147). Mahwah, NJ: Lawrence Erlbaum Associates.

Aubrey, C. (1997). Children's early learning of number in school and out. In I. Thompson (Ed.), *Teaching and learning early number* (pp. 20–29). Philadelphia: Open University Press.

Ball, D. L., & Bass, H. (2000). Interweaving content and pedagogy in teaching and learning to teach: Knowing and using mathematics. In J. Boaler (Ed.), *Multiple perspectives on the teaching and learning of mathematics* (pp. 83–104). Westport, CT: Ablex.

Baroody, A. J. (1993). *Problem solving, reasoning, and communicating (K–8): Helping children think mathematically.* New York: Merrill/Macmillan.

Baroody, A. J., with Coslick, R. T. (1998). *Fostering children's mathematical power: An investigative approach to K–8 mathematics instruction.* Mahwah, NJ: Lawrence Erlbaum Associates.

Battista, M. T., & Clements, D. H. (2000). Mathematics curriculum development as a scientific endeavor. In A. E. Kelly & R. A. Lesh (Eds.), *Handbook of research design in mathematics and science education* (pp. 737–760). Mahwah, NJ: Lawrence Erlbaum Associates.

Beilin, H., Klein, A., & Whitehurst, B. (1982). *Strategies and structures in understanding geometry.* New York: City University of New York. (ERIC Document Reproduction Service No. ED ED 225808)

Boulton-Lewis, G. M., Wilss, L. A., & Mutch, S. L. (1996). An analysis of young children's strategies and use of devices of length measurement. *Journal of Mathematical Behavior, 15,* 329–347.

Bowman, B. T., Donovan, M. S., & Burns, M S. (Eds.). (2001). *Eager to learn: Educating our preschoolers.* Washington, DC: National Academy Press.

Brown, M., Blondel, E., Simon, S., & Black, P. (1995). Progression in measuring. *Research Papers in Education, 10*(2), 143–170.

Carpenter, T. P., & Levi, L. (1999, April). *Developing conceptions of algebraic reasoning in the primary grades.* Paper presented at the meeting of the American Educational Research Association, Montreal, Canada.

Chittenden, E. (1991). Authentic assessment, evaluation and documentation of student performance. In V. Perrone (Ed.), *Expanding student assessment* (pp. 22–31). Alexandria, VA: Association for Supervision and Curriculum Development.

Chittenden, E. (1999). Science assessment in early childhood programs. In G. D. Nelson (Ed.), *Dialogue on early childhood science, mathematics, and technology education* (pp. 106–114). Washington, DC: American Association for the Advancement of Science.

Clements, D. H. (1984). Training effects on the development and generalization of Piagetian logical operations and knowledge of number. *Journal of Educational Psychology, 76,* 766–776.

Clements, D. H. (1999). Young children and technology. In G. D. Nelson (Ed.), *Dialogue on early childhood science, mathematics, and technology education* (pp. 92–105). Washington, DC: American Association for the Advancement of Science.

Clements, D. H. (2001). Mathematics in the preschool. *Teaching Children Mathematics, 7,* 270–275.

Clements, D. H. (2002). Linking research and curriculum development. In L. D. English (Ed.), *Handbook of international research in mathematics education* (pp. 599–630). Mahwah, NJ: Lawrence Erlbaum Associates.

Clements, D. H., & Battista, M. T. (2000). Designing effective software. In A. E. Kelly & R. A. Lesh (Eds.), *Handbook of research design in mathematics and science education* (pp. 761–776). Mahwah, NJ: Lawrence Erlbaum Associates.

Clements, D. H., & Sarama, J. (1999). *Preliminary report of building blocks—foundations for mathematical thinking, pre-kindergarten to grade 2: Research-based materials development (NSF Grant No. ESI-9730804).* Buffalo: State University of New York.

Clements, D. H., Swaminathan, S., Hannibal, M. A. Z., & Sarama, J. (1999). Young children's concepts of shape. *Journal for Research in Mathematics Education, 30,* 192–212.

Cooper, R. G., Jr. (1984). Early number development: Discovering number space with addition and subtraction. In C. Sophian (Ed.), *Origins of cognitive skills* (pp. 157–192). Mahwah, NJ: Lawrence Erlbaum Associates.

Copley, J. (1999). *The early childhood mathematics collaborative project: Year one.* Unpublished manuscript, University of Houston, Houston, TX.

Fennema, E. H., Carpenter, T. P., & Franke, M L. (1997). Cognitively guided instruction. In S. N. Friel & G. W. Bright (Eds.), *Reflecting on our work: NSF teacher enhancement in K–6 mathematics* (pp. 193–196). Lanham, MD: University Press of America.

Friel, S. N., & Curcio, F. R., & Bright, G. W (2001). Making sense of graphs: Critical factors influencing comprehension and instructional implications. *Journal for Research in Mathematics Education, 32,* 124–158.

Fuson, K. C. (1988). *Children's counting and concepts of number.* New York: Springer-Verlag.

Fuson, K. C., Carroll, W. M., & Drueck, J. V. (2000). Achievement results for second and third graders using the *Standards*-based curriculum. *Everyday Mathematics. Journal for Research in Mathematics, 31,* 277–295.

Fuson, K. C., Smith, S. T., & Lo Cicero, A. (1997). Supporting Latino first graders' ten-structured thinking in urban classrooms. *Journal for Research in Mathematics Education, 28,* 738–760.

Gagatsis, A., & Patronis, T. (1990). Using geometrical models in a process of reflective thinking in learning and teaching mathematics. *Educational Studies in Mathematics, 21,* 29–54.

Geary, D. C. (1994). *Children's mathematical development: Research and practical applications.* Washington, DC: American Psychological Association.

Geary, D. C., Bow-Thomas, C. C., Fan, L., & Siegler, R. S. (1993). Even before formal instruction, Chinese children outperform American children in mental addition. *Cognitive Development, 8,* 517–529.

Ginsburg, H. P., Choi, Y. E., Lopez, L. S., Netley, R., & Chi, C.-Y. (1997).Happy birthday to you: The early mathematical thinking of Asian, South American, and U.S. children. In T. Nunes, & P. Bryant (Eds.), *Learning and teaching mathematics: An international perspective* (pp. 163–207). East Sussex, England: Psychology Press.

Ginsburg, H. P., Inoue, N., & Seo, K.-H. (1999). Young children doing mathematics: Observations of everyday activities. In J. V. Copley (Ed.), *Mathematics in the early years* (pp.88–99). Reston, VA: National Council of Teachers of Mathematics.

Goodlad, J. I. (1984). *A place called school.* New York: McGraw-Hill.

Grant, S. G., Peterson, P. L., & Shojgreen-Downer, A. (1996). Learning to teach mathematics in the context of system reform. *American Educational Research Journal, 33*(2), 509–541.

Gravemeijer, K. P. E. (1999). How emergent models may foster the constitution of formal mathematics. *Mathematical Thinking and Learning, 1,* 155–177.

Griffin, S., & Case, R. (1997). Re-thinking the primary school math curriculum: An approach based on cognitive science. *Issue in Education, 3*(1), 1–49.

Griffin, S., Case, R., & Capodilupo, A., (1995). Teaching for understanding: The importance of the Central Conceptual Structures in the elementary mathematics curriculum. In A. McKeough, J. Lupart, & A. Marini (Eds.), *Teaching for transfer: Fostering generalization in learning* (pp. 121–151). Mahwah, NJ: Lawrence Erlbaum Associates.

Guskey, T. R., & Huberman, M. (Eds.). (1995). *Professional development in education: New paradigms and practices.* New York: Teachers College Press.

Haith, M. M., & Benson, J. B. (1998). Infant cognition. In W. Damon, D. Kuhn, & R. S. Siegler (Eds.), *Handbook of child psychology: Cognition, perception, and language* (5th ed., Vol. 2, pp. 199–254). New York: Wiley.

Hannibal, M. A. Z., & Clements, D. H. (2000). *Young children's understanding of basic geometric shapes.* Manuscript submitted for publication.

Heck, D. J., Weiss, I. R., Boyd, S., & Howard, M. (2002, April). *Lessons learned about planning and implementing statewide systemic initiatives in mathematics and science education.* Paper presented at the meeting of the American Educational Research Association, New Orleans, LA.

Hiebert, J. C. (1999). Relationships between research and the NCTM *Standards. Journal for Research in Mathematics Education, 30,* 3–19.

Holly, P. (1991). Action research: The missing link in the creation of schools as centers of inquiry. In A. Liberman & L. Miller (Eds.), *Staff development for education in the 90's: New demands, new realties, new perspectives* (pp. 133–157). New York: Teachers College Press.

Huttenlocher, J., & Newcombe, N. (1984). The child.s representation of information about location. In C. Sophian (Ed.), *The origin of cognitive skills* (pp. 81–111). Hillsdale, NJ: Lawrence Erlbaum Associates.

Jordan, N. C., Huttenlocher, J., & Levine, S. C. (1992). Differential calculation abilities in young children from middle- and low-income families. *Developmental Psychology, 28,* 644–653.

Kamii, C. K., & Housman, L. B. (1999). *Young children reinvent arithmetic: Implications of Piaget's theory* (2nd ed.). New York: Teachers College Press.

Kellman, P. J., & Banks, M. S. (1998). Infant visual perception. In W. Damon, D. Kuhn, & R. S. Siegler (Eds.), *Handbook of child psychology: Cognition, perception, and language* (5 ed., Vol. 2, pp. 103–146). New York: Wiley.

Kilpatrick, J., Swafford, J., & Findell, B. (2001). *Adding it up: Helping children learn mathematics.* Washington, DC: National Academy Press.

Kronholz, J. (2000, May 16). See Johnny jump! Hey, isn't it math he's really doing? *The Wall Street Journal,* pp. A1, A12.

Lehrer, R., Jenkins, M., & Osana, H. (1998). Longitudinal study of children's reasoning about space and geometry. In R. Lehrer & D. Chazan (Eds.), *Designing learning environments for developing understanding of geometry and space* (pp. 137–167). Mahwah, NJ: Lawrence Erlbaum Associates.

Lehrer, R., Osana, H., Jacobson, C., & Jenkins, M. (1993, April). *Children's conceptions of geometry in the primary grades.* Paper presented at the meeting of the American Educational Research Association, Atlanta, GA.

Ma, L. (1999). *Knowing and teaching elementary mathematics: Teachers' understanding of fundamental mathematics in China and the United States.* Mahwah, NJ: Lawrence Erlbaum Associates.

Malaguzzi, L. (1997). *Shoe and meter.* Reggio Emilia, Italy: Reggio Children.

McLaughlin, M. W. (1990). The Rand Change Agent study revisited: Macro perspectives and micro realities. *Educational Researcher,19*(9), 3.

Miller, K. F., Smith, C. M., Zhu, J., & Zhang, H. (1995). Preschool origins of cross-national differences in mathematical competence: The role of number-naming systems. *Psychological Science, 6,* 56–60.

Moll, L. C., Amanti, C., Neff, D., & Gonzalez, N. (1992). Funds of knowledge for teaching: Using a qualitative approach to connect homes and classrooms. *Theory Into Practice, 31,* 132–141.

Murphy, C. (1995). Whole-faculty study groups: Doing the seemingly undoable. *Journal of Staff Development, 16*(3), 37–44.

National Association for the Education of Young Children and the International Reading Association. (1998, July). Learning to read and write: Developmentally appropriate practices for young children. *Young Children*, pp. 30–46.

National Council of Teachers of Mathematics. (1989). *Curriculum and evaluation standards for school mathematics.* Reston, VA: Author.

National Council of Teachers of Mathematics. (2000). *Principles and standards for school mathematics.* Reston, VA: Author.

Papert, S. (1980). *Mindstorms: Children, computers, and powerful ideas.* New York: Basic Books.

Piaget, J., & Inhelder, B. (1967). *The child's conception of space* (F. J. L. J. L. Lunzer, Trans.). New York: Norton.

Piaget, J., Inhelder, B., & Szeminska, A. (1960). *The child's conception of geometry.* London: Routledge & Kegan Paul.

Piaget, J., & Szeminska, A. (1952). *The child's conception of number.* London: Routledge & Kegan Paul.

Presson, C. C., & Somerville, S. C. (1985). Beyond egocentrism: A new look at the beginnings of spatial representation. In H. M. Wellman (Ed.), *Children's searching: The development of search skill and spatial representation* (pp. 1–26). Mahwah, NJ: Lawrence Erlbaum Associates.

Russell, S. J. (1991). Counting noses and scary things: Children construct their ideas about data. In D. Vere-Jones (Ed.), *Proceedings of the Third International Conference on Teaching Statistics.* Voorburg, Netherlands: International Statistical Institute.

Saxe, G. B., Guberman, S. R., & Gearhart, M. (1987). Social processes in early number development. *Monographs of the Society for Research in Child Development, 52*(2, Serial No. 216).

Shipley, E. F., & Shepperson, B. (1990). Countable entities: Developmental changes. *Cognition, 34,* 109–136.

Showers, B., & Joyce, B. (1996). The evolution of peer coaching. *Educational Leadership, 53*(6), 12–16.

Simon, M. A. (1995). Reconstructing mathematics pedagogy from a constructivist perspective. *Journal for Research in Mathematics Education, 26*(2), 114–145.

Sparks, D., & Loucks-Horsley, S. (1989). Five models of staff development for teachers. *Journal of Staff Development, 10*(4), 40–45.

Starkey, P., & Klein, A. (1992). Economic and cultural influence on early mathematical development. In F. L. Parker, R. Robinson, S. Sombrano, C. Piotrowski, J. Hagen, S. Randoph, & A. Baker (Eds.), *New directions in child and family research: Shaping Head Start in the 90s* (pp. 4–40). New York: National Council of Jewish Women.

Starkey, P., Klein, A., Chang, I., Qi, D., Lijuan, P., & Yang, Z. (1999, April). *Environmental supports for young children's mathematical development in China and the United States.* Paper presented at the meeting of the Society for Research in Child Development, Albuquerque, NM.

Starkey, P., Spelke, E. S., & Gelman, R. (1990). Numerical abstraction by human infants. *Cognition, 36,* 97–128.

Steffe, L. P. (1992). Children's construction of meaning for arithmetical words: A curriculum problem. In D. Tirosh (Ed.), *Implicit and explicit knowledge: An educational approach* (pp. 131–168). Norwood, NJ: Ablex.

Steffe, L. P., & Cobb, P. (1988). *Construction of arithmetical meanings and strategies.* New York: Springer-Verlag.

Thompson, S. (2001). The authenic standards movement and its evil twin. *Phi Delta Kappan, 82,* 358–362.

Tibbals, C. (2000, May). *Standards for preschool and kindergarten mathematics education.* Paper presented at the meeting of the Conference on Standards for Preschool and Kindergarten Mathematics Education, Arlington, VA.

Weiss, I. R. (2002, April). *Systemic reform in mathematics education: What have we learned?* Paper presented at the meeting of the Research presession of the 80th annual meeting of the National Council of Teachers of Mathematics, Las Vegas, NV.

# II

## Elaboration of Major Themes and Recommendations

# Section 1

# Standards in Early Childhood Education

# 2

# Standards for Preschool and Kindergarten Mathematics Education

Sue Bredekamp
*Council for Professional Recognition*

The standards-based accountability movement that has dominated elementary and secondary education reform for the last decade has now reached preschool and kindergarten. The most obvious manifestation of this trend is the requirement for child-outcome-based accountability in the 1998 reauthorization of Head Start. Other evidence is readily available as increasing numbers of states develop guidelines for prekindergarten learning. Professional organizations are also extending their learning standards down to preschool, while technical reports such as the National Research Council's *Preventing Reading Difficulties in Young Children* include statements of literacy accomplishments for children, even below the age of 3 (Snow, Burns, & Griffin, 1998). In its revised standards, the National Council of Teachers of Mathematics (NCTM, 2000) for the first time includes prekindergarten mathematics standards.

This chapter addresses the advantages and disadvantages of such standards-based accountability strategies with very young children, and the particular implementation issues involved in the field of early childhood education.

# WHAT ARE THE DISADVANTAGES
# AND ADVANTAGES OF HAVING SPECIFIC
# MASTERY GOALS FOR YOUNG CHILDREN?

Historically, early childhood educators have been resistant to specifying learning goals for very young children for several reasons. Their frequently voiced concerns mirror the basic disadvantages of having specific mastery goals for young children's learning. A major concern has arisen from the fact that children develop and learn at individually different rates so that no one set of age-related goals can be applied to all children. A specific learning timeline may create inaccurate judgments and categorizations of individual children. Early childhood educators are wary that outcomes will not be sensitive to individual, cultural, and linguistic variation in young children. These concerns are not without basis in reality given that readiness testing for preschool and/or kindergarten entrance and exit are common, and negative consequences are more frequent for certain groups of children.

A second common concern has been that specifying learning outcomes would limit the curriculum to those outcomes and would also lead to inappropriate teaching of narrowly defined skills. This concern is similar to the "teach to the test" phenomenon that occurs with older children. It arises in early childhood education primarily because the field has a long, valued tradition of emergent curriculum and following individual children's interests and needs in teaching. A related concern is that the learning outcomes will be limited to a few academic areas without adequately addressing the development of the "whole child." Early childhood educators are especially concerned that the physical, social, emotional, and aesthetic dimensions will be neglected, and these are critical areas of development during the earliest years of life. Finally, a fundamental concern is that mastery goals set for young children will be developmentally inappropriate; that is, they will *not* be achievable as well as challenging for the majority of children within a given age range, nor will they be responsive to individual, cultural, and linguistic diversity.

Though all these potential disadvantages are real and warrant attention, each of them is based on the same assumption: that the mastery goals set will be the wrong goals. If this assumption could be confronted and changed, then many of the potential disadvantages could be turned into advantages.

Just as there are potential disadvantages, there are several potential advantages to specific mastery goals. First, teachers of young children need guidance about what are appropriate expectations for children's learning. When goals are achievable and challenging, that is, developmentally appropriate, they provide a valuable and useful framework for planning and implementing curriculum and individualizing teaching. A common criticism of early childhood programs is that the curriculum lacks depth and intellectual rigor (Bowman, Donovan, & Burns, 2001). Designing curriculum using agreed-upon, empirically based goals would undoubtedly raise the bar on the learning experiences and outcomes for children.

Precedents are now arising in several arenas of work in early childhood education. For example, the International Reading Association (IRA) and the National Association for the Education of Young Children (NAEYC) recently published a joint position statement on developmentally appropriate practices in early literacy (IRA & NAEYC, 1998; Neuman, Copple, & Bredekamp, 2000). In working on the position statement, we found that teachers welcomed more specific guidance on learning goals linked to age/grade levels. Such information not only helps guide planning and instruction, but also helps teachers identify children whose learning progress is outside the typical range.

The assumption that goals will be inappropriate or unachievable is unfair. As long as goals are developed drawing on research and the wisdom of practice, goals can be excellent contributions, as the NCTM standards have been. However, for specific mastery goals to truly be useful guides for teachers, they need to be more closely connected to age/grade levels than the NCTM standards have been. The NCTM (2000) standards list mathematics accomplishments that cover the broad range of prekindergarten through second grade and each section states: "all children should." This format makes sense when the emphasis is on indicating the full range of development and learning in a particular mathematics area. It also makes sense from the point of view of not wanting to put limits on children's learning nor on lowering our expectations for their achievement. These are very important considerations; however, for most teachers the more fundamental questions are what to teach and when to teach it. Teachers need a clearer picture of the overall developmental/learning continuum from which to assess children's learning. The NCTM standards do not intend that every prekindergartner "should" have mastered all the math content listed, and yet they could easily be interpreted that way. The intent of the standards needs to be as clear as possible. Providing guidance about appropriate mastery goals for children's learning is especially crucial in the area of mathematics where teachers' own knowledge of the discipline is usually inadequate to make these judgments.

## HOW DO STANDARDS TAKE
## INTO CONSIDERATION THE WIDE RANGE
## OF WHAT IS DEVELOPMENTALLY APPROPRIATE?

Any standards document must acknowledge at the outset that there is a wide range of individual variation, and there is a wide range of expectations that are well within the range of typical, that is, developmentally appropriate. Such statements commonly appear on most standards documents, but unfortunately, they are essentially ignored when standards are implemented in assessments or decisions about children. Therefore, a more useful strategy is to articulate goals/standards for young children as a developmental or learning continuum. Certain subject areas including language, literacy, and mathematics lend themselves more easily to such treatment.

The IRA/NAEYC (1998) position statement emphasized the concept of learning to read and write as a developmental continuum rather than an all-or-nothing phenomenon. The concept has been well accepted by early childhood educators as well as reading specialists. A comparable collaboration between experts in mathematics and early childhood would be a useful strategy to promote understanding. The emphasis should come from mathematics educators, however, because the message of individual variation may be more expected from early childhood educators and therefore, less influential.

## HOW DO WE IMPLEMENT SUCH STANDARDS CONSIDERING SUCH A WIDE RANGE OF ADULTS WHO CARE FOR CHILDREN, ESPECIALLY PRESCHOOL CHILDREN?

The biggest challenge to implementing any set of learning goals for very young children is the range of qualifications of the adults who teach them. Preschool-age children are served in a variety of settings including family child-care homes, child-care centers (which vary widely in quality), and public schools. (In addition, many children do not experience an out-of-home educational program.) The qualifications of workers in these settings range from a high school diploma (or less) in child-care centers to a CDA (child development associate) or associate degree in Head Start to a baccalaureate degree with a teaching certificate for public schools. Most state child-care licensing standards require very little preservice training. Texas, for example, requires eight clock hours! Therefore, the challenge of implementing early childhood curriculum reform and standards-based accountability is overwhelming. It is also important to point out that even among better educated teachers, very few have taken more than one course in mathematics and perhaps part of a course in math methods for young children.

The low qualifications of the early childhood workforce are directly linked to very low salaries which are, in turn, related to high rates of turnover in the field. To significantly raise educational qualifications of early childhood teachers, it will be necessary to raise compensation significantly. Setting high standards for children's learning will have little effect unless high standards are also set for teachers. However, we cannot wait until the intransigent problem of compensation is solved before we act to improve the quality of learning experiences and outcomes for young children.

In the meantime, the target for such standard-setting efforts such as that of NCTM needs to be teacher educators, curriculum developers, trainers, and others who influence the quality of practice in programs for children. For instance, Head Start has an entire infrastructure of training and technical assistance providers, most of whom are blissfully unaware of NCTM, not to mention new knowledge about mathematics learning in young children. Commercial developers continue to offer the same, shallow "mathematics" worksheets with numbers 1–10 and sell that as a math curriculum.

A concerted effort needs to be made to come to consensus among early childhood educators and mathematics educators about what the standards should be for preschool and kindergarten. Then an implementation plan is needed to move the standards into practice by reeducating teacher educators and making sure classroom teachers have the materials and knowledge they need to implement well-designed curricula. Math is one area of the early childhood curricula that if left to emerge is likely to be limited to passing out napkins and counting attendance.

## SHOULD WE HAVE STANDARDS FOR CHILDREN OR STANDARDS FOR PROGRAMS, OR BOTH?

Early childhood education has a history of program standards. These are usually licensing standards for child care, but the field also has more than 15 years experience with NAEYC accreditation criteria, and more recently family day-care accreditation by the National Association for Family Child Care (NAFCC). These systems set the parameters within which a program should operate. They do not specify any one curriculum, but they do have curriculum implementation standards. For the most part, such standards are based on research on the effects of various program components on outcomes for children. Recently such outcome research has focused more on child care and found that higher quality programs result in learning benefits into elementary school, including in mathematics (Cost, Quality, and Child Outcomes Study Team, 1999).

Given the diversity of regulators, funders, and auspices in the field of early childhood education, it remains necessary for the foreseeable future to establish program standards, at least in part because programs that meet such standards don't just protect children from harm but actually contribute to their development and learning. Program standards in early childhood provide the opportunity for adults to learn standards and, therefore, are essential to provide the context for child-outcome standards to be applied.

But we can no longer rely on program standards alone to ensure quality. We need to be sure that what we're doing with children is making a difference for them. We also need to test program standards against outcomes. Are children making expected progress? Are we accelerating learning progress for those children who come to preschool far behind the typical expectation for their peer group? To answer these questions, we must know what the expected standard is, we must know what to do to help children achieve it, and we must know how to assess what children have learned. So setting standards is only the first step. Connecting standards to curriculum, teaching, and assessment is essential if the standards are to be implemented.

The NCTM (2000) standards recognize these connections admirably and address them to a large extent, but not in the area of preschool. There is minimal attention to teaching the child below kindergarten and little clarity about what appropriate expectations should be. For the document to be really useful, it must take the next step and get even more specific. Admittedly, by doing so, other problems will arise, such as were referred to earlier under disadvantages. But if this work is done very carefully and followed up by training and technical assistance through early childhood networks, the results could be quite positive. We have already begun to see both positive and negative effects on the field of the new information coming out of the early literacy work. Compared to mathematics, language and literacy were well-explored areas of the early childhood curriculum. So the potential to create change is great. But the time is now, while there is still motivation and before the curriculum becomes totally consumed by reading.

## CONCLUSION

Perhaps, a bigger question than any of the four addressed here is how to distinguish between what children can learn and what they should learn. Standards should be research based and a growing body of research in early mathematics education demonstrates that we have greatly underestimated children's cognitive capacities (Bowman et al., 2001). For example, research demonstrates that children can learn numbers up to 100; but should every child in preschool be expected to know numbers to 100? Children tend to exhibit these competencies under particular conditions. How can those conditions be translated into the average preschool or kindergarten classroom? Any further work on setting more specific mathematics learning goals for preschool/kindergarten needs to pass the *can versus should* filter. The NCTM standards state "all children *should*" for each standard. If that's the verb, then we know how the standards will probably be used and should act accordingly.

## REFERENCECS

Bowman, B. T., Donovan, S., & Burns, S. (Eds.). (2000). *Eager to learn: Educating our preschoolers.* Washington, DC: National Academy Press.

Cost, Quality, and Child Outcomes Study Team. (1999). *Cost, quality, and child outcomes children go to school.* Chapel Hill, NC: Frank Porter Graham Publications.

International Reading Association & National Association for the Education of Young Children. (1998). *Learning to read and write: Developmentally appropriate practices for young children. Position statement.* Washington, DC: National Association for the Education of Young Children.

National Council of Teachers of Mathematics. (2000). *Principles and standards for school mathematics.* Reston, VA: Author.

Neuman, S., Copple, C., & Bredekamp, S. (2000). *Learning to read and write: Developmentally appropriate practices for young children.* Washington, DC: National Association for the Education of Young Children.

Snow, C., Burns, S., & Griffin, P. (1998). *Preventing reading difficulties in young children.* Washington, DC: National Academy Press.

# 3

# Mathematics Curriculum in the Early Childhood Context

Carol E. Copple
*National Association for the Education of Young Children*

As we turn our attention to math curriculum and an array of exciting experiments in curriculum development, we should pause a moment to consider the context—actually, the enormously varied contexts—within which children 5 and under spend their days.

## VARIATION IN CHILD-CARE SETTINGS

Education and care settings for children through age 5 are highly diverse. Of all children under 5 in the United States, almost a quarter are at home with a parent. Others are cared for by a relative (23%), family child-care provider (16%), or nanny/individual (6%). Finally, about a third of under-5 children—and nearly half of all 3- and 4-year-olds—are in some kind of center-based program.[1]

Dramatic differences exist in the training and skills of those who care for young children, even if only those caring for children in group settings are considered. In the early childhood workforce, teacher/caregiver backgrounds range from a bachelor's degree or beyond (31%) to a high school

---

[1] Jeffery Capizzano, Gina Adams, & Freya Sonenstein (2000). "Child Care Arrangements for Children Under Five: Variation Across States." Number B-7 of *New Federalism: National Survey of America's Families* series. Washington, DC: The Urban Institute.

diploma or less (24%).[2] This variegated picture of the contexts in which young children in the United States spend their time must be taken into account by curriculum developers and others seeking to shape young children's mathematical experiences. Such innovators should be asking themselves, for instance:

- Is this curriculum or resource accessible for caregivers or teachers with relatively little background in child development, early childhood education, and math? Can they understand and make effective use of it? If not, what experiences and resources will they need in order to do so?

- What can be done to bring aspects of this curriculum into the home and other informal settings? How can the value of mathematics in general—and this curriculum approach in specific—be communicated to parents and other lay persons? Are there some simple things families can do with their children to enhance the impact of the curriculum?

## COMMON FEATURES OF THE EARLY CHILDHOOD CONTEXT

In the majority of programs, even across the quite varied landscape of early childhood care and education, certain practices are likely to be found. Although varying from program to program and teacher to teacher, these practices are far more typical in settings for children up through age 5 than they are in classrooms for elementary and higher grades. Each of the following practices—and the overall context they create for children—is relevant in developing effective curriculum design and implementation:

- Throughout much of the day children are free to move about the room and go to any of the learning centers or activity areas—blocks, dramatic play, and so on. As they do so, **children manipulate a wide variety of things,** including materials in mass (e.g., sand, rice, water); discrete objects that may be sorted, classified, arranged in patterns, and counted; and materials/activities in which shapes are salient (puzzles, tangrams, and the like). Teachers generally provide **opportunities for children to "mess about"** with materials and processes—allowing time to explore and experiment—especially when things are first introduced.

---

[2]Whitebook, M., Howes, C., & Phillips, D. (1998). *Worthy Work, Unlivable Wages: The National Child Care Staffing Study, 1988–1997.* Washington, DC: Center for the Child Care Workforce; Current Population Surveys (1995), Bureau of Labor Statistics, U.S. Department of Labor.

**However,** teachers need more knowledge of the kinds of materials and experiences that would be most valuable for children for mathematical learning.

- As children **pursue their own interests and investigations** in art, construction, dramatic play, sand and water play, and other activities, many teachers (with varying levels of skill) look for opportunities to help them extend and elaborate their pursuits. Early childhood teachers tend to talk and **interact with children** individually and in small and large groups, typically conversing *with* them rather than "lecturing." They **ask open-ended questions and make comments** in order to get children to notice, think, and express their ideas. **However,** because many teachers are not proficient in following up on initial questions or remarks, their questions often make little impact on children's thinking and construction of knowledge. Sustained interactions relating to math ideas are scarce indeed.

- Most early childhood teachers do not divide the day by subject or discipline (math, science, language and literacy, etc.). Rather, they plan an **integrated curriculum,** often organizing classroom activity around a theme, unit, or project in the course of which children will use and learn in all or most of the learning domains. **However,** integrated curriculum has risks as well as strengths. The mathematics that comes up in a given project or unit—for example, children ringing up groceries on a cash register—may be very superficial or so far from where the children are in their math understanding that they get almost nothing mathematical from the experience. Many teachers say that "math is everywhere" in their classroom and curriculum, yet little of it registers with children because teachers lack developmental knowledge of children's math learning.

- Children are continually **interacting with one another;** as they engage in cooperative play they communicate, negotiate, debate, and work together to achieve joint purposes. Too often, **however,** the learning environment and experiences are not designed to spark mathematical conversations and investigations; when these do occur, teachers rarely follow up on children's comments and actions to deepen and extend their awareness of the mathematics:

- Teachers or caregivers have **closer contact with families,** and parents tend to feel more at home with them, than is the case with teachers in higher grades. **However,** the vast potential afforded by this rapport and daily communication is too rarely put to use by involving parents in promoting children's learning and development at home, or even sharing with them much about what the child is learning and doing in the program, in mathematics, for instance. As for promoting children's enthusiastic engagement with math, parents are almost never used as a resource.

In sum, there are a number of ways in which early childhood programs are well suited to children's math learning. Children are not sitting passively; they are actively involved with materials, and they are talking with one another and with teachers. All this is good, but it is not enough to ensure children's acquisition of mathematical knowledge and concepts. Much of the potential offered by the early childhood context with respect to mathematics learning is not being fully realized.

## WHAT DO EARLY CHILDHOOD TEACHERS NEED FROM US?

Staff working in early childhood settings need extensive training, sometimes even in the rudiments of safety and caring for children, not to mention the fostering of children's learning. As we work to improve the quality of math curriculum and instruction in the early years, we need to remember that this is the reality: There are hundreds of thousands of virtually untrained early childhood workers, along with hosts of teachers with basic early childhood training but little if any preparation relating to math teaching and learning.

For the least trained personnel, it will be well to focus on a few core messages. In the reading area, by analogy, a simple but powerful message is "Read to children every day." We need to think about what such simple and potent messages or practices might be for math.

Another fruitful direction of exploration is developing or identifying materials—from simple toys and games to software—that take children into interesting mathematical avenues without sophisticated teachers on the spot (Nelson, 1999). Unquestionably, teachers' knowledge and skill are vital to educational effectiveness. But as programs work to improve the mathematics curriculum, teachers will have their own learning curve. In the meantime, good materials add to teachers' learning as well as children's by giving them excellent opportunities to observe what children do and understand.

As for published curriculum resources, they certainly have a role to play in improving early childhood mathematics. When knowledgeable experts develop and extensively field-test a curriculum, they are providing a resource that few teachers could develop on their own. Yet without a degree of professional development for teachers, most curricula will fall far short of achieving their goals. We need to think a lot more about this problem.

Practically all teachers need to know more about mathematics—the nature of the beast—and how to work with children in math. They need to know much more about what math young children are interested in and capable of doing; many vastly underestimate the range of young children's interests and the extent of their capabilities. Other chapters in this volume address the critical issues of professional development for early childhood teachers, to improve their own understanding and their knowledge of how to further children's mathematical knowledge and understanding.

For our part, we should not underestimate early childhood teachers. When they have this awareness and knowledge about mathematics and the rich potentials for early math learning, a great many will think of wonderful ways to "mathematize" their classroom and curriculum.

## REFERENCES

Nelson, G. (1999). Within easy reach: Using a shelf-based curriculum to increase the range of mathematical concepts accessible to young children. In J. V. Copley (Ed.), *Mathematics in the early years* (pp. 135–145). Reston, VA, and Washington, DC: National Council of Teachers of Mathematics and the National Association for the Education of Young Children.

# Section 2

# Math Standards and Guidelines

# What is Developmentally Appropriate in Early Childhood Mathematics Education? Lessons from New Research

Kyoung-Hye Seo
*Ewha University, Seoul, Korea*

Herbert P. Ginsburg
*Teachers College, Columbia University*

What is developmentally appropriate for early mathematics education? On the one hand, we want to help children get ready for school and succeed there. We know that children—especially low-income, minority children—often have difficulty with school mathematics and science, usually beginning around the third grade. Perhaps intensive early mathematics education can provide the "basics" that can help prepare them to achieve at an acceptable level. At the same time, we do not wish to pressure young children, to subject them to harsh forms of instruction, and to impose on them material they are not ready to learn. We do not want a "push-down curriculum" forcing young children to engage in developmentally inappropriate forms of written drill and practice in mathematics.

Our desire to prepare children for school success (and to avoid school failure) thus clashes with our reluctance to impose inappropriate forms of teaching on young children. This conflict then raises several basic questions: Are there approaches to early mathematics instruction that are developmentally appropriate for young children and that can help prepare

91

them for school? Can these approaches be both enjoyable and effective for *all* children—including low-income minority children?

We believe that in order to determine what is developmentally appropriate for early mathematics education, early childhood educators need to begin with a deeper understanding of children's mathematical interests, motivations, and competence. Our recent research illuminates these issues (Ginsburg, Inoue, & Seo, 1999). We observed young children's everyday activities and attempted to learn about their spontaneous mathematical interests and questions. We studied children from several income and ethnic groups. This research on young children's everyday mathematical activities provides useful information about what might be developmentally appropriate in early mathematics education.

Several basic questions framed our research:

- How often do young children engage in mathematical activities during their free play?

- In what kinds of mathematical activities do young children spontaneously engage during their free play?

- Does the everyday mathematics of low-income African-American and Latino children differ from that of middle-income African-American and Latino children and from that of White upper-income children?

## METHOD

The participants were 90 4- and 5-year-old children drawn from five schools (see Table 4.1). Of the 90 children, 30 were from low-income families (mean age = 4.92). The low-income group consisted of 18 African Americans and 12 Latinos, 17 boys and 13 girls. The second group included 30 children from middle-income families (mean age = 4.86). The middle-income group consisted of 13 African Americans, 13 Latinos, and 4 Whites; there were 16 boys and 14 girls. The last group consisted of 30 White children from upper-income families (mean age = 4.98). The upper-income group consisted of 16 boys and 14 girls. The groups were unevenly distributed by ethnicity. Such is social reality in this country.

We began by observing these 90 children during their free play, one at a time. We then introduced the video camera and cordless microphone to their classrooms. After familiarizing the children with us and with the video equipment, we videotaped the target child's play for 15 minutes without interruption. A total of 90 15-minute episodes of children's free play was collected.

To analyze children's everyday mathematical activities, mathematical content codes were developed. The codes were developed inductively. Instead of imposing conceptual categories derived from the literature, we attempted to draw analytic constructs from our pilot data, explored many

TABLE 4.1

*Participants in the Study*

| Categories | Centers | A | B | C | D | E | Total |
|---|---|---|---|---|---|---|---|
| Income Level | Low Income | 9 | 14 | 7 | 0 | 0 | 30 |
| | Middle Income | 4 | 7 | 0 | 19 | 0 | 30 |
| | Upper Income | 0 | 0 | 0 | 0 | 30 | 30 |
| Ethnic | African-Americans | 9 | 11 | 4 | 7 | 0 | 31 |
| | Latinos | 3 | 10 | 3 | 9 | 0 | 25 |
| | Whites | 1 | 0 | 0 | 3 | 30 | 34 |
| Gender | Boys | 10 | 12 | 4 | 7 | 16 | 49 |
| | Girls | 3 | 9 | 3 | 12 | 14 | 41 |
| Total | | 13 | 21 | 7 | 19 | 30 | 99 |

possible explanatory categories, and looked for the best of several alternative accounts. Progressively newer analytic schemes emerged as we went through lengthy and repetitive processes of coding, revision, and recoding. The mathematical content codes involve the following categories:

- Classification: Systematic arrangement in groups according to established criteria.
- Magnitude: Statement of magnitude or comparison of two or more items to evaluate relative magnitude.
- Enumeration: Numerical judgment or quantification.
- Dynamics: Exploration of the process of change or transformation.
- Pattern and Shape: Exploration of patterns and spatial forms.
- Spatial Relations: Exploration of positions, directions, and distances in space.

*Classification* involves sorting, grouping, or categorizing activities. For example, Anna takes out all the plastic bugs from the container, places them on a table, and sorts them by types and then by colors. In the block area, Aaron cleans up the blocks on the rug. He picks out one block at a time and puts it into one of the boxes that contains the same size and shape of blocks.

*Magnitude* involves activities such as describing the global magnitude of the objects, making direct or side-by-side comparison of objects, or making magnitude judgments with or without quantification. For example, Briana brings a newspaper and puts it on an art table. Amy says to her, "This isn't big enough to cover the table." Abdul and Michael build structures with Legos. Abdul says to Michael, "Look at mine. Mine is big!" Michael says, "Mine is bigger!" They place their Lego structures side by side and compare whose is taller.

*Enumeration* activity involves saying number words, counting, subitizing, or reading or writing numbers. For example, Kasheef takes out all the beads in a box and puts them on a table. He says to Britney, "Look! I got 100!" He starts counting them as if to find out if he really has 100 beads. He picks the beads out one by one and counts out loud, "one, two, three...." Britney joins in counting and they manage to count up to 100, with only a few errors. At another table, three girls draw the pictures of their families. They talk about how many brothers and sisters they have and how old their siblings are.

*Dynamics* involves activities such as putting things together, taking them away or apart, or exploring motions like flipping or rotations. For example, Jessica and three girls play with play-dough at a table. She presses her dough with her hand, stretches it, and makes a flat circular shape. She then cuts it in half with a stick and cuts each half again in half. She says, "I made a pizza for all of us."

*Pattern and Shape* activities involve identifying or creating patterns or shapes, or exploring geometric properties and relationships. For example, Jennie makes a bead necklace, putting plastic beads into a string one by one. She uses only yellow and red beads for her necklace and makes a yellow-red color pattern. Jose plays with wooden blocks. He puts a double-unit block on the rug, two unit blocks on the double-unit block, and a triangle unit on the middle of two unit blocks. He builds a symmetrical structure with rectangular and triangular prisms.

Finally, *Spatial Relations* involves activities such as telling a location or direction, or representing a location in three-dimensional space or on paper. For example, Cory comes to Alex who is playing with a button puzzle and asks him where he found it. "There," Cory says, pointing to a storage unit in the block area. Alex goes to the storage unit and asks him again, "Where?" Cory replies, "Second ones ... right side, no, the left side." Teresa and Katie rearrange the furniture in a dollhouse. When Teresa puts a couch beside a window, Katie moves it to the center of the living room, saying, "The couch should be in front of the TV."

In coding the videotaped data, we divided each child's 15-minute-long episode into 1-minute segments. We watched a minute-long segment and then coded it in terms of the occurrence and the type of mathematical activity (whether the target child engaged in mathematical activity and if so, what kind of mathematical activity the child engaged in). Pairs of independent judges coded the 15-minute-long episodes of 30 children and achieved satisfactory agreement in coding (89% perfect agreement for mathematical content).

## RESULTS

### Frequency of Everyday Mathematics

How often do young children engage in mathematical activities in everyday settings? When children play, they do not appear to be doing mathematics. But our results show otherwise. We found that 79 children out of 90 (88%) engaged in at least one mathematical activity during their play. We also examined the average percentage of minutes (recall that each of the 90 children was taped for 15 minutes) in which mathematical activity occurred. The result showed that children exhibited at least one mathematical activity during an average of 43% of the minutes (about 7 of the 15 minutes). The result shows that young children engage in a considerable amount of mathematical activity during their free play.

We then considered income-level differences (Fig. 4.1). Statistical analyses showed that income level was not related to overall frequency of mathemati-

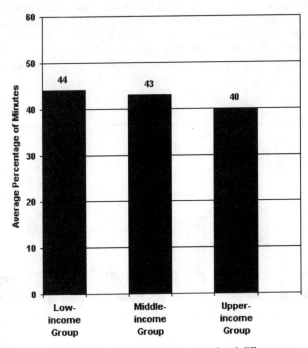

FIG. 4.1.   Frequency of mathematical activity: income-level differences.

cal activity. Low- and middle-income children showed virtually identical average percentages of minutes spent in mathematical activity (43.8% and 43.2%, respectively) and upper-income children slightly less (39.8%).

We also examined gender differences. Statistical analysis showed that gender was not associated with overall frequency of mathematical activity. Boys and girls engaged in similar amounts of mathematical activity, (41.3% and 43.5%, respectively, were the average percentages of minutes of mathematical activity).

## Relative Frequency of Different Types of Mathematical Activity

We were also interested in how frequently different types of mathematical activity occurred. We examined the average percentage of minutes during which a particular category of mathematical activity occurred within a 15-minute episode. The results showed that the most frequently occurring mathematical activity was Pattern and Shape (21%), and then Magnitude (13%), Enumeration (12%), Dynamics (5%), Spatial Relations (4%), and Classification (2%) (see Fig. 4.2).

Age was related to the overall frequency of mathematical activity. Older children engaged in more mathematical activity than younger. Consider next whether and how age was related to specific types of mathematical activity. Statistical analyses showed that two of the three most frequent categories of mathematical activity, Pattern and Shape and Enumeration, were related to age, whereas other categories of mathematical activity were not. Older children in this study dealt with patterns and shapes and enumerated to a slightly greater extent than did younger children.

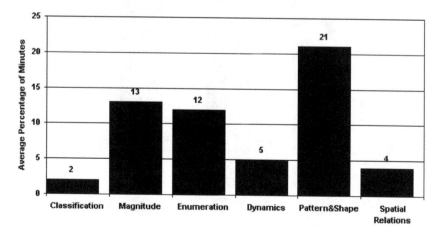

FIG. 4.2.   Relative frequency of six types of mathematical activity: average percentage of minutes within a 15-minute episode.

What about income-level differences in specific types of mathematical activity? As shown in Fig. 4.3, the relative frequency of different types of mathematical activity was very similar across income groups. In all three groups, Pattern and Shape, Magnitude, and Enumeration were the most frequent types of mathematical activity. Statistical analyses showed that there was no relation between income level and any of the categories of mathematical activity with the exception of Spatial Relations, which middle- and upper-income children engaged in to a small extent and low-income children almost not at all. But this result should be evaluated with caution because the frequency of Spatial Relations was very small (4% overall).

We also examined gender differences in specific types of mathematical activity. The relative frequency of different types of mathematical activity was similar across gender (see Fig. 4.4). Statistical analyses showed that boys and girls did not differ in specific types of mathematical activity except for Spatial Relations, where boys exhibited 7% on the average percentage of minutes and girls 1%. Again, the results should be treated with caution because the frequency of Spatial Relations was so low.

In brief, our findings revealed that the frequency of overall mathematical activity and the relative frequency of different types of mathematical activity were related to age, but not to income level and gender. Older children engaged in mathematical activity more often than did younger children, particularly in Enumeration and Pattern and Shape. But different in-

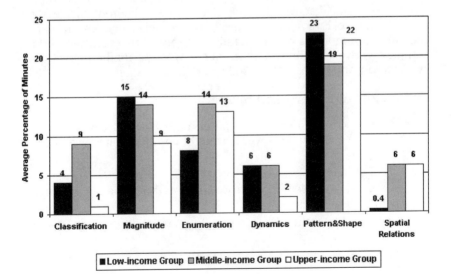

FIG. 4.3. Relative frequency of six types of mathematical activity: income-level differences in the average percentage of minutes.

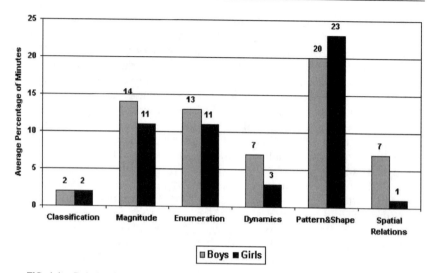

FIG. 4.4.    Relative frequency of six types of mathematical activity: gender differences.

come-level groups and also boys and girls did not differ in their everyday mathematical activities.

However, these results do not capture possible differences in complexity of mathematical activity. It is possible that two children engage in the same amounts of Enumeration activity, or any other categories, and yet engage in different levels of Enumeration activity. Thus, we examined the complexity levels of three most frequent types of mathematical activity—Patterns and Shapes, Magnitude, and Enumeration.

## Complexity of Pattern and Shape

Consider first the most frequent type of mathematical activity, Patterns and Shapes. We examined several levels of complexity involving Pattern and Shape:

- Level I—Figure Identification: Beth names the shapes as she plays with pattern blocks.
- Level II—Patterning: Horace makes a line of alternating red and blue blocks.
- Level III—Symmetry: Anna builds a simple block tower like the letter U.
- Level IV—Shape Matching: Jose combines two triangles and makes a rhombus. He then changes the position of one of the triangle, adds another triangle, and makes a trapezoid.

First, we examined the relative frequency of four levels of Patterns and Shapes (Fig. 4.5). The most frequently occurring level of Pattern and Shape activity was Level I, Figure Identification (47%), and then Level III (22%), Level II (17%), and Level IV (14%). In other words, about 50% of the children's Pattern and Shape activities involved recognizing, sorting, or naming shapes.

Secondly, income-level differences in the complexity of Pattern and Shape were examined in all 39 children who engaged in Pattern and Shape activity. In all three groups, Level I Figure Identification was most frequent. Statistical analysis indicated a lack of income-level differences in frequency of Level I activity. However, the three groups exhibited some differences in Level III Symmetry activity. Whereas Type III was the second most frequent one in low- and middle-income groups (35% and 25%, respectively), it was the least frequent type in the upper-income group (9%). Because the number of cases was insufficient, no statistical analysis was conducted to examine the differences in Level III activity.

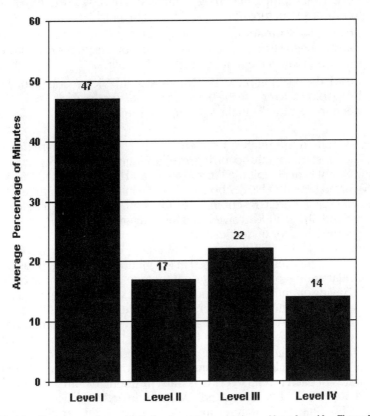

FIG. 4.5.   Frequency of complexity levels: pattern and shape. Note: Level I = Figure Identification; Level II = Patterning; Level III = Symmetry; Level IV = Shape Matching.

Finally, gender differences were examined. Again, Level I was most frequent in both groups, amounting to 56% of boys' and 37% of girls' Pattern and Shape activity. Statistical analysis indicated a lack of gender differences in frequency of Level I activity. Level III Symmetry, however, presented some differences. Though it was the second most frequent type in girls' Pattern and Shape activity (32%), it was the least frequent one in boys' (13%). Because of insufficient number of cases, no statistical analysis was conducted to further examine the differences in Level III activity.

## Complexity of Magnitude

We also examined the complexity of children's Magnitude activities:

- Level I—Saying Quantity or Magnitude Words: Emily says, "Oh, this is really big."
- Level II—Empirical Matching: John places his Lego structure next to Aaron's structure and says, "Mine is bigger."
- Level III—Estimation without Quantification: John looks at Aaron's Lego structure, adds more Lego pieces to his own structure, and makes it equal in height to Aaron's.
- Level IV—Estimation with Quantification: Victor and Paul lay down blocks to create the base of a house. Victor says to Paul, "We need three more" blocks to complete the base.

We examined the relative frequency of four levels of Magnitude (Fig. 4.6). The most frequently occurring level of Magnitude activity was Level I, Saying Quantity or Magnitude Words (49%), and then Level III (24%), Level II (15%), and Level IV (11%). About half of the children's Magnitude activity involved saying words describing the global quantity or magnitude of the objects; and about 30% involved making magnitude judgements without direct comparison or quantification.

Then, income-level differences in complexity of Magnitude were examined in all 55 children who engaged in Magnitude. All three groups exhibited similar scores on the average percentage of minutes of each level. Level I, Saying quantity or magnitude words, was most frequent in all three groups, 44% (low-income children), 53% (middle-income children), and 51% (upper-income children). Statistical analyses showed that income level was not associated with the frequency of Level I, Saying quantity or magnitude words, and Level III, Estimation without quantification.

Finally, boys and girls showed similar scores on the average percentage of minutes of each level. Level I was most frequent in both groups and involved about half of boys' and girl's Magnitude activity (45% and 52%, respectively). Statistical analyses indicated a lack of gender differences in the frequency of Level I activity.

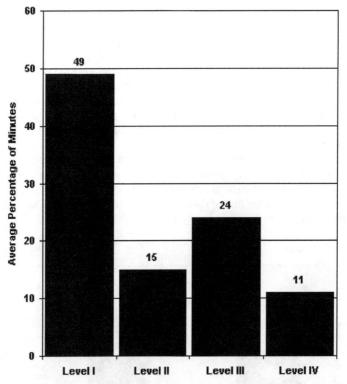

FIG. 4.6. Frequency of complexity levels: magnitude. Note: Level I = Saying Quantity or Magnitude Words; Level II = Empirical Matching; Level III = Estimation without Quantification; Level IV = Estimation with Quantification.

## Complexity of Enumeration

We also examined complexity levels for Enumeration:

- Level I—Saying Number Words: Ann says, "I'm 5 years old."
- Level II—Counting: Laura counts some chips, tagging each of them, "One, two, three, four, five." She says, "I got five."
- Level III—Subitizing/Estimation: Subitizing involves immediately seeing that a set has a particular number, without overt counting. Jack looks at the puzzle pieces on the table and quickly says, "I got five." Zoe estimates, "I think there are about seven there."
- Level IV—Reading/Writing Numbers: Lucy points to the numbers on the calendar and reads them out loud to her friend.

The most frequently occurring level of Enumeration activity was Level III, Subitizing/Estimation (39%), and then Level I (38%), Level II (13%), and Level IV (10%). Children's Enumeration activity involved for the most part subitizing, estimation, and saying number words (Fig. 4.7).

Income-level differences in complexity of Enumeration were examined in all 49 children who engaged in Enumeration. In all three groups, Level I, Saying number words, and III, Subitizing/estimation, were prevalent, amounting to 70% to 80% of their Enumeration activity. Statistical analyses showed that income level was not related to the frequency of Levels I and III Enumeration activity.

Boys and girls also showed similar scores on the average percentage of minutes of each level. In both groups, Levels I and III were more prevalent than Levels II and IV. Statistical analyses indicated a lack of significant differences between boys and girls in the frequency of Level I and Level III Enumeration activity.

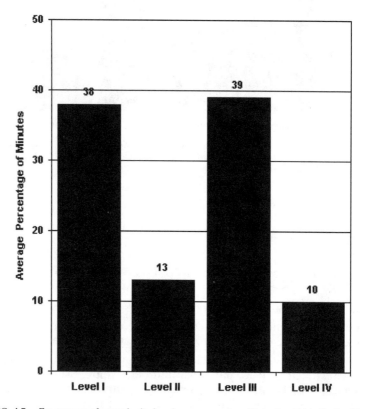

FIG. 4.7.   Frequency of complexity levels: enumeration. Note: Level I = Saying Number Words; Level II = Counting; Level III = Subitizing/Estimation; Level IV = Reading/Writing Numbers.

In brief, we find a lack of income-level and gender differences in the complexity of three most frequent types of mathematical activity, Pattern and Shape, Magnitude, and Enumeration.

## CONCLUSIONS

Our findings show that preschool and kindergarten children engage in a significant amount of mathematical activity during free play. Young children's everyday mathematics involves various types of mathematical activity. Children often explore patterns and shapes, compare magnitudes, and enumerate. Less frequently, they explore dynamic changes, classify, and examine spatial relations. We also find a lack of income-level and gender differences in the frequency of overall mathematical activity, the relative frequency of different types of mathematical activity, and the complexity of specific mathematical activities such as Pattern and Shape, Magnitude, and Enumeration. The bottom line is that preschool and kindergarten children's mathematics is more advanced and powerful than is often realized, and that children from different income-level groups display similar amounts, patterns, and complexities of mathematical behavior.

### What are the Implications of This for Educational Practice and Policy?

Most important, educators should revise views about what is developmentally appropriate. They should create State standards and policies that serve to engage preschool and kindergarten children in challenging and exciting mathematics programs. These can use children's spontaneous interests as a starting point, and help them—with what we call "artful guidance" (see Greenes, 2000)—to learn about patterns and shapes, about numbers and their transformations, about symmetries, and about mathematical relations.

Educators should not limit early mathematics to play alone. Yes, children do learn from play, but it appears that they can learn much more with artful guidance and challenging activities provided by their teachers. At the same time, educators should remember that children deserve more than mindless drill sheets or workbook pages. They need to engage in diverse and challenging mathematical activities.

Educators should institute challenging and exciting mathematics programs for *all* children—not only the privileged. Low-income minority children can profit greatly from programs like these.

Finally, the field of early childhood should support programs of professional development that will help teachers to implement new programs in mathematics. Teachers of young children need to learn new forms of pedagogy, new mathematical content, and new psychological insights. Consequently, it is necessary to help teachers to learn how to implement new mathematics programs. Teachers need to learn the necessary mathematics if they don't know it already. Teachers also need assistance in understanding the mental lives and learning potential of young children—including poor, minority children.

## ACKNOWLEDGMENTS

This research was supported by a generous grant from the Spencer Foundation (199800041).

## REFERENCES

Ginsburg, H. P., Inoue, N., & Seo, K. H. (1999). Preschoolers doing mathematics: Observations of everyday activities. In J. Copley (Ed.), *Mathematics in the early years* (pp. 88–99). Reston, VA: National Council of Teachers of Mathematics.

Greenes, C. (2000, May). *Mathematics curricula for young children: Panel discussion.* Presented at the Conference on Standards for Preschool and Kindergarten Mathematics Education, National Science Foundation, Arlington, VA.

# 5

# Pre-K to Grade 2 Goals and Standards: Achieving 21st-Century Mastery for All

Karen C. Fuson
*Northwestern University*

Nationwide tests and international comparisons have repeatedly indicated that many students in the United States are falling short of the mathematical proficiency required for the 21st century (National Research Council, 2001). Robust mathematical learning by all young children is a necessary base for later learning and is necessary to keep children from falling permanently behind in mathematics. To accomplish such early mastery by all, we must restructure the goals, standards, instruction, and assessments for Pre-K through Grade 2 mathematics. This chapter summarizes central issues involved in doing this so that we can attain mastery by all children at the end of Grade 2.

This chapter is drawn from the extensive research literature, from my service on the National Academy of Sciences National Research Council committee on mathematics learning, and from my curricular research experience during 10 years in urban and suburban classrooms designing and revising a research-based world-class mastery curriculum for kindergarten through Grade 5. More detailed discussion of the research literature in this domain can be found in Fuson (1992a, 1992b, 2003) and in *Adding It Up* (National Research Council, 2001). Examples and discussion of teaching can be found in Fuson, Lo Cicero et al. (1997), Fuson et al. (2000), Lo Cicero, De La Cruz, and Fuson (1999), and Lo Cicero, Fuson, and Allexaht-Snider (1999).

The research evidence suggests that it is possible for all children to leave Grade 2 with higher levels of understanding and skill than even children in affluent areas presently demonstrate. It is vital that we increase the mastery by all through Grade 2 because at present many children leave Grade 2 already so far behind that it is difficult to catch up. Some of these children are in every school, but disproportionate numbers of such children are in schools of poverty. Changing the present situation will enable our country to have many more students successful at upper grades because they will have a strong foundation in the early grades.

This paper is divided into three major parts. Part A focuses on curricular and testing issues. It identifies two central issues: organizing the U.S. mathematics curriculum into big coherent conceptual chunks and relating these to mastery standards-based testing rather than to standardized testing. Part B overviews research concerning teaching for mastery by all. Part C provides design principles, outlines curricular conceptual chunks, and proposes mastery goals and process standards for a mastery curriculum that can support mastery teaching for all.

The research overviewed in Part B focuses on the domains of number systems (number words and written numbers), addition and subtraction situations, and algebraic problem solving. These are the core topics of prekindergarten through Grade 2. The goals and standards proposed in Part C do include geometry, measure, and graphing data. The balance among these various topics is discussed in Part C.

## PART A: CURRICULAR AND TESTING ISSUES
## THAT CAN FACILITATE ACHIEVING MASTERY FOR ALL

### The Need to Focus on Big Coherent
### Conceptual Grade-Level Chunks

Several current aspects of U.S. mathematics education coalesce to require that U.S. mathematics curricula become reorganized into big coherent conceptual grade-level chunks that are related over grade levels.

We first need to acknowledge that the goal of mastery for all, even in the area of computational fluency, has been an elusive goal at least since the 1950s. It is not the case that the United States has had a successful computational curriculum that is now at risk of being thrown over by "math reform." National reports, national research studies, and international studies have for decades identified many aspects of computation in which results were disappointing. These results were sometimes overshadowed by even worse results for problem solving or applications of calculations, making calculation seem less of an issue than it has consistently been. Many of the calls for math reform focused on understanding have been at least partially focused on teaching for understanding as a way to eliminate computational errors and thus increase computational performances. For example, on standardized tests national Grade 2 norms for two-digit subtraction requiring borrowing (e.g., 62 − 48) are 38% correct. Many children subtract the smaller from the larger number in each column to get 26 as the answer to 62 − 48. This top-from-bottom error is largely eliminated when children learn to subtract with understanding (e.g., Fuson & Briars, 1990; Fuson, Wearne et al., 1997; Hiebert et al., 1997). Building on a foundation of understanding can help all students achieve computational fluency.

***Problems With Present U.S. Math Curricula.***    In comparisons with the curricula of countries achieving well on international comparisons, the U.S. curriculum has been characterized as "underachieving" and as "a mile wide and an inch deep" (McKnight et al., 1989; McKnight & Schmidt, 1998; Peak, 1996). Successful countries select vital grade-level topics and devote enough time so that students can gain initial understandings and mastery of those topics. They do not engage in repetitive review of those topics in the next year; they move on to new topics. In the United States no teacher and no grade level is responsible for a given topic. Topics such as multidigit computations are distributed over several years, doing one digit larger each year. Large amounts of time are devoted at the beginning of each year and of each new topic to teach what was not learned or was learned incorrectly in the year before.

This wastes huge amounts of learning time and bores the students who have mastered concepts. It is also counterproductive because it is much easier to help students build initial correct computational methods than to correct errors. For example, second graders using base-10 blocks for initial learning of multidigit addition and subtraction explained answers and achieved high levels of accuracy that were maintained over time (Fuson, 1986a; Fuson & Briars, 1990). This is in contrast to the usual national performance of second graders at only 38% correct on two-digit subtraction involving regrouping. Older students who had been making subtraction errors for years did learn in one session with base-10 blocks to correct their errors, but many later fell back to their old errors (Resnick & Omanson, 1987). Carefully designed practice, help during learning, and other aspects described later are important for computational fluency. But the most crucial necessity at this point is helping students learn in a timely fashion one correct generalizable method that they understand. Such initial learning must be deep and accurate. Only with understanding can interference from later similar notations and methods be reduced.

Most people think that we do not have a national curriculum in the United States. At one level this is true—each of the 50 states has its own grade-level math learning goals, and each district within a state may (and usually does) further specify goals. These goals vary hugely across different states. Furthermore, the National Council of Teachers of Mathematics (NCTM) Standards (2000) also is not a national curriculum. It specifies only loosely defined topics within wide grade bands and articulates perspectives of balancing across mathematical topics and across goals such as problem solving, communication, and computational fluency.

However, we do have a functional national curriculum, at least at the Kindergarten to Grade 8 level. That curriculum is the topics that are in each grade in the major commercial textbooks published by the for-profit sector. An examination across these textbooks reveals remarkable similarity. This similarity results from the necessity to sell textbooks across all of the different states, with their differing state goals. Even if a company focuses on the most populous states, where it is possible to sell the most textbooks, the total topics across these states results in a large list of topics for the grade level. Even though the books are large, the number of topics means that few days can be allocated to each topic. There is not time to develop understanding deeply. Because most teachers use a commercial for-profit textbook, most students experience these cursory treatments of most topics.

Furthermore, this national curriculum is heavily influenced by large states that require textbooks to go through an approval process to appear on a state-approved list. Some of the largest of these states have large numbers of non-English-speaking students and students living in poverty. This results in reducing expectations of reading and complexity because of low expectations about what is possible for such students to learn.

There are no requirements that commercial textbooks have data about the success of their programs. Because of the rapidly changing nature of state goals, textbook companies are under difficult time lines to produce learning materials. They cannot produce thoughtful materials or try out their materials in classrooms. Furthermore, recent takeovers of many textbook companies and present economic conditions result in much textbook writing being done by short-term writers or development houses rather than by experienced in-house writers, further reducing coherence of the learning materials. Finally, the physical appearance and the availability of many peripheral materials are often the bases of a choice of a textbook rather than the quality of the learning experiences it provides. Art is often used to entertain and is irrelevant rather than being used to convey mathematical ideas.

***Equity Issues.*** Research indicates that children from diverse backgrounds can learn mathematics if it is organized into big coherent chunks (Kameenui & Carnine, 1998) and if children have opportunity and time to understand each domain deeply. A three-phase model (Dixon et al., 1998) can enable students to learn deeply over a sustained period in one domain. Children from diverse backgrounds can learn mathematics. But they need sustained and supported learning time in connected areas.

***New Learning Goals for the 21st Century.***    Technology and the information age have created new learning goals for mathematics all over the world. Now adults in many situations must understand computational methods and be able to use them in a range of situations rather than just get correct answers.

These new learning goals are accessible to high-poverty classrooms as well as to more affluent classrooms. Knapp and associates (Knapp, 1995; Zucker, 1995) found that successful teachers in high-poverty classrooms supported conceptual understanding by focusing students on alternative solution methods (not just on answers), elicited thinking and discussion about solution methods, used multiple representations and real-life situations to facilitate meaning making, and modeled ways to probe meaning of mathematical problems or methods. We used similar approaches to obtain above-grade-level understanding with multidigit computation in high-poverty Latino classrooms (Fuson, Smith, & Lo Cicero, 1997).

***Organizing U.S Curricula Into Big Coherent Conceptual Chunks.***    There is sufficient research information in many areas about what is accessible to students, especially at the Pre-K to Grade 2 levels, to outline ambitious but attainable mastery goals for all children at each of these levels. Mastery goals focus on the most appropriate and most central concepts and skills for these grade levels. They could result in mastery for all children that is beyond the present levels of achievement in schools with few students living in poverty. If states would work together to agree on some core of goals (say 80% of the goals for each level), then several different high-quality programs could be developed to focus on these goals. States could vary the remaining 20% of goals if agreement could not be reached beyond the 80%. Such research-based ambitious goals would provide all states with a solid foundation of successful children at the lower grades who would not be permanently out of the mathematics-learning pipeline.

These mastery goals would be grade-level specific, not by grade band (e.g., Grades 3–5). Grade-band goals such as used by NCTM and by states can lead to excessive review and non-mastery at any grade level because the grade-band specification is taken to mean "do at each Grade 3, 4, and 5" rather than to mean "do well somewhere within the three Grades 3, 4, and 5."

These goals would also not limit what children would or could learn. They would simply be the baseline goals for which schools would be held accountable. Research indicates that U.S. children can learn more than they do at present. Increasing learning in the early grades will make it easier to be more ambitious at the upper grades where U.S. students are considerably behind.

# PART B: RESEARCH CONCERNING TEACHING
# FOR MASTERY BY ALL

## Achieving Mastery for All: The Necessity to Move From "Standardized" to Mastery Testing

U.S. children's learning has a scattershot "mile wide inch deep" nature for another reason. Many school districts give standardized norm-referenced tests to assess how students are achieving. Many people think that a "standardized" test is curriculum-fair, reflects important learning goals in a balanced way, and assesses what students know about the content for that grade level. Most standardized tests have none of these characteristics. Profit-making companies develop them with no oversight concerning what items they test. Different tests vary considerably in the topics they cover and in the proportion of topics at each grade level.

The goal of standardized tests is to determine which half of the students are above average and which half are below average (and which schools and districts are above average or below average). To rank order students in this way, many items must be difficult or complex. They must use difficult vocabulary or have 2 steps or have difficult formats or be complex in other ways. Otherwise most students would get them right, and the tests could not scale students.

Standardized tests are secret. Teachers, parents, and students are not allowed to know what is on the test. This is supposedly to keep the test "objective." But in mathematics, it is easy to make parallel items that are similar. The secrecy really just results in standardized tests not being curriculum-fair. Teachers do not even know what to teach, so students may fail items because they did not have an opportunity to learn those items.

All of these aspects of standardized tests render it difficult to prepare for them sensibly. Frenzied test-preparation time reviewing and practicing many different topics further reduces the chance for sustained learning time on central topics, which could enable students to answer questions that are complex rather than simple.

A further problematic aspect of standardized tests is the nature and timing of their results. They do not give sufficient information about performance on particular items so that those can be remediated for individual students (or such information is expensive). Results often are not returned until the following year or at the very end of the school year, so results cannot be used for instruction for the class in general or for specific students.

Many states have begun to shift to mastery testing—testing for specified mastery topics that all students should master. This type of testing is more appropriate. But the number and types of items must be sensible and not overwhelming. Also, these are usually given at Grade 3 at the earliest, where many children may already be too far behind. Districts meanwhile often continue to use at many grade levels standardized tests that have all of the problems described earlier. The combination of standardized tests and state mastery tests is overwhelming for teachers, who must prepare for two kinds of high-stakes tests about which they necessarily have inadequate information.

Research-based grade-level tests that were public would enable a whole community to work together to help all children in a school achieve mastery of those goals. In the early years, such tests would need to include some interview components because much early mathematical competence depends on counting skills and on whether children understand and can explain their methods. Periodic mastery testing throughout the year, including some interviewing, would enable teachers to use the testing information for instruction and to obtain extra help for those students who need it. The money now used for standardized testing could be used to organize such extra helping for students in various ways, including family out reach programs to help families learn how to help their children in mathematics.

Mastery for all will require additional learning time for some children who enter preschool or kindergarten with less mathematical experience than other children. There are many ways in which such extra learning time might be organized. It might even take as much time as an extra year in the earliest grades for some children who enter way behind and have no prekindergarten experience. In Russia, this is acknowledged by organizing some schools and some classes within schools to take 4 years to do the content of the first 3 years of school. Children learn the same content—they just have more time to do so. This is in contrast to the United States, where we often pass children with weak backgrounds along and do not allow them to learn the same content as children who enter with stronger backgrounds. They get a "dumbed down" curriculum.

We must not confuse educatedness (present school-relevant knowledge) with educatability (how much a child can learn). At present we often confound these by lowering the goals for those who enter with less school knowledge (low educatedness) by assuming that they are less educatable. Mastery rather than standardized testing, extra help and learning time for those who need it, high ambitious goals for all, reorganized curricula, and teaching as discussed later can greatly increase the amount of mathematics learned by all U.S. children.

## Instruction That Facilitates Mastery by All

*Helpful Instructional Phases.*    What features of classrooms can contribute to mastery by all? A recent review of the literature summarizes the many studies that found an experimental instructional method superior to a traditional control method (Dixon et al., 1998). The less-effective traditional methods involved two phases: a teacher presentation of some topic (with students observing passively) followed by independent student practice of that topic, with or without teacher monitoring, giving feedback, and so on.

Superior learning was achieved by effective methods that had three phases. In the initial *orienting phase,* teachers initially involved students in the introduction of the topic through explanations, questions, and discussion: Students were *active learners* whose *initial knowledge* about a domain was *elicited.* In the second *supporting learning* phase, students were helped *during a long period* to move from teacher-regulated to self-regulated solving. Teachers structured a significant period of help that was gradually phased out. This helping was accomplished in different ways: by scaffolded problems and visual or other supports, by peers, and by the teacher or aides. During this sustained helping period, students received feedback on their performance, got corrective help so that they did not practice errors, and received (and often gave) explanations. The third phase of effective instruction focused on *long-term remembering.* This involved a brief assessment of students' ability to apply knowledge to untaught problems *(near transfer)* in which students worked independently. Such assessments were then followed by help in seeing how the untaught problems were like the earlier problems so that transfer could occur meaningfully. This third phase of long-term remembering—practicing taught and untaught problems—needs to be distributed over time. Such distributed practice has been found to facilitate remembering in a wide range of studies, as has experiencing similar but related problems and situations. Only a couple such problems are necessary, so remembering work can involve a mixture of different kinds of problems.

Many textbooks now provide ideas to teachers about the orienting phase; they describe introductory activities or manipulatives to help the concepts become meaningful. The crucial aspect of this phase, however, is that the teacher help the new concepts become related to the knowledge of the particular learners in that classroom. Textbooks seldom help teachers structure the long second phase of supporting learning. Pictures, quantity drawings, or manipulatives may be used initially for one or two pages, but they are dropped much too quickly. This second long phase also requires more active helping than the teacher walking around helping individuals as they solve problems.

One easy way to structure such a supported learning phase is using a solve-and-explain blackboard structure. We use this structure frequently in my project classrooms. The teacher sends as many students as possible to the board to solve a given problem while the rest of the class solves that problem at their seats. Early in a given domain students make math drawings to show the quantities in their problem as well as showing numerical solutions. The teacher can watch student problem solving much better when it is on the board than at the seat, and students at the board often interact and help each other. Different solution methods are visible on the board in the drawings and in the numerical methods. The teacher then asks two (or three) students to explain their solution. These students are chosen because explaining their methods will be helpful to the class at that point in learning. Problems with typical errors may be chosen to illuminate and correct those errors in a supportive climate. Classmates listen carefully to the explanations and ask questions to clarify their own understandings and to improve the specificity of (help edit) the explanation. Students can follow the discussion even with weak language skills because the drawings and numerical solutions are visible and are pointed to during the explanations. This process greatly improves communication skills of all kinds. Building such a classroom structure takes initial teacher modeling of explaining and of questioning, developing a helping classroom community, and practice over time for students to improve in explaining and questioning. Early on, the teacher must move to the side or back of the classroom and "bite her tongue" to facilitate direct student-to-student talk. We have found that teachers can build such a classroom even for first graders and for children from any background. Teachers become amazed at the solution methods their children develop and explain.

Other relevant results from the studies reviewed in Dixon et al. (1998) were that instruction on learning particular mathematical strategies was superior to not giving such instruction, working fewer problems in depth was more effective than working more problems quickly, writing as well as solving problems was helpful, and solving concept examples sequenced to facilitate generalization and discrimination was helpful.

The implications of all of these results are that all students had sustained supported time to learn a given domain deeply and accurately. Such deep sustained accurate learning over time is necessary for complex domains requiring multistep solution methods. Students need to learn the central principles of a domain (e.g., in multidigit addition and subtraction, that you add or subtract like multiunits), learn the overall shape of a given method, learn in detail the steps of the method, and weave this developing knowledge together so that it operates fluidly and accurately. This is true whether the students invent the method or learn it from other students or from the teacher. Practice was important, but effective practice was supported by monitoring and help focused on doing and on understanding. In contrast, "drill and practice" frequently carries the connotation of rote practice, has little sense of monitoring or feedback, and no sense of helping or of visual, conceptual, psychological, or motivational support for learning throughout the practicing phase.

A textbook issue that at present interferes with the more effective three-phase method (and interferes with effective teacher presentation of topics even in the less-effective two-phase traditional approach) is the common misuse of art (i.e., photographs, drawings, cartoons, etc.) in U.S. math textbooks. In many other countries the art is designed to support conceptual thinking. In the United States, art frequently distracts from conceptual understanding because it is irrelevant or overwhelmingly busy. All visual aspects of learning materials need to support learning, not interfere with it.

***Helping Diverse Learners.***    A related review of literature concerning school success of diverse learners (Kameenui & Carnine, 1998) identified six crucial aspects of successful teaching and of learning materials for diverse learners: structuring around big ideas, teaching conspicuous strategies, priming (e.g., eliciting or stimulating) background knowledge, using mediated scaffolding (e.g., peer tutoring, giving feedback about thinking, providing visual supports that provide cues for correct methods), using strategic integration (integration into complex applications to provide distributed practice in more complex situations), and designing judicious review. Diverse learners are those who may experience difficulties in learning because of low-income backgrounds, speaking English as a second language (or not at all), or other background reasons.

The first of these six crucial aspects for diverse learners, structuring around big ideas, has been discussed previously. The next three—teaching conspicuous strategies, stimulating background knowledge, and using mediated scaffolding (specific helpful supports)—are crucial in the initial active learning phase and in the helping phase in the three-phase effective teaching model outlined earlier. The final two crucial aspects—using strategic integration and designing judicious review—follow deep and effective initial learning in a domain. Strategic integration of various computational methods into moderately complex problems increases problem-solving competence by increasing the range of situations in which students use that computational method. It also provides for practice that is effective because it is distributed over time.

Judicious review is defined as being plentiful, distributed, cumulative, and appropriately varied. It follows initial deep learning. Distributed and monitored practice requires working one or two examples occasionally, with immediate help for wrong answers. This is important even after successful meaningful learning because the nonsupportive or misleading mathematical words or notations in many domains continually suggest wrong methods (e.g., aligning a one-digit and a two-digit number on the left because you write from left to right). Furthermore, many computational domains are similar, and learning new domains creates interference with old domains (e.g., you do *multiply* the tops and bottoms of fractions but you do not add or subtract them if the bottoms are different). Therefore, after deep and successful initial learning, distributed practice of a couple of problems of a given kind can check whether errors are creeping in. Frequently, helping students correct their methods is as simple as suggesting they remember their original supports. For example, as some errors crept into multidigit methods learned with base-10 blocks, asking students to "think about the blocks" was sufficient for them to self-correct their errors in subtracting with zeroes in the top number (Fuson, 1986a).

The research of Knapp and associates (Knapp, 1995; Zucker, 1995) on attributes of successful high-poverty classrooms underscores these results. They found that a balance between conceptual understanding and skill practice resulted in higher computational and problem-solving results by lower achieving and higher achieving students.

*Individual Differences.* As in other subject-matter areas, substantial social-class and ethnicity differences exist in mathematics achievement (e.g., Ginsburg & Russell, 1981; Secada, 1992). Kerkman and Siegler (1993) found that low-income children had less practice in solving problems and they executed strategies less well. Strategy instruction and monitored practice were therefore recommended for such students. Individual differences as early as first grade cut across gender and income levels to differentiate children into what Siegler (1988) termed good students, not-so-good students, and perfectionists. Roughly half of the not-so-good students went on to be identified as having mathematical disabilities by fourth grade versus none of the other groups. On single-digit addition tasks, these students were characterized by use of more primitive methods and by more production of errors on problems on which they could have used (but did not use) more accurate but effortful strategies (e.g., counting with their fingers). These students were producing incorrect answers more often, thereby creating responses that competed with their experiences of correct answers. Perfectionists and good students had similar positive long-term outcomes, but the perfectionists were much more likely to use slower and effortful methods even on simpler problems than were the good students.

These results emphasize that methods of practice should facilitate individuals in understanding their own growth and progress rather than comparing individuals. Practice should also be varied so that sometimes speed is important but, at other times, use of the practiced method in a complex situation is important. An overemphasis on either could lead to rigidity rather than computational fluency. Not-so-good students need help to learn and use more accurate strategies.

There has been less work on mathematics disability than on reading disability, especially with younger children. Different kinds of mathematics disability have been identified. Geary's (1994) review identifies four types and recommends different kinds of learning supports for each kind. His results and recommendations are quite consistent with the research described earlier. They emphasize using visual conceptual supports with extra conceptual cues, teaching more-advanced solution methods, drawing the problem situation, and using accessible algorithms that are easy to learn conceptually and carry out procedurally.

Students with semantic memory disabilities have difficulty with verbal, and especially phonetic, memory but many have normal visuo-spatial skills. These students have great difficulty memorizing basic computations because these rely on a phonetic code. Therefore instructional supports that use visual rather than phonetic cues and teaching strategies for basic calculations are recommended for these students.

Students with procedural deficits use less-advanced methods than their peers. Though many eventually catch up, this long period of using primitive methods may be detrimental. Such children do not seem to invent more-advanced methods as readily as do their peers. Therefore, conceptually based strategy instruction that helps them use and understand more-advanced strategies such as counting on can be helpful.

Students with visuo-spatial disabilities have difficulties with concepts that use spatial representations, such as place value. Research is not clear about the developmental prognosis of such children, but suggested methods of remediation are to support visual processing with extra cues. Because distinguishing left–right directionality is a special problem with such students, the accessible methods described later in this chapter that can be carried out in either direction might be especially helpful for such students.

Difficulties with mathematical problem solving that go beyond arithmetic deficits also characterize some students. Supports for problem solving such as drawing the problem situation are suggested as useful for these students. Technology may also help provide complex problem-solving situations that are nevertheless accessible to students with math disabilities (Goldman, Hasselbring, & the Cognition and Technology Group at Vanderbilt, 1997).

## Achieving Both Sense-Making and Computational Fluency

### *Real-World Situations, Problem Solving, and Computation Need to Be Continually Intertwined.*   Traditionally in the United States, computation of whole numbers has been taught first, and then problems using that kind of computation have been presented as applications. This approach has several problems. First, less-advanced students sometimes never reached the application phase, limiting greatly their learning. Second, word problems are usually put at the end of each computational chapter, so sensible students never read the problems: They just do the operation practiced in that chapter. This, plus the focus on teaching students to focus on key words in problems rather than building a complete mental model of the problem situation, leads to poor problem solving by students because they never learn to read and model the problems themselves. Third, seeing problem situations only after learning computations does not enable the meanings in the problem situations to become linked to those computations. This limits the meaningfulness of the computations and the ability of children to use the computations in a variety of situations.

Research has indicated that beginning with problem situations yields higher problem-solving competence and equal or better computational competence. Children who start with problem situations directly model solutions to these problems. They later move on to more advanced mathematical approaches as they move through levels of solutions and of problem difficulty. Thus, the development of computational fluency and problem solving is intertwined when both are codeveloping with understanding.

Problem situations can also provide vital kinds of numerical experiences. We identify later four kinds of core arithmetical real-world situations. In each of these, children can learn mathematical language involved in that kind of situation (e.g., "altogether," "the rest," "less than"), and they can learn central numerical operations to use with numbers (e.g., decomposing, counting on, grouping).

Research for many years has contrasted conceptual and procedural aspects of learning mathematics. Which should come first has been debated for a long time. The current state of the research presents a much more complex relationship between conceptual and procedural aspects than one preceding the other. Rather, they are continually intertwined and facilitating each other. As a given child comes to understand more, the given method becomes more integrated within itself and in relation to other methods. As a method becomes more automatic, reflection about some aspect may become more possible, leading to new understanding. These conceptual and procedural intertwinings take place within individuals in individual ways. It may not even be useful to distinguish between these two aspects because doing and understanding are always intertwined in complex ways.

Furthermore, different researchers may refer to the same method as a procedure or as a concept, depending on whether the focus is on carrying out the method or on its conceptual underpinnings. And, in a given classroom at a given time, some students may be carrying out what looks like the same method, but they may well have different amounts of understanding of that method at that time. This is what the helping aspects of classroom teaching is all about—helping everyone to relate their methods to their knowledge in ways that give them fluency and flexibility.

### *The Importance of Children Experiencing the Range of Real-World Addition and Subtraction Situations to Build Meanings for Addition and Subtraction Operations.*

Researchers around the world have identified three main types of real-world addition and subtraction situations. Each type involves three different quantities (a total and two addends), and each of these quantities can be unknown. Learning to solve all of these problem variations by focusing on the problem meaning and modeling it, and eventually writing an algebraic equation with an unknown, provides vital experience in rich algebraic problem solving that can prepare all children for algebra. Research indicates that almost all of these problems are accessible to Grade 1 children and all can be mastered by Grade 2 children. However, typically in U.S. textbooks, only the simplest variation of each problem type has been included, those that most children can already solve in kindergarten. In contrast, in the texts of the former Soviet Union, problems were given equally across the various types and unknowns, and 40% of first-grade problems and 60% of second-grade problems were two-step problems (Stigler, Fuson, Ham, & Kim, 1986).

One type of addition and subtraction situation is what mathematicians call a binary operation situation: You have two groups of objects and you want to put them together (Put Together) or you have one group of objects and you want to take them apart (Break Apart) to make two groups. This type is sometimes called Combine; it may or may not have any physical action in it. For example, you may have four dogs and three cats and ask how many animals there are.

The second type is what mathematicians call a unary operation: You have one group of objects (an initial state) and you want to add a group of objects to it (Add To) or you want to take a group of objects away from it (Take Away). These problems are sometimes called Change problems because there is an initial state, a change (plus or minus), and a resulting state. Solutions to these change problems undergo abbreviation over time that creates more-advanced methods (these are discussed in a later section).

The third type compares two groups of objects to find out how much more (Compare More) or how much less (Compare Less) one group has than the other. There are many ways to ask the comparing sentence, and most ways have a pair of sentences that reverse the direction of comparison. This type is particularly difficult for young children for three reasons. First, the quantity more or less is not actually physically there in the situation. Second, the language is complex for children. Third, it is difficult to understand the direction of a given comparison.

There are also several different types of multiplication and division real-world situations. Some of these are accessible to children as young as kindergarten or even Pre-K if the language is simple, the numbers are small, and objects are available to model the problem. Equal-partitioning situations seem to be particularly easy. These give rise to multiplication (e.g., two groups of three), measurement division (e.g., six total partitioned into groups of three), and fraction division (e.g., six total partitioned into two equal groups).

Such situations in the form of word problems and real situations brought into the classroom by students can provide contexts within which operations of addition, subtraction, multiplication, and division can come to take on their whole range of required mathematical meanings. These real-world meanings can be acted out, modeled with objects, and drawn with simplified math drawings. Students can tell and write as well as read and solve problems. Rich language use by retelling a story in your own words can build listening, vocabulary, and comprehension skills. Children in bilingual or ESL classes can learn mathematics in these ways. Preschool children can solve and tell simple stories. Older children gradually come to represent and solve stories using larger numbers and more-advanced representations such as math drawings that show quantities but not the actual things in the situation, equations, and numerical solution methods.

There is an important distinction between a situation representation (an equation or a drawing) and a solution representation. The most powerful problem-solving approach is to understand the situation deeply—draw it or otherwise represent it to oneself. This is the natural method used by young students. But textbooks, and teachers under their influence, push students to write solution representations that are not consistent with their view of the situation. Students will write $8 + = 14$ for a problem like "Erica had \$8. She babysat last night and now has \$14. How much did she earn babysitting?" Textbooks often push students to write $14 - 8 =$ , but this is not how most students will represent or solve that problem. Allowing students to represent the situation in their own way communicates that the goal of problem solving is to understand the problem deeply. With this view, students can experience success and move on to more difficult problems throughout their school and out-of-school life.

### Using in Classrooms the Research on Learning Progressions, Multiple Solution Methods, and Advantages and Disadvantages of Different Algorithms.

Over the past 30 years, there has been a huge amount of research all over the world concerning children's solution methods in single-digit and multidigit addition and subtraction. This research indicates that we need to change substantially our present classroom teaching and learning practices in these areas. For Pre-K through Grade 2 children, most classrooms usually contain children who solve a given kind of problem in different ways, and most children have more than one available method for some kinds of problems. This is quite a different picture from the usual vision of mathematics problems as having one kind of solution that must be taught by the textbook and by the teacher and then learned and used by all children. This does not say that children learn methods in an experiential vacuum. Their experiences are vital, and teachers and classroom experiences are central to enabling children to learn various methods.

Within each computational domain, individual learners move through progressions of methods from initial transparent, problem-modeling, concretely represented methods to less transparent, more problem-independent, mathematically sophisticated and symbolic methods. At a given moment, each learner knows and uses a range of methods that may vary by the numbers in the problem, by the problem situation, and by other individual and classroom variables. A learner may use different methods even on similar problems, and any new method competes for a long time with older methods and may not be used consistently. Typical errors can be identified for each domain and for many methods. Ways to help students overcome these errors have been designed and studied. Detailed understandings of methods in each domain enable us to identify prerequisite competencies that can be developed in learners to make those methods accessible to all learners.

The constant cycles of mathematical doings and knowings in a given domain lead to learners' construction of representational tools that are used mentally for finding solutions in that domain. For example, the counting word list initially is just a list of words used to find how many objects there are in a given group. Children use that list many times for counting, adding, and subtracting. Gradually, the list itself becomes a mathematical object. The words themselves become objects that are counted, added, and subtracted; other objects are not necessary. For students who have opportunities to learn with understanding, the written place-value notation can become a representational tool for multidigit calculations as the digits in various positions are decomposed or composed.

Learners invent varying methods regardless of whether their classrooms have been focused on teaching for understanding or on rote memorizing of a particular method. However, a wider range of effective methods is developed in classrooms teaching for understanding. In classrooms in which teachers help students move through progressions to more-advanced methods, children are more advanced. In rote classrooms, incomplete or little understanding is frequent. But students do reflect on patterns they abstract from the rotely learned methods, and different students make different kinds of errors carrying out partially correct methods. Thus, even in traditional classrooms focused on memorizing standard computational methods, learners are not passive absorbers of knowledge. They build and use their own meanings and doings, and they generalize and reorganize these meanings and doings.

Because most people in the United States were taught only one method to do multidigit addition, subtraction, multiplication, and division, they think that there is only one way to do each of these (the way they were taught). These methods are called algorithms—a general multistep procedure that will produce an answer for a given class of problems. Computers use many different algorithms to solve different kinds of problems. Inventing new algorithms for new kinds of problems is an increasingly important area of applied mathematics. Throughout history and at the present time around the world, many different algorithms have been invented and taught for multidigit addition, subtraction, multiplication, and division. Different algorithms have been taught at different times in U.S. schools. Many immigrant children are taught one method at school and a different method at home, and children who immigrate are often forced to learn a new method that interferes with the old method they learned originally. This is difficult for them and is unnecessary.

Each algorithm has advantages and disadvantages. Therefore, part of the decision making around mastery for all concerns which algorithms might be supported in classrooms and the bases for selecting those algorithms. Research has now identified some accessible algorithms that are easier for children to understand and to carry out than the algorithms usually taught at present in the United States. These are described in a later section and more fully in Fuson (2003), Fuson and Burghardt (in press), and Fuson, Wearne et al. (1997).

## Single-Digit Addition and Subtraction: Much More Than "Learning the Facts"

Learning single-digit addition and subtraction has for much of this century been characterized in the United States as "learning math facts." The predominant learning theory was of these facts as rote paired-associate learning in which each pair of numbers was a stimulus (e.g., 7 + 6) and the answer (13) needed to be memorized as the response to this stimulus. "Memorizing the math facts" has been a central focus of the mathematics curriculum, and many pages of textbooks presented these stimuli to which children were to respond with their "memorized" response.

This view of how children learn basic single-digit computations was invalidated by one line of research earlier this century (by Brownell, 1987) and by much research from all over the world during the last 30 years. We now have robust knowledge of how children in many countries actually learn single-digit addition and subtraction.

The unitary progression of methods used all over the world by children stems from the sequential nature of the list of number words. This list is first used as a counting tool, and then it becomes a representational tool in which the number words themselves are the objects that are counted (Bergeron & Herscovics, 1990; Fuson, 1986b; Steffe, Cobb, & von Glasersfeld, 1998). Counting becomes abbreviated and rapid. Children begin to count on in addition situations (e.g., solve 8 + 6 by counting "8, 9, 10, 11, 12, 13, 14" rather than counting from 1 to 14). They also begin to count up to solve subtraction situations, which is much easier and much more accurate than is counting down, which is subject to errors. So to solve 14 – 8, they think, "8 have been taken away, so 9, 10, 11, 12, 13, 14, that is 6 more left." Children use this same strategy to solve unknown addend situations (8 + ? = 14). Some (or in some settings, many) children later go on to chunk numbers using thinking strategies, These chunkings turn additions children do not know into additions they do know. Some of these use doubles (e.g., I know 6 + 6 = 12, so 6 + 7 is 1 more than 12, which is 13), and some use 10 (e.g., I know 8 + 2 = 10, so 8 + 6 is 4 more than 10, so 14). Of course, all during this learning progression, children also learn some additions and subtractions automatically, especially for smaller numbers.

During this progression, which may last into third or even into fourth or fifth grade for some children (because they are not helped through the progression), individual children use a range of different methods on different problems. Learning-disabled children and others having difficulty with math do not use methods that differ from this progression. They are just slower than others in this progression (Geary, 1994; Ginsburg & Allardice, 1984; Goldman, Pellegrino, & Mertz, 1988; Kerkman & Siegler, 1993).

Most of these methods are not ordinarily taught in the United States or in many other countries. However, when these more-advanced methods are not supported in the classroom, several years separates the earliest and latest users of advanced methods. In contrast, helping children progress through methods can lead all first graders to methods efficient enough to use for all of later multidigit calculation. Counting on can be made conceptually accessible to first graders; it makes rapid and accurate addition of all single-digit numbers possible. Single-digit subtraction is usually more difficult than is addition for U.S. children, primarily because children model taking away by inventing counting-down methods, which are difficult and error-prone. Children can easily learn to think of subtraction as counting up to the known total if they think of (or draw) taking away the first objects, e.g., $8 - 5$ is : ⊙⊙⊙⊙⊙ o o o "I've taken away 5 so 3 more to make 8: "6, 7, 8." Teachers in many other countries help students see that subtraction can be solved by forward counting and adding methods. Such methods make subtraction as easy as, or easier than, addition. But at present, counting up to solve subtraction rarely appears in U.S. textbooks.

Children's tools for beginning understandings of addition and subtraction are the counting word list ("one, two, three, four, etc."), the ability to count objects, some indicating act (e.g., pointing, moving objects) tying words said and objects counted together (one at a time), and the count-cardinal knowledge that the last count word said tells how many objects there are in all. These tools are learned in the preschool years by many but not all children in the United States. Focused help in pre-K and in kindergarten with all of this prerequisite knowledge could help all children come to mastery more rapidly. With these tools, addition can be done orally using concrete situations comprehensible to young learners. They count out objects for the first addend, count out objects for the second addend, and then count all of the objects (count all). This general counting-all method then becomes abbreviated, interiorized, chunked, and abstracted, as discussed earlier.

The widely reported superiority of East Asian students over U.S. students in the early grades does not result from a focus on rote memorized addition and subtraction "facts." It results from systematic visual and oral work that provides the underpinnings for strategies that are then explicitly taught. East Asian students, as well as students in many other parts of the world, are taught a general thinking strategy: making a 10 by giving some from one addend to the other addend. This method is facilitated by the number words in some countries (e.g., China, Japan, Korea, and Taiwan): 10, 11, 12, 13, and so on, are said as "Ten, ten one, ten two, ten three, and so on."

Many of these children also learn numbers and addition using a 10-frame: an arrangement of small circles into two rows of five. This pattern emphasizes 6, 7, 8, and 9 as $5 + 1$, $5 + 2$, $5 + 3$, and $5 + 4$. Work with this visual pattern enables many children to "see" these small additions under 10 using a five-pattern. For example, some Japanese and Chinese adults report adding $6 + 3$ by thinking/seeing $(5 \text{ and } 1) + 3 = 5 \text{ and } 4 = 9$. This reduction of $6 + 3$ to $5 + 1 + 3 = 5 + 4 = 9$ is done rapidly and without effort, as automatically as is recall. The 10-frame is also used to teach the "make a 10" method. For example, for $8 + 6$, 8 has 2 missing in the 10-frame, so $8 + 6$ requires 2 from the 6 to fill the 10-frame, leaving 4 to make $10 + 4 = 14$. By the end of first grade, most children in these countries rapidly use these 5-patterns or 10-patterns mentally to add and subtract single-digit numbers. The "make a 10" method is also taught in some European countries.

There are three prerequisites that children must learn in order to use the "make a 10" method effectively. They must know what number makes 10 with each number (e.g., $10 = 8 + 2$ or $6 + 4$ or $7 + 3$), be able to break apart any number into any of its two addends (to make ten and the rest over ten), and know $10 + n$ (e.g., $10 + 5 = 15$). In countries that teach the "make a 10" method, these prerequisites are developed before the "make a 10" method is introduced. Children age 4 and 5 in China and Japan may have extensive experiences in breaking apart a number into different numbers hiding inside that number (e.g., $5 = 3 + 2 = 4 + 1$). Many U.S. first and even second graders do not have all of these prerequisites consolidated, and they are rarely developed sufficiently in textbooks. Consequently few children invent this strategy. The strategy also is rarely taught in this country.

Textbooks in the United States have in the past typically shown little understanding of children's progression of methods. They moved directly from counting all (e.g., $4 + 3$ shows four objects and then three objects) to pages with only numbers, where children are to begin to "memorize their facts" (which they can not do because no answers are given). Children responded by inventing the experiential trajectory of methods discussed previously, what I often call the "secret under-the-table worldwide progression of solution methods." Some textbooks do now support some children's methods. However, in the midst of so many other topics, textbooks rarely provide sufficient time for children to master these methods.

This lack of fit between what is in textbooks and how children think is exacerbated by other features of textbook treatment of addition. Compared to other countries, the United States has had a delayed placement of topics in the elementary school curriculum (Fuson, 1992a; Fuson, Stigler, & Bartsch, 1988). Almost all of first grade was spent on addition and subtraction below 10, and problems with totals above 12 were often in the last chapters (which many teachers never reached). Such simple problems below 10 were then also emphasized and reviewed in Grade 2, resulting overall in many more of the easier additions and relatively fewer of the more difficult single-digit additions (Hamann & Ashcraft, 1986). Thus, in contrast to East Asian children who are shown in first grade effective methods for solving the difficult additions over 10 (i.e., with totals between 10 and 18) in visually and conceptually supported ways, many U.S. children had little opportunity to solve such problems in first grade and were not supported in any effective methods to do so.

Clearly U.S. children need more support than most of them receive at present to move through the developmental progression of solution methods. Many would also benefit from more work with visual patterns and with seeing the numbers 6 through 10 as a five and some extra. Visual quantity supports and language supports can help children understand the teen numbers as one 10 and some extra ones. Teachers can use visual quantity supports such as 10-frames or penny/dime strips (10 pennies on one side grouped to show two fives and on the other side one dime) with pennies to make teen numbers. Number cards can show the 10 inside each teen number if the 10 card is twice as wide as the single-digit cards so that they can be placed over the zero on the 10 card (see Fuson, Grandau, & Sugiyama, 2001). First graders can learn counting on for addition and counting up to for subtraction, and second graders can use methods that make a 10 in multidigit addition and subtraction. Specific grade-level goals in this domain are given in Part C.

## Multidigit Addition and Subtraction: The Need for Using Accessible Algorithms

There is considerable research on various ways in which children learn various multidigit addition and subtraction methods, though not nearly as much research as on single-digit addition and subtraction. In single-digit addition and subtraction, the earliest steps in the learning progression are similar in many different countries. In contrast, the multidigit addition and subtraction domain seems to consist much more of different pieces that are put together in different orders and in different ways by different children (e.g., Hiebert & Wearne, 1986). Different children even within the same class may see different patterns in the complex whole and thus follow different learning progressions and use different methods. Furthermore, children learn less about aspects of multidigit numbers and methods at home, so multidigit addition and subtraction depend much more on what is taught in school.

***Difficulties With Words and Numbers.***   As with teen numbers, the English number words between 20 and 100 complicate the teaching/learning task for multidigit addition and subtraction. English names the hundreds and thousands regularly, but does not do so for the tens. For example, 3,333 is said "3 thousand 3 hundred thirty 3" not "3 ten 3." English-speaking children must learn and use a special sequence of decade words for 20, 30, 40, and so on. This sequence, like the teens, has irregularities. Furthermore, teens words and decade words sound alike: In a classroom it is often difficult to hear the difference between "eighteen" and "eighty." The same numbers one through nine are reused to write how many tens, hundreds, thousands, and so forth. Whether 3 tens or 3 hundreds or 3 thousands, it is shown by the relative position of the 3: The 3 is how many positions to the left of the number farthest to the right? Relative position is a complex concept.

The written place-value system is an efficient system that lets us write large numbers, but it is also abstract and misleading: The numbers in every position look the same. To understand the meaning of the numbers in the various positions, first- and second-grade children need experience with some kind of size visual quantity supports: manipulatives or drawings that show tens to be collections of 10 ones and show hundreds to be simultaneously 10 tens and 100 ones, and so on. Various kinds of such size visual quantity supports have been designed and used in teaching our written system of place value. However, classrooms rarely have enough of such supports for children themselves to use them (and many classrooms do not use anything). Such supports are rarely used in multidigit addition and subtraction, or they are used alone to get answers without sufficient linking to a written method related to the manipulative method.

As a result, many studies indicate that many U.S. first and second graders do not have or use quantity understandings of multidigit numbers (see reviews in Fuson, 1990, 1992a, 1992b). Instead, many children view numbers as single digits side by side: 827 is functionally "eight two seven" and not eight groups of 100, two groups of 10, and seven single ones. Children make many different errors in adding and subtracting multidigit numbers, and many who do add or subtract correctly cannot explain how they got their answers.

***Teaching for Understanding and Fluency.***          In contrast, research instructional programs in the United States, Europe, and South Africa indicate that focusing on understanding multidigit addition and subtraction methods results in much higher levels of correct multidigit methods and produces children who can explain how they got their answers using quantity language (Beishuizen, 1993; Beishuizen, Gravemeijer, & van Lieshout, 1997; Carpenter, Franke, Jacobs, & Fennema, 1998; Fuson & Briars, 1990; Fuson & Burghardt, 1997, in press; Fuson, Smith et al., 1997; Fuson, Wearne et al., 1997; McClain, Cobb, & Bowers, 1998). Characteristics of all of these approaches are that students used some kind of visual quantity support to learn meanings of hundreds, tens, and ones, and these meanings were related to the oral and written numerical methods developed in the classrooms.

Many different addition and subtraction methods were developed in these studies, often in the same classrooms (see Fuson, Wearne et al., 1997, and Fuson & Burghardt, in press, for summaries of many methods). In most of these studies children invented various methods and described them to each other, but in some studies conceptual supports were used to give meaning to a chosen algorithm. Many studies were intensive studies of children's thinking in one or a few classrooms, but some studies involved 10 or more classrooms including one study of all second-grade classrooms in a large urban school district (Fuson & Briars, 1990). In all studies a strong emphasis was placed on children understanding and explaining their method using quantity terms (e.g., using hundreds, tens, ones, or the names of the object supports being used).

The function of visual quantity supports is to suggest meanings that can be attached to the written numbers and to the steps in the solution method with numbers. Therefore, methods of relating the visual quantity supports and the written number method through linked actions and through verbal descriptions of numerical method are crucial. However, in the classroom, supports often are used without recording anything except the answer at the end, and then students are shifted to written methods without linking to the steps taken with the supports. Thus, the written numerals do not necessarily take on meanings as tens, hundreds, and so on, and the steps in the numeral method may be thought of as involving only single digits rather than their actual quantity meanings. This leaves them vulnerable to the many errors created by students without the meanings to direct or constrain them. Even for students who initially learn a meaningful method, the appearance of multidigit numbers as single digits may cause errors to creep in. An important step in maintaining the meanings of the steps is to have students occasionally explain their method using the names for their quantity support (e.g., big cubes, etc., or money).

***Solution Methods and Accessible Algorithms.*** Many different methods of multidigit addition and subtraction are invented by children and are used in different countries. There is not space here to describe all of them or to analyze their respective advantages and disadvantages. However, two addition methods and one subtraction method have been selected for discussion. These are especially clear conceptually, are easy for even less-advanced students to carry out, and are less prone to errors than are many other methods. We also show the addition and the subtraction algorithms that are currently taught most frequently in textbooks in the United States. These methods are all shown in Fig. 5.1.

In Fig. 5.1 the algorithm on the top left is the addition method currently appearing in most U.S. textbooks. It starts at the right, in contrast to reading, which starts at the left. Most methods that children invent start at the left, perhaps because of reading from the left and perhaps because we read our number words starting at the left. The current addition algorithm has two major problems. One is that many children object initially (if they are in a position in which mathematical objections can be voiced) to putting the little 1s above the top number. They say that you are changing the problem. And in fact, this algorithm does change the numbers it is adding by adding in these carries to the top numbers. The second method in the top row of Fig. 5.1 does not change the top number: The new 1 ten is written down in the space for the total on this line. Children using base-ten blocks (Fuson & Burghardt, 1993, in press) invented this method so that they did not change the answer as they went. It is also easier to see the total 14 ones when the 1 is written so close to the 4. The second problem with

| Typical U.S. Algorithms | Accessible Generalizable Methods | | Drawings to Show Quantities |
|---|---|---|---|

**Drawings to Show Quantities**

Hundred = ☐ or ▯ | Ten = ▮ or | | One = ▪ or ▫ | 1 ten

**Accessible Generalizable Methods**

**Method A: New Groups Below**

```
  1 1
  568        568        568
+ 876   →  + 876   →  + 876
              1 1         1 1
    4        44         1444
```

Move right to left

1 new group goes below in answer space of next left column, keeping total together

Add 2 numbers you see, then increase that number by 1 to add the new group

**Method B: See Place Values**

```
  568
+ 876
 1300
  130
   14
 1444
```

Can be done in either direction

Add each kind of unit first, then add those totals

**Typical U.S. Algorithms**

```
  1 1
  568
+ 876
 1444
```

Move right to left

Add ones, carry 1 to above left; add tens, carry 1 to above left

Usually add carry to top number, remember that number while adding it to bottom number

**Ungroup Everything First (As Necessary) Then Subtract Everywhere**

```
 13 13         13            13
 3̶. 3̶. 14     13 14         13 3̶. 14
 X̶ X̶ X̶ X̶    1̶ 4̶ 4̶ 4̶     X̶ X̶ X̶ X̶
 - 5 6 8     - 5 6 8        - 5 6 8
   8 7 6       8 7 6          8 7 6
             Left-to-right   Right-to-left
             ungrouping      ungrouping
```

Do all ungrouping, in any order, until every top number is larger than the bottom number. Then subtract each kind of multiunit, in any order.

Move right to left

Alternate ungrouping and subtracting

Stage 1: Sustained linking of quantities to written algorithm to build understanding of quantity meanings in drawings.

Stage 2: Only do numerical algorithm but occasionally explain using quantity words (thousands, hundreds, tens, ones) to elicit mental images of quantity drawings.

FIG. 5.1.  Multidigit addition and subtraction.

127

the present U.S. algorithm is that it makes the single-digit adding in each column difficult. You must add in the 1 to the top number, remember it even though it is not written, and add that remembered number to the bottom number. If instead you add the two numbers you see, you may forget to go up to add on the 1 ten (or 1 hundred). The second method solves this problem: You just add the two numbers you see and then increase that total by 1. This makes the adding much easier for less-advanced children.

Method B in Fig. 5.1 separates the two major steps in multidigit adding. The total for adding each kind of multiunit is written on a new line, emphasizing that you are adding each kind of multiunit. The carrying-regrouping-trading is just done as part of the adding of each kind of multiunit: The new 1 ten of the next larger multiunit is just written in the next-left column. One then does the final step of multidigit adding: Add all of the partial additions to find the total. Method B can be done in either direction (Fig. 5.1 shows the left-to-right version). Because you write out the whole value of each addition (e.g., 500 + 800 = 1,300), this method facilitates children's thinking about and explaining how and what they are adding.

The drawings at the far right can be used with any of the three methods to support understanding of the major components of the methods. The different sizes of the ones, tens, and hundreds in the drawings support the first component: adding of those like quantities to each other. Ten of a given unit can be encircled to make 1 of the next higher unit (10 ones = 1 ten, 10 tens = 1 hundred, 10 hundreds = 1 thousand). Circling the new 10 units can support the general "make a 10" single-digit methods. The components each algorithm must also show are: (a) how to record the adding of each kind of unit, the making of each 1 new larger unit from 10 of the smaller units, and (b) the adding of the partial additions to make the total.

Under the drawing are summarized the two vital elements of using drawings or objects to support understanding of addition methods. First is a long Stage 1 in which the objects or drawings are linked to the steps in the algorithms to give meanings to the numerical notations in those algorithms. A second but crucial Stage 2 then lasts over an even longer period (over years) in which students only carry out the numerical algorithm but they occasionally explain it using words describing quantity objects or drawings so that meanings stay attached to the steps of the algorithm. Stage 2 is vital because of the single-digit appearance of our written numerals; these do not direct correct methods or inhibit incorrect methods, as the objects and drawings do, and errors can creep into understood methods, especially as children learn other solution methods in other domains.

Two subtraction methods are shown in Fig. 5.1. The method on the left is the most widely used current U.S. algorithm. It moves from right to left, and it alternates between the two major subtraction steps: Step 1: regrouping (borrowing, trading) to get 10 more of a given unit so that unit can be subtracted (necessary when the top unit is less than the bottom unit); and Step 2: subtracting after the top number has been fixed. The regrouping may be written in different ways (e.g., as a little 1 beside the 4 instead of crossing out the 4 and writing 14 above). The alternating between the two major subtracting steps presents three kinds of difficulties to students. One is initially learning this alternation. Two is then remembering to alternate the steps. The third is that the alternation renders students susceptible to the pervasive subtracting error: subtracting a smaller top number from a larger bottom number (e.g., doing 62 – 15 as 53). When moving left using the current method, a solver sees two numbers in a column while primed to subtract. For example, after regrouping in 1,444 – 568 to get 14 in the rightmost column and subtracting 14 – 6 to get 8, one sees 3 at the top and 6 at the bottom of the next column. Automatically the answer 3 is produced (6 – 3 = 3). This answer must be inhibited while one thinks about the direction of subtracting and asks whether the top number is larger than the bottom (i.e., asks oneself whether regrouping or borrowing is necessary).

The accessible subtraction method shown in the bottom middle of Fig. 5.1 separates the two steps used in the current method, thus making each conceptually clearer as well as procedurally easier. First, a student asks the regrouping (borrowing) question for every column, in any direction. The goal here is to rewrite the whole top number so that every top digit is larger than the bottom digit. This makes the conceptual goal clearer: You are rearranging the units in the top number so that they are available for subtracting like units. Because this step is not intermixed with subtraction, it makes it easier to discuss why you are not changing the top number when you regroup. Regrouping the whole top number at once also prevents the ubiquitous top-from-bottom error because each top number will be as large as the bottom number when you begin to do all of the subtracting. Doing the regrouping in any direction allows children to think in their own way. The second major step then is to subtract every column. This also can be done in any order. The separation into two major steps makes the process easier than alternating between the steps.

The drawing at the bottom right of Fig. 5.1 shows how a size drawing or size objects can support the two aspects of multidigit subtracting. There are not enough ones, or tens, or hundreds to do the needed subtracting, so 1 larger unit is opened up to make 10 of the needed units. The subtraction can be done from this 10, facilitating the "take from 10" single-digit subtraction method. Or students can count up to find the difference in the written number problem.

The irregular structure of the English words between 20 and 99 continues to present problems in multidigit problems because all single-digit and multidigit calculation is done using the words as oral intermediaries for the written numbers, and these words do not show the tens in the numbers. Using English forms of the regular East Asian words ("1 ten 4 ones" for 14) along with the ordinary English number words has been reported to be helpful (Fuson et al., 1997). This permits children to generalize single-digit methods meaningfully. For example, for 48 + 36, students can use their single-digit knowings and think, "4 tens + 3 tens is 7 tens" rather than having to think "forty plus thirty is?" or use only single-digit language ("four plus three is seven"), and thus ignoring the values of the numbers.

*Textbook and Curricular Issues.*   U.S. textbooks have several problematic features that complicate children's learning of multidigit addition and subtraction methods. The grade placement of topics is delayed compared to that of other countries (Fuson et al., 1988), and problems generally have one more digit each year so that this topic continues into Grade 5 or even 6. In contrast, multidigit addition and subtraction for large numbers are completed in some countries by Grade 3. In the first grade in the United States, two-digit addition and subtraction problems with no regrouping (carrying or borrowing) are given but no problems requiring regrouping are given until almost a year later, in second grade. Problems with no regrouping set children up for making the most common errors, especially subtracting the smaller number from the larger even when the larger number is on the bottom (e.g., 72 – 38 = 46). This error is one major reason that on standardized tests only 38% of U.S. second graders are accurate on problems such as 72 – 38.

Accessibility studies indicate that first graders can solve two-digit addition problems with trading if they can use drawings or visual quantity supports (Carpenter et al., 1998; Fuson, Smith et al., 1997). Because knowing when to make one new ten is an excellent use of place-value knowledge, such problems can be thought of as consolidating place-value ideas, not just as doing addition. Giving from the beginning subtraction problems that require regrouping would help children understand the general nature of two-digit subtraction. This might well be delayed until second grade because children find two-digit subtraction much more difficult than addition. But second graders learning with visual quantity supports and with a focus on understanding their methods can have high levels of success.

This review suggests some central features for effective learning materials. Any algorithms that are included need to be accessible to children and to teachers, and support needs to be provided so that they are learned with understanding. The research-based accessible methods in Fig. 5.1 were included here to indicate algorithms that are more accessible than those presently appearing in most U.S. textbooks. Furthermore, children need to use visual quantity supports in initial experiences with multidigit solving and multidigit algorithms so that these can be learned with meaning. Finally, students and teachers need to use referents when discussing methods so that everyone can follow the discussion. Drawing quantities can be helpful here. Methods children learn at home can be discussed in the classroom and analyzed to see how they work to add or subtract accurately.

*Conclusion.*   Recent research clearly indicates that nontraditional approaches can help U.S. children come to carry out, understand, and explain methods of multidigit addition and subtraction rather than only carry out a method. This higher level of performance can also be done at earlier grades than is presently expected only for answers. Features of classrooms engendering this higher level of performance are: an emphasis on understanding and explaining methods; initial use by children of visual quantity supports or drawings that show the different sizes of ones, tens, and hundreds in order to give meanings to methods with numbers; and sufficient time and support for children to develop meanings for methods with numbers and for prerequisite understandings (these may be developed alongside the development of methods) and to negotiate and become more skilled with the complexities of multistep multidigit methods.

The most effective approach at present seems to be to make the learning of algorithms more mathematical by considering it an important arena of mathematical pattern finding and invention that will use and contribute to robust understandings of our place-value system of written numeration. Meaningful discussion of various standard algorithms brought into the classroom from children's homes (e.g., the subtraction algorithm widely used in Latin America and Europe; see Ron, 1998) has an important role. Seeking to discover why each one works provides excellent mathematical investigations. It also is important to share accessible methods with less-advanced children so that they have a method they understand and can use. However, the focus should be on their understanding and explaining, not just on rote use.

All three of the accessible methods in Fig. 5.2 were invented by children but also have been shared with and learned meaningfully by many children. There may well be other methods not as yet discovered (or rediscovered) that will be even more powerful. Comparing methods to see how they take care of the crucial issues of that domain facilitates reflection by everyone on the underlying conceptual and notational issues of that domain. This seems a much more appropriate focus in the 21st century, where new machine algorithms will be needed and new technology will require many people to learn complex multistep algorithmic processes. If this focus is accompanied by a continual focus on testing and teaching accessible methods as well as on fostering invention, all children should be able to learn and explain a multidigit addition and subtraction method as well as carry it out accurately.

## PART C: DESIGN PRINCIPLES, CURRICULAR CONCEPTUAL CHUNKS, AND A PROPOSAL FOR MASTERY GOALS FOR ALL

One of the major themes in this chapter has been the need to reorganize U.S. curricula into coherent chunks and spend more time on each of these chunks. I now briefly outline a specific research-based proposal about how to do this. This proposal is not the only way that coherent foci could be developed. But it is an obvious one based on present research. It

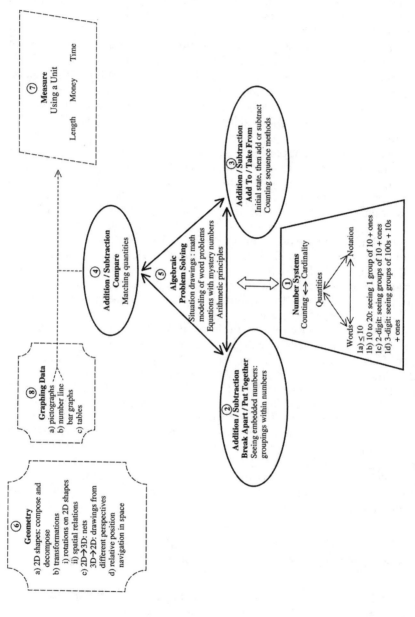

FIG. 5.2.　Conceptual chunks in Pre-K to Grade 2 curricula.

has also been worked out in considerable detail in my own classroom curricular research, and developing versions of it have been used in a wide range of classrooms. This proposal is overviewed in Tables 5.1 and 5.2 and in Fig. 5.3. Table 5.1 outlines design principles concerning aspects of the coherent chunks and how they are related. Table 5.2 further specifies goals at each grade level from Pre-K through Grade 2 to indicate how these goals build from grade to grade without excessive repetition.

Figure 5.2 expresses in a schematized fashion the proposed eight coherent chunks. Five chunks form the numerical core. The other three related core chunks are geometry, measure, and graphing data. More specific goals within each chunk are specified by grade/age level in Table 5.2. Table 5.2 assumes mastery of goals at the preceding age, so goals are not repeated. This is how goals in many other countries are structured. Many of the goals in Table 5.2 take repeated experiencing over many days to come to understanding and fluency.

The foundational chunk within the numerical core is number systems. The systems of number words and of written number notations are developed and related to each other and to quantities in the world. This is shown by the quantities, word, and notation triangle. The three types of addition/subtraction situations discussed earlier form three of the chunks of the numerical core. Algebraic problem solving brings in number systems as a problem-solving tool and relates the three types of real-world addition/subtraction situations. All of these take on related meanings through problem solving. Language is used extensively as children pose and solve problems and learn to use mathematical situational language. The blackboard structure described earlier for multidigit calculation works well for story problem solving and posing as children make math drawings at the board and explain their solutions. Children are helped to move through the developmental progression of solution strategies.

Though some elementary ideas in multiplication/division domains can be introduced early, it is much more cohesive and developmentally appropriate to concentrate heavily and deeply on the whole range of addition/subtraction situations and obtain mastery on them for quantities as large as three-digit numbers in Pre-K to Grade 2. Time that could be spent on multiplication and division is better spent on developing some notions of geometry (see later discussion). In Grade 3 and beyond students can then begin substantive and deep examination of the whole range of multiplication/division situations and the extensions to rational numbers, decimals, and integers.

The five core numerical chunks, and their specific goals in Table 5.2, represent a more ambitious curriculum than is at present achieved even in most of the higher socioeconomic schools in the United States. Concentrating on this core, and experiencing lots of language for addition/subtraction situations and for explaining solution methods, can bring mastery of this ambitious core for students from all backgrounds.

Substantial geometric experiences are appropriate in Pre-K through Grade 2. We in this country have not yet developed a coherent research-

TABLE 5.1

## *Design Principles for Mastery Curricula and Mastery Teaching*

**Real-world situations, problem solving, and computation need to be continually intertwined in order to achieve sense-making and computational fluency.**

Each of the three types of addition/subtraction real-world situations (Break Apart/Put Together, Add To/Take Away, Compare) forms one of the coherent curricular chunks (Chunks 2, 3, and 4). Each of these is also integrated with other related topics.

Algebraic problem solving (Chunk 5) relates all of these by coordinating children's

   a) use of situation drawings,

   b) reading/writing/solving of word problems of each of the three types using varying language,

   c) use of equations with one unknown that varies (by Grade 2) across all of the three possible unknowns,

   d) explaining solution methods.

Computation is integrated with problem solving throughout Chunks 2, 3, 4, and 5, but is also a special focus of number system activities in Chunk 1.

   a) For single-digit addition and subtraction, children are helped to move through a learning progression of general methods to more-advanced methods (at least to counting on for addition and counting up for unknown addend and subtraction).

   b) For multidigit addition and subtraction, children build mastery by

      i) using visual and language conceptual supports for learning the quantity triad so that they can invent, understand, and explain methods,

      ii) examining accessible research-based algorithms,

      iii) discussing and explaining algorithms children bring from home,

      iv) explaining their own solution method.

Practice is varied, distributed over time, cumulative, monitored with feedback, and help is given as necessary. Practice first focuses on working enough in a given domain so that a child "gets it" and then is distributed over time so that a child is able to "keep it" (remember and use knowings built earlier).

Work in Pre-K through Grade 2 concentrates on building mastery in the addition and subtraction domains that is more ambitious than at present. Some geometry is introduced, as are some measure and graphing data ideas. Mastery in Chunks 1 through 5 means that Grades 3, 4, and 5 can concentrate on build

*(continued on next page)*

TABLE 5.1 (*continued*)

ing mastery in multiplication and division domains, including rational numbers and integers. Substantial understandings in measure and geometry will also be able to be built at those grade levels. All of this will be possible because of the strong foundations from Chunks 1 through 8 in Pre-K to Grade 2 with little need for repeating those chunks. The algebraic problem solving will continue in multiplication and division situations and will provide a strong foundation for Grade 8 algebra for all.

Note.    The teaching of topics in Fig. 5.2 and Table 5.2 follows the process standards in Table 5.3 and the core connections in Fig. 5.3.

based stream of activities that develop over grade levels (but see other chapters in this volume for what is now known). Some kinds of graphing (pictographs and bar graphs) can be understood in Grades 1 and 2; these are listed in Table 5.2. However, research and my own experiences in many classrooms indicate that few concepts of measure are appropriate to Pre-K through Grade 2. Developing the concepts of units for each kind of measure is difficult and takes much special equipment. Even working correctly with length units takes time and special equipment. So length is included as a goal, but it is not developed deeply until Grade 2, where students have the conceptual numerical underpinnings and the physical coordination to do many interesting geometric activities using rulers and length. Area can be developed nicely and deeply along with multiplication/division in Grade 3, and volume, liquid capacity, weight/mass, and temperature can follow in the other higher grades. This is not to say that children cannot understand anything about these ideas at Pre-K through Grade 2. But many states list many kinds of measures at each grade level, contributing to the "mile wide inch deep" U.S. curricular problem. Postponing these as goals to a grade level where they can be mastery goals is the most sensible course.

An example of the conceptual difficulties caused by length is the number line. The number line is used in many textbooks and classrooms as a representational tool for adding and subtracting small whole numbers. But many children (and some curricular materials) do not understand that the number line is a length model. The fiveness is a length of five units. Many children can only conceptualize discrete quantities, so the five to them is the little mark above the 5 on the number line. Confusion about the source of the fiveness (there are six little marks for the length of five units) leads many children to be off by one when they add or subtract using the number line. This discrete object versus length notion is the same differ-

TABLE 5.2

*Mastery Goals for All: Toward World-Class Mathematics Learning*

| Coherent conceptual chunk | Pre-K: Age 4/5 | Kindergarten: Age 5/6 | Grade 1 | Grade 2 |
|---|---|---|---|---|
| | 1. Number Systems and Meanings: Counting, Cardinality, Groups of 10, Word-Quantity-Notation links | | | |
| a) ≤ 10, counting | a) count, cardinality, 1-1 correspondence 1→10; fingers ≤ 5, recognize numerals 1→10 | a) write #'s 1→10, say next number fingers ≤ 10 | | |
| b) 10 to 20, place value | b) count to 20 with fingers (also flash 10 fingers one time for teens, two times for 20) | b) teens as tens and ones: objects, fingers; write numbers 11→20, dime = 10 pennies | b) which is closer to x? | |
| c) 2-digit, 3-digit +/- | c) count to 100 with flashes of 10 fingers | c) two-digit #s as tens and ones; count dimes and pennies; two-digit addition with re-grouping; drawing objects | c) two-digit –, three-digit +/– invented and accessible algorithms; explain method you use |

## 2. Break Apart/Put Together Situations and Embedded Numbers (Total & Partners)

| Word problem language Embedded numbers | oral use | oral use | oral, read/write | oral, read/write |
|---|---|---|---|---|
| a) all break-apart partners of a number (e.g, $6 = 5 + 1 = 4 + 2 = 3 + 3$) | a) break-apart partners $\le 5$ (e.g., $5 = 4 + 1 = 2 + 3$, $4 = 3 + 1 = 2 + 2$) | a) break-apart partners of 6, 7, 10 | a) break-apart partners of 9, 8 | |
| b) using 5s in 6, 7, 8, 9, 10 (e.g., $9 = 5 + 4$) | b) fingers, objects, drawings | b) nickel as 5 pennies | | b) & c) count coins P, N, D |
| c) using 10 for +/− | | c) see with objects, fingers, drawings | c) introduce "make a 10" strategies for +/− | c) many use "make a 10" in multidigit +/− |

## 3. Add To/Take Away: Change + and − Situations

| Word problem language: Addition and subtraction methods | oral | oral | oral, read/write | oral, read/write |
|---|---|---|---|---|
| | direct model solutions: objects, fingers for totals ≤ 5 | direct model solutions: objects, fingers for totals ≤ 10 | count on to find total or part (count up to for subtraction and mystery addends) use 2 b, 2 c, 2 d in Ch +/− situations | see 5 |

TABLE 5.2 (cont.)

| Coherent conceptual chunk | Pre-K: Age 4/5 | Kindergarten: Age 5/6 | Grade 1 | Grade 2 |
|---|---|---|---|---|
| | | | 4. Compare: Match Situations | |
| Word problem language | oral | oral | oral, read/write | oral, read/write |
| More/less | more, less, equal matching 1→6 objects make an = set by matching, by counting | activities for 6→10 with objects | | |
| How many more/less? | | | for 1→18, all types but inconsistent language | for 1→18 all types including inconsistent language for 1→1,000 |
| Pictographs | | read pictographs 1→10 | for 1→18 | |
| | | | 5. Algebraic Problem Solving | |
| situation equations for | | | | |
| a) Chunks 2, 3, 4 | a) Oral, object, and finger direct modeling problem solving in conceptual Chunks 2 and 3 to prepare for 5) in kindergarten; easy problem types | a) Continue oral, object, finger, and drawing problem solving in conceptual Chunks 2 and 3: write and solve +/− equations for easy problem types | a) Link situations, math drawings and equations for Chunks 2, 3, 4; all problem types except Unknown Start and Compare Inconsistent language | a) Link situations, math drawings and equations for Chunks 2, 3, 4 for all problem types; also all types for two-digit numbers |

| | | | b) begin these | b) all types |
|---|---|---|---|---|
| b) two-step, extra information problems | | | | |
| c) arithmetic principles: commutativity, +/- as inverse operations (subtraction as an unknown addend), associativity | | subtraction as taking away a break-apart partner | discuss all of these for totals ≤20; notate with letters | discuss all of these for totals ≤ 1,000; notate with letters |

**6. Geometry**

| | | | b) begin these | b) all types |
|---|---|---|---|---|
| 2D shapes: compose, decompose squares, arrays, patterns; △: pattern blocks | see shapes; compose, decompose shapes | cut out and draw more complex patterns and compositions with squares and pattern blocks | draw on square arrays; draw pattern blocks on grids | what lengths make a triangle? |
| Transformation geometry: rotate, reflect, translate | turn shapes | turn + draw | rotate and draw shapes; flip and draw shapes | rotate and draw midpoints of shapes, diagonals |
| 2D→3D: nets 3D→2D: drawings from viewpoints | | see surfaces of cube, boxes (rectangular prisms) | cube: many nets for a cube | buildings from cubes→ drawings from 5 views |
| Relative position, navigation in space | block play, spatial language | body in space activities, spatial language | | |

TABLE 5.2 (cont.)

| Coherent conceptual chunk | Pre-K: Age 4/5 | Kindergarten: Age 5/6 | Grade 1 | Grade 2 |
|---|---|---|---|---|
| **7. Measure** | | | | |
| Money | penny as 1¢ | nickel as 5 pennies dime = 10 pennies | make amounts with pennies, nickels, dimes; $1, $10 | P, N, D, Q; $1, $10, $100 |
| Length | | experience cm and inch lengths | draw inch and cm lengths for objects; count inches, centimeters | measure using in, ft, yd, cm, dm, meter; measure perimeters |
| Time | | | | time to 1 min; $\frac{1}{4}$, $\frac{1}{2}$ past and before |
| **8. Graphing Data** | | | | |
| Pictographs (social studies, science): use for comparing and for other +/– problems | | pictographs for numbers 1 to 10 | pictographs for numbers 1 to 20 | pictographs for comparing |
| Number line, bar graph | | | | number line, bar graph |
| Table | | | table: 1 row or column | table: 2 rows and 2 columns |

*Note.* We as a nation lose a great deal of learning time if we must accomplish the previous year's learning goals. The goals in this table assume mastery by all at each grade without repetition. We need substantive and substantial math learning in day care, half-day Pre-K and kindergartens, and full-day kindergartens to close that gap in Grade 1.

140

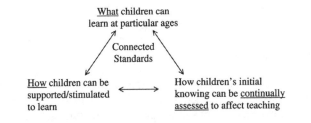

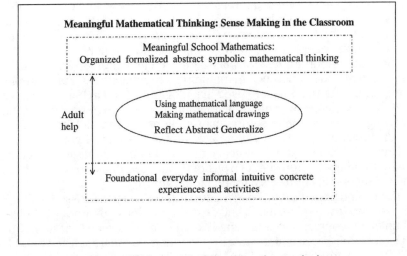

FIG. 5.3.    Core connections for meaningful mathematics standards.

ence between pictographs (where the objects each fill a square and the squares—the objects—are numbered) and bar graphs (where a length scale is used and the numbers are at the end of the little length marks). For Pre-K, kindergarten, and Grade 1, discrete object models are more developmentally appropriate than is the number line. A discrete object number sequence model like a board game where numbers appear on each square is more accessible than the number line. The number line is important when fractions are introduced (in Grade 3, under our core grade-level concepts principle), because one can no longer label in the middle of lengths because that is now a fractional part that requires its own label.

Understanding money can build upon and contribute to deep understanding of our number systems, so 5¢ and 10¢ (the nickel and dime) can be understood first (see Table 5.2 for age/grade levels). Mastery of money, especially of coins, takes a great deal of time because children have to learn all of the different kinds of counting (by fives, by 10s, by 25s), learn to shift among types of counting, and learn how the types of counting match with the coins in the face of misleading size cues (e.g., the dime is smaller than the penny and the nickel but the dime has a larger value). The placement of money topics in Table 5.2 reflects my extensive classroom-based research concerning when these topics are accessible and sensibly related to other appropriate grade-level topics.

Time is like many topics in U.S. curricula: It appears every year, and each year one more small piece is supposed to be learned (e.g., time to the hour in kindergarten, time to the hour and half hour in first grade, and time to five minutes in second grade). As with other types of measures, time takes special equipment (which poorer schools do not have) and considerable class time to learn deeply with meaning. It is more readily accessible at Grade 2, and for these reasons we suggest postponing time as a topic until it can be done deeply (time to single minutes) in Grade 2.

There are important relations across these eight chunks. Emphasizing these can provide coherence to mathematical experiences. For example, comparing and matching are used in pictographs (and in bar graphs that are scaled versions of counted pictographs), and pictographs and length drawings can help make comparing situations clearer. All kinds of addition/subtraction questions can be asked of tables and of graphed data. Building meaning and coherence is the most important task in teaching math. Helping children see all types of relations within and across these eight conceptual chunks is a foundational goal.

The design principles in Table 5.1 summarize issues discussed in Part B concerning results of research and describe relationships among the eight chunks. Of course, how teaching is carried out is crucial for achieving mastery by all. Process standards to guide such teaching are listed in Table 5.3. The top group is the NCTM Standards. The others emerged from discussions at the smaller conference following the large May 2000 conference on Pre-K to Grade 2 standards. Figure 5.3 outlines some further discussion at the smaller conference concerning the necessary connectedness of standards for early childhood. What children learn, how they learn it, and how learning is assessed (particularly how teacher assessment can be used to improve teaching) are fundamentally interconnected. The connections specified at the bottom of Fig. 5.3 are important at all ages, but they feel absolutely central for young children just beginning school experiences. Children must learn from the beginning that mathematical learning and teaching are about making sense of their world. The formal mathematical language, notations, and methods must be connected to children's everyday informal experiences to facilitate continual sense making. The ideas in these process standards are discussed more in the Equity Pedagogy developed in my classroom research (see Fuson et al., 2000).

The process goals are particularly important when teaching particular strategies. Some mathematics educators are so concerned that children's natural strategies like counting on and counting up to will be

TABLE 5.3
**_Process Standards for Pre-K to Grade 2_**

_General Process Standards_

Problem Solving

Representation

Reasoning

Communication

Connections

_Mathematical Processes Used Across Domains_

Organizing information

Patterning

Decomposing/composing

Unitizing

Describing one's thinking

Learning and using the language of mathematical situations

_Orienting Mathematical Questions for Children to Learn to Use_

Where is it in my world?

How can I describe it?

How can I represent it?

What happens when I break it apart?

What happens when I put it together?

What happens when I compare it?

What kind of quantity is it?

What kind of units are there?

Do I see a pattern?

taught rotely and imposed on children before they are ready that they advocate not teaching strategies at all. My experience after helping teachers teach thousands of first graders to count on for addition and count up to for subtraction and for mystery addends is that teaching such strategies helps to close the gap between more-advanced and less-advanced students and it makes subtraction easier than addition. Of course, not all students can do these strategies when they are first discussed. The strategies can come from the more-advanced students who have already invented them. These strategies do need to be related to the groups of quantities involved. For example, for 8 + 6, one can make groups of 8 and 6 and then count the group of 8. You discover that the last counting word you say is "eight." So children can see that they do not have to count from 1 to 8; they can abbreviate the count and begin the count of the total at 8 and count on 6 more (keeping track with fingers or other means of the six more counts): "8, 9, 10, 11, 12, 13, 14." Many children when first beginning to count on do not trust that final cardinal number and need to do a running quick count "12345678" before counting the six added on more slowly: "9, 10, 11, 12, 13, 14." For subtraction such as 14 – 8, taking away the first 8 facilitates counting up to: "Take away 8, so now 9, 10, 11, 12, 13, 14, that's 6 left from the 14." If sense making is emphasized continuously, and children are supported but not forced to use strategies, the dangers of learning rotely can be minimized and less-advanced children can learn to use more effective strategies.

A chief assumption of mastery goals learned by all children is that all children are given an opportunity to learn the mastery goals in a sense-making way. Children who are not reached in the prekindergarten years may enter kindergarten with much less relevant mathematical experience. They may require extra time and support during the kindergarten year to catch up and learn the mastery goals. My experience is that rich structured kindergarten experiences can enable many children to catch up, especially in a full-day program. However, for both mathematical and literacy goals, it may make sense to form 3-year programs for some children to learn deeply the kindergarten and Grade 1 goals. If children enter second grade as nonreaders, it is difficult to catch up and accomplish Grade 2 goals in math or in literacy. For children who are in Head Start and other prekindergarten programs, it is essential that their programs be organized to meet the prekindergarten goals. Efforts must also be made to reach parents who do not send their children to preschools so that they can carry out mathematical activities at home.

It should be underscored that the concentration of time and energy on these eight chunks enables considerably more to be learned in all areas by the end of Grade 2 than is the case at present. Thus the foundation will be stronger and will also enable more substantive mathematics to be learned in Grades 3 and above.

# CONCLUSION

A new more coherent view of goals, standards, and testing for Pre-K through Grade 2 is necessary to achieve the new more complex goals of mathematics learning and teaching necessary for the 21st century. These goals, standards, and testing require focused concentrated ambitious grade-level topics that build across the age levels. Replacing "standardized" testing with mastery testing linked to coherent and ambitious grade-level goals can help focus everyone's energies on the same developmentally appropriate teaching/learning goals and facilitate mastery for all. Some children may need additional learning time and support to achieve mastery goals. This is more equitable than the present practice of allowing children to move on with quite different amounts of learning with some falling increasingly behind. Instruction organized into three phases—orienting, supporting learning, and long-term remembering—can facilitate learning by all. Real-world situations, problem solving, and computation need to be continually intertwined to achieve sense-making and computational fluency. Children can be helped to learn more-advanced and rapid single-digit methods that can also be understood. Accessible multidigit addition and subtraction algorithms can enable more children to learn with understanding and achieve high levels of mastery. Finally, a specific proposal to organize the Pre-K through Grade 2 curriculum into eight research-based coherent chunks was outlined. This permits deep coherent learning in each of the areas with strong articulation and building across the grade levels. All of the attributes summarized here can coalesce into truly achieving mastery by all children of ambitious world-class goals by the end of Grade 2.

# REFERENCES

Beishuizen, M. (1993). Mental strategies and materials or models for addition and subtraction up to 100 in Dutch second grades. *Journal for Research in Mathematics Education, 24*, 294–323.

Beishuizen, M., Gravemeijer, K. P. E., & van Lieshout, E. C. D. M. (Eds.). (1997). *The role of contexts and models in the development of mathematical strategies and procedures.* Utretch, Netherlands: CD-B Press/The Freudenthal Institute.

Bergeron, J. C., & Herscovics, N. (1990). Psychological aspects of learning early arithmetic. In P. Nesher & J. Kilpatrick (Eds.), *Mathematics and cognition: A research synthesis by the International Group for the Psychology of Mathematics Education.* Cambridge, England: Cambridge University Press.

Brownell, W. A. (1987). AT Classic: Meaning and skill—Maintaining the balance. *Arithmetic Teacher, 34*(8), 18–25.

Carpenter, T. P., Franke, M. L., Jacobs, V., & Fennema, E. (1998). A longitudinal study of invention and understanding in children's multidigit addition and subtraction. *Journal for Research in Mathematics Education, 29*, 3–20.

Dixon, R. C., Carnine, S. W., Kameenui, E. J., Simmons, D. C., Lee, D-S., Wallin, J., & Chard, D. (1998). *Executive summary: Report to the California State Board of Education: Review of high quality experimental research.* Eugene, OR: National Center to Improve the Tools of Educators.

Fuson, K. C. (1986a). Roles of representation and verbalization in the teaching of multi-digit addition and subtraction. *European Journal of Psychology of Education, 1,* 35–56.

Fuson, K. C. (1986b). Teaching children to subtract by counting up. *Journal for Research in Mathematics Education, 17,* 172–189.

Fuson, K. C. (1990). Conceptual structures for multiunit numbers: Implications for learning and teaching multidigit addition, subtraction, and place value. *Cognition and Instruction, 7,* 343–403.

Fuson, K. C. (1992a). Research on learning and teaching addition and subtraction of whole numbers. In G. Leinhardt, R. T. Putnam, & R. A. Hattrup (Eds.), *The analysis of arithemetic for mathematics teaching* (pp. 53–187). Hillsdale, NJ: Lawrence Erlbaum Associates.

Fuson, K. C. (1992b). Research on whole number addition and subtraction. In D. Grouws (Ed.), *Handbook of research on mathematics teaching and learning* (pp. 243–275). New York: Macmillan.

Fuson, K. C. (2003). Developing mathematical power in whole number operations. In J. Kilpatrick, W. Martin, & D. Shifter (Eds.), *A research companion to Principles and Standards for School Mathematics* (pp. 68–94). Reston, VA: National Council of Teachers of Mathematics.

Fuson, K. C., & Briars, D. J. (1990). Base-ten blocks as a first- and second-grade learning/teaching approach for multidigit addition and subtraction and place-value concepts. *Journal for Research in Mathematics Education, 21,* 180–206.

Fuson, K. C., & Burghardt, B. H. (1993). Group case studies of second graders inventing multidigit addition procedures for base-ten blocks and written marks. In J. R. Becker & B. J. Pence (Eds.), *Proceedings of the Fifteenth Annual Meeting of the North American Chapter of the International Group for the Psychology of Mathematics Education* (pp. 240–246). San Jose, CA: The Center for Mathematics and Computer Science Education, San Jose State University.

Fuson, K. C., & Burghardt, B. H. (1997). Group case studies of second graders inventing multidigit subtraction methods. In J. A. Dossey, J. O. Swafford, M. Parmantie, & A. E. Dossey (Eds.), *Proceedings of the 19th Annual Meeting of the North American Chapter of the International Group for the Psychology of Mathematics Education* (Vol. 1, pp. 291–298). Columbus, OH: ERIC Clearinghouse for Science, Mathematics, and Environmental Education.

Fuson, K. C., & Burghardt, B. H. (in press). Multi-digit addition and subtraction methods invented in small groups and teacher support of problem solving and reflection. In A. Baroody & A. Dowker (Eds.), *The development of arithmetic concepts and skills: Constructing adaptive expertise.* Mahwah, NJ: Lawrence Erlbaum Associates.

Fuson, K. C., De La Cruz, Y., Smith, S., Lo Cicero, A., Hudson, K., Ron, P., & Steeby, R. (2000). Blending the best of the 20th century to achieve a Mathematics Equity Pedagogy in the 21st century. In M. J. Burke & F. R. Curcio (Eds.), *Learning mathematics for a new century* (pp. 197–212). Reston, VA: National Council of Teachers of Mathematics.

Fuson, K. C., Grandau, L., & Sugiyama, P. (2001). Achievable numerical understandings for all young children. *Teaching Children Mathematics, 7*(9), 522–526.

Fuson, K. C., Lo Cicero, A., Hudson, K., & Smith, S. T. (1997). Snapshots across two years in the life of an urban Latino classroom. In Hiebert, J., Carpenter, T., Fennema, E., Fuson, K. C., Wearne, D., Murray, H., Olivier, A., & Human, P. (Eds.), *Making sense: Teaching and learning mathematics with understanding* (pp. 129–159). Portsmouth, NH: Hienemann.

Fuson, K. C., Smith, S. T., & Lo Cicero, A. (1997). Supporting Latino first graders' ten-structured thinking in urban classrooms. *Journal for Research in Mathematics Education, 28,* 738–760.

Fuson, K. C., Stigler, J., & Bartsch, K. (1988). Grade placement of addition and subtraction topics in Japan, mainland China, the Soviet Union, Taiwan, and the United States. *Journal for Research in Mathematics Education, 19*(5), 449–456.

Fuson, K. C., Wearne, D., Hiebert, J., Murray, H., Human, P., Olivier, A., Carpenter, T., & Fennema, E. (1997). Children's conceptual structures for multidigit numbers and methods of multidigit addition and subtraction. *Journal for Research in Mathematics Education, 28,* 130–162.

Geary, D. C. (1994). *Children's mathematical development: Research and practical applications.* Washington, DC: American Psychological Association.

Ginsburg, H. P., & Allardice, B. S. (1984). Children's difficulties with school mathematics. In B. Rogoff & J. Lave (Eds.), *Everyday cognition: Its development in social contexts* (pp. 194–219). Cambridge, MA: Harvard University Press.

Ginsburg, H. P., & Russell, R. L. (1981). Social class and racial influences on early mathematical thinking. *Monographs of the Society for Research in Child Development, 44*(6, Serial no. 193).

Goldman, S. R., Hasselbring, T. S., & the Cognition and Technology Group at Vanderbilt (1997, March/April). Achieving meaningful mathematics literacy for students with learning disabilities. *Journal of Learning Disabilities, 30*(2), 198–208.

Goldman, S. R., Pellegrino, J. W., & Mertz, D. L. (1988). Extended practice of basic addition facts: Strategy changes in learning-disabled students. *Cognition and Instruction, 5*(3), 223–265.

Hamann, M. S., & Ashcraft, M. H. (1986). Textbook presentations of the basic addition facts. *Cognition & Instruction, 3,* 173–192.

Hiebert, J., Carpenter, T., Fennema, E., Fuson, K. C., Wearne, D., Murray, H., Olivier, A., & Human, P. (1997). *Making sense: Teaching and learning mathematics with understanding.* Portsmouth, NH: Hienemann.

Hiebert, J., & Wearne, D. (1986). Procedures over concepts: The acquisition of decimal number knowledge. In J. Hiebert (Ed.), *Conceptual and procedural knowledge: The case of mathematics* (pp. 199–223). Hillsdale, NJ: Lawrence Erlbaum Associates.

Kameenui, E. J., & Carnine, D. W. (Eds.). (1998). *Effective teaching strategies that accommodate diverse learners.* Upper Saddle River, NJ: Prentice-Hall.

Kerkman, D. D., & Siegler, R. S. (1993). Individual differences and adaptive flexibility in lower-income children's strategy choices. *Learning and Individual Differences, 5*(2), 113–136.

Knapp, M. S. (1995). *Teachng for meaning in high-poverty classrooms.* New York: Teachers College Press.

Lo Cicero, A., De La Cruz, Y., Fuson, K. C. (1999). Teaching and learning creatively with the Children's Math Worlds Curriculum: Using children's narratives and explanations to co-create understandings. *Teaching Children Mathematics, 5*(9), 544–547.

Lo Cicero, A., Fuson, K. C., & Allexaht-Snider, M. (1999). Making a difference in Latino children's math learning: Listening to children, mathematizing their stories, and supporting parents to help children. In L. Ortiz-Franco, N. G. Hernendez, & Y. De La Cruz (Eds.), *Changing the faces of mathematics: Perspectives on Latinos* (pp. 59–70). Reston, VA: National Council of Teachers of Mathematics.

McClain, K., Cobb, P., & Bowers, J. (1998). A contextual investigation of three-digit addition and subtraction. In L. Morrow (Ed.) *Teaching and learning of algorithms in school mathematics* (pp. 141–150). Reston, VA: National Council of Teachers of Mathematics.

McKnight, C. C., Crosswhite, F. J., Dossey, J. A., Kifer, E. Swafford, J. O., Travers, K. T., & Cooney, T. J. (1989). *The underachieving curriculum: Assessing U.S. school mathematics from an international perspective.* Champaign, IL: Stipes.

McKnight, C. C., & Schmidt, W. H. (1998). Facing facts in U.S. science and mathematics education: Where we stand, where we want to go. *Journal of Science Education and Technology, 7*(1), 57–76.

National Research Council. (2001). *Adding it up: Helping children learn mathematics.* Washington, DC: National Academy Press.

Peak, L. (1996). *Pursuing excellence: A study of the U.S. eighth-grade mathematics and science teaching, learning, curriculum, and achievement in an international context.* Washington, DC: National Center for Educational Statistics.

Resnick, L. B., & Omanson, S. F. (1987). Learning to understand arithmetic. In R. Glaser (Ed.), *Advances in instructional psychology* (Vol. 3, pp. 41–95). Hillsdale, NJ: Lawrence Erlbaum Associates.

Ron, P. (1998). My family taught me this way. In L. J. Morrow & M. J. Kenney (Eds.), *The teaching and learning of algorithms in school mathematics* (pp. 115–119). Reston, VA: National Council of Teachers of Mathematics.

Secada, W. G. (1992). Race, ethnicity, social class, language, and achievement in mathematics. In D. Grouws (Ed.), *Handbook of research on mathematics teaching and learning* (pp. 623–660). New York: Macmillan.

Siegler, R. S. (1988). Individual differences in strategy choices: Good students, not-so-good students, and perfectionists. *Child Development, 59*(4), 833–851.

Steffe, L. P., Cobb, P., & von Glasersfeld, E. (1988). *Construction of arithmetical meanings and strategies.* New York: Springer-Verlag.

Stigler, J. W., Fuson, K. C., Ham, M., & Kim, M. S. (1986). An analysis of addition and subtraction word problems in American and Soviet elementary mathematics textbooks. *Cognition and Instruction, 3*(3), 153–171.

Zucker, A. A. (1995). Emphasizing conceptual understanding and breadth of study in mathematics instruuction. In M. S. Knapp (Ed.), *Teaching for meaning in high-poverty classrooms* (pp. 47–63). New York: Teachers College Press.

# The Role of Psychological Research in the Development of Early Childhood Mathematics Standards

Arthur J. Baroody
*University of Illinois at Urbana-Champaign*

How important is it for early childhood and special educators to be knowledgeable about children's mathematical teaching and learning? Current teaching practices and teacher-training efforts suggest that it is not a priority or even important. Consider, for instance, that at the University of Illinois at Urbana-Champaign (UIUC), elementary education majors are required to take two mathematics methods courses for a total of six credits (in addition to two mathematics content courses required of all majors). In contrast, early childhood education majors take a single combination mathematics-science methods course. In effect, they take 1.5 credits of mathematics methods, less if science education faculty teach the course. Even more grievously, before the Illinois State Board of Education revised certification requirements effective 2002, special education majors were not required to take even a single mathematics methods course. (They are now required to take one.) Unfortunately, an inadequate preparation for teaching young and special children mathematics is not unique to the early childhood and special education programs at UIUC.

The premise of this chapter is that early childhood and special education teachers need a powerful and practical framework for teaching young children and those with special needs. This framework should include a deep understanding of the following:

149

- The *mathematics* taught and how it relates to subsequent mathematics instruction (**content**).
- Effective *techniques for teaching mathematics* (**methods**).
- The development of *children's mathematical thinking and knowledge* (**mathematical psychology**).

In this chapter, I focus on the third component in this list because it is the area of my research specialization. In Part I, I draw some conclusions about the role of psychological research in changing early childhood mathematics instruction. In Part II, I discuss why and how the early childhood standards should help early childhood and special education teachers construct a powerful developmental framework. Next, I outline how this could be accomplished in a practical manner. I end the chapter with a conclusion about the importance of ensuring a truly professional training for early childhood and special education practitioners—one that includes a sound developmental framework.

## PART I: THE ROLES OF PSYCHOLOGICAL RESEARCH IN IMPROVING EARLY CHILDHOOD MATHEMATICS INSTRUCTION

Psychological theory and research can play at least two important roles in promoting mathematics education reform: (a) changing beliefs about the learning and teaching of young children and (b) providing a powerful developmental framework for developing and guiding better instructional practices. In this part of the chapter, I note how recent psychological research has helped foster beliefs that early childhood mathematics instruction is possible and that a "child-centered" approach is not only feasible, but desirable. I then delineate the reasons why early childhood and special education teachers need a powerful developmental framework. Next, I describe an example of how recent psychological research can help mold beliefs about how young children are taught mathematics and why knowledge of such research is necessary to teach early childhood mathematics effectively.

### Fostering Beliefs About the Possibility and Nature of Early Childhood Mathematics Learning

In this section, I discuss (a) the impact psychological research has already had on educational leaders' beliefs about young children's mathematical potential and how best to foster this potential and (b) some impediments to reaching a wider audience.

#### *Recognition of Young Children's Potential*

Recent research indicates that preschoolers do have impressive informal mathematical strengths in a variety of areas. In particular, it appears that young children—despite important limitations—are capable of understanding much more about number and arithmetic than previously or commonly thought possible.

*Recognition by Educational Leaders.* In her comments on the National Council of Teachers of Mathematics (NCTM) symposium "Linking Research and New Early Childhood Mathematics Standards" (April 11, 2000), Maggie Myers correctly noted that psychological research has already had an impact on educational, governmental, and industrial leaders, namely promoting the belief that mathematics development should be an important component of early childhood education and prompting efforts to create standards to guide this development. For example, on page 79 of chapter 4 ("Standards for Grades Pre-K–2") of the *Principles and Standards for School Mathematics* (*PSSM*), the following point is emphasized: "Teachers should not underestimate what young students can learn" (NCTM, 2000). In brief, psychological research has created a climate where discussing and developing early childhood mathematics standards is now possible.

*The Challenge Remaining.* What remains is, perhaps, a greater challenge—changing the belief of teachers, school administrators, and the public at large about mathematics learning in early childhood. This task is made more difficult because elementary education majors, overall, have relatively high levels of mathematics anxiety and mathematics avoidance (Hembree, 1990) and those of early childhood and special educators may be particularly high (see, e.g., Ashcraft, Kirk, & Hopko, 1998, for a review of the literature). The difficulty of the task is compounded by the largely negative attitude toward mathematics by the general public (e.g., Ashcraft et al., 1998; McLeod, 1992). Nevertheless, it is essential that early childhood and special education teachers and their supporting cast (which should include administrators and parents) need to be informed about young children's mathematical capabilities.

### Recognition of How Best to Foster Young Children's Potential

It is important not only to change teachers', other educators', and the public's view of young children's mathematical potential, but to change their views about how it can be fostered. Following, I briefly summarize four different views of mathematics instruction and then discuss the challenge of changing the conventional or traditional view of teaching.

*Four Views of Mathematics Teaching.* Table 6.1 summarizes four qualitatively different approaches to instruction. The skills approach

TABLE 6.1

*Four Approaches to Mathematics Instruction*

| Instructional Approach | Philosophical View | | Teaching Style | Aim of Instruction |
|---|---|---|---|---|
| | Name | Nature of Knowledge | View of Authority | | |

| Instructional Approach | Name | Nature of Knowledge | View of Authority | Teaching Style | Aim of Instruction |
|---|---|---|---|---|---|
| Skills Approach | Dualism | Right or wrong with no shades of gray: There is *one* correct procedure or answer. | Absolute external authority: As the expert, the teacher is *the* judge of correctness. Procedures or answers that differ from those advocated by the teacher are wrong and not tolerated. Teacher provides definitive feedback (e.g., praise for the correct answer). | Completely authoritarian and extremely teacher centered: Direct instruction (teaching by imposition). | Foster routine expertise: the rote memorization of basic skills (arithmetic and geometric facts, definitions, rules, formulas, and procedures). |
| Conceptual Approach | Pluralism | Continuum from right to wrong: There is a choice of possible but not equally valid procedures or answers. Objectively, there is one best possibility. | Tolerant external authority: Teacher accepts diverse procedures and answers but strives for perfection, namely, learning of the best procedure or answer. Teacher provides feedback (e.g., praises all ideas, particularly the conventional one). | Semiauthoritarian and teacher centered: Direct and semidirect instruction (teaching by "careful" imposition). | Foster adaptive expertise: the meaningful memorization of facts, definitions, rules, formulas, and procedures. |

| | | | | |
|---|---|---|---|---|
| Investigative Approach | Instru- mentalism | Many right choices: There is a choice of possible procedures or answers and often many are good. | Open internal authority: Teacher or student remains committed to a method or viewpoint as long as it is effective. Teacher responds to incorrect procedures or answers by posing a question, problem, or task that prompts stu- dent reflection. | Semidemocratic and student cen- tered: Semiindirect instruction (guided participatory democracy). | Foster all aspects of mathematical profi- ciency: productive disposition (e.g., in- terest, confidence and constructive be- liefs about learning and using mathe- matics), conceptual understanding (the basis for adaptive expertise), compu- tational fluency, and strategic mathemati- cal thinking (the ca- pacity to conduct mathematical in- quiry including problem solving and reasoning). |
| Problem- Solving Approach | Extreme Relativism | No right or wrong: There are many possible, equally valid possibilities. | No external authority: Teacher and each stu- dent define his or her own truth. Children evaluate their own conclusions. | Completely democratic and extremely student centered: Indirect instruction (teach- ing by negotiation). | Foster mathemati- cal thinking—the ability to conduct mathematical inquiry. |

| | Focus of Instruction | Teacher's/Students' Roles | Organizing Principle | Methods |
|---|---|---|---|---|
| Skills Approach | Procedural content (e.g., how to add multidigit numbers). | Teacher serves as a director: an information dispenser (informer) and taskmaster (manager). Because children are viewed as uninformed and helpless, students must be spoonfed knowledge. | Bottom-up (logically): Sequential instruction from most basic skills to most complex skills such as problem solving. | • Teacher lectures and demonstrates.<br>• Textbook-based and largely symbolic.<br>• Children work in isolation.<br>• Practice with an emphasis on written, sterile worksheets.<br>• Little or no use of manipulatives or technology. |
| Conceptual Approach | Procedural and conceptual content (e.g., why you carry when adding multidigit numbers). | Teacher serves as a shepherd: information dispenser (informer) and up-front guide (conductor). Because children are seen as capable of understanding mathematics if helped, they are engaged in quasi-independent activities and discussions. | Bottom-up (psychologically): Sequential instruction based on the readiness of students to construct understanding. | • Didactic instruction supplemented by guided discovery-learning.<br>• Textbook-based, but teacher uses, e.g., meaningful analogies and concrete models to explain procedures.<br>• Whole-class, small group, and individual instruction.<br>• Children imitate manipulative procedures demonstrated by the teacher. |
| Investigative Approach | Procedural content, conceptual content, and the | Teacher serves as a mentor: activity organizer (instigator) and guide-on-the-side (moderator). Because | Top-down (guided): Teacher usually poses a "worthwhile task" (one that is challenging | • Various methods with an emphasis on indirect techniques that involve students in exploring, conjecturing about, and debating ideas (e.g., semi-guided discovery learning). |

| | | |
|---|---|---|
| processes of mathematical inquiry (problem solving, reasoning, conjecturing, representing and communicating). | children have informal knowledge and an inherent need to understand, they are capable of inventing their own solutions and making (at least some) sense of mathematical situations themselves (i.e., students are engaged in semi-independent activities and discussions). and complex) as way of exploring, learning and practicing basic concepts and skills; teacher may take advantage of teachable moments (e.g., question or problem posed by student). | • Projects, problems, everyday situations, activities, science experiments, children's literature, math games, etc., create a need for learning and practicing math; textbooks serve a supporting role (e.g., a source of worthwhile tasks and resolving disagreements over definitions). <br>• Children often work together in groups. <br>• Students encouraged to invent, share, and streamline their own concrete models and, later, written procedures (including the conventional one or equally or more efficient nonconventional ones). <br>• Practice done purposefully. <br>• Use of technology is a key aim and central to many learning tasks. |
| Problem-Solving Approach | Processes of mathematical inquiry: problem solving, reasoning, conjecturing, representing, and communicating. | Teacher serves as a partner: participant, monitor, and devil's advocate. Students engage in relatively independent activities and discussions. Top-down (unguided): Class tackles problems of their own choosing, whether or not students have received formal instruction on the content involved. | • Open-ended or unstructured discovery learning. <br>• Content instruction done incidentally as needed; little or no use of textbooks. <br>• Students encouraged to invent, share, and streamline their own concrete models and, later, written procedures. |

*Note.*  Based on Baroody with Coslick (1998) and Baroody (2003). Copyright © 1998 and 2003, respectively by Lawrence Erlbaum Associates. Adapted by permission.

is the traditional lecture-and-drill approach, which Brownell (1935) labeled "drill theory." The conceptual approach is essentially what Brownell called "meaning theory" and embodied his ideas for reforming the traditional skills approach. The problem-solving approach is basically what Brownell called "incidental-learning theory," which was embodied in John Dewey's early progressive-education movement and later in "Free or Open Schools" (e.g., Silberman, 1973) and some Piagetian (radical constructivists') curricula (e.g., Furth & Wachs, 1974; Neill, 1960). The investigative approach, in effect, is a composite of what Brownell called the meaning and incidental-learning theories. This purposeful, meaningful, and inquiry-based approach embodies the NCTM's (1989, 1991, 2000) standards and "developmentally appropriate practices" (Bredekamp & Copple, 1997). (See, e.g., Baroody, 2003, and Baroody with Coslick, 1998, for a detailed comparison of these four approaches.)

Both psychological and educational research and practical consider-ations suggest that the investigative approach is the best bet for promoting all aspects of mathematical proficiency: conceptual understanding (well-connected or meaningful learning), computational fluency (the effi-cient, appropriate, and flexible use of basic skills), strategic mathematical thinking (e.g., problem solving and reasoning), and a productive disposi-tion (e.g., the interest, confidence, and persistence to learn mathematics and to solve challenging problems; Baroody, 2003; Baroody with Coslick, 1998). (For a detailed discussion of mathematical proficiency, see Kilpat-rick, Swafford & Findell, 2001; Schoenfeld, 1985, 1992.) Furthermore, al-though more research is needed to settle the issue, there is some reason to believe that even children with severe learning difficulties might benefit from the investigative approach (Baroody, in press; see Baroody, 1996, 1999, for reviews of the literature).

*The Challenge.* As Ginsburg, Klein, and Starkey (1998) noted, psychological research has had and can have an important impact on educators' and the public's view of how mathematics should be taught. Unfortunately, its impact on educational practice has not, to date, been entirely positive. Indeed, Ginsburg et al. argued that although William Brownell (1935) won the hearts and minds of mathematics educators with his meaning theory, Thorndike (1922) won the hearts and minds of practitioners with his drill theory. Many teachers and other adults cling to the view that teaching involves talking and learning involves imitating and practicing facts, definitions, procedures, and formulas until they are memorized by rote. Indeed, many teachers and other adults believe that mathematics should be taught the way they were taught, even if they found it unappealing, anxiety-provoking, and/or largely unhelpful. In brief, the conventional view of mathematics is the skills approach, not the conceptual approach, let alone the more effective but more complicated standards-based investigative approach. The challenge remaining is convincing teachers and the public at large that the standards-based investigative approach is more effective than the traditional skills approach, or even the conceptual approach. (See Baroody, 2003, for a comparison of the investigative and conceptual approaches and why reform efforts based on the latter may not be effective.)

## Reasons Teachers Need a Deep Understanding of Mathematical Psychology

Changing the beliefs of teachers (e.g., convincing them of the merits of a child-centered approach), however, is not enough. Indeed, many early childhood educators already believe in such an approach. Early childhood and special education teachers need a powerful and practical framework in order to make the innumerable decisions needed to implement the investigative approach effectively. In the following sections, I outline the general rationale for why teachers need an extensive knowledge base, one that includes a deep understanding of mathematical psychology. I then outline three important ways this developmental framework can help educators.

### General Reasons Why Early Childhood Educators Need a Powerful Developmental Framework

John Dewey (1963), the father of the progressive-education movement, recognized that his early efforts to implement a child-centered approach were not successful and concluded that simply providing children experiences in the form of free play or unstructured discovery learning (the problem-solving or incidental approach) did not ensure learning. He came to the following conclusions:

1. Educational reform cannot simply be a knee-jerk reaction to traditional instruction (the skills approach). That is, new teaching methods cannot be substituted for traditional methods simply because they are different from the latter. New teaching approaches, methods, or tools must have their own (theoretical, empirical, and practical) justification. The *PSSM* (NCTM, 2000), particularly chapters 1 ("A Vision for School Mathematics") and 2 ("Principles for School Mathematics")—along with previous NCTM (1989, 1991, 1995) standards documents—provides a well-articulated justification for current reform efforts.

2. Teachers must strive to provide *educative experiences* (experiences that lead to learning or a basis for later learning), not *mis-educative experiences* (experiences for experience's sake and that may impede development). This sentiment is reflected in the following statement in the *PSSM* (NCTM, 2000): "High-quality learning results from formal and informal experiences during the preschool years. 'Informal' does not mean un-

planned or haphazard" (p. 75).[1] It is further reflected in the "curriculum principle": "A curriculum is more than a collection of activities; it must be coherent, focused on important mathematics, and well articulated across the grades" (NCTM, 2000, p. 14).

3. Educative experiences result "from an interaction of external factors, such as the nature of the subject matter and teaching practices, and internal factors, such as a child's [developmental readiness] and interests" (Baroody, 1987, p. 37). The importance of both external and internal factors is emphasized throughout the *PSSM* (NCTM, 2000). For instance, the following quotes are clear allusions to the latter factor: "Teachers of young students ... need to be knowledgeable about the many ways students learn mathematics" (p. 75). "Teachers must recognize that young students can think in sophisticated ways" (p. 77).

***Teachers Need to Understand the Whys and Hows of the Investigative Approach.*** In regard to Item 1 from the preceding list, early childhood and special education teachers need to understand the rationale for the reform movement (the standards-based investigative approach) and its recommended methods. This includes the psychological reasons why a purposeful, meaningful, and inquiry-based approach makes more sense than a traditional skills approach, or even the conceptual approach (as embodied, e.g., in the "California Standards," California Department of Education, 1999; see, Baroody, 2003, in press, and Baroody with Coslick, 1998, for a more complete discussion of this argument). Such knowledge will permit educators to substitute innovative methods for traditional ones in a thoughtful and reflective manner—that is, to use new educational tools flexibly, selectively, and adaptively. Parenthetically, it will also enable teachers to justify their methods effectively to interested others such as parents.

***Teachers Need to Be Able to Critically Analyze Activities.*** In regard to Item 2, educators must be provided with more than a bag of tricks. They must be helped to construct the knowledge that enables them to distinguish between worthwhile activities and those that are not. This requires an extensive understanding of young children's mathematical development. For instance, the still highly useful *Mathematics Their Way* program (Baratta-Lorton, 1976) includes a number of physical activities (e.g., hand clapping, foot stomping, and finger snapping) to "provide

---

[1]A popular view is that "play is children's work" (NCTM, 2000, p. 74; see also Bruner, Jolly, & Sylva, 1976). Dewey's (1963) distinction between educative and mis-educative experience can be interpreted to mean that not all play is the former—of equal value developmentally. Although this qualification is important for practitioners to keep in mind, common sense dictates that play for the sake of fun is valuable for young children and has a place in early childhood education. In other words, some balance between play for learning and play simply for joy seems a reasonable goal for young children.

experience saying one number with one motion" (p. 90). This one-to-one correspondence between a physical action such as finger pointing and uttering a count term is a key basis for object counting (enumeration). Early childhood teachers who are knowledgeable about developmental research would know that children typically master this prerequisite for enumeration quite early—about 2 to 3 years of age. Thus, they might choose the *Mathematics Their Way* activities just described as precounting lessons for toddlers and children hampered by a developmental delay, because it would be an educative experience for them. They would not choose to do this activity for most 4- to 6-year-olds, because it would be an unnecessary and hence, a mis-educative experience for these children (Baroody with Coslick, 1998).

***Teachers Must Understand Children's Knowledge and Thinking in Order to Provide Worthwhile Activities.*** Item 3 from the earlier list underscores the point made previously in this chapter's introduction. As the example in the preceding paragraph illustrates, the powerful and practical framework necessary to make effective teaching decisions must include knowledge of mathematical psychology (internal factors) as well as knowledge of content and methods (external factors). By understanding what young children know about these foundational concepts and what they can do with them, teachers can better incorporate developmentally appropriate activities to nurture their students' mathematical development.

### *What Mathematical Psychology Can Tell Early Childhood Educators*

A deep understanding of mathematical psychology can help educators decide what to teach, when to teach it, and how to teach. This point is illustrated by the example discussed in the next section.

***What to Teach.*** As documented in subsequent chapters, young children display a surprising array of informal mathematical competencies. For example, not only do they seem ready to solve simple nonverbal and, later, verbal addition and subtraction problems, many preschoolers also seem capable of solving simple division (fair-sharing) problems. Not only do they seem capable of reasoning about whole numbers, but they may be capable of reasoning qualitatively about fractions.

***When to Teach.*** As the *Math Their Way* example about one-to-one counting discussed in the previous section demonstrates, a familiarity with developmental psychology can be indispensable deciding when a particular concept or skill should be the focus of instruction.

***How to Teach.*** Mathematical psychology can also provide educators invaluable clues about how to teach young children, in general, and how to help them learn specific skills, concepts, and inquiry competencies in particular.

## A Case in Point

Recent findings regarding children's informal addition strategy of counting on (e.g., for 5 + 3, counting: "5; 6 [is one more], 7 [is two more], 8 is three more]") illustrates how psychological research can be used to justify the investigative approach in efforts to change beliefs about early childhood instruction and to illustrate a general (constructivist) teaching principle. That is, it can help teachers, administrators, and parents recognize how children can construct meaningful mathematical knowledge in a purposeful and inquiry-based manner, and why this is ultimately more beneficial to students than the traditional lecture-and-drill method. The recent psychological research regarding counting on can also provide specific guidelines for facilitating key achievements in young children's informal addition development by specifying what to teach, when to teach it, and, perhaps most important, how to teach it.

### The General Principle: Guiding Children's Mathematical Discoveries

Because psychological research has brought the relatively efficient counting-on strategy to the attention of educators, various efforts have been made to incorporate instruction on it into early childhood mathematics curricula and textbooks. Often, these efforts involve direct instruction, such as modeling by a teacher or a textbook example and imitation by students (see, e.g., p. 92 of Eicholz et al., 1991).

I agree with Les Steffe (2000) that imposing such a strategy on children does not make sense. Children who do not understand the underlying conceptual basis for this strategy may learn counting on by rote but not apply it when needed (i.e., they may forsake its use in favor of a more meaningful strategy). Such children may also misapply the meaningless strategy by, for instance, starting the keeping-track process too soon (e.g., for 5 + 3, counting: "5 [*is one more*], 6 [*is two more*], 7 [*is three more*]—the sum is 7"; Baroody & Tiilikainen, 2003; Hopkins, 1998). Other children may simply reject the strategy outright and not use it.

Consider, for instance, the case of Felicia (Baroody, 1984), who typically used a counting-all procedure (e.g., for 3 + 5, counted: "1, 2, 3, 4, 5; 6 [*is one more*], 7 [*is two more*], 8 [*is three more*]—the sum is 8"). Although this child used an abstract counting-on or counting-on-like strategy with large addends (e.g., for 25 + 3, counted "25, 26, 27, 28" or "20, 21, 22, 23, 24, 25,

26, 27, 28"), when counting on was modeled for her using single-digit combinations, she noted that you can't add that way. Furthermore, she persisted in using counting-all strategies with such combinations, even after several demonstrations.

The case of Brianna illustrates the possible conceptual barriers to accepting and adopting a counting-on procedure (Baroody & Tiilikainen, 2003; Baroody, Tiilikainen, & Tai, 2000). This kindergartner consistently considered as "smart" a concrete counting-all strategy (e.g, for 3 + 5, count out three items and next five items to represent the addends 3 and 5, respectively, and then count all eight items put out to determine the sum). However, she considered the counting-on strategy as "not smart." For instance, when this strategy was modeled using 6 + 8, she explained, "You're wrong. You started [counting the second addend] at nine. You are supposed to start at one." This explanation is consistent with Fuson's (1992) argument that to invent a verbal or abstract strategy, children must recognize that both addends can be represented in a single count: "the embedded integration of both addends." For the other demonstration of counting on with 7 + 5, Brianna commented, "Maybe we should count out seven blocks [represent the first addend]." This explanation is consistent with Fuson's observation that children must recognize that it is unnecessary to produce the first addend sequence: "the embedded cardinal-count principle."

Nevertheless, I also agree with Karen Fuson's (2000) commentary on Steffe's (2000) paper—that it can be helpful and sometimes even necessary to promote the learning of counting on. Fortunately, recent research suggests a way that teachers can *guide* children's *invention* of this procedure, one that involves helping students make the conceptual breakthrough needed to understand the procedure. Put differently, the approach takes into account the concerns raised by both Steffe and Fuson.

### Specific Guidance About What, When, and How

Baroody (1995) found that children with normal or below-normal IQs typically began counting on soon after discovering the *number-after rule for* n + 1 *combinations*: "The sum of a n + 1 combination is simply the number after *n* in the counting sequence" (e.g., the sum of 5 + 1 is the number after *five*: *six*). Bråten (1996), likewise, found this pattern with children with learning difficulties. Apparently, this induced rule provided a conceptual basis or scaffold for counting on. For example, children seem to reason that if the sum of 5 + 1 is the number after *five* in the counting sequence, then the sum of 5 + 3 must be three numbers after *five* in the counting sequence: "six, seven, eight." Furthermore, as might be expected if the number-after rule served as a scaffold for inventing counting

TABLE 6.2
*Adding by Counting on—Specific Guidelines About What,*
*When, and How to Teach*

| | Developmental prerequisite for counting on | Addition strategy of counting on |
|---|---|---|
| What to teach: | The number-after rule for $n + 1$ combinations. | The extension of the number-after for $n + 1$ combinations rule to larger $(n + m)$ combinations. |
| When to teach: | Once children have developed and mastered the number-after skill (e.g., can efficiently specify that after five comes six, without counting from one). | Once children can consistently use their existing number-after knowledge to answer any $n + 1$ combination. |
| How to teach: | Encourage children to discover and to discuss (share) the connection between their number-after knowledge and $n + 1$ combinations by providing purposeful opportunities to compute $n + 1$ sums and to look for shortcuts. | Encourage children to discover and to discuss (share) the connection between their number-after rule for $n + 1$ combinations by providing purposeful opportunities to compute somewhat larger $n + m$ sums and to look for shortcuts. |

on, the majority (6 of 10) of children described in the Baroody (1995) report first used this strategy (or first extended this strategy beyond $n + 1$ or $1 + n$ combinations) with $n + 2$ or $2 + n$ combinations, which require minimal attention to the keeping-track process.

This research suggests the specific guidelines in Table 6.2 for helping children invent counting on for themselves (Baroody with Coslick, 1998). Prompting children to discover patterns and relations and then apply them in somewhat novel contexts is psychologically sound because it encourages them to construct their own understandings and procedures (Steffe, 2000). It is pedagogically sound because it involves children in mathematical inquiry and thinking (e.g., looking for patterns, using logical reasoning, communicating with peers). This approach also allows teachers to discharge their responsibility of promoting more advanced concepts and procedures in a nondidactic but a reasonably efficient manner (cf. Fuson & Secada, 1986; Secada, Fuson, & Hall, 1983).

## CONCLUSIONS

In brief, as the discussion of how to teach counting on illustrates, psychological research can help make a powerful and convincing case for the standards-based investigative approach by illustrating how it can be effective in promoting the learning of specific content, including basic skills (facts, procedures, and formulas), concepts or principles, and inquiry competencies (e.g., inductive and deductive reasoning; see Baroody with Coslick, 1998, for additional examples). Psychological knowledge can also be invaluable to educators as a guide for how to implement the investigative approach, in general, and to how to use it to teach specific content, in particular. It can also provide teachers the detailed knowledge about what, when, and how to guide the development of these specific mathematical competencies.

Even so, William James' (1939) caution to educators about using psychological knowledge is still relevant:

> I say moreover that you make a great, a very great mistake, if you think that psychology, being the science of the mind's laws, is something from which you can deduce definite programmes and schemes and methods of instruction for immediate schoolroom use. Psychology is a science, and teaching is an art, and sciences never generate arts directly out of themselves. An intermediary inventive mind must make the application, by using its originality. (pp. 7–8)

As illustrated in the "Number and Operations" chapter (Baroody, chap. 7, this volume), psychological knowledge is also constantly changing as more effective measures are devised, new facts are discovered, and theories change to accommodate the new evidence. Moreover, psychological findings are not the only basis for making educational decisions. Even if young children are capable of constructing a particular concept, such as fraction addition and subtraction, it does not necessarily follow that it should be taught. Educators must weigh the relative advantages and disadvantages of doing so because, among other practical considerations, teaching time is limited.

## PART II: USING STANDARDS AS A VEHICLE
## FOR PROFESSIONAL DEVELOPMENT

In this part of the chapter, I make a case for using national and state early childhood standards as basis for helping educators, including teachers, supervisors, and curriculum developers construct the powerful developmental framework necessary to devise or implement effective child-centered mathematics instruction for all young children. I conclude with comments on the roles detailed psychological knowledge can and should play in early childhood mathematics standards and the feasibility of including such information in these documents.

## Using Standards Documents to Disseminate Knowledge About Mathematical Learning

### *The Rationale*

National and state standards can and, I believe, should play a role in teacher professional development—in the belief-changing and framework-building processes necessary to implement the investigative approach. This can be done, in part, by developing research-based standards that create new and more accurate expectations of young children. Including brief summaries of recent research or, better yet, vignettes illustrating their findings could also serve this purpose. A broad and concerted effort by the federal and state governments, the NCTM, and other interested parties should be undertaken to educate teachers, administrators, curriculum developers, and the public about the national and state early childhood standards and the evidence that supports them.

### *Using Numeral Reading and Writing as an Example*

In an NCTM research presession talk (Baroody, 2000), I used the development of numeral-reading and -writing skills to illustrate the value of psychological knowledge for early childhood and special education teachers. In the following subsections, I briefly summarize my key points, the reaction of one of the discussants of this paper, and some conclusions about the value of psychological knowledge to professional development.

### *Implications for Early Childhood Standards.* 
Reading and writing numerals involves constructing an accurate mental image of these symbols, a mental representation that includes their parts and how these parts fit together to make a whole. Writing numerals also requires a motor plan, a step-by-step plan of execution for translating a mental image into appropriate motor actions. Although young children typically construct a mental image and motor plan with little help, this process—as the more detailed discussion in my next chapter suggests—is not an uncomplicated process. To ensure that instructional efforts are well directed and children receive the guidance they need, teachers must be familiar with the details

of this process.[2] Furthermore, children with learning difficulties frequently need more than a little guidance but, unfortunately, often do not get it because their teachers are unaware of the psychological processes underlying numeral-reading and -writing skills.

Given the points just made, I (Baroody, 2000) concluded that it is not sufficient for national or state standards for early childhood mathematics to simply state the goal, "Kindergartners should master reading and writing numerals from 0 to 9." Such a statement does not provide teachers any guidance on how to achieve the goal. I went on to conclude that national and state early childhood standards could and should be used a vehicle for helping teachers construct a better understanding of children's mathematical learning (e.g., how they learn to read and write numerals).

*A Counterargument.* In her discussion of my (Baroody, 2000) paper, Mary Lindquist noted that she never thought about sticks and loops (analogies for the component parts of the numeral 6) when writing 6s and implied that the psychological model for learning how to read and write numerals was not important. She concluded that caring about and listening carefully to children is sufficient to overcome the problems we face in mathematics education. She further argued that (national or state) standards are not an appropriate forum to educate practitioners and not the place for detailed developmental information.

*Psychological Knowledge: A Key But Sometimes Overlooked Component of Professional Development.* Few would argue with the proposition that the professional development of teachers should include a solid grounding in mathematical content and pedagogy (Howe, 1999; Ma, 1999; NCTM, 1991). The third critical component of such development—an understanding of how children's mathematical thinking and knowledge develop (e.g., Baroody with Coslick, 1998; NCTM, 1991)—is not always considered in reform efforts (Baroody, 1987; Kline, 1974; cf. Howe, 1999; Ma, 1999).

As I suggested earlier in this chapter, Dr. Lindquist was correct to imply that practitioners and those responsible for training them should not accept psy-

---

[2]Without a powerful psychological framework to guide them, teachers may blindly follow teacher guides or curricula. In *Mathematic Their Way*, for instance, Baratta-Lorton (1976) suggested having children copy a numeral with finger motions in the air or in the palm of their hand. Unfortunately, such a procedure leaves no visible record for a child or a teacher to evaluate the child's successful execution of a motor plan. As a result, a child who is using an inaccurate or incomplete motor plan may not receive the feedback needed to prompt a correction to this plan. Furthermore, the authors of one elementary mathematics education textbook (D'Augustine & Smith, 1992) recommended delaying numeral-writing instruction until first grade—until after children developed the fine-motor coordination necessary for this skill. This advice disregards the fact that the numeral-writing difficulties of kindergartners are typically due to an incomplete or an inaccurate motor plan, not the lack of fine-motor coordination.

chological theories or evidence uncritically. However, whether or not she has ever thought of a 6 as being composed of a stick and a loop is not relevant to gauging the value of the numeral-reading and -writing model I (Baroody, 2000) discussed. For most adults and even many children, the mental images (knowledge of the parts and part–whole relations) and motor plans for numerals are nonconscious and may be largely or entirely nonverbal. "Sticks and loops" is merely an analogy for this underlying knowledge—an analogy that can be useful to parents and teachers, especially when a child asks, "What does a 6 look like?" or "How do you make a 6?"

Even if a psychological model is not entirely accurate or complete—as is inevitably the case—its educational value depends on whether or not it yields useful predictions, insights, or guidelines. The numeral-reading and -writing model described earlier does effectively explain why, for instance, children are more prone to confuse some numerals (2 and 5 or 6 and 9) but not others, and why some children are prone to reversals, even with a model numeral in front of them. Moreover, this model is extremely helpful—as empirical evidence shows—in providing direction on how to overcome these difficulties. In fact, I have used the model with good results with typical children, including my own (Baroody with Coslick, 1998), children diagnosed as learning disabled (Baroody & Kaufman, 1993), and those diagnosed as mentally retarded (Baroody, 1987, 1988). This model and its supporting evidence is merely one example of the considerable body of psychological theory and research that has proven to be useful in teaching young children mathematics.

Caring about and listening carefully to children are unarguably crucial for effective teaching. However, by themselves, they are not enough; effective teaching also requires competence, which includes a powerful developmental framework (Baroody with Coslick, 1998). Without such knowledge, teachers are not in a good position to help children no matter how much they care or how carefully they listen.

Consider the case of a second-grade teacher whose own son was diagnosed as learning disabled and was having considerable difficulty writing numerals. This woman, who cared deeply about her son, was unable to respond effectively to his pleas for help because her training did not include an effective model of numeral reading and writing. When he asked, for instance, "How do you make a 7?" she responded by drawing a 7. Unfortunately, such demonstrations were not enough for him to decipher where to start and in which direction to head, where to stop, and what to do next (i.e., to construct an accurate and complete motor plan). Despite his mother's (and teachers') best efforts, then, the boy continued to have numeral-writing difficulties throughout the elementary grades and beyond. If his mother (and teachers) had had the theoretical framework to understand that his question (e.g., "How do you make a seven?") was, in effect, a request for a motor plan, it is likely he could have been spared a great deal of unnecessary anguish.

If early childhood and special education teachers are ever to achieve the status of genuine professionals, they must be helped to secure an accurate and detailed understanding of young children's mathematical learning. The proposed early childhood standards should be a beginning of this professional development. These documents are and should be inherently educational in nature. Why the standards should include specific psychological knowledge and how this can be achieved is discussed next.

## The Roles of Detailed Psychological Knowledge in Early Childhood Standards and the Feasibility of Its Inclusion in Such Documents

Fuson (2000) raised several important questions about the inclusion of detailed psychological information in national or state standards documents: (a) What purpose would it serve? and (b) Is it practical? I address these questions in turn.

### Purposes

Using detailed developmental knowledge to develop specific standards is useful, indeed, necessary for the following reasons:

* To serve as a guide for developing, maintaining, and evaluating the high-quality pre-service teacher education programs necessary to produce truly professional teachers who are capable of implementing an NCTM standards-based investigative approach.
* To serve as a guide for developing, maintaining, and evaluating the high-quality in-service teacher education programs necessary to upgrade or maintain a truly professional teaching corps that is capable of implementing an NCTM standards-based investigative approach.
* To develop and evaluate state, district, or school mathematics curricula that are consistent with an NCTM standards-based investigative approach.
* To develop and evaluate assessment means consistent with the NCTM (1991) *Assessment Standards* at all levels (commercial, national, state, district, school, or classroom levels).
* To serve as a resource for curriculum coordinators or classroom teachers who are interested in implementing the NCTM standards-based investigative approach or who wish to further their professional development on their own.

### Feasibility

Fuson (2000) suggested that developing specific standards would result in hundreds of statements and would make standards documents so overwhelming that they would, by and large, go unread. A practical solution is to have four levels of standards within each conceptual domain: (a) global standards that reflect the really big ideas, (b) general standards that indicate the big ideas, (c) specific standards that summarize the basic developmental components, and (d) detailed standards that delineate the developmental progression within each developmental component. An attempt to lay out these levels of standards for a portion of the number and operations domain, for example, is summarized in Table 7.1 of chapter 7 of this volume.

A main standards document could lay out the first three levels of standards. That is, it could consist of a relatively few global standards, a number of general standards, and include tables, figures, or appendices that summarize the specific standards. This document could also indicate where an interested party could go for the more-detailed standards. The detailed standards could be laid out in a series of supplemental standards (e.g., one for each of the global standards). In addition to or in place of printed supplemental standards, a Web site could include the detailed standards for each specific standard. Indeed, the Web site could be designed to start with the global standards and provide increasing specific standards. Visitors would explore an area as deeply as they needed or desired.

## CONCLUSION

In conclusion, federal and state governments now spend millions of dollars on special education to, for example, provide children with special needs small classes and, in many cases, a personal aide. Unfortunately, the teachers of these smaller classes and the personal teaching aides—by and large—do not have a deep understanding of how special children learn mathematics. The result is that most mathematics instruction of special children is ineffective. Put differently, much of the federal and state investment in special education is simply wasted.

We risk the same result with our efforts to improve early childhood instruction, if a concerted effort is not made to help early childhood educators construct a powerful and practical framework that includes a deep understanding of how young children learn mathematics. In order to help remedy the insufficient attention paid to the mathematics instruction and learning of young children, particularly those with special needs, the NCTM, state education departments, and the federal government—through their publications, the proposed national and state early childhood mathematics standards, and other efforts—need to help early childhood and special pre- and in-service teachers construct an accurate and extensive knowledge of the mathematical teaching and learning of all children.

Helping pre- and in-service teachers construct a deep understanding of the mathematics they need to teach, how children learn mathematics, and how to foster this learning effectively is necessary for elevating teaching to the level of a true profession (one comparable to medicine or law) and for the success of the current reform movement. Many anti-NCTM-standards proponents, including some supporters of the California Standards, believe that it is not practical or even possible to help teachers achieve professional-level knowledge—a deep understanding of mathematics, psychology, and pedagogy. For this reason, they propose a different approach to reform: skills-focused standards, "teacher-proof" curricula, high-stakes standards-based testing, and accountability. The aim is to eliminate incompetent teachers or ineffective schools (rather than support their redevelopment).

I was disturbed to hear again and again at our October meeting in Dallas that the early childhood standards should not be too complicated because, for example, teachers would be overwhelmed. By advocating "dumbed down" standards, we are conceding that anti-NCTM-standards proponents' premise is correct, namely that the vast majority of teachers are not bright or sufficiently motivated enough to acquire the knowledge necessary to implement sophisticated instruction, such as the investigative approach, effectively (cf. Brownell, 1935). (I am ashamed that there were times during the meeting when I concluded that this pessimistic conclusion was, in fact, a realistic assessment of the situation.) By focusing on global and general standards to the exclusion of specific and detailed standards, we help to set in concrete *what is*, not on *what could* or *should be*.

Developing a simplified list of goals for each grade level has its uses and should be done. However, it should be clearly tied to big mathematical ideas and to more specific and detailed research-based goals. The latter is necessary to counter the charges of anti-NCTM-standards proponents that current reform efforts are merely "fuzzy math" and based on ideology rather than science. In brief, the development of a coherent multilevel set of standards as illustrated in chapter 7 of this volume is necessary to empower teachers to foster the mathematical power of all children.

## ACKNOWLEDGMENTS

This chapter is based on papers presented at the symposium "Linking Research and the New Early Childhood Mathematics Standards" at the Research Presession of the annual meeting of the National Council of Teachers of Mathematics, Chicago, April 2000; the Conference on Standards for Preschool and Kindergarten Mathematics Education (sponsored by the National Science Foundation and ExxonMobil Foundation), Arlington, Virginia, May 2000; and a follow-up conference in Dallas, Texas, October, 2000.

The preparation and writing of this chapter was supported, in part, by a Faculty Fellowship awarded by the Bureau of Educational Research (College of Education, University of Illinois at Urbana-Champaign) and a grant from the National Science Foundation (BCS-0111829). The opinions expressed are solely those of the author and do not necessarily reflect the position, policy, or endorsement of the National Science Foundation.

# REFERENCES

Ashcraft, M. H., Kirk, E. P., & Hopko, D. (1998). On the cognitive consequences of mathematics anxiety. In C. Donlan (Ed.), *The development of mathematical skills* (pp. 175–196). Hove, England: Psychology Press.

Baratta-Lorton, M. (1976). *Mathematics their way.* Menlo Park, CA: Addison-Wesley.

Baroody, A. J. (1984). The case of Felicia: A young child's strategies for reducing memory demands during mental addition. *Cognition and Instruction, 1,* 109–116.

Baroody, A. J. (1987). *Children's mathematical thinking: A developmental framework for preschool, primary, and special education teachers.* New York: Teachers College Press.

Baroody, A. J. (1988). A cognitive approach to writing instruction for children classified as mentally handicapped. *Arithmetic Teacher, 36*(2), 7–11.

Baroody, A. J. (1995). The role of the number-after rule in the invention of computational short cuts. *Cognition and Instruction, 13,* 189–219.

Baroody, A. J. (1996). An investigative approach to teaching children labeled learning disabled. In D. K. Reid, W. P. Hresko, & H. L. Swanson (Eds.), *Cognitive approaches to learning disabilities* (3rd ed., pp. 545–615). Austin, TX: Pro-Ed.

Baroody, A. J. (1999). The development of basic counting, number, and arithmetic knowledge among children classified as mentally retarded. In L. M. Glidden (Ed.), *International review of research in mental retardation* (Vol. 22, pp. 51–103). New York: Academic Press.

Baroody, A. J. (2000, April*). Key transitions in the mathematical development of typical and special children.* Paper presented as part of the symposium titled, "Linking research and the new early childhood mathematics standards" at the Research Presession of the annual meeting of the National Council of Teachers of Mathematics, Chicago.

Baroody, A. J. (2003). The development of adaptive expertise and flexibility: The integration of conceptual and procedural knowledge. In A. J. Baroody & A. Dowker (Eds.), *The development of arithmetic concepts and skills: Constructing adaptive expertise* (pp. 1–34). Mahwah, NJ: Lawrence Erlbaum Associates.

Baroody, A. J. (in press). Framework. In F. Fennell (Ed.), *Special education and mathematics: Helping children with learning difficulties achieve mathematical proficiency.* Reston, VA: National Council of Teachers of Mathematics.

Baroody, A. J., with Coslick, R. T. (1998). *Fostering children's mathematical power: An investigative approach to K–8 mathematics instruction.* Mahwah, NJ: Lawrence Erlbaum Associates.

Baroody, A. J., & Kaufman, L. C. (1993). The case of Lee: Assessing and remedying a numerical-writing difficulty. *Teaching Exceptional Children, 25*(3), 14–16.

Baroody, A. J., & Tiilikainen, S. (2003). Two perspectives on addition development. In A. J. Baroody & A. Dowker (Eds.), *The development of arithmetic concepts and skills: Constructing adaptive expertise* (pp. 75–125). Mahwah, NJ: Lawrence Erlbaum Associates.

Baroody, A. J., Tiilikainen, S. H., & Tai, Y. (2000). The application and development of an addition goal sketch. In M. L. Fernández (Ed.), *Proceedings of the Twenty-Second Annual Meeting of the North American Chapter of the International Group for the Psychology of Mathematics Education* (Vol. 2, pp. 709–714). Columbus, OH: ERIC Clearinghouse for Science, Mathematics, and Environment Education.

Bråten, I. (1996). *Cognitive strategies in mathematics. Report No. 10, 1996.* Oslo, Norway: University of Oslo, Institute for Educational Research.

Bredekamp, S., & Copple, C. (1997). *Developmentally appropriate practice in early childhood programs.* Washington, DC: National Association for the Education of Young Children.

Brownell, W. A. (1935). Psychological considerations in the learning and the teaching of arithmetic. In D. W. Reeve (Ed.), *The teaching of arithmetic* (10th Yearbook of the National Council of Teachers of Mathematics, pp. 1–31). New York: Bureau of Publications, Teachers College, Columbia University.

Bruner, J. S., Jolly, A., & Sylva, K. (1976). *Play: Its role in development and evolution.* New York: Basic Books.

California Department of Education. (1999). *Mathematics framework for California schools.* Sacramento, CA: Author.

D'Augustine, C., & Smith, C. W., Jr. (1992). *Teaching elementary school mathematics.* New York: HarperCollins.

Dewey, J. (1963). *Experience and education.* New York: Collier.

Eicholz, R. E., O'Daffer, P. G., Charles, R. I., Young, S. L., Barnett, C. S., & Fleenor, C. R. (1991). *Grade 1 Addison-Wesley mathematics.* Menlo Park, CA: Addison-Wesley.

Furth, H. G., & Wachs, H. (1974). *Thinking goes to school: Piaget's theory in practice.* New York: Oxford University Press.

Fuson, K. C. (1992). Research on whole number addition and subtraction. In D. Grouws (Ed.), *Handbook of research on mathematics teaching and learning* (pp. 243–275). New York: Macmillan.

Fuson, K. C. (2000, April). *Goals and standards for prek-grade 2: Toward mastery by all.* Discussion of papers presented at the symposium "Linking research and new early childhood mathematics standards," National Council of Teachers of Mathematics Research Presession, Chicago.

Fuson, K. C., & Secada, W. G. (1986). Teaching children to add by counting-on with one-handed finger patterns. *Cognition and Instruction, 3,* 229–260.

Ginsburg, H. P., Klein, A., & Starkey, P. (1998). The development of children's mathematical knowledge: Connecting research with practice. In I. E. Sigel & K. A. Renninger (Eds.), *Handbook of child psychology: Vol. 4. Children psychology in practice* (5th ed., pp. 401–476). New York: Wiley.

Hembree, R. (1990). The nature, effects, and relief of mathematics anxiety. *Journal for Research in Mathematics Education, 21,* 33–46.

Hopkins, S. (1998). *The simple addition performances of learning disabled adolescent students. An explanation of how the moving-on process for developing reliance on retrieval is impeded by pressure.* Unpublished doctoral thesis, Flinders University, South Australia.

Howe, R. (1999). Knowing and teaching elementary mathematics. *Journal for Research in Mathematics Education, 30,* 579–589. (Reprinted from *Notices of the American Mathematical Society, 46,* 881–887)

James, W. (1939). *Talks to teachers on psychology.* New York: Holt.

Kilpatrick, J., Swafford, J., & Findell, B. (Eds.). (2001). *Adding it up: Helping children learn mathematics.* Washington, DC: National Academy Press.

Kline, M. (1974). *Why Johnny can't add.* New York: Vintage.

Ma, L. (1999). *Knowing and teaching elementary mathematics: Teachers' understanding of fundamental mathematics in China and the United States.* Mahwah, NJ: Lawrence Erlbaum Associates.

McLeod, D. B. (1992). Research on affect in mathematics education: A reconceptualization. In D. A. Grows & D. B. McLeod (Eds.), *Handbook of research on mathematics teaching and learning* (pp. 575–596). New York: Macmillan.

National Council of Teachers of Mathematics. (1989). *Curriculum and evaluation standards for school mathematics.* Reston, VA: Author.

National Council of Teachers of Mathematics. (1991). *Professional standards for teaching mathematics.* Reston, VA: Author.

National Council of Teachers of Mathematics. (1995). *Assessment standards for school mathematics.* Reston, VA: Author.

National Council of Teachers of Mathematics. (2000). *Principles and standards for school mathematics.* Reston, VA: Author.

Neill, A. S. (1960). *Summerhill: A radical approach to child rearing.* New York: Hart.

Schoenfeld, A. H. (1985). *Mathematical problem solving.* New York: Academic Press.

Schoenfeld, A. H. (1992). Learning to think mathematically: Problem solving, metacognition, and sense making in mathematics. In D. A. Grouws (Ed.), *Handbook of research on mathematics teaching and learning* (pp. 334–370). New York: Macmillan.

Secada, W. G., Fuson, K. C., & Hall, J. (1983). The transition from counting-all to counting-on addition. *Journal for Research in Mathematics Education, 14,* 47–57.

Silberman, C. E. (Ed.). (1973). *The open classroom reader.* New York: Vintage Books.

Steffe, L. P. (2000, April). *PSSM from a constructivist perspective.* Paper presented at the symposium "Linking research and the new early childhood mathematics standards," National Council of Teachers of Mathematics Research Presession, Chicago.

Thorndike, E. L. (1922). *The psychology of arithmetic.* New York: Macmillan.

# Appendix

## SOME RESOURCES ON EARLY CHILDHOOD MATHEMATICS EDUCATION

Baratta-Lorton, M. (1976). *Mathematics their way.* Menlo Park, CA: Addison-Wesley.

Baroody, A. J. (1987). *Children's mathematical thinking: A developmental framework for preschool, primary, and special education teachers.* New York: Teachers College Press.

Baroody, A. J. (1989). *A guide to teaching mathematics in the primary grades.* Boston: Allyn & Bacon.

Baroody, A. J., with Coslick, R. T. (1998). *Fostering children's mathematical power: An investigative approach to K-8 mathematics instruction.* Mahwah, NJ: Lawrence Erlbaum Associates.

Bereiter, C., & Engelmann, S. (1966). *Teaching disadvantaged children in the preschool.* Englewood Cliffs, NJ: Prentice-Hall.

Bredekamp, S., & Copple, C. (1997). *Developmentally appropriate practice in early childhood programs.* Washington, DC: National Association for the Education of Young Children.

Burns, M. (1992). *Math and literature (K-3).* Sausalito, CA: Math Solutions Publication.

Copley, J. (Ed.). (1999). *Mathematics in the early years, birth to five.* Reston, VA: National Council of Teachers of Mathematics.

Fromboluti, C. S., & Rinck, N. (1999). *Early childhood, where learning begins, mathematics: Mathematical activities for parents and their 2- to 5-year-old children.* Jessup, MD: U.S. Department of Education.

Smith, S. S. (1997). *Early childhood mathematics.* Boston: Allyn & Bacon.

Thiessen, D., & Mathias, M. (Eds.) (1992). *The wonderful world of mathematics.* Reston, VA: National Council of Teachers of Mathematics.

Whitin, D. J., & Wilde, S. (1992). *Read any good math lately: Children's books for mathematical learning, K-6.* Portsmouth, NH: Heinemann.

# 7

# The Developmental Bases
# For Early Childhood Number
# and Operations Standards

Arthur J. Baroody
*University of Illinois at Urbana-Champaign*

"Historically, number [and operations on them have] been a cornerstone of the entire mathematics curriculum" (National Council of Teachers of Mathematics [NCTM], 2000, p. 32). Indeed, "all the mathematics proposed for prekindergarten through grade 12 is strongly grounded in number.... Young children's earliest reasoning is likely to be about number situations, and their first mathematical representation will probably be of numbers" (NCTM, 2000, p. 32). Furthermore, number and operations on them are essential for most everyday activities. That is, understanding their applications is a basic survival skill in our highly technological and information-dependent society and, thus, a key basis of a mathematical literacy, which is now as important as language literacy.

In Part I of this chapter, I describe a general developmental framework that includes three key transitions. In Part II, I summarize some of what researchers have recently discovered about the development of young children's number and arithmetic as they make these transitions. This knowledge can provide early childhood and special education practitioners with the specific developmental framework necessary to make policy, curriculum, and instructional decisions about early childhood mathematics education.

# PART I: THREE KEY TRANSITIONS IN YOUNG CHILDREN'S NUMERICAL AND ARITHMETIC COMPETENCIES

According to the Mental Models View proposed by Huttenlocher and her colleagues (e.g., Huttenlocher, Jordan, & Levine, 1994; Mix, Huttenlocher, & Levine, 2002a), how children represent number changes. The first key change (transition) involves supplementing inexact, nonverbal representations with exact ones; the second entails the development of counting-based number and arithmetic competencies; and the third encompasses the learning of written symbols (Baroody, 2000, 2002).

## Transition 1: The Development of Exact Precounting Numerical and Arithmetic Processes

Proponents of the Mental Models View (e.g., Mix et al., 2002a) argue that the development of a numerical representation is more complicated than that suggested by the currently popular nativists' view (e.g., Wynn, 1998). According to the latter, infants can differentiate between discrete quantities (collections of items quantified by counting) and continuous quantities (e.g., length, area, weight, time, and other quantities quantified by measurement) and can nonverbally "count" and mentally represent small collections with surprising precision. Nativists also assume that the development of conventional counting knowledge is guided by this innate precounting knowledge and builds directly on it.

According to the Mental Models View, children in the pre-Transition 1 phase do not initially differentiate between discrete and continuous quantities and may represent both inexactly in terms of one or more perceptual cues, such as contour length (Mix, Huttenlocher, & Levine, 2002b). Two factors may account for Transition 1:

1. The evolution of object individuation provides precounters a basis for constructing an understanding of one-to-one correspondence, which, in turn, provides them a basis for identifying and representing discrete quantities and the groundwork for an informal understanding of numerical equivalence and number. For instance, Mix (2001) noted that her 21-month-old son retrieved two dog treats for two pet dogs in another room while saying, in effect, This [one] is for [the name of the first dog], and this [one] is for [the name of the second dog].

2. Huttenlocher et al. (1994) hypothesized that children's ability to create mental models of numbers and, thus, to represent them exactly should start to develop at about age 2, when they begin to exhibit a variety of symbolic activities, such as symbolic play (see also Piaget, 1951). Children between 2 and 3 years of age, for example, become capable of using a picture to understand the layout of a real room or inferring the location of a hidden toy in a room from a model of a miniature toy and room (DeLoache, 1987, 1991).

Pre-Transition 1 and Transition 1 phases in the Mental Models View are consistent with Piaget's (e.g., 1965; Piaget & Inhelder, 1969) view of number development.[1] He too concluded that children's earliest understanding of number was nonverbal, tied to perception, and imprecise. That is, Piaget argued that number development begins before children acquire language or other conventional knowledge, stems from (reflections on) perceptual cues or actions, and, thus, at first, is essentially an estimation process. He also argued that one-to-one correspondence (rather than verbal-based counting) is the psychological basis for the construction of a number concept.[2]

A key intermediate step to the next transition is recognizing that—like color, size, and weight—numbers are an important basis for categorizing and, thus, identifying and comparing items (Mix et al., 2002). Learning the first few count words might focus children's attention on the attribute of number and help them see a numerical commonality among even otherwise (physically) dissimilar collections. That is, knowing number words might serve to promote abstract quantitative thinking and an understanding of numerical equivalence. Some evidence (Baroody, 2002; Baroody & Benson, 2001) indicates that learning number words, in conjunction with subitizing (immediate number recognition), indeed, may play an important role in constructing an understanding of one to four, the intuitive numbers (cf. Klahr & Wallace, 1973; von Glasersfeld, 1982; Wagner & Walters, 1982; Wynn, 1990, 1992).

---

[1]Constance Kamii, in her discussion of my paper presented at the Conference on Standards for Preschool and Kindergarten Mathematics Education (Baroody, 2000), noted that Piaget distinguished between the form of representation and mental structures (e.g., the conceptual content represented) and that he argued that the latter was more important. She concluded her comments by dismissing the Mental Models view as unimportant and useless. Although knowing only the form of number representation, for instance, does not necessarily indicate the extent of a child's understanding of number, it is, in fact, important and useful to understand. For one thing, the type of representation may limit a child's understanding of number or their ability to reason about number in critical ways. As will be illustrated later in the text, the development of more advanced number representation can provide children with a more powerful means of thinking about and using numbers.

Indeed, Piaget (1951) himself devoted considerable effort to describing the development of a symbolic function and how this development built on but differed from sensory-motor intelligence. As Ginsburg and Opper (1969) noted:

"The ability to form mental symbols is an achievement of great magnitude. In the sensorimotor period this capacity was lacking.... By contrast, the older child can use mental symbols to stand for absent events or things. Things no longer need to be present for the child to act on them. In this sense, the ability to symbolize eventually liberates the child from the immediate present" (p. 78).

For a discussion of how representational intelligence (through the use of the symbolic function) differs from sensory-motor intelligence, see Flavell (1963, pages 151 and 152, including the footnote at the bottom of page 151).

[2]Unlike the Mental Models view, though, Piaget (1965) believed that children did not construct an operational or genuine understanding of one-to-one correspondence until they were about seven. This was signaled by the ability to conserve number—an achievement that occurs well after children have learned verbal- and object-counting skills. In Piaget's view, these counting skills were merely learned and used by rote, a view subsequent research largely suggests is inaccurate.

## Transition 2: The Development of Counting-Based Numerical and Arithmetic Competencies

Children's nonverbal and precounting numerical and arithmetical competencies probably provide a scaffold or basis for assimilating counting-based numerical and arithmetical knowledge (Transition 2). Existing evidence indicates that young children are, in fact, more successful on nonverbal versions of arithmetic tasks than on verbally presented story problems, as well as symbolic "number-fact" tasks (Huttenlocher et al., 1994; Jordan, Huttenlocher, & Levine, 1992, 1994; Levine, Jordan, & Huttenlocher, 1992; see Jordan, Hanich, & Uberti, 2003, for a detailed discussion).

## Transition 3: The Development of Written Representations

In this third major transition, children assimilate written representations to nonverbal and verbal-based knowledge of number and arithmetic (Ginsburg, 1977). Transition 3 begins as early as about 3 years of age and, typically, is gradual. For reviews of the literature on this topic, see Donlan (2003), Munn (1998), and Sinclair and Sinclair (1986).

## PART II: RECENT DEVELOPMENTAL RESEARCH AND ITS EDUCATIONAL IMPLICATIONS

In this part of the chapter, I summarize the developmental research and its educational implications regarding two really big ideas that are the basis for the number and operations standard for Grades Pre-K to 2 in chapter 4 of the NCTM's (2000) *Principles and Standards for School Mathematics* (*PSSM*):

- Really Big Idea 1: One of the most essential of human tools, numbers can play several roles, involve numerous relations, and can be represented in various ways.
- Really Big Idea 2: Numbers can be operated on (used to perform computations) in various interrelated ways to model a variety of real-world transformations or situations.

More specifically, I examine six key areas of early number and arithmetic development, namely, using numbers to quantify collections, using numbers to compare collections, adding and subtracting single-digit numbers, understanding part–whole relations, equal partitioning or grouping, and grouping and place value. These concepts form the core of young children's number sense and provide a key basis for understanding and assimilating school-taught mathematics. For each area/concept, I first note the "big idea" underlying it. I then summarize the recent research findings about how each of the basic competencies develop between toddlerhood and the third year of formal number and arithmetic instruction (i.e., second grade) and how each is related to the developmental transitions discussed in Part I. Next, I comment on whether the number and operations standard (and other relevant standards) for Grades Pre-K to 2 mentioned in chapter 3 and delineated in chapter 4 of the *PSSM* (NCTM, 2000) adequately emphasize crucial components of these six competencies. Finally, I make recommendations regarding number and operation standards for early childhood. Four levels of proposed goals (standards) for the first two big ideas (based on the developmental research reviewed in this chapter) are delineated in Table 7.1. Note that these goals range from highly general to highly specific.

## Understanding, Representing, and Using Cardinal Numbers

- Big Idea 1.1: Counting can be used to find out how many items a collection contains or to make a collection of a particular size.

Numbers have four meanings or roles. A key and, perhaps, the earliest developing meaning is the cardinal meaning. A *cardinal number* identifies *how many* items there are in a collection (e.g., This sentence has *five* words). Numbers can also be used to specify *how much* (i.e., a measurement meaning indicating size such as, My grading pencil is only *two* inches long), *where* (i.e., an ordinal meaning indicating position or order, as in Go to Room *34*), or *what* (a nominal meaning in which a number serves as a name, as in Player *21* is really good).

Like physical characteristics such as color or other abstract categories such as fair versus unfair, cardinal numbers are an extremely useful tool for classifying things and, thus, identifying and comparing them (e.g., "Get mommy the cup with two flowers on it"; Mix et al., 2002a). Object counting (enumeration) provides a systematic means for applying number words to items and enhances or enables children to represent mentally and exactly collections, particularly those of more than about four items. Counting further enhances or enables children to create a given number of items (production). An understanding of cardinal number also includes an ability to identify equivalent

collections (e.g., recognizing ■ ■, ★ ★, * * and ■ ■ all as pairs or "*two*," recognizing ■ ■, ★ ★ ★, * * * and ■ ■ ■ all as trios or "*three*," and so forth). Both informal and formal written representations of cardinal numbers (e.g., representing a collection of three items as | | | or 3) can greatly extend our use of numbers (e.g., serve as a memory aid or represent large numbers such as 198,253 compactly).

## Table 7.1

## A Sample of Possible Early Childhood Number and Operations Goals

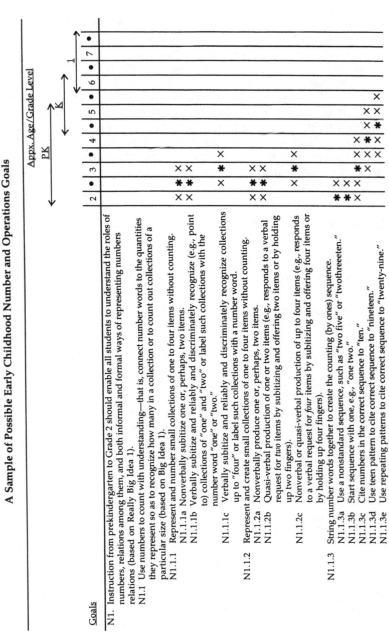

| Goals | \|← PK →\| | \|← K →\| | \|← 1 →\| | | | |
|---|:---:|:---:|:---:|:---:|:---:|:---:|
| **Appx. Age/Grade Level** | 2 | 3 | 4 | 5 | 6 | 7 |
| N1. Instruction from prekindergarten to Grade 2 should enable all students to understand the roles of numbers, relations among them, and both informal and formal ways of representing numbers relations (based on Really Big Idea 1). | | | | | | |
| N1.1 Use numbers to count with understanding—that is, connect number words to the quantities they represent so as to recognize how many in a collection or to count out collections of a particular size (based on Big Idea 1). | | | | | | |
| N1.1.1 Represent and number small collections of one to four items without counting. | | | | | | |
| N1.1.1a Nonverbally subitize one or, perhaps, two items. | X | * | | | | |
| N1.1.1b Verbally subitize and reliably and discriminately recognize (e.g., point to) collections of "one" and "two" or label such collections with the number word "one" or "two." | X | * | | | | |
| N1.1.1c Verbally subitize and reliably and discriminately recognize collections up to "four" or label such collections with a number word. | | X | X | | | |
| N1.1.2 Represent and create small collections of one to four items without counting. | | | | | | |
| N1.1.2a Nonverbally produce one or, perhaps, two items. | X | * | | | | |
| N1.1.2b Quasi-verbal production of one or two items (e.g., responds to a verbal request for *two* items by subitizing and offering two items or by holding up two fingers). | X | * | | | | |
| N1.1.2c Nonverbal or quasi-verbal production of up to four items (e.g., responds to a verbal request for *four* items by subitizing and offering four items or by holding up four fingers). | | X | X | | | |
| N1.1.3 String number words together to create the counting (by ones) sequence. | | | | | | |
| N1.1.3a Use a nonstandard sequence, such as "two five" or "twothreeeiten." | * | X | X | | | |
| N1.1.3b Start sequence with one, e.g., "one two." | * | * | X | | | |
| N1.1.3c Cite numbers in the correct sequence to "ten." | X | X | X | | | |
| N1.1.3d Use teen pattern to cite correct sequence to "nineteen." | | | X | X | | |
| N1.1.3e Use repeating patterns to cite correct sequence to "twenty-nine." | | | * | * | | |

178

| | | | | | | | |
|---|---|---|---|---|---|---|---|
| | | | | | | | × |
| | | | | | | × × | * |
| × | | | × | | × | | × | × * | × |
| × | | | × × * | | × * | | × * | × * × |
| * | | × × × * × | | * × × | | × * × | * × |
| × | | × × × * × | | × * | | × * × | * × |
| × | | * * × | × | × | | * * × | |
| | × | × × | × | | × | * | × |
| | × | | * | | * | | × |
| * | × | | × | × | | × | |

N1.1.4   Use the counting sequence to enumerate collections—that is, to count objects to identify the number of items in a collection.

N1.1.3f   Use repeating patterns to cite correct sequence to "one hundred."

N1.1.4a   Pair a number word of the count sequence with each item of a small collection and identify a collection by repeating the count.

N1.1.4b   Construct the count-cardinal concept—that is, recognize that the last number word used to label items in a collection also represents the total.

N1.1.4c   Accurately enumerate any type of collection of up to five items.

N1.1.4d   Recognize the identity-conservation or number-constancy principle.

N1.1.4e   Recognize the order-irrelevance principle.

N1.1.4f   Accurately enumerate collections to 10.

N1.1.4g   Accurately enumerate collections to 20.

N1.1.5   Use the counting sequence to produce (count out) collections of a specified size.

N1.1.5a   Construct the cardinal-count concept—that is, recognize that a cardinal label for a collection such as "four" is equivalent to actually counting the collection.

N1.1.5b   Accurately produce up to five items in response to a verbal request (verbal production).

N1.1.5c   Verbal production of up to 10 items.

N1.1.5d   Verbal production of up to 20 items.

N1.1.6   Flexibly start verbal count-by-one sequence from any point—that is, start a count from a number other than "one."

N1.1.7   Flexibly cite the number after a specified count term.

N1.1.7a   State number after 1 to 9 with a running start (e.g., "What comes after 1, 2, 3, 4, 5?").

N1.1.7b   State number after 1 to 9 with an abbreviated running start (e.g., "What comes after 3, 4, 5?").

N1.1.7c   State number after 1 to 9 without any running start.

N1.1.7d   State the number after 10 to 28.

N1.1.7e   State the number after 29 to 99.

N1.1.8   Flexibly cite the number before a specified count term.

N1.1.8a   State number before 2 to 10.

N1.1.8b   State number before 11 to 29.

N1.1.9   Verbally count backward.

N1.1.9a   Verbally count backward form "five."

N1.1.9b   Verbally count backward from "ten."

N1.1.9c   Verbally count backward form "twenty."

N1.1.10   Apply decade-count skills.

N1.1.10a   Skip count by tens to 100.

179

## Goals

| Goal | | 2 | • | 3 | • | 4 | • | 5 | • | 6 | • | 7 | • |
|---|---|---|---|---|---|---|---|---|---|---|---|---|---|
| N1.1.11 | Flexibly use other skip counts. | | | | | | | | | | | | |
| N1.1.10b | Flexibly state the decade after 10 to 90. | | | | | | | × | × | × | × | × | ✱ |
| N1.1.11a | Verbally count by fives to 100. | | | | | | | | × | ✱ | ✱ | ✱ | ✱ |
| N1.1.11b | Verbally count by twos to 20. | | | | | | | ✱ | × | × | × | × | |
| N1.1.11c | Count objects by fives. | | | | | | | | | × | × | × | |
| N1.1.11d | Count objects by twos. | | | | | | | | | | | | |
| N1.1.11e | Verbally count odd numbers to 19. | | | | | | | | | | | × | |
| N1.1.12 | Explicitly distinguish between the cardinal meaning/use of number and other (ordinal, measurement, and nominal) meanings/uses of number. | | | | | | | | | | | | |
| N1.2 | Use numbers to compare quantities by developing an understanding of the relative position and magnitude of whole numbers and the connection between ordinal and cardinal numbers. | | | | | | | | | | | | |
| N1.2.1 | Visually (qualitatively) identify which collection is "more." | | | | | | | | | | | | |
| N1.2.1a | Correctly indicate "same" or "more" with collections that are obviously equal or not equal (perception of "same" or "more"). | ✱ | | | | | | | | | | | |
| N1.2.1b | Correctly indicate "more" with collections up to about four that differ in number by one (perception of fine differences). | × | | ✱ | | | | | | | | | |
| N1.2.2 | Use (nonverbal or verbal) subitizing (overt or covert) counting to make equivalence judgments of small collections. | | | | | | | | | | | | |
| N1.2.2a | Nonverbally identify as equivalent or nonequivalent static (simultaneously presented) collections consisting of one to four items. | × | | ✱ | | | | | | | | | |
| N1.2.2b | Nonverbally match equivalent sets of disks and dots—two homogeneous sets consisting of highly similar items. | | | × | | ✱ | × | | | | | | |
| N1.2.2c | Match equivalent sets of shells and dots—two homogeneous sets consisting of dissimilar items. | | | ✱ | | × | × | | | | | | |
| N1.2.2d | Identify a (static) collection (e.g., three dots) with a sequential presentation (e.g., three successively presented dots). | | | | | ✱ | × | | | | | | |
| N1.2.2e | Make a cross-modal match (e.g., match three dots with three bell rings). | | | × | | ✱ | × | | | | | | |
| N1.2.2f | Match a static collection with a sequentially repeated event (e.g., match three dots with three puppet jumps). | | | | | ✱ | × | | | | | | |
| N1.2.2g | Match equivalent sets of random objects and dots—a heterogeneous collection and a set of dissimilar items. | | | | | × | ✱ | | | | | | |
| N1.2.3 | Recognize equivalent collections of more than four items despite appearances. | | | | | | | | | | | | |
| N1.2.3a | Recognize equivalent collections despite appearances. Apply the same-number (number-identity) principle: Two collections with same cardinal designation are equal in number regardless of appearances. | | | × | | × | | | | | | × | |
| N1.2.3b | Conserves number. | | | | | | | | | ✱ | | × | |

N1.2.4 Use larger-number principle (the later a number appears in the counting sequence, the larger the quantity represented) to make gross comparisons—that is, to order widely separated numbers.
  N1.2.4a Make gross comparisons of "more" up to "ten."
  N1.2.4b Make gross comparisons of "less" up to "ten."
  N1.2.4c Make gross comparison of "more" up to "one hundred."
N1.2.5 Use larger-number principle and number after knowledge to make fine comparisons—that is, to order two adjacent numbers in the counting sequence.
  N1.2.5a Make fine comparisons of more up to "five."
  N1.2.5b Make fine comparisons of more up to "ten."
  N1.2.5c Make fine comparisons of more up to "one hundred."
  N1.2.5d Make fine comparisons of less up to "ten."
  N1.2.5e Make fine comparisons of less up to "one hundred."
N1.2.6 Understand and effectively apply verbal ordinal terms.
  N1.2.6a Recite the ordinal terms (first, second, third . . .) to "tenth."
  N1.2.6b Describe the parallels and differences between the ordinal and cardinal sequences.
  N1.2.6c Recognize that ordinal terms are relational—are meaningful only if a point of reference is specified.
  N1.2.6d Recite and apply effectively ordinal terms to "twenty-ninth."
N1.3 Represent collections up to 10 and numerical relations by connecting numerals to number words and the quantities both represent.
  N1.3.1 Draw pictographic symbols (drawings of objects) or iconic symbols (e.g., tallies) to respond to a spoken number (nonfunctional use of informal numerical symbols).
  N1.3.2 Use pictographic or iconic symbols to represent the cardinal value of a collection (functional use of informal numerical symbols).
  N1.3.3 Execute and apply numeral skills.
    N1.3.3a Recognize/identify one-digit numerals (e.g., is able to point out a "three" given a choice of fine one-digit numerals).
    N1.3.3b Read one-digit numerals.
    N1.3.3c Copy or write one-digit numerals.
    N1.3.3d Use one-digit written numbers to represent the cardinal value of a collection (functional use of numerals).
    N1.3.3e Identify the larger of two written numerals.
  N1.3.4 Use relational symbols effectively.
    N1.3.4a Informally represent the equivalence or inequivalence of two collections.
    N1.3.4b Correctly identify and use the formal relational symbols $=, \neq, >, <$ with single-digit numbers.

181

## Goals

Appx. Age/Grade Level

| Goal | 2 | 3 | 4 | 5 | 6 (PK) | 7 (K) | 1 |
|---|---|---|---|---|---|---|---|
| **N1.3.5** Use written number words and relational terms effectively. | | | | | | | |
| N1.3.5a Identify written number words *one, two, three, … nine* with their corresponding verbal words and numerals and use them to represent the cardinal value of a collection. | | | | | × | ? | ? |
| N1.3.5b Describe the parallels between abbreviated ordinal terms (1st, 2nd, 3rd … 9th) and cardinal terms. | | | | | * | × | × |
| N1.3.5c Identify written ordinal terms *first, second, third, … ninth* with their corresponding verbal words and use them to represent ordinal relations. | | | | | × | * | ? |
| N1.3.5d Identify written relational terms *equals, unequal, greater than,* and *less than* with their corresponding verbal terms and written symbols. | | | | | | × | * |
| **O2. Instruction from pre-kindergarten to Grade 2 should enable all students to understand the various meanings of operations, to recognize how the operations are related, to compute fluently, and to make reasonable estimates (Really Big Idea 2).** | | | | | | | |
| O2.1 Understand the change meaning of addition and subtraction of whole numbers (Big Idea 1) and use this knowledge to make sensible estimates and to develop calculational proficiency. | | | | | | | |
| O2.1.1 Nonverbally and mentally determine sums and differences. | × | × | | | | | |
| O2.1.1a Nonverbally add one item and another or subtract one item from two. | × | * | × | | | | |
| O2.1.1b Nonverbally estimate sums up to five and their subtraction complements (e.g., for "3 + 2" put out four to six items as the answer). | | × | × | × | | | |
| O2.1.1c Nonverbally determine sums up to three and differences up to "3 − 2." | | | × | * | | | |
| O2.1.1d Nonverbally determine sums up to five and their subtraction counterparts. | | | × | × | × | | |
| O2.1.2 Estimate the sums of addition word problems and their subtraction complements up to … | | | | | * | | |
| O2.1.2a 10; | | | | | | | |
| O2.1.2b 20. | | | | | | | |
| O2.1.3 Use direct-modeling strategies (concrete counting all or take away) to solve addition and subtraction word problems with … | | | | × | × | × | |
| O2.1.3a Sums to 10 and corresponding differences; | | | | | × | × | × |
| O2.1.3b Sums to 18 and corresponding differences. | | | | | × | × | |
| O2.1.4 Use more-advanced counting strategies to solve addition word problems with sums to 18. | | | | | × | × | × |
| O2.1.4a Use the embedded-addend concept to indirectly model addition (i.e., use verbal counting all). | | | | | × | × | × |
| O2.1.4b Use the number-after rule to determine sums for $n + 1$ and $1 + n$ combinations | | | | | * | × | × |
| O2.1.4c Use the embedded cardinal-count concept to solve addition problems by counting on and subtraction problems by counting down or up. | | | | | × | * | × |

| | | | | |
|---|---|---|---|---|
| O2.1.5 | Connect formal addition and subtraction to concrete or informal knowledge. | ✳ | × | ✳ |
| O2.1.5a | Translate addition and subtraction word problems (and their solutions) into a number sentence and vice versa. | × | × | × |
| O2.1.5b | Solve symbolic expression using a variety of strategies. | ✳ | ✳ | × |
| O2.1.6 | Use thinking strategies and existing knowledge to reason out unknown sums to 18 and their subtraction counterparts (e.g., $7 + 8 = 7 + 7 + 1 = 14 + 1 = 15$ or $15 - 7 = ? \rightarrow 7 + ? = 15 \rightarrow$ so $? = 8$). | × | × | |
| O2.1.7 | Achieve fluency with basic addition and subtraction combinations regardless of strategy used. | × | × | |

Note. Asterisks (*) indicate the average age in which children learn a skill. The xs indicate the age range children normally learn the skill.

183

## Development

An understanding of cardinal number (Big Idea 1.1; Goal N1.1 in Table 7.1) deepens gradually over the course of early childhood. It can begin by recognizing the number of items in small collections (e.g., ● ● seeing as "two"), even before children learn to count objects reliably. The use of object counting and then written numbers develops.

***Transition 1.*** The development of an ability to mentally represent small collections exactly by means of a mental image, mental marker, or other nonverbal means—without number-word labels (*nonverbal subitizing*) and in conjunction with number-word labels (*verbal subitizing*)—provides the foundation of a cardinal number concept (Goal N1.1.1 in Table 7.1). Nonverbal subitizing (Goal N1.1.1a) may permit *nonverbal production* of small collections—the ability to create a collection that matches (is equivalent to) their mental representation of a previously viewed collection (Goal N1.1.2a and possibly Goal N1.1.2c in Table 7.1; Huttenlocher et al., 1994). Children typically start recognizing small collections of one to about four items and identifying them reliably with a number word between 2 and 4 years of age (Goals N1.1.1b and N1.1.1c; e.g., Baroody, 2002; Ginsburg & Baroody, 2003; Wagner & Walters, 1982). Verbal subitizing may underlie nonverbal production of four, three, or even two items and *quasi-verbal production,* which involves creating a collection of a specified size (e.g., "give me two cookies") without counting (N1.1.2b and N1.1.2c; Baroody, 1986, 2002; Wilkins & Baroody, 2000). In brief, the key finding is that 3-year-olds typically have already developed reasonably accurate ways of representing, labeling, and creating small collections before learning to count collections in a reliable manner.

***Transition 2.*** Between 3.5 and 4 years of age, children develop verbal- and object-counting skills, which provide them a more powerful tool for representing and using numbers.

For children to verbally count to 100 (Goal N1.1.3 in Table 7.1), they need to know (a) the single-digit sequence 1 to 9, (b) a 9 signals a transition (e.g., 19 signals the end of the teens and the need to begin a new series), (c) the decade terms for the new series (e.g., 20 follows 19), (d) the rules for generating the new series (e.g., the 20s and all subsequent series are generated by combining the decade term with, in turn, each term in the single-digit sequence, and (e) the exceptions to the rules (Baroody, 1989a). Learning the counting sequence, then, requires both memorizing arbitrary terms or rote counting (e.g., the first nine single-digit terms and the first three decade terms) and pattern recognition or rule-governed counting (e.g., the aforementioned points b and d and the decade sequence starting with *forty*).

Counting a collection (*enumeration*; Goal N1.1.4 in Table 7.1) involves matching counting words one for one with each item in the collection. To enumerate a collection of objects correctly, a child must (a) generate the correct counting-word sequence, (b) label each object in a set with a single counting word (one-for-one tagging), and (c) keep track of counted and uncounted objects so that each object is tagged only once.

The development of object-counting ability in the preschool years is marked by a growing or deepening understanding of cardinality. The construction of a cardinality principle (Gelman & Gallistel, 1978), sometimes called the *count-cardinal concept* (Fuson, 1988, 1992), is an important first step in meaningful object counting (see Goal N1.1.4b in Table 7.1). Perhaps by comparing the outcome of enumerating a small collection with the number label generated by verbal subitizing, preschoolers discover the cardinality principle: The last number word in the enumeration process has special significance because it represents the total number of items in a collection and can be used to answer the *How many?* questions posed by others (Fuson, 1988; Fuson & Hall, 1983; Gelman & Gallistel, 1978; Schaeffer, Eggleston, & Scott, 1974; von Glasersfeld, 1982). The reverse concept, namely the *cardinal-count concept* (Goal N1.1.5a in Table 7.1), appears to be a key prerequisite for verbal (counting-based) production—counting out a specified number of objects (Goal N1.1.5b in Table 7.1; Baroody, 1987a; Wilkins & Baroody, 2000). A counting-based cardinality concept is further deepened when children discover the *identity-conservation* or *number-constancy principle*—that the cardinal value of a collection does not change despite changes in appearances (e.g., a linear array of five items is still "five" if arranged in a circular pattern; Goal N1.1.4d; e.g., Ginsburg & Baroody, 2003; Piaget, 1964). A relatively deep understanding of a counting-based cardinality concept is achieved when they discover the *order-irrelevance principle*—that the order in which the items of a collection are enumerated does not matter as long as each item is counted once and only once (Goal N1.1.4e, e.g., Baroody, 1992b, 1993; Piaget, 1964). An understanding of cardinality is further deepened as children's understanding of comparing two (or more) collections grows (Goal N1.2), which is discussed later.

***Transition 3.*** The third major transition in children's number knowledge is learning how to use written symbols to represent numerical situations or meanings. This transition may begin as early as 3 years of age or as late as 6 years, depending on a child's home and preschool environment. Sinclair and Sinclair (1986) noted that there are two important aspects of this symbolic competence: (a) children's personal production of these symbols when needed and (b) their understanding or ideas about written symbols. The former can be equated with knowledge of form; the latter, knowledge of function:

- *Knowledge of form*. Knowledge of form includes constructing a mental image of a symbol. This entails recognizing the component parts of a symbol (e.g., noticing that a 6 consists of a "stick" and a "loop") and part–whole relations (e.g., knowing how the parts of a 6 fit together to make the whole, such as the loop is attached to the bottom of the stick). Knowledge of the component parts and part–whole relations enables children to distinguish one written symbol from another and, thus, to identify and to read them. For instance, the implicit or explicit knowledge that a 6 consists of a "loop" and "stick" enables a child to distinguish a 6 from all other numerals except 9. Although 6 and 9 share the same parts, children can distinguish between them because the loop of each is attached to the stick in two distinct ways: bottom versus top and right versus left, respectively. The fact that the numerals such as 2 and 5 or 6 and 9 share common parts helps explain why some children—particularly those with learning difficulties—confuse these numerals.

  Knowledge of form also involves constructing an implicit or explicit motor plan for symbols, a step-by-step plan of execution for translating a mental image into motor actions (Goodnow & Levine, 1973). A motor plan—which specifies where to start, what direction to proceed, when to stop, how to change direction, and where to stop—is necessary for copying and writing numerals. A plan for the numeral 6, for instance, specifies start at the top right and draw a stick that slants to the left; then make a loop by first going right.

  Even if a child's mental image for a written symbol is complete or accurate, he or she will not be able to write it correctly and may repeatedly make the same mistake if his or her motor plan is incomplete or inaccurate. This can even happen when children have a model numeral in front of them (i.e., when "merely" copying a numeral). Reversals (i.e., writing a symbol backward) are often the result of an incomplete or inaccurate motor plan. Writing 6 backwards some of the time indicates that a child may be unsure whether to start on the (top) right and draw a slanted line toward the left or vice versa. A child who consistently writes a 6 backwards may well have an inaccurate motor plan, one that specifies "start on the (top) left and draw a slanted line toward right." Children with learning difficulties, particularly, may have such writing problems (Baroody, 1987a, 1988a; Baroody & Kaufman, 1993).

- *Knowledge of function*. Knowledge of function includes knowing the various meanings of a numeral (namely cardinal, measurement, nominal, and ordinal meanings). It also involves knowing when and why written representations would be useful and how they can be used effectively.

  Hughes' (1986) study indicates "that children do have personally meaningful ways of writing quantity before they use the conventional notation" (Munn, 1998, p. 60). He found that 3- and 4-year-olds most often used idiosyncratic representations (interpretable only to the child), pictographic representations (drawing of objects involved), iconic representations (e.g., tally marks), or a combination of pictographic and iconic representations.

## Implications for Early Childhood Standards

***Transitions 1 and 2.*** The *PSSM* (NCTM, 2000) correctly suggests that a major goal of the early childhood education should be building on and extending children's rich and varied intuitive and informal knowledge of number. A mention of infants' ability to recognize and discriminate small numbers (pre-Transition 1) accurately implies that number development begins before children acquire conventional knowledge such as counting. Furthermore, the importance of counting experiences is justifiably emphasized with such comments as "counting is a foundation for students' early work with number" (p. 79). The importance of Transitions 1 and 2 is clearly implied by statements such as children "connect number words [and] the quantities they represent" (p. 78) and "can associate number words with small collections of objects" (p. 79).

Although (a) estimation, (b) mental representation of number, and (c) automatic recognition of number (subitizing) are discussed, their mention seems to be in reference to verbal-based number skills, not their possible predecessors (nonverbal number skills):

1. The only direct mention of number estimation (estimating the size of a collection) suggests that children use benchmarks (a known smaller quantity) to gauge the size of a relatively large collection. Recognizing that a collection of 12 items is a little more than 10 by visually noticing two groups of five, for instance, is likely only after children can readily identify and verbally label collections of five items and efficiently determine the sum of $5 + 5$. Pre-Transition 1 and many Transition 1 children might benefit from estimation experiences with intuitive numbers, and Transition 1 and early Transition 2 children might do so from estimation experiences with five to nine items (Baroody & Gatzke, 1991).
2. The following statement about mentally representing number is potentially misleading because of the research cited: "In these early years, students develop the ability to deal with numbers mentally and to think about numbers without having a physical model (Steffe[,] Cobb, [& von Glasersfeld,] 1988)" (p. 80). If the *PSSM* writers had intended this statement to refer to Transition 1, then they should have cited Huttenlocher and colleagues (e.g., 1994). This transition in number-representation ability and even Transition 2 comes well before the more abstract representational abilities (e.g., mentally solving relatively difficult missing-addend problems)

discussed by Steffe, Cobb, and von Glasersfeld (1988). Put differently, Goals N1.1.1 and N1.1.2 in Table 7.1 are achievable before the age of 6 years or so—before children are successful on Steffe et al.'s missing-addend task.

The general guidelines for promoting Transition 2 are crucial but do not provide the detailed direction teachers need to help young children achieve this transition. For example, no mention is made of integrating the critical components for enumerating collections: (a) generating a correct verbal number sequence, (b) creating a one-to-one correspondence between verbal numbers and items in a collection, and (c) keeping track of which items have been counted and which have not. Furthermore, there is no indication at what age children face these various challenges. (Three-year-olds often have difficulty coordinating the first two components, particularly when beginning or ending a count; whereas, 4.5- to 5.5-year-olds have the most difficulty with the aforementioned third component; Fuson, 1988.)

Early childhood standards should include clear and explicit expectations about Transitions 1 and 2 (e.g., in Table 7.1, see Goals N1.1.1 and N1.1.2 and N1.1.3 to N1.1.7, respectively)—including the development of *verbal-based* number estimation, mental representation, and subitizing. Moreover, some mechanism or mechanisms must be found to help educate early childhood and special education teachers, curriculum developers, and so forth about the specifics underlying both Transitions 1 and 2.

***Transition 3.***    In a clear reference to Transition 3, the *PSSM* (NCTM, 2000) includes the following expectation for Pre-K to 2 students: "connect … numerals to the quantities they represent" (p. 78). It is further noted that "concrete models can help students … bring meaning to [their] use of written symbols" (p. 80).

The *PSSM* (NCTM, 2000) also includes the expectation that young children should "develop understanding of … the ordinal and cardinal numbers and their connections" (p. 78). It further implies that they should understand the measurement meaning of number. No mention, however, is made of the nominal meaning (using numbers as names, such as "Your bus is number 24").

The *PSSM* (NCTM, 2000) includes the clear expectation that children initially be allowed to use their own written representations of number (see, e.g., Fig. 1.30 on p. 131 and the second and third paragraphs on p. 136). Their use of pictographic or iconic representations, at least, is consistent with existing research (e.g., Hughes, 1986) and makes sense. If children use idiosyncratic representations, which are uninterpretable by others and, perhaps, in some cases, even by themselves later, then they miss the point about why we use written representations for numbers. Such children need help appreciating the communicative function of written representations.

Furthermore, the *PSSM* (NCTM, 2000) is silent about symbol-form instruction. The issues of how to help children construct a mental image of numerals or a motor plan for these symbols is not mentioned. Given that written representations of numerals and other mathematical concepts are indispensable aspects of nearly all mathematics instruction and innumerable everyday activities, it is essential that early childhood standards include some discussion of this topic.

Early childhood standards, then, should include the expectation that young students understand all meanings of number, including the nominal meaning (Goal N1.1.12 in Table 7.1). They should also include the recommendation that children develop and use their own invented written representations of numbers before learning conventional symbols—with the caveat that they be helped to understand the communicative function of symbols (Goal N1.3.2). Additionally, mechanisms must be found to help practitioners understand the mechanics of helping children learn to read and write conventional symbols (e.g., Goal N1.3.3). (For a detailed discussion of how instruction can help children construct an accurate mental image and motor plan for each numeral, see Unit 4•2 in Baroody with Coslick, 1998.)[3]

## Understanding, Representing, and Using Ordinal Relations or Numbers

- Big Idea 1.2: Two (or more) collections can be compared or ordered, and numbers are one useful tool for doing so.

---

[3]In her critique of my paper presented at the Conference on Early Math Standards (Baroody, 2000), Connie Kamii noted that reversing numerals was common among pre-second-graders and not a cause of concern because children naturally outgrow such errors. She concluded that students do not need help writing numerals correctly. In general, Kamii's comments are all true. However, many children recognize for themselves that they are writing numerals incorrectly (e.g., in reverse), are puzzled or concerned about this, and ask for help (e.g., How do you make an 8?). Teachers should recognize that such questions are a request for an accurate motor plan. Furthermore, children with learning difficulties frequently do not spontaneously discover or invent correct motor plans and, in such cases, reversals (or other errors) may persist for years (Baroody, 1987a, 1988a; Baroody & Kaufman, 1993). For such children, remedial efforts, including help with constructing a motor plan, are necessary.

Coincidentally, a request from Diane Goodman, a Senior Editor at Riverside Publishing (via Doug Clements and Danny Breidenbach of NCTM), several weeks after the NCTM presession underscores the value of the psychological model for numeral-reading and -writing discussed above and in the text of this chapter. The question asked was, "Which format of the 4 [open versus closed] is most (sic) appropriate for Grades K-2 and why?

Without a theoretical model, the choice between an open 4 and a closed 4 is arbitrary or difficult to make. It follows from the model discussed that the open 4 is somewhat more preferable, because it does not involve a diagonal. Although this may not be a factor in forming a mental image of the numeral or reading it, the mental image children do form may impact the ease with which they master a motor plan. Writing numerals (and letters) composed only of horizontal and vertical lines is easier than doing so for those that involve a diagonal. A motor plan for the latter requires orienting in two directions at once. For instance, for the closed 4, the plan for the diagonal would be to start at the *upper right* and *slant down* to the lower left (would involve both up-down and right-left directions). Theoretically, the most efficient way to teach reading and writing 4s, then, would be to use open 4s. This way, children's mental image would be consistent with the easier motor plan for written 4s.

Comparing quantities (numerical relations) can involve determining whether two (or more) collections of distinct items are equal, which one is the larger (largest) or which one is the smaller (smallest). Comparing collections is a basic survival skill used, for example, to determine whether everyone in a group got a fair share of candies, which team got more points and won a game, or which brand is cheaper for a given unit price. Comparing two obviously different collections can be done visually. Numbers allow us to compare two collections close in size (e.g., 11 versus 12 items) or even huge collections precisely (e.g., 1,000,214 is greater than 1,000,213).

## Development

***Transition 1.*** Children first develop an intuitive (nonverbal and imprecise) sense of number order (for collections of up to three or four items). This occurs between 12 and 18 months, somewhat later than they do that of cardinal number (Cooper, 1984; Strauss & Curtis, 1981, 1984). Currently, little is known about the transition from an inexact to an exact ordinal sense of numerosity. A possible basis of Transition 1 is learning relational terms such as *more* and *less*. Children about 2 years of age can reliably identify as *more* the larger of two collections, as long as the perceptual cue(s) for the difference are salient—that is, one row of items is clearly longer, denser, or covers more area than another (Goal N1.2.1a in Table 7.1). This appears to be the beginning of assimilating language-based number knowledge to their nonverbal knowledge of numerosity. Gauging which of two collections is *less* is more difficult and develops later because, in part, children rarely hear or use the term (e.g., Donaldson & Balfour, 1968; Kaliski, 1962; Weiner, 1974). Transition 1 may permit preschoolers to nonverbally and reliably identify as equivalent or non-equivalent two small, static (simultaneously presented) collections, both consisting of identical elements (N1.2.2a in Table 7.1; Mix, 1999a; Siegel, 1973) or highly similar elements, such as one collection of disks and one of dots (N1.2.2b; Mix, 1999b).

***Transition 1 or 2.*** The development of verbal-based number representations of number appears to account for three important extensions in children's ability to make equivalence judgments with small collections, all of which are consistent with Resnick's (1992) model of increasing generality of thinking.

1. The first is the ability to compare collections of increasingly dissimilar elements (Mix, 1999b). Specifically, children older than 3.5 years or so can compare two homogeneous collections of *dissimilar* objects, such as a collection of shells and a collection of dots (Goal N1.2.2c in Table 7.1; Mix, 1999b). Between 4 and 4.5, children can compare heterogeneous collections of dissimilar items (Goal N1.2.2g; Mix, 1999b; cf. Gelman & Gallistel, 1978).

2. The second important extension is that after 3.5 years, children become capable of making nonstatic comparisons—that is those that occur over time (Mix, 1999a). This includes comparing a collection presented simultaneously with one in which the items are presented successively (Goal N1.2.2d in Table 7.1; Mix, 1999a; Mix, Huttenlocher, & Levine, 1996), comparing a (simultaneous) visual display and a sequential auditory display (N1.2.2e; Mix et al., 1996), and a (simultaneous) visual display and a sequential event (N1.2.2f; Mix, 1999a).

3. The third is cross-model transfer such as the ability to recognize equivalent visual and auditory displays (again see Goal N1.2.2e; Mix et al., 1996).

A key element in the transition to using the counting sequence as a useful tool is recognizing that numbers can be used to identify equivalent collections. Specifically, by counting and visually comparing small collections, children can recognize the *same number-name principle*: Two collections are equal if they share the same number name, despite differences in the physical appearance of the collection (see N1.2.3a; Baroody with Coslick, 1998). Because it is a general (abstract) principle, young children can use it to compare any size collection that they can count.

Construction of the same number-name principle appears to underlie the later development of a relatively sophisticated or advanced understanding of numerical equivalence, what Piaget (1965) called *number conservation*. Number conservation involves recognizing the numerical equivalence of two uncounted and nonsubitizeable collections over time and despite appearances—that is, over a number-irrelevant physical transformation that results in a misleading perceptual cue (N1.2.3b in Table 7.1). Initially, children do not realize that if one collection put into one-to-one correspondence with another is then physically, but not numerically, changed (e.g., lengthened or shortened), then it is still equivalent to the other collection. Even counting the collections may not help. After children construct the same number-name principle and gain confidence in this counting-based knowledge, they can then apply it in relatively complicated contexts such as the number-conservation task. That is, once they trust that this principle is applicable, children can disregard misleading perceptual cues and "conserve" equivalence relations (e.g., recognize that two previously matched collections still have the same number, even though one is longer and looks like it has "more"). In time, children construct the following general (qualitative) principle: If nothing is added to or subtracted from two equivalent collections, then they continue to have the same number (despite appearances). This relatively abstract principle allows children to conserve number with logical certainty—that is, without counting or rematching the items in the collections (see Baroody, 1987a, for a review of the research supporting this position).

***Post-Transition 2.***    After Transition 2, children learn how to use the counting sequence to compare collections or numbers. By verbally subitizing or counting two small and (obviously) unequal collections, they may discover the *larger-number principle*: The later a number word appears in the counting sequence, the larger the collection it represents (e.g., *four* represents a larger collection than *two* does because it comes later in the counting sequence than *two*; Schaeffer et al., 1974). This permits them to use numbers to mentally make gross comparisons—determine the larger of two widely separated numbers (Goal N1.2.4 in Table 7.1). Once children can automatically cite the number after another in the counting sequence (e.g., The number after *four* is *five*), they can use the larger-number principle to *mentally* compare two adjacent numbers (e.g., Who is older, someone 9 or someone 8?—the 9-year-old because 9 comes after 8; Goal N1.2.5 in Table 7.1). This relatively abstract number skill has many everyday applications and can be used for even huge numbers (1,000,129 is greater than 1,000,128 because, according to our counting rules, the former comes after the latter). Typically, children can cite the number after another up to *ten* and can use this knowledge and the larger-number principle to mentally compare any two numbers up to *five* before they enter kindergarten (are 4.5 to 5.5 years of age; Goal N1.2.5a). By the time they leave kindergarten (are 5.5 to 6 years old), children typically can compare any two numbers at least up to *ten* (Goal N1.2.5b).

Another important aspect of the Post-Transition 2 phase is learning and applying the ordinal-number sequence ("First, second, third, ..."; Goal N1.2.6 in Table 7.1). The process of learning the ordinal terms (Goal N1.2.6a) can be facilitated by noticing the parallels (and dissimilarities) with the counting (cardinal) sequence (e.g., *sixth*→six + th; *seventh*→seven + th; Goal N1.2.6b). The key to understanding and applying ordinal terms is recognizing, at least implicitly, that they are relational terms—defined relative to a reference point (Goal N1.2.6c). For example, the "first in line" can be defined by which direction a line of children is facing or its direction of movement, such as toward the classroom door. Unfortunately, this defining attribute of ordinal numbers is often not made clear to children.

**Transition 3.**    By assimilating written numerals to their knowledge of the verbal counting sequence, children can quickly recognize that written numbers embody an ordinal relation and choose the larger of two numerals (within their known counting sequence; Goal N1.3.3e in Table 7.1). Likewise, by connecting written representations for ordinal numbers (first, second, third, ... or 1st, 2nd, 3rd ...) or ordinal relations (< and >) to their existing (verbal-based) understanding of numerical relations, children can readily understand and use these formal terms. Learning difficulties arise when children have not had the opportunity to learn prerequisite skills and concepts or when written representations for ordinal numbers are not related to this knowledge.

## *Implications for Early Childhood Standards*

No mention is made of Transition 1 (Goal N1.2.1 and possibly Goal N1.2.2) in the *PSSM* (NCTM, 2000). General guidelines are provided for promoting Transitions 2 and 3 (e.g., "develop understanding of the relative position and magnitude of whole numbers and of ordinal ... numbers and their connection [to cardinal numbers]"; p. 78). Again, though, these guidelines are not sufficiently detailed to help teachers plan instruction. Consider, for instance, the critical but often overlooked skill of comparing numbers. The *PSSM* clearly lays out the expectation that students need to "develop understanding of the relative position and magnitude of whole numbers" (p. 78) and that they should be encouraged to discover that "the next whole number in the counting sequence is ... more than the number just named" (p. 79). However, there are few clues about the developmental progression and prerequisites necessary to make such a discovery. (The prerequisites for fine-number comparisons [Goal N1.2.5], for example, are the larger-number principle [Goal N1.2.4] and automatically citing the number after another [Goal N1.1.7c]). In brief, the same conclusions made about the early childhood standards regarding cardinal number apply here also. (See Unit 4•1 in Baroody with Coslick, 1998, for guidelines and recommendations on teaching this topic.)

## Single-digit Addition and Subtraction

- Big Idea 2.1: A collection can be made larger by adding items to it and made smaller by taking some away from it.

An understanding of addition and subtraction (a key aspect of Really Big Idea 2 noted earlier) includes Big Idea 2.1 and is fundamental to success with school mathematics. For example, the former is essential for understanding more advanced and related topics such as multiplication (e.g., $3 \times 5 = 5 + 5 + 5$, which equals 15) or fractions (e.g., $\frac{3}{5}$ is literally $\frac{1}{5} + \frac{1}{5} + \frac{1}{5}$). An understanding that a collection of items can be made larger by adding additional items or smaller by taking some away is also fundamental to countless aspects of everyday life (e.g., combining a team's scores for each of four quarters to determine its final score, adding sales tax to a price to determine total costs, or subtracting the dollars spent from a checking account). Clearly, addition and subtraction of whole numbers should be a core topic of any early childhood curriculum.

### *Development*

Recent research indicates that children start constructing an understanding of these arithmetic operations long before school. Whether this starts in infancy (pre-Transition 1) as nativists claim (e.g., Wynn, 1998) or not, an intuitive understanding of addition and subtraction (Goal O2.1.1 in Table 7.1) clearly seems to develop before children are capable of counting-based arithmetic efforts (post-Transition 2), which, in turn, develops before written arithmetic competencies (post-Transition 3).

As with making number comparisons, then, children's informal addition is initially relatively concrete (in the sense that they are working nonverbally with real collections or mental representation of them) and limited to small collections of four or fewer. Later, as they master and can apply their counting skills, they extend their ability to engage in informal arithmetic both in terms of more abstract contexts (word problems and, even later, symbolic expressions such as 2 + 1 = ?) and more abstract numbers (namely, numbers greater than four).

***Transition 1.*** Transition 1 children develop the ability to solve simple nonverbal addition or subtraction problems (e.g., Huttenlocher et al., 1994). Such problems involve showing a child a small collection (one to four items), covering it, adding or subtracting an item or items, and then asking the child to indicate the answer by producing a matching number of disks. For one item plus another item ("1 + 1"), for instance, a correct response would involve putting out two disks rather than, say, one disk or three disks. In the Huttenlocher et al. study, for example, most children who had recently turned 3 years old could correctly solve problems involving "1 + 1" or "2 – 1" (i.e., they could imagine adding one object to another or could mentally subtract one object from a collection of two objects). Most who were about to turn 4 years old could solve "1 + 2," "2 + 1," "3 – 1," "3 – 2" as well, and at least a quarter could also solve "1 + 3," "2 + 2," "3 + 1," "4 + 1," "4 – 1," and "4 – 3." By the age of 4, children typically can mentally add or subtract any small number of items (Ginsburg & Baroody, 2003).

How do children so young manage these feats of simple addition and subtraction? They apparently can reason about their mental representations of numbers. For "2 + 1," for instance, they form a mental representation of the initial amount (before it is hidden from view), form a mental representation of the added amount (before it is hidden), and then can *imagine* the added amount added to the original amount to make the latter larger. In other words, they understand the most basic concept of addition—it is a transformation that makes a collection larger. Similarly, they understand the most basic concept of subtraction—it is a transformation that makes a collection smaller.

***Transition 2.*** Later—but typically before they receive formal arithmetic instruction in school—children can solve simple addition and subtraction word problems by using counting strategies (e.g., Carpenter & Moser, 1982, 1984; DeCorte & Verschaffel, 1987; Fuson,

1992; Huttenlocher et al., 1994), including those involving numbers larger than four. How do they manage this? Basically, children decipher the meaning of the story by relating it to their informal understanding of addition as a "make-larger" transformation ("change add-to" view) or their informal understanding of subtraction as a "make-smaller" transformation ("change take-away" view; e.g., Baroody with Coslick, 1998; Carpenter, Hiebert, & Moser, 1983). They then—at least initially—use objects (e.g., blocks, fingers, or tallies) to model the meaning (type of transformation) indicated by the word problem. Consider the following problem: *Rafella helped her mom decorate three cookies before lunch. After lunch, she helped decorate five more cookies. How many cookies did Rafella help decorate altogether?* Young children might model this problem by using a concrete counting-all procedure: counting out three items to represent the initial amount, counting out five more items to represent the added amount, and then counting all the items put out to determine the solution.

Research further reveals that children invent increasingly sophisticated counting strategies to determine sums and differences (e.g., Baroody, 1984, 1987b; Carpenter & Moser, 1982, 1983, 1984; Resnick & Ford, 1981; Steffe et al., 1988). At some point, children abandon using objects to directly model the meaning of a problem and rely on verbal (abstract) counting procedures, which require a keeping-track process: keeping track of how far to count beyond the first addend. To solve the aforementioned problem, for instance, they might count up to the number representing the initial amount ("1, 2, 3") and continue the count five more times to represent the amount added ("4 [*is one more*], 5 [*is two more*], 6 [*is three more*], 7 [*is four more*], 8 [*is five more*]—8 cookies altogether"; the keeping-track process is the italicized portion). One shortcut for this strategy, disregarding addend, can reduce the effort required to keep track. For 3 + 5, for instance, counting the larger addend first reduces the keeping-track process from five steps (as shown in the previous example) to two steps ("1, 2, 3, 4, 5; 6 [*is one more*], 7 [*is two more*], 8 [*is three more*]—the sum is 8"). Another shortcut many children spontaneously invent is counting on: starting with the number representing the initial (or larger) amount, instead of counting from *one*. For 3 + 5, for example, this would involve starting with the cardinal value of *five* and counting three more times: "5; 6 (*is one more*), 7 (*is two more*), and 8 (*is three more*)—8 cookies altogether." (See Baroody & Tiilikainen, 2003, for a detailed discussion of addition-strategy development.)

***Transition 3 and Post-Transition 3.*** Research evidence makes clear that instruction needs to ensure that written arithmetic representations should be connected to children's informal arithmetic knowledge (e.g., Baroody, 1987a; Baroody with Coslick, 1998; Ginsburg, 1977; Hughes, 1986).

Probably one of the greatest concerns to early childhood educators is "number-fact" mastery. How the basic number combinations such as 7 + 1 = 8 and 4 x 5 = 20 are registered in, represented by, and retrieved from long-term memory (LTM) are still baffling issues (see, e.g., Ashcraft, 1985, versus Baroody, 1985; and Brownell, 1935, versus Thorndike, 1922). Almost two decades ago, Mark Ashcraft (1982) published an article in *Developmental Review* summarizing the state of the knowledge in the area. Specifically, he concluded that:

1. Addition number facts were organized in LTM in a manner analogous to the addition tables studied by schoolchildren,

2. Rules involving 0 or 1 (e.g., any number plus 0 is simply that number) served merely as slow backup strategies in case fact retrieval failed.

Research indicates that both these assumptions are probably wrong (see, e.g., Baroody, 1985, 1994, for reviews of the literature). For example, a series of training experiments (Baroody, 1988b, 1989a, 1992a) demonstrated that rules involving 0 and 1 transferred to unpracticed addition combinations, allowing children to answer such combinations efficiently. In a more recent review of the literature, Ashcraft (1992) himself concluded that the consensus in the field was (a) his original table-analogy model was no longer viable and (b) combinations involving 0 or 1 might well be produced by *fast* rules.

Research further indicates that other relational knowledge may play a key role in both number-combination learning *and* representation (e.g., Baroody, 1999; Baroody, Ginsburg, & Waxman, 1983). For instance, research indicates that knowledge of commutativity may affect how basic combinations are mentally represented or organized (Butterworth, Marschesini, & Girelli, 2003; Rickard & Bourne, 1996; Rickard, Healy, & Bourne, 1994; Sokol, McCloskey, Cohen, & Aliminosa, 1991). In and of itself, then, practice, is not THE key factor determining what number combinations children remember (e.g., Baroody, 1988b, 1999), as suggested by information-processing models (e.g., Siegler, 1988; Siegler & Shipley, 1995). Another important finding is that even adults use a variety of strategies to determine sums and differences efficiently (e.g., LeFevre, Sadesky, & Bisanz, 1996; LeFevre, Smith-Chant, Hiscock, Daley, & Morris, 2003). In brief, new research suggests that internalizing the basic number combinations is not simply a matter of memorizing individual facts by rote but may also involve automatizing relational knowledge and that experts do not simply retrieve facts from LTM but may use a variety of automatic or near-automatic strategies, including efficient rules and reasoning strategies.

## Implications for Early Childhood Standards

Given its importance for school mathematics and everyday life, early childhood instruction should also focus on helping children devise and share increasingly efficient strategies for generating sums and differences.

***Transitions 1 and 2.*** The *PSSM* (NCTM, 2000) does not explicitly address the development of precounting (Pre-Transition 2) addition and subtraction or how this might provide a basis for verbal-counting-based arithmetic (Transition 2).

In regard to post-Transition 2 developments, general, but not specific, guidelines are provided. Children's use of informal addition strategies is encouraged. For instance, it is explicitly noted that "they often solve addition and subtraction problems by counting concrete objects, and many ... invent problem-solving strategies based on counting strategies" (NCTM, 2000, pp. 79–80). Other general guidelines explicitly, or at least implicitly, noted include "students should encounter a variety of meanings for addition and subtraction" (p. 34; see, e.g., Baroody with Coslick, 1998, for a taxonomy of operation meanings), children should be "encouraged to develop, record, explain, and critique one another's strategies for solving computational problems" (p. 35; see also p. 84) and instruction and practice should be done in context (in a purposeful manner). However, practitioners are not provided specific guidelines. For example, although teachers are encouraged to foster the relatively sophisticated counting-on strategy, no advice is provided on how this can be accomplished (for such advice, see pp. 160–163 of chap. 6 in this volume).

Early childhood standards should include expectations regarding the development of nonverbal addition and subtraction and how their verbal counterparts can build on this knowledge (see Goals O2.1.1 to O2.1.4 in Table 7.1). Mechanisms must also be found to help teachers learn specific guidelines for fostering young children's nonverbal and verbal addition and subtraction.

***Transition 3 and Post-Transition 3.*** In regard to Transition 3, instruction should build on and extend children's informal knowledge by helping them (a) to "connect ... formal expressions or equations such as 5 + 3 [and] 5 + ? = 8" to problem situations and their informal solutions for them and (b) to "relate symbolic expressions to various problems" (Baroody with Coslick, 1998, pp. 5-11 and 5-12). The *PSSM* (NCTM, 2000) implicitly, if not explicitly, includes the first recommendation by underscoring the importance of solving problems and connecting various representations of problem strategies and solutions. It clearly and explicitly makes the aforementioned second recommendation in several places (see, e.g., pp. 34, 83, and 139).

The recommendations regarding mastery of basic number combinations made in chapters 3 and 4 of the *PSSM* (NCTM, 2000) are not entirely consistent, which may reflect the conflicting views held by the *PSSM* writers on this surprisingly complicated issue. The expectations for Pre-K to 2 outlined in chapter 4 include "develop fluency with basic number combinations for addition and subtraction," where *fluency* is defined as "using efficient and accurate methods for computing" (p. 78). Not equating fluency with the retrieval of isolated facts memorized by rote but equating it with various speedy and reliable methods is clearly consistent with recent research that even adults do so to determine basic sums (e.g., LeFevre et al., 1996). Substituting *basic number* **combinations** for the misleading term *basic number* **facts** further reinforces this key point.

Important to note, chapter 4 of the *PSSM* (NCTM, 2000) includes the recommendation that "students should develop strategies for knowing basic number combinations that build on their thinking about, and understanding of, numbers" and that they be provided tasks that "help them develop the relationships within addition and subtraction" (p. 84; see, e.g., Baroody, 1999; Fuson, 1992; Steinberg, 1985). A search of *PSSM* uncovered two examples of these recommendations: discovery of (a) the number-after rule ("the next whole number in the counting sequence is one more than the number just named"; p. 79) and (b) the complementary relation between addition and subtraction (e.g., $5 - 3 = ?$ can be thought of as $3 + ? = 5$; p. 138).

In *PSSM* (NCTM, 2000) chapter 3, references are also made to "knowing basic number combinations" (pp. 32 and 33), but this appears to imply a different meaning than that suggested in chapter 4. In contrast to the later chapter where *knowing the basic number combinations* is, at least implicitly, equated with *fluency*, a distinction between the two terms appears to be made in the earlier chapter. After the former is identified as essential comes the statement "equally essential is computational fluency" (p. 32). This same apparent distinction appears on page 35: "By the end of grade 2, students should *know* the basic addition and subtraction combinations, should be *fluent* in adding two-digit numbers ... (italics added).[4]

Early childhood standards should include explicit expectations about how written addition and subtraction can be linked to children's existing knowledge, including the recommendation that they be encouraged to represent as equations word problems and their informally determined solutions (see Goal O2.1.5 in Table 7.1). Given the common misconceptions and confusion about the issue of combination mastery, these stan-

---

[4]An almost identical sentence appeared in the *PSSM* draft (NCTM, 1998), except that *recall* was used instead of *know*, and *facts* was used instead of *combinations*. Although these changes appear to contradict the argument that knowing is not being contrasted with fluency, they seem to be a Clintonian gambit to use words ambiguously when compared with the clear-cut statement from page 78 in Chapter 4 quoted earlier.

dards should also include (above and beyond the general Goals O2.1.6 and O2.1.7) the following explicit and clear-cut expectations:

1. *Fluency* with each *family* of number combinations should build on two requisite developmental phases: (a) counting-based strategies for determining sums and differences (e.g., counting on) and (b) reasoning-based strategies for doing so (e.g., $7 + 8 = 7 + 7 + 1 = 14 + 1 = 15$). (A family of combinations consists of combinations that share a common pattern or relation. A combination may belong to more than one family.)

2. To promote the second (reasoning-based) phase and lay the groundwork for the third (fluency), teachers should encourage children to look for patterns and relations and use them to devise, implement, and share reasoning ("thinking") strategies.

3. To promote the third phase (fluency) and to minimize the amount of practice required to achieve it, practice should focus on helping students automatize reasoning (thinking) strategies, not memorizing individual facts by rote.

4. Practice should be done in a purposeful, meaningful, and—when possible—inquiry-based manner.

5. Fluency can embody a variety of strategies, including—but not limited to—the recall of (isolated) facts.

Furthermore, the general principles just listed should be *accompanied* by at least one example. For instance, Principle 2 could be illustrated by the examples cited in the *PSSM* (NCTM, 2000; the number-after rule for $n + 1$ combinations or translating subtraction combinations into known complementary addition combinations) or any one of the examples listed in Box 5.6 on pages 5-31 and 5-32 in Baroody with Coslick (1998). Principle 4 could be illustrated by cases where problems, games, and other activities can be used to provide purposeful, meaningful, and inquiry-based practice (see, e.g., Box 5.4 and Activity Files 5.6 to 5.8 on pp. 5-28 and 5-29 of Baroody with Coslick, 1998).

## Part–Whole Relations

• Big Idea 1.3/2.2: A quantity (a whole) can consist of parts and can be "broken apart" (decomposed) into them, and the parts can be combined (composed) to form the whole.

An understanding of how a whole is related to its parts—what Piaget (1965) termed "additive composition"—includes recognizing that a whole is the sum of its parts (Part 1 + Part 2 = Whole) and that the whole is larger than any single part (Whole > Part 1 or Part 2). The construction of a part–whole concept is an enormously important achievement (e.g., Resnick & Ford, 1981). Some scholars consider it to be the basis for a *deep* understanding of number (Really Big Idea 1) and arithmetic (Really Big Idea 2) and a key link between these two concepts (e.g., Piaget, 1965; Resnick, 1992). (This is why this big idea is represented above by the combined designation 1.3/2.2.)

***Deep Understanding of Number.*** A part–whole concept may be the foundation for understanding the following more advanced concepts of number: (a) place-value representation (e.g., the whole 123 can be decomposed into the parts 1 one hundred, 2 tens, and 3 ones; 12 tens and 3 ones; 1 one hundred, 1 ten, and 13 ones; and so forth), (b) common fractions (in the representation $a/b$, the numerator $a$ indicates the number of equal-size parts of a whole of interest, and the denominator $b$ indicates the total number of equal parts into which the whole is subdivided), and (c) ratios—including probability (the probability of an outcome = its frequency/frequency of all outcomes = frequency of the part of interest/frequency of all parts or the whole).

***More Advanced Understanding of Arithmetic.*** A part–whole concept is assumed to underlie a more formal part–whole ("binary") meaning of addition and subtraction (Resnick, 1992). Unlike children's informal change add-to view of addition (embodied in Problem A as follows), part–whole situations do not involve a physical action that results in increasing an initial amount (see, e.g., Problem B as follows).

■ **Problem A.** *Arillo had three candies. His mom gave him two* **more**. *How many candies does Arillo have now?*

■ **Problem B.** *Bree held three of her candies in her left hand and two in her right hand. How many candies did she have in all?*

A part–whole concept is considered to be a conceptual basis for understanding and solving missing-addend word problems such as the following Problems C and D and missing-addend equations such as ? + 3 = 5 and ? – 2 = 7 (Resnick, 1992; Riley, Greeno, & Heller, 1983):

■ **Problem C.** *Angie bought some candies. Her mother bought her three more candies. Now Angie has five candies. How many candies did Angie buy?*

■ **Problem D.** *Blanca had some pennies. She lost two pennies playing. Now she has seven pennies. How many pennies did Blanca have before she started to play?*

A part–whole concept may be the psychological basis for arithmetic concepts such as the principles of additive commutativity (Part 1 + Part 2 = Part 2 + Part 1) and associativity ([Part 1 + Part 2] + Part 3 = Part 1 + [Part 2 + Part 3]; Resnick, 1992; Riley et al., 1983). Furthermore, an understanding of part–whole relations may serve to connect the operations of addition and subtraction in the following three ways: the basic complement principle (Whole – Part 1 = ?, which is related to Part 1 + ? = Whole), the advanced complement principle (Part 1 + Part 2 = Whole, which is related to Whole – Part 1 = Part 2 or Whole – Part 2 = Part 1), and the inverse principle (Part 1 + Part 2 – Part 2 = Part 1 or Part 1 – Part 2 + Part 2 = Part 1; e.g., Baroody, 1999).

***A Link between Number and Arithmetic.*** Finally, a part–whole concept may underlie an understanding of "number families" or the different-names-for-a-number concept (a number can be represented in various ways because a whole can be composed or decomposed in various ways) and is one key link between number and arithmetic. The number represented by 5 can also be represented by, for example, $0 + 5$, $1 + 4$, $2 + 3$, $3 + 2$, $4 + 1$, $5 + 0$, $6 - 1$, $7 - 2$ (as well as | | | | |, ╫╫, V, *five*, and ●●●●● ).

### Development

***Part–Whole Concept.*** Using a matching task to eliminate the need for verbal responses, Boisvert, Standing, and Moller (1999) found that a majority of children as young as 2.5 years of age could correctly identify a composite figure (the whole) made up of conceptually different units (the parts). For instance, asked to find a "cat made of triangles," participants more often pointed to the corresponding picture than they did to a picture of a cat, a picture of triangles, and a picture of a giraffe made of triangles. The results contradicted earlier evidence that preschoolers cannot pay attention to both the whole and its parts simultaneously (e.g., Elkind, Koegler, & Go, 1964).

The construction of a part–whole concept may begin with inexact nonverbal (pre-Transition 1) experiences, such as putting together interlocking blocks or pieces of playdough and taking them apart. This could lead to an intuitive understanding that a whole is larger than its composite parts. Transition 1 could result in a more precise understanding of additive composition, at least with quantities children could nonverbally subitize and mentally represent. Specifically, it may provide the basis for recognizing that one discrete quantity and another invariably make a particular total (e.g., two items and one more item always yield three items) and, even perhaps, that the order in which these particular discrete amounts are combined does not affect the total.

Irwin (1996) examined the following two key aspects of a proto-quantitative part–whole concept identified by Resnick (1992) and found that the majority of children as young as 4 years old understood both:

1. The *co-variation principle* entails recognizing the equivalence of adding the same number of items to a part and its whole (If Part 1 + Part 2 = Whole, then [Part 1 + a number] + Part 2 = Whole + the number) or subtracting the same number of items from a part and the whole [Part 1 – a number] + Part 2 = Whole – the number).

2. The *compensation principle* involves understanding the effect of taking a number of items from one part and adding the same number of items to the other part (If Part 1 + Part 2 = Whole, then [Part 1 + a number] + [Part 2 – the number] = Whole).

Irwin's (1996) participants were significantly less successful on corresponding tasks with counted wholes and utterly unsuccessful on a symbolic version involving verbally stated numbers. Her results, then, *appear* to be consistent with Resnick's (1992) model.[5]

***Class Inclusion.***     One task Piaget (1965) used to study the development of part–whole knowledge was the "class-inclusion" task. This task entailed showing children two collections such as five roses and three daisies and asking them if there were more flowers or more roses. Children before about 7 years of age typically responded that there were more of the latter.

---

[5]Three problems with Irwin's (1996) methodology, however, render her results inconclusive. It is not clear that she really measured part-whole understanding at Resnick's (1992) protoquantities level. For example, 4-year-olds compared an experimenter's collection of three items with their own three-item collection, which was subdivided into parts of two items and one item. These collections could easily have been non-verbally subitized, verbally subitized, or subvocally or surreptitiously counted. In other words, children could easily have been using any of several exact-number processes, instead of an inexact process that characterizes Resnick's protoquantities level. Second, it is not clear whether Irwin was actually measuring part-whole-knowledge or something else with the so-called protoquantities task. Her participants could have been responding correctly to the co-variation trials simply by noticing that an item was added or taken away rather than considering the effects on the child's whole relative to the tester's (cf. Brush, 1978). In effect, the children might have been interpreting the task in terms of a change add-to view of addition, not in terms of part-whole view. Third, the putative variable of interests, namely the conceptual level, was not the only way the protoquantities-level task differed from the quantities- and numbers-level tasks. With the first task, a child could readily see (by nonverbal or verbal subitizing or by subvocal counting) that a collection of items was split evenly between the tester and him- or herself. With the quantities-level task, for example, the child was asked to give the tester a specified number of items, which the latter then hid in one hand. The tester next placed an unspecified number of items in the other hand, which was then operated on in various ways. The participant could, then, not be sure that the collections in the two hands, were, in fact, equal and may not have been thinking in terms of a specific number of items. Furthermore, unlike the so-called protoquantities task, children did not see both parts in the quantities task.

However, subsequent analyses and research strongly indicate that Piaget (1965) underestimated young children's part–whole knowledge, in part, because the wording of his class-inclusion task was unfamiliar and confusing to them (Brainerd, 1978; Kohnstamm, 1967; Markman, 1979; Trabasso et al., 1978; Winer, 1980). When collective terms such as *family* or *army* are used in class-inclusion questions, children as young as 4 are successful on the task (Fuson, Lyons, Pergament, Hall, & Kwon, 1988; Markman, 1973). Controlling for a variety of extraneous difficulties, Sophian and McCorgray (1994, Experiment 2) found that 5- and 6-year olds, but not 4-year-olds were successful on a class-inclusion task.

Sophian and McCorgray (1994, Experiment 1) and Sophian and Vong (1995), likewise, found that 5- and 6-year-olds, but not 4-year-olds, recognized that the starting amount (Part 1) in a missing-start change add-to problem had to be less than the numerical total of two numbers (the Whole). Irwin (1996) noted that this accomplishment apparently reflects the transition from protoquantitive knowledge about class-inclusion relations to quantitative knowledge about it. This research is discussed further in the next subsection.

***Missing-Addend Problems.*** Young children's inability to solve missing-addend word problems and equations has been taken as yet more evidence that they lack a part–whole concept (e.g., Riley et al., 1983). Some have interpreted such evidence as support for Piaget's (1965) conjecture that the pace of cognitive development determines the mathematical concepts children can and cannot learn and have concluded that instruction on missing addends is too difficult to be introduced in the early primary grades (Kamii, 1985).

The results of several recent studies suggest otherwise (e.g., Sophian & Vong, 1995). Sophian and McCorgray (1994, Experiment 1), for instance, gave 4-, 5-, and 6-year-olds problems like Problems C and D discussed earlier. Problems were read to a participant and acted out using a stuffed bear and pictures of items. When reference was made to the initial unknown amount, the participant was shown a round box covered by an envelope. When reference was made to adding objects, a picture of their objects was shown to the child and then put in the envelope (out of sight). For problems involving subtraction, a picture of the objects taken was removed from the box, shown to the child, and then placed out of sight. When the result was mentioned, the participant was shown a picture of the corresponding items. Although 5- and 6-year-olds typically had great difficulty determining the exact answers of such problems, they at least gave answers that were in the right direction. For Problem C, for instance, children knew that the answer (a part) had to be less than five (the whole). For Problem D, for example, they recognized that the answer (the whole) had to be larger than seven (the larger of the two parts). These results suggest that 5- and 6-year-olds can reason (qualitatively) about missing-addend situations and, thus, have a basic understanding of part-whole relations.

***Related Number and Arithmetic Concepts.*** The available evidence does not provide a clear indication of when children construct a more formal part–whole view of addition and subtraction (see Baroody, Wilkins, & Tiilikainen, 2003, for a review). Moreover, efforts to trace the development of additive commutativity from a protoquantitative level to general abstract reasoning have, to date, not confirmed the progression of levels hypothesized by Resnick (1992; again see Baroody et al., 2003, for a review). What is known is that, between 5 and 7 years of age, children discover that whether Part 2 is added to Part 1 or vice versa, the sum is the same—whether the task involves unknown quantities, known quantities, or symbolic expressions (Baroody, 1987b; Baroody & Gannon, 1984; Baroody et al., 1983; Bermejo & Rodriguez, 1993; Cowan & Renton, 1996; Sophian, Harley, & Martin, 1995). Furthermore, children appear to recognize commutativity earlier when the task involves part–whole problems than when it entails change add-to problems (Wilkins, Baroody, & Tiilikainen, 2001). The latter may be more difficult because change add-to problems imply adding in a particular order. Children who can overcome this implied order constraint (e.g., recognize that five and three more has the same sum as three and five more) have constructed a relatively deep understanding of additive commutativity.

Even the basic complementary relation between addition and subtraction (Whole – Part 1 = Part 2, which is related to Part 1 + Part 2 = Whole) appears to be far less salient to young children than is additive commutativity (Baroody, 1999; Baroody et al., 1983). This principle may be a basis for a reasoning out difference (e.g., 5 – 3 = ? can be thought of as 3 + ? = 5), discussed earlier.

Furthermore, many prefirst graders may not recognize that a quantity (a whole) can be decomposed or created in various ways (e.g., Baratta-Lorton, 1976; Baroody with Coslick, 1998). Young children's change add-to view of addition and change take-away view of subtraction may contribute to this incomplete understanding of part–whole relations (Baroody, 1987a). For instance, a child may believe that five and two more is seven (Part 1 + Part 2 = a Whole) and not realize that four and three more can have the same outcome ([Part 1 – 1] + [Part 2 + 1] = the Whole). In effect, children may have to rediscover the compensation principle at the level of abstract number. This may occur about the age of 7 years, when children begin to compute and either mentally compare sums and differences or compare written equations.

## Implications for Early Childhood Standards

In the *PSSM* draft (NCTM, 1998), part–whole relations are mentioned in two passages, the first implicitly and the second explicitly: (a) "develop an understanding of multiple relationships among whole numbers by ... composing [and] decomposing number" (p. 109); (b) "Children gradually develop part-part-whole concepts. For example, in a situation where there are 4 red balls and 3 blue balls, three and four are parts and seven is the whole" (p. 111). Nothing is explicitly said, however, about why a part–whole concept is important (e.g., providing a basis for assimilating missing-addend problems) or how a teacher might foster its development.

The preceding Point a was retained in the *PSSM* (NCTM, 2000) in a revised form as one of the Pre-K to 2 expectations. Inexplicably, though, the direct mention of the part–whole concept (Point b, preceding) was not. As was the case in the *PSSM* draft (NCTM, 1998), the *PSSM* (NCTM, 2000) does not include direct mention of how a part–whole concept underlies an understanding of key concepts and skills. The discussions of the concepts of additive commutativity and associativity, missing-addend addition, the relations between addition and subtraction, measurement, place value, and other names for a number concept (e.g., see pp. 33, 34, 80, and 82–84), for instance, are not tied to a part–whole understanding. A discussion of fractions only implicitly makes a connection to this key idea: "Young children can be encouraged ... to see fractions as part of a unit whole or of a collection" (p. 33).

The early childhood standards should explicitly identify the part–whole concept as one of the "big ideas" that forms the nucleus of early mathematics instruction, one that holds this nucleus together as a coherent body of knowledge. It should further illustrate why it is important (see, e.g., Resnick, 1992) and how this key knowledge can be fostered (see, e.g., chap. 6 in Baroody with Coslick, 1998).

## Grouping and Place Value

- Big Idea 1.4/2.3: Items can be grouped to make a larger unit and, in a written multidigit number, the value of a digit depends on its position because different digit positions indicate different units.

Grouping items by larger units such as making groups of ten, hundreds, and so forth can make counting large collections easier (e.g., instead of counting a collection of 63 items by one, counting: "10, 20, 30, 40, 50, 60, 61, 62, 63"). Along with place-value concepts (e.g., the position of a digit indicates its value), grouping concepts serve as the underlying rationale for our system of written, multidigit numbers (e.g., the 2 in 258 represents two groups of one hundred; the 5, five groups of ten; the 8, eight singles). These concepts are also the basis for multidigit arithmetic procedures with either whole numbers or decimals, including renaming ("carrying" and "borrowing"; e.g., for 97 + 48, the sum of the units place digits 15 can be thought of as a group of 10 and 5 singles and so a 1 can be placed atop the tens column to represent 1 group of ten and the 5 can be recorded in the units place).

A grouping concept, which includes other base systems (grouping by numbers other than 10), also has a variety of everyday applications. For example, money equivalents are based on groupings of 5 (5 pennies = 1 nickel, 5 nickels = 1 quarter, 5 dimes = 1 half dollar, etc.) and 10 (10 pennies = 1 dime, 10 dimes = 1 dollar, etc.), electronic devices such as calculators or computers operate on a base-2 system, and produce retailers regularly use groups of 12 to quantify their purchases and sales (12 items = 1 dozen, 12 dozen = 1 gross, 12 grosses = 1 great gross; see Baroody with Coslick, 1998, 2000, for examples and explanations).

## Development

Unlike Asian counting sequences, the English sequence does not clearly underscore grouping and place-value concepts (Big Idea 1.4/2.3 listed earlier; see, e.g., Fuson & Burghardt, 2003; Miura & Okamoto, 2003). Thus, although English-speaking children may begin to construct some understanding of these concepts before school, most probably do not develop a deep understanding of them without effective instruction. The normal course of development in this country, then, is to move from a counting-based view of number (e.g., view a verbal number such as *twenty-three* or a multidigit written number such as 23 as a collection of 23 items, not as two groups of ten and three units) to one based on grouping and place value at least to some degree. The development of a grouping and a place-value concept is intertwined with each other and other concepts.

### Transitions 1 and 2. After Transition 1, preschoolers may engage in intuitive grouping activities, such as repeatedly add two blocks to a toy pickup truck to create a "full load" (a larger unit of blocks), which is transported to make a house (an even larger unit of blocks). Transition 2 makes it more likely that children will construct a broader, more accurate, and more explicit understanding of grouping. With the advent of meaningful counting (enumeration and production), children can create equal groups of even larger numbers and use numbers to ensure their equality. Dealing with larger numbers, in turn, can create a real need for forming groups of groups (i.e., even larger units). For example, in keeping track of hundreds of points, it behooves children to make piles of 10 (treat 10 items as a single group of ten) and to group 10 groups of ten into a hundred. This may lead to recognizing "hierarchical grouping"—that *each* larger unit is composed in the same way (e.g., tens are composed of *10* ones; hundreds, of *10* tens; thousands, of *10* hundreds; and so forth). Children take another important step when they recognize that grouping can be reversed (e.g., that a ten can be decomposed into 10 ones; e.g., Cobb & Wheatley, 1988).

The construction of a place-value concept may begin in pre-Transition 2 form when a young child, for instance, plays target games. A child in this phase of development may know that hitting the target is good and that hitting the bull's-eye of the target is even better. Transition 2, especially, can result in associating a particular value with, say, hitting the target and hitting the bull's-eye.

**Transition 3.**   The transition to written representations of numbers, particularly informal ones (*twelve* = ||||||||||||), can further facilitate the development of a grouping concept. It can be especially important for the construction of place-value understanding. A step toward an understanding that the position of a digit in a multidigit nu meral defines its value may be recognizing that 23 and 32 represent different amounts or that the latter is larger than the former (Donlan, 2003). Furthermore, children need to learn that (a) items can be grouped, and grouped items are treated differently from ungrouped items; (b) the group size (10 in base-10) is used repeatedly to group smaller groups (e.g., ten 10s are grouped to make 100, ten 100s make 1,000, and so forth); and (c) successively larger groups are arranged from right to left and the number in each group is denoted by a single-digit numeral (Hendrickson, 1983). Furthermore, when adding or subtracting multidigit numbers, only digits of the same group size can be combined or subtracted (Fuson, 1992).

Children who have not been given the opportunity to construct grouping and place-value concepts may have difficulty learning multidigit skills. The symptoms of such difficulties have been widely observed and include "writing numerals as they sound" (e.g., writing *twenty-three* as 203; e.g., Ginsburg, 1977), making "face-value errors" (e.g., interpreting 23 as two of something, such as two uncircled items, and three of something else, such as three circled items; e.g., Ross, 1989), and using "buggy algorithms" (e.g., subtracting the smaller digit from the larger regardless of position, as in 254 – 67 = 213; Ashlock, 1998; Brown & Burton, 1978; Buswell & Judd, 1925).

## Implications for Early Childhood Standards

Grouping and place-value concepts are emphasized in the *PSSM* (NCTM, 2000) and justifiably so. The importance of using various models to help children construct these concepts is mentioned in a number of places. For example, one of the expectations for Grades Pre-K to 2 is that children "use multiple models to develop initial understandings of place value and the base-ten number system" (NCTM, 2000, p. 78). Also clearly emphasized is the need to develop flexibility in thinking about numbers. The example of students modeling *twenty-five* with 25 beans and two dimes and a nickel, for instance, could be interpreted as helping children see that multidigit numbers have both a counting-based meaning and a grouping-based meaning. Key connections between place-value/grouping concepts and counting and written multidigit numbers are also discussed.

There is little mention, though, about the earliest forms of grouping and place-value concepts (Transition 1 experiences) in the *PSSM* (NCTM, 2000). Also not discussed are the relative merits of different models that can provide bases for Transitions 2 and 3 (see Fig. 7.1) or the pedagogical

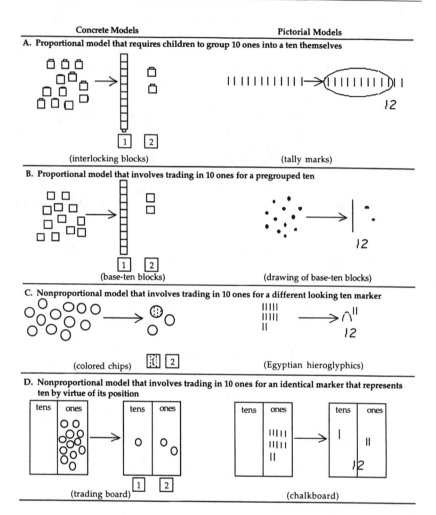

FIG. 7.1.   Models for grouping and place-value concepts. These are increasing abstract models of multidigit numbers using objects or pictures.

benefits of introducing other bases (see chapter 6 in Baroody with Coslick, 1998 and 2000, for a discussion of both of these issues). Although the *PSSM* (NCTM, 2000) includes the caution that using concrete materials, especially in a rote manner, does not ensure understanding (e.g., Baroody 1989b; Clements & McMillen, 1996), it does not lay out adequate guidelines for using manipulative in a meaningful manner (see, e.g., Baroody, with Coslick, 1998; Fuson & Burghardt, 2003; Miura & Okamoto,

2003). The early childhood standards should address all the issues raised in the preceding discussion.

## Equal Composing and Decomposing

- Big Idea 1.5/2.4: A whole can be composed from or decomposed into equal size parts.

Like a part–whole concept, equal composing and decomposing is another big idea in that it provides the conceptual basis for important aspects of number (Really Big Idea 1) and operations on numbers (Really Big Idea 2) and further connects these major domains. Equal composing (e.g., combining collections of *equal size* to form a whole) is a conceptual basis for multiplication, which is simply a special case of addition (namely combining collections of *equal size*). Analogously, decomposing a whole into equal-size groups (equal partitioning) is a conceptual basis of division. For example $14 \div 4 = 3$ r2 can be thought of as 14 items shared fairly among four people would result in shares of 3 items each with 2 items left over (unshared). Equal partitioning is also the conceptual basis for fractions (and measurement). For example, the fraction 3/8 can represent taking 3 pieces of a pizza (a whole), which has been subdivided into 8 equal pieces.

### *Development*

Even before they learn to count, children may be interested in sharing or splitting up (more or less) equally small, discrete (and continuous) quantities. With the development of counting, children secure another method of ensuring or checking on equal shares, particularly for quantities larger than four items.

*Multiplication.*   Many children find multiplication to be easier than subtraction because the former builds on addition and the latter involves informal calculations that are relatively difficult to do mentally (see Baroody, 1987a, for a detailed discussion). Specifically, multiplication is relatively easy to understand if instruction helps students see that it is simply repeated addition—the addition of a like term.

*Division.*   Research has shown that many children of kindergarten age can respond appropriately to fair-sharing problems involving divvying-up situations, such as Problem E as follows:

■ **Problem E.** *Three sisters Martha, Marta, and Marsha were given a plate of six cookies by their mom. If the three sisters shared the six cookies fairly, how many cookies would each sister get?*

Some children solve this type of problem by using a dealing-out strategy: Count out objects to represent the amount; then deal out the cookies one at a time into piles; repeat the process until all the objects have been passed out; and then count the number of items in each pile to determine the solution (e.g., Davis & Pitkethly, 1990; Hiebert & Tonnessen, 1978; Hunting & Davis, 1991; Miller, 1984). For the aforementioned Problem E, this would entail counting out six items, dealing out one item at a time to each of three piles, repeating the dealing-out process, and finally counting the two items in one of the piles to determine the answer. Even the operation of division, then, can be introduced at a concrete level to children as early as kindergarten.

Fair-sharing problems can also involve measuring-out situations, as Problem F illustrates:

■ **Problem F.** *Jerry has 12 cookies. If he made shares of 3 cookies each, how many children could share the cookies fairly?*

An understanding of measure-out division is important for (a) a more complete understanding of the operation and, in time, how division is related to a groups-of multiplication and (b) making sense of fraction and decimal division. Research suggests, though, that many children are not familiar with and have more difficulty solving measure-out problems (Fischbein, Deri, Nello, & Marino, 1985). Because they are inclined to relate symbolic division to a divvy-up meaning exclusively, students are puzzled by expressions such as $\frac{1}{2} \div \frac{1}{8}$ or $0.75 \div 0.25$ (Baroody with Coslick, 1998).

*Fractions.* Equal partitioning of both discrete and continuous quantities to solve fair-sharing problems can provide a key informal basis for understanding fractions (e.g., Baroody with Coslick, 1998; Hunting & Davis, 1991; Mack, 1990, 1993; Streefland, 1993). For instance, trying to share three cookies between two children can give rise to dividing each of the cookies into two equal-size pieces (halves) and giving each child a half of each cookie, or one whole cookie and half of another ($\frac{1}{2} + \frac{1}{2} + \frac{1}{2} = \frac{3}{2}$ or $1\frac{1}{2}$). Some children might solve the same problem by giving each child a whole cookie and half of the third cookie ($1\frac{1}{2}$). A class discussion could make explicit the following fundamental fraction concepts: (a) the shares must be fair or equal in size (fractions involve a special situation in which all the parts of a whole are equal in size), (b) *three halves* literally means *three one-halves* (fractions embody multiplicative reasoning; e.g., $= \frac{3}{2} = \frac{1}{2} + \frac{1}{2} + \frac{1}{2} = 3 \times \frac{1}{2}$), and (c) *three halves* and *one and a half* represent the same amount (a fractional amount can have different names—which we call *equivalent fractions* ). Unfortunately, formal instruction on fractions typically moves too quickly with abstract symbols and, thus, does not provide an adequate conceptual basis for understanding fractions (e.g., the idea that parts must be equal; e.g., Behr, Harel, Post, & Lesh, 1992).

Fraction addition and subtraction may not deserve emphasis in early childhood education. However, as with an understanding of whole numbers (Piaget, 1965), a relatively complete and accurate understanding of fractions depends, in part, on understanding the role of additive composition. For instance, an accurate understanding of one half includes recognizing that a half is less than a whole and that two halves ($\frac{1}{2} + \frac{1}{2}$) make a whole.

Perhaps most surprising of all is the research indicating that preschoolers may understand simple fraction addition and subtraction. Mix, Levine, and Hutlenlocher (1999) presented 3-, 4-, and 5-year-olds nonverbal problems that involved, for instance, first showing half of a circular sponge and then putting it behind a screen, next showing half of another circular sponge and then also putting it behind the screen, and finally presenting four choices (e.g., one fourth of a sponge, one half of a sponge, three fourths of a sponge, and a whole sponge) and asking which was hidden by the screen. The 3-year-olds were correct only 25% of the time (i.e., responded at a chance level—no better than could be expected by random guessing). The 4- and 5-years olds, though, responded at an above-chance level. For instance, over half were correct on trials involving "$\frac{1}{4} + \frac{1}{2}$," "$\frac{1}{4} + \frac{3}{4}$," "$\frac{1}{2} - \frac{1}{4}$," and "$1 - \frac{1}{4}$."

In his discussion of my paper presented at the Conference on Standards for Preschool and Kindergarten Mathematics Education (Baroody, 2000), Kevin Miller correctly cautioned that Mix and her colleagues' (1999) evidence does not necessarily mean that their participants understood fractions (e.g., as a part of a whole subdivided into equal-size parts), let alone fraction addition and subtraction. He noted that children could be responding to perceptual cues such as area. Clearly, further research is needed to assess whether most or even some 5-year-olds understand fraction addition and subtraction.

## Implications for Early Childhood Standards

**Multiplication.** The *PSSM* (NCTM, 2000) includes explicit mention of the conceptual basis of multiplication (equal composing). "Through work situations involving equal subgroups within a collection, students can associate multiplication with the repeated joining (addition) of groups of equal size" (p. 84).

**Division.** The *PSSM* (NCTM, 2000) includes explicit mention of division and its conceptual basis (equal partitioning): "Understand situations that entail ... divisions, such as equal groupings of objects and sharing equally" (p. 78). This document also clearly indicates that fair-sharing problems can provide a conceptual basis for developing these ideas: "Division can begin to have meaning for students in prekindergarten through grade 2 as they solve problems that arise in their environment, such as how to share a bag of raisins fairly among four people" (p. 34). The *PSSM* (NCTM, 2000) does not distinguish between *divvy-up* fair-sharing problems (like the one in the previous sentence or the earlier Problem E) and *measure-out* fair-sharing problems (such as the earlier Problem F).

The proposed EC standards should not only recommend the use of fair sharing, in general, but the use of such problems involving both divvy-up and measuring-out situations. For a detailed discussion of the distinction between these two types of division problems and how a teacher can use everyday situations to introduce each, see pages 5-17 to 5-24, particularly Fig. 5.4 on page 5-20 and Activity 5.5 on page 5-21 in Baroody with Coslick (1998).

**Fractions.** The *PSSM* (NCTM, 2000) does include specific mention of fractions. For instance, page 33 includes the statement: "Beyond understanding whole numbers, young children can be encouraged to understand and represent commonly used fractions in context, such as $\frac{1}{2}$ of a cookie or $\frac{1}{8}$ of a pizza, and to see fractions as part of a unit whole or of a collection." The list of expectations for Pre-K to Grade 2 regarding number and operations on page 78 echoes the first portion of the previous statement ("understand and represent commonly used fractions, such as ($"\frac{1}{4}, \frac{1}{3},$ and $\frac{1}{2}"$). Unfortunately, this key goal is not clearly related to the foundational concept of equal partitioning. The proposed early childhood standards should not only include the expectations about fractions outlined earlier but explicitly link this expectation to providing young children with equal-partitioning experience with discrete quantities first and then with continuous quantities. The former involves using a single divvy-up strategy for all problems, whereas the latter entails using different strategies for different problems (e.g., subdividing a cookie between two people requires finding a diameter; subdividing it among three does not).

For Pre-K to Grade 2, the *PSSM* (NCTM, 1998) mentions operations on whole numbers only. Gaining understanding of fraction relations, including addition of fractions, is a goal for Grades 3 to 5 (see, e.g., *PSSM*, p. 33). Given that young children may be successful on nonverbal fraction addition and subtraction tasks (Mix et al., 1999), it may make sense that—at the very least—early childhood instruction should involve them in qualitative reasoning about such operations using concrete models and, later, fraction words and written representations. Even if the 5-year-old participants in the Mix et al. study were merely responding to area, this may provide a basis for qualitative reasoning about the effects of adding and subtracting fractions (halves at least). Along with equal-partitioning experience, this may provide a basis for an understanding of commonly used fractions such as $\frac{1}{4}, \frac{1}{3}$ and $\frac{1}{2}$, including the recognition that two one fourths ("$\frac{1}{4} + \frac{1}{4}$") or two one thirds ("$\frac{1}{3} + \frac{1}{3}$") is less than a whole, and three halves is greater than a whole.

## CONCLUDING COMMENTS

Advocating a detailed level of standards should not be interpreted as suggesting a laundry list of lessons or units for teachers to implement. That is, I am not advocating that teachers have one lesson or unit for each detailed standard. Typically, several detailed goals could be addressed in an integrated lesson or unit. For example, consider the game *Animal Spots* (Wynroth, 1986). On each turn, a player rolls a die with, for example, 0 to 5 dots on a side. The player counts the dots (Goals N1.1.3b, N1.1.3c, N1.1.4a, N1.1.4b, and N1.1.4c in Table 7.1) or subitizes the number of dots (Goals N1.1.1b and N1.1.1c), counts out a corresponding number of pegs (Goals N1.1.5a and N1.1.5b), and puts the pegs ("spots") into the holes of board cut out in the form of a leopard or giraffe. The first player to fill all the holes in his or her animal board is the winner.

Note also that playing this game is consistent with an investigative approach described earlier in chapter 6 (this volume). Children are engaged in an activity that is purposeful to them (i.e., it involves learning and practicing mathematical competencies in an inherently real, interesting, and meaningful manner). Because it involves using mathematical competencies in context, children can better understand why and how the competencies are used (i.e., the games provide a basis for meaningful or conceptual learning). For example, if one child counts five dots and another sees four, the discrepancy can provide an opportunity for discussing one-to-one counting and keeping-track strategies (strategies for distinguishing between already-counted items and items yet to be counted). The discrepancy can also provide an opportunity for engaging in mathematical inquiry. For instance, a teacher might ask if both answers could be correct, how the group could decide which was correct, and why the incorrect answer is incorrect and how it came about.

## ACKNOWLEDGMENTS

This chapter is based on papers presented at the symposium "Linking Research and the New Early Childhood Mathematics Standards" at the

Research Presession of the annual meeting of the National Council of Teachers of Mathematics, Chicago, April 2000; the Conference on Standards for Preschool and Kindergarten Mathematics Education (sponsored by the National Science Foundation and ExxonMobil Foundation), Arlington, Virginia, May 2000; and a follow-up conference in Dallas, Texas, October, 2000.

The preparation and writing of this paper was supported, in part, by a Faculty Fellowship awarded by the Bureau of Educational Research (College of Education, University of Illinois at Urbana-Champaign) and a grant from the National Science Foundation (BCS-0111829). The opinions expressed are solely those of the author and do not necessarily reflect the position, policy, or endorsement of the National Science Foundation.

## REFERENCES

Ashcraft, M. H. (1982). The development of mental arithmetic: A chronometric approach. *Developmental Review, 2,* 213–236.

Ashcraft, M. H. (1985). Is it farfetched that some of us remember arithmetic facts? *Journal for Research in Mathematics Education, 16,* 99–105.

Ashcraft, M. H. (1992). Cognitive arithmetic: A review of data and theory. *Cognition, 44,* 75–106.

Ashlock, R. B. (1998). *Error patterns in computation* (7th ed.). Upper Saddle River, NJ: Prentice-Hall.

Baratta-Lorton, M. (1976). *Mathematics their way.* Menlo Park, CA: Addison-Wesley.

Baroody, A. J. (1984). The case of Felicia: A young child's strategies for reducing memory demands during mental addition. *Cognition and Instruction, 1,* 109–116.

Baroody, A. J. (1985). Mastery of the basic number combinations: Internalization of relationships or facts? *Journal of Research in Mathematics Education, 16,* 83–98.

Baroody, A. J. (1986). Basic counting principles used by mentally retarded children. *Journal for Research in Mathematics Education, 17,* 382–389.

Baroody, A. J. (1987a). *Children's mathematical thinking: A developmental framework for preschool, primary, and special education teachers.* New York: Teachers College Press.

Baroody, A. J. (1987b). The development of counting strategies for single-digit addition. *Journal for Research in Mathematics Education, 18,* 141–157.

Baroody, A. J. (1988a). A cognitive approach to writing instruction for children classified as mentally handicapped. *Arithmetic Teacher, 36*(2), 7–11.

Baroody, A. J. (1988b). Mental-addition development of children classified as mentally handicapped. *Educational Studies in Mathematics, 19,* 369–388.

Baroody, A. J. (1989a). Kindergartners' mental addition with single-digit combinations. *Journal for Research in Mathematics Education, 20,* 159–172.

Baroody, A. J. (1989b). One point of view: Manipulatives don't come with guarantees. *Arithmetic Teacher, 37*(2), 4–5.

Baroody, A. J. (1992a). The development of kindergartners' mental-addition strategies. *Learning and Individual Differences, 4,* 215–235.

Baroody, A. J. (1992b). The development of preschoolers' counting skills and principles. In J. Bideaud, C. Meljac, & J. P. Fischer (Eds.), *Pathways to number* (pp. 99–126). Hillsdale, NJ: Lawrence Erlbaum Associates.

Baroody, A. J. (1993). The relationship between the order-irrelevance principle and counting skill. *Journal for Research in Mathematics Education, 24,* 415–427.

Baroody, A. J. (1994). An evaluation of evidence supporting fact-retrieval models. *Learning and Individual Differences, 6,* 1–36.

Baroody, A. J. (1999). Children's relational knowledge of addition and subtraction. *Cognition and Instruction, 17,* 137–175.

Baroody, A. J. (2000, May). *Number and operations: Key transitions in the numerical and arithmetic development of typical and special children between the ages of 2 and 6 years.* Paper presented at the Conference on Standards for Preschool and Kindergarten Mathematics Education, Arlington, VA.

Baroody, A. J. (2002, May). *The developmental foundations of number and operation sense.* Presentation and poster presented at the EHR/REC (NSF) Principal Investigators' Meeting ("Learning and Education: Building Knowledge, Understanding Its Implications"), Arlington, VA.

Baroody, A. J., & Benson, A. (2001). Early number instruction. *Teaching Children Mathematics, 8,* 154–158.

Baroody, A. J., with Coslick, R. T. (1998). *Fostering children's mathematical power: An investigative approach to K–8 mathematics instruction.* Mahwah, NJ: Lawrence Erlbaum Associates.

Baroody, A. J., with Coslick, R. T. (2000). *Instructor's guide to fostering children's mathematical power: An investigative approach to K–8 mathematics instruction.* Mahwah, NJ: Lawrence Erlbaum Associates. (Available in electronic form at www.erlbaum.com or http://www.ed.uiuc.edu/facstaff/baroody/newbook.html.)

Baroody, A. J., & Gannon, K. E. (1984). The development of commutativity principle and economical addition strategies. *Cognition and Instruction, 1,* 321–329.

Baroody, A. J., & Gatzke, M. S. (1991). The estimation of set size by potentially gifted kindergarten-age children. *Journal for Research in Mathematics Education, 22,* 59–68.

Baroody, A. J., Ginsburg, H. P., & Waxman, B. (1983). Children's use of mathematical structure. *Journal for Research in Mathematics Education, 14,* 156–168.

Baroody, A. J., & Kaufman, L. C. (1993). The case of Lee: Assessing and remedying a numerical-writing difficulty. *Teaching Exceptional Children, 25(3),* 14–16.

Baroody, A. J., & Tiilikainen, S. H. (2003). Two perspectives on addition development. In A. J. Baroody & A. Dowker (Eds.), *The development of arithmetic concepts and skills: Constructing adaptive expertise* (pp. 75–125). Mahwah, NJ: Lawrence Erlbaum Associates.

Baroody, A. J., Wilkins, J. L. M., & Tiilikainen, S. (2003). The development of children's understanding of additive commutativity: From protoquantitative concept to general concept? In A. J. Baroody & A. Dowker (Eds.), *The development of arithmetic concepts and skills: Constructing adaptive expertise* (pp. 127–160). Mahwah, NJ: Lawrence Erlbaum Associates.

Behr, M. J., Harel, G., Post, T., & Lesh, R. (1992). Rational number, ratio, and proportion. In D. Grouws (Ed.), *Handbook of research on mathematics teaching and learning* (pp. 296–333). New York: Macmillan.

Bermejo, V., & Rodriguez, P. (1993). Children's understanding of the commutative law of addition. *Learning and Instruction, 3,* 55–72.

Boisvert, M., Standing, L., & Moller, L. (1999). Successful part-whole perception in young children using multiple-choice tests. *The Journal of Genetic Psychology, 160,* 167–180.

Brainerd, C. J. (1978). *Piaget's theory of intelligence.* Englewood Cliffs, NJ: Prentice-Hall.

Brown, J. S., & Burton, R. B. (1978). Diagnostic models for procedural bugs in basic mathematical skills. *Cognitive Science, 2,* 155–192.

Brownell, W. A. (1935). Psychological considerations in the learning and the teaching of arithmetic. In D. W. Reeve (Ed.), *The teaching of arithmetic* (Tenth yearbook, National Council of Teachers of Mathematics, pp. 1–50). New York: Bureau of Publications, Teachers College, Columbia University.

Brush, L. (1978). Preschool children's knowledge of addition and subtraction. *Journal for Research in Mathematics Education, 9,* 44–54.

Buswell, G. T., & Judd, C. H. (1925). Summary of educational investigations relating to arithmetic. *Supplementary Educational Monographs, No. 27.* Chicago: University of Chicago Press.

Butterworth, B., Marschesini, N., & Girelli, L. (2003). Development of multiplication skills: Rote learning or reorganization? In A. J. Baroody & A. Dowker (Eds.). *The development of arithmetic concepts and skills: Constructing adaptive expertise* (pp. 189–202). Mahwah, NJ: Lawrence Erlbaum Associates.

Carpenter, T. P., Hiebert, J., & Moser, J. (1983). Problem structure and first grade children's initial solution processes for simple addition and subtraction problems. *Journal for Research in Mathematics Education, 12,* 27–39.

Carpenter, T. P., & Moser, J. M. (1982). The development of addition and subtraction problem-solving skills. In T. P. Carpenter, J. M. Moser, & T. A. Romberg (Eds.), *Addition and subtraction: A cognitive perspective* (pp. 9–24). Hillsdale, NJ: Lawrence Erlbaum Associates.

Carpenter, T. P., & Moser, J. M. (1983). The acquisition of addition and subtraction concepts. In R. Lesh & M. Landau (Eds.), *Acquisition of mathematical concepts and procedures* (pp. 7–44). New York: Academic Press.

Carpenter, T. P., & Moser, J. M. (1984). The acquisition of addition and subtraction concepts in grades one through three. *Journal for Research in Mathematics Education, 15,* 179–202.

Clements, D. H., & McMillen, S. (1996). Rethinking "concrete" manipulatives. *Teaching Children Mathematics, 2*(5), 270–279.

Cobb, P., & Wheatley, G. (1988). Children's initial understanding of ten. *Focus on Learning Problems in Mathematics, 10*(3), 1–28.

Cooper, R. G. (1984). Early number development: Discovering number space with addition and subtraction. In C. Sophian (Ed.), *Origins of cognitive skills* (pp. 157–192). Hillsdale, NJ: Lawrence Erlbaum Associates.

Cowan, R., & Renton, M. (1996). Do they know what they are doing? Children's use of economical addition strategies and knowledge of commutativity. *Educational Psychology, 16,* 407–420.

Davis, G., & Pitkethly, A. (1990). Cognitive aspects of sharing. *Journal for Research in Mathematics Education, 21,* 145–153.

DeCorte, E., & Verschaffel, L. (1987). The effects of semantic structure on first graders' strategies for solving addition and subtraction word problems. *Journal for Research in Mathematics Education, 18,* 363–381.

DeLoache, J. S. (1987). Rapid change in the symbolic functioning of very young children. *Science, 238,* 1556–1557.

DeLoache, J. S. (1991). Symbolic functioning in very young children: Understanding of picture models. *Child Development, 62,* 736–752.

Donaldson, M., & Balfour, G. (1968). Less is more. *British Journal of Psychology, 59,* 461–471.

Donlan, C. (2003). Numeracy development in children with specific language impairments: The interaction of conceptual and procedural knowledge. In A. J. Baroody & A. Dowker (Eds.), *The development of arithmetic concepts and skills: Constructing adaptive expertise* (pp. 337–358). Mahwah, NJ: Lawrence Erlbaum Associates.

Elkind, D., Koegler, R. R., & Go, E. (1964). Studies in perceptual development: II. Part–whole perception. *Child Development, 35,* 81–90.

Fischbein, E., Deri, M., Nello, M. S., & Marino, M. S. (1985). The role of implicit models in solving verbal problems in multiplication and division. *Journal for Research in Mathematics Education, 16,* 3–17.

Flavell, J. H. (1963). *The developmental psychology of Jean Piaget.* New York: Van Nostrand.

Fuson, K. C. (1988). *Children's counting and concepts of number.* New York: Springer-Verlag.

Fuson, K. C. (1992). Research on whole number addition and subtraction. In D. Grouws (Ed.), *Handbook of research on mathematics teaching and learning* (pp. 243–275). New York: Macmillan.

Fuson, K. C., & Burghardt, B. H. (2003). Multidigit addition and subtraction methods invented in small groups and teacher support of problem solving and reflection. In A. J. Baroody & A. Dowker (Eds.), *The development of arithmetic concepts and skills: Constructing adaptive expertise* (pp. 267–304). Mahwah, NJ: Lawrence Erlbaum Associates.

Fuson, K. C., & Hall, J. W. (1983). The acquisition of early number word meanings: A conceptual analysis and review. In H. P. Ginsburg (Ed.), *The development of mathematical thinking* (pp. 49–107). New York: Academic Press.

Fuson, K. C., Lyons, B. G., Pergament, G. G., Hall, J., & Kwon, Y. (1988). Effects of collection terms on class-inclusion and on number tasks. *Cognitive Psychology, 20,* 96–120.

Gelman, R., & Gallistel, C. R. (1978). *The child's understanding of number.* Cambridge, MA: Harvard University Press.

Ginsburg, H. P. (1977). *Children's arithmetic.* New York: Van Nostrand.

Ginsburg, H. P., & Baroody, A. J. (2003). *Test of Early Mathematics Ability—Third Edition (TEMA-3).* Austin, TX: Pro-Ed.

Ginsburg, H. P., & Opper, S. (1969). *Piaget's theory of intellectual development: An introduction*. Englewood Cliffs, NJ: Prentice-Hall.

Goodnow, J., & Levine, R. A. (1973). "The grammar of action": Sequence and syntax in children's copying. *Cognitive Psychology, 4*, 82–98.

Hendrickson, A. D. (1983). Prevention or cure? Another look at mathematics learning problems. In D. Carnine, D. Elkind, A. D. Hendrickson, D. Meichenbaum, R. L. Sieben, & F. Smith (Eds.), *Interdisciplinary voices in learning disabilities and remedial education* (pp. 93–107). Austin, TX: Pro-Ed.

Hiebert, J., & Tonnessen, L. H. (1978). Development of the fraction concept in two physical contexts: An exploratory investigation. *Journal for Research in Mathematics Education, 9*, 374–378.

Hughes, M. (1986). *Children and number*. New York: Basil Blackwell.

Hunting, R. P., & Davis, G. (Eds.). (1991). *Early fraction learning*. New York: Springer-Verlag.

Huttenlocher, J., Jordan, N. C., & Levine, S. C. (1994). A mental model for early arithmetic. *Journal of Experimental Psychology: General, 123*, 284–296.

Irwin, K. C. (1996). Children's understanding of the principles of covariation and compensation in part-whole relationships. *Journal for Research in Mathematics Education, 27*, 25–40.

Jordan, N. C., Hanich, L. B., & Uberti, H. Z. (2003). Mathematical thinking and learning difficulties. In A. J. Baroody & A. Dowker (Eds.), *The development of arithmetic concepts and skills: Constructing adaptive expertise* (pp. 359–383). Mahwah, NJ: Lawrence Erlbaum Associates.

Jordan, N. C., Huttenlocher, J., & Levine, S. C. (1992). Differential calculation abilities in young children from middle- and low-income families. *Developmental Psychology, 28*, 644–653.

Jordan, N. C., Huttenlocher, J., & Levine, S. C. (1994). Assessing early arithmetic abilities: Effects of verbal and nonverbal response types on the calculation performance of middle- and low-income children. *Learning and Individual Differences, 6*, 413–432.

Kaliski, L. (1962). Arithmetic and the brain-injured child. *Arithmetic Teacher, 9*, 245–251.

Kamii, C. (1985). *Young children reinvent arithmetic: Implication of Piaget's theory*. New York: Teachers College Press.

Klahr, D., & Wallace, J. G. (1973). The role of quantification operators in the development of conservation of quantity. *Cognitive Psychology, 4*, 301–327.

Kohnstamm, G. A. (1967). *Piaget's analysis of class inclusion: Right or wrong?* The Hague, Netherlands: Mouton.

LeFevre, J., Sadesky, G. S., & Bisanz, J. (1996). Selection of procedures in mental addition: Reassessing the problem size effect in adults. *Journal of Experimental Psychology: Learning, Memory, and Cognition, 22*, 216–230.

LeFevre, J., Smith-Chant, B. L., Hiscock, K., Daley, K. E., & Morris, J. (2003). Young adults' strategic choices in simple arithmetic: Implications for the development of mathematical represented. In A. J. Baroody & A. Dowker (Eds.), *The development of arithmetic concepts and skills: Constructing adaptive expertise* (pp. 203–228). Mahwah, NJ: Lawrence Erlbaum Associates.

Levine, S. C., Jordan, N. C., & Huttenlocher, J. (1992). Development of calculation abilities in young children. *Journal of Experimental Child Psychology, 53*, 72–103.

Mack, N. K. (1990). Learning fractions with understanding: Building on informal knowledge. *Journal for Research in Mathematics Education, 21*, 16–32.

Mack, N. K. (1993). Learning rational numbers with understanding: The case of informal knowledge. In T. P. Carpenter, E. Fennema, & T. A. Romberg (Eds.), *Rational numbers: An integration of research* (pp. 85–105). Hillsdale, NJ: Lawrence Erlbaum Associates.

Markman, E. (1973). The facilitation of part-whole comparisons by use of the collective noun "family." *Child Development, 44*, 837–840.

Markman, E. (1979). Classes and collections: Conceptual organization and numerical abilities. *Cognitive Psychology, 11*, 395–411.

Miller, K. (1984). Child as a measurer of all things: Measurement procedures and the development of quantitive concepts. In C. Sophian (Ed.), *Origins of cognitive skills* (pp. 193–228). Hillsdale, NJ: Lawrence Erlbaum Associates.

Miura, I. T., & Okamoto, Y. (2003). Language supports for mathematics understanding and performance. In A. J. Baroody & A. Dowker (Eds.), *The development of arithmetic con-*

*cepts and skills: Constructing adaptive expertise* (pp. 229–242). Mahwah, NJ: Lawrence Erlbaum Associates.

Mix, K. S. (1999a). Preschoolers' recognition of numerical equivalence: Sequential sets. *Journal of Experimental Child Psychology, 74,* 309–332.

Mix, K. S. (1999b). Similarity and numerical equivalence: Appearances count. *Cognitive Development, 14,* 269–297.

Mix, K. S. (2001, April). The differentiation of continuous and discrete quantification. In K. S. Mix (Chair), *The role of overall amount in early quantification.* Symposium conducted at the biennial meeting of the Society for Research in Child Development, Minneapolis, MN.

Mix, K. S., Huttenlocher, J., & Levine, S. C. (1996). Do preschool children recognize auditory-visual numerical correspondences? *Child Development, 67,* 1592–1608.

Mix, K. S., Huttenlocher, J., & Levine, S. C. (2002a). *Math without words: Quantitative development in infancy and early childhood.* New York: Oxford University Press.

Mix, K. S., Huttenlocher, J., & Levine, S. C. (2002b). Multiple cues for quantification in infancy: Is number one of them? *Psychological Bulletin, 128,* 278–294.

Mix, K. S., Levine, S. C., & Huttenlocher, J. (1999). Early fraction calculation ability. *Developmental Psychology, 35,* 164–174.

Munn, P. (1998). Number symbols and symbolic function in preschoolers. In C. Donlan (Ed.), *The development of mathematical skills* (pp. 47–71). Hove, England: Psychology Press.

National Council of Teachers of Mathematics. (1998). *Principles and standards for school mathematics: Discussion draft.* Reston, VA: Author.

National Council of Teachers of Mathematics. (2000). *Principles and standards for school mathematics.* Reston, VA: Author.

Piaget, J. (1951). *Play, dreams, and imitation in childhood.* New York: Norton.

Piaget, J. (1964). Development and learning. In R. E. Ripple & V. N. Rockcastle (Eds.), *Piaget rediscovered* (pp. 7–20). Ithaca, NY: Cornell University.

Piaget, J. (1965). *The child's conception of number.* New York: Norton.

Piaget, J., & Inhelder, B. (1969). The gaps in empiricism. In A. Koestler & J. R. Smythies (Eds.), *Beyond reductionism* (pp. 118–160). Boston: Beacon Press.

Resnick, L. B. (1992). From protoquantities to operators: Building mathematical competence on a foundation of everyday knowledge. In G. Leinhardt, R. Putnam, & R. A. Hattrup (Eds.), *Analysis of arithmetic for mathematics teaching* (pp. 373–425). Hillsdale, NJ: Lawrence Erlbaum Associates.

Resnick, L. B., & Ford, W. W. (1981). *The psychology of mathematics for instruction.* Hillsdale, NJ: Lawrence Erlbaum Associates.

Rickard, T. C., & Bourne, L. E., Jr. (1996). Some tests of an identical elements model of basic arithmetic skills. *Journal of Experimental Psychology: Learning, Memory, and Cognition, 22,* 1281–1295.

Rickard, T. C., Healy, A. F., & Bourne, L. E., Jr. (1994). On the cognitive structure of basic arithmetic skills. Operation, order, and symbol transfer effects. *Journal of Experimental Psychology: Learning, Memory, and Cognition, 20,* 1139–1153.

Riley, M. S., Greeno, J. G., & Heller, J. I. (1983). Development of children's problem-solving ability in arithmetic. In H. P. Ginsburg (Ed.), *The development of mathematical thinking* (pp. 153–200). New York: Academic Press.

Ross, S. H. (1989). Parts, wholes, and place value: A developmental review. *Arithmetic Teacher, 36*(6), 47–51.

Schaeffer, B., Eggleston, V. H., & Scott, J. L. (1974). Number development in young children. *Cognitive Psychology, 6,* 357–379.

Siegel, L. S. (1973). The role of spatial arrangement and heterogeneity in the development of concepts of numerical equivalence. *Canadian Journal of Psychology, 27,* 351–355.

Siegler, R. S. (1988). Strategy choice procedures and the development of multiplication skill. *Journal of Experimental Psychology: General, 117,* 258–275.

Siegler, R. S. (1997). Beyond competence—Toward development. *Cognitive Development, 12,* 323–332.

Siegler, R. S., & Shipley, C. (1995). Variation, selection, and cognitive change. In G. Halford & T. Simon (Eds.), *Developing cognitive competence: New approaches to process modeling* (pp. 31–76). Hillsdale, NJ: Lawrence Erlbaum Associates.

Sinclair, H., & Sinclair, A. (1986). Children's mastery of written numerals and the construction of basic number concepts. In J. Hiebert (Ed.), *Conceptual and procedural knowledge: The case of mathematics* (pp. 59–74). Hillsdale, NJ: Lawrence Erlbaum Associates.

Sokol, S. M., McCloskey, M., Cohen, N. J., & Aliminosa, D. (1991). Cognitive representations and processes in arithmetic: Inferences from the performance of brain-damaged subjects. *Journal of Experimental Psychology: Learning, Memory, and Cognition, 17,* 355–376.

Sophian, C., Harley, H., & Martin, C. S. M. (1995). Relational and representational aspects of early number development. *Cognition and Instruction, 13,* 253–268.

Sophian, C., & McCorgray, P. (1994). Part-whole knowledge and early arithmetic problem-solving. *Cognition and Instruction, 12,* 3–33.

Sophian, C., & Vong, K. I. (1995). The parts and wholes of arithmetic story problems: Developing knowledge in the preschool years. *Cognition and Instruction, 13,* 469–477.

Steffe, L. P., Cobb, P., & von Glasersfeld, E. (1988). *Construction of arithmetical meanings and procedures.* New York: Springer-Verlag.

Steinberg, R. M. (1985). Instruction on derived fact strategies in addition and subtraction. *Journal for Research in Mathematics Education, 16,* 337–355.

Strauss, M. S., & Curtis, L. E. (1981). Infant perception of numerosity. *Child Development, 52,* 1146–1152.

Strauss, M. S., & Curtis, L. E. (1984). Development of numerical concepts in infancy. In C. Sophian (Ed.), *Origins in cognitive skills* (pp. 131–155). Hillsdale, NJ: Lawrence Erlbaum Associates.

Streefland, L. (1993). Fractions: A realistic approach. In T. P. Carpenter, E. Fennema, & T. A. Romberg (Eds.), *Rational numbers: An integration of research* (pp. 289–325). Hillsdale, NJ: Lawrence Erlbaum Associates.

Thorndike, E. L. (1922). *The psychology of arithmetic.* New York: Macmillan.

Trabasso, T., Isen, A. M., Dolecki, P., McLanahan, A. G., Riley, C. A., & Tucker, T. (1978). How do children solve class-inclusion problems? In R. S. Siegler (Ed.), *Children's thinking: What develops?* (pp. 151–180). Hillsdale, NJ: Lawrence Erlbaum Associates.

von Glasersfeld, E. (1982). Subitizing: The role of figural patterns in the development of numerical concepts. *Archives de Psychologie, 50,* 191–218.

Wagner, S., & Walters, J. (1982). A longitudinal analysis of early number concepts: From numbers to number. In G. Forman (Ed.), *Action and thought* (pp. 137–161). New York: Academic Press.

Weiner, S. L. (1974). On the development of more and less. *Journal of Experimental Child Psychology, 17,* 271–287.

Wilkins, J. L. M., & Baroody, A. J. (2000). An additional explanation for production deficiencies. In M. L. Fernández (Ed.), *Proceedings of the Twenty-Second Annual Meeting of the North American Chapter of the International Group for the Psychology of Mathematics Education* (Vol. 2, p. 740). Columbus, OH: ERIC Clearinghouse for Science, Mathematics, and Environment Education.

Wilkins, J. L. M., Baroody, A. J., & Tiilikainen, S. H. (2001). Kindergartners' understanding of additive commutativity within the contexts of word problems. *Journal of Experimental Child Psychology, 79,* 23–36.

Winer, G. A. (1980). Class-inclusion reasoning in children: A review of the empirical literature. *Child Development, 51,* 309–328.

Wynn, K. (1990). Children's understanding of counting. *Cognition, 36,* 155–193.

Wynn, K. (1992). Children's acquisition of the number words and the counting system. *Cognitive Psychology, 20,* 220–251.

Wynn, K. (1998). Numerical competence in infants. In C. Donlan (Ed.), *Development of mathematical skills* (pp. 3–25). Hove, England: Psychology Press.

Wynroth, L. (1986). *Wynroth math program—The natural numbers sequence.* Ithaca, NY: Wynroth Math Program.

# 8

## *PSSM* From a Constructivist Perspective

Leslie P. Steffe
*University of Georgia*

Affirmation of the equity principle (PSSM; National Council of Teachers of Mathematics [NCTM], 1998) that mathematics instructional programs should promote the learning of mathematics by *all* students is not only necessary, but also critical in the mathematics education of children. It has widespread and pervasive implications for school mathematics that can be enacted by teachers through what they understand as mathematics for children and as children's learning of that mathematics. The disposition toward mathematics in *PSSM* is clearly stated in the discussion of the mathematics curriculum principle: "Mathematics curriculum as enacted at multiple levels—teacher lesson plans, a year-long instructional program, school or district curriculum guidelines, and state or province frameworks or standards—provides the basis from which teachers make decisions about what content to address, what emphases to choose, [etc.]" (p. 27).

It is customary for mathematics educators to speak in this way and to regard mathematics curriculum as content for children to learn quite apart from the children who are to learn it and quite apart from the teachers who are to teach it. There are passages in the *PSSM*, however, that recognize that young children think in ways that are different from that of an adult:

> Young children make sense of the world by reasoning and problem solving, and teachers should recognize that young children think in ways that can be sophisticated. At the same time, it should be recognized that a child's ways

of knowing and communicating is different from that of an adult. Children will find their own ways of representing and communicating their ideas. (NCTM, 1998, p. 106)

I find the preceding passage compatible with my concept of *the mathematics of children*. But in keeping with the mathematics curriculum principle, the authors of *PSSM* continue the cited passage with the sentence, "By the end of the second grade, children should begin to use many conventional representations with understanding" (NCTM, 1998, p. 106). So, the mathematics curriculum principle, when juxtaposed with the cited passage, does create an unavoidable tension between children's mathematical ways of knowing and communicating and what is regarded as mathematics curricula for children. Is it the case that such things as school or district curriculum guidelines, and state or province frameworks or standards should provide *the* basis from which teachers make decisions about what content to address? My argument is that teachers' decisions should be based on their understanding of children's mathematics and that this understanding should constitute the primary basis for their decisions. In saying this, my interest is in mathematics as a living subject rather than in mathematics as a subject of being. That is, my interest is in the ways and means of operating mathematically by human beings and in constituting those ways and means as the basis for mathematical curricula. In my way of thinking, we can certainly formulate such things as yearlong "curriculum guidelines" in order to communicate expectations, but in doing so, these instruments of communication should include children as coauthors.

I did not mention teachers as coauthors of curriculum guidelines because I assume that the writers of curriculum guidelines themselves should be mathematics teachers who deeply understand children's mathematics. In any case, children's knowledge as well as teachers' knowledge should be taken into account in the design of mathematics curricula, and the way children's knowledge can be taken into consideration is through the curriculum designers' knowledge of children's mathematics. My basic goal in this chapter is to discuss some of the knowledge of children's mathematics that I have learned as a result of teaching children and to present that knowledge as legitimate mathematical knowledge.

## THE MATHEMATICS OF CHILDREN

Shouldn't we consider children as rational beings whose mathematical knowledge is as legitimate as the mathematical knowledge of the adults who teach them?[1] I don't see how we can take the equity principle seriously unless we adults are willing to attribute mathematical concepts and operations to children that are rational and coherent but, yet, may

---

[1]The question of what it means to be legitimate has several parts. Perhaps the most basic part is that an adult can formulate an internally consistent and explanatory model of children's mathematical knowledge.

differ from those of an adult. Even if such an attribution is made, it is not unusual for the mathematical concepts and operations of children to be viewed as being eventually *replaced* by more conventional concepts and operations rather than as being *modified, reorganized, and enlarged* as a result of children's mathematical interactions within their social and cultural milieu. In my view, this is unfortunate because then the conventional mathematical concepts and operations of school mathematics serve as the ultimate source of validation of the explanations that are offered of children's mathematical knowledge. Such practices led the authors of *PSSM* to comment that: "School mathematics has been viewed as a sorting machine, in which many students are considered unlikely to study higher mathematics and in which a few students are identified as capable of succeeding in the discipline of mathematics or in mathematically related fields of study" (NCTM, 1998, p. 24). This view of school mathematics as independent of the children who are to learn it starts at the very beginning of children's mathematics education and proceeds on throughout their school years. In fact, children who are at risk in their mathematics education can be identified at the very beginning of their first grade in school (Wright, 2000).

Constructing a mathematics of children is especially crucial in cases where the equity principle is taken seriously. Perhaps an example best illustrates what I mean. In a course on children's mathematical learning I offered in the fall semester of 1999, each student in the course spent 1 hour in each of 10 weeks teaching a first-grade child. My request to the assistant principal of the school that the students be permitted to teach first-grade children resulted in 31 of the 32 students being assigned a child who was termed by the school as "developmentally delayed".[2] The 31 children amounted to approximately 40% of the first-grade population of the school. Although this percentage of students might seem greater than one would expect, it is not at all out of the ordinary in the southeastern region of the United States.

There are a host of questions that immediately arise concerning these developmentally delayed children. Among them are the following:

1. Is there a model to explain these children's mathematics other than the phrase "developmentally delayed" that would be useful to a mathematics teacher?

2. What does it mean for teachers to have high expectations for these students (NCTM, 1998)?

These children were indeed developmentally delayed in mathematics. Only 1 of the 32 children that my students worked with could count on, and

---

[2]By using this term, the school did not mean special education students requiring special services and placement into self-contained classrooms. Rather, the term referred to the fact that the cognitive development of the children was delayed.

this child could count on before the student to whom he was assigned started to work with him.[3] The 31 other children did not learn to count on over the 10 week period that my students worked with them, and it was not at all apparent to me that they would learn to count on in the near future. So, although I am in great sympathy with the equity principle that "Mathematics instructional programs should promote the learning of mathematics by *all* students" (NCTM, 1998, p. 23), it is also obvious to me that major modifications in our conception of what constitutes school mathematics and mathematics learning are necessary.

I use the phrase "children's mathematics" to refer to the mathematical concepts and operations that I assume children have constructed before I attempt to teach them. This phrase is important because I start with the assumption as a mathematics teacher that children do not come to the classroom as blank slates. Rather, they come with complex ways and means of operating mathematically, and I assume that it is my job to learn these ways and means and to learn how to affect them productively. Such an assumption, however, is not helpful to a mathematics teacher without an understanding of what those concepts and operations might consist of. Consequently, I introduce the phrase "mathematics of children" to refer to those models that I make to explain my observations of children's mathematical language and actions. Mathematics of children is a construction of the observer, and it is a kind of mathematics that can be learned in the context of teaching children.

## COUNTING SCHEMES AS MATHEMATICS OF CHILDREN

When formulating a model of children's mathematics within a domain of their mathematical activity, I use the concept of scheme (Piaget, 1980; von Glasersfeld, 1981). The notion of scheme has proven to be a particularly useful concept in explaining children's mathematics because it is based on the observable activity of children. However, what the child establishes as a situation of a scheme is often not observable, in which case, the situation must be inferred from the activity and from the results of the activity. It is this kind of situation that most concerns me in this chapter.

There are three parts of a scheme: the situation, the child's activity, and the results of the child's activity. The child's activity is regarded as purposeful activity in that the child engages in the activity to attain a goal.

### Situations of Counting

Two of my most basic observations in teaching children are (a) that they count in a variety of situations when it is their goal to find how many or to make comparisons and/or judgments concerning how many and (b) that, even though I might observe a child counting, the child may not be able to

---

[3]This child's mathematical development was not delayed.

count on.[4] So, I begin the discussion of children's counting schemes by discussing two primitive schemes that precede counting on. First, I consider the countable unit items that children establish prior to counting that occur in composite wholes. The first such composite whole children establish are perceptual collections, and I sketch the main events in the construction of the elements of such collections. I also distinguish among perceptual collections, figurative collections, and the first composite whole that I consider numerical.

***Perceptual Collections.***     Children construct conceptual items very early on in life that they use in establishing an experience, such as a "dog experience." When the conceptual item can be used in generating a visualized image of a past experience, I regard it as an *object concept*. When an object concept attains permanence, the child believes that an object still exists after it is hidden from view (von Glasersfeld, 1995).[5] When a child has constructed an object as permanent, this permits the child to form a collection of perceptual items (like the houses on the hill or the boats in the harbor). These examples imply that the child has already learned to categorize the items together on the basis of some common features.

Just because the items of a collection are permanent objects for a child, this does not necessarily imply that the collection per se has been established as a permanent object. This distinction between an object concept that a child uses to constitute what an observer would say are *permanent objects*, and one that a child uses to constitute what an observer would say is a *permanent collection* of such objects is rarely made. But the distinction is crucial in the child's progress toward the construction of *numerical concepts*, because a numerical concept is based on collections of objects.

The houses on the hill or the boats in the harbor both afford the child an opportunity to construct an awareness of *perceptual plurality*. That is, when classifying the objects together, the child establishes an awareness of more than one perceptual item, which is an awareness of perceptual plurality. This awareness is a *quantitative property* that is introduced into the perceptual collection by the acting child. In fact, it is one of the first quantitative properties and is essential in the construction of a counting scheme because it serves the child in establishing a goal of making an awareness of more than one perceptual item definite by counting.[6] However, an awareness of perceptual plurality is to be distinguished from an awareness of numerosity, which we see later is a quantitative property of a more abstracted composite whole than a perceptual collection.

A perceptual collection is an *experiential* composite whole that exists for a child in the *immediate here and now*. How it might come to be estab-

---

[4]As I explain later, I consider *counting on* as the first numerical counting scheme.

[5]Piaget (1934/1955) demonstrated that a child can *recognize* an object long before he or she is aware of the object after it leaves his or her visual field.

[6]In other words, the child forms the goal of finding how many items are in the perceptual collection.

lished as permanent involves the ability of the child to regenerate an experience of the collection in the absence of the items of the collection. We know that during the first 2 years of a child's life, the child establishes object permanence (Piaget, 1934/1955), and this involves using the object concept in generating a visualized image of a past object experience. However, using an object concept to generate *more than* two or three images—a collection of images—does not follow immediately on from the ability to use it in generating a single image (Steffe, 1994).

***Collections of Perceptual Unit Items.*** There is a distinction between a perceptual item and a perceptual *unit* item. Perceptual items are produced by compounding sensory material from various sensory channels together, and the records of this operation constitute the beginnings of an object concept. In the construction of an object concept, say, "ball," the child might compound the sensory material produced by visually scanning a rolling thing, hitting the ball while the lying on his or her back, rolling over the ball on his or her tummy, pushing the ball, throwing the ball, and so forth. The construction of the object concept does not happen in one fell swoop, but entails many encounters in which the object concept is modified in its use. In any event, compounding sensory material together marks the beginning of the *unitizing* operation, an operation that continues to function throughout our lifetimes.

In that case where the object concept, ball, is used in establishing a "ball experience," one can think of the object concept as being active in the experience much like a resonating tuning fork. I don't think of an object concept as simply constituting a current experience that is identical to one past, but instead as being modified in its use. Each new ball experience is not exactly like a past ball experience to which it might be compared. Because the object concept is continually modified in its use, it is legitimate to say that it is used in processing sensory material in constituting an experience. If the child establishes *several* perceptual items using an object concept, an occasion may arise where the child reconsiders the perceptual items, that is, where the child reviews the perceptual items already established using the object concept that was used in establishing them. In this case, the child may unitize each perceptual item and produce perceptual unit items. For example, if a child establishes a perceptual collection like the houses on the hill, the child may return to this experience and compare, say, an adjacent pair of houses. In fact, the child may focus, not on particular sensory features of the houses, but rather on the houses as *unitary things,* thus essentially ignoring the sensory features of the houses that were used in classifying them together.

In constituting the houses as unitary things, the basis of the classification changes from particular recurrent sensory features to the unitariness of the perceptual items. *A result of this change is that classification based on recurrent sensory features is not the basic element in the construction of number* as many authors often suggest (Reys, Suydam, Lindquist, & Smith, 1999).

When a child can establish perceptual *unit* items, perceptual items of no particular kind can be taken together as unit items to be counted. An example might be a small red triangular logic block, a ball, a pipe cleaner, a marble, a doll, and a bracelet. There may still be a need for perceptual items to use in making unit items, but what these perceptual items might be is not relevant for the classification. They simply become *things* that form a collection of *things*. Perceptual unit items certainly can be established outside of the counting context. In fact, the child's ability to make a collection of perceptual unit items is assumed as the most elementary composite whole that should be considered as a situation of a counting scheme.

## The Perceptual and Figurative Stages of the Counting Scheme

Children who can count collections of perceptual unit items but who also require such collections to be in their perceptual field in order to count are called *counters of perceptual unit items*. Of the 31 children I mentioned earlier, at least 25 were counters of perceptual unit items. These children were in the *perceptual stage* of their counting scheme and the others were in the *figurative stage*. It is easy to distinguish between children in these two stages because those in the figurative stage can count items that are not in their immediate perceptual field. What this means is that the collections of perceptual unit items that the children establish are for the first time constituted by the children as permanent.

When the child can use his or her object concepts in producing an image of more than two or three perceptual unit items, I refer to the composite whole the child produces as a collection of figurative items.[7] When counting a collection of perceptual items that are hidden from view, some children just entering the figurative stage of their counting scheme point to or otherwise indicate places on the screening device behind or under which they think perceptual items are hidden, and coordinate the pointing act with the utterances of number words (which is counting). What these children are doing is extending the activity of counting from counting perceptual unit items to counting their images of perceptual unit items, which is a major advancement in the children's counting scheme. Because counting propels them forward, they often create figurative items *in the activity of counting*. But they are usually consumed by the counting activity and stop fortuitously, usually when reaching a boundary of the screening device (cf. Steffe, von Glasersfeld, Richards, & Cobb, 1983).

Making visualized images of perceptual unit items is a dynamic operation, and the child is considered as being *in* the activity of making the images.[8] There is a result of the activity (the visualized perceptual unit items),

---

[7] Sometimes I say "figurative collection" in abbreviation.

[8] To imagine what it means to be in the experience of visualizing several perceptual unit items that are hidden from view, the experience of visualizing the inside of a box might be comparable in that one has to "go inside" of the box and imagine what it might look like.

but one should not assume that the child can set these visualized items "at a distance" and unitize each of them, making figurative unit items that can be counted. For example, a child might be able to make separate images of two hidden collections of perceptual unit items, but be quite incapable of using these separate images to make an image of one collection of perceptual unit items separated into two hidden parts. In this case, if the child was asked to count all of the hidden items, the child would count the items hidden in the two locations by starting with "one" each time. To start with "one" only once, and count the items in the two hidden collections as if they were the items of one collection hidden in two separate locations, requires an additional operation. Other than producing two figurative collections, the child would also need to take these two figurative collections together to form one figurative collection. This entails the child setting the figurative collections at a distance[9] and then taking them together. The means by which this is accomplished is unitizing the items of the two figurative collections, creating figurative unit items.[10]

The results of taking two figurative collections together (I call taking two figurative collections together a figurative join of the two collections) are easy to observe. First, the child creates *substitute countable items* in the activity of counting, such as the motoric acts of repeatedly pointing with a finger or sequentially putting up fingers.[11] Second, the children count the items of the first hidden collection and then count the items of the second collection as a continuation of counting the items of the first collection. For example, to find how many items are hidden in two locations, six in one location and seven in the other, such a child might utter "1, 2, 3, 4, 5, 6" in synchrony with sequentially putting up six fingers, and then continue on counting in this way, "7, 8, 9, 10, 11, 12, 13" and stop when they recognize a finger pattern for "seven." They still need to count to establish meaning for a number word, but the items the children actually count differ from those they intended to count. Counting is still a sensorimotor activity and the children cannot take it as a given. They necessarily count to establish meaning for number words that are beyond the range of their figurative patterns. These children are yet to count on and always start to count from "one."

I consider the perceptual and figurative stages of the children's counting schemes as prenumerical stages. These children do produce unit items, but the unit items are perceptual or figurative unit items rather than arithmetical unit items. The children are yet to construct a *number sequence,* although they do produce sequences of counted items as re-

---

[9]"Setting the collections at a distance" means that the child is aware of the visualized items of the collection as if the child were actually looking at them.

[10]Unitizing the items of the two figurative collections is an act of categorization that is analogous to how a child categorizes items together on the basis of their unitariness—as *things* that are *taken* together.

[11]If the child simultaneously puts up fingers to establish a finger pattern, I consider the child as replacing one perceptual collection for another. In this case, the child counts his or her fingers as perceptual items.

sults of using their counting schemes. However, these are experiential sequences that exist for the child in the immediate here and now and have no permanence.

## NUMERICAL COUNTING SCHEMES

The major advance the child makes in constructing *counting on* is that the child can use its counting scheme to generate an experience of counting without actually counting. Imagine that two collections of perceptual items are screened from view, that a child is told how many items are behind each screen, and that the child is asked to find how many items are behind both screens. A child who has constructed counting on can generate an experience of counting the items behind one of the two screens without actually counting, and then extend counting beyond this imagined experience when counting the items behind both screens. There is still a certain restriction in how the child keeps track of the counting acts in the extension of counting in that the child stops when recognizing a numerical pattern. The child is yet to learn to explicitly count the counting acts of the extension. Nevertheless, a major advancement has been made in the child's counting scheme in that the scheme has been constituted as a number sequence.

### Construction of Counting-On

One might feel compelled to ask how the child learns to generate an experience of counting without actually counting because, prior to this event, an experiential sequence of counted items constituted the child's "number sequence." When considering that a child, in principle, can generate the experience of counting up to any number word, say, "ninety-nine" that it might know without actually counting, it is not at all easy to explain such learning. But monitoring counting is the key (Steffe, 1991). Monitoring counting—intentionally keeping track of the counting acts in an extension of counting—has to be learned, and learning it involves the coordination of two operations. First, the child re-presents[12] the counting acts of an extension of counting and, second, the child unitizes each re-presented counting act. This produces a sequence of *arithmetical unit items*. Similar to the way in which an object concept can be used to produce an object experience, an arithmetical unit item can be willfully used to produce a counting experience—an experience of a counting act. The experience may be a sensorimotor or an imagined action. In either case, the action has the status of an operation. So after the construction of arithmetical units, it is legitimate to speak of counting operations rather than simply counting acts. It is easy to observe the difference between counting acts that have been constituted as operations and those that haven't, and I elaborate on that difference in the next section.

---

[12]A re-presentation of a counting act is a regeneration of a past counting act in visualized imagination.

The emergence of monitoring counting can occur for children who have constructed the figurative counting scheme. For example, I observed a child, Tyrone, learn to monitor his counting acts "8, 9, 10, 11, 12," which were a continuation of his already completed counting acts, "1, 2, 3, 4, 5, 6, 7." However, it wasn't until some time later that he reorganized his counting scheme in such a way that he could count on, which constitutes indication that he constructed the *initial number sequence*.

To illustrate how I decided that Tyrone's counting scheme was a figurative scheme, I present a protocol from a teaching episode with him that I held in October of his first grade in school (Steffe, 1991). In the protocol, "T" stands for "Teacher" and "Ty" for "Tyrone".

Protocol I:   *Tyrone's figurative counting scheme.*

T:         (Places a card covered by two cloths in front of Tyrone) There are eight squares here (touches one of the cloths), and three here (touches the other cloth).

Ty:       (Utters 1, 2, 3, 4, 5, 6, 7, 8 while looking at at and synchronously touching the first cloth. Continues uttering 9, 10, 11 while looking at and synchronously touching the second cloth.) Eleven.

There are several important indications that Tyrone had constructed the figurative counting scheme. His activity of looking at and touching the first cloth at distinct locations each time he performed a counting act indicates that he was aware of the items of the hidden collection of squares. This in turn indicates that he used his object concept, square, to create images of the squares he intended to count. Furthermore, his continuation of counting, "9, 10,11" indicates that he took the items of the two hidden collections as belonging to one collection in the way that I previously explained. So, I infer that Tyrone had constructed at least figurative unit items. That Tyrone did not count on three more past eight—"Eight; 9, 10, 11. Eleven"—constitutes contraindication that he had constructed a numerical concept, eight, and the initial number sequence.

Whatever the nature of the items were that Tyrone established prior to counting, he coordinated the utterance of the number *word* sequence "1, 2, 3, 4, 5, 6, 7, 8" with repeatedly touching the cloth. These counting acts served in isolating possible locations of hidden perceptual items, and the pointing acts he created in the activity of counting were substitutes for these hidden items. As such, it is no exaggeration to say that Tyrone was counting his pointing acts, and that he created the items he counted in the activity of counting. Still, it is possible that the pointing acts were implementations of arithmetical unit items even though his failure to count on starting at "eight" can be used as a contraindication. So, for clarification, I presented him with another task of the same kind:

Protocol II:   *Tyrone's construction of monitoring counting.*

T:          Tyrone, there are seven here (points to one cloth), and five here (points to the other cloth).

Ty:         (Touches the first cloth seven times while whispering) 1, 2, 3, 4, 5, 6, 7. (His points of contact form no identifiable pattern. He continues on, touching the second cloth six times in a row while whispering) 8, 9, 10, 11, 12, 13.

Ty:         (Starts over from "one" without suggestion. In the midst of touching the second cloth, he loses track, so he starts over from "one" again. This time, he deliberately touches the second cloth five times in a row while looking intently at his points of contact) 8, 9, 10, 11, 12 (looks up) 13, 14. Fourteen!

T:          How many are there under this cloth (pointing to the cloth hiding five squares).

Ty:         Five. (Again counts over the first cloth, and then continues touching the second cloth five times in a row, but this time he stares into space) 8, 9, 10, 11, 12—(looks at T) Twelve!

Tyrone obviously did not have a five pattern available that he could use to keep track of counting five more times beyond counting to "seven," though he did have an available pattern for "three" that he used to keep track of counting three more times beyond counting to "eight." But in the case of a continuation of counting five more times beyond counting to "seven," he actually constructed a pattern for "five" in the activity of counting that he used to keep track of counting five more times. These observations indicate that, prior to constructing a pattern for "five," Tyrone's pattern for "three" was a figurative rather than a numerical pattern.

I infer that it was a figurative pattern because, first, even though he could use it to keep track of counting three items "9, 10, 11," there was no necessity for him to monitor counting to keep track of counting. And, second, when there was a necessity for him to keep track of counting five more times beyond counting to seven, he did not monitor his counting acts in his first trial. Rather, he simply continued counting beyond counting to seven until he apparently realized that he didn't know when to stop. This observation corroborates my earlier inference that Tyrone's counting scheme was a figurative scheme, and that his counting acts were not counting operations. He was yet to construct arithmetical unit items.

The fact that he experienced an ambiguity in knowing when to stop counting is critical because it led to self-regulation of counting activity. Self-regulation emerges from within the child, and is a critical precursor to monitoring counting. Without the self-regulation that Tyrone exemplified (he independently started over twice), there could be no monitoring of counting and, hence, no construction of counting on or of arithmetical unit items. The act of simply recognizing a row of five squares does not require an intentional monitoring of the activity that produces a numerical pattern, five. When Tyrone was producing a pattern consisting of the records of his points of contact of his finger on the cloth, he had to establish what pattern he produced after each touch because there were no visible traces of his touches (it is not indicated in the protocol, but Tyrone was in deep concentration as he looked intently at the cloth). This involves the construction of a feedback system in the counting scheme in which the counted items feed back into and are constituted as a part of the countable items.

The first time Tyrone made a continuation of counting, he produced counted items (a pointing act along with the utterance of a number word[13]). There was no indication in the two first trials that Tyrone constituted the counted items he established as belonging to the items he intended to count, items that I call countable items. It is important here to reestablish that Tyrone produced a visualized image of the squares that were hidden under the second cloth even though his visualization initially was indefinite in that he did not "see" five co-occurring squares.[14] But he was aware of squares, and this made it possible for him to intend to count the hidden squares. As he counted, his acts of pointing were coordinated with uttering number words, and these coordinated acts served in locating hidden squares. In that he was not able to see the squares he intended to count, he substituted his pointing acts for the hidden squares as his countable items as he went along. In this case, what Tyrone actually counted (his point acts) differed from what he intended to count (the squares).

Tyrone's residual experience of counting acts constituted his counted items. But, given that it was his goal to count five hidden squares beyond counting seven of them, his production of counted items did not close the counting episode because he could not recognize having touched the cloth five times. This explains the ambiguity he experienced while counting. The feedback system that he created amounted to asking himself, "How many have I counted?" after each counting act. For example, after touching the cloth and saying, "ten," Tyrone would need to re-present the counted items "eight, nine, ten", and "look at" the re-presented result as if it were a trio of perceptual items. This "looking" involves Tyrone *unitizing* each re-presented counting act, which is the operation that permits "placing the counting acts at a distance and looking at them."

Unitizing means that he focused his attention on each item he re-presented. Focusing attention on a regeneration of the first item he counted, then the second, then the third, permitted him to become explicitly aware of the trio of counted items. Unitizing a re-presented counting act creates what I have called an arithmetical unit item, which is an abstracted unit pattern that contains records of the experience of the sensorimotor count-

---

[13]In that Tyrone intently focused on the cloth in his first two trials, I infer that he was focusing on the places he touched. Still, the pointing acts were involved, and were at least an auxiliary part of the counted items.

[14]Had he been able to imagine five co-occurring squares, he could have used this pattern in knowing when to stop counting, which would have closed off the need to monitor counting.

ing act that was re-presented. The abstracted unit pattern is simply a permanently recorded *unitizing operation,* which, when implemented, constitutes a *counting operation.* A counting operation consists of an implementation of the records of counting that are contained in the unit pattern along with unitizing the implemented sensory material.

After Tyrone constituted "8, 9, 10" as a sequence of three arithmetical unit items, he was "above" his counting activity looking down at it, which is another way of saying that he was aware of having just counted three times. Being aware that his trio of counting acts was not five led to his awareness that he needed to count again. In this way, he constituted the items he already counted as a part of the items he intended to count, and so one could say that the partial results of his counting scheme (his counted items) fed back into the (again) partial situation (his countable items) of his counting scheme. He could consider the items he counted as counted items as well as a part of those items he intended to count in the activity of counting. This is what I call a feedback system in his counting scheme, and it is foundational in the construction of monitoring counting.

Tyrone created a numerical pattern consisting of five arithmetical unit items in linear sequence as a result of his activity, as indicated in the last trial of Protocol II. He had learned to regulate his counting acts by monitoring counting in specific uses of his counting scheme. However, it would not be plausible that this accommodation would be sufficient for him to a priori establish any five adjacent counting acts of his figurative counting scheme as a numerical pattern (e.g., "48, 49, 50, 51, 52), nor would it be plausible that he constructed similar numerical concepts for other number words. Nevertheless, by early January of his first grade he had reorganized his counting scheme and could now count on! Prior to the Christmas holidays, he was never observed counting on, so it was likely that he reorganized his counting scheme while he was on vacation. Such observations are not at all unusual and they speak toward a developmental process only the results of which are observable. After Christmas vacation, he definitely had constructed numerical concepts to which his number words referred, and I call these numerical concepts *numerical composites.*

A numerical composite is a sequence of arithmetical unit items. Before they are actually carried out, the counting acts symbolized by the number word "seven," for example, are what I mean by a numerical composite. So, I regard the numerical composite, seven, as a sequence of arithmetical unit items that contain records of counting acts. A numerical composite is a mathematics-of-children concept, as are the notions of the perceptual, the figurative, and the numerical counting scheme that is indicated by counting on.

## Counting-On as a Nonteachable Scheme

As stated earlier, the 31 first-grade children did not learn to count on over the 10-week period my students worked with them. And as we've learned from the previous discussion, self-regulation of counting activity by children who are in the figurative stage of their counting scheme initiates learning to count-on (cf. Steffe, Cobb, & von Glasersfeld, 1988, for a more extensive discussion). Self-regulation emerges from within the child, and it can be only indirectly brought forth by a teacher through presenting problematic situations for children to solve. So, if "teaching" is interpreted as direct teaching, then counting on is surely a nonteachable scheme.

When regarding school mathematics as consisting of important mathematics like place value, function, scaling and similarity, or the structure of the number system, important mathematics-of-children concepts such as the perceptual counting scheme, the figurative counting scheme, and the counting scheme that is indicated by counting on—the initial number sequence—are in danger of being suppressed in favor of the conventional concepts. Place value, for example, is regarded in *PSSM* (NCTM, 1998) as a teachable mathematical concept much like van Oers (1996) regarded the cultural practice of mathematics. According to van Oers, the cultural practice of mathematics "can be transformed into curriculum content and, as such, it can be taught" (p. 94). Following Vygotsky, he did take the personal meanings that students may attach to the "actions, rules, methods, and values as provided by a school subject" into account, and they are a constitutive part of his basis for instructional practice in mathematics education. However, the personal meanings of which he spoke are in the main left unspecified because they are conceptualized *relative to the cultural practices of mathematics*. In van Oers' system, the teacher embodies the mathematical practices of a wider society and children's personal meanings of mathematics are gauged relative to that mathematics. In my way of thinking, the mathematics-of-children is also a construction of the mathematics teacher. By means of teaching children, the teacher constructs important mathematics of children concepts like numerical composite and initial number sequence[15] that she would not regard as a part of her understanding of the mathematical practices of a wider society, which are adult practices and are not based on children's mathematics.

My advocacy that the mathematics of children be the primary mathematics of interest in mathematics teaching might seem to suppress the cultural practices of mathematics that are known to the teacher in favor of an overemphasis on children's methods. It might be thought that I am advocating that children be left with immature mathematical ways and means of operating that would prove insufficient as they encounter cultural practices of mathematics. However, this is not my advocacy at all be-

---

[15]Neither of these two concepts should be regarded as misconceptions. There are situations in which a mathematics teacher might observe children counting on to solve a situation in which counting on is not adequate to solve. In such cases, children would make "mistakes" like counting nine more past six when asked to find how many of nine items are hidden when six of them are visible. Although such "mistakes" are valuable indicators of what the child can't currently do, from the child's point of view, there is no awareness of a "mistake" when solving the task. I categorize such mistakes as "necessary mistakes."

cause of my view of mathematics as an integral part of living systems. I regard teachers' mathematical knowledge much in the same way that I regard children's mathematical knowledge. One difference is that I believe that the teacher's mathematical knowledge should include the mathematics of children. It should be the goal of the teacher to learn the mathematical knowledge of children, what mathematical knowledge might be placed into their zones of potential construction[16], and situations of learning that might transform the children's zones of potential construction into zones of actual construction. It also should be the goal of the teacher to learn how to interact mathematically with children in order to bring forth, sustain, and modify their children's mathematical knowledge. This opens mathematics teaching into a creative and problem-solving enterprise, where the basic problem is to learn how to bring forth in children the mathematical concepts and operations that would enable them to solve the problems they are not currently able to solve.

The boundary between the mathematical knowledge of the teacher that she would say is knowledge of children's mathematics, and the mathematical knowledge that she would not currently attribute to the children she is teaching is a very fuzzy and constantly changing boundary. I fully appreciate that constructing a mathematics of children is very demanding, but it is one of the things that marks a mathematics teacher as a professional. Constructing a mathematics of children empowers mathematics teachers in a way that is not possible when the focus is on teaching a predetermined and a priori mathematics curriculum. There, the focus is often on transferring the teacher's mathematical knowledge from the head of the teacher to the heads of children by means of the words of the language. In contrast, the mathematics of children emerges from within children and it must be constructed by children.

A very experienced mathematics educator for whom I have great respect once asked me if I thought counting on could be taught. Should it be considered as a part of the mathematics curriculum? I was apprehensive then and I still am that if we agree that counting on is an important kind of counting scheme (the initial number sequence), teachers will consider it as teachable in the transfer sense in which I have been speaking. For children who have constructed the initial number sequence, counting on does not need to be taught, and for children in the stage of the figurative (or perceptual) counting scheme, it should not be a goal of the teacher to teach the children to count on in the transfer sense. In other words, it should never be a goal of a teacher to directly teach children to count on. I would prefer that a teacher not demonstrate how to count on unless there is good reason for the teacher to believe that the involved children can already count on or can easily curtail always count-

---

[16]A zone of potential construction is determined by the teacher. It consists of those mathematical concepts and operations that the teacher has experienced other children learn who are like the current children (cf. Olive, 1994).

ing from one. In my experience teaching children, a demonstration of how to count-on is rarely effective.[17]

## Double Counting

The mathematics of children certainly does not stop with counting on (the initial number sequence). In fact, the construction of the initial number sequence is a *starting point* rather than an end point. Nevertheless, it opens possibilities that are not available to children in the figurative stage of the counting scheme. Double counting is one of these possibilities, and concerns how children keep track of counting in an extension of the counting acts that are symbolized by a number word. For example, in that case where nine items are hidden from view and, say, eight more are put with them, if a child counts: "Nine. 10 is 1, 11 is 2, 12 is 3, 13 is 4, 14 is 5, 15 is 6, 16 is 7, 17 is 8; Seventeen," the child counts his or her counting acts in the extension of the first nine counting acts that are symbolized by "nine." The important thing in the example of double counting is that the child uses "eight" to symbolize counting acts from "nine" onward and uses them as input for making countable items. The child knows that he or she is going to count eight more times beyond nine, and uses his or her number sequence to generate an image of counting beyond "nine" prior to counting.

Just as counting on should not be regarded as directly teachable, neither should double counting. Like counting on, double counting is not a procedural aspect of counting. But again, I introduce the caveat that a teacher may have good reason to believe that a child is on the verge of double counting and thereby may create a sequence of learning situations that may afford the child the opportunity to construct double counting *on his or her own.*

One reason a teacher might believe that a child is on the verge of constructing double counting is if the child's method of keeping track of counting carries the force of double counting. For example, if the child continues to count on beyond "nine" by sequentially putting up eight fingers in synchrony with uttering "ten, eleven, twelve, thirteen, fourteen, fifteen, sixteen, seventeen" and stops after recognizing a finger pattern for "eight," this is an indication that keeping track of counting carries the force of double counting, because the child generates an experience of the continuation of counting *before actually counting.* In the extension of counting beyond "nine," the child takes the counting scheme *as its own input* because what the child counts are not images of perceptual items, but rather images of counting acts.

Double counting in this way indicates that the child has constructed a number sequence beyond the initial number sequence. I call this number sequence the *tacitly nested number sequence.* The major advancement in

---

[17]I have encouraged children to "put six in my [the child's] head" and then count on, say, four more. In my judgment, these children were in transition to the initial number sequence.

the construction of the tacitly nested number sequence is that the child can take the number sequence as its own input for making countable items. The child is no longer constrained to counting objects that are perceptually present nor to counting her or his images of such objects when they are hidden from view. It is as if the child has two number sequences, one to use as material to make countable items, and the other to use in counting these countable items.

## The Explicitly Nested Number Sequence

The major importance of double counting is that it opens the way for children to construct strategic reasoning in additive and subtractive situations. For example, I asked a child named Johanna (Steffe, 1992) to take 12 blocks, told her that together we had 19, and asked her how many I had. After sitting silently for about 20 seconds, she said, "seven" and explained, "Well, ten plus nine is nineteen; and I take away the two—I mean, ten plus two is twelve, and nine take away two is seven!" This kind of strategic reasoning is well beyond double counting from "twelve" up to and including "nineteen" and it is in the province of a child who has constructed the explicitly nested number sequence. But it should not be regarded as a necessary consequence of that construction. Strategic reasoning is a goal for children who have constructed the explicitly nested number sequence and is a good example of what I mean by mathematics *for* children. Children who have constructed the explicitly nested number sequence may not engage in strategic reasoning unless it is encouraged by a teacher or another adult who has responsibility for the mathematical education of children.

An indication that a child has constructed the explicitly nested number sequence that is less demanding than strategic reasoning is where a child has put a handful of pennies with, say, 19 pennies, and then counts all of the pennies and finds that there are 27. If the child double counts from "nineteen" up to and including "twenty-seven" to find how many pennies were added to the 19, this would be an indication that the child has constructed the explicitly nested number sequence. A more solid indication would be where the child takes a handful of pennies away from the 27 pennies and counts those that remain and finds that there are 16. If the child counts from 27 *down to* 16 to find how many pennies were taken away (e.g., the child might utter "27, 26, ..., 17" synchronously with putting up fingers and recognize the fingers put up as "eleven"), this would be a corroboration that the child has constructed the explicitly nested number sequence.[18] Still another indication would be where the child takes away the same 8 pennies that he or she added right after counting to solve the original situation, and knows that 17 are left without counting.

---

[18] A child might also count, "26, 25, ..., 16" synchronously with putting up fingers.

# ADDING AND SUBTRACTING SCHEMES

Counting up to, counting down to, and strategic reasoning cannot be directly taught any more than counting on or double counting can, because they all involve monitoring actual or symbolized counting activity in their construction. They all constitute ways of adding or subtracting in the stage of the explicitly nested number sequence. There are ways of adding and subtracting that precede those that I also consider adding and subtracting schemes. In the perceptual and figurative stages of children's counting schemes, perhaps we should not say that children engage in adding because that term is normally reserved for a numerical scheme. But for the sake of simplicity, I use "adding" to refer to certain ways of operating in which I have observed children in those stages engage.

## Adding Scheme in the Perceptual Stage: Counting All

In the perceptual and figurative stages of the counting scheme, we have to consider the whole of the counting scheme in order to formulate a model of children's adding. In the perceptual stage, it is important for the involved collections of perceptual items to have category names, like marbles or toys, so that an adding language may be developed along with the particular actions. The situations that can be imagined are inexhaustible, so I present only example situations and leave it to the reader to contextualize them.

At the most basic level, I involve children in the perceptual stage in sensorimotor action. For example, I might ask one child to count out four toys and another child three toys. I might then ask each child how many toys the other child counted out, and then ask each to find how many toys would be in a box *if they put all of the toys into the box*. Asking the children to find how many toys the other child counted out is done to encourage the children to decenter and to take the other's results of counting into consideration. Asking how many toys would be in a box if they put all of them into the box is done to encourage the children to take the two perceptual collections of toys together as countable items. Taking the two separate collections together to form a single collection of perceptual unit items is the basic meaning of addition in this stage, and I call it a *perceptual join*. It is a joining action that in my opinion is far more important than physically placing the toys together.

The sequence in which the questions are asked does encourage counting at each step. As each child counts out four or three toys, as the case may be, counted collections of perceptual unit items are produced. Then, asking each child to find how many toys the other child counted out again encourages establishing a second counted collection of perceptual unit items. Finally, asking the last question of the sequence of three questions encourages the children to reprocess the collections of *counted perceptual unit items* by scanning the collections when taking them together.

This is an important point because the children conceptually join four counted perceptual unit items and three counted perceptual unit items. In that case, children in the perceptual stage do make and maintain a distinction between the two collections of perceptual unit items and count them, "1, 2, 3, 4 (pointing to each item of the quadriad of perceptual unit items); 5, 6, 7 (pointing to the trio of perceptual unit items). Seven." I refer to the adding scheme as *counting all* if I can also observe it in other situations like the one in the example.

It is not unusual to find children in the perceptual stage of the counting scheme who simply count their own collection of perceptual items when asked to find how many toys there would be in a box if both children put all of their toys into the box. In this case, I encourage these children to work alone and actually enact putting the two collections of toys they count out into a box and then count the toys in the box. These children usually establish no relationship between the counted collection of toys in the box and the two counted collections of toys prior to placing them into the box. No claim of an adding scheme on the part of these children should be made.

## Adding Scheme in the Figurative Stage: Counting All with Intuitive Extension

In the figurative stage of the counting scheme, the goal is to encourage children to categorize the items of two collections of counted perceptual unit items together *after the items have been placed into an opaque container,* and then count the items of the two hidden collections together. An example might be where a child counts out seven discs and places them into an opaque container, counts out five more discs and places them into the container, and then counts all of the discs in the container without looking at them. The child might touch the container seven times at specific places in synchrony with uttering the number words "one, two, ..., seven", and then continue on counting, touching the container five more times in synchrony with uttering the number words "eight, nine, ten, eleven, twelve." The child knows to stop when recognizing a spatial pattern for "five" formed by the locations of the points of contact with the container.

The child might also sequentially put up fingers in synchrony with uttering "one, two, ..., seven" and then continue on sequentially putting up fingers in synchrony with uttering "eight, nine, ten, eleven, twelve" and stop when recognizing a finger pattern for "five." In this case, the child reuses two fingers to make a finger pattern for "five." In both cases, however, the child counts the elements of a pattern for "five," a spatial pattern in the first case and a finger pattern in the second case, and stops when completing the pattern. Because the child is not monitoring counting but simply coordinating the elements of a pattern with uttering number words, I call the child's adding scheme *counting all with intuitive extension.*

## Adding Scheme in the Stage of the Initial Number Sequence: Counting-On With Numerical Extension

The adding scheme of children in the stage of the initial number sequence involves numerical composites rather than collections of perceptual or figurative unit items. The difference is relatively easy to observe. Consider, for example, the following situation:

> There are seven marbles in this cup (rattling marbles in the cup). Here are eight more marbles (places eight more marbles in the cup). How many marbles are there in the cup?

If the child says there are seven marbles in the cup and then proceeds to count the additional marbles—"8, 9, 10, 11, 12, 13, 14, 15—fifteen!"—it suggests that in uttering "seven" the child knows that the number word, in the given context, stands for a specific collection of individual perceptual unit items that satisfy the child's concept "marble" and that, if counted, they could be coordinated with utterances of the number words from "one" to "seven." The child knows this and therefore does not have to run through the counting activity that would actually implement it. This is another way of saying that the child has constructed a numerical composite, seven.

But there is more going on in the child's adding scheme than his or her meaning of "seven." First, the child's meaning of "eight" is quite similar to his or her meaning of "seven" in that "eight" refers to eight counting acts that the child could carry out without actually doing it. That is, I assume the child established two numerical composites, one corresponding to "seven" and the other to "eight" prior to counting. The child then juxtaposes these two sequences together, where the sequence for eight extends beyond the sequence for seven. The child then counts to specify the unknown numerosity of this juxtaposed sequence. The reader might wonder why I didn't simply model this as the child taking the two collections of marbles together into one collection. The reason is that the child's number words now refer to numerical structures that I call numerical composites. Based on the way the child counted (counting on rather than counting all), I infer that the number words "seven" and "eight" referred to these numerical structures and I call the observed adding scheme *counting on with numerical extension*. I use "numerical extension" because counting on eight more times was an implementation of a numerical composite, eight. The goal of the child in counting "8, 9, 10, 11, 12, 13, 14, 15—fifteen!" is to specify the numerosity of the numerical composite established by juxtaposing the two numerical composites seven and eight. It is in this sense that counting on with numerical extension is regarded as a *child-generated addition algorithm*. I also regard the adding schemes of children in the two preceding stages as child generated.

## Subtracting Scheme in the Stage of the Initial Number Sequence: Its Purposes

There are no compelling arguments that I know for attempting to bring forth a counting-all scheme for subtracting in the case of children in the perceptual and figurative stages of their counting schemes. For those children who can count on with numerical extension, however, there are good reasons for developing very particular learning situations involving what is commonly known as *take-away* subtraction. An example situation is to ask the child to place, say, 15 blocks into an opaque container and then to take out 3 of them and put them into another opaque container so they can't be seen. The child is to find how many blocks remain in the first container. In presenting this situation, I assume that the child can count backward from at least "twenty."

There are two goals in presenting the situation. The first is for the child to re-present the forward-counting acts to "fifteen" and use these counting acts starting from "fifteen" as material for making countable items in counting backward: "fifteen, fourteen, thirteen."[19] This is done to encourage the child to take the initial number sequence as his or her own input material, which is what is necessary for children to construct the next number sequence after the initial number sequence—the tacitly nested number sequence. The second goal is to encourage the children to *unite the three counting acts together into a composite unit* after they reach "thirteen is three." If the child has the goal to find how many blocks are left in the container, the child could stop at "thirteen," "step out" of the sensory experience of counting, and "look at" what he or she has just done. By "looking at" what he or she has just done, the child sets the three counting acts at a distance and takes them as one thing. That is, the child compounds (or unites) the trio of re-presented counting acts together into a unitary thing, and produces a unit containing three units.

If the child does in fact unite a re-presentation of "fifteen, fourteen, thirteen" together into a unit, this moves the child[20] to a plane above counting. The child is now looking backward toward 1 from 13. There are three possibilities now for how the child operates and I have observed all of them.

First, the child may re-present the counting acts backward from "twelve" to "one" and then change their direction from backward- to forward-counting acts. In this case, the child simply says "twelve" to indicate how many blocks are left. This bidirectionality of counting indicates that the child takes the counting acts as material of the uniting operation and unites them together into a composite unit because then the child would

---

[19]Note that I used a number small enough so that the child can use a numerical pattern to keep track of how many times he or she counts backward. It may be necessary to ask the child to take out one item at a time rather than three items together in order for them to initiate counting backward to find how many items are left after taking more than one item out at a time.

[20]It is important to remember that the child is working wholly in re-presentation. From the observer's perspective, the child is engaging in thought.

be "above" the counting acts and operating on them. The child knows that the counting acts from "twelve" down to "one" are the self-same counting acts as counting from "one" up to "twelve," but in a different direction.

Second, the child may continue to count from "twelve" down to "one." Here, there are two possibilities:

1. The child may simply utter the number words without keeping track. This is important, because the child will not have reached his or her goal after counting. Consequently, the child may independently reinitialize counting, this time keeping track by sequentially putting up fingers in synchrony with uttering the number-word sequence.

2. The child keeps track of her or his counting acts by putting up fingers upon initializing counting starting from "twelve."

In both cases the child monitors counting and thereby takes each counting act as a unit item. This is what I call *reinteriorizing counting acts* and it leads to the next number sequence. After the child completes its counting activity, there is a distinct possibility that the child will unite the records of counting into a composite unit.

Third, the child may introduce a novelty—double counting. That is, the child might count "twelve is one, eleven is two, ..., one is twelve. Twelve!" By saying "twelve," the child indicates that he or she unites the counting acts into a composite unit. So, introducing take-away subtraction to children in this stage in the way I have explained is done not to teach subtraction, but rather for the purpose of the children making vertical progress in the construction of their number sequence.

Additive situations where the numerosity of the numerical extension is beyond the range of the child's numerical patterns also can be used to encourage the construction of the next number sequence. In sum, the main goal of the teacher for children whose adding scheme is counting on with numerical extension should be for the children to make vertical progress to the next number sequence. Of course, there are many subsidiary goals (which I refer to as *lateral learning goals*) that can be elaborated in a mathematical scope and sequence which do entail important mathematics for these children to learn that is within their learning level.

## The Construction of Subtracting as the Inversion of Adding

The tacitly nested number sequence is essentially a transitional sequence between the initial and the explicitly nested number sequences. In fact, a teacher may not even realize that a child is undergoing such a transition even though the transition may last as long as 3 and sometimes even up to 5 months (Steffe et al., 1988). But as soon a child can make a numerical extension that carries the force of double counting (or else actually double count), the teacher can present tasks, which I call "hidden items" tasks, to find out if the child can find how many items of a collection of items of known numerosity are hidden from view. For example, a child might be presented with a situation where 9 of 16 items are hidden from view and asked to find how many are hidden. If the child solves the task by first counting the visible items, and then counting from "eight" up to "sixteen" while keeping track of how many times he or she counted, this would be in the province of the tacitly nested number sequence.

Counting up to does not necessarily indicate that the child disembeds the remainder of the counting acts past "eight" up to and including "sixteen" from the whole of the sequence of counting acts from "one" to "sixteen." After counting the visible items up to "seven," the child is in the midst of counting, and may make a distinction between the first seven counting acts and those yet to be carried out to "sixteen." That is, the child may make two composite units, one containing the first seven counting acts and the others that remain, but the child may not disembed either of the two composite units from the containing unit. Disembedding is analogous to how an adult might take the even numbers to 100 out of all of the numbers to 100 while leaving the numbers to 100 intact. Disembedding is a conceptual act that takes elements out of a given composite unit and uses them to make a new composite unit. But the elements that are taken out of the composite unit are left in the composite unit, so disembedding does not conceptually destroy the composite unit from which elements are taken. One might think of disembedding as creating new elements identical to some of those contained in a composite unit.

Rather than being content with the child counting from "eight" up to and including "sixteen" to find how many items are hidden, the teacher might ask the child if he or she can find out how many items are hidden by counting backwards. The purpose of doing so is to encourage the child to take the sequence of counting acts he or she has just produced in the forward direction as input for counting backwards. This encourages the child to take the counted items as countable items and to count them again. These counting operations are similar to the operations that are involved in disembedding in that the child posits a composite unit and then mentally extracts part of the elements from all of the elements. By "mentally extract," I mean that the child "lifts" an element from itself while leaving the element in place, thus creating two elements. This is precisely what happens when a child takes a counted item as a countable item—the child creates two identical unit items, one already counted and one to count. The main goal is for the child to be able to decide when to count forward and when to count backwards when solving hidden-items tasks.[21]

The reader may wonder why I haven't mentioned conventional notation like "7 + _ = 16" as an important step in solving the missing-items situations, or other conventional notation like "16 − 7 = _." It is not that I haven't or

---

[21]For example, if 47 of 52 items were hidden in one location and 5 in another, and if the child knows how many are hidden in both locations together and in one of the two locations, the goal is for the child to make decisions concerning the easiest way to count to find how many items are hidden in the other location.

wouldn't encourage children to learn to use such conventional notation. The reason is that initially, in the construction of the concepts and operations that constitute children's mathematics, children's natural language serves as their primary symbol system and it is the means whereby children maintain the spontaneity of their spontaneous development.

When the child learns to disembed the composite unit containing the remainder of the first seven elements of the number sequence to 16 from the whole-number sequence without destroying the sequence, I refer to the child's number sequence as *explicitly nested*. There is a second feature of the explicitly nested number sequence which, when coupled with the disembedding operation, produces great economy in the child's reasoning. In the case of the tacitly nested number sequence, a number word like "seven" refers to a composite unit containing a sequence of seven unit items, which I symbolize using conventional notation for the purposes of illustration: $\{1, 2, 3, 4, 5, 6, 7\}$. In the case of the explicitly nested number sequence, "seven" refers to a composite unit containing a singleton unit that can be iterated seven times to fill out the composite unit.[22] These two advancements permit the child to collapse 16 into two unitary items—a unit containing the first seven items of the sequence and a unit containing the remaining items of the sequence to 16.[23] The child can then disembed both the unit of 7 and the unit containing the sequence of units following 7 to 16 and consider them as two unitary and component parts of 16 both apart from 16 and in 16. So, the child can produce three numbers—7, the remainder of 7 in 16, and 16—and establish relationships among them. This permits the child to construct subtracting as the inversion of adding because the child has only three unitary items to deal with—7, 9, and 16. It also permits the child to establish subtraction as the *difference of two numbers* rather than as the more primitive concept of take away. To understand what is meant by the difference of 16 and 7, say, a child maintains 7 as embedded in 16 but also as a number apart from 16. The difference of the two numbers can then be conceptualized as the gap between them—how many units of one follow 7 in 16? These operations also permit the child to construct strategic reasoning as exemplified by Johanna.

---

[22]The unit of one takes on the characteristic of being iterable if, first, it refers to a sequence of units of one such as $\{1, 2, 3, 4, 5, 6, 7\}$, and second, if it can be repeated to produce the sequence. The unit of one produced upon each repetition can be taken together with those that precede it to form an intermediate sequence of units of one. It is also possible for the child to unite the units of each intermediate sequence into a composite unit even though the child may not engage in these operations while iterating the unit.

[23]When the child regards the unit to which "seven" refers as if it were a unit of one, this frees the child to consider what follows 7 in the number sequence to 16. In that consideration, the child can use the iterable unit of one as a symbol for all of the units that follow 7. This frees the child from producing an image of a sequence of units of one, and so the child can easily focus his or her attention on the composite unit that contains the sequence. In this way, the child can be aware of two composite units that he or she can treat as if they were units of one; the composite unit to which "seven" refers and the composite unit containing the sequence of units which follow 7 in the number sequence to 16.

## Constructing Composite Units as Iterable

After children have constructed the explicitly nested number sequence, the tendency might be to head as quickly as possible toward such learning objectives as "adding or subtracting numbers through 999 + 999." If this is interpreted as meaning the children should learn standard computational algorithms, I would consider it as a major disaster in their mathematical education. But if it is interpreted to mean that the children produce child-generated algorithms, then there is a chance for them to maintain their insight and creativity in mathematics while learning what all too often is considered as procedures. The children certainly have constructed some very powerful ways and means of operating and it should be the teacher's goal to bring forth accommodations of these ways and means so that the children's methods blossom into ever more powerful and spontaneous methods.

The children's explicitly nested number sequence is a number sequence involving the unit of 1 and those who have constructed this number sequence essentially live in a "ones world." "One hundred," for example, refers to 1 iterated 100 times; but not to 50 iterated twice, to 25 iterated 4 times, to 10 iterated 10 times, to 5 iterated 20 times, and so forth. A major goal for children who have constructed the explicitly nested number sequence is for them to construct composite units as iterable in the way that their unit of one is iterable. An illustrative task is to ask the children a question like "If you count up to 12 by threes, how many threes would you count?" The typical first attempt is "1, 2, 3, that is one; 4, 5, 6, that is two; 7, 8, 9, that is three; 10, 11, 12, that is four. Four." This may be one of the first times the child repeats a composite unit more than once. Nevertheless, the child has already constructed one as an iterable unit, so it would seem that the construction of three as an iterable unit would be within their zone of potential construction.

In any case, a child who has recently constructed the explicitly nested number sequence is yet to construct three or any other composite unit as an iterable unit. This realization is staggering, because in conceptually reorganizing, say, 60 into a unit of six units of 10, it is of great advantage for 10 to be available to children as an iterable unit. Bringing forth the construction of the operations that produce a unit of units of units (a unit containing six units of 10, e.g.) is a major goal for the children in the stage of the explicitly nested number sequence. This goal, when elaborated within the mathematics of children, supersedes all conventional learning objectives concerned with place value; because in learning numeration, it is conventional for children to begin by interpreting a two-digit numeral as so many tens and so many ones without first constructing the operations necessary to reorganize, say, a unit containing a sequence of 37 units of one into a unit containing three units of 10 and one unit of 7. To accomplish such a reorganization, the child must have established the units of 10 and 1 as units to measure other composite units. This means that 10 and 1 must be constructed at least as iterable units that are embedded in a way of operating that the child can use to measure other composite units.

***Establishing 10 as an Iterable Unit.*** Children in the stage of the explicitly nested number sequence can produce the number-word sequence "ten, twenty, thirty, ..., one hundred" before they have constructed the unit of 10 as iterable. This introduces a practical difficulty because such children often circumvent constructing an iterable unit of 10 simply because they can solve most of the tasks they encounter in school mathematics without doing so. For example, when asked to find how many dimes could be traded for 100 pennies, I have observed children simply utter "10, 20, ..., 100" in synchrony with putting up fingers and answer "ten," but yet have no idea how to find how many stacks of pennies with 10 pennies per stack could be made out of 100 pennies without actually making the stacks. Because they treat a dime as a unit of one rather than a unit that symbolizes a unit containing 10 units of one, I refer to their apparent counting-by-10 activity as pseudo counting by 10. I have observed a similar phenomenon in the case of counting by two.

Because of pseudo counting by 10, it might seem easier for children to find how many stacks with 10 blocks per stack *could* be made from, say, 70 blocks than how many stacks with 3 blocks per stack *could* be made from, say, 15 blocks. But I have not found this to be the case at all because pseudo counting by 10 is usually not activated by such conceptual tasks. Rather, such tasks appear to the child to be a novel problems that have to be solved. One of my goals in presenting these tasks is for the children to use double counting in solving them. For example, after counting to 10, my goal is to bring forth double counting in the following way; "11 is one, 12 is two, 13 is three, ..., 20 is ten. Two tens. 21 is one, 22 is two, 23 is three, ..., 30 is ten. Three tens...." Upon reaching "seventy," the child would know that seven tens have been counted. This encourages abstracting that each decade in the number sequence for one is of numerosity 10, a number sequence for the unit of 10 (10, 20, 30, 40, ...) whose elements can be counted and whose elements refer to a decade in the corresponding number sequence for one, and a unit of 10 that can be iterated.

Once children have constructed 10 as an iterable unit, they can take counting by 10 as a given in a way that is quite analogous to how they can take counting by 1 as a given in the case of units of 1. That is, "seventy" or "70" can symbolize counting by 10 seven times and what this counting activity produces—a unit containing seven units of 10. This permits the child to construct child-generated algorithms for finding sums and differences of numbers in the decades. For example, when finding how many blocks in a container containing 73 blocks after 47 more are placed into the container, the child who can take counting by 10 and 1 (a slight modification of counting by 10) as a given can count on by 10 and 1 to find how many blocks there are. For example, the child might count "73; 83, 93, 103, 113—114, 115, 116, 117, 118, 119, 120. One hundred twenty." Such child-generated algorithms permit the child to maintain ownership of their mathematics and to build great confidence in their own ways and means of operating.[24]

Are child-generated algorithms to be considered as a step in the construction of standard paper-and-pencil algorithms? I consider standard computational algorithms as neolithic devices that should not regulate what is emphasized in the mathematics curriculum as was the case in 1930 (National Society for the Study of Education, 1930). Rather, child-generated algorithms should be emphasized along with the construction of *systems of units* that are relevant for the decimal system of numeration. Until children have constructed the relevant systems of units, the standard algorithms should not be of concern because there is a grave danger of the standard algorithms providing the children with a way of operating in which constructing and reasoning with systems of units is not necessary. Once reasoning with systems of units and the reflective thought they imply are available to children, they will be ready to creatively generate more or less conventional ways of operating as productive thought.

### *Criteria for Judging When a Composite Unit Is Iterable.*

For a composite unit to be judged as iterable, the child must be aware of such composite units prior to operating. That is, the child must have constructed a composite unit containing another composite unit that can be iterated so many times, a structure that is strictly analogous to the numerical structure the child constructs in the case of the iterable unit of one. Rather than speak of seven ones, for example, the child can also speak of seven fours because the child is aware of a unit containing a composite unit of four that can be iterated seven times. The ability to solve the following missing-composite-units task is an excellent indication that the child has constructed the composite unit of four as iterable if the child solves it as I explain.

> There are six strings of four toys each under this cover. Some more toys are put under the cover. There are now 44 toys under the cover. How many strings of four can be made from the toys added?

If the child proceeds to find how many toys originally were under the cover by counting by four six times, and then continues on making units of four while keeping track of how many more units of four could be made, this is a strong indication that the child has constructed four as an iterable composite unit. For example, the child might proceed as follows: "Four,

---

[24]I advocate that such child-generated algorithms be constructed by children for numbers up to 1,000. In this context, I encourage children to engage in strategic reasoning of the sort in which Johanna engaged. Strategic reasoning is critical because it is by this means that children can curtail their child-generated algorithms. For example, to find the sum of 73 and 47 strategically, children might reason as follows: "Seven tens and four tens are eleven tens. Eleven tens is one hundred and ten. Seven and three is ten, so one hundred and twenty."

that is one; eight, that is two; twelve, that is three; sixteen, that is four; twenty, that is five; twenty-four, that is six. Twenty-eight, that is one; thirty-two, that is two; thirty-six, that is three; forty, that is four; forty-four, that is five. Five!" In the solution, I would infer that the child could imagine *making a continuation* of counting by four six times prior to counting. In this continuation, the child would be aware of an unknown numerosity of fours that could be made from the toys added.

So, in situations designed to bring forth the construction of composite units as iterable, rather than simply ask children to count by four up to a certain number, I ask them, for example, how many stacks of four they could make out of, say, 24 blocks. I ask this question because I want to encourage the children to imagine a sequence of stacks of four blocks each, and I might encourage them to describe what they intend to do as they solve the task before they engage in solving activity. In this way, I encourage them to visualize the results of making stacks of four and, in doing so, to use their numerical concept of four several times in producing visualized images of stacks of four blocks. If I am successful, the child usually refers to these visualized images as they engage in keeping track of counting by four.

Once I establish with the children that they can, in fact, find how many stacks of two, three, four, or five blocks can be made from given numbers of blocks without actually making the stacks, several options open up. First, I can ask the children to regenerate parts of their solutions. For example, in the case of the 24 blocks, I might ask the children how many blocks are in the six stacks they made. This orients the children to take the results of their solution as input for further operating, which should be regarded as the primary means of children making progress. It is also the very beginnings of recursion, a process that the authors of *PSSM* emphasize along with iteration and the comparison of algorithms "because of their utility in a technological world" (NCTM, 1998, p. 28). Throughout this chapter, I have emphasized all three of these processes as basic in the mathematics of children, not only as a product of the mental operations that constitute this mathematics, but also in the construction of these mental operations.

## FINAL COMMENTS AND SUMMARY

My purpose in writing this chapter was to sketch out a possibility for the mathematics of children to become the rational bridgehead[25] of school mathematics. I have certainly not exhausted this topic nor have I attempted to be exhaustive. There are many more things that need to be discussed in the topics considered herein, as well as other topics that must be considered. I regard the mathematics of children as a mathematics that only children can bring to life through their interactions. As Tom Kieren (1994) has reminded us many times, an adult can only provide the

---

[25]A rational bridgehead consists of allegedly unique common core beliefs (Konold & Johnson, 1991).

occasions for bringing such a mathematics forth, sustaining it, and modifying it. But in doing so, the adult is coimplicated in the mathematics of children. So, I regard teachers as playing an incontestable functional role in the mathematical education of children. There are several places in the chapter where I have tried to suggest that role, but I know these suggestions are merely that—suggestions.

Making the mathematics of children the rational bridgehead of school mathematics not only involves a change of paradigm, but also a willingness to open oneself to the world of children's mathematics and to assume that, within that world, children's mathematical thinking is every bit as coherent and rational as the thinking of the adult. In fact, I have always found children to be internally consistent in how they operate mathematically, an observation that serves as a foundation for my advocacy that we take their mathematics seriously.

It is often difficult to imagine what the mathematical concepts and operations of children might be like and how they might be constructed in establishing a coherent view of children's mathematics under the assumption that children are indeed rational beings. Starting with the object concepts that human beings construct during the first 2 years of life, I traced a constructive itinerary that begins with perceptual unit items, then proceeds to figurative unit items, arithmetical unit items, the iterable unit of one, and finally to iterable composite units. Furthermore, I identified the operations that produce these five different unit types as re-presenting, unitizing, monitoring, and uniting. By unitizing the items of a perceptual collection, a child constructs perceptual unit items. Because the child learns to focus on the unitary aspect of the perceptual items rather than on some specific sensory feature, the child can classify what would otherwise be quite disparate perceptual items together on the basis of their unitariness. This is the first abstraction in the construction of the numerical units I have called arithmetical units. In this itinerary, classifying does not produce numerical structure. It is unitizing re-presented perceptual items that produces numerical structure.

A numerical composite is a sequence of arithmetical unit items that have been constructed as a result of monitoring counting. Unitizing the elements of a re-presented sequence of counted perceptual unit items is involved in monitoring, and the unit items that are produced, called arithmetical units, can be used in producing countable units because they contain records of the experience of counting acts. Consequently, a numerical composite is simply a number sequence that is symbolized by a number word like "seven." As children make progress, they construct composite units containing these number sequences and operations with these composite units. Moreover, they learn to operate with these composite units in ways that enable an adult to guide and shape the operations into quite advanced ways of reasoning mathematically.

Children's number sequences are fundamental in their mathematical education, but they are not to be regarded as being constituted in the same way as the conventional concept of a number sequence in mathematics. I traced the construction of children's counting schemes through essentially four stages: the perceptual, the figurative, the initial number sequence, and the explicitly nested number sequence. The tacitly nested number sequence is a more or less transitional stage between the preceding and succeeding number sequences. The first number sequence that I mentioned, the initial number sequence, is nothing but an interiorization of the figurative counting scheme, and each succeeding number sequence is an interiorization of the one preceding. This understanding of children's number sequences provides us with a new insight into children's construction of number and extends it into the province of their mathematics education. The explanation offered by Piaget and Szeminska (1952) for children's construction of number culminated with a structure similar to the initial number sequence. Although this is a crucial structure in children's conceptual development, it is only a beginning point in the children's constructive itineraries. At every stage, I stressed counting as a scheme rather than as an activity. In fact, a number sequence is nothing but a numerical counting scheme. As a scheme, counting is goal directed and purposeful. It serves in the construction of adding and subtracting schemes, child-generated algorithms, the structure of a unit of units of units, and the establishment of a scheme for measuring numbers, among other things.

## ACKNOWLEDGMENTS

This chapter is a revision of the paper that was written for the Research Symposium *Linking Research and the New Early Childhood Mathematics Standards* held at the 2000 NCTM Research Presession, Chicago, Illinois.

This chapter was written as part of the Activities of the project Interdisciplinary Research on Number (IRON) of which NSF Project No. REC 9814853 is a part. All opinions are those of the author.

## REFERENCECS

Kieren, T. (1994). Play and mathematical understanding. *Journal of Research in Childhood Education, 8*(2), 132–141.
Konold, C., & Johnson, D. K. (1991). Philosophical and psychological aspects of constructivism. In L. P. Steffe (Ed.), *Epistemological foundations of mathematical experience* (pp. 1–13). New York: Springer-Verlag.
National Council of Teachers of Mathematics. (1998). *Principles and standards for school mathematics: Discussion draft.* Reston, VA: Author.
National Society for the Study of Education. (1930). *Twenty-ninth yearbook of the society's committee on arithmetic.* Bloomington, IL: Public School Publishing.
Olive, J. (1994). Building a new model of mathematical learning. *Journal of Research in Childhood Education, 8*(2), 162–173.
Piaget, J. (1955). *The child's construction of reality.* London: Routledge and Kegan Paul. (Original work published 1934)

Piaget, J. (1980). Opening the debate. In M. Piattelli-Palmarini (Ed.), *Language and learning: The debate between Jean Piaget and Noam Chomsky* (pp. 23–34). Cambridge, MA: Harvard University Press.

Piaget, J., & Szeminska, A. (1952). *The child's conception of number.* London: Routledge and Kegan Paul.

Reys, R. E., Suydam, M. N., Lindquist, M., & Smith, N. L. (1999). *Helping children learn mathematics.* New York: Wiley.

Steffe, L. P. (1991). The learning paradox: A plausible counterexample. In L. P. Steffe (Ed.), *Epistemological foundations of mathematical experience* (pp. 26–44). New York: Springer-Verlag.

Steffe, L. P. (1992). Schemes of action and operation involving composite units. *Learning and Individual Differences, 4*(3), 259–309.

Steffe, L. P. (1994). Children's construction of meaning for arithmetical words: A curriculum problem. In D. Tirosh (Ed.), *Implicit and explicit knowledge: An educational approach* (pp. 131–168). Norwood, NJ: Ablex.

Steffe, L. P., Cobb, P., & von Glasersfeld, E. (1988). *Construction of arithmetical meanings and strategies.* New York: Springer-Verlag.

Steffe, L. P., von Glasersfeld, E., Richards, J., & Cobb, P. (1983). *Children's counting types: Philosophy, theory, and application.* New York: Praeger.

van Oers, B. (1996). Learning mathematics as a meaningful activity. In L. P. Steffe & P. Nesher (General Eds.), *Theories of mathematical learning* (pp. 91–114). Mahwah, NJ: Lawrence Erlbaum Associates.

von Glasersfeld, E. (1981). An attentional model for the conceptual construction of units and number. *Journal for Research in Mathematics Education, 12*(2), 33–96.

von Glasersfeld, E. (1995). *Radical constructivism: A way of knowing and learning.* Washington, DC: Falmer Press

Wright, R. J. (2000). Professional development in recovery education. In L. P. Steffe & P. W. Thompson (Eds.), *Radical constructivism in action: Building on the pioneering work of Ernst von Glasersfeld* (pp. 134–151). New York: RoutledgeFalmer.

# 9

# A Prospective Developmental Perspective on Early Mathematics Instruction

Catherine Sophian
*University of Hawaii*

A developmental perspective on early instruction is often equated with the notion of age-appropriateness or readiness. On this view, a developmentally appropriate curriculum is one that is well matched with the cognitive abilities and/or learning styles of the age group for which it is intended. Another kind of developmental perspective, one that I call a prospective developmental perspective, is concerned with the impact of early mathematics instruction on aspects of mathematics learning that become important *later* in development. In this chapter, I address the significance of incorporating a prospective developmental perspective in the formulation of standards for early mathematics instruction. The modes of instruction that produce the greatest immediate learning may not always be the ones that are best for the long term. Accordingly, instructional standards should be directed toward maximizing the long-term as well as the short-term effectiveness of early mathematics instruction.

I focus on the arena of fraction learning to develop this idea. In doing so, I am not necessarily advocating the inclusion of fractions in preschool or kindergarten mathematics curricula. Rather, my recommendation is that in deciding how and what to teach young children about whole numbers we should keep in mind the conceptual foundation that they need to acquire in order to be in a position to make sense of fractions whenever they are introduced.

Instruction in fractions in the middle to late elementary school years is widely considered a watershed, a transition point at which many children begin to have serious trouble with mathematics. It is often argued that fractions are difficult because they do not fit well with children's intuitive ideas about numbers, which are a good foundation for learning about counting and related whole-number operations but not for fractions. A troubling implication of this view is that the early years of mathematics instruction, in which the focus is on whole numbers, cannot prepare children for the transition to fractions and rational number concepts. The prospective developmental perspective suggests another possibility, however. It may be that prevalent modes of instruction in the first years of school, though effective for beginning mathematics content, actually contribute to the difficulty children experience in making the transition to fractions or, at least, fail to pave the way for that transition as effectively as they might. If so, it is important to rethink the ways we teach whole-number concepts to children in the first years of school in light of long-term as well as short-term educational objectives.

I suggest that much of the difficulty in fraction learning stems from conceptual issues that are not unique to fractions, but that have their origins in the way very young children think about counting and whole-number quantities. In particular, I suggest that limitations on the ways young children think about units of quantification in their early counting are the source of much of the difficulty they later have in making sense of fractions. I present three kinds of evidence that bear on this idea.

First, in order to clarify the nature of the difficulties that so often plague fraction learning, I take a close look at a basic but problematic aspect of fraction knowledge in older children and adults—understanding the ordinal relations among fractions with different denominators. I report comparisons across groups of students ranging from fourth graders to university undergraduates. The university students no longer show a misconception that is common among fourth and fifth graders—the belief that a larger denominator makes for a greater fractional value. Despite this progress, however, they make other systematic errors, indicating that the mathematics education they have received has not succeeded in establishing a solid understanding of how the value of a fraction is related to the values of the numbers that make up its numerator and denominator. I liken these errors to the well-known "bugs" in multidigit subtraction (Van Lehn, 1983). Like those bugs, I suggest, the ordinality errors reflect an inadequate grasp of the semantics or meaning of mathematical representations, in this case representations of fractional values.

Second, I review research on young children's understanding of units of quantification in counting that I believe helps to illuminate the difficulties older children (and even adults) have in understanding the values of fractions. The main point I want to draw from this research is that young children tend to conflate units of quantification with physically bounded entities (everyday objects). Thus, although their counting performance is good as long as objects are an appropriate unit of enumeration, they have difficulty as soon as it is necessary to work with other kinds of units. This limitation has strong ramifications for fraction learning, because fractions entail the coordination of alternative levels of quantification (the unit and the fractional part).

Finally, in support of the idea that difficulties in reasoning about fractions and ratios are closely related to limitations on children's understanding of mathematical units, I present evidence from recent research on children's judgments about spatial proportionality. In particular, the results show that, whereas even preschool and kindergarten children can make judgments of spatial proportionality, the availability of numerical units disrupts rather than facilitates proportional comparison at early ages. This finding, I believe, is symptomatic of the overly restricted range of numerical activities and relations typically presented to young children.

In the concluding sections of the chapter, I address the question of how the perspective I have articulated can be put into practice. I report a very short-term training study that illustrates the malleability of young children's thinking about number and quantity. Then, I briefly describe an experimental Pre-K mathematics curriculum that was recently implemented on an experimental basis in several Head Start classrooms. And finally, I offer some closing reflections on the ramifications of recognizing that children can know something in many different ways for efforts to formulate appropriate standards and put them into practice. Even the best-motivated set of instructional objectives can be counterproductive if the emphasis shifts from engendering particular kinds of understanding to eliciting correct performance on particular tasks.

## MISCONCEPTIONS ABOUT ORDINAL RELATIONS AMONG FRACTIONS

The errors that children—and even adults—make in comparing the values of fractions with unlike denominators are a telling indication of the nature of the difficulties that plague fraction learning. They are not just random errors but reflect specific ways of interpreting fraction values that change developmentally and yet that often remain erroneous even in adulthood.

In one research project (Sophian & Dulloog, 2000), we asked students in Grades 4, 5, and 7 and university undergraduates to judge which fraction in each of a series of pairs was the larger. In one problem set, the fractions appeared in their "base" (nonreducible) form; in the other, the same fractional values were presented using a common denominator (12ths). The common-denominator problems, not surprisingly, elicited predominantly correct performance at every grade level; it was the pattern of performance on the different-denominator problems that was of primary interest.

Within the different-denominator problems, patterns of performance across grade levels were very different for problems that involved comparing two unit fractions (e.g., $\frac{1}{12}$ vs. $\frac{1}{3}$, or $\frac{1}{2}$ vs. $\frac{1}{6}$) than for problems that involved the "complements" of those fractions—the values obtained by subtracting each fraction from 1 (e.g., $\frac{11}{12}$ vs. $\frac{2}{3}$, or $\frac{1}{2}$ vs. $\frac{5}{6}$). On the unit-fraction problems, the seventh graders and the university students did markedly better than the fourth or fifth graders, $M = 95\%$ correct for seventh graders and 94% correct for university students, versus 41% correct for fourth graders and 54% correct for fifth graders. However, on the complement problems, the performance of the university students was substantially lower, $M = 78\%$ correct, whereas that of the fourth and fifth graders was higher, $M = 80\%$ and 81% correct, respectively. The seventh graders' performance remained high, $M = 92\%$ correct, as it had been on the unit-fraction problems.

The greater difficulty of the unit fractions than of their complements for fourth and fifth grade students likely reflects the often-observed misconception that the value of a fraction increases as the sizes of the numbers of which it is comprised increase. The greater difficulty of the complements than of the unit fractions for university students is more surprising, however, and suggests that although students eventually overcame the misconceptions that were evident at early ages, they did not acquire a firm grasp of how fraction values are related. Whatever they did learn that allowed them, by seventh grade, to respond correctly to the full range of problems presented, soon faded and left them prone to new kinds of errors. Two undergraduates were systematically incorrect on the complement pairs, suggesting that they incorrectly extended the rule that a large denominator makes for a small fractional value from the unit fractions, for which it is always true, to the complement pairs, for which it is not true (because the numerators of those fractions covary in size with the denominators). The rest of the undergraduates showed less marked error patterns, but the fact that they erred predominantly on complement problems suggests that many of them were also influenced by this kind of reasoning, albeit to a smaller degree. Altogether 13 university students made more errors on the complement problems than on the unit problems, whereas only 2 made more errors on the unit problems.

The regularities in the errors the undergraduates made on common-denominator problems are reminiscent of the "buggy arithmetic" errors noted in schoolchildren's performance of complex whole-number operations such as subtraction with borrowing (cf., Resnick, 1982; Van Lehn, 1983). Although the students in this research were not asked to produce a computational result, such as a difference, clearly they had to carry out some sequence of numerical operations to arrive at their responses to the different-denominator problems. And the systematic differences in error rates between unit problems and complement problems make it clear that the mistakes they made in doing so were not just random but stemmed from systematically incorrect comparison processes. In particular, it seems likely that students sometimes considered only the relative magnitude of the denominators, without considering the value of the numerators. However, the observed errors could also have resulted from other forms of faulty reasoning. More detailed information about students' comparison processes and not just their final judgments would be needed to identify the specific bugs in their reasoning (and also the specific forms of reasoning through which correct responses were generated).

Regardless of those specifics, however, what is important about the erroneous comparison processes that resulted in incorrect judgments here, like the "bugs" identified in earlier research on arithmetic computations, is that they clearly do not respect the semantics of the problems—that is, the quantitative relations that are being represented. Buggy arithmetic appears to result from an effort to extend known rules to new problem situations, without grasping the quantitative relations that constrain the ways the numbers are manipulated. In a similar way, the errors we have found in university students' judgments about fraction magnitudes appear to reflect the overextension of a rule that works when only the denominators differ (as is the case for unit fractions) to problems in which numerators as well as denominators vary. But, as is the case with buggy subtraction (Resnick, 1982), this overgeneralization would not be plausible if students grasped the semantics of what they were doing. Because the value of a fraction depends on its numerator as well as its denominator, it is semantically as well as procedurally wrong to base a magnitude judgment only on the denominator. What the "bugs" in students' magnitude judgments imply, then, is that they have not achieved an understanding of the semantics of fractions, the way in which their numerators and denominators together specify particular quantitative values.

Fundamentally, the principle that is involved in understanding how the numerator and the denominator of a fraction together determine its value is the iteration of units of measurement: The denominator specifies the size of the units and the numerator specifies how many of those units there are. The key to understanding that, for unit fractions, the size of the denominator is inversely related to the value of the fraction is understanding that fractional units are obtained by partitioning, and the more parts one creates from a given whole the smaller each individual part will be. Coming to understand this is the conceptual foundation for overcoming the misconception that big denominators make for large fractional values. But what if a child does not acquire this conceptual foundation? Such children may still learn the correct ordering of unit fractions, but in doing so all they will have acquired is an arbitrary rule. As a result, they are likely to have trouble extending what they have learned to the more complex case of nonunit fractions, particularly fractions in which numerators as well as denominators vary.

The general point that emerges from this analysis is that to learn about fractions effectively, children need to understand the semantics of fractions, not just the procedural rules that apply to them. And the foundation for the semantics of fractions is the idea of generating a new unit of measurement by partitioning the original one (Davydov, 1991). It is here that I believe there is a fundamental connection between fraction learning and the learning about counting and whole-number operations that occurs as children are just beginning their schooling.

## THE CONFLATION OF PHYSICAL OBJECTS AND UNITS IN EARLY COUNTING

In counting, children generally take individual objects as units—each item is counted once and only once in order to arrive at the cardinal value of the set. At early ages, they find it quite difficult to adopt other counting units—for instance, to count the number of different shapes in a collection where each shape appears more than once, or to count two separated parts of an object as a single thing (Gal'perin & Georgiev, 1969; Shipley & Shepperson, 1990; Sophian & Kailihiwa, 1998). But, as Gal'perin and Georgiev pointed out, there is a profound difference between an individual and a mathematical unit:

> Mastery of the initial concept of the unit is the most important step in the formation of elementary arithmetic concepts (they are all built on the unit or presuppose it). But the prevailing idea of the unit as an entity (a separate thing) ... is mathematically incorrect and psychologically wrong. It orients children to the visual properties of magnitudes and to their evaluation through direct comparison ... [and] hinders the correct formation of elementary mathematical notions. (p.197)

They noted that, although children eventually come to distinguish spontaneously between units and individuals, this distinction is likely to be fragile and easily lost if it is not systematically established through instruction.

One limitation associated with treating individuals as units is that children do not recognize the significance of variations in the size of units when they form individual items out of a continuous quantity. For instance, Gal'perin and Georgiev (1969) had 6- to 7-year-old children carry out a subtraction activity in which they put five spoonfuls of rice in a pile, then removed four from it and were asked how many spoonfuls remained in the original pile. Because children tended not to take care to fill the spoons completely when removing rice from the pile, many of them ended up with more than one spoonful left. Moreover, for the most part they were not able to make sense of what had happened. Eighteen children estimated by sight that three or four spoonfuls were left, failing to connect the problem with the mathematical relation $5 - 4 = 1$. Ten others insisted that only one spoonful was left and were unable to explain why it looked like so much. Only four children were able to connect the unduly large remainder to the fact that they had not completely filled the spoon when removing the four spoonfuls.

Another line of research that vividly illustrates young children's indifference to variations in item size is work on sharing problems, in which children are asked to divide materials among two or three recipients making sure that each gets an equal share. A common approach to this type of problem is distributive sharing—giving one item to each recipient in turn, and then another and another until all the items have been distributed (Frydman & Bryant, 1988; Miller, 1984). This behavior makes use of one-to-one correspondence to ensure that each recipient gets the same number of items. It is effective in generating equal shares so long as all the items are the same size and every round of distribution is completed (i.e., the items do not run out on the last round, leaving someone short-changed). But when Miller asked children to create equal shares of continuous quantities, the children cut the material into pieces to be distributed with little regard for the sizes of the pieces. Even more strikingly, when they came up short in passing out the last round of pieces, several children solved the problem by taking one of the pieces the shortchanged individual had received earlier in the process and cutting it in two to create another piece for him! Obviously (to an adult eye), this action did not change the overall amount that individual received; but so indifferent were the children to the ramifications of differences in the sizes of the pieces that they were content to have equated the numbers of pieces each recipient got in this way.

Clearly, there are situations in which the number of discrete items is the focus of interest and not their size or other characteristics. What is important about young children's focus on discrete objects in counting is not that this is the wrong unit, but that it is based on a failure to differentiate between physical and quantitative units (Gal'perin & Georgiev, 1969). The conflation of physical and quantitative units is profoundly limiting for mathematical development because it precludes the consideration of alternative units of quantification and the relations between them, relations that are essential for understanding measurement, place value, fractions, and much more.

Sophian and Kailihiwa (1998) obtained direct evidence that young children are inflexible in their choice of units of quantification by asking children to quantify arrays of objects that lent themselves well to two different levels of quantification. The arrays were composed of objects that were made up of two separable pieces (like the halves of an Easter egg), and some of the objects were presented intact whereas others were separated into their pieces. Children were asked two alternative questions about these arrays: "How many pieces can we get from all these things?" versus "How many whole eggs [e.g.] can we get from all these things?" As in Shipley and Shepperson's (1990) work, some children counted discrete items (this was most common among the 4-year-olds, the youngest age group tested). Many, however, did generate either counts of the component pieces (treating the separable parts of the objects as separate items, even when they were joined to form intact objects) or counts of aggregates (treating pairs of pieces as single items, even when they had not been put together). Yet, the children were strikingly poor at adapting their choice of counting unit to the question that was posed.

In an initial study, most 4- and 5-year-old children (and even a substantial minority of 7-year-olds) selected one type of counting unit and stuck with it from trial to trial regardless of which question the experimenter posed. A follow-up study endeavored to make the contrast between the two questions more salient by asking both questions, one right after the other, about each array that was presented. This procedure was successful in eliciting a more differentiated choice of counting units from 5-year-olds but not from 4-year-olds. These results are interesting from an instructional perspective because, even though they indicate important limitations on early quantitative reasoning, they also demonstrate the impact that even small variations in problem presentation can have on that reasoning. The finding that kindergarten children can be induced to adopt different counting units by simply juxtaposing alternative quantification questions about the same array of objects suggests that there is considerable potential for early instruction to help children discover the fundamental distinction between a mathematical unit and an individual.

## SPATIAL RATIOS AND NUMERICAL UNITS

The idea that childrqen have difficulty understanding numerical ratios because they lack an appropriate understanding of mathematical units raises the possibility that young children may be better able to grasp ratio relations if they are introduced in a form that does not entail the use of units. For instance, even young children have an idea of what it means for something (or someone) to be fat or skinny, and it seems likely that such judgments are not based on width alone but on how wide something is relative to its height.

Several recent studies have provided evidence that children as young as 4 and 5 years of age can successfully compare spatial ratios that do not entail the use of fractional units. For instance, in one study (Sophian, 2000, Experiment 2) 4- and 5-year-old children were asked to identify which of two small rectangles matched a larger sample in shape, that is, in how elongated or close to square it was. The children responded correctly to 93% of problems on which there was a large contrast between the choice stimuli (e.g., the small rectangles embodied width-to-height ratios of .25:1 vs. .5:1) and to 82% of problems on which the contrast was not as great (e.g., .33:1 vs. .5:1).

To more directly investigate the idea that units are a source of difficulty in ratio reasoning, a subsequent study compared children's performance on ratio comparison problems in which spatial stimuli were constructed either of continuous regions or of regions that were visibly partitioned into units (Sophian & Yamashita, 2000). Examples of the stimuli for the two conditions can be seen in Fig. 9.1. Children were asked to compare the sizes of two differently colored regions that together comprised a sample figure, and then to complete a new figure, given one of its two regions, so that the balance or mix of the two colors in it was the same as that in the sample.

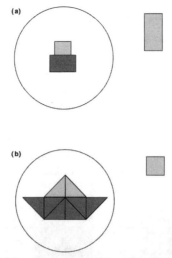

FIG. 9.1. Examples of (a) continuous and (b) partitioned stimuli used in the study by Sophian and Yamashita (2000). In each example, the figure on the left is a sample stimulus composed of two regions (light and dark), and the rectangular figure on the right is one region of a test stimulus that the child is to complete.

This task was quite difficult for young children. Children averaged less than 10% correct responses at both 5 and 7 years, and only 27% correct even at 10 years (fifth grade). A common error, particularly at the younger ages, was to disregard the ratio relations in the problem and simply make the region being generated the same size as the correspondingly colored region in the sample. These size-match errors accounted for 26% of children's responses at 5 years, 29% at 7 years, and 19% at 10 years. But what was illuminating was that both correct responses and size-match errors varied substantially across the conditions, and in different ways at different ages. The means for each condition are plotted in Fig. 9.2. Whereas 10-year-olds benefited from numerical information, in that they were more likely to respond correctly and less likely to make size-match errors in working with partitioned regions than in working with continuous ones, both 5- and 7-year-olds showed just the opposite pattern. The availability of numerical information appears to have diverted young children's attention away from global spatial relations that they were able to utilize (to some degree) in the continuous condition to construct a proportional match to the sample. It exacerbated the tendency, which was pronounced even in the continuous condition, to respond nonproportionally, reproducing the absolute size of the corresponding region in the sample rather than the relation between the two regions.

These negative effects of partitioning, like the limitations on children's reasoning about numerical units that other studies have identified, indi-

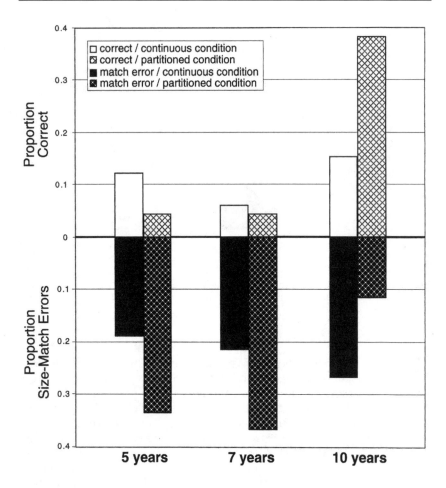

FIG. 9.2.   Correct responses and size-match errors on problems involving continuous versus partitioned stimuli (data from Sophian and Yamashita, 2000).

cate that the ways young children use numbers are too restricted to support the kinds of mathematical learning that will be expected of them in future years. Early mathematics education, therefore, must go beyond "standard" numerical activities in which discrete objects are the unit and absolute magnitude is the focus. From the very beginning of mathematics instruction, learning activities should be designed to expand the ways in which children use and understand numbers, to move them beyond routine procedures to an exploration of the quantitative relations and concepts on which mathematical meaning depends.

## TEACHING CHILDREN ABOUT UNITS
## THROUGH MEASUREMENT

In order to determine the feasibility of addressing profound mathematical concepts such as that of a unit in early childhood mathematics instruction, I conducted an experimental study (Sophian, 2002) that examined pre-schoolers' reasoning about effects of unit size. In the study, 3- and 4-year-old children were asked questions such as whether more small bears or more large bears (examples provided) would be able to sit to-gether on a given bench. In addition to evaluating children's initial under-standing of the relation between unit size and number, the study also evaluated how responsive their thinking was to a series of demonstration trials on which they were shown what happened as different sizes of ob-jects were put in the space. On these trials, the experimenter began, as she did on regular test trials, by asking the child whether more of one kind of object or more of the other would fit into a given space. As soon as the child answered, however, she said, "Let's see," and began putting small and large objects, one at a time, into corresponding spaces. (E.g., she first put a large bear on one bench and a small bear on a second identical bench; then she put a second large bear beside the first one and a second small bear beside the first of those.) As she did so, she drew the child's attention to how the two spaces were filling up, saying, for example, "There's not much more room here now, is there? But there is still plenty of room over here." When one of the spaces was full, she again asked whether more of one kind of object or more of the other fit; then she stated the correct an-swer if the child had not, and asked the child why that was so.

On average, children responded correctly to just 36% of the pretest prob-lems. In other words, they incorrectly judged that more large than small items would fit in a given space almost twice as often (on 64% of the prob-lems) as they correctly judged that more small items would fit. After six demonstration trials, however, their performance rose to 64% correct—still far from errorless but substantially better than it had been on corresponding problems at the start of the study. Because the specific types of containers and objects used for the posttest problems were ones that the child had not seen before, this improvement cannot be attributed simply to learning about the relation between particular objects and particular containers. Rather, the results of the study indicate that, although uninstructed pre-school children have little understanding of the significance of unit size for measurement-related problems, their understanding grows rapidly when they have the opportunity to make relevant observations.

These results, and the broader prospective developmental perspective advanced in this chapter, are the foundation for a Pre-K mathematics curric-ulum that I recently deveoped as part of a project funded by the Head Start—University Partnerships program[1]. This curriculum engages children

---

[1] Barbara DeBaryshe was the principal investigator for this project.

in hands-on activities involving counting, comparing, transforming, and measuring that are designed to address both the concept of unit and the idea of additive composition (that parts combine to form wholes and wholes can be decomposed into parts). For example, in several activities children explore the impact of using alternative measurement units (small vs. larger cups to measure volume; longer vs. shorter handprints to measure length) on the numerical values obtained. In others, they put together duplicates of one geometric shape to make new shapes (e.g., two identical right triangles can be combined to form either another triangle or a rectangle) and then consider how the areas of the different shapes created in this way compare. Measurement is at the heart of the curriculum because it is indispensable for understanding units, which are fundamentally a means of measuring. In addition, because measurement activities give children a way to experiment with units and quantities, they provide an ideal bridge between the hands-on exploration that comes naturally to young children and the abstractions of mathematics toward which they are heading.

## CONCLUSION: APPLYING A PROSPECTIVE DEVELOPMENTAL PERSPECTIVE IN EARLY CHILDHOOD CLASSROOMS

A major challenge in formulating appropriate standards for early childhood mathematics education, and also for using the standards appropriately once they have been formulated, stems from the fact that there are many ways of knowing (Sophian, 1999). Learning to solve a set of problems by adhering to a prescribed procedural sequence is a very different thing from being able to generate an appropriate procedure oneself or understanding the quantitative significance of each step in the procedure and its relationship to the goal specified in the problem.

Adopting a prospective developmental perspective is largely a matter of thinking carefully about how to teach the content we already teach, so as to ensure that children come to know it in a way that they can build on as their learning advances. But because correct performance on any given task may be obtained in a number of ways, the goal of fostering developmentally important ways of knowing cannot be satisfied by simply adding new tasks to the early childhood curriculum and ensuring that children learn to perform them correctly. The inclusion of greater diversity in the counting activities we present to young children can be valuable, but it is critical to keep the focus on how children think about the activities they are engaged in and not just on whether or not they get the right answers.

In part because of the historical emphasis on performance rather than understanding in schools, a widespread view is that it is important not to confront children with problems that are too difficult for them. But, insofar as the goal of instruction is to promote new ways of thinking, this approach may do more harm than good. Mathematical problems that are sufficiently rich to stimulate advances in children's thinking are not likely to fit neatly within prescribed levels of difficulty. Instead, they will generally be amenable to analysis at a range of levels, some of which are certain to be beyond a young child's grasp. Thus, in developing a curriculum that addresses the development of mathematical thinking, it is important to recognize that children need not be able to understand a problem at all levels in order to benefit from working with it.

For instance, consider the suggestion I have made that young children be encouraged to explore the results of using different sizes of objects as measurement units. There are many aspects of this activity that are unlikely to be fully understood by preschool or kindergarten-age children. Measurement is a complex concept, involving conservation, transitive inference, and indeed the notion of a unit itself. But children do not need to understand all of this in order to make sense of the activity and to learn from it. They do not even need to realize that what they are doing is measuring objects, albeit with unconventional units. What matters is that the activity gives them an opportunity to discover that, for certain kinds of numerical activities, the sizes of objects are critically important. Likewise, observing the numerical consequences of applying different-size units to a series of objects is a concrete way of stimulating children's thinking about numerical relations. Multiplicative relationships among numbers are unlikely to be familiar to preschool and kindergarten children, but some children may gain insight into them by seeing the patterns of numbers they get as they apply different sizes of units to various objects (especially if the unit sizes are chosen so that one unit is a simple multiple of the other, e.g., twice as long or twice as heavy). Others may only notice the ordinal regularities in the results—for example, that when the smaller counters were used, more of them were needed to cover a given length. This too is a valuable discovery, as an understanding of inverse relations is critical to making sense of ratios and fractions.

Though I have focused here on the problems students have with fraction learning and on how looking ahead to that challenge might inform the design of early mathematics instruction, in closing I want to underscore that the notion of a prospective developmental perspective is much broader than this. In general terms, the recommendation I am making is that the design of mathematics instruction for early childhood be informed by consideration of the long-range goals and challenges of mathematics education as well as by an analysis of what very young children know and can learn. Thinking about what children will need to know in order to make sense of fractions served as a useful illustration of this idea because we know enough about the difficulties children have with fractions to make some tangible suggestions about how early childhood mathematics instruction could help. In other arenas, too, we need to look closely at our long-term instructional goals, at where difficulties arise as we undertake to meet those goals, and at how we might prepare children for those challenges in the ways we teach them in the very first years of schooling. Where we do not have sufficient knowledge to answer these questions, the prospective developmental perspective may serve as a useful tool in framing a research agenda as well as in formulating instructional goals.

## ACKNOWLEDGMENTS

The author gratefully acknowledges support received from National Institutes of Health Grant 1 RO1 HD37378 and from a Head Start—University Partnerships grant (B. DeBaryshe, PI), which made possible the research reported here.

## REFERENCES

Davydov, V. V. (1991). The object sources of the concept of fractions. In V. V. Davydov (Ed.), *Soviet studies in mathematics education* (Vol. 6, pp. 86–147). Reston, VA: National Council of Teachers of Mathematics.

Frydman, O., & Bryant, P. (1988). Sharing and the understanding of number equivalence by young children. *Cognitive Development, 3,* 323–339.

Gal'perin, P., & Georgiev, L. S. (1969). The formation of elementary mathematical notions. In J. Kilpatrick & I. Wirszup (Eds.), *Soviet studies in the psychology of learning and teaching mathematics: Vol. 1. The learning of mathematical concepts* (pp. 189–216). Chicago: University of Chicago Press.

Miller, K. F. (1984). The child as the measurer of all things: Measurement procedures and the development of quantitative concepts. In C. Sophian (Ed.), *Origins of cognitive skills* (pp. 193–228). Hillsdale, NJ: Lawrence Erlbaum Associates.

Resnick, L. B. (1982). Syntax and semantics in learning to subtract. In T. P. Carpenter, J. M. Moser, & T. A. Rombert (Eds.), *Addition and subtraction: A cognitive perspective* (pp. 25–38). Hillsdale, NJ: Lawrence Erlbaum Associates.

Shipley, E. F., & Shepperson, B. (1990). Countable entities: Developmental changes. *Cognition, 34,* 109–136.

Sophian, C. (1999). Children's ways of knowing: Lessons from cognitive development research. In J. Copley (Ed.), *Mathematics in the early years* (pp. 11–20). Reston, VA: National Council of Teachers of Mathematics.

Sophian, C. (2000). Perceptions of proportionality in young children: Matching spatial ratios. *Cognition, 75,* 145–170.

Sophian, C. (2002). Learning about what fits: Preschool children's reasoning about effects of object size. *Journal for Research in Mathematics Education, 33,* 290–302.

Sophian, C., & Dulloog, L. (2000). *Persisting semantic errors in judgments about fraction magnitudes.* Unpublished manuscript.

Sophian, C., & Kailihiwa, C. (1998). Units of counting: Developmental changes. *Cognitive Development, 13,* 561–585.

Sophian, C., & Yamashita, E. (2000). *Developmental changes in the impact of numerical information on children's proportionality judgments.* Unpublished manuscript.

Van Lehn, K. (1983). On the representation of procedures in repair theory. In H. P. Ginsburg (Ed.), *The development of mathematical thinking* (pp. 197–252). New York: Academic Press.

# 10

# Geometric and Spatial Thinking in Early Childhood Education

Douglas H. Clements
*University at Buffalo, State University of New York*

Geometry and spatial reasoning are inherently important because they involve "grasping ... that space in which the child lives, breathes and moves ... that space that the child must learn to know, explore, conquer, in order to live, breathe and move better in it" (Freudenthal, in National Council of Teachers of Mathematics [NCTM], 1989, p. 48). In addition, especially for early childhood, geometry and spatial reasoning form the foundation of much learning of mathematics and other subjects.

Although our knowledge of young children's geometric and spatial thinking is not as extensive as that of their numerical thinking, it has grown substantially and can be used as a basis for curriculum development and teaching. Here, we briefly review these two main areas of this research: shape and transformation (two-dimensional [2-D] figures; angle; three-dimensional [3-D] figures; congruence, symmetry, and transformations; composition and decomposition) and spatial thinking (spatial orientation: maps and navigation; and spatial visualization and imagery). We conclude with implications for curriculum and instruction in early childhood geometry.

## SHAPE AND TRANSFORMATION

### 2-D Geometric Figures

Too often, teachers and curriculum writers assume that children in early childhood classrooms have little or no knowledge of geometric figures.

267

Furthermore, teachers have had few experiences with geometry in their own education or in their professional development. Thus, it is unsurprising that most classrooms exhibit limited geometry instruction. One early study found that kindergarten children had a great deal of knowledge about shapes and matching shapes before instruction began. Their teacher tended to elicit and verify this prior knowledge but did not add content or develop new knowledge. That is, about two thirds of the interactions had children repeat what they already knew in a repetitious format as in the following exchange (Thomas, 1982):

Teacher:     Could you tell us what type of shape that is?
Children:    A square.
Teacher:     Okay. It's a square.

A more recent study confirmed that current practices in the primary grades also promote little conceptual change: First-grade students in one study were more likely than older children to differentiate one polygon from another by counting sides or vertices (Lehrer, Jenkins, & Osana, 1998). Over time, children were *less* likely to notice these attributes, given conventional instruction of geometry in the elementary grades.

Such neglect evinces itself in student achievement. Students are not prepared for learning more sophisticated geometry, especially when compared to students of other nations (Carpenter, Corbitt, Kepner, Lindquist, & Reys, 1980; Fey et al., 1984; Kouba et al., 1988; Stevenson, Lee, & Stigler, 1986; Stigler, Lee, & Stevenson, 1990). In the recent TIMMS work, U.S. students scored at or near bottom in every geometry task (Beaton et al., 1996; Lappan, 1999).

Such comparisons may be present even among preschoolers in various countries (Starkey et al., 1999). On a geometry assessment, 4-year-olds from America scored 55% compared to those from China at 84%. Thus, cultural supports are lacking from the earliest years in the United States.

How do children think and learn about shapes? It is possible they are born with a tendency to form certain mental prototypes. People in a Stone Age culture with no geometric concepts were asked to choose a "best example" of a group of shapes[1], such as a group of quadrilaterals and near-quadrilaterals (Rosch, 1975). People chose a square and circle more often, even when close variants were in the group. For example, the group with squares included squarelike shapes that were not closed, had curved sides, and had nonright angles. So, people might have "built-in" preferences for closed, symmetric shapes (cf. Bornstein, Ferdinandsen, & Gross, 1981).

Culture shapes these preferences. We conducted an extensive examination of materials that teach children about shapes from books, toy stores, teacher supply stores, and catalogs. With few exceptions (and with

---

[1]Of course, all physical shapes are 3-D; however, we follow common usage in referring to, for instance, a triangle pattern block as a "triangle" (instead of a pattern block with a triangle face).

signs that this is changing in recent years), these materials introduce children to triangles, rectangles, and squares in rigid ways. Triangles are usually equilateral or isosceles and have horizontal bases. Most rectangles are horizontal, elongated shapes about twice as long as they are wide. No wonder so many children, even throughout elementary school, say that a square turned is "not a square anymore, it's a diamond" (cf. Lehrer et al., 1998). Research indicates that such rigid visual prototypes can rule children's thinking throughout their lives (Burger & Shaughnessy, 1986; Fisher, 1978; Fuys, Geddes, & Tischler, 1988; Kabanova-Meller, 1970; Vinner & Hershkowitz, 1980; Zykova, 1969).

Specifically, what visual prototypes and ideas do preschool children form about common shapes? Decades ago, Fuson and Murray (1978) reported that by 3 years of age more than 60% of children could name a circle, square, and triangle. More recently, Klein, Starkey, and Wakeley (1999) reported shape-naming accuracy of 5-year-olds as: circle, 85%; square, 78%; triangle, 80%; rectangle, 44%.

We recently conducted several studies with hundreds of children, ages 3 to 6 years. In the first study (Clements, Swaminathan, Hannibal, & Sarama, 1999), we used the same line drawings we previously used with elementary students for comparison purposes. Children identified circles quite accurately: 92%, 96%, and 99% for 4-, 5-, and 6-year-olds, respectively. Only a few of the youngest children chose the ellipse and curved shape (Fig. 10.1). Most children described circles as "round," if they described them at all. Thus, the circle was easily recognized but relatively difficult to describe for these children. Evidence suggests that they matched the shapes to a visual prototype.

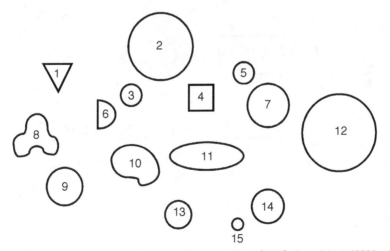

FIG. 10.1.   Student marks circles. From Razel and Eylon (1991). Copyright © 1991 by the authors. Adapted by permission.

Children also identified squares fairly well: 82%, 86%, and 91% for 4-, 5-, and 6-year-olds, respectively. Younger children tended to mistakenly choose nonsquare rhombi ("diamonds" such as No. 3 in Fig. 10.2). However, they were no less accurate in classifying squares without horizontal sides (Nos. 5 and 11). Children were more likely to be accurate in their square identification when their justifications for selection were based on the shape's attributes (e.g., number and length of sides).

They were less accurate at recognizing triangles and rectangles. However, their scores were not low; about 60% correct for triangles (see Fig. 10.3). Children's visual prototype seems to be of an isosceles triangle.

Young children tended to accept "long" parallelograms or right trapezoids (Shapes 3, 6, 10, and 14 in Fig. 10.4) as rectangles. Thus, children's visual prototype of a rectangle seems to be a four-sided figure with two long parallel sides and "close to" square corners.

Although young children in this study were less accurate recognizing triangles and rectangles, their results are not remarkably smaller than those of elementary students (Clements, Battista, & Sarama, 2001) as shown in Figs. 10.5 and 10.6 (in addition, many of the elementary students were from relatively high socioeconomic status [SES] populations). Indeed, for all shapes assessed two trends were evident. First, as discussed previously, very young children possess knowledge of geometric figures. Second, children show a steady, but hardly remarkable, improvement from preschool through the elementary grades.

In the second study, we asked children ages 3 to 6 to sort a variety of manipulative forms. We found that certain mathematically irrelevant characteristics affected children's categorizations: skewness, aspect ratio, and,

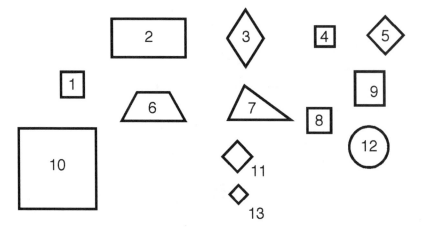

FIG. 10.2.   Student marks squares. From Razel and Eylon (1991). Copyright © 1991 by the authors. Adapted by permission.

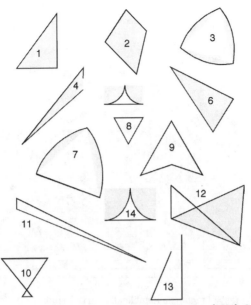

FIG. 10.3.   Student marks triangles. From Clements and Battista (1991). Copyright © 1991 by the authors. Adapted by permission from Burger and Shaughnessy (1986), Journal for Research in Mathematics Education, copyright © 1986 by the National Council of Teachers of Mathematics.

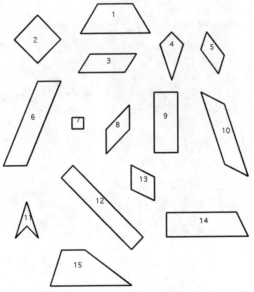

FIG. 10.4.   Student marks rectangles. From Clements and Battista (1991). Copyright © 1991 by the authors. Adapted by permission from Burger and Shaughnessy (1986), Journal for Research in Mathematics Education, copyright © 1986 by the National Council of Teachers of Mathematics.

Rectangles

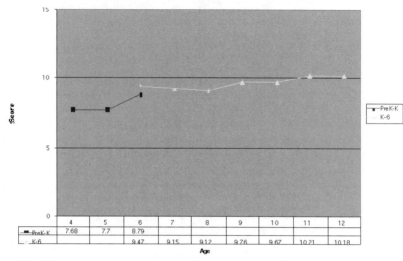

| Age | 4 | 5 | 6 | 7 | 8 | 9 | 10 | 11 | 12 |
|---|---|---|---|---|---|---|---|---|---|
| PreK-K | 7.68 | 7.7 | 8.79 | | | | | | |
| K-6 | | | 9.47 | 9.15 | 9.12 | 9.76 | 9.67 | 10.21 | 10.18 |

FIG. 10.5.   Accuracy of rectangle identification in two studies

Triangles

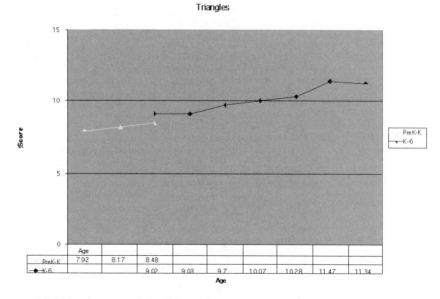

| Age | | | | | | | | | |
|---|---|---|---|---|---|---|---|---|---|
| PreK-K | 7.92 | 8.17 | 8.48 | | | | | | |
| K-6 | | | 9.02 | 9.03 | 9.7 | 10.07 | 10.28 | 11.47 | 11.34 |

FIG. 10.6.   Accuracy of triangle identification in two studies.

for certain situations, orientation. With these manipulatives, orientation had the least effect. Most children accepted triangles even if their base was not horizontal, although a few protested. Skewness, or lack of symmetry, was more important. Many rejected triangles because "the point on top is not in the middle." For rectangles, on the other hand, many children accepted nonright parallelograms and right trapezoids. Also important was aspect ratio, the ratio of height to base. Children preferred an aspect ratio near one for triangles, that is, about the same height as width. Other forms were "too pointy" or "too flat." Children rejected both triangles and rectangles that were "too skinny" or "not wide enough."

These are simple tasks, chosen initially for their consistency with other research-based tasks and traditional curricular goals. Yet they do illustrate both the strength of children's initial competencies and the weakness of the cultural and instructional support for building upon them. Further, children's capabilities exceed naming, describing, and sorting shapes. We turn to additional aspects of children's knowledge of shape and spatial structure.

## Angle and Turn

Angles are turning points in the study of geometry and spatial relationships. Unfortunately, one does not have to turn far for examples of children's difficulty with the angle concept (Lindquist & Kouba, 1989). Children have many different ideas about what an angle is. These ideas include "a shape," a side of a figure, a tilted line, an orientation or heading, a corner, a turn, and a union of two lines (Clements & Battista, 1990). Students do not find angles to be salient attributes of figures (Clements, Battista, Sarama, & Swaminathan, 1996; Mitchelmore, 1989). When copying figures, students do not always attend to the angles.

Similarly, regarding the size of angles, children frequently focus on the length of the line segments that form its sides, the tilt of the top line segment, the area enclosed by the triangular region defined by the drawn sides, the length between the sides, or the proximity of the two sides (Clements & Battista, 1989). Some misconceptions decrease over the elementary years, such as orientation; but others, such as the effect of segment length, do not change, and some, such as the distance between end points, increase (Lehrer et al., 1998).

Nevertheless, there are some initial competencies on which instruction might build. Preschoolers use angles intuitively in their play, such as block building (Ginsburg, Inoue, & Seo, 1999). In an early study, though 5-year-olds showed no evidence of attention to angle in judging congruence, they could match angles in correspondence tasks (Beilin, 1984; Beilin, Klein, & Whitehurst, 1982). Some primary-grade children can distinguish between angles based on size (Lehrer et al., 1998).

There is some research on instructional approaches that attempt to develop these early abilities. One uses multiple concrete analogies (Mitchelmore, 1993). Practical experience in various situations (e.g., turns, slopes, meetings, bends, directions, corners, opening) helps children understand angular relationships in each situation individually. Gradually, children develop general angle concepts by recognizing common features of these situations. Research on teaching activities based on these ideas revealed that most elementary-age students understood physical relations. Turn, or rotation, was a difficult concept to understand in concrete physical contexts.

Other research supports the importance of integration across situations and ideas. One study took as the starting point children's experience with physical rotations, especially rotations of their own bodies (Clements et al., 1996). During the same time, they gained limited knowledge of assigning numbers to certain turns, initially by establishing benchmarks. A synthesis of these two domains—turn-as-body-motion and turn-as-number—constituted a critical juncture in learning about turns for many elementary students. This and other studies have used the Logo turtle to help children mathematize[2] their physical experiences.

Related topics include parallel and perpendicular lines. Both are difficult concepts for students in some applications. However, children as young as 3 and 4 years use parallelism in alignment tasks and 6-year-olds can name parallel and nonparallel lines, although they have difficulty locating parallels in complex figures (Mitchelmore, 1992).

Teaching Australian Grade 1 students about perpendicular lines was abandoned because students were unable to conceptualize perpendiculars as lines in a special angular relationship (Mitchelmore, 1992). However, as noted, preschoolers deliberately use parallelisms and perpendicularly intuitively in their block-building play (Ginsburg et al., 1999). It remains to be seen if curricula and teaching approaches that build on these early beginnings can effectively facilitate lasting learning outcomes.

## 3-D Figures

Similar to findings regarding 2-D figures, students do not perform well with 3-D shapes. Most intermediate-grade students have difficulty naming solids (Carpenter, Coburn, Reys, & Wilson, 1976). South African first graders used different names for solids (such as "square" for cube) but were capable of understanding and remembering features they discussed (Nieuwoudt & van Niekerk, 1997). U.S. students' reasoning about solids was much like that about plane figures; they referred to a variety of characteristics, such as "pointyness" and comparative size or slenderness (Lehrer et al., 1998). Students also treated the solid wooden figures as

---

[2]We define mathematization as representing and elaborating mathematically—creating models of an everyday activity with mathematical objects, such as numbers and shapes; mathematical actions, such as counting or transforming shapes; and their structural relationships. Mathematizing involves reinventing, redescribing, reorganizing, quantifying, structuring, abstracting, and generalizing that which is first understood on an intuitive and informal level in the context of everyday activity.

malleable, suggesting that the rectangular prism could be transformed into a cube by "sitting on it."

Use of plane figure names for solids may indicate a lack of discrimination between two and three dimensions (Carpenter et al., 1976). Learning only plane figures in textbooks during the early primary grades may cause some initial difficulty in learning solids. Construction activities involving nets (foldout shapes of solids) may be valuable as they require children to switch between more-analytic 2-D and synthetic 3-D situations (Nieuwoudt & van Niekerk, 1997).

## Congruence, Symmetry, and Transformations

Young children develop beginning ideas not just about shapes, but also about congruence and transformations. Although many young children judge congruence (Are these two shapes "the same"?) based on whether they are, on the whole, more similar than different (Vurpillot, 1976), even 4-year-olds and some younger children can generate strategies for verifying congruence for some tasks. Preschoolers often try to judge congruence using an edge-matching strategy, although only about 50% can do it successfully (Beilin, 1984; Beilin et al., 1982). They gradually develop a greater awareness of the type of differences between figures that are considered relevant and move from considering various parts of shapes to considering the spatial relationships of these parts (Vurpillot, 1976). In about first grade, they consider both multiple attributes and their spatial relationships and begin to use superposition. Thus, strategies supercede one another in development (e.g., motion-based superposition) becoming more powerful, sophisticated, geometrical, and accurate.

Other studies have focused on geometric motions. Some have reported that younger students' abilities are slight. For example, one study showed that second graders learned manual procedures for producing transformation images but did not learn to mentally perform such transformations (Williford, 1972). In contrast, other studies indicate that even young children can learn something about these motions and appear to internalize them, as indicated by increases on spatial ability tests (Clements, Battista, Sarama, & Swaminathan, 1997; Del Grande, 1986). Slides appear to be the easiest motions for students, then flips and turns (Perham, 1978); however, the direction of transformation may affect the relative difficulty of turn and flip (Schultz & Austin, 1983). Results depend on specific tasks, of course; even 4- to 5-year olds can do turns if they have simple tasks and orientation cues (Rosser, Ensing, Glider, & Lane, 1984). Furthermore, some studies indicate that second-grade students are capable of mental rotation involving imagery (Perham, 1978; Rosser, Lane, & Mazzeo, 1988).

Under the right conditions, children of all ages can apply similarity transformations to shapes. Even 4- and 5-year-olds can identify similar shapes in some circumstances (Sophian & Crosby, 1998). The coordination of height and width information to perceive the proportional shape of a rectangle (fat vs. skinny, wide or tall) might be a basic way of accessing proportionality information. This may serve as a foundation for other types of proportionality, especially fractions. Similarly, other research shows first graders can engage in and benefit from similarity tasks (Confrey, 1992).

Children have intuitive notions of symmetry from the earliest years (Vurpillot, 1976). Symmetric stimuli are not only preferred but are consistently detected faster, discriminated more accurately, and often remembered better than asymmetrical ones. Preference for vertical symmetry develops between 4 and 12 months of age (Bornstein et al., 1981) and vertical bilateral symmetry remains easier for students to handle than horizontal symmetry (Genkins, 1975). However, many concepts of symmetry are not firmly established before 12 years of age (Genkins, 1975). Julie Sarama has noticed that children often use and refer to rotational symmetry as much as they do line symmetry in working with pattern blocks (Sarama, Clements, & Vukelic, 1996).

Computer environments can be particularly helpful in learning congruence, transformations, and symmetry (Clements, Battista et al., 2001). Indeed, the effects of Logo microworlds on symmetry were particularly strong for young (kindergarten) students. Writing Logo commands for the creation of symmetric figures, testing symmetry by flipping figures via commands, and discussing these actions apparently encouraged students to build richer and more general images of symmetric relations (with possibly some overgeneralization). Students had to abstract and externally represent their actions in a more explicit and precise fashion in Logo activities than, say, in free-hand drawing of symmetric figures.

## Composition and Decomposition

Another of the many processes young children can perform with geometric shapes is composition. I take this opportunity here to both overview the research on children's composing and decomposing competencies and illustrate how research can be used to go beyond "checklist" approaches to curriculum. The following is a research-based developmental sequence, or learning trajectory, that approximately spans ages 4 to 8 years. (This learning trajectory, first noted in Sarama et al., 1996, has been explicated by these researchers in and for the *Building Blocks* project; Clements, Sarama, & Wilson, 2001.) The basic competence is combining shapes to produce composite shapes.[3] At each level, a child does the following (see Table 1.2 in chap. 1, this volume for a synopsis and illustrations):

1. *Precomposer.* Children manipulate shapes as individuals, but are unable to combine them to compose a larger shape. For example, children

---

[3]The notion of creating and then iterating units and higher order units to construct patterns, measure, or compute has been established as a basis for mathematical understanding and analysis (Steffe & Cobb, 1988).

might use a single shape for a sun, a separate shape for a tree, and another separate shape for a person.

2. *Piece Assembler.* Children at this level are similar to precomposers, but they can concatenate shapes to form pictures. In free-form "make a picture" tasks, for example, each shape used represents a unique role, or function in the picture (e.g., one shape for one leg). Children can fill simple frames using trial and error (Mansfield & Scott, 1990; Sales, 1994), but have limited ability to use turns or flips to do so; they cannot use motions to see shapes from different perspectives (Sarama et al., 1996). Thus, children at the first two levels view shapes only as wholes and see few geometric relationships between shapes or between parts of shapes (i.e., a property of the shape).

3. *Picture Maker.* Children can concatenate shapes to form pictures in which several shapes play a single role (e.g., a leg might be created from three contiguous squares), but use trial and error and do not anticipate creation of new geometric shapes. Shapes are chosen using gestalt configuration or one component such as side length (Sarama et al., 1996). If several sides of the existing arrangement form a partial boundary of a shape (instantiating a schema for it), the child can find and place that shape. If such cues are not present, the child matches by a side length. The child may attempt to match corners, but does not possess angle as a quantitative entity, so they try to match shapes into corners of existing arrangements in which their angles do not fit. Rotating and flipping are used, usually by trial and error, to try different arrangements (a "picking and discarding" strategy). Thus, they can complete a frame that suggests that placement of the individual shapes but in which several shapes together may play a single semantic role in the picture.

4. *Shape Composer.* Children combine shapes to make new shapes or fill puzzles, with growing intentionality and anticipation ("I know what will fit"). Shapes are chosen using angles as well as side lengths. Eventually, the child considers several alternative shapes with angles equal to the existing arrangement. Rotation and flipping are used intentionally (and mentally, i.e., with anticipation) to select and place shapes (Sarama et al., 1996). They can fill complex frames (Sales, 1994) or cover regions (Mansfield & Scott, 1990). Imagery and systematicity grow within this and the following levels. In summary, there is intentionality and anticipation, based on the shapes' attributes, and thus, the child has imagery of the component shapes, although imagery of the composite shape develops within this level (and throughout the following levels).

5. *Substitution Composer.* Children deliberately form composite units of shapes (Clements, Battista, Sarama, & Swaminathan, 1997) and recognize and use substitution relationships among these shapes (e.g., two pattern block trapezoids can make a hexagon).

6. *Shape Composite Iterater.* Children construct and operate on composite units intentionally. They can continue a pattern of shapes that leads to a "good covering," but without coordinating units of units (Clements, Battista, Sarama, & Swaminathan, 1997).

7. *Shape Composer with Superordinate Units.* Children build and apply (iterate and otherwise operate on) units of units of units.

These levels represent a synthesis across divergent studies. We are in the process of empirically evaluating the validity of this sequence with a cross-sectional approach and designing off- and on-computer activities for each level for evaluation with teaching experiments (see Sarama, chap. 15, this volume).

## SPATIAL THINKING

Why do we need to develop children's "spatial sense," especially in mathematics classes? Spatial ability and mathematics achievement are related (Fennema & Sherman, 1977, 1978; Guay & McDaniel, 1977; Lean & Clements, 1981; Wheatley, 1990). Though we do not fully understand why and how, children who have strong spatial sense do better at mathematics. To have spatial sense you need spatial abilities. Two major abilities are spatial orientation and spatial visualization (Bishop, 1980; Harris, 1981; McGee, 1979).

### Spatial Orientation: Maps and Navigation

Spatial orientation—knowing the shape of one's environment—represents a domain of early cognitive strength for young children. It is probably a "core domain"—a "built-in" area of knowledge that includes the ability to actively and selectively seek out pertinent information and certain interpretations of ambiguous information (Gelman & Williams, 1997). Toddlers, for example, eschew other cues and instead use geometric information about the overall shape of their environment to solve location tasks.

Spatial orientation is knowing where you are and how to get around in the world, that is, understanding and operating on relationships between different positions in space, especially with respect to your own position. Young children learn practical navigation early—as all adults responsible for their care will attest. Channeling that experience is valuable. For example, when nursery school children tutor others in guided environments, they build geometrical concepts (Filippaki & Papamichael, 1997).

Young children can mathematize their experiences with navigation. They can use and create simple maps and begin to build mental representations of their spatial environments. This is illustrated in 3-year-olds' building of simple, but meaningful maps with landscape toys such as houses, cars, and trees (Blaut & Stea, 1974); however, we know less about what specific abilities and strategies they use to do so. For example, kindergarten children making models of their classroom cluster furniture correctly (e.g., they put the furniture for a dramatic play center together), but may not relate the clusters to each other (Siegel & Schadler, 1977). Also unclear is what kind of "mental maps" young children possess. Some researchers believe that people first learn to navigate only by noticing landmarks, then by routes, or connected series of landmarks, then by scaled routes, and finally by putting many routes and locations into a kind of "mental map." Only older preschoolers learn scaled routes for familiar paths; that is, they know about the relative distances between landmarks (Anooshian, Pascal, & McCreath, 1984). Even young children, however, can put different locations along a route into some relationship, at least in certain situations. For example, they can point to one location from another even though they never walked a path that connected the two (Uttal & Wellman, 1989). A significant proportion (40%) of 4-year-olds only can not identify that a direct and indirect route to a given location are not the same distance, but can explain why the direct route was shorter (Fabricius & Wellman, 1993).

Developing spatial orientation competencies, and eventually understanding maps, is a long-term process. Children slowly develop many different ways to represent the locations of objects in space. Infants associate objects as being near a person such as a parent (Presson & Somerville, 1985), but cannot associate objects to distance landmarks. Toddlers and 3-year-olds can place objects in prespecified locations near distant landmarks, but "lose" locations that are not specified ahead of time once they move. Children as young as 3.5 years were able, like adults, to accurately walk along a path that replicated the route between their seat and the teacher's desk in their preschool classroom (Rieser, Garing, & Young, 1994). They can build imagery of locations and use it, but they must physically move to show their competence. So, they may be able to form simple frameworks, such as the shape of the arrangement of several objects, that has to include their own location. With no landmarks, even 4-year-olds make mistakes (Huttenlocher & Newcombe, 1984). Kindergartners build local frameworks that are less dependent on their own position. They still rely, however, on relational cues such as being close to a boundary. By third grade, children can use larger, encompassing frameworks that include the observer of the situation.

Neither children nor adults actually have "maps in their heads"—that is, their "mental maps" are not like a mental picture of a paper map. Instead, they are filled with private knowledge and idiosyncrasies and actually consist of many kinds of ideas and processes. These may be organized into several frames of reference. The younger the child, the more loosely linked these representations are. These representations are spatial more than visual. Blind children are aware of spatial relationships by age 2, and by 3 begin to learn about spatial characteristics of certain visual language (Landau, 1988).

What about physical maps? We have seen that 3-year-olds have some capabilities building simple "maps." There are many individual differences in such abilities. In one study, most preschoolers rebuilt a room better using real furniture than toy models. For some children, however, the difference was slight. Others placed real furniture correctly, but grouped the toy models only around the perimeter. Some children placed the models and real furniture randomly, showing few capabilities (Liben, 1988). Even children with similar mental representations may produce quite different maps due to differences in drawing and map-building skills (Uttal & Wellman, 1989).

Most children can learn *from* maps. For example, 4- to 7-year-olds had to learn a route through a playhouse with six rooms. Children who examined a map beforehand learned a route more quickly than those who did not (Uttal & Wellman, 1989). Similarly, 5- to 6-year-olds can use maps to navigate their way out of a cave (Jovignot, 1995). As with adults, then, children learn layouts better from maps than from navigation alone. Even preschoolers know that a map represents space (Liben & Yekel, 1996). More than 6- or 7-year-olds, however, they have trouble knowing where they are in the space. Therefore, they have difficulty using information available from the map relevant to their own position (Uttal & Wellman, 1989). Preschoolers, like older people, could preserve the configuration of objects when reconstructing a room depicted on a map. However, preschoolers placed objects far from correct locations and performed worse with asymmetric than symmetric configurations (Uttal, 1996). They have difficulty aligning maps to the referent space (Liben & Yekel, 1996). They may understand that symbols on maps represent objects but have limited understanding of the geometric correspondence between maps and the referent space; both understandings are developing, but have far to go, by the end of the preschool years (Liben & Yekel, 1996). By the primary grades, most children are able to draw simple sketch maps of the area around their home from memory. They also can recognize features on aerial photographs and large-scale plans of the same area (Boardman, 1990).

What accounts for differences and age-related changes? Maturation and development are significant. Children need mental processing capacity to update directions and location. The older they get, the more spatial memories they can store and transformations they can perform. Such increase in processing capacity, along with general experience, determines how a space is represented more than the amount of experience with the particular space (Anooshian et al., 1984). Both general development and learning are important. Instruction on spatial ability, symbolization, and metacognitive skills (consciously self-regulated map-reading behavior through strategic map referral) can increase 4- to 6-year-olds' competence with reading route maps, although it does not overcome age-related differences; Frank, 1987) .

Though young children possess impressive initial abilities, they have much to learn about maps. For example, preschoolers recognized roads on a map, but suggested that the tennis courts were doors (Liben & Downs, 1989)! In addition, older students are not competent users of maps. School experiences fail to connect map skills with other curriculum areas, such as mathematics (Muir & Cheek, 1986).

Fundamental is the connection of primary to secondary uses of maps (Presson, 1987). Even young children form primary, direct relations to spaces on maps. They must grow in their ability to treat the spatial relations as separate from their immediate environment. These secondary meanings require people to take the perspective of an abstract frame of reference ("as if you were there") that conflicts with the primary meaning. You no longer imagine yourself "inside," but rather must see yourself at a distance, or "outside," the information. Such meanings of maps challenge people into adulthood, especially when the map is not aligned with the part of the world it represents (Uttal & Wellman, 1989). Using oblique maps (e.g., tables are show with legs) aids preschoolers' subsequent performance on plan ("bird's-eye view") maps (Liben & Yekel, 1996). However, these must not be overly simple iconic picture maps, but must challenge children to use geometric correspondences. Adults need to connect the abstract and concrete meanings of map symbols. Similarly, many of young children's difficulties do not reflect misunderstanding about space, but the conflict between such concrete and abstract frames of reference. In summary, children (a) develop abilities to build relationships among objects in space, (b) extend the size of that space, and (c) link primary and secondary meanings and uses of spatial information.

These findings reemphasize that we must be careful how we interpret the phrase "mental map." Spatial information may be different when it is garnered from primary and secondary sources, such as maps.

What about the mathematics of maps? Developing children's ability to make and use mental maps is important, and so is developing geometric ideas from experiences with maps. We should go beyond teaching isolated "map skills" and geography to engage in actual mapping, surveying, drawing, and measuring in local environments (Bishop, 1983). Such activities can begin in the early years.

Our goal is for children to both read and make maps meaningfully. In both of these endeavors, four basic questions arise: direction—which way?, distance—how far?, location—where?, and identification—what objects? To answer these questions, students need to develop a variety of skills. Children must learn to deal with mapping processes of abstraction, generalization, and symbolization. Some map symbols are icons, such as an airplane for an airport, but others are more abstract, such as circles for cities. Children might first build with objects such as model buildings, then draw pictures of the objects' arrangements, then use maps that are "miniaturizations" and those that use abstract symbols. Some symbols may be beneficial even to young children. Overreliance on literal pictures and icons may hinder understanding of maps, leading children to believe, for example, that certain actual roads are red (Downs, Liben, & Daggs, 1988).

Similarly, children need to develop more sophisticated ideas about *direction* and *location*. Young children should master environmental directions, such as above, over, and behind. They should develop navigation ideas, such as left, right, and front, and global directions such as north, east, west, and south, from these beginnings. Perspective and direction are particularly important regarding the alignment of the map with the world. Some children of any age will find it difficult to use a map that is not so aligned. Teachers should introduce such situations gradually and perhaps only when necessary.

Young children can learn to relate various reference frames, which brings us to the notion of coordinates. The Piagetian position is that coordinate frameworks are analogical to a container made up of a network of sites or positions (Piaget & Inhelder, 1967). Objects within this container may be mobile, but the positions are stationary. From the simultaneous organization of all possible positions in three dimensions emerges the coordinate system. This involves the gradual replacement of relations of order and distance between objects with similar relations between the positions themselves. The space is "emptied of objects." Thus, intuition of space is not an innate apprehension of the properties of objects, but a system of relationships borne in actions performed on these objects.

In this arena, as in others, we see there is a long developmental process, but some early competencies on which to build. For example, very young children can orient a horizontal or vertical line in space (Rosser, Horan, Mattson, & Mazzeo, 1984). Similarly, 4- to 6-year-old children (a) can extrapolate lines from positions on both axes and determine where they intersect, (b) are equally successful going from point to coordinate as going from coordinate to point, and (c) can extrapolate as well with or without grid lines (Somerville & Bryant, 1985). Piagetian theory seems correct in postulating that the coordination of relations develops after such early abilities. Young students fail on double-axis orientation tasks even when misleading perceptual cues are eliminated (Rosser, Horan et al., 1984). Similarly, the greatest difficulty is coordinating two extrapolations, which has its developmental origins at the 3- to 4-year-old level, with the ability to extrapolate those lines developing as much as a year earlier (Somerville, Bryant, Mazzocco, & Johnson, 1987). These results suggest an initial inability to utilize a conceptual coordinate system as an organizing spatial framework (Liben & Yekel, 1996). Some 4-year-olds can use a coordinate reference system, whereas most 6-year-olds can (Blades & Spencer, 1989). However, 4-year-olds can coordinating dimensions if the task is set in a meaningful context in which the orthogonal dimensions are cued by the line of sights of imaginary people (Bremner, Andreasen, Kendall, & Adams, 1993).

Coordinate of coordinates is not limited to two orthogonal dimensions. Children as young as 5 years can metrically represent spatial information in a polar coordinate task, using the same two dimensions as adults radius and angle, although children do not use categorizations of those dimensions until age 9 (Sandberg & Huttenlocher, 1996).

In summary, even young children can use coordinates that adults provide for them. However, when facing traditional tasks, they and their older peers may not yet be able or predisposed to spontaneously make and use coordinates for themselves.

Computer activities can facilitate learning of navigational and map skills. Young children can abstract and generalize directions and other map concepts working with the Logo turtle (Borer, 1993; Clements, Battista, Sarama, Swaminathan, & McMillen, 1997; Clements & Meredith, 1994; Goodrow, Clements, Battista, Sarama, & Akers, 1997; Kull, 1986; Try, 1989; Watson, Lange, & Brinkley, 1992; Weaver, 1991) although results are not guaranteed . The interface must be appropriate and activities must be well planned (Watson & Brinkley, 1990/1991). Giving the turtle directions such as forward 10 steps, right turn, forward 5 steps, they learn orientation, direction, and perspective concepts, among others. Walking paths and then re-creating those paths on the computer help them abstract, generalize, and symbolize their experiences navigating. For example, one kindergartner abstracted the geometric notion of "path" saying, "A path is like the trail a bug leaves after it walks through purple paint."

Logo can also control a floor turtle robot, which may have special benefits for certain populations. For example, blind and partially sighted children using a computer-guided floor turtle developed spatial concepts such as right and left and accurate facing movements (Gay, 1989).

Other simple (non-Logo) navigational programs may have similar benefits. For example, using such software (with on-screen navigation) has shown to increase kindergartners' understanding of the concepts of left and right (Carlson & White, 1998).

Coordinate-based games on computers can help older children learning location ideas (Clements, Sarama, Gòmez, Swaminathan, & McMillen, in press). When children enter a coordinate to move an object but it goes to a different location, the feedback is natural, meaningful, nonevaluative, and so particularly helpful.

Many people believe that maps are "transparent"—that anyone can "see through" the map immediately to the world that it represents. This is not true. Clear evidence for this is found in students' misinterpretations of maps. For example, some believe that roads colored red on a map are red in the real world; others may believe that a river is a road or that a pictured road is *not* a road because "it's too narrow for two cars to go on." Even *adults* do not really understand maps. They believe that maps are simply miniaturizations of the world.

Students should see that maps do not show what "is"; rather, they communicate a certain "view." They should understand that maps are different ways of viewing the world, in a way that is comparable to different artistic interpretations. They are models that help us see what we often can not see in the real world. Different models show the world in different ways—"This is what the world would look like if...." In the long term, students should understand that maps let us "see" aspects of the world that we could not see without them. They allow us to inspect and transform the larger world in new ways. They empower us in perceiving relationships about the world that we would not have noticed without the structural characteristics of the map.

## Spatial Visualization and Imagery

Spatial visualization is the ability to generate and manipulate images. Kosslyn (1983) defined four classes of image processes: generating an image, inspecting an image to answer questions about it, maintaining an image in the service of some other mental operation, and transforming and operating on an image. Thus, spatial visualization involves understanding and performing imagined movements of 2-D and 3-D objects. To do this, you need to be able to create a mental image and manipulate it. An image is not a "picture in the head." It is more abstract, more malleable, and less crisp than a picture. It is often segmented into parts. As we saw, some images can cause difficulties, especially if they are too inflexible, vague, or filled with irrelevant details.

People's first images are static. They can be mentally re-created, and even examined, but not transformed. For example, you might attempt to think of a group of people around a table. In contrast, dynamic images can be transformed. For example, you might mentally "move" the image of one shape (such as a book) to another place (such as a bookcase, to see if it will fit). In mathematics, you might mentally move (slide) and rotate an image of one shape to compare that shape to another one. Piaget argued that most children cannot perform full dynamic motions of images until the primary grades (Piaget & Inhelder, 1967, 1971). However, preschool children show initial transformational abilities, as we discussed in previous sections.

## Spatial Sense

Spatial sense includes two main spatial abilities: spatial orientation and spatial visualization and imagery. Other important knowledge includes how to represent ideas in drawing and how and when you can use such abilities.

This view clears up some confusion regarding the role of spatial sense in mathematics thinking. "Visual thinking" and "visual strategies" are not the same as spatial sense. Spatial sense as we describe it—all the abilities we use in "making our way" in the spatial sphere—is related to mathematical competencies (Brown & Wheatley, 1989; Clements & Battista, 1992; Fennema & Carpenter, 1981; Wheatley, Brown, & Solano, 1994).

Visual thinking, as in the initial levels of geometric thinking, is thinking that is tied down to limited, surface-level, visual ideas. Children move beyond that kind of visual thinking as they learn to manipulate dynamic images, as they enrich their store of images for shapes, and as they connect their spatial knowledge to verbal, analytic knowledge. Teachers might encourage children to describe why a shape does or does not belong to a shape category.

# EARLY CHILDHOOD GEOMETRY: IMPLICATIONS FOR INSTRUCTION

These findings have substantial implications for curriculum and instruction in early childhood education. This section describes these implications. (This research review was generated to inform the *Building Blocks* curriculum project—see Sarama, chap. 15, this volume—so its main goal was to generate research-based guidelines for curriculum and teaching. It should be noted that Table 1.2 in chap. 1 of this book was created from the review.)

## Geometric Figures

The belief that children are geometric tabula rasa is untenable; preschool children exhibit working knowledge of shapes. Instruction should build on this knowledge and move beyond it. Unfortunately, present curriculum and practice (including the home and preschool) rarely does so. Very young children can learn rich concepts about shape if provided with varied examples and nonexamples, discussions about shapes and their characteristics, and interesting tasks. Let us consider each of these in more depth.

Research indicates that curricula should ensure that children experience many different examples of a type of shape. For example, Fig. 10.3 shows a rich variety of triangles and distractors that would be sure to generate discussion. We should also show nonexamples that, when compared to similar examples, help focus attention on the critical attributes.

Discussions should encourage children's descriptions while encouraging the development of precise language. Early talk can clarify the meanings of terms. With such clarification, children can learn to explain why a shape belongs to a certain category—"It has three straight sides." Eventually, they can internalize such arguments; for example, thinking, "It is a weird, long, triangle, but it has three straight sides!" Finding and identifying shapes by feeling is one useful activity (see Fig. 10.7; Sarama, chap.15, this volume).

We should encourage children to describe why a figure belongs or does not belong to a shape category. Visual (prototype-based) descriptions should, of course, be expected and accepted, but attribute and property responses should also be encouraged. They may initially appear spontaneously for shapes with stronger and fewer prototypes (e.g., circle, square). They should be especially encouraged for those shape categories with more possible prototypes, such as triangles. In all cases, the traditional, single-prototype approach must be extended.

Early childhood curricula traditionally introduce shapes in four basic-level categories: circle, square, triangle, and rectangle. The idea that a square is not a rectangle is rooted by age 5 (Clements et al., 1999; Hannibal & Clements, 2000). It is time to rethink our presentation of squares as an isolated set. If we try to teach young children that "squares are rectangles,"

FIG. 10.7.   Children build polygons with plastic sticks.

especially through direct telling, confusion is likely. If, on the other hand, we continue to teach "squares" and "rectangles" as two separate groups, we will block children's transition to more flexible categorical thinking.

In our study (Clements et al., 1999), 4-year-olds were more likely to accept the squares as rectangles, possibly because they were less predisposed (because their prototype of rectangles was less distinguished from that of squares) or able to judge equality of all sides. Although the squares were included in the rectangle-recognition task (by the original task designers) to assess hierarchical inclusion, we did not expect or find such thinking in these young children. Their responses do show, however, that the path to such hierarchical thinking is a complex and twisting one with changes at several levels. This again raises the question of whether the strictly visual-prototype approach to teaching geometric shapes is a necessary prerequisite to more flexible categorical thinking or a detriment to the early development of such thinking. Kay (1987) provided first graders with instruction that (a) began with the more general case, quadrilaterals, proceeded to rectangles, and then to squares; (b) addressed the relevant characteristics of each class and the hierarchical relationships among classes; and (c) used terms embodying these relationships ("square-rectangle"). At the end of instruction, most students identified characteristics of quadrilaterals, rectangles, and squares, and about half identified hierarchical relationships among these classes, although none had done so previously. Although the depth of these first graders' understanding (especially of hierarchical relations) and the generalizations made on the basis of the empirical results must be questioned (Clements & Battista, 1992), so too should we question the wisdom of the traditional, prototype-only approach, which may lay groundwork that must be overturned to develop hierarchical thinking.

Probably the best approach is to present many examples of squares and rectangles, varying orientation, size, and so forth, including squares as examples of rectangles. If children say "that's a square," teachers might respond that it is a square, which is a special type of rectangle, and they might try double-naming ("it's a square-rectangle"). Older children can discuss "general" categories, such as quadrilaterals and triangles, counting the sides of various figures to choose their category. Also, teachers might encourage them to describe why a figure belongs or does not belong to a shape category. Then, teachers can say that because a triangle has all equal sides, it is a special type of triangle, called an equilateral triangle. Children might also "test" right angles on rectangles with a "right angle checker" (angle as turn is addressed in the following section).

Logo microworlds can be evocative in generating thinking about squares and rectangles for young children. In one large study (Clements, Battista et al., 2001), some kindergartners formed their own concept (e.g., "it's a square rectangle") in response to their work with the microworlds. This concept was applied only in certain situations: Squares were still squares, and rectangles, rectangles, unless you formed a square while working with procedures—on the computer or in drawing—that were designed to produce rectangles. The concept was strongly visual in nature, and no logical classification per se, such as class inclusion processes, should be inferred. The creation, application, and discussion of the concept, however, were arguably a valuable intellectual exercise.

Also, children can and should discuss the parts and attributes of shapes. Activities that promote such reflection and discussion include building shapes from components. For example, children might build squares and other polygons with toothpicks and marshmallows or other objects (see Fig. 10.7). They might also form shapes with their bodies, either singly or with their friends (see Fig. 10.8). Again, computer-based shape manipulation and navigation (including turtle geometry and simpler) environments can help mathematize these experiences.

Shape concepts begin forming in the preschool years and stabilize as early as age 6 (Gagatsis & Patronis, 1990; Hannibal & Clements, 2000). It is therefore critical that children be provided better opportunities to learn about geometric figures between 3 and 6 years of age. Curricula should develop early ideas aggressively, so that by the end of Grade 2 children can identify a wide range of examples and nonexamples of a wide range of geometric figures; classify, describe, draw, and visualize shapes; and describe and compare shapes based on their attributes.

FIG. 10.8.   Children make a rhombus with their bodies.

## Angle and Turn

Students struggle with angles. To understand angles, they must understand the various aspects of the angle concept, overcome difficulties with orientation, discriminate angles as critical parts of geometric figures, and construct and represent the idea of turns. Furthermore, they must construct a high level of integration between these aspects. Some argue that this difficult concept should not be a component of the early childhood mathematics curriculum. In contrast, the research reviewed here indicates that children do have initial competencies in the domain of turns and angles, and that the long developmental process is best begun in the early and elementary classrooms, as children deal with corners of figures, comparing angle size, and turns. Computers can help children quantify turns and angles (Fig. 10.9).

The role parallelism and perpendicularity should play are less clear. It may be that embedded in an overall approach to angle, turn, shape, and spatial structure, these ideas can be successfully nurtured, but whether they should be abstracted and discussed as separate concepts (e.g., lessons on perpendicular lines) requires additional research-based curriculum development.

FIG. 10.9. Turning shapes with computer tools helps children *quantify* turns.

## 3-D Figures

As with 2-D figures, children need more and richer experiences with solids. Research indicates that construction activities involving nets (foldout shapes of solids) may help students learn to discriminate between 2-D and 3-D figures. Practitioners and curriculum developers report success providing many other experiences; we need research to better describe, explain, and develop these approaches.

## Congruence, Symmetry, and Transformations

Beginning as early as 4 years of age, children can create and use strategies for judging whether two figures are "the same shape." In the Pre-K to Grade 2 range, they can develop sophisticated and accurate mathematical procedures for determining congruence.

There is mixed evidence regarding young children's ability with geometric motions. Pre-K–K, and even Grade 1–2 children, may be limited in their ability to mentally transform shapes, although there is evidence that even these sophisticated processes are achievable. Furthermore, they can learn to perform rotations on objects (physical or virtual), and a rich curriculum, enhanced by such manipulatives and computer tools, may reveal that knowledge and mental processes are valid educational goals for most young children.

Similarity is a surprising area of competence for young children. Young children can identify similar shapes in certain situations and use computers to create similar shapes. First and second graders can identify similar shapes and use scaling transformations to check their predictions.

Symmetry is also an area of strength (see Fig. 10.10). There is undeveloped potential in generating curricula that seriously consider children's intuitions, preference, and interest in symmetry.

## Composition and Decomposition

Preschool children move through levels in the composition and decomposition of 2-D figures. From lack of competence in composing geometric shapes, they gain abilities to combine shapes into pictures, then synthesize combinations of shapes into new shapes (composite shapes), eventually operating on and iterating those composite shapes. Few curricula challenge students to move through these levels. See Sarama (chap. 15, this volume) for an elaborated example of the *Building Blocks* approach to this critical area.

FIG. 10.10.   Children intuitively use symmetry in their block buildings.

## Spatial Orientation: Maps and Navigation

Spatial orientation—knowing the shape of one's environment—is perhaps even more an area of early intuitive knowledge than the domain of small shapes. Very young children know and use the shape of their environment in navigation activities, and, with guidance, can learn to mathematize this knowledge. They can learn about direction, perspective, distance, symbolization, location, and coordinates. Some studies have identified first grade as the period of most efficient learning of maps, but informal experiences in preschool and kindergarten are also beneficial, especially those that emphasize building imagery from physical movement. (See Fig. 10.11.)

## Spatial Visualization and Imagery

Even preschool and kindergarten children show initial transformational abilities in certain settings (see the "Transformations" section). All children should work on developing their ability to create, maintain, and represent mental images of mathematical objects.

FIG. 10.11. Walking around a rectangular rug, and talking about the experience, helps children build imagery and knowledge of two-dimensional shapes.

## Final Words

Research has clearly identified that children's informal numerical knowledge develops through the preschool years. Though not as extensively documented, there is sufficient research indicating that informal geometric knowledge similarly develops throughout the early childhood years. There is some evidence that there is little to lose, and much to gain, by fostering that development. Especially given children's affinity toward, knowledge of, and ability to gain geometric and spatial knowledge, it would be an educational shame to allow the U.S. obsession with number (both in practice and research) to reinstantiate itself in the nascent domain of early childhood mathematics education.

## ACKNOWLEDGMENTS

This chapter is based on work supported in part by the National Science Foundation under Grant ESI-9730804, "Building Blocks—Foundations for Mathematical Thinking, Pre-Kindergarten to Grade 2: Research-based Materials Development" and Grant REC-9903409, "Technology- Enhanced Learning of Geometry in Elementary Schools." Any opinions, findings, and conclusions or recommendations expressed in this material are those of the author(s) and do not necessarily reflect the views of the National Science Foundation. It is adapted from a paper presented at the 78th Annual Meeting of the National Council of Teachers of Mathematics, San Francisco, California, April 2000; symposium: "Linking Research and the New Early Childhood Mathematics Standards," J. Sarama, organizer.

## REFERENCES

Abravanel, E. (1977). The figural simplicity of parallel lines. *Child Development, 48,* 708–710.
Anooshian, L. J., Pascal, V. U., & McCreath, H. (1984). Problem mapping before problem solving: Young children's cognitive maps and search strategies in large-scale environments. *Child Development, 55,* 1820–1834.
Beaton, A. E., Mullis, I. V. S., Martin, M. O., Gonzalez, E. J., Kelly, D. L., & Smith, T. A. (1996). *Mathematics achievement in the middle school years: IEA's third international mathematics and science study (TIMSS).* Retrieved January 19, 1997, from http://wwwcsteep.bc.edu/timss
Beilin, H. (1984). Cognitive theory and mathematical cognition: Geometry and space. In B. Gholson & T. L. Rosenthanl (Eds.), *Applications of cognitive-developmental theory* (pp. 49–93). New York: Academic Press.
Beilin, H., Klein, A., & Whitehurst, B. (1982). *Strategies and structures in understanding geometry.* New York: City University of New York. (ERIC Document Reproduction Service No. ED ED 225808)
Bishop, A. J. (1980). Spatial abilities and mathematics achievement—A review. *Educational Studies in Mathematics, 11,* 257–269.
Bishop, A. J. (1983). Space and geometry. In R. Lesh & M. Landau (Eds.), *Acquisition of mathematics concepts and processes* (pp. 7–44). New York: Academic Press.
Blades, M., & Spencer, C. (1989). Young children's ability to use coordinate references. *The Journal of Genetic Psychology, 150,* 5–18.
Blaut, J. M., & Stea, D. (1974). Mapping at the age of three. *Journal of Geography, 73*(7), 5–9.

Boardman, D. (1990). Graphicacy revisited: Mapping abilities and gender differences. *Educational Review, 42,* 57–64.

Borer, M. (1993). *Integrating mandated Logo computer instruction into the second grade curriculum.* M.S. Practicum Report, Nova University (ERIC Document No. ED367311).

Bornstein, M. H., Ferdinandsen, K., & Gross, C. G. (1981). Perception of symmetry in infancy. *Developmental Psychology, 17,* 82–86.

Bremner, J. G., Andreasen, G., Kendall, G., & Adams, L. (1993). Conditions for successful performance by 4-year-olds in a dimensional coordination task. *Journal of Experimental Child Psychology, 56*(2), 149–172.

Brown, D. L., & Wheatley, G. H. (1989). Relationship between spatial knowledge and mathematics knowledge. In C. A. Maher, G. A. Goldin, & R. B. Davis (Eds.), *Proceedings of the eleventh annual meeting, North American Chapter of the International Group for the Psychology of Mathematics Education* (pp. 143–148). New Brunswick, NJ: Rutgers University Press

Burger, W. F., & Shaughnessy, J. M. (1986). Characterizing the van Hiele levels of development in geometry. *Journal for Research in Mathematics Education, 17,* 31–48.

Carlson, S. L., & White, S. H. (1998). The effectiveness of a computer program in helping kindergarten students learn the concepts of left and right. *Journal of Computing in Childhood Education, 9*(2), 133–147.

Carpenter, T. P., Coburn, T., Reys, R., & Wilson, J. (1976). Notes from National Assessment: Recognizing and naming solids. *Arithmetic Teacher, 23,* 62–66.

Carpenter, T. P., Corbitt, M. K., Kepner, H. S., Lindquist, M. M., & Reys, R. E. (1980). National assessment. In E. Fennema (Ed.), *Mathematics education research: Implications for the 80s* (pp. 22–38). Alexandria, VA: Association for Supervision and Curriculum Development.

Clements, D. H., & Battista, M. T. (1989). Learning of geometric concepts in a Logo environment. *Journal for Research in Mathematics Education, 20,* 450–467.

Clements, D. H., & Battista, M. T. (1990). The effects of Logo on children's conceptualizations of angle and polygons. *Journal for Research in Mathematics Education, 21,* 356–371.

Clements, D. H., & Battista, M. T. (Artist). (1991). *Logo geometry.* Morristown, NJ: Silva, Burdett, & Ginn.

Clements, D. H., & Battista, M. T. (1992). Geometry and spatial reasoning. In D. A. Grouws (Ed.), *Handbook of research on mathematics teaching and learning* (pp. 420–464). New York: Macmillan.

Clements, D. H., Battista, M. T., & Sarama, J. (2001). Logo and geometry. *Journal for Research in Mathematics Education Monograph Series, 10.*

Clements, D. H., Battista, M. T., Sarama, J., & Swaminathan, S. (1996). Development of turn and turn measurement concepts in a computer-based instructional unit. *Educational Studies in Mathematics, 30,* 313–337.

Clements, D. H., Battista, M. T., Sarama, J., & Swaminathan, S. (1997). Development of students' spatial thinking in a unit on geometric motions and area. *The Elementary School Journal, 98*(2), 171–186.

Clements, D. H., Battista, M. T., Sarama, J., Swaminathan, S., & McMillen, S. (1997). Students' development of length measurement concepts in a Logo-based unit on geometric paths. *Journal for Research in Mathematics Education, 28*(1), 70–95.

Clements, D. H., & Meredith, J. S. (1994). *Turtle math.* Montreal, Quebec: Logo Computer Systems, Inc. (LCSI).

Clements, D. H., Sarama, J., Gòmez, R. M. G., Swaminathan, S., & McMillen, S. (in press). Development of mathematical concepts of two-dimensional space in grid environments: An exploratory study. *Cognition and Instruction.*

Clements, D. H., Sarama, J., & Wilson, D. C. (2001). Composition of geometric figures. In M. van den Heuvel-Panhuizen (Ed.), *Proceedings of the 21st Conference of the International Group for the Psychology of Mathematics Education* (pp. ??). Utrecht, Netherlands: Freudenthal Institute.

Clements, D. H., Swaminathan, S., Hannibal, M. A. Z., & Sarama, J. (1999). Young children's concepts of shape. *Journal for Research in Mathematics Education, 30,* 192–212.

Confrey, J. (1992, April). *First graders' understanding of similarity.* Paper presented at the meeting of the American Educational Research Association, San Francisco.

Del Grande, J. J. (1986). Can grade two children's spatial perception be improved by inserting a transformation geometry component into their mathematics program? *Dissertation Abstracts International, 47,* 3689A. (UMI No. ??)

Downs, R. M., Liben, L. S., & Daggs, D. G. (1988). On education and geographers: The role of cognitive developmental theory in geographic education. *Annuals of the Association of American Geographers, 78,* 680–700.

Fabricius, W. V., & Wellman, H. M. (1993). Two roads diverged: Young children's ability to judge distances. *Child Development, 64,* 399–414.

Fennema, E., & Carpenter, T. P. (1981). Sex-related differences in mathematics: Results from National Assessment. *Mathematics Teacher, 74,* 554–559.

Fennema, E., & Sherman, J. (1977). Sex-related differences in mathematics achievement, spatial visualization and affective factors. *American Educational Research Journal, 14,* 51–71.

Fennema, E. H., & Sherman, J. A. (1978). Sex-related differences in mathematics achievement and related factors. *Journal for Research in Mathematics Education, 9,* 189–203.

Fey, J., Atchison, W. F., Good, R. A., Heid, M. K., Johnson, J., Kantowski, M. G., & Rosen, L. P. (1984). *Computing and mathematics: The impact on secondary school curricula.* College Park: Universty of Maryland.

Filippaki, N., & Papamichael, Y. (1997). Tutoring conjunctions and construction of geometry concepts in the early childhood education: The case of the angle. *European Journal of Psychology of Education, 12*(3), 235–247.

Fisher, N. D. (1978). Visual influences of figure orientation on concept formation in geometry. *Dissertation Abstracts International, 38,* 4639A. (UMI No. 7732300)

Frank, R. E. (1987). *The emergence of route map reading skills in young children.* Baltimore: Society for Research in Child Development. (ERIC Document Reproduction Service No. ED 288 785)

Fuson, K. C., & Murray, C. (1978). The haptic-visual perception, construction, and drawing of geometric shapes by children aged two to five: A Piagetian extension. In R. Lesh & D. Mierkiewicz (Eds.), *Concerning the development of spatial and geometric concepts* (pp. 49–83). Columbus, OH: ERIC Clearinghouse for Science, Mathematics, and Environmental Education.

Fuys, D., Geddes, D., & Tischler, R. (1988). The van Hiele model of thinking in geometry among adolescents. *Journal for Research in Mathematics Education Monograph Series, 3.*

Gagatsis, A., & Patronis, T. (1990). Using geometrical models in a process of reflective thinking in learning and teaching mathematics. *Educational Studies in Mathematics, 21,* 29–54.

Gay, P. (1989). Tactile turtle: Explorations in space with visually impaired children and a floor turtle. *British Journal of Visual Impairment, 7*(1), 23–25.

Gelman, R., & Williams, E. M. (1997). Enabling constraints for cognitive development and learning: Domain specificity and epigenesis. In D. Kuhn & R. Siegler (Eds.), *Cognition, perception, and language: Vol. 2. Handbook of child psychology* (5th ed., pp. 575–630). New York: Wiley.

Genkins, E. F. (1975). The concept of bilateral symmetry in young children. In M. F. Rosskopf (Ed.), *Children's mathematical concepts: Six Piagetian studies in mathematics education* (pp. 5–43). New York: Teachers College Press.

Ginsburg, H. P., Inoue, N., & Seo, K.-H. (1999). Young children doing mathematics: Observations of everyday activities. In J. V. Copley (Ed.), *Mathematics in the early years* (pp. 88–99). Reston, VA: National Council of Teachers of Mathematics.

Goodrow, A., Clements, D. H., Battista, M. T., Sarama, J., & Akers, J. (1997). *How long? How far? Measurement.* Palo Alto, CA: Dale Seymour Publications.

Guay, R. B., & McDaniel, E. (1977). The relationship between mathematics achievement and spatial abilities among elementary school children. *Journal for Research in Mathematics Education, 8,* 211–215.

Hannibal, M. A. Z., & Clements, D. H. (2000). *Young children's understanding of basic geometric shapes.* Manuscript submitted for publication.

Harris, L. J. (1981). Sex-related variations in spatial skill. In L. S. Liben, A. H. Patterson, & N. Newcombe (Eds.), *Spatial representation and behavior across the life span* (pp. 83–125). New York: Academic Press.

Howell, R. D., Scott, P. B., & Diamond, J. (1987). The effects of "instant" Logo computing language on the cognitive development of very young children. *Journal of Educational Computing Research, 3*(2), 249–260.

Huttenlocher, J., & Newcombe, N. (1984). The child's representation of information about location. In C. Sophian (Ed.), *The origin of cognitive skills* (pp. 81–111). Hillsdale, NJ: Lawrence Erlbaum Associates.

Jovignot, F. (1995). Can 5–6 year old children orientate themselves in a cave? *Scientific Journal of Orienteering, 11*(2), 64–75.

Kabanova-Meller, E. N. (1970). The role of the diagram in the application of geometric theorems. In J. Kilpatrick & I. Wirszup (Eds.), *Soviet studies in the psychology of learning and teaching mathematics* (Vols. 4, pp. 7–49). Chicago: University of Chicago Press.

Kay, C. S. (1987). Is a square a rectangle? The development of first-grade students' understanding of quadrilaterals with implications for the van Hiele theory of the development of geometric thought. *Dissertation Abstracts International, 47*, 2934A. (UMI No. DA8626590)

Klein, A., Starkey, P., & Wakeley, A. (1999, April). *Enhancing pre-kindergarten children's readiness for school mathematics*. Paper presented at the meeting of the American Educational Research Association, Montreal.

Kosslyn, S. M. (1983). *Ghosts in the mind's machine*. New York: Norton.

Kouba, V. L., Brown, C. A., Carpenter, T. P., Lindquist, M. M., Silver, E. A., & Swafford, J. O. (1988). Results of the fourth NAEP assessment of mathematics: Measurement, geometry, data interpretation, attitudes, and other topics. *Arithmetic Teacher, 35*(9), 10–16.

Kull, J. A. (1986). Learning and Logo. In P. F. Campbell & G. G. Fein (Eds.), *Young children and microcomputers* (pp. 103–130). Englewood Cliffs, NJ: Prentice-Hall.

Landau, B. (1988). The construction and use of spatial knowledge in blind and sighted children. In J. Stiles-Davis, M. Kritchevsky, & U. Bellugi (Eds.), *Spatial cognition: Brain bases and development* (pp. 343–371). Hillsdale, NJ: Lawrence Erlbaum Associates.

Lappan, G. (1999). Geometry: The forgotten strand. *NCTM News Bulletin, 36*(5), 3.

Lean, G., & Clements, M. A. (1981). Spatial ability, visual imagery, and mathematical performance. *Educational Studies in Mathematics, 12*, 267–299.

Lehrer, R., Jenkins, M., & Osana, H. (1998). Longitudinal study of children's reasoning about space and geometry. In R. Lehrer & D. Chazan (Eds.), *Designing learning environments for developing understanding of geometry and space* (pp. 137–167). Mahwah, NJ: Lawrence Erlbaum Associates.

Liben, L. S. (1988). Conceptual issues in the development of spatial cognition. In J. Stiles-Davis, M. Kritchevsky, & U. Bellugi (Eds.), *Spatial cognition: Brain bases and development* (pp. 145–201). Hillsdale, NJ: Lawrence Erlbaum Associates.

Liben, L. S., & Downs, R. M. (1989). Understanding maps as symbols: The development of map concepts in children. In H. W. Reese (Ed.), *Advances in child development and behavior* (Vol. 22, pp. 145–201). San Diego: Academic Press.

Liben, L. S., & Yekel, C. A. (1996). Preschoolers' understanding of plan and oblique maps: The role of geometric and representational correspondence. *Child Development, 67*(6), 2780–2796.

Lindquist, M. M., & Kouba, V. L. (1989). Geometry. In M. M. Lindquist (Ed.), *Results from the Fourth Mathematics Assessment of the National Assessment of Educational Progress* (pp. 44–54). Reston, VA: National Council of Teachers of Mathematics.

Mansfield, H. M., & Scott, J. (1990). Young children solving spatial problems. In G. Booker, P. Cobb, & T. N. deMendicuti (Eds.), *Proceedings of the 14th annual conference of the International Group for the Psychology of Mathematics Education* (Vol. 2, pp. 275–282). Oaxlepec, Mexico: International Group for the Psychology of Mathematics Education.

McGee, M. G. (1979). Human spatial abilities: Psychometric studies and environmental, genetic, hormonal, and neurological influences. *Psychological Bulletin, 86*, 889–918.

Mitchelmore, M. C. (1989). The development of children's concepts of angle. In G. Vergnaud, J. Rogalski, & M. Artique (Eds.), *Proceedings of the Thirteenth Conference of the International Group for the Psychology of Mathematics Education* (pp. 304–311). Paris: City University.

Mitchelmore, M. (1992). Children's concepts of perpendiculars. In W. Geeslin & K. Graham (Eds.), *Proceedings of the Sixteenth PME Conference* (Vol. 2, pp. 120–127). Durham, NH: Program Committee of the 16th PME Conference.

Mitchelmore, M. C. (1993). The development of pre-angle concepts. In A. R. Baturo & L. J. Harris (Eds.), *New directions in research on geometry* (pp. 87–93). Brisbane, Australia: Centre for Mathematics and Science Education, Queensland University of Technology.

Muir, S. P., & Cheek, H. N. (1986). Mathematics and the map skill curriculum. *School Science and Mathematics, 86,* 284–291.

National Council of Teachers of Mathematics. (1989). *Curriculum and evaluation standards for school mathematics.* Reston, VA: Author.

Nieuwoudt, H. D., & van Niekerk, R. (1997, March). *The spatial competence of young children through the development of solids.* Paper presented at the meeting of the American Educational Research Association, Chicago.

Perham, F. (1978). An investigation into the effect of instruction on the acquisition of transformation geometry concepts in first grade children and subsequent transfer to general spatial ability. In R. Lesh & D. Mierkiewicz (Eds.), *Concerning the development of spatial and geometric concepts* (pp. 229–241). Columbus, OH: ERIC Clearinghouse for Science, Mathematics, and Environmental Education.

Piaget, J., & Inhelder, B. (1967). *The child's conception of space* (F. J. Langdon & J. L. Lunzer, Trans.). New York: Norton.

Piaget, J., & Inhelder, B. (1971). *Mental imagery in the child.* London: Routledge and Kegan Paul.

Presson, C. C. (1987). The development of spatial cognition: Secondary uses of spatial information. In N. Eisenberg (Ed.), *Contemporary topics in developmental psychology* (pp. 77–112). New York: Wiley.

Presson, C. C., & Somerville, S. C. (1985). Beyond egocentrism: A new look at the beginnings of spatial representation. In H. M. Wellman (Ed.), *Children's searching: The development of search skill and spatial representation* (pp. 1–26). Hillsdale, NJ: Lawrence Erlbaum Associates.

Razel, M., & Eylon, B.-S. (1991, July). *Developing mathematics readiness in young children with the Agam Program.* Paper presented at the meeting of the Fifteenth Conference of the International Group for the Psychology of Mathematics Education, Genova, Italy.

Rieser, J. J., Garing, A. E., & Young, M. F. (1994). Imagery, action, and young children's spatial orientation: It's not being there that counts, it's what one has in mind. *Child Development, 65*(5), 1262–1278.

Rosch, E. (1975). Cognitive representations of semantic categories. *Journal of Experimental Psychology: General, 104,* 192–233.

Rosser, R. A., Ensing, S. S., Glider, P. J., & Lane, S. (1984). An information-processing analysis of children's accuracy in predicting the appearance of rotated stimuli. *Child Development, 55,* 2204–2211.

Rosser, R. A., Horan, P. F., Mattson, S. L., & Mazzeo, J. (1984). Comprehension of Euclidean space in young children: The early emergence of understanding and its limits. *Genetic Psychology Monographs, 110,* 21–41.

Rosser, R. A., Lane, S., & Mazzeo, J. (1988). Order of acquisition of related geometric competencies in young children. *Child Study Journal, 18,* 75–90.

Sales, C. (1994). *A constructivist instructional project on developing geometric problem solving abilities using pattern blocks and tangrams with young children.* Unpublished master's thesis, University of Northern Iowa, Cedar Falls.

Sandberg, E. H., & Huttenlocher, J. (1996). The development of hierarchical representation of two-dimensional space. *Child Development, 67*(3), 721–739.

Sarama, J., Clements, D. H., & Vukelic, E. B. (1996). The role of a computer manipulative in fostering specific psychological/mathematical processes. In E. Jakubowski & D. Watkins & H. Biske (Eds.), *Proceedings of the eighteenth annual meeting of the North America Chapter of the International Group for the Psychology of Mathematics Education* (Vol. 2, pp. 567–572). Columbus, OH: ERIC Clearinghouse for Science, Mathematics, and Environmental Education.

Schultz, K. A., & Austin, J. D. (1983). Directional effects in transformational tasks. *Journal for Research in Mathematics Education, 14,* 95–101.

Siegel, A. W., & Schadler, M. (1977). The development of young children's spatial representations of their classrooms. *Child Development, 48,* 388–394.

Somerville, S. C., & Bryant, P. E. (1985). Young children's use of spatial coordinates. *Child Development, 56,* 604–613.

Somerville, S. C., Bryant, P. E., Mazzocco, M. M. M., & Johnson, S. P. (1987, April). *The early development of children's use of spatial coordinates.* Paper presented at the meeting of the Society for Research in Child Development, Baltimore.

Sophian, C., & Crosby, M. E. (1998, August). *Ratios that even young children understand: The case of spatial proportions.* Paper presented at the meeting of the Cognitive Science Society of Ireland, Dublin.

Starkey, P., Klein, A., Chang, I., Qi, D., Lijuan, P., & Yang, Z. (1999, April). *Environmental supports for young children's mathematical development in China and the United States.* Paper presented at the meeting of the Society for Research in Child Development, Albuquerque.

Steffe, L. P., & Cobb, P. (1988). *Construction of arithmetical meanings and strategies.* New York: Springer-Verlag.

Stevenson, H. W., Lee, S.-Y., & Stigler, J. W. (1986). Mathematics achievement of Chinese, Japanese, and American children. *Science, 231,* 693–699.

Stigler, J. W., Lee, S.-Y., & Stevenson, H. W. (1990). *Mathematical knowledge of Japanese, Chinese, and American elementary school children.* Reston, VA: National Council of Teachers of Mathematics.

Thomas, B. (1982). *An abstract of kindergarten teachers' elicitation and utilization of children's prior knowledge in the teaching of shape concepts.* Unpublished manuscript, School of Education, Health, Nursing, and Arts Professions, New York University, New York.

Try, K. M. (1989). *Cognitive and social change in young children during Logo activities: A study of individual differences.* Unpublished doctoral dissertation, The University of New England, Armidale, New South Wales, Australia.

Uttal, D. H. (1996). Angles and distances: Children's and adults' reconstruction and scaling of spatial configurations. *Child Development, 67*(6), 2763–2779.

Uttal, D. H., & Wellman, H. M. (1989). Young children's representation of spatial information acquired from maps. *Developmental Psychology, 25,* 128–138.

Vinner, S., & Hershkowitz, R. (1980). Concept images and common cognitive paths in the development of some simple geometrical concepts. In R. Karplus (Ed.), *Proceedings of the Fourth International Conference for the Psychology of Mathematics Education* (pp. 177–184). Berkeley: Lawrence Hall of Science, University of California.

Vurpillot, E. (1976). *The visual world of the child.* New York: International Universities Press.

Watson, J. A., & Brinkley, V. M. (1990/1991). Space and premathematic strategies young children adopt in initial Logo problem solving. *Journal of Computing in Childhood Education, 2,* 17–29.

Watson, J. A., Lange, G., & Brinkley, V. M. (1992). Logo mastery and spatial problem-solving by young children: Effects of Logo language training, route-strategy training, and learning styles on immediate learning and transfer. *Journal of Educational Computing Research, 8,* 521–540.

Weaver, C. L. (1991). *Young children learn geometric and spatial concepts using Logo with a screen turtle and a floor turtle.* Unpublished doctoral dissertation, State University of New York, Buffalo.

Wheatley, G. H. (1990). Spatial sense and mathematics learning. *Arithmetic Teacher, 37*(6), 10–11.

Wheatley, G. H., Brown, D. L., & Solano, A. (1994). Long term relationship between spatial ability and mathematical knowledge. In D. Kirshner (Ed.), *Proceedings of the sixteenth annual meeting of North American Chapter of the International Group for the Psychology of Mathematics Education* (Vol. 1, pp. 225–231). Baton Rouge: Louisiana State University.

Williford, H. J. (1972). A study of transformational geometry instruction in the primary grades. *Journal for Research in Mathematics Education, 3,* 260–271.

Zykova, V. I. (1969). Operating with concepts when solving geometry problems. In J. Kilpatrick & I. Wirszup (Eds.), *Soviet studies in the psychology of learning and teaching mathematics* (Vol. 1, pp. 93–148). Chicago: University of Chicago.

# Measurement in Pre-K to Grade 2 Mathematics

Douglas H. Clements
*University at Buffalo, State University of New York*

Michelle Stephan
*Purdue University Calumet*

Primary-grade students were making a simple map of their classroom. They began by saying that they needed to measure the room. Pleased, the teacher passed out meter sticks. They began laying these down but soon stopped, puzzled. "We need more." Teacher: "More meter sticks?" "Yeah. There's not enough." Teacher: "Maybe you could work together and solve that." "No. Even all of 'em wouldn't reach." Teacher: "I mean is there a way you could measure with just the meter sticks you have?" Silence. Teacher: "How about this? Can you lay a meter stick down, mark the end with your finger, and then move it?" "Wow! Good idea!" (Clements, 1999). It was a new idea that, apparently, not one of the students had apparently encountered before.

Is this apparent lack of knowledge of measurement a "fluke"? It may not be. Many students use measurement instruments or count units in a rote fashion (Clements & M. T. Battista, 1992). In international comparisons, U.S. students score lower in measurement and geometry than in other topics (National Center for Education Statistics, 1996). We need much stronger measurement instruction in the early years. Fortunately, we know quite a bit about the concepts and skills children need to develop and how they develop them. Here, we briefly review young children's understanding of measurement then consider their development of length, area, and angle and turn measurement in more depth. We conclude with implications for curriculum and instruction in early childhood measurement.

## YOUNG CHILDREN AND MEASUREMENT

Children's understanding of measurement has its roots in the preschool years. Preschool children know that continuous attributes such as mass, length, and weight exist, although they cannot quantify or measure them accurately. Even 3-year-olds know that if they have some clay and then are given more clay, they have more than they did before. Preschoolers cannot reliably make judgments about which of two amounts of clay is more; they use perceptual cues such as which is longer. At age 4–5 years, however, most children can learn to overcome perceptual cues and make progress in reasoning about and measuring quantities.

Young children naturally encounter and discuss quantities (Ginsburg & Seo, chap. 4, this volume). They first learn to use words that represent quantity or magnitude of a certain attribute. Then they compare two objects directly and recognize equality or inequality (Boulton-Lewis, Wilss, & Mutch, 1996). At this point, they are ready to learn to measure, connecting number to the quantity. (Measurement is defined as assigning a number to continuous quantities.) We next examine this development in more detail for the case of length.

## LENGTH MEASUREMENT

As a first simple definition, we can say that length is a characteristic of an object and can be found by quantifying how far it is between the endpoints of the object. Distance refers to the empty space between two points. Measuring length and distance, and learning about length measurement, is more complex. Measuring consists of two aspects, identifying a unit of measure and *subdividing* (mentally and physically) the object by that unit, placing that unit end to end (*iterating*) alongside the object. Subdividing and unit iteration are complex mental accomplishments that are too often ignored in traditional measurement curriculum materials and instruction. Therefore, many researchers go beyond the physical act of measuring to investigate students' understandings of measuring as covering space and quantifying that covering.

We discuss length in the following two sections. First, we identify several key concepts that underlie measuring (adapted from Stephan & Clements, in press). Second, we describe research-based instructional approaches that were designed to help students develop concepts and skills of length measurement.

### Concepts in Linear Measurement

Several important concepts underpin children's learning of length measurement. We can use these concepts to understand how students are thinking about space as they go through the physical activity of measuring. These concepts are: (a) partitioning, (b) unit iteration, (c) transitivity, (d) conservation, (e) accumulation of distance, and (f) relation to number.

*Partitioning* is the mental activity of slicing up an object into the same-sized units. This idea is not obvious to children. It involves mentally seeing the object as something that can be partitioned (or "cut up") before even physically measuring. Asking students what the hash marks on a ruler mean can reveal how they understand partitioning length (Clements & Barrett, 1996; Lehrer, in press). Some students, for instance, may understand "five" as a hash mark, not as a space that is cut into five equal-size units. As students come to understand that units can also be partitioned, they come to grips with the idea that length is continuous (e.g., any unit can itself be further partitioned).

*Unit iteration* is the ability to think of the length of a small block as part of the length of the object being measured and to place the smaller block repeatedly along the length of the larger object (Kamii & Clark, 1997). Students initially may iterate a unit leaving gaps between subsequent units or overlapping adjacent units (Lehrer, in press). For these students, iterating is a physical activity of placing units end to end in some manner, not an activity of covering the space/length of the object with no gaps. When students count each unit iteration, teachers should focus students' conversations on that to which they are referring. For example, if a student iterates a unit five times, the "five" represents five units of length. For some students "five" signifies the hash mark next to the numeral five instead of the amount of space covered by five units (see Stephan, Cobb, Gravemeijer, & Estes, in press). In this way, the marks on a ruler "mask" the intended conceptual understanding involved in measurement. Many students see no problem mixing units (e.g., using both paper clips and pen tops) or using different-size units (e.g., small and large paper clips) as long as they cover the entire length of the object in some way (Clements, M. Battista, & Sarama, 1998; Lehrer, in press).

Furthermore, students often begin counting at the numeral "1" on a ruler (i.e., 1 as the zero point; Lehrer, in press) or, when counting paces heel to toe, start their count with the movement of the first foot (i.e., they miss the first foot and count the "second" foot as one from an adult perspective; Lehrer, in press; Stephan et al., in press). Students probably are not thinking about measuring as covering space. Rather, the numerals on a ruler (or the placement of a foot) signify when to start counting, not an amount of space that has already been covered (i.e., "one" is the space from the beginning of the ruler to the hash mark, not the hash mark itself). Finally, many students initially find it necessary to iterate the unit until it "fills up" the length of the object and will not extend the unit past the endpoint of the object they are measuring (Stephan et al., in press).

*Transitivity* is the understanding that if the length of Object 1 is equal to (or greater/less than) the length of Object 2 and Object 2 is the same length as (or greater/less than) Object 3, then Object 1 is the same length as (or greater/less than) Object 3. Children might, for example, use a stick to judge whether two towers, one on the floor and one on a table, are the same height. A child who can reason in this manner can take a third or middle item (the stick) as a referent by which to compare the heights or lengths of other objects. Given this definition, most researchers argue that students must reason transitively before they can understand measurement (Boulton-Lewis, 1987; Hiebert, 1981; Kamii & Clark, 1997). Some researchers conclude that the ruler is useless as a measuring tool if a student cannot yet reason transitively (Kamii & Clark, 1997). This may only be partially true, as we discuss in a following section.

*Conservation* of length is the understanding that as an object is moved, its length does not change. For example, if children are shown two equal-length rods aligned, they say they are the same length. If one is moved to project beyond the other, children 4.5 to 6 years will say the projecting rod is longer. At 5 to 7 years, many children hesitate or vacillate; beyond that, they answer immediately, as if it were obvious. Conservation of length is not equivalent to the concept of measurement but rather develops as the child learns to measure (Inhelder, Sinclair, & Bovet, 1974). Some researchers hold that conservation is essential for, but not equivalent to, a full conception of measurement (Copeland, 1974). For example, Piaget, Inhelder, and Szeminska (1960) argued that transitivity is impossible for students who do not conserve lengths because once they move a unit, it is possible, in the student's view, for the length of the unit to change. Most researchers agree that students develop the notion of conservation before transitivity (Boulton-Lewis, 1987). Though researchers agree that conservation is essential for a complete understanding of measurement, several articles caution that students do not necessarily need to develop transitivity and conservation before they can learn some measurement ideas (Boulton-Lewis, 1987; Clements, 1999; Hiebert, 1981). Two measurement ideas that do seem to require conservation and transitivity are: (a) the inverse relation between the size of the unit and the number of those units and (b) the need to use equal-length units when measuring. On many tasks that *appear* to require general logical reasoning, children find their own strategy to measure, and they do so correctly. These solution strategies do not necessarily match the structural logic of the task. For example, children use intermediate measurements to compare two lengths without explicitly asking the transitivity question. They move a unit to measure the length of an object and do not worry about whether the length is being conserved. Finally, children of all developmental levels solve simple measurement tasks that do not appear to rely heavily on general reasoning.

*Accumulation of distance* is the understanding that as you iterate a unit along the length of an object and count the iteration, the number words signify the space covered by all units counted up to that point. Piaget et al. (1960) characterized students' measuring activity as an accumulation of distance when the result of iterating forms nesting relationships to each other. That is, the space covered by three units is nested in or contained in the space covered by four units. For example, in Stephan et al. (in press), students measured the lengths of objects by pacing heel to toe and counting their steps. As one student paced the length of a rug, the teacher stopped the student midmeasure and asked her what she meant by "8." Some students claimed that 8 signified the space covered by the eighth foot whereas others argued that it was the space covered from the beginning of the first foot to the end of the eighth. These latter students were measuring by accumulating distances. Most researchers have observed this type of interpretation in 9 to 10-year-olds (Clements, 1999; Copeland, 1974; Kamii & Clark, 1997; Piaget et al., 1960). However, Stephan et al. (in press) showed that, with meaningful instruction, children as young as 6 years old construct an accumulation of distance interpretation.

*Relation between number and measurement:* Children's chief experience with mathematics in elementary school is often that of counting objects (e.g., blocks). This type of counting can be thought of as measuring discrete units. Students must reorganize their understanding of the objects they are counting to measure continuous units. Thus, it is not surprising that students' counting plays a role in their development of measuring conceptions. They make measurement judgments based on counting ideas. For example, Inhelder et al. (1974) showed students two rows of matches that were the same length but each row was composed of a different number of matches (See Fig. 11.1).

Although, from the adult perspective, the lengths of the rows were the same, many children argued that the row with 6 matches was longer because it had more matches. Other studies have also found that children draw on their counting experiences to interpret their measuring activity. Anyone who has taught measurement knows that students often start measuring with the numeral "1" as the starting point instead of 0. After all, when we measure, the first number word we say is "one." Lehrer (in press) argues that measurement assumes a "zero point," a point from which a measurement begins. The zero point need not be 0, but if students understand measuring only as "reading the ruler," then they will not understand this idea. Lubinski and Thiessan (1996) found that with meaningful instruction focusing on students' interpretations of their measuring activity, students were able to use flexible starting points on a ruler to indicate measures successfully.

A

B

FIG. 11.1.   A task assessing children's use of counting ideas in measurement situations.

Although researchers debate the order of the development of these concepts and the ages at which they are developed, they agree that these ideas form the foundation for measurement and should be considered during any measurement instruction. When a teacher has these ideas in mind during instruction, she is better able to interpret students' understanding and ask questions that will lead them to construct these ideas. It is clear, however, that traditional measurement instruction is insufficient for helping students build these conceptions. What kinds of instructional activities does a teacher use to build these ideas?

## Learning and Teaching Linear Measurement

Traditionally, the goal of measurement instruction has been to help students learn the skills necessary to use a conventional ruler. In contrast, research and recent reform curricula suggest developing the conceptual building blocks that lead to estimating and measuring meaningfully. Different approaches have been taken to achieve these goals.

Kamii and Clark (1997) stressed that comparing lengths is at the heart of developing the notions of conservation, transitivity, and unit iteration, but most textbooks do not have these types of tasks. Textbooks tend to ask questions such as "How many paper clips does the pencil measure?" rather than "How much longer is the blue pencil than the red pencil?" Although Kamii and Clark advocated beginning instruction by comparing lengths with nonstandard or standard units (not a ruler), they cautioned that such an activity is often done by rote. Teachers must focus students on the mental activity of transitive reasoning and accumulating distances. One type of task that involves indirect comparisons is to ask students if the doorway is wide enough for a table to go through. This involves an indirect comparison (and transitive reasoning) and therefore de-emphasizes physical measurement procedures.

Most recent curricula advise a sequence of instruction in which students compare lengths, measure with nonstandard units, incorporate the use of manipulative standard units, and measure with a ruler (Clements, 1999; Kamii & Clark, 1999). The basis for this sequence is, explicitly or implicitly, Piaget et al.'s (1960) developmental theory of measurement. The argument is that this approach motivates students to see the need for a standard measuring unit. Researchers who advocate this approach argue that, when classroom discussions focus on students' meaning during measuring, they are able to construct sophisticated understanding (Lehrer, in press; Lubinski & Thiessan, 1996; Stephan et al., in press).

For example, such an approach might begin with children pacing from one point to another. As students discussed their measuring activity, ideas concerning unit iteration and identical units emerge (Lehrer, in press; McClain, Cobb, Gravemeijer, & Estes, 1999; Stephan et al., in press). Students progress from counting paces to constructing a unit of units, such as a "footstrip" consisting traces of their feet glued to a roll of adding-machine tape. Students may then confront the idea of expressing their result in different-size units (e.g., 15 paces or three footstrips each of which has 5 paces). They also discuss how to deal with leftover space, to count it as a whole unit or as part of a unit. Measuring with units of units helps students think about length as a composition of these units. Furthermore, it provided the basis for constructing rulers.

A somewhat different approach is suggested by other research (Boulton-Lewis, 1987; Clements, 1999; Clements, M. T. Battista, Sarama, Swaminathan, & McMillen, 1997; Nunes, Light, & Mason, 1993) that questions the wisdom of concentrating first on nonstandard units. For example, Boulton-Lewis et al. (1996) found that children used nonstandard units unsuccessfully. They were successful at an earlier age with standard units and measuring instruments. The researchers concluded that nonstandard units is not a good way to initially help children understand the need for standardized conventional units in the length measuring process. Just as interesting were students' strategy preferences. Students of every age, especially in Years 1 and 3, preferred to use standard rulers, even though their teachers were encouraging them to use nonstandard units. One teacher did not allow use of rulers in her classroom, saying they had become a distraction because children wanted to use them!

Another study (Nunes et al., 1993) suggests that children can meaningfully use rulers before they "reinvent" such ideas as units and iteration. They had 6- to 8-year-old children communicate about lengths using string, centimeter rulers, or one ruler and one broken ruler starting at 4 cm. The traditional ruler supported the children's reasoning more effectively than the string; children's performance almost doubled. Their strategies and language (it is as long as the "little line [half] just after three") indicated that children gave "correct responses based on rigorous procedures, clearly profiting from the numerical representation available through the ruler" (p. 46). They even did better with the *broken* ruler than the string, showing that they were not just "reading numbers off" the ruler. The unusual situation confused children only 20% of the time. The researchers concluded that conventional units already chosen and built into the ruler do not make measurement more difficult. Indeed, children benefited from the numerical representation provided even by the broken ruler.

The Piagetian-based argument, that children must conserve length before they can make sense of ready-made systems such as rulers (or computer tools, such as those discussed in the following section), may be an overstatement. Findings of these studies support a Vygotskian perspective, in which rulers are viewed as cultural instruments children can appropriate. That is, children can use rulers, appropriate them, and so build new mental tools. Not only do children prefer using rulers, but they can use them meaningfully and in combination with manipulable units to develop understanding of length measurement.

Based on research such as this, Clements (1999) suggested the following sequence of instruction. Students should be given a variety of experiences comparing the size of objects (e.g., finding all the objects in the classroom longer than their forearm). Next, students should engage in experiences that allow them to connect number to length. Teachers should provide students with both conventional rulers and manipulative units using standard units, such as centimeter cubes. As they explore with these tools the ideas of unit iteration (not leaving space between successive units, e.g.), correct alignment, (with a ruler) and the zero-point concept can be developed. He cautioned that teachers should focus on the meaning that the numerals on the ruler have for students, such as enumerating lengths rather than discrete numbers. In other words, classroom discussions should focus on "What are you counting?" Using manipulable units to make their own rulers helps children connect their experiences and ideas. In second or third grade, teachers might introduce the need for standard units and the relation between the size and number of units. The relationship between the size and number of units, the need for standardization of units, and additional measuring devices can be explored.

In a related vein, children should develop *measurement sense*. Teachers should present problems involving drawing and estimating lengths and observe children's strategies for solving these problems. Length tasks such as sketching a rectangle with particular dimensions may be presented, and teachers can observe whether students partition the lengths. Students who draw marks may need to have such perceptible units to quantify the length. These children can be presented with similar tasks, such as drawing a 10-by-5-cm rectangle, with an emphasis on equal-interval partitioning and the creation of different units of length. Students who do not and cannot segment lines to iterate units and partition lengths can be guided to continually tie the results of that activity to their counting. For example, they might draw a toy, measure it, and draw it again using the same (and later, a smaller) measure. They could measure distances by counting their steps along a path. Teachers should emphasize experiences and ideas of motion and distance. Finally, some students show sophisticated strategies. They draw proportional figures and visually partition line segments to assign them a length measure. These students can visually segment distances and use part-whole strategies to find unknown lengths. They have an "internal" measurement tool. This is not a static image, but a mental process of moving along an object, segmenting it, and counting the segments, even along complex paths, such as the perimeter of a shape. Students can impose such a "conceptual ruler" onto objects and geometric figures (Steffe, 1991). This is a critical point in their development of measurement sense. They might be given more complex "missing measures" problems such as determining the all the measures in Fig. 11.2.

Turtle geometry experiences especially help students link number and geometry in measurement activities and build measurement sense. Turtle geometry provides both motivation and meaning for many length measurement activities. This illustrates an important general guideline: Students should use measurement as a means for achieving a goal, not as an

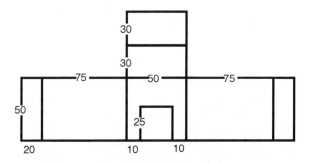

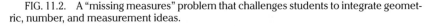

FIG. 11.2. A "missing measures" problem that challenges students to integrate geometric, number, and measurement ideas.

end in itself only. Note that even young children can abstract and generalize measurement ideas working with computers (Clements et al., 1997; Clements & Meredith, 1994; Kull, 1986; Try, 1989) if the interface is appropriate and activities are well planned (Watson & Brinkley, 1990/1991). Giving the turtle directions such as forward 10 steps, right turn 90°, forward 5 steps, they learn both length and turn and angle concepts.

Finally, Clements and Barrett (1996) found that introducing perimeter tasks not only teaches that important concept, but introduces children to the need for coordinating measures of parts of paths with the measure around the entire path. Perimeter tasks also emphasize measurable attributes of units as children examine grids and other ways of partitioning the sides and perimeter of a shape; by setting tasks that require a child to identify measured features, like focusing on the edges of a square tile rather than the entire tile as a unit, children learn to discriminate length from area. These researchers found that when children had to relate length units (e.g., cm) to side length and to perimeter within the same figure, they began to forge an invariant, multiplicative relation—they begin to define each line segment with reference to a particular set of repeated images of smaller, unit-size segments chained together—resulting from the iteration of the units. As the children "measured on" around a perimeter and then coordinated the value to a sum of individual sides, they developed coordinated images of collections of units. In this way, students internalize the process of iteration along paths and learn to relate measures of line segments with the iteration of unit-size segments as a basis for quantitative comparisons of perimeter.

Although different approaches have been suggested by research, several conclusions are consistent across most studies. First, measurement should not be taught as a simple skill; instead, it is a complex combination of concepts and skills that develops slowly over years. We have discussed six of these concepts. Second, initial informal activities should establish the attribute of length and develop concepts such as "longer," "shorter," and "equal in length" and strategies such as direct comparison. Third, emphasis on children solving real measurement problems, and, in so doing, building and iterating units, as well as units of units, helps children development strong concepts and skills. Fourth, teachers should help children closely connect the use of manipulative units and rulers. Even though research suggests varying instructional strategies, some convergence might be detected. For example, research does not support the early use of *multiple* nonstandard units. Either standard units and rulers might be used, or nonstandard units such as footsteps introduced in a carefully designed sequence of activities that leads to the use of standard units.

## AREA MEASUREMENT

Area is an amount of two-dimensional surface that is contained within a boundary and that can be quantified in some manner (Baturo & Nason, 1996). Area measurement assumes that: (a) a suitable two-dimensional region is chosen as a unit, (b) congruent regions have equal areas, (c) regions do not overlap, and (d) the area of the union of two regions is the sum of their areas (Reynolds & Wheatley, 1996). Thus, finding the area of a region can be thought of as tiling (or partitioning) a region with a two-dimensional unit of measure. Such understandings are complex, and children develop them over time. For example, they must develop the understanding that decomposing and rearranging shapes does not affect their area. Perhaps most challenging is developing the ability to use two linear dimensions to build the idea of a two-dimensional space. Without such understandings and abilities, children often learn a rule, such as multiplying two lengths, without meaning.

Although area measurement is typically stressed in Grades 3–5 (National Council of Teachers of Mathematics, 2000), the literature suggests that there are some less formal aspects of area measurement that can be introduced in earlier grades. We describe some of the important concepts that form the foundation for area measurement and then describe some instructional approaches that promote these ideas.

### Concepts of Area Measurement

There are at least five foundational concepts that are involved in learning to measure area: (a) partitioning, (b) unit iteration, (c) conservation, (d) structuring an array, and (e) linear measurement. As with linear measurement, *partitioning* is the mental act of cutting two-dimensional space with a two-dimensional unit. Teachers often assume that the product of two lengths structures a region into an area of two-dimensional units for students. However, the construction of a two-dimensional array from linear units is nontrivial. Students' first experiences with area might include tiling a region with a two-dimensional unit of choice and, in the process, discuss issues of leftover spaces, overlapping units, and precision. Discussions of these ideas lead students to mentally partition a region into subregions that can be counted.

As they cover regions with area units with no gaps or overlapping, children can also develop the concept of *unit iteration* to measure area. As with length measurement, children often cover space, but do not extend units over the boundaries (Stephan et al., in press). Also, children often choose units that physically resemble the region they are covering, for example, choosing bricks to cover a rectangular region and beans to cover an outline of their hands (Lehrer, in press; Nunes et al., 1993). They also mix unit shapes, rectangular and triangular, to cover the same region. Once these problems have been solved, students need to structure two-dimensional space into an organized array of units, a concept to which we return later.

Similar to linear measurement, *conservation* of area is an important idea that is often neglected in instruction. Students have difficulty accepting that when they cut a given region and rearrange its parts to form another shape, the area remains the same (Lehrer, in press). Students should explore and discuss the consequences of folding or rearranging pieces to establish that one region, cut and reassembled, covers the same space. Related research shows that young children use different strategies to make judgments of area. For example, 4- and 5-year-olds may match only one side of figures when attempting to compare their areas. They also use height + width rules to make area judgments (Cuneo, 1980). Children from 6 to 8 years use a linear extent rule, such as the diagonal of a rectangle. Only after this age to most children move to multiplicative rules. This leads to our next concept.

Students need to *structure an array* to understand area as truly two-dimensional. Children develop through a series of levels in developing this difficult competence, including the following: (a) little or no ability to organize, coordinate, and structure two-dimensional space (cannot represent covering a rectangle with tiles without overlaps or gaps); (b) complete covering, but counting incorrectly (cannot keep track of which units were counted; e.g., counts around the border and then unsystematically counts internal units); (c) covering and counting but again with no row or column structuring; (d) the local, incomplete use of rows or columns (e.g., counts some, but not all, rows as a unit); (e) structuring the rectangle as a set of rows; (f) iterating those rows (e.g., counting each row of 5, "5, 10, 15 ..."; (g) iterating the rows in coordination with the number of squares in a column (e.g., counting by 5); (h) understanding that the rectangle's dimensions provide the number of squares in rows and columns and thus meaningfully calculating area from these dimensions (M. T. Battista, Clements, Arnoff, K. Battista, & Borrow, 1998; Outhred & Mitchelmore, 1992, 2000). Without this competence, students cannot use the area formula meaningfully. They are also more likely to confuse concepts such as perimeter and area, for example, believing that counting the units around a figure gives its area.

Finally, most articles explicitly mention that a good foundation in *linear measurement* is a necessary condition for understanding area measurement. This is obviously the case because area measurement, in its more sophisticated form, is the product of two linear measurements.

## Teaching Area Measurement

What kind of activities help students learn initial area concepts, structure arrays, and finally learn all five concepts to form a complete foundation for measuring area meaningfully? First, students should investigate covering regions with a unit of measure. They should realize that there are to be no gaps or overlapping and that the entire region should be covered.

Second, they should learn how to structure arrays. This is a long-term process, but second graders can make significant gains. Figuring out how many squares in pictures of arrays, with less and less graphic information of clues, is an excellent task (see Akers, M. T. Battista, Goodrow, Clements, & Sarama, 1997; M. T. Battista et al., 1998). Students can also tile rectangular regions and keep count. However, only using square manipulatives may eventually provide too much support; for example, students may not be able to overlap them (Outhred & Mitchelmore, 2000). Instead, as students create arrays, they should also be encouraged to draw the results of their covering (cf. Akers et al. , 1997; Reynolds & Wheatley, 1996). Such drawings can reveal how students are actually structuring the array—or not. For example, some students draw a series of square tiles within the region they were measuring, yet there were obvious gaps between tiles. Other students draw an array that had unequal number of units in each row. Students need to be provided tasks and instruction that leads them through the levels of learning this structuring (Akers et al., 1997; M. T. Battista et al., 1998).

Third, students should learn that the length of the sides of a rectangle can determine the number of units in each row and the number of rows in the array. Fourth—and this usually is appropriate only in the intermediate grades—children can meaningfully learn to multiply the two dimensions as a shortcut for determining the total number of squares. An appropriate understanding of linear measurement (that the length of a side specifies the number of unit lengths that will fit along it) is essential. Only then can students construct the area formula.

Thus, instruction in area should not begin with rulers. In one study (Nunes et al., 1993), children failed to solve area problems when they used a ruler but were able to devise multiplicative solutions when given a chance to cover with a unit. If instruction begins with a ruler, one of the most common mistakes is for children to measure the length of each side and add the two linear measures. Lehrer, Jenkins, and Osana (1998) suggested engaging students in tasks requiring them to find the area of an irregular surface with a unit of their choice. For example, their students were asked to trace their hands and find their area using a variety of manipulatives (e.g., centimeter cubes, beans). Though most children chose objects that most physically resemble the shape of their hands (i.e., beans), this task provided the opportunity for students to discuss how to deal with leftover space that is uncovered. Because the students were unsure how to solve the dilemma of counting the extra space, the teacher introduced a square grid as a measurement device. They gradually accepted this notation and used it to estimate and combine partial units.

As a follow-up task, students can be asked to draw and measure islands with their newly constructed square grids. This type of task gives students more opportunity to measure with square units and to combine parts of units together to form whole units. The teacher should not focus on the calculation processes students develop but rather on the meaning that their procedures have for them. Finally, students may be moved toward building arrays with tasks such as finding the area of zoo cages. Students in Lehrer's study (in press) were given a set of various, polygonal outlines that represented the floor plan of different zoo cages. Students were provided with rulers if they found them necessary. Though some students measured the lengths of each side of a rectangle, they incorrectly argued that the resulting area would be 40 *inches*. Other students partitioned the rectangular cages into array structures and argued that they really meant 40 *square* units. In this way, students were provided a chance to relate the familiar array structure to ideas of length.

In summary, the too-frequent practice of simple counting of units to find area (achievable by preschoolers) leading directly to teaching formulas is a recipe for disaster. Instead, educators should build upon young children's initial spatial intuitions and appreciate the need for students to: (a) construct the idea of measurement units (including development of a measurement sense for standard units; e.g., finding common objects in the environment that have a unit measure), (b) have many experiences covering quantities with appropriate measurement units and counting those units, (c) spatially structure the object they are to measure (e.g., linking counting by groups to the structure of rectangular arrays; building two-dimensional concepts); and eventually (often in the intermediate grades), (d) construct the inverse relationship between the size of a unit and the number of units used in a particular measurement, and (e) construct two-dimensional space and corresponding multiplicative relations.

## ANGLE AND TURN MEASURE

Mathematically, angle has been defined in distinct but related ways. For example, an angle can be considered the figure formed by two rays extending from the same point. Angle also can be defined as the amount of turning necessary to bring one line or plane into coincidence with or parallel to another. Methods of measuring the size of angles are based on the division of a circle. The degree, one 360th of a full angle, is the most common unit used in elementary school.

As with length and area, children need to understand concepts such as partitioning and unit iteration to understand angle and turn measure. Due to the nature of this domain of measurement, and our focus on young children, we emphasize basic concepts of understanding what is being measured.

Angle and turn measure are difficult concepts for students. When judging the size of angles, students frequently focus on the length of the line segments that form its sides, the tilt of the top line segment, the area enclosed by the triangular region defined by the drawn sides, the length between the sides, or the proximity of the two sides (Clements & M. T. Battista, 1989). Some misconceptions decrease over the elementary years, such as orientation; but others, such as the effect of segment length, do not change, and some, such the distance between endpoints, increase (Lehrer et al., 1998).

One might argue that angle and turn measure are both difficult and relatively esoteric mathematical concepts and therefore need not be introduced to young children. However, there are valid reasons to include these as goals for early childhood mathematics education. First, children can and do use angle and turn measures informally. Second, use of angle size, at least implicitly, is necessary to work with shapes; for example, children who distinguish a square from a nonsquare rhombus are recognizing angle size relationships. Third, angle measure plays a pivotal role in geometry throughout school, and laying the groundwork early is a sound curricular goal. Fourth, there is research evidence that young children can learn these concepts successfully (Lehrer et al., 1998).

As noted in the previous chapter on geometry (Clements, chap. 10, this volume), however, there are initial foundations on which children can build. (That chapter discusses several studies related to angle concepts that we do not repeat here.) For example, children in preschool use angles implicitly as in block building (Ginsburg, Inoue, & Seo, 1999). Children as young as 5 appear to use angles to represent locations of objects in a circle (i.e., an intuitive use of polar coordinates; Sandberg & Huttenlocher, 1996). In an early study, though 5-year-olds showed no evidence of attention to angle in judging congruence, they could match angles in correspondence tasks (Beilin, 1984; Beilin, Klein, & Whitehurst, 1982). Some primary-grade children can distinguish between angles based on size (Lehrer et al., 1998). So, helping children mathematize their intuitive use of angle size, matching shapes by angles, and using angles to complete puzzles are all within the competence of most children from a very young age.

Children do much more than recognize that geometric figures have corners. They appear to reliably distinguish among angles of different measure, and can mentally decompose a figure into separate attributes of length and angle (Lehrer et al., 1998). Still, as noted previously, they often confound angle and length measures, so careful instructional attention must be given to angle and turn measure. They especially need help learning to integrate turns, and, in general, a dynamic understanding of angle measure-as-rotation, into their understandings of angles.

One particularly useful instructional tool to accomplish these goals is through the use of the computer. Certain computer environments help children quantify angles and especially turns, attaching numbers to these quantities to achieve true measurement. Here we examine two types of computer environments.

The first type is the computer manipulative, perhaps the more appropriate of the two for younger children. In *Shapes,* for example, children work with on-screen geometric figures. They use turn-and-flip tools to make pictures and designs and to solve puzzles (see Fig. 11.3).

Just using these tools helps children bring the concept of a turn to an explicit level of awareness (Sarama, Clements, & Vukelic, 1996). For example, 4-year-old Leah first called the tool the "spin" tool, which made sense—she clicked it repeatedly, "spinning" the shape. Within 1 week, however, she called it the turn tool and used the left or right tool deliberately. Similarly, when Mitchell worked off-computer, he quickly manipulated the pattern block pieces, resisting answering any questions as to his intent or his reasons. When he finally paused, a researcher asked him how

FIG. 11.3.    A computer shapes manipulative, from the *Building Blocks* project (DLM Math Software, see Clements & Sarama, 2003a. 2003b).

he had made a particular piece fit. He struggled with the answer and then finally said that he "turned it." When working on-computer, he seemed aware of his actions, in that when asked how many times he turned a particular piece, he said," Three," without hesitation (Sarama et al., 1996).

A second computer environment is Logo's turtle geometry. Logo can also assist children in learning ideas of angle and turn measurement. A first grader explained how he turned the turtle 45°: "I went 5, 10, 15, 20 ... 45! [rotating her hand as she counted]. It's like a car speedometer. You go up by fives!" (Clements & M. T. Battista, 1991). This child is mathematizing turning: She is applying a unit to an act of turning and using her counting abilities to determine a measurement.

Research indicates that the traditional Logo philosophy of body syntony—or connections with one's physical movements—is a critical instructional component. One study showed that children learned turn measure first through physical rotations, especially rotations of their own bodies (Clements, M. T. Battista, Sarama, & Swaminathan, 1996). During the same time, they gained limited knowledge of assigning numbers to certain turns with turtle geometry, initially by establishing benchmarks. A synthesis of these two domains—turn-as-body-motion and turn-as-number—constituted a critical juncture in learning about turns for many primary-grade students. This and other studies have used the Logo turtle to help children mathematize[1] their physical experiences. In one study across Grades K–6, the youngest children improved on certain turn and angle tasks the most relative to controls (Clements & M. T. Battista, 2001). These tests involved difficult distractors, which demanded, for example, that children differentiate between greater angle measure and greater side length. Thus, thinking about angles and turns in turtle geometry helped children as young as kindergarten develop robust concepts of their measure.

To understand angles, students must understand the various aspects of the angle concept. They must overcome difficulties with orientation, discriminate angles as critical parts of geometric figures, and construct and represent the idea of turns, among others. Furthermore, they must construct a high level of integration among these aspects. This is a difficult task that is best begun early, as children deal with corners of figures, comparing angle size, and turns.

## CONCLUSION

Measurement is one of the principal real-world applications of mathematics. It bridges two critical realms of mathematics: geometry or spatial

---

[1]We define mathematization as representing and elaborating mathematically—creating models of an everyday activity with mathematical objects, such as numbers and shapes; mathematical actions, such as counting or transforming shapes; and their structural relationships. Mathematizing involves reinventing, redescribing, reorganizing, quantifying, structuring, abstracting, and generalizing that which is first understood on an intuitive and informal level in the context of everyday activity.

relations and real numbers. Number and operations are essential elements of measurement. The measurement process subdivides continuous quantities such as length to make them countable. Measurement provides a model and an application for both number and arithmetic operations. In this way, measurement helps connect the two realms of number and geometry, each providing conceptual support to the other.

Research on linear, area, and angle and turn measurement indicates that measuring in general is more complex than learning the skills or procedures for determining a measure. The conceptual, mental activities of children as they engage in measuring situations should be the focus of instruction. Table 1.3 in chapter 1 of this book provides research-based guidelines for curriculum goals and learning trajectories in early childhood measurement based on the research reviewed here.

## ACKNOWLEDGMENTS

This chapter was supported in part by the National Science Foundation under Grants ESI-9730804, "Building Blocks—Foundations for Mathematical Thinking, Pre-Kindergarten to Grade 2: Research-Based Materials Development" and ESI-98-17540: "Conference on Standards for Preschool and Kindergarten Mathematics Education," as well as a grant from the ExxonMobil Foundation. Any opinions, findings, and conclusions or recommendations expressed in this material are those of the author and do not necessarily reflect the views of either foundation.

## REFERENCES

Akers, J., Battista, M. T., Goodrow, A., Clements, D. H., & Sarama, J. (1997). *Shapes, halves, and symmetry: Geometry and fractions*. Palo Alto, CA: Dale Seymour Publications.

Battista, M. T., Clements, D. H., Arnoff, J., Battista, K., & Borrow, C. V. A. (1998). Students' spatial structuring of 2D arrays of squares. *Journal for Research in Mathematics Education, 29*, 503–532.

Baturo, A. & Nason, R. (1996). Student teachers' subject matter knowledge within the domain of area measurement. *Educational Studies in Mathematics, 31*, 235–268.

Beilin, H. (1984). Cognitive theory and mathematical cognition: Geometry and space. In B. Gholson & T. L. Rosenthanl (Eds.), *Applications of cognitive-developmental theory* (pp. 49–93). New York: Academic Press.

Beilin, H., Klein, A., & Whitehurst, B. (1982). *Strategies and structures in understanding geometry*. New York: City University of New York. (ERIC Document Reproduction Service No. ED ED 225808)

Boulton-Lewis, G. (1987). Recent cognitive theories applied to sequential length measuring knowledge in young children. *British Journal of Educational Psychology, 57*, 330–342.

Boulton-Lewis, G. M., Wilss, L. A., & Mutch, S. L. (1996). An analysis of young children's strategies and use of devices of length measurement. *Journal of Mathematical Behavior, 15*, 329–347.

Clements, D. (1999). Teaching length measurement: Research challenges. *School Science and Mathematics, 99*(1), 5–11.

Clements, D. H., & Barrett, J. (1996). Representing, connecting and restructuring knowledge: A micro-genetic analysis of a child's learning in an open-ended task involving perimeter, paths and polygons. In E. Jakubowski, D. Watkins, & H. Biske (Eds.), *Proceedings of the eighteenth annual meeting of the North America Chapter of the International Group for the Psychology of Mathematics Education* (Vol. 1, pp. 211–216). Columbus, OH: ERIC Clearinghouse for Science, Mathematics, and Environmental Education.

Clements, D. H., & Battista, M. T. (1989). Learning of geometric concepts in a Logo environment. *Journal for Research in Mathematics Education, 20,* 450–467.

Clements, D. H., & Battista, M. T. (1991). *Logo geometry.* Morristown, NJ: Silver Burdett & Ginn.

Clements, D. H., & Battista, M. T. (1992). Geometry and spatial reasoning. In D. A. Grouws (Ed.), *Handbook of research on mathematics teaching and learning* (pp. 420–464). New York: Macmillan.

Clements, D. H., & Battista, M. T. (2001). Logo and geometry. *Journal for Research in Mathematics Education Monograph Series, 10.*

Clements, D. H., Battista, M. T., & Sarama, J. (1998). Development of geometric and measurement ideas. In R. Lehrer & D. Chazan (Eds.), *Designing learning environments for developing understanding of geometry and space* (pp. 201–225). Mahwah, MJ: Lawrence Erlbaum Associates.

Clements, D. H., Battista, M. T., Sarama, J., & Swaminathan, S. (1996). Development of turn and turn measurement concepts in a computer-based instructional unit. *Educational Studies in Mathematics, 30,* 313–337.

Clements, D. H., Battista, M. T., Sarama, J., Swaminathan, S., & McMillen, S. (1997). Students' development of length measurement concepts in a Logo-based unit on geometric paths. *Journal for Research in Mathematics Education, 28*(1), 70–95.

Clements, D. H., & Meredith, J. S. (1994). *Turtle math.* Montreal, Quebec: Logo Computer Systems, Inc.

Clements, D. H., & Sarama, J. (2003a). *DLM early childhood express math resource guide.* Columbus, OH: SRA/McGraw-Hill.

Clements, D. H., & Sarama, J. (2003b). *DLM math software* [software]. Columbus, OH: SRA/McGraw-Hill.

Copeland, R. (1974). *How children learn mathematics: Teaching implications of Piaget's research* (2nd ed.). New York: Macmillan.

Cuneo, D. (1980). A general strategy for quantity judgments: The height + width rule. *Child Development, 51,* 299–301.

Ginsburg, H. P., Inoue, N., & Seo, K. H. (1999). Young children doing mathematics: Observations of everyday activities. In J. V. Copley (Ed.), *Mathematics in the early years* (pp. 87–99). Reston, VA: National Council of Teachers of Mathematics.

Hiebert, J. (1981). Cognitive development and learning linear measurement. *Journal for Research in Mathematics Education, 12*(3), 197–211.

Inhelder, B., Sinclair, H., & Bovet, M. (1974). *Learning and the development of cognition.* Cambridge, MA: Harvard University Press.

Kamii, C., & Clark, F. (1997). Measurement of length: The need for a better approach to teaching. *School Science and Mathematics, 97*(3), 116–121.

Kull, J. A. (1986). Learning and Logo. In P. F. Campbell & G. G. Fein (Eds.), *Young children and microcomputers* (pp. 103–130). Englewood Cliffs, NJ: Prentice-Hall.

Lehrer, R. (in press). Developing understanding of measurement. In J. Kilpatrick, W. G. Martin, & D. E. Schifter (Eds.), *A research companion to principles and standards for school mathematics.* Reston, VA: National Council of Teachers of Mathematics.

Lehrer, R., Jenkins, M., & Osana, H. (1998). Longitudinal study of children's reasoning about space and geometry. In R. Lehrer & D. Chazan (Eds.), *Designing learning environments for developing understanding of geometry and space* (pp. 137–167). Mahwah, NJ: Lawrence Erlbaum Associates.

Lubinski, C., & Thiessan, D. (1996). Exploring measurement through literature. *Teaching Children Mathematics, 2*(5), 260–263.

McClain, K., Cobb, P., Gravemeijer, K. & Estes, B. (1999). Developing mathematical reasoning within the context of measurement. In L. Stiff (Ed.), *Developing mathematical reasoning, K–12* (pp. 93–106). Reston, VA: National Council of Teachers of Mathematics.

National Center for Education Statistics. (1996). *Pursuing excellence, NCES 97-198 (initial findings from the Third International Mathematics and Science Study)* [Online]. Retrieved January 19, 1997, from www.ed.gov/NCES/timss

Nunes, T., Light, P., & Mason, J. (1993). Tools for thought: The measurement of length and area. *Learning and Instruction, 3,* 39–54.

Outhred, L. N., & Mitchelmore, M. (1992). Representation of area: A pictorial perspective. In W. Geeslin & K. Graham (Eds.), *Proceedings of the sixteenth Psychology in Mathematics Education Conference* (Vol. 2, pp. 194–201). Durham, NH: Program Committee of the sixteenth Psychology in Mathematics Education Conference.

Outhred, L., & Mitchelmore, M. (2000). Young children's intuitive understanding of rectangular area measurement. *Journal for Research in Mathematics Education, 31*(2), 144–167.

Piaget, J., Inhelder, B., & Szeminska, A. (1960). *The child's conception of geometry.* London: Routledge and Kegan Paul.

National Council of Teachers of Mathematics. (2000). *Principles and standards for school mathematics.* Reston, VA: Author.

Reynolds, A., & Wheatley, G. (1996). Elementary students' construction and coordination of units in an area setting. *Journal for Research in Mathematics Education, 27*(5), 564–581.

Sandberg, E. H., & Huttenlocher, J. (1996). The development of hierarchical representation of two-dimensional space. *Child Development, 67*(3), 721–739.

Sarama, J., Clements, D. H., & Vukelic, E. B. (1996). The role of a computer manipulative in fostering specific psychological/mathematical processes. In E. Jakubowski, D. Watkins, & H. Biske (Eds.), *Proceedings of the eighteenth annual meeting of the North America Chapter of the International Group for the Psychology of Mathematics Education* (Vol. 2, pp. 567–572). Columbus, OH: ERIC Clearinghouse for Science, Mathematics, and Environmental Education.

Steffe, L. P. (1991). Operations that generate quantity. *Learning and Individual Differences, 3,* 61–82.

Stephan, M., & Clements, D. H. (in press). Linear, area, and time measurement in grades pre-K to 2. In D. H. Clements (Ed.), *Learning and teaching measurement.* Reston, VA: National Council of Teachers of Mathematics.

Stephan, M., Cobb, P., Gravemeijer, K., & Estes, B. (in press). The role of tools in supporting students' development of measurement conceptions. In *2001 NCTM Yearbook.* Reston, VA: National Council of Teachers of Mathematics.

Try, K. M. (1989). *Cognitive and social change in young children during Logo activities: A study of individual differences.* Unpublished doctoral dissertation, University of New England, Armidale, New South Wales, Australia.

Watson, J. A., & Brinkley, V. M. (1990/1991). Space and premathematic strategies young children adopt in initial Logo problem solving. *Journal of Computing in Childhood Education, 2,* 17–29.

# Section 3

## Curriculum, Learning, Teaching, and Assessment

# 12

# Making Sense

Kathy Richardson
*Mathematical Perspectives Teacher Development Center*

Making sense is at the heart of mathematics and so it must also be at the heart of the mathematics we do with young children. Mathematical competence develops in children, who learn that mathematics makes sense and who learn to trust their own abilities to make sense of it. Asking children to perform without understanding interferes with their development of mathematical ideas. It is not always obvious which experiences help build understanding in young children and which do not. We often make assumptions that children are thinking what we are thinking when they perform correctly. For example, when I taught preschool, I had my children work with dot cards. I would show them cards with the same dot arrangements that we find on dice, and they learned to recognize these arrangements. One day, I asked them to use counters and build what they saw on the card. To my amazement, I found that they did not use the correct number of counters. Instead they made an X shape to match the shape of the five dots and they made a "squarish" shape to match the arrangement of the nine dots. I thought I was teaching them quantity but they were focused on what the card looked like. I learned from this that I must always interact with children in ways that ask them to show me what they know.

The experience with the dot cards is not unique. In my 30 years of studying the thinking of young children, I have observed many situations in which children appear to understand but, upon further examination, I find they do not. This "illusion" of learning can mislead those charged with the task of helping children develop foundational mathematical understandings. When teachers assume children understand more than they do, they do not provide the experiences necessary for the development of an understanding of these ideas. And even more detrimental, children approach the learning of mathematics as tasks to complete rather than as a sense-making process.

Consider the task of learning to count to 10. Children can appear to know more than they do about counting if situations are set up to prevent errors. It is not uncommon for adults to create situations that help children get the right answer rather than to bump up against the underlying ideas. I met one of the children who helped me understand this problem during her first week of kindergarten. Stephanie appeared eager to work with me as she joined me at the back of her classroom. I placed a group of 15 counters on the table and asked her to find out how many there were. Stephanie very carefully touched each counter as she said, "One, two, three, four, five, six, seven, eight, nine, ten...." Without any hesitation at all, she continued to count the remaining counters saying, "One, two, three, four, five." When she finished counting, I asked, "How many are there?" Stephanie replied, "Five." In order to see what would happen when Stephanie did not face the problem of running out of words with which to count, I asked her to hand me five. This time she started counting aloud, but the counting faded away and she ended up handing me the whole pile of 15 counters. I asked her how many she had handed me and she answered, "Five." Then I asked her to place five counters on a paper that had 10 dots on it, arranged in two rows of 5. She proceeded to cover each of the 10 dots with a counter. I again asked her how many counters were on the paper and she answered, "Five." At this point, I decided to see what she would do if I had her work with a smaller number. I removed some of the counters leaving seven on the table and asked Stephanie to count this pile. All the time we were working, Stephanie was watching my face for clues to whether she was right or wrong. Now, it seemed as though she finally remembered what she was supposed to do. Before counting the pile of seven, she carefully lined up the counters in a row and then very precisely and deliberately touched each one saying, "One, two, three, four, five, six, seven." I asked her, "How many?" and she responded, "Seven."

It appeared that Stephanie had been taught the behaviors necessary to get the right answer when counting but she hadn't learned the underlying idea or essence of what counting is about. She had been shown how to line up the counters so she would be able to keep track easily. She had been taught to say one counting word as she touched each object and she knew she had to repeat the last word she said when asked, "How many?" If I had not asked her to apply what she knew to an unfamiliar situation, I might have assumed she not only could get right answers but that she understood as well. However, when Stephanie was given more than 10 to count, she had no way to approach this. Children who understand more about counting than Stephanie did might respond with "I can't count that high." Or they often just stop when they run out of words they know. But even more revealing of her lack of understanding than starting over with "one" when she ran out of words, was her inability to deal with the requests to count smaller amounts when the situations varied from what she had been taught. The problem was not that she couldn't count past 10 but that she had misconceptions about what the task of counting is about.

When children understand counting, they are able to count in many different situations. We can't assume children understand what they need to know about counting if we only see them count in one kind of setting. I learned this from another child whom I observed filling a small plastic container with cubes. He counted each cube as he dropped it into the container. When he put the eighth cube into the container, the container was full so he stopped counting and wrote 8 on his paper. Because this task didn't seem to challenge him, I decided to make the task a bit harder by having him fill the container without counting, dump out the counters onto the table and then count and see how many he had. This would require him to organize and keep track of the objects, something unnecessary when he was counting as he filled the container. He chose a smaller container and filled it as I had directed him to do. I could see that the container held four objects. He dumped the counters out and proceeded to count them. He pointed at the objects and said the counting sequence but he didn't stop when he had counted them all. Instead, he continued to count the objects over and over again. I realized then that filling the container was the cue he needed to stop counting and now he didn't have that support. I stopped him while he was counting and asked him to hand me three of the four objects. He handed me one. I then asked him to hand me two objects. He gave me the rest of the counters in the pile. At first, I thought it might be a language problem so I had his teacher repeat the assessment in the child's native language. He showed he still couldn't count competently unless the situation were structured for him.

Conscientious parents and teachers work hard to prepare children for kindergarten but they do not always give the children the experiences that will help them most in the long run. My experiences working with kindergarten children bear this out. I am reminded of one particular group of kindergarten children who had been identified and placed in a class designed to provide them with extra help in mathematics. Most of them had attended a preschool for at-risk children before coming to kindergarten. Through my assessments, I found that most of them knew how to count by rote and recognize numerals to 10 or even to 20. However, only one of them could actually count three or four objects. Though what they had learned was important, it was not what they most needed in order to make the expected progress in kindergarten. Children who have been identified as at risk who leave their preschool experience appearing to know what is necessary but without the underlying ideas to build on will continue to fall behind if these needs are not met.

Undeveloped ideas and misconceptions are a normal part of the child's evolving understanding. We can't prevent these misconceptions by teaching children to say words or perform procedures they don't understand. If we want children to make sense of mathematics, we must provide a variety of experiences that ask the children to think about what they are doing and to focus on critical elements of the concept. It is through encountering an idea in different settings and in many different ways over time that generalizations begin to form. If we insist that children must always have correct responses for concepts they are not ready to understand, they must resort to rote memory of these correct responses, as they will not be able to make sense of the situations by themselves. When we try to teach children our way of thinking or our way of getting answers before they can understand, we only interfere with their sense-making process. They stop looking for their own meaning and instead look to the teacher to see if they are right or wrong. As long as teachers think their job is to make sure children "do it right," children will be limited in their ability to understand and make sense of concepts.

Children can say the right answer and not know what they are saying, as with the dot cards. They can also give the "wrong" answer and still be pondering an important idea. We do not need to know ahead of time when giving a child a task or a question whether it will be out of reach or not. If we are willing to learn from the children's honest responses, we will be able to present ideas to them in all their complexity rather than oversimplifying them in order to ensure "success." Another experience comes to mind. A group of children were asked to figure out which jar held the most rice. In the set were three mustard jars that were the same shape but of different sizes. One of the children was convinced that they should all hold the same amount of rice. Even after pouring the rice from one jar to the other, he said, "I see it. But I don't believe it!" This response indicates that the child is still searching and trying to make sense. He is not content with accepting something just because "teacher said."

As I worked with children over the years, I had to redefine what it meant to be a good teacher. Being a good teacher is not about getting all your children to perform at a particular level at a particular time. Being a good teacher is about knowing what your children already know and what they are still grappling with. It is valuing where each child is on their own personal journey and not comparing them to anyone else. Standards and goals give me an idea of what I must be working toward with my children. One child may be a long way from achieving a particular standard whereas another child may have reached this standard long ago. My job is to challenge all my children no matter if they are just figuring out how to hand me 2 jellybeans or if they are figuring out how to share 12 jellybeans with two people. I don't need to be reluctant to find out what a child really knows but to be excited by the process they are engaged in.

The opportunity is here to develop mathematics programs that enhance and maximize the children's learning rather than those that promote the kinds of learning that give the appearance of high expectations but that in reality result in inappropriate practices that interfere with the real work and growth of children.

# 13

# Number Worlds: A Research-Based Mathematics Program for Young Children

Sharon Griffin
*Clark University*

Imagine for a moment that you are 3 or 4 years old and the world you experience is not the single, integrated entity known to adults but rather, is a multitude of separate, independent, and unrelated worlds. We can call one such world, the "world of counting numbers." Already, in your 4 or 5 years on this earth, you have learned quite a bit about this world. You can count from 1 to 5 (or 1 to 10), you know that you must touch one and only one object in a set as you do so, and you probably also know that the last number word said "tells" you how many are in the set. You may even be able to count backward from five to one and to count on from the bigger number when asked to figure out how many there are when you add two small numbers. As yet, however, you may have little idea of the uses to which these skills can be put to help you make sense of another world you are also intimately familiar with: the "world of quantity," in all its physical manifestations.

In your few years on earth, you have also learned quite a bit about this quantitative world. You can recognize and describe global, perceptually salient, differences in the world of objects (e.g., one group is "bigger" or "smaller" than another), in the world of dot sets (e.g., one pattern has "more" dots), in the world of paths and lines (e.g., one position is "farther" along), and in the world of scale measures (e.g., on a thermometer, one position is "higher" up). You may even be able to recognize global differences in the world of dials (e.g., one point is "farther around" than another is). As yet, however, you may have no idea that the counting words you have learned can help you describe these different manifestations of quantity more precisely or help you describe changes in these quantity arrays. Lacking this overarching concept, it is very likely that these representations of quantity may themselves seem to reside in separate, unrelated worlds.

A third world that you have very likely been exposed to but that is probably still mysterious is the "world of formal symbols." Although you may be able to say the names of the written numerals and possibly even of the operation signs (e.g., "plus," "minus"), you may have little idea of the quantities associated with each symbol or the operations (e.g., addition, subtraction) each entails. A major goal of the Pre-K–2 Number Worlds program (Griffin, 1997, 1998, 2000; Griffin & Case, 1995) is to help children broaden and deepen their understanding of each of these worlds and establish a rich set of connections among them.

How will we know if children have achieved this integrated set of understandings? Consider the following situations:

- John bought four candies. Then he bought three more.
- John drove four miles. Then he drove three miles farther.
- Yesterday the temperature was four degrees. Today it went up by three degrees.
- Yesterday the show came on at 4 o'clock. Today it will come on 3 hours later.

If children have constructed the interconnected set of understandings referred to previously, they will have no difficulty representing these problem situations, seeing the equivalence among them, solving the problem, and writing a number sentence $(4 + 3 = 7)$ to record the process.

Consider what they have learned to make this possible. In each of these situations, numbers are represented in different ways: as objects in the first example, as segments along a path in the second, as positions on a scale in the third, and as points on a dial in the fourth. Although adults and older children immediately see these situations as equivalent and as entailing a simple addition operation, when we consider the physical operations involved in each, they can be seen to be quite different—so different that they might seem to be from different worlds. In the first situation, one has a number of small objects (candies) that one can physically move from one location to another. One can see a larger group of objects at the end of one's work and count up the number of units it contains. In the second situation, however, the object that moves is oneself and the only result that one can see at the end is that one occupies a different location.

To solve the aforementioned addition problems, children must not only appreciate the equivalence of the different forms of representation but they must also understand that the language used to talk about numbers and about change in magnitude differs, as well, across these representational contexts. Finally, children must understand that each quantity and each change in magnitude indicated in the aforementioned situations can be represented symbolically with a common symbol system. This is a substantial developmental achievement and it is typically not mastered until the first or second grade, marking one milestone among many in the development of children's mathematical understanding.

The name of the Number Worlds program was specifically chosen to capture several aspects of the developmental progression alluded to in the foregoing and to capture several features of the Pre-K–2 program that was developed, over a period of 12 years, to facilitate this process. Although many children appear to make this transition quite naturally, supported by their early home and school experiences, there are many children in the United States who do not and who start their first formal learning of arithmetic without the knowledge needed to make sense of the instruction that is provided (Griffin, Case, & Siegler, 1994). It was with these children in mind—children who typically live in low-income communities, children who are at risk for school failure—that an early version of the Number Worlds program called Rightstart was developed. The program has subsequently been expanded to include four grade levels and to serve the needs of *all* children, from a variety of cultures, linguistic backgrounds, and income levels. The new name reflects this broader scope.

More specifically, the name "Number Worlds" captures three overarching goals of the program. First, it was designed to help children integrate the three worlds referred to earlier, namely: the world of counting numbers, the world of quantity, and the world of formal symbols. Second, it was designed to expose children to the major ways number and quantity are represented, and talked about, in our culture. Third, it was designed to provide visual–spatial learning environments, "worlds to explore" in the classroom, that encourage children to construct the desired knowledge in a hands-on, interactive fashion. In the remainder of this chapter, these goals are described in greater detail along with several other features of the program that support their realization.

## KNOWLEDGE GOALS

The informal description of the knowledge goals of the program provided earlier suggests that the Number Worlds program is, above all else, a developmental approach. It is based on careful research on the manner in which children spontaneously construct mathematical knowledge between the ages of 4 and 8 years, given a "good-enough" environment in which to do so; on the ways this knowledge is sequenced and organized in children's thought across this age range; and on the learning opportunities that provide the best fit for young children's sense-making capabilities within this age range (see Griffin & Case, 1997, for a review of this research).

The learning objectives that are built into the Number Worlds program at each grade level reflect this natural developmental progression. This makes good sense, educationally, because the knowledge that is targeted at each grade level is knowledge that is known (a) to be within the developmental capabilities of most, if not all, children within each age group and (b) to provide a natural building block for knowledge at the next level. The knowledge that is targeted at each grade level can also be seen to be foundational for success in school math because the children on whom this developmental progression is based (i.e., the typical subjects in developmental research) are typically children from middle- to upper-middle-income homes who do well in school math. Finally, because many children from all income levels are known to struggle with school math, having an opportunity to broaden, deepen, and consolidate knowledge that may be acquired quite naturally, at least in a bare-bones fashion, can be seen to be highly beneficial.

The developmental milestones that research has identified as crucial building blocks for success in school math have been described, in part, in the opening paragraphs. They can be summarized as follows. By the age of 4 years, most children have constructed an initial *counting schema* (i.e., a well-organized knowledge structure for counting), which enables them to verbally count from one to five, to use the one-to-one correspondence rule, and to use the cardinality rule (Gelman, 1978). By the same age, most children have also constructed an initial *quantity schema*, which gives them an intuitive understanding of relative amount (they can compare two groups of objects that differ in size and tell which has a lot or a little) and of the transformations that change this amount (they know that one group will get bigger or smaller if objects are added to it or taken away). Most preschoolers can also use words to talk about these quantity relations and transformations (Starkey, 1992). As suggested earlier, however, most preschoolers do not use these schemas in a coordinated or integrated fashion (Siegler & Robinson, 1982). It is as if they were stored in separate files in children's minds.

Around the age of 5–6 years, as children's knowledge of counting and quantity becomes more elaborate and differentiated, their knowledge also gradually becomes more integrated, eventually merging in a single knowledge network called a *central conceptual structure for number* (Case & Griffin, 1990; Griffin, Case, & Siegler, 1994). With this higher order knowledge structure (referred to elsewhere as a "central organizing scheme"), children come to realize that a question about addition or subtraction can be answered, in the absence of any concrete set of objects, simply by counting forward or backward along the counting string. They also come to realize that a simple verbal statement about a transformation such as "I have four things, then I get one more" has an automatic entailment with regard to quantity. One does not even need to see the objects that are involved or know anything else about them. These simple understandings actually betoken a major revolution in children's understanding that changes the world of formal mathematics from something that can occur only "out there" to something that can occur inside their own heads, and under their own control. As this change takes place, children begin to use their counting skills in a wide range of other contexts. In effect, children realize that counting is something one can do to determine the relative value of two objects on a wide variety of dimensions (e.g., width, height, weight, musical tonality) (Griffin, Case, & Capodilupo, 1995).

Around 6–7 years, supported by their entry to formal schooling, children learn the written numerals that represent numbers. When this new understanding is linked to their central conceptual structure for number, children understand that the numerals stand as symbols for number words as both ordered "counting tags" and as indicators of numerical cardinality simultaneously. Finally, around the age of 7–8 years, children construct a more elaborate *bidimensional central conceptual structure for number*, which permits them to represent two quantitative dimensions in a coordinated fashion and solve problems requiring this level of complexity (e.g., place value and problems involving double-digit numbers in the domain of arithmetic; problems involving hours and minutes in the domain of time; problems involving dollars and cents in the domain of money) (Griffin, Case, & Sandieson, 1992).

The major goals of the Number Worlds program at four grade levels are informed by these research findings. Thus, in the Pre-K program, the major focus is on ensuring that children acquire well-developed counting and quantity schemas. In the kindergarten program, the major focus is on ensuring that children develop a well-consolidated central conceptual structure (for single-digit numbers). In the Grade 1 program children are given ample opportunity to link this structure to the formal symbol system and to construct the more elaborated knowledge network this entails. Finally, the focus of the Grade 2 program is on helping children construct the bidimensional central conceptual structure (for double-digit numbers), which underlies a solid understanding of the base-10 system and operations within this system.

In addition to these explicit grade-level objectives, there are two additional objectives that span all grade levels. The first is to ensure that children are exposed to the major ways that numbers are represented and talked about in developed societies. As mentioned earlier, numbers can be represented as a group of objects, as a position on a line, or as a point on a dial, for example, and the language used to describe quantity and changes in quantity varies considerably across these contexts. In order to maximize the chances that children will develop a good intuitive sense of numbers, including their spatial magnitude—and that they will be able to relate these intuitions to their explicit knowledge of written numerals—it is important that they understand the equivalence of different ways of representing numbers and that they are able to match and/or produce such representations. This objective and the ways it is addressed in the Number Worlds program is described further in the following section.

The second additional objective is to ensure that all children have ample opportunity to move forward at their own pace once they have acquired the foundational knowledge for the next level. To accomplish the latter objective, a set of implicit knowledge objectives is built into each level of the program. These make knowledge that is explicitly targeted at the next level available at the current level for children who are ready to take advantage of it. Thus, in the Pre-K program, activities that teach counting are always taught in the context of quantity representations. In the kindergarten program, activities that teach elements of the central conceptual structure for number are always taught in the context of written numerals, and so on. Making higher level knowledge available in an implicit fashion serves two purposes in the program. It not only allows individual children to move forward at their own pace but it also scaffolds higher order learning for all children.

## REPRESENTATIONS FOR NUMBER IN DIFFERENT LANDS

The Number Worlds program is divided into five different "lands" at each grade level, with each land exposing children to a particular form of number representation. Learning activities developed for each land (an average of 15 activities per land at each grade level) share a particular form of number representation while they simultaneously address specific knowledge goals for each grade level. The five forms of representation and the Lands in which they appear are illustrated in Fig. 13.1. As the figure suggests, the first land children are exposed to is Object Land, where numbers are represented by the bundling of several objects such as pennies or fingers into groups. This is the first way in which numbers were represented historically (Schmandt-Basserat, 1978) and the first one that children naturally learn. In Object Land, children first work with real objects (e.g., "How many crackers will you have left after you eat one?" "After you eat one more?") and then move to working with pictures of objects (e.g., "Are there enough hats so that each clown will have one?" "How many more do you need?" "How do you know?").

The second land children are introduced to is Picture Land, where numbers are represented as sets of stylized, semiabstract dot set patterns. These patterns provide a link between the world of moveable objects and the world of abstract symbols. Unlike the real objects they represent, dot set pictures cannot be physically placed in one-to-one correspondence for easier comparison. Instead, a child must make a mental correspondence between two sets, for example by noticing that the pattern for five is the same as four, but the five pattern has one extra dot in the center. As children engage in Picture Land activities (e.g., by playing an assortment of card games and dice games similar in format to War, Fish, and Concentration) they gradually come to think of these patterns as forming the same sort of ordered series as do the number worlds themselves. Numerals, another way of representing numbers, are also part of Picture Land and they

# D:Representation for Numbers in Different Lands

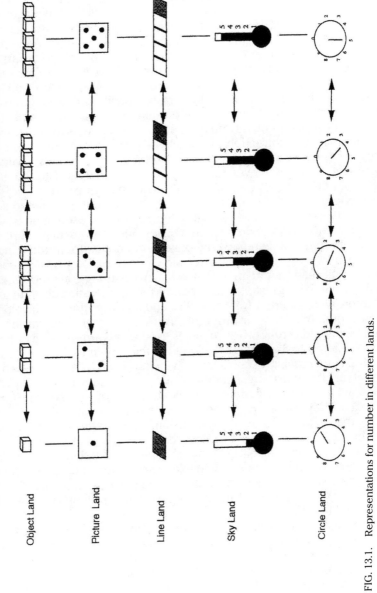

FIG. 13.1. Representations for number in different lands.

are used extensively in the activity props that are provided and by the children themselves, in the upper levels of the program, as they create written records to describe the quantity transactions they have been enacting.

A third way to represent numbers is as segments along a line, such as the lines that are found on board games like Chutes and Ladders. The language that is used for numbers in this context is the language of distance. In Line Land (by playing games on a Human Game Mat and on an assortment of smaller number line game boards), children come to understand that a number such as four can refer not only to a particular place on a line, but also to a number of moves *along* the line. One can talk about going four numbers forward, from the number four, on one's fourth turn! Perhaps the most important transition that children must make, as they move from the world of small countable objects to the world of abstract numbers and numerical operations, is to treat the physical addition or subtraction of objects as equivalent to movement forward or backward along a line. All children eventually make this correspondence; however, until they do, they are unable to move from physical operations to mental operations with any insight.

Yet another way to represent numbers is with bar graphs and scales, such as thermometers. In Sky Land, this sort of representation is always used in a vertical direction, such that bigger numbers are higher up. These forms of representation make a convenient context for introducing children to the use of numbers as a measure, as a way to keep track of continuous quantity in standard units. Systems for measuring continuous quantity have the same long history as do systems for enumerating discrete objects (Damerow, Englund, & Nissen, 1995), and it is important to develop children's intuitions for their properties from the outset. A lesson from the Number Worlds Pre-K program that is used as a warm-up activity to introduce children to Sky Land is included in the Appendix. This lesson is repeated in increasingly sophisticated versions in all levels of the program.

Dials are the final representation of number included in Number Worlds. Sundials and clocks are more sophisticated ways of representing numbers because they incorporate the cyclic quality—a path that repeats itself—that certain real-world dimensions such as time and the natural rhythm of the seasons possess. Children develop spatial intuitions in Circle Land (e.g., by playing games on a skating rink configuration, which requires them to chart progress within and across revolutions in order to determine a winner) that become the foundation for understanding many concepts in mathematics that deal with circular motion (e.g., pie charts, time and number bases).

Although the lands have been introduced in a fixed order here, from easiest to most difficult, an important goal of the Number Worlds program is to help children appreciate the equivalence of these forms of representation and of the language used to talk about number in these contexts. To achieve this, Level 1 activities in each land (i.e., activities that target knowledge objectives that are foundational for higher level learning) are introduced early in the school year, followed by Level 2 activities in each land, and finally Level 3 activities. As the year progresses, warm-up activities from each land are increasingly used in conjunction to facilitate the construction of the interconnected knowledge network illustrated in Fig. 13.1.

## PROCESS GOALS (DESIGN PRINCIPLES)

The process goals of the Number Worlds program (i.e., the learning processes children are expected to engage in and teachers are expected to encourage) are entirely consistent with those recommended in the National Council of Teachers of Mathematics (NCTM; 2000) standards. In previous publications (e.g., Griffin & Case, 1997), we have referred to these process goals as design principles to reflect our efforts, as the developers of this curriculum, to ensure that each activity we created for the program not only made these processes possible but also actively scaffolded them. Four of the most important process goals of the program are described next.

### Problem Solving

As has been suggested in the foregoing discussion, most of the activities included in the program provide opportunities for children to explore a variety of visual–spatial worlds in which elements of the number system (which vary in complexity across levels of the program) are salient. Most of the activities are also set in a game format. The problems children encounter as they move through these environments, motivated by the goals of the game, require them to actively interact with (and often to use) components of the number system (and/or representations of quantity) that have been built into the game. In many activities, success in the game is dependent on efficient use of the number system, or success in solving the number problems that the situation presents. In the sample activity provided in the Appendix (one of the simplest activities in the whole program), children are unable to blast off—an action they never tire of—until they successfully count down from five to one (or from a higher number selected by the teacher) *and* until the red liquid in thermometer correspondingly drops and reaches the zero (blast-off) mark. The game format that is provided for most of the activities engages children emotionally and motivates them to actively participate in solving the increasingly complex number problems that the activities present.

### Communication

Communication is vital in a Number Worlds classroom and it has been built into the program in many ways. Most of the activities are collaborative ones, which have been developed for small-group work. In these activities, as well as in many whole-class activities, communication is required to move the activity or game forward. For example, in the Line Land Number Line Game, which a group of four children play on a game board displaying four numbered paths (from 1 to 10), children take turns rolling a die, computing the quantity shown, asking the banker to give them that many counting chips, aligning the chips along their path (counting out loud as they do so), and moving their pawn that many spaces along the path (counting out loud once more) until it rests on the final chip that has been placed. At each point in this process, children are encouraged to challenge each other if they think the count is wrong, in terms of the number of chips asked for, the number provided by the banker, the placement of the chips along the path (e.g., skipping a numbered square), or the movement of the pawn along the path (e.g., starting to count from the square you start from instead of the next numbered square in the sequence). Because the first child to reach the winner's circle (in the 10th square) is the winner, children are motivated to watch and listen closely as others take their turns and to challenge each other if the need arises.

This basic game format is repeated in the Sky Land Elevator Up and Elevator Down Games, where children take turns moving their elevator man pawn up (or down) an elevator in a 10-story building, and in the Circle Land Skating Party Game, where children move their pawns around a circular skating rink (numbered from 0—the Start position—to 9) to see how many times they can skate around the rink in the allotted amount of time, and how many Award Cards (picked up each time they pass through the Start position) they can collect. To scaffold a high level of mathematical talk—as opposed to talk about who is winning, losing, or cheating—a set of question cards has been developed for most small-group games. Dialogue suggestions have also been included in the activity descriptions prepared for teachers. Both of these props focus attention on the sorts of questions that might prove useful at various points in game play (e.g., Where are you now? Where will you be when you make that move? Who is closer to the goal? How many more do you need? How do you know? How did you figure it out?). Although teachers will initially pose these questions, it is expected that children will eventually learn many of them "by heart" and use them independently to guide their own learning. Additional dialogue suggestions help teachers to ensure that children will learn the standard linguistic terms that are used for referring to numbers in different contexts (e.g., larger numbers are "farther along" in Line Land, are "higher up" in Sky Land, and are "farther around" in Circle Land). Communication is also "institutionalized" in the Wrap-Up component of a typical Number Worlds lesson (described in the following section).

## Reasoning

Reasoning is so much a part of problem solving and communication that it is somewhat redundant to give it a separate heading. However, there are at least two ways that the Number Worlds program fosters reasoning that may not be implied in the foregoing discussion. First, the program places a heavy emphasis on helping children integrate implicit and explicit knowledge. The activities encourage children to build up representations that involve a strong global–spatial component, and they help children move back and forth between these intuitive representations to representations that are more explicit, and that involve a strong verbal component. By doing so, they encourage children to reason with both sides of their brain and to create links across them, possibly strengthening neural pathways across brain hemispheres in the process (Dehaene & Cohen, 1995). Second, one of the ways it accomplishes this is to place a heavy emphasis on prediction (e.g., How far along will you be when you make that move?) as well as explanation, in contexts that allow predictions to be tested soon after they are framed and articulated.

## Universal Empowerment (Equity)

Most Number Worlds activities were designed to be multileveled: to allow for multiple levels of understanding so children with different entering knowledge, and different learning rates, can all learn something from each activity. For example, in the Skating Party Game described earlier, children who have not yet learned to identify quantity in dot-set patterns will receive repeated opportunities to develop this basic understanding as they count the dots on each die configuration they roll. Children who have mastered this basic skill are given opportunities to make relative quantity estimates (e.g., Who is farther around? Who has gone the shortest distance? How do you know?) and children who are adept at these comparisons are given opportunities to solve more challenging prediction problems (e.g., How much farther do you need to go to get an Award Card? How did you figure it out?). The activities are also designed to be appropriate for children with a wide range of talents, as well as children from a wide range of cultural, social, and economic backgrounds. They are intended to give *all* children the opportunity to advance on a broad number of fronts, at a rate that is appropriate for them.

## USING THE NUMBER WORLDS PROGRAM

Each day's lesson usually starts with a *Warm-Up* activity. In the Pre-K and kindergarten levels of the program, these activities often give children practice counting up and counting down in one (or more) of the five Number Worlds lands. These activities are typically short, lasting about 5 to 10 minutes depending on the number of children who wish to take turns participating. They are always taught in a whole-class format, often with children sitting in a circle around the teacher.

The Warm-Up activity is followed by a longer period of *Large-Group or Small-Group Work*, which lasts about 20 minutes in the lower levels of the program and about 40 minutes in the upper levels. The large-group games and activities can be used with the whole class. The small-group games and activities are played by small groups of four children working together. Once children become familiar with the small-group games, they can play them by themselves, without teacher supervision. However, whenever possible it is always better to have the teacher or another adult assigned to each small group to foster communication and to facilitate learning. During any particular lesson, small groups of children may play different games, depending on their level of understanding and their learning needs. This becomes easier to manage as children gain familiarity with the rules and procedures of different games and can play them more or less independently.

Group Work is always followed by a *Wrap-Up* period, which gives children a chance to reflect on and to discuss what they did during math time that day and what they learned. Wrap-Up is always conducted in a whole-class setting. When it follows Whole-Group work, it typically takes the form of a general discussion, with volunteers describing what they did during the activity and what they learned. When it follows Small-Group Work, a Reporter from each group usually takes the lead describing what his or her group did that day and what they learned. As with all the other components of each day's math lesson, Wrap-Up is facilitated by careful teacher questioning to encourage children to focus on the knowledge the lesson was designed to teach and to help them deepen and broaden their understanding.

For example, in the activity that was most recently mentioned (The Skating Party Game), a teacher might follow up a child's description of the number of award cards collected by each member of his or her group with the questions: Did everyone in your group have the same number of turns? If so, how come one member of your group skated around the rink three times (collecting three award cards) and another member of your group skated around the rink only two times (collecting two award cards)? If the Reporter canvasses the group and responds that the child who covered the greatest distance must have skated faster (as opposed to rolling high numbers on several turns), the group can be encouraged to test their hypothesis on subsequent rounds of game play and "to pay careful attention to what helps you go farther (or less far) in this game."

Teachers are also encouraged to take advantage of many opportunities that arise each day to teach math in *informal situations*. Lining up for recess or for lunch in groups that share a certain feature (e.g., all children wearing dresses and all children wearing pants) provides opportunities to count the number in each group, to compare quantity, and to become familiar with ordinal position (e.g., first, second, third). Counting stairs as you ascend and descend, sorting and counting snacks, and counting Number Worlds materials before putting them away provide other opportunities.

Most of the activities included in Number Worlds program were designed to be used over and over. In fact, the learning opportunities they provide are greatly enhanced by this repetition. Several games and activities also have extension activities in the form of *Challenges and Variations* that introduce children to higher level concepts and skills, and that provide opportunities for them to deepen and broaden their knowledge. (Note: The activity included in the Appendix provides an example of both of these features of the program.)

## PROGRAM EVALUATION

The Number Worlds program has now been tried out in several different communities in Canada and in the United States. For research purposes, the samples we have followed have always been drawn from schools serving low-income, predominantly inner-city communities. This decision was based on the assumption that if the program works for children known to be at risk for school failure, there is a good chance that it will work as well, or even better, for children from more affluent communities. Several different forms of evaluation have also been conducted.

In the first form of evaluation, children who received the kindergarten level of the program (formerly called Rightstart) were compared with matched controls, who received a readiness program of a different sort. On tests of mathematical knowledge, on a set of more general developmental measures, and on a set of experimental measures of learning potential, children who received the Number Worlds program consistently outperformed those in the control groups (Griffin et al., 1992, 1995). In a second type of study, children who received the kindergarten level of the program (and who graduated into a variety of more traditional first-grade classrooms) were followed up 1 year later, and evaluated on an assortment of mathematical and scientific tests, using a double-blind procedure. Once again, those who had received the Number Worlds program in kindergarten were found to be superior on virtually all measures, including teacher evaluations of "general number sense" (Griffin & Case, 1996; Griffin et al., 1994).

The expansion of the Number Worlds program to include curricula for Grades 1 and 2 permitted a third form of evaluation: a longitudinal study in which children were tracked over a 3-year period. At the beginning of the study and the end of each year, children who received the Number Worlds program were compared with two other groups: (a) a second low-SES (socioeconomic status) group who were originally tested as having superior achievement in mathematics, and (b) a mixed-SES (largely middle-class) group who also showed a higher level of performance at the outset and who attended an acclaimed magnet school with a special mathematics coordinator and an enriched mathematics program. Over the course of this study, which extended from the beginning of kindergarten to the end of Grade 2, children who received the Number Worlds program gradually outstripped both other groups on the major measure used throughout this study: a developmental test of number knowledge (i.e., the Number Knowledge Test; see Griffin & Case, 1997).

On this measure, as well as on a variety of other mathematics tests (e.g., measures of number sense), the Number Worlds group outperformed the second low-SES group from the end of kindergarten onward. On tests of procedural knowledge (i.e., the Computation Test; see Stigler, Lee, & Stevenson, 1990) administered at the end of Grade 1, they also compared very favorably with groups from China and Japan that were tested on the same measures (Griffin, in press; Griffin & Case, 1997).

These findings provide clear evidence that the Number Worlds program works for the population of children most in need of effective school-based instruction: children living in poverty. In a variety of studies, it enabled children from diverse cultural backgrounds to start their formal learning of arithmetic on an equal footing with their more advantaged peers. It also enabled them to keep pace with their more advantaged peers (and even outperform them on some measures) as they progressed through the first few years of formal schooling, and to acquire the higher level mathematics concepts that are central for continued progress in this area. In addition to the mathematics learning and achievement demonstrated in these studies, two other findings are worthy of note. Both teachers and children who have used the Number Worlds program consistently report a positive attitude to the teaching and learning of math. For teachers, this often represents a dramatic change in attitude. Doing math is now seen as fun, as well as useful, and both teachers and children are eager to do more of it.

## RELATIONSHIP TO NCTM 2000 STANDARDS

To those familiar with the NCTM (2000) standards, it must by now be apparent that the Number Worlds program and the standards share a number of features. A high level of consistency is present in: (a) their general philosophy; (b) their explicit grounding in current research on how children think, and know, and come to understand mathematics; (c) their knowledge objectives for Pre-K to Grade 2; and (d) their process goals. Although the general framework of the standards and the program is remarkably consistent, there are two differences that should be noted.

First, the Number Worlds program is narrower in scope. It seeks to teach the first two content standards (i.e., the Number & Operations Standard and the Algebra Standard) in considerable depth. Though it lays a foundation for learning in the remaining content areas (i.e., the Geometry Standard, the Measurement Standard, and the Data Analysis Standard), it does not explicitly address the complete set of learning objectives listed for these standards. This was a deliberate choice in emphasis and it was based on three factors: (a) the central role that number and algebra (e.g., quantity) concepts play in all areas of the discipline, (b) the amount of number knowledge many children still need to acquire when they start school, and (c) the amount of time most teachers have to teach mathematics.

Second, what the Number Worlds program sacrifices in scope, it makes up for in depth as well as breadth in the knowledge it chooses to teach. For example, a primary goal of the program—ensuring that *all* children acquire well-consolidated central conceptual structures for number—is given depth as well as breadth by the program's additional emphasis on exposing children systematically to multiple representations for number and to the standard and nonstandard ways numbers are talked about in these representational contexts.

Finally, as suggested by the program evaluation findings, the Number Worlds program provides a powerful way to address the content standards it "privileges" and that it was developed to teach. The strength of the findings may be attributed to the more limited focus of the program. However, it may also be due to the sorts of learning opportunities it provides. Number World activities not only foster the five process goals recommended in the standards (e.g. Problem Solving, Reasoning & Proof, Communication, Connections) but they *require* that these processes be enacted in order for the activities to work. Although this often creates challenges for novice teachers—who must learn how to structure and facilitate collaborative, small-group learning; how to turn control for learning over to the children; how to scaffold children's mathematical talk—it also creates an opportunity to implement these processes in their classroom, and to discover the rich sorts of learning they make possible. This journey is sometimes a struggle for teachers. However, it usually proves to be an exhilarating and rewarding adventure, one that teachers are committed to perpetuate and one they find was well worth the effort it took to achieve.

## ACKNOWLEDGMENTS

The research that is reported in this chapter was made possible by the generous support of the James S. McDonnell Foundation. The author gratefully acknowledges this support as well as the contributions of all the teachers and children who have used the Number Worlds programs in various stages of their development, and who have helped shape their final form.

## REFERENCES

Case, R., & Griffin, S. (1990). Child cognitive development: The role of central conceptual structures in the development of scientific and social thought. In E. A. Hauert (Ed.), *Developmental psychology: Cognitive, perceptuo-motor, and neurological perspectives* (pp. 193–230). Amsterdam: Elsevier.

Dehaene, S., & Cohen, L. (1995). Towards an anatomical and functional model of number processing. *Mathematical cognition, 1,* 83–120.

Damerow, P., Englund, R. K., & Nissen, H. J. (1995). The first representations of number and the development of the number concept. In R. Damerow (Ed.), *Abstraction and representation: Essays on the cultural evolution of thinking* (pp. 275–297). Dordrecht, Netherlands: Kluwer Academic.

Gelman, R. (1978). Children's counting: What does and does not develop. In R. S. Siegler (Ed.), *Children's thinking: What develops* (pp. 213–242). Hillsdale, NJ: Lawrence Erlbaum Associates.

Griffin, S. (1997). *Number Worlds: Grade one level.* Durham, NH: Number Worlds Alliance.

Griffin, S. (1998). *Number Worlds: Grade two level.* Durham, NH: Number Worlds Alliance.

Griffin, S. (2000). *Number Worlds: Preschool level.* Durham, NH: Number Worlds Alliance.

Griffin, S. (in press). Evaluation of a program to teach number sense to children at risk for school failure. *Journal for Research in Mathematics Education.*

Griffin, S., & Case, R. (1995). *Number Worlds: Kindergarten level.* Durham, NH: Number Worlds Alliance.

Griffin, S., & Case, R. (1996). Evaluating the breadth and depth of training effects when central conceptual structures are taught. *Society for Research in Child Development Monographs, 59*, 90–113.

Griffin, S., & Case, R. (1997). Re-thinking the primary school math curriculum: An approach based on cognitive science. *Issues in Education, 3*(1), 1–49.

Griffin, S., Case, R., & Capodilupo, A. (1995). Teaching for understanding: The importance of central conceptual structures in the elementary mathematics curriculum. In A. McKeough, I. Lupert, & A. Marini (Eds.), *Teaching for transfer: Fostering generalization in learning* (pp. 121–151). Hillsdale, NJ: Lawrence Erlbaum Associates.

Griffin, S., Case, R., & Sandieson, R. (1992). Synchrony and asynchrony in the acquisition of children's everyday mathematical knowledge. In R. Case (Ed.), *The mind's staircase: Exploring the conceptual underpinnings of children's thought and knowledge* (pp. 75–97). Hillsdale, NJ: Lawrence Erlbaum Associates.

Griffin, S., Case, R., & Siegler, R. (1994). Rightstart: Providing the central conceptual prerequisites for first formal learning of arithmetic to students at-risk for school failure. In K. McGilly (Ed.), *Classroom lessons: Integrating cognitive theory and classroom practice* (pp. 24–49). Cambridge, MA: Bradford Books MIT Press.

National Council of Teachers of Mathematics. (2000). *Curriculum and evaluation standards for school mathematics.* Reston, VA: Author.

Schmandt-Basserat, D. (1978). The earliest precursor of writing. *Scientific American, 238*, 40–49.

Siegler, R. S., & Robinson, M. (1982). The development of numerical understanding. In H. W. Reese & L. P. Lipsitt (Eds.), *Advances in child development and behavior* (pp. 241–312). New York: Academic Press.

Starkey, P. (1992). The early development of numerical reasoning. *Cognition and instruction, 43*, 93–126.

Stigler, J. W., Lee, S. Y., & Stevenson, H. W. (1990). Mathematical knowledge of Japanese, Chinese, and American elementary school children. *Monographs of the National Council of Teachers of Mathematics.*

# Appendix

## 2
## Blastoff!

Sky Land

**WHOLE** GROUP   **1-2** DIFFICULTY

### Learning Objectives
- Count down from 5 to 1 and from 10 to 1
- Associate counting down with decreases in the height of a scale measure

### Materials
- Sky Land Classroom Thermometer

### Prepare Ahead
- Use a red grease pencil to color the thermometer from the bulb up to 5.
- An eraser to use with the grease pencil on the thermometer

*Seeing the level of the mercury drop in a thermometer while counting down will give children a good foundation for subtraction.*

### Activity
Play Blastoff! to give the children practice counting down from 5 to 1.
- Tell the children to pretend they are on a rocket ship, getting ready to blast off.
- Explain that you will erase the level of the red pencil on the thermometer as the children count backwards from 5 to 1, and when you reach the bottom, everyone should call "Blastoff!" and jump up out of their seats.
- If necessary, model this for the children by erasing the level of the red pencil on the

thermometer down from 5 to 1, one notch at a time, while you say each number in the countdown sequence, and then jumping up while calling "Blastoff!"
- Have the children count down while you erase the pencil on the thermometer.
- Make sure everyone counts down correctly and waits for the blastoff signal before jumping up.

Once the children are familiar with the procedure, invite volunteers to erase the level of the red pencil on the thermometer while the other children count down and get ready to jump up.
- If anyone jumps up too soon or too late, have the children repeat the sequence.
- If a counting mistake is made, have the children begin the sequence over.

### Challenge
Once the children are comfortable counting down from 5 to 1, repeat the procedure having the children count down from 10 to 1.

### Teacher's Note
Blastoff! is played in each of the five Number Worlds™ lands, in a format appropriate to each land. Playing this game in the different lands will help to reinforce the idea that the lands are not entirely separate entities, but rather that they all share important number concepts. Each land represents a different way of expressing aspects of the number system that are common to all the lands.

# Blastoff!
## Variation 1: It's a Chilly Day

### Learning Objectives
- Identify the next number down in sequence
- Associate counting down with decreases in the height of a scale measure

### Materials
- Sky Land Classroom Thermometer

### Prepare Ahead
- Use a red grease pencil to color the thermometer from the bulb up to 5.
- An eraser to use with the grease pencil on the thermometer

### Activity
Tell the children to pretend that it is getting colder and the temperature is dropping from 5 down to 1.
- Sit in a semicircle with the children.
- Have the children take turns around the circle saying the next number down in the countdown sequence, starting with 5.
- Each time that a child says the next number down correctly, erase the level of the red pencil on the thermometer by one to correspond with the number counted.
- If a child makes a mistake or cannot remember the next number down, have the child begin the sequence over by saying the number 5.

### Challenge
Each time the group successfully counts down to 1, repeat the procedure starting with the next number up to 10 as the children become ready for each new step. If the children are not ready to count down from a higher number, wait until they are ready.

# Blastoff!
## Variation 2: The Incredible Shrinking People

### Learning Objectives
- Count down from 5 to 1 and from 10 to 1

### Activity
Tell the children to pretend that they are Incredible Shrinking People.
- Have the children stand up and reach their hands up in the air.
- Have the children slowly count backwards from 5 to 1 while they lower themselves to the floor so that after saying the number 1, they are in a crouching position.

### Challenge
If the children are comfortable with counting down the number sequence, have the children count up and grow after counting down and shrinking, so that after saying the number 5 the children are standing straight up again with their hands in the air.

342

# 14

# Fostering Preschool Children's Mathematical Knowledge: Findings From the Berkeley Math Readiness Project

Alice Klein
Prentice Starkey
*University of California, Berkeley*

Comparative studies of mathematics achievement in different countries over the past 15 years have revealed that the achievement of American students compares unfavorably with that of students from several other nations, particularly East Asian nations, at the middle and high school levels (e.g., Peak, 1996; Takahira, Gonzales, Frase, & Salganik, 1998). Cross-national differences in mathematics achievement have been found in the early elementary school grades as well (e.g., Frase, 1997; Stevenson, 1987; Stevenson, Lee, & Stigler, 1986). Moreover, there is evidence that specific aspects of mathematical knowledge, such as number words and addition, are more developed in East Asian children than in American children prior to their entry into elementary school (e.g., Geary, Bow-Thomas, Fan, & Siegler, 1993; Ginsburg, Choi, Lopez, Netley, & Chi, 1997; Miller, Smith, Zhu, & Zhang, 1995; Starkey et al., 1999). Taken together, cross-national research on mathematics achievement has had a significant impact on the education reform movement in the United States by focusing attention on the need to raise standards for mathematics education in this country.

When we examine mathematics achievement within the United States, studies have found considerable achievement differences across socioeconomic strata. In general, students from low-income families are at risk for underachievement in mathematics. Moreover, this achievement gap between students from low-income and middle-income families has been documented not just in high school (Dorsey, Mullis, Lindquist, & Chambers, 1988), but from the earliest grades of elementary school, including kindergarten (Entwisle & Alexander, 1990; Griffin, Case, & Siegler, 1994; Jordan, Huttenlocher, & Levine, 1992).

How can we interpret this evidence of cross-SES (socioeconomic status) differences in mathematics achievement from the beginning of elementary school? One view is that these SES-related achievement differences are due to differences in mathematics instruction in school. An alternative view, however, is that there is an earlier developmental basis for differences in mathematics achievement observed later in school. According to this view, cross-SES differences in young children's mathematical thinking develop during the preschool years, and then these differences are either increased or reduced by instructional practices in school.

Research has revealed that preschool children construct informal mathematical knowledge about the world around them. This knowledge depends on the presence or mental representation of sets of concrete entities such as objects (e.g., Baroody, 1992; Clements, Swaminathan, Hannibal, & Sarama, 1999; Gelman & Gallistel, 1978; see Ginsburg, Klein, & Starkey, 1998, for a recent review). Furthermore, findings indicate that at least some aspects of numerical knowledge, such as simple addition and the use of counting strategies, are more developed in middle-income preschoolers than in their low-income peers (e.g., Jordan, Huttenlocher, & Levine, 1994; Saxe, Guberman, & Gearhart, 1987; Starkey & Klein, 1992). This socioeconomic gap in children's numerical cognition is evident even for children attending Head Start during the prekindergarten year (Klein & Starkey, 1995; Starkey & Klein, 2000). In summary, the evidence that there are cross-SES differences in children's informal mathematical knowledge before kindergarten supports the view that there is an earlier, developmental basis for subsequent differences in school mathematics achievement.

Cross-socioeconomic differences in mathematical development are especially problematic for the goal of equity in early mathematics instruction. Because children from different socioeconomic backgrounds do not possess a comparable foundation of informal mathematical knowledge, they enter elementary school at different levels of readiness to learn school mathematics. Thus, there is a need to intensify our efforts to support young children's informal mathematical development so that all children will be ready to learn a standards-based mathematics curriculum in school.

The remainder of this chapter focuses on an early mathematics intervention project, the Berkeley Math Readiness Project, which we recently conducted. In particular, we discuss some findings from this project that bear on the issue of a socioeconomic gap in preschool children's mathematical development. Our project had two principal objectives. The first was to conduct a comprehensive study of low- and middle-income children's informal mathematical knowledge during the prekindergarten year. We expected that this study not only would broaden the knowledge base on socioeconomic differences in early mathematical development, but also would reveal specific mathematical concepts that need greater support during the preschool years. The second objective was to develop a conceptually broad prekindergarten mathematics curriculum and implement it in a variety of preschool programs to determine its effectiveness at fostering preschool children's mathematical knowledge.

## THE BERKELEY MATH READINESS PROJECT

The Berkeley Math Readiness Project sought to support young children's mathematical development by developing an early childhood mathematics curriculum for use in classrooms and at home. Prekindergarten children enrolled in 10 preschool classrooms, 5 serving middle-income families and 5 serving low-income families, participated in the project. At each socioeconomic level, both Intervention and Comparison Groups of children were included in the design.

Children in the Intervention Groups received the mathematics curriculum during their prekindergarten year. By contrast, children in the Comparison Groups, who were selected from the same preschool classrooms with the same teachers during the year preceding the intervention, did not receive the math curriculum. The number and mean age of each group of children at the end of the prekindergarten year were as follows: Middle-Income Intervention Group ($n = 41$; mean age, 4 years, 11 months); Middle-Income Comparison Group ($n = 42$; mean age, 4 years, 11 months); Low-Income Intervention Group ($n = 37$; mean age, 5 years, 0 months); Low-Income Comparison Group; $n = 43$; mean age, 4 years, 10 months).

A pretest–posttest design was employed to examine the effectiveness of the curricular intervention at enhancing prekindergarten children's mathematical knowledge. Children in the Intervention Groups were tested in the fall and the spring of their prekindergarten year with the Child Math Assessment (CMA, described later). Children in the Comparison Groups were given the CMA in the spring of their prekindergarten year.

The basic pedagogical approach taken in the intervention was to provide all prekindergarten children in a classroom with a broad mathematics curriculum over the course of the year. The content of our prekindergarten mathematics curriculum (Klein, Starkey, & Ramirez, 2002) was consistent with NCTM's (National Council of Teachers of Mathematics) new *Principles and Standards for School Mathematics* (NCTM, 2000) and with the findings of developmental research concerning the composition of early mathematical knowledge (e.g., Clements, 2000; Ginsburg et al., 1998). It was designed to foster children's informal mathematical knowledge in the domains of numerical and spatial-geometric cognition. There were teacher-guided small-group activities for use in the preschool classrooms as well as parent-guided dyadic activities for use at home. The curriculum was organized into seven topical units, each with multiple sets of math activities accompanied by concrete materials. It included the following units: (a) Enumeration and Number Sense, (b) Arithmetic Reasoning, (c) Spatial Sense, (d) Geometric Reasoning, (e) Pattern Sense and Unit Construction, (f) Nonstandard Measurement and (g) Logical Relations. The math activities were designed to be sensitive to the needs of individual children. They could be extended downward for children who were not developmentally ready for a particular activity, and upward for children who were developmentally ready for a more challenging activity.

Teachers were given a curriculum manual containing instructions for each math activity and descriptions of materials to use. They learned how to implement the mathematics curriculum by attending summer and winter workshops and by receiving on-site assistance throughout the year from a staff member of the project. Moreover, in the workshops and end-of-the-year meetings, teachers discussed their classroom experiences and provided feedback about specific math activities that needed further development.

We also developed a new instrument, the Child Math Assessment (CMA), to assess young children's informal mathematical knowledge across a broad range of concepts. Sixteen tasks comprising the CMA were informed by the basic research literature on young children's mathematical development. The CMA assessed knowledge of number, arithmetic, space and geometry, patterns, and nonstandard measurement, and the tasks encompassed a range of difficulty (e.g., tasks involving smaller and larger set sizes, visible and hidden objects). Furthermore, it should be noted that there was a conceptual, but not an identical, overlap between math activities in the curriculum and tasks from the CMA. For example, *Imagine a Shape* was a curriculum activity that supported spatial visualization. It involved the completion of different shapes in customary and rotated orientations. In contrast, the *Triangle Transformation* task from the CMA assessed spatial visualization. It involved matching corresponding sides of congruent triangles that differed by a spatial transformation (slide, rotation, or flip).

## RESULTS

We first report analyses of the overall effect of the curricular intervention on the development of children's mathematical knowledge. These include comparisons of the extent of informal mathematical knowledge in low-income and middle-income children who received the curriculum (the Intervention Groups) and those who did not (the Comparison Groups). We then report findings on three specific tasks that assessed children's knowledge of addition and patterns.

## Children's Overall Accuracy

We examined children's mathematical knowledge across a broad range of concepts by computing a composite mathematics score on the CMA for each child. This score represented the mean proportion of correct solutions across all mathematical problems presented to the child. Children's knowledge of number, arithmetic, geometry, nonstandard measurement, and patterns were reflected in the composite score.

We performed a two-way repeated measures ANOVA (analysis of variance) on the composite scores of low-income and middle-income intervention children during the fall (pretest) and spring (posttest) assessments. There was a significant main effect for socioeconomic group, $F(1/76) = 32.10, p < .001$, with the composite scores of middle-income children being higher than those of low-income children (Fig. 14.1). Note that at the beginning of the prekindergarten year, middle-income children solved more than one half of the problems assessed by the CMA, whereas low-income children solved only one third of the problems. There also was a significant

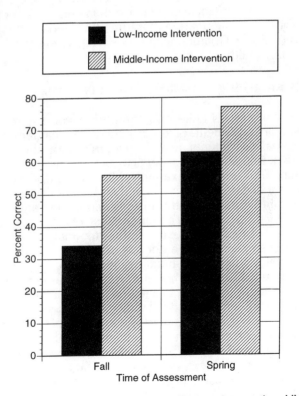

FIG. 14.1.   Composite scores of low- and middle-income intervention children.

main effect for time of assessment, $F(1/76) = 267.89, p < .001$, with children's scores in the spring being higher than their fall scores. In addition, the Group × Time interaction was significant, $F(1/76) = 6.61, p < .02$. Low-income children's scores increased more in the spring relative to their starting point in the fall (from 34% to 63% correct) than middle-income children's scores (from 56% to 77% correct). This finding indicates that low-income children in particular experienced rapid mathematical development by participating in this curricular intervention.

We then performed a two-way between-groups ANOVA with age as a covariate to compare the spring composite scores of children in the Intervention Groups with children in the Comparison Groups. Again there was a significant main effect for socioeconomic group, $F(1/158) = 44.95, p < .001$. Mathematical knowledge over all tasks was more developed in middle-income children than in low-income children.

However, there was also a significant main effect for curriculum group (Intervention vs. Comparison), $F(1/158) = 26.12, p < .001$. Children in the Intervention Groups had higher scores than children in the Comparison Groups. When presented with a broad prekindergarten math curriculum, both middle-income and low-income intervention children exhibited more extensive mathematical knowledge than comparison children did at the end of their prekindergarten year. Thus, the intervention significantly enhanced the informal mathematical knowledge of both middle-income and low-income children.

## Children's Knowledge of Addition and Patterns

Although our analyses of children's composite scores demonstrate the general need for and benefits of an early childhood mathematics curriculum, these analyses do not reveal children's informal mathematical knowledge at a sufficient level of detail to inform mathematics standards or instruction. Thus, we now examine children's performance on three specific tasks that assessed aspects of their knowledge of addition and patterns: Two-Set Addition, Pattern Duplication, and Pattern Extension. After examining the accuracy of children's answers (correct vs. incorrect) on these tasks, we report the results from error analyses to illustrate developmental changes that were not apparent in the accuracy analyses. We argue that if mathematics standards and instruction aspire to be developmentally sensitive, they should reflect an awareness of the sometimes subtle changes that occur in children's early mathematical thinking as they progress toward full understanding of a concept.

A two-set addition task was used to assess children's ability to judge the effects of an addition operation on the relative number of objects in two sets. This task required children to use one-to-one correspondence to represent the initial sets of objects and to solve the addition problem. The experimenter simultaneously constructed two sets of objects (marbles) using one-to-one correspondence and saying, "I am putting a marble in this container and a marble in that container, and another marble in this container and another marble in that container." As the experimenter spoke, she dropped a marble through a hole in each of two opaque containers until the two initial sets contained unequal numbers of marbles (four vs. six). Then the child was asked whether the containers had the same number of marbles or whether one container had more. If one container was judged to have more, the child was asked to indicate which one. Next, the experimenter added one marble to the set with four marbles, resulting in final sets that contained unequal numbers of marbles (four plus one vs. six). The child was then asked whether the containers had the same number of objects or whether one container had more.

A pattern duplication task assessed children's ability to copy a linear repeating pattern of small colored blocks. A simple ABAB pattern was presented in this task. The experimenter placed a preconstructed pattern of blocks on her side of the table and asked the child to make a pattern that "looks just like mine." The child was given a source set of colored blocks that contained more than the minimum number needed to copy the pattern.

A pattern extension task assessed children's ability to complete a linear repeating pattern of small colored blocks. The same type of ABAB pattern was presented in this task as in pattern duplication. The experimenter began by constructing two repetitions (units) of the pattern of blocks in front of the child, and then asked the child to "finish making the pattern." The experimenter gestured to the last block placed to indicate where the child should continue to extend the pattern. The child was given a source set of colored blocks that contained more than the minimum number needed to extend the pattern.

Children's solutions to the two-set addition, pattern duplication, and pattern extension problems were scored as correct/incorrect. Accuracy scores were calculated for middle-income and low-income Intervention and Comparison Groups. Table 14.1 presents the mean percentage correct on two-set addition, pattern duplication, and pattern extension problems for these groups. This table includes data for the Intervention Groups of children in the fall (pretest) and spring (posttest) as well as for the Comparison Groups of children in the spring of their prekindergarten year.

The general pattern of results on these problems was consistent with the analyses of children's composite scores. A strong effect of socioeconomic group on early math knowledge was evident. Middle-income children exhibited more extensive mathematical knowledge on these problems than low-income children did in the fall as well as in the spring. However, the pervasive effect of the curricular intervention on children's mathematical development was also evident. Specifically, both middle-income and low-income Intervention Groups exhibited significant progress in their addition and pattern knowledge after participating in the curriculum activities. Furthermore, their knowledge on these problems was greater than in the corresponding Comparison Groups. Two-way between-group ANOVAs with age as a covariate revealed that the accuracy scores of inter-

## TABLE 14.1

**Mean Percentage Correct on *Two-Set Addition, Pattern Duplication,* and *Pattern Extension Problems:* Middle-Income and Low-Income Groups**

| | Two-Set Addition | Type of Problem Pattern Duplication | Pattern Extension |
|---|---|---|---|
| Group | Inequality Problem | ABAB Problem | ABAB Problem |
| MI Intervention—Pretest | 44 | 56 | 27 |
| MI Intervention—Posttest | 80 | 95 | 34 |
| MI Comparison[a] | 62 | 76 | 14 |
| LI Intervention—Pretest | 16 | 24 | 0 |
| LI Intervention—Posttest | 51 | 78 | 32 |
| LI Comparison[a] | 33 | 53 | 14 |

*Note.* MI = middle-income. LI = low-income.
[a]MI and LI Comparison groups were assessed at the same time of the year (spring) as the MI and LI Intervention groups at the posttest.

vention and comparison children differed significantly on two-set addition, pattern duplication, and pattern extension, all $ps < .02$.

One unanticipated finding was that children's performance on the pattern extension task was markedly lower than their performance on pattern duplication. Low-income children in the fall were unable to extend even a simple ABAB pattern, and only 27% of the middle-income children could do so. Although individual accuracy scores on pattern extension indicated that some children clearly benefited from the intervention, the majority of children did not improve at the posttest. Thus, pattern extension is a later development than pattern duplication.

Accuracy scores are useful indicators of learning, but they have at least two limitations. First, they are insensitive to developmental progress that does not yet produce correct answers. Second, they do not reveal the specific nature of children's misunderstandings when an incorrect answer is given. Yet, this is precisely the kind of information that teachers need in order to foster young children's informal mathematical knowledge. Consequently, we conducted error analyses to specify the difficulties that preschool children exhibited as they were learning about two-set addition, pattern duplication, and pattern extension.

*Two-Set Addition Errors.* Table 14.2 presents the percentage of error types made by low- and middle-income intervention children on the two-set addition inequality problem at the pretest and posttest. Error analyses revealed that at both socioeconomic levels children made several distinct types of errors. Response perseveration was the most developmentally immature type of error. For children making this error, the occurrence of addition did not alter their judgments of the relative number of objects in the sets. The typical form this error took was for children to judge incorrectly that the initial sets (four vs. six) were the "same number". Then, the experimenter added one object to the four-object set, but children perseverated by responding "same number" to the final sets.

Primitive errors were also developmentally immature, but they were more advanced than simple response perseveration. For children making this error, the occurrence of addition did alter their judgments, but their judgments did not take into account the absolute number of objects in the initial sets. Children used one-to-one correspondence to judge correctly that the six-object set contained more than the four-object set. Then the experimenter added one object to the four-object set, but children judged incorrectly that this set now contained more objects than the other set. That is, they judged that if addition is performed on Set A, it has more objects (Set A + 1 > Set B). They had failed to integrate the number of objects added (+1) with the numerical value of the initial sets (Set A has four and Set B has six).

Qualitative errors were more advanced developmentally than the other error types. Children correctly judged the initial sets to be unequal, and they attempted to integrate addition with the number of objects in

TABLE 14.2

**Percentage of Error Types on the Two-Set Addition Inequality Problem: Middle-Income and Low-Income Intervention Groups—Pretest Versus Posttest**

| Group | Time of Assessment | Total Errors | Error Types | | |
| --- | --- | --- | --- | --- | --- |
| | | | Perseverative | Primitive | Qualitative |
| Middle-Income | Pretest | 26 | 43% | 12% | 46% |
| Middle-Income | Posttest | 8 | 12% | 0% | 88% |
| Low-Income | Pretest | 31 | 48% | 7% | 45% |
| Low-Income | Posttest | 17 | 0% | 18% | 82% |

the initial sets. They erred because they apparently integrated the addition operation with an imprecise representation of the initial inequality (Set A has fewer objects than Set B) rather than a precise representation (Set A has two fewer objects than Set B). Consequently, they went on to judge (incorrectly) that the addition of one object to the four-object set compensated for the initial inequality, producing equal sets (if Set A < Set B, then Set A + 1 = Set B).

Children who produced a correct solution to the problem apparently represented the initial inequality precisely. They judged that the smaller set had fewer objects than the larger set, even after the addition of one object (e.g., if Set A has two fewer objects than Set B, then Set A + 1 has fewer than Set B).

The distribution of errors children made changed over the course of the intervention. At the pretest, low-income children made response perseveration or primitive errors frequently and more often than middle-income children did (46% vs. 34% of children, respectively). Both groups of children made these errors more often at the pretest prior to the intervention (40%) than at the posttest after the intervention (5%). Thus, during the intervention many children learned to use one-to-one correspondence to judge correctly the initial sets, and they learned to take the addition operation into account in attempting to solve two-set addition problems.

The overall percentage of children who made qualitative errors did not change a great deal from the pretest (32%) to the posttest (28%), but the composition of the group making these errors did change. Several children who made response perseveration or primitive errors at the pretest progressed to qualitative errors at the posttest, and several who made qualitative errors at the pretest correctly solved the two-set addition problem at the posttest. In the latter case, children had learned to integrate the addition operation with the number of objects in the initial sets in order to solve the problem. The principal effect of the intervention was to develop more advanced arithmetic problem solving strategies.

***Pattern Duplication Errors.*** We next analyze the errors children made on the pattern duplication problem. Table 14.3 presents the percentage of error types made by low- and middle-income intervention children on the pattern duplication ABAB problem at the pretest and posttest. Children's errors were classified into three principal types that reflected different developmental levels of pattern knowledge.

The first type of error, No Initial Unit, reflected the least developed knowledge of patterns. In attempting to duplicate the model pattern, children did not even begin their construction with the initial unit AB. Examples of this error type included BAAB and AABA. A more developmentally advanced type of error, Only Initial Unit, reflected a partial knowledge of repeating patterns. Children who made this type of error apparently understood that the pattern began with the initial unit AB, but they did not systematically iterate this initial unit throughout their construction. Examples of this error type included ABBA and ABAAB.

TABLE 14.3

**Percentage of Error Types on the Pattern Duplication ABAB Problem: Middle-Income and Low-Income Intervention Groups—Pretest Versus Posttest**

| Group | Time of Assessment | Total Errors | Error Types | | |
|---|---|---|---|---|---|
| | | | No Initial Unit AB | Only Initial Unit AB | Model Pattern + Extra Blocks |
| Middle-Income | Pretest | 18 | 50% | 33% | 17% |
| Middle-Income | Posttest | 2 | 100% | 0% | 0% |
| Low-Income | Pretest | 28 | 75% | 18% | 7% |
| Low-Income | Posttest | 8 | 25% | 38% | 38% |

The most advanced type of pattern duplication error we observed was the Model Pattern plus Extra Blocks error. In this error, children correctly constructed the initial unit AB and then systematically iterated the initial unit until they duplicated the model pattern. However, after duplicating the model pattern, they did not stop. Children incorrectly added one or two extra blocks from the source set. Examples of this error type included ABABA and ABABAA.

Error analyses at the pretest revealed that low-income children made a greater number of errors than middle-income children. However, both groups of children made the same predominant error type, No Initial Unit, on pattern duplication. This finding suggests that many 4-year-old children at the beginning of the prekindergarten year find it difficult to analyze the unit of a repeating pattern.

The intervention had a significant effect on the number and type of errors made by middle-income and low-income children at the posttest. There was a marked decrease in the overall number of errors for both groups. Although 44% of the children in the middle-income group made pattern duplication errors at the pretest, only 5% did so at the posttest. An even steeper decrease was observed for the low-income children, dropping from 76% of the children at the pretest to 22% at the posttest. Furthermore, those low-income children who still made errors at the posttest exhibited a shift from the least advanced error type (No Initial Unit) to the more advanced error types over the course of the intervention.

*Pattern Extension Errors.*    Table 14.4 presents the percentage of error types made by middle-income and low-income intervention children on the pattern extension ABAB problem at the pretest and posttest. Note that children made the same three types of errors as they had on pattern duplication. Error analyses at the pretest demonstrated that both groups of children made a greater number of errors on pattern extension (86% of children) than on pattern duplication (59% of children). Nevertheless, the same predominant error type, No Initial Unit, occurred on both tasks. This converging finding from pattern duplication and pattern extension supports the view that the majority of prekindergarten children, regardless of socioeconomic background, experienced difficulty at the beginning of the year with a fundamental property of repeating patterns—identification of the core unit of the pattern.

Posttest analyses of pattern extension errors revealed that the intervention produced a qualitative shift in children's predominant error types, but it did not significantly reduce the number of errors made by middle-income and low-income children. The percentage of children making the least advanced error type (No Initial Unit) decreased from 32% to 2% among middle-income children and from 51% to 14% among low-income children. In contrast, the percentage of children making developmentally more advanced errors (Only Initial Unit and Model Pattern plus Extra Blocks) rose

TABLE 14.4

**Percentage of Error Types on the Pattern Extension ABAB Problem: Middle-Income and Low-Income Intervention Groups—Pretest Versus Posttest**

| | | | Error Types | | |
|---|---|---|---|---|---|
| Group | Time of Assessment | Total Errors | No Initial Unit AB | Only Initial Unit AB | Model Pattern + Extra Blocks |
| Middle-Income | Pretest | 30 | 43% | 20% | 37% |
| Middle-Income | Posttest | 27 | 4% | 11% | 85% |
| Low-Income | Pretest | 37 | 51% | 27% | 22% |
| Low-Income | Posttest | 25 | 20% | 8% | 72% |

from 41% to 63% in the middle-income group and from 49% to 54% in the low-income group. It appears that over the course of the intervention, many children became able to analyze the unit of a repeating pattern.

In summary, more errors were made on the two-set addition, pattern duplication, and pattern extension tasks by low-income children than by middle-income children, but both groups of intervention children made the same types of errors. The principal qualitative difference between these groups was that low-income children exhibited less advanced types of errors than middle-income children, especially at the pretest.

The error analyses also revealed developmental progress in children's informal mathematics knowledge that was not evident from accuracy scores alone. Many children in the Intervention Groups who were not yet able to correctly solve the addition or pattern problems nevertheless made more advanced types of errors at the posttest. This reduction in the percentage of children making immature types of errors from the pretest to the posttest was a robust effect of the intervention. Thus, the error analyses provided valuable evidence of and insight into the development of preschool children's understandings of addition and patterns.

## CONCLUSIONS AND IMPLICATIONS FOR EARLY MATHEMATICS STANDARDS

A broad socioeconomic gap in informal mathematical knowledge was present at the beginning of the prekindergarten year. This gap included not just numerical concepts and arithmetic reasoning, but also spatial concepts and geometric reasoning, knowledge of patterns, and nonstandard measurement. Preschool teachers who participated in the curricular intervention received training in early mathematical development and education through workshops, and they were provided with ongoing support throughout the year. These teachers learned to deliver a conceptually broad mathematics curriculum that significantly enhanced children's informal mathematical knowledge in all areas assessed. General analyses revealed that both low- and middle-income children in the Intervention Groups made significant developmental progress in their mathematical thinking relative to children in the Comparison Groups. Moreover, low-income children made more progress during the prekindergarten year, relative to their starting point at the pretest, than middle-income children did. Consequently, by the end of the prekindergarten year, the socioeconomic gap in informal mathematical knowledge was reduced.

Our error analyses of addition and pattern knowledge revealed important details about children's mathematical development. Both socioeconomic groups made the same types of errors on the addition and pattern tasks, but the low-income children made less advanced types of errors more frequently. A principal outcome of the intervention was a developmental shift in children's understandings from less advanced error types either to more advanced error types or to correct solutions. Finally, although the develop- ment of children's understandings of two-set addition and pattern duplication were found to be well under way during the prekindergarten year, their understanding of pattern extension was just beginning to develop. Our findings indicate that curricular enhancements during the prekindergarten year are feasible and produce beneficial developmental outcomes for young children.

In conclusion, these analyses demonstrated that it is not sufficient to assess children's knowledge of a mathematical concept on the basis of accuracy scores alone. It is also important to assess the types of errors that individual children make. This deeper level of assessment will reveal difficulties that children encounter while learning specific mathematical concepts. Data on the nature of children's misunderstandings are potentially very useful to preschool teachers and others who want to support children's informal mathematical development.

In creating mathematics standards for young children and planning their learning opportunities, our research suggests a need for greater specificity along two dimensions—children's developmental status and their socioeconomic status. Consider first the developmental dimension. There is a need for further differentiation within the Pre-K to Grade 2 band of the *PSSM* (NCTM, 2000) regarding the expectations for mathematical knowledge at specific age or grade levels. As shown in our intervention study, considerable development in mathematical knowledge can occur within the span of one school year. Thus, the expectations for younger children in the Pre-K to Grade 2 band should differ from those for older children. This differentiation would facilitate curriculum planning and teaching that accommodate to developmental differences in children's early mathematical knowledge.

The second dimension concerns socioeconomic differences in young children's informal mathematical knowledge. Given the existence of a socioeconomic gap in this knowledge, there is a need to specify the full developmental range of mathematical knowledge manifested in the preschool population. This specification will help teachers plan ways to support effectively the mathematical development of all young children. By creating early mathematics standards and curricula that reflect the developmental and socioeconomic variation in early mathematical knowledge that exists in the population, we will be taking a major step toward achieving the goal of equal educational opportunity for all children.

## ACKNOWLEDGMENTS

Preparation of this chapter was supported by OERI/U.S. Department of Education Grant R307F60024 and by National Science Foundation (IERI) Grant REC-9979974 to the authors. This chapter is based on a paper presented at the 78th Annual Meeting of the NCTM, April 2000.

# REFERENCES

Baroody, A. J. (1992). The development of preschoolers' counting skills and principles. In J. Bideau, C. Meljac, & J. P. Fischer (Eds.), *Pathways to number* (pp. 99–126). Hillsdale, NJ: Lawrence Erlbaum Associates.

Clements, D. H. (2000, April). Geometric and spatial thinking in early childhood education. In J. Sarama (Chair), *Linking research and the new early childhood mathematics standards*. Paper presented at the 78th Annual Meeting of the National Council of Teachers of Mathematics, Chicago, IL.

Clements, D. H., Swaminathan, S., Hannibal, M. A. Z., & Sarama, J. (1999). Young children's concepts of shape. *Journal for Research in Mathematics Education, 30,* 192–212.

Dorsey, J. A., Mullis, I. V. S., Lindquist, M. M., & Chambers, D. L. (1988). *The mathematics report card: Are we measuring up?* (NAEP Report No. 17-M-01). Princeton, NJ: Educational Testing Service.

Entwisle, D. R., & Alexander, K. L. (1990). Beginning school math competence: Minority and majority comparisons. *Child Development, 61,* 454–471.

Frase, M. (1997). *Pursuing excellence: a study of U.S. fourth-grade mathematics and science achievement in international context. Initial findings from the Third International Mathematics and Science Study* (GPO Report No. 065-000-00959-5). Washington, DC: U.S. Government Printing Office. (ERIC Document Reproduction Service No. ED410098)

Geary, D. C., Bow-Thomas, C. C., Fan, L., & Siegler, R. S. (1993). Even before formal instruction, Chinese children outperform American children in mental addition. *Cognitive Development, 8,* 517–529.

Gelman, R., & Gallistel, C. R. (1978). *The child's understanding of number.* Cambridge, MA: Harvard University Press.

Ginsburg, H. P., Choi, Y. E., Lopez, L. S., Netley, R., & Chi, C.-Y. (1997). Happy birthday to you: The early mathematical thinking of Asian, South American, and U.S. children. In T. Nunes & P. Bryant (Eds.), *Learning and teaching mathematics: An international perspective* (pp. 1–45). East Sussex, England: Lawrence Erlbaum Associates/Taylor & Francis.

Ginsburg, H. P., Klein, A., & Starkey, P. (1998). The development of children's mathematical thinking: Connecting research with practice. In W. Damon, I. E. Sigel, & K. A. Renninger (Eds.), *Handbook of child psychology* (5th edition), *Child psychology in practice* (Vol. 4, pp. 401–476). New York: Wiley.

Griffin, S., Case, R., & Siegler, R. S. (1994). Rightstart: Providing the central conceptual prerequisites for first formal learning in arithmetic to students at risk for school failure. In K. McGilly (Ed.), *Classroom lessons: Integrating cognitive theory and classroom practice* (pp. 25–49). Cambridge, MA: MIT Press.

Jordan, N. C., Huttenlocher, J., & Levine, S. C. (1992). Differential calculation abilities in young children from middle- and low-income families. *Developmental Psychology, 28,* 644–653.

Jordan, N. C., Huttenlocher, J., & Levine, S. C. (1994). Assessing early arithmetic abilities: Effects of verbal and nonverbal response types on the calculation performance of middle- and low-income children. *Learning and Individual Differences, 6,* 413–432.

Klein, A., & Starkey, P. (1995, April). Preparing for the transition to school mathematics: The Head Start Family Math Project. In P. Starkey (Chair), *School readiness and early achievement of impoverished children.* Symposium conducted at the meeting of the Society for Research in Child Development, Indianapolis, IN.

Klein, A., Starkey, P., & Ramirez, A. (2002). *Pre-K mathematics curriculum.* Glendale, IL: Scott, Foresman.

Miller, K. F., Smith, C. M, Zhu, J. J., & Zhang, H. C. (1995). Preschool origins of cross-national differences in mathematical competence: The role of number-naming systems. *Psychological Science, 6,* 56–60.

National Council of Teachers of Mathematics. (2000). *Principles and standards for school mathematics.* Reston, VA: Author.

Peak, L. (1996). *Pursuing excellence: a study of U.S. eighth-grade mathematics and science teaching, learning, curriculum, and achievement in international context. Initial findings from the Third International Mathematics and Science Study* (GPO Report No.

065-000-01018-6). Washington, DC: U.S. Government Printing Office. (ERIC Document Reproduction Service No. ED400209)

Saxe, G. B., Guberman, S. R., & Gearhart, M. (1987). Social processes in early number development. *Monographs of the Society for Research in Child Development, 52,* (2, Serial No. 216).

Starkey, P., & Klein, A. (1992). Economic and cultural influences on early mathematical development. In F. L. Parker, R. Robinson, S. Sombrano, C. Piotrowski, J. Hagen, S. Randolph, & A. Baker (Eds.), *New directions in child and family research: Shaping head start in the 90s* (p. 440). New York: National Council of Jewish Women.

Starkey, P., & Klein, A. (2000). Fostering parental support for children's mathematical development: An intervention with Head Start families. *Early Education and Development, 11,* 659–680.

Starkey, P., Klein, A., Chang, I., Dong Q., Pang L., & Zhou, Y. (1999, April). Environmental supports for young children's mathematical development in China and the United States. Paper presented at the biennial meeting of the Society for Research in Child Development, Albuquerque, NM.

Stevenson, H. W. (1987). The Asian advantage: The case of mathematics. *American Educator, 47,* 26–31.

Stevenson, H. W., Lee, S. Y., & Stigler, J. W. (1986). Mathematics achievement of Chinese, Japanese, and American children. *Science, 231,* 693–699.

Takahira, S., Gonzales, P., Frase, M., & Salganik, L. H. (1998). *Pursuing excellence: A study of U.S. twelfth-grade mathematics and science achievement in international context. Initial findings from the Third International Mathematics and Science Study* (National Center for Educational Statistics Report No. 98-049). Washington, DC: U.S. Government Printing Office. (ERIC Document Reproduction Service No. ED419717)

# 15

## Technology in Early Childhood Mathematics: *Building Blocks* as an Innovative Technology-Based Curriculum

Julie Sarama
*University at Buffalo, State University of New York*

*Building Blocks* is a new Pre-K to Grade 2, software-enhanced, mathematics curriculum designed to comprehensively address the year 2000 standards of the National Council of Teachers of Mathematics, *Principles and Standards for School Mathematics*. In this chapter, I describe the basic features of the *Building Blocks* program, including the research on which it was based, and specific activities from the program, including the results of field tests of those activities with a range of teachers and children.

### THE DESIGN OF *BUILDING BLOCKS*

*Building Blocks* is designed to enable all young children to build solid content knowledge and develop higher-order, or critical, thinking. To achieve this, we (Douglas H. Clements and I) needed to consider the audience, determine the basic approach to learning and teaching, and draw from theory and research in each phase of the design and development process. In this section, I briefly overview these three areas; I describe them in more detail in the following sections.

The demographics of the early end of the age range imply that materials should be designed for home, day care, and classroom environments, and

361

for children from a variety of backgrounds, interests, and ability levels. To reach this broad spectrum, the materials are progressively layered—users will be able to "dig deeper" into them to reach increasingly rich, but demanding, pedagogical and mathematical levels.

Based on theory and research on early childhood learning and teaching (Bowman, Donovan, & Burns, 2001; Clements, 2001), we determined that *Building Blocks'* basic approach would be *finding the mathematics in, and developing mathematics from, children's activity*. The materials are designed to help children extend and mathematize their everyday activities, from building blocks to art to songs and stories to puzzles. Activities are designed based on children's experiences and interests, with an emphasis on supporting the development of *mathematical* activity. So, the materials do not rely on technology alone, but integrate three types of media: computers, manipulatives (and everyday objects), and print.

Many claim a research basis for their materials, but these claims are often vacuous, citing vague theories without specifics (Sarama & Clements, in press). *Building Blocks* is research based in several fundamental ways. Our design process is based on the assumption that curriculum and software design can and should have an explicit theoretical and empirical foundation, beyond its genesis in someone's intuitive grasp of children's learning. It also should interact with the ongoing development of theory and research—reaching toward the ideal of testing a theory by testing the software and the curriculum in which it is embedded. Our model includes specification of mathematical ideas (computer objects) and processes/skills (computer tools) and extensive field-testing from the first inception through to large summative evaluation studies (Clements, 2002; Clements & Battista, 2000; Sarama & Clements, in press). Phases of this nine-step design process model are: drafting curriculum goals, building an explicit model of children's knowledge and learning in the goal domain, creating an initial design, investigating components of the software design, assessing prototypes and curriculum (with one-on-one interviews with students and teachers), conducting pilot tests (in a few classrooms), conducting field tests in numerous classrooms, and publishing the materials. All the while, feedback from the field results in further refinement to the design of the software and activities, which then results in further testing. In this way, we continually loop through the earlier phases of the model.

Several steps deserve a bit more elaboration. The step of "building an explicit model of children's knowledge and learning in the goal domain" involves the adaptation, creation, and use of learning trajectories. *Building Blocks* is structured on empirically based learning trajectories through the big ideas and skill areas of mathematics (Clements & Battista, 1992; Fuson, 1997). The step of "creating an initial design" is based largely on these learning trajectories (which are discussed in detail in Part I and several chapters of this volume), but also on other bodies of research. For example, what mathematics is included is based on research on what topics are developmentally appropriate for, generative for, and interesting to young children. As another example, the design directly applies research on making computer software for young children motivating and educationally effective (Clements, Nastasi, & Swaminathan, 1993; Clements & Swaminathan, 1995). It is to this last issue that I next turn.

## DEVELOPMENTALLY APPROPRIATE PRESCHOOL MATHEMATICS SOFTWARE

The extensive use of software in *Building Blocks* requires mining the existing research for what it tells us about young children's use of, and learning from, computer programs. Although the basic question of whether computers are "developmentally appropriate" for young children at all is still debated, I do not discuss it in detail, as the research is clear that, *used wisely*, computer use can be meaningful, motivating, and beneficial for children 3 years of age and above (Davidson & Wright, 1994; Haugland, 2000; Haugland & Wright, 1997; Sarama & Clements, 2002; Shade, 1994).

The research also indicates that not all uses of computers are valuable and that teachers must work hard to integrate technology effectively (Wright, 1998). As an example of the first finding, although hundreds of products are now available for young children that include mathematics, most of these products fall into one of three categories (Clements & Nastasi, 1992; Sarama & Clements, 2002). The first category is drill programs, often disguised by multimedia "bells and whistles." Such programs can be effective at their intended purpose, providing practice, but they do not develop conceptual knowledge. Too often, the drill in these packages is not optimally designed (e.g., not using the computer's management capabilities to provide targeted practice). The second, related, category, often called "Edutainment," also has attractive multimedia features, but limited mathematics content and pedagogy. The third category, exploratory environments, has potential for mathematical investigations, but unfortunately young children usually explore them only on the surface level. For both the second and third categories, there is little learning, by children or educators (Sarama & Clements, 2002).

In contrast, programs with focused goals and coherent pedagogy can help young children develop both concepts and skills (Clements & Nastasi, 1992; Sarama & Clements, 2002). For example, the flexibility of computer technologies allows the creation of a vision not limited by traditional materials and pedagogical approaches (cf. Confrey, 1996). As just one illustration, computer-based communication can allow representations and actions not possible with other media. As an example of the latter, blocks can be actually glued together, trucks can leave paths in the sand, and these paths can be changed, moved, saved, and used later with other vehicles. The *Building Blocks* materials not only ensure that the actions and objects mirror concepts and procedures, but also that they are embedded in tasks and developmentally appropriate settings (e.g., narratives, fantasy worlds, building projects).

The second research finding is that guidance by the teacher is essential for effective integration of technology. Teachers must introduce, monitor, and mediate children's interactions with computer programs (Clements & Nastasi, 1992; Sarama & Clements, 2002). *Building Blocks* integrates technology activities with off-computer activities, and helps the teacher provide such mediation by providing pedagogical guidance for both off- and on-computer activities in the teachers' materials.

We designed *Building Blocks* within this general research framework. We also looked at the research on particular uses of computers to teach mathematics to young children. One decision was to use computer manipulatives. Some early childhood educators may argue that young children benefit much more from the tactile experience of interacting with concrete manipulates. But can on-screen manipulatives still be "concrete"? One has to examine what *concrete* means. Sensory characteristics do not adequately define it (Clements & McMillen, 1996; Wilensky, 1991).

First, it cannot be assumed that children's conceptions of the manipulatives are similar to adults' (Clements & McMillen, 1996). For example, a student working on place value with beans and beansticks used the bean as 10 and the beanstick as 1 (Hiebert & Wearne, 1992). Second, physical actions with certain manipulatives may suggest different mental actions than those we wish students to learn. For example, researchers found a mismatch among students using the number line to perform addition. When adding five and four, the students located 5, counted "one, two, three, four," and read the answer. This did not help them solve the problem mentally, for to do so they have to count "six, seven, eight, nine" and at the same time count the counts—6 is 1, 7 is 2, and so on. These actions are quite different (Gravemeijer ,1991). Thus, manipulatives themselves do not carry the meaning of the mathematical idea. Students must act on these manipulatives in the context of well-planned activities, and ultimately reflect on these actions. Later, we expect them to have a "concrete" understanding that goes beyond these physical manipulatives.

It appears that there are different ways to define *concrete* (Clements & McMillen, 1996). We define Sensory-Concrete knowledge as that in which students must use sensory material to make sense of an idea. For example, at early stages, children cannot count, add, or subtract meaningfully unless they have actual things. They build Integrated-Concrete knowledge as they learn. Such knowledge is connected in special ways. This is the root of the word *concrete*—"to grow together." What gives sidewalk concrete its strength is the combination of separate particles in an interconnected mass. What gives Integrated-Concrete thinking its strength is the combination of many separate ideas in an interconnected structure of knowledge (Clements & McMillen, 1996).

For example, computer programs may allow children to manipulate on-screen pattern blocks. Children working with physical pattern blocks may develop sophisticated ideas of symmetry and geometric relationships, but research has shown they often do not (Sarama,

Clements, & Vukelic, 1996). The computer manipulatives offer several mathematical and practical benefits. The software encourages explicit awareness of the geometric motions used in creating a design. Specific tools can allow children to dynamically explore composition and decomposition of shapes. The "flatness" of the on-screen manipulatives facilitates exploration of relationships between shapes (e.g., Matthew became frustrated working off-computer after working with the software because he was unable to cover half of his blue rhombus to get a much desired blue triangle).

Practical benefits include being able to easily move a design when more space is needed. Off-computer, moving the physical manipulatives often results in the design falling apart. On-computer, children can glue the shapes together before quickly sliding the entire design to another part of the screen. Similarly, most children simply destroy their pattern block designs when it is "clean-up" time. Children working on computer can save their work and later come back to reflect, reproduce, or extend.

Computers encourage students to make their knowledge explicit, which helps them build Integrated-Concrete knowledge. Specific theoretically and empirically grounded advantages of using computer manipulatives include (Clements & McMillen, 1996): providing a manageable, clean manipulative; offering flexibility; changing arrangement or representation; storing and later retrieving configurations; recording and replaying students' actions; linking the concrete and the symbolic with feedback; dynamically linking multiple representations; changing the very nature of the manipulative; linking the specific to the general; encouraging problem posing and conjecturing; scaffolding problem solving; focusing attention and increasing motivation; and encouraging and facilitating complete, precise explanations.

Of course, multimedia and other computer capabilities should be (and, in *Building Blocks* are) used when they serve educational purposes. Features such as animation, music, surprise elements, and especially consistent interaction get and hold children's interest (Escobedo & Evans, 1997). They can also aid learning, *if* designed to be consistent with, and supporting, the pedagogical goals. In addition, access to technology is an important equity issue. We plan on having much of our materials running on the widely available Internet (Word Wide Web).

In summary, we designed the *Building Blocks* project to combine the art and science of teaching and learning with the science of technology, with the latter serving the former. Such synthesis of (a) curriculum and technology development as a scientific enterprise and (b) mathematics education research will reduce the separation of research and practice in mathematics and technology education. This will produce materials based on research and research based on effective and ecologically sound learning situations. Moreover, these results will be immediately applicable by practitioners (parents, teachers, and teacher educators), administrators and policymakers, and curriculum and software developers.

# MATHEMATICAL CONTENT

What mathematics should we teach? Basic mathematics for preschool children can be organized into two areas: (a) geometric and spatial ideas and skills and (b) numeric and quantitative ideas and skills. Research shows that young children are endowed with intuitive and informal capabilities in both these areas (Bransford, Brown, & Cocking, 1999; Clements, 1999a). Three mathematical themes should be woven through both these main areas: (a) patterns, (b) data, and (c) sorting and sequencing. These are children's *mathematical building blocks*, or ways of knowing the world mathematically. We illustrate one approach to developing these concepts through our *Building Blocks* project.[1]

As stated, we believe a good mathematics curriculum is based on *finding the mathematics in, and developing mathematics from, children's activity.* In this approach, children extend and mathematize their everyday activities, from art to songs to puzzles to, of course, building blocks (this is another meaning behind the *Building Blocks* name). So, we designed activities based on children's experiences and interests, with an emphasis on supporting the development of *mathematical* activity. Mathematization emphasizes representing—creating models of activity with mathematical objects, such as numbers and shapes, and mathematical actions, such as counting or transforming shapes. Our materials embody these actions-on-objects in a way that mirrors what research has identified as critical *mental actions*—children's *cognitive building blocks* (the third meaning of the name). These cognitive building blocks include creating, copying, and combining objects such as shapes or numbers. A following section illustrates how such actions-on-objects are embedded in the activities.

# ROLE OF THE COMPUTER

An illustration of mathematical actions-on-objects, and how they are embodied in both off-computer and computer activities, builds on young children's experiences with and love of puzzles. This set of activities is briefly described in Fig. 15.1. Children fill in outline puzzles using an extended set of pattern blocks. The *objects* they use are basic geometric shapes. The *actions* they perform on these objects include sliding, turning, flipping, and combining or composing. They initially solve outline puzzles with physical pattern blocks off the computer (Fig. 15.1a). They solve similar puzzles at the computer, enjoying that the blocks "snap" and stay together accurately (Fig. 15.1b). More importantly, they use the computer's tools to perform actions on the shapes (Fig. 15.1c). Because they have to figure out how to move the blocks and *choose* a motion such as

[1]"Building Blocks—Foundations for Mathematical Thinking, Pre-Kindergarten to Grade 2: Research-Based Materials Development." is being developed at the State University of New York at Buffalo and Wayne State University, where Julie Sarama is the codirector. See http://www.gse.buffalo.edu/org/buildingblocks/.

FIG. 15.1a.  Children solve puzzles by filling a puzzle outline with pattern blocks. They solve each one in several different ways if they are interested.

FIG. 15.1b.  Then children do a similar activity on the computer, where the pattern blocks snap together in a satisfying manner and stay put.

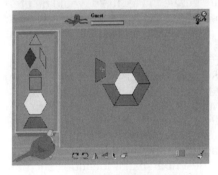

FIG. 15.1c.  Also, the computer's tools for actions such as sliding and turning help children become more aware of these mathematical processes.

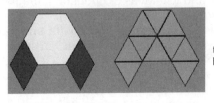

FIG. 15.1d.  Children might be challenged to find a way to use the fewest (or the most) blocks to fill an outline.

FIG. 15.1a-15.1d.  The "Shape Puzzles" activity.

367

slide or turn, they are more conscious of these geometric motions. Four-year-old Leah initially referred to the "spinning" tools, but later called them the "turn shapes" tools, and after several months was describing directions and quantities, such as "OK, get *this* [right or clockwise] turn tool and turn it three times!" Such choices also encourage children to be more *deliberate*. They "think ahead" and talk to each other about what shape and action to choose next. In these ways, the computer slows down their actions and increases their reflection. Just as important, using the motion tools deliberately helps children become familiar with seeing shapes in different orientations and realizing that changing the orientation does not affect the shape's name or class. In a related activity, children are challenged to build a picture or design with physical blocks and copy it onto the computer. Again, this requires the use of specific tools for the geometric motions of slide, flip, and turn and encourages children to reflect on the orientation of the shapes. Children who are experienced or advanced may be challenged in several ways. Some might enjoy finding a way to use the fewest blocks to fill an outline (Fig. 15.1d).

How are learning trajectories embodied in this activity? Our theoretical learning trajectory (see Clements, chap. 10, this volume) guides the selection of puzzles for children at different levels of the trajectory. For example, the puzzle in Fig. 15.2a would be presented to the child at the level of *Pre-Composer,* whereas the puzzle in Fig. 15.2b would be presented to the child at the level of *Picture Maker* (just to be sure you know what it is, Fig. 15.2c shows the final picture), and the puzzle in Fig. 15.2d would be presented to the child at the level of *Shape Composer.*

These are powerful mathematical processes to perform on shapes, but not out of the reach of preschoolers (although some will reach only the lower levels). Research shows that preschoolers know a considerable amount about shapes (Clements, Swaminathan, Hannibal, & Sarama, 1999; Lehrer, Jenkins, & Osana, 1998), and they can do more than we assume, especially working with computers (Sarama et al., 1996). In the broad area of geometry and space, they can do the following: recognize, name, build, draw, describe, compare, and sort two- and three-dimensional shapes, investigate putting shapes together and taking them apart, recognize and use slides and turns, describe spatial locations such as "above" and "behind," and describe and use ideas of direction and distance in getting around in their environment (Clements, 1999a).

In the area of number, preschoolers can learn to count with understanding (Fuson, 1988; Gelman, 1994), recognize "how many" in small sets of objects (Clements, 1999b; Reich, Subrahmanyam, & Gelman, 1999), compare numbers (Griffin, Case, & Capodilupo, 1995), and learn simple ideas of addition and subtraction (Aubrey, 1997; Clements, 1984; Siegler, 1996). They can count higher and generally participate in a much more exciting and varied mathematics than usually considered (Ginsburg, Inoue, & Seo, 1999; Trafton & Hartman, 1997). Challenging number activities don't just develop children's number sense; they can

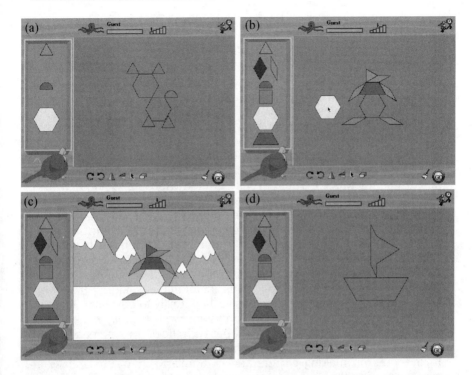

FIG. 15.2. Screens from the "Shape Puzzles" computed activity.

also develop children's competencies in such logical competencies as sorting and ordering (Clements, 1984).

As an illustration, *Building Blocks* includes a set of activities in which children learn one-to-one correspondence, counting, and equality. For example, children "get just enough" treats or scissors for the children at their table and in other real-world situations throughout the day. A computer activity challenges them to help a character get ready for a party, beginning with setting the table. At a higher level of the same activity, an on-screen character requests a certain number of items to add to the table. If a dish is missing, a character at the table may say, "I don't have a dish!" This type of natural feedback helps young children learn. In related activities, children decide how to share a given number of treats among those sitting at the table. Teachers might talk to the children about the way they are figuring out how many items they will need. Do they "deal out" the supplies each time? Or do they count the number of people, and use that number when getting supplies?

# IN CLASSROOMS

We have completed the first three of the steps of classroom testing investigating components of the software design, assessing prototypes and curriculum (with one-on-one interviews with students and teachers), conducting pilot tests (in a few classrooms). In this section, I provide summaries and examples of the results of these tests.

The first pilot test for the geometry materials was limited in time—we had only 6 weeks (27 sessions) and so we attempted to condense the main *Building Blocks* activities for geometry. Pre- and posttests were given to the students. The children's average pretest score was 69. Their average posttest score was 84. Thus, despite limited exposure to the activities, there was a substantial average gain.

On what specific items did children make the greatest gains? They increased their scores on several difficult paper-and-pencil items in which they had to identify shapes, especially increasing in their ability not to be "fooled" by shapes that "looked like" triangles, squares, rectangles, and especially rhombi and quadrilaterals, but were not. In a similar vein, although they made only small gains in identifying figures that were congruent, they significantly increased their ability to correctly state that certain figures that looked to be congruent were actually not. On four items that asked children to make shapes with sticks, they increased moderately on initially choosing the correct number of sticks, while tripling their scores on making correct angles. Similarly, they substantially increased their ability to copy a complex design of three embedded shapes by manipulating transparent versions of the individual shapes.

What activities engendered this learning? The children in this group interacted with shapes in many different ways. They made pictures with paper cutouts of shapes, completed pattern block puzzles, searched for shapes in their environment and recorded what they saw (with adult help, if needed), sorted shapes, built shapes with straws and blocks, and identified shapes in storybooks. On computer they matched shapes, explored pattern block puzzles (including the use of geometric transformations), and identified shapes in the context of building Mystery Toys.

Let's look at a specific example. When sorting rectangles and nonrectangles, the teacher focused the children's attention on the sides. Chandra was able to tell the teacher which pile to put a new shape in, but was unable to articulate her sorting rule. Her partner, Marnie, similarly said, "It matches," while pointing to the correct pile. For the next shape (a right trapezoid), Chandra again pointed to the correct pile but gave color as her reason for doing so. Alethea joined the group and disagreed, saying the shape should go in the rectangle pile. Mitchell joined, pointed to the nonperpendicular side and said, "No, [it's not a rectangle, because] someone cut it right here."

Later, the teacher asked Tiffany if she knew the *name* of the trapezoid. She immediately said, "trapezoid," and pointed to the computer, indicating where they had learned that vocabulary term. In the computer activity Mystery Toys, each shape name is pronounced as children match shapes. Later, the children are asked to click on the correct shape when the computer pronounces its name. This was a popular activity with the children and they enjoyed imitating the "computer" voice when they named shapes. Throughout the study, discussions encouraged children's descriptions while encouraging the development of precise language. Early talk clarified the meanings of terms. With such clarification, children learned to explain why a shape belongs to a certain category—"It has three straight sides." Eventually, they internalized such arguments, for example, thinking, "It is a weird, long triangle, but it has three straight sides!" Finding and identifying shapes by feeling was one particularly useful activity (see Fig. 15.3).

We piloted the number activities in another classroom of eight children; we altered the assessment extensively, so averages were not computed. Children made gains on all but a couple of items (most of which showed a "ceiling" or "floor" effect; e.g., counting verbally to 10) that remained the same from pre- to posttest. Increases were small (e.g., average gain of .25 points or more) on the following items:

- Recognizing the number of objects in collections of one to five (four children could recognize the number of small collections of one to five at pretest; the other four could recognize about half; all could recognize all collections on the posttest).

FIG. 15.3. "Feely box" activities support both physical exploration and the development of vocabulary and communication competencies.

- Counting 8 objects.
- Adding and subtracting small numbers (totals < 4) without objects.
- Ordering "towers" of 6 to 12 connecting cubes.
- Identifying the number between two numbers (e.g., "What number is between 5 and 7?").

Children made moderate gains (average of 1/3 to ½ point) on the following items:

- Comparing the number in small collections (e.g., shown cards with ● ● ● and ● ● ● and asked, "Are these the same number?").
- Recognizing counting mistakes that a doll made (moderate gains on two subitems; small gains on two subitems).
- Counting out (producing) sets of 6.
- Labeling sets of one to five with numerals.
- Recognizing which hidden set was larger when they were initially equal and items were added or subtracted.

Children made moderate gains (average above ½ point) on the following items:

- Quickly recognizing the number in small collections (i.e., subitizing; one to six objects).
- Adding and subtracting with objects (e.g., "If there were six dogs and only four bones, how many dogs wouldn't get a bone?").

What activities facilitated children's learnings on the number items? Children counted objects continually throughout the study. Reading "non-math" books as well as books showing numerals were part of circle time, but books also became part of the centers. It was in the centers that children were able to interact with the books more extensively. Tanya was looking at the book *One Hungry Monster* and wanted to figure out how much food the monster ate on one of the pages. She put cubes near each numeral counting as she did, "1, ... 1,2 ... 1,2,3." She then counted, "1,2,3,4,5,6 ... 6!" On computer, children's counting was supported by the management system, which automatically adjusted the activity for difficulty and provided appropriate feedback and help.

The children had multiple opportunities to perform simple addition and subtraction. A toy dinosaur shop was set up in the socio-dramatic play area of the classroom. As Geri played with Janelle and Andre, she filled many "dinosaur orders." This involved reading a numeral on a card and counting out the correct quantity for her "customers" and collecting the correct amount of play money. Eventually, Janelle wanted to "trick" Geri and gave her two cards, a 2 and a 5. The teacher suggested Geri give Janelle two of one kind and five of another. She carefully counted out the two piles, put them together and counted the total. She then asked Janelle for $7.

Ordering towers of connecting cubes became part of pretend play when children were "making stairs" for small characters to climb. On the computer, children moved along the learning trajectory built into the software, first "finding the next stair," then building an entire staircase, then finding missing stairs.

Counting out sets of objects was another activity that the children had multiple opportunities to engage in throughout the year. In small groups, children placed the requested number of objects in play scenes, made cookies with chips, and filled dinosaur orders as previously described. In the beginning of the study, some children could only count out two objects. In these small groups, children worked on counting out different quantities depending on their capabilities. On computer, the children counted out chips on a cookie, silverware and plates for a party, or the correct number of dinosaurs to fill an order. The management system automatically adjusted the difficulty level (the number of items requested).

## SUMMARY

Although mentioned briefly, it is easy to overlook the power of our combined strategies. Research-based computer tools stand at the base, providing computer analogs to critical mathematical ideas and processes. These are used, or implemented, with activities and a management system that guides children through fine-grained, research-based learning trajectories (developed over years of synthesizing our own and others' empirical work). These activities-through-trajectories connect children's informal knowledge to more formal school mathematics. The result is a package that will be motivating for children, but is also *comprehensive* in that it includes both exploratory environments that include specific tasks and guidance, building concepts and well-managed practice building skills, a full set of critical curriculum components, and a full range of mathematical activities. The initial pilot tests results indicate that such an approach can result in significant assessed learning gains consistent with the new *Standards* of the National Council of Teachers of Mathematics (a complete field test is being completed at the time of this writing).

## ACKNOWLEDGMENTS

This chapter is based on work, coauthored with Douglas H. Clements, supported in part by the National Science Foundation under Grant No. ESI-9730804, "Building Blocks—Foundations for Mathematical Thinking, Pre-Kindergarten to Grade 2: Research-Based Materials Development," and Grant REC-9903409, "Technology- Enhanced Learning of Geometry in Elementary Schools." Any opinions, findings, and conclusions or recommendations expressed in this material are those of the author(s) and do not necessarily reflect the views of the National Science Foundation.

# REFERENCES

Aubrey, C. (1997). Children's early learning of number in school and out. In I. Thompson (Ed.), *Teaching and learning early number* (pp. 20–29). Philadelphia: Open University Press.

Bowman, B. T., Donovan, M. S., & Burns, M. S. (Eds.). (2001). *Eager to learn: Educating our preschoolers.* Washington, DC: National Academy Press.

Bransford, J. D., Brown, A. L., & Cocking, R. R. (Eds.). (1999). *How people learn.* Washington, DC: National Academy Press.

Clements, D. H. (1984). Training effects on the development and generalization of Piagetian logical operations and knowledge of number. *Journal of Educational Psychology, 76,* 766–776.

Clements, D. H. (1999a). Geometric and spatial thinking in young children. In J. V. Copley (Ed.), *Mathematics in the early years* (pp. 66–79). Reston, VA: National Council of Teachers of Mathematics.

Clements, D. H. (1999b). Subitizing: What is it? Why teach it? *Teaching Children Mathematics, 5,* 400–405.

Clements, D. H. (2001). Mathematics in the preschool. *Teaching Children Mathematics, 7,* 270–275.

Clements, D. H. (2002). Linking research and curriculum development. In L. D. English (Ed.), *Handbook of international research in mathematics education* (pp. 599–630). Mahwah, NJ: Lawrence Erlbaum Associates.

Clements, D. H., & Battista, M. T. (1992). Geometry and spatial reasoning. In D. A. Grouws (Ed.), *Handbook of research on mathematics teaching and learning* (pp. 420–464). New York: Macmillan.

Clements, D. H., & Battista, M. T. (2000). Designing effective software. In A. E. Kelly & R. A. Lesh (Eds.), *Handbook of research design in mathematics and science education* (pp. 761–776). Mahwah, NJ: Lawrence Erlbaum Associates.

Clements, D. H., & McMillen, S. (1996). Rethinking "concrete" manipulatives. *Teaching Children Mathematics, 2*(5), 270–279.

Clements, D. H., & Nastasi, B. K. (1992). Computers and early childhood education. In M. Gettinger, S. N. Elliott, & T. R. Kratochwill (Eds.), *Advances in school psychology: Preschool and early childhood treatment directions* (pp. 187–246). Hillsdale, NJ: Lawrence Erlbaum Associates.

Clements, D. H., Nastasi, B. K., & Swaminathan, S. (1993). Young children and computers: Crossroads and directions from research. *Young Children, 48*(2), 56–64.

Clements, D. H., & Swaminathan, S. (1995). Technology and school change: New lamps for old? *Childhood Education, 71,* 275–281.

Clements, D. H., Swaminathan, S., Hannibal, M. A. Z., & Sarama, J. (1999). Young children's concepts of shape. *Journal for Research in Mathematics Education, 30,* 192–212.

Confrey, J. (1996). The role of new technologies in designing mathematics education. In C. Fisher, D. C. Dwyer, & K. Yocam (Eds.), *Education and technology, reflections on computing in the classroom* (pp. 129–149). San Francisco: Apple Press.

Davidson, J., & Wright, J., L. (1994). The potential of the microcomputer in the early childhood classroom. In J. L. Wright & D. D. Shade (Eds.), *Young children: Active learners in a technological age* (pp. 77–91). Washington, DC: National Association for the Education of Young Children.

Escobedo, T. H., & Evans, S. (1997, March). *A comparison of child-tested early childhood education software with professional ratings.* Paper presented at the meeting of the American Educational Research Association, Chicago.

Fuson, K. C. (1988). *Children's counting and concepts of number.* New York: Springer-Verlag.

Fuson, K. C. (1997). Research-based mathematics curricula: New educational goals require programs of four interacting levels of research. *Issues in Education, 3*(1), 67–79.

Gelman, R. (1994). Constructivism and supporting environments. In D. Tirosh (Ed.), *Implicit and explicit knowledge: An educational approach* (Vol. 6, pp. 55–82). Norwood, NJ: Ablex.

Ginsburg, H. P., Inoue, N., & Seo, K. H. (1999). Young children doing mathematics: Observations of everyday activities. In J. V. Copley (Ed.), *Mathematics in the early years* (pp. 87–89). Reston, VA: National Council of Teachers of Mathematics.

Gravemeijer, K. P. E. (1991). An instruction-theoretical reflection on the use of manipulatives. In L. Streefland (Ed.), *Realistic mathematics education in primary school* (pp. 57–76). Utrecht, Netherlands: Freudenthal Institute, Utrecht University.

Griffin, S., Case, R., & Capodilupo, A. (1995). Teaching for understanding: The importance of the Central Conceptual Structures in the elementary mathematics curriculum. In A. McKeough, J. Lupart, & A. Marini (Eds.), *Teaching for transfer: Fostering generalization in learning*. Hillsdale, NJ: Lawrence Erlbaum Associates.

Haugland, S. W. (2000). What role should technology play in young children's learning? Part 2. Early childhood classrooms in the 21st century: Using computers to maximize learning. *Young Children, 55*(1), 12–18.

Haugland, S. W., & Wright, J. L. (1997). *Young children and technology: A world of discovery*. Boston: Allyn & Bacon.

Hiebert, J. C., & Wearne, D. (1992). Links between teaching and learning place value with understanding in first grade. Journal for Research in Mathematics Education, *23*, 98–122.

Lehrer, R., Jenkins, M., & Osana, H. (1998). Longitudinal study of children's reasoning about space and geometry. In R. Lehrer & D. Chazan (Eds.), *Designing learning environments for developing understanding of geometry and space* (pp. 137–167). Mahwah, NJ: Lawrence Erlbaum Associates.

Reich, S., Subrahmanyam, K., & Gelman, R. (1999, April). *Children's use of number and amount information when making judgments about quantity.* Paper presented at the meeting of the Society for Research in Child Development, Albuquerque, NM.

Sarama, J., & Clements, D. H. (2002). Learning and teaching with computers in early childhood education. In O. N. Saracho & B. Spodek (Eds.), *Contemporary perspectives in early childhood education* (pp. 171–219). Greenwich, CT: Information Age Publishing.

Sarama, J., & Clements, D. H. (in press). Linking research and software development. In K. Heid & G. Blume (Eds.), *Technology in the learning and teaching of mathematics: Syntheses and perspectives.* New York: Information Age Publishing.

Sarama, J., Clements, D. H., & Vukelic, E. B. (1996). The role of a computer manipulative in fostering specific psychological/mathematical processes. In E. Jakubowski, D. Watkins, & H. Biske (Eds.), *Proceedings of the eighteenth annual meeting of the North America Chapter of the International Group for the Psychology of Mathematics Education* (Vol. 2, pp. 567–572). Columbus, OH: ERIC Clearinghouse for Science, Mathematics, and Environmental Education.

Shade, D. D. (1994). Computers and young children: Software types, social contexts, gender, age, and emotional responses. *Journal of Computing in Childhood Education, 5*(2), 177–209.

Siegler, R. S. (1996). *Emerging minds: The process of change in children's thinking.* New York: Oxford University Press.

Trafton, P. R., & Hartman, C. L. (1997). Developing number sense and computational strategies in problem-centered classrooms. *Teaching Children Mathematics, 4*(4), 230–233.

Wilensky, U. (1991). Abstract mediations on the concrete and concrete implications for mathematics education. In I. Harel & S. Papert (Eds.), *Constructionism* (pp. 193–199). Norwood, NJ: Ablex.

Wright, J. (1998). A new look at integrating technology into the curriculum. *Early Childhood Education Journal, 26*(2), 107–109.

# 16

# Mathematics Problem-Solving Adventures: A Language-Arts-Based Supplementary Series for Early Childhood That Focuses on Spatial Sense

Beth Casey
*Boston College*

## THE MAJOR ELEMENTS OF THIS EARLY CHILDHOOD SUPPLEMENTARY MATHEMATICS SERIES, 'ROUND THE RUG MATH

Two key elements of this new 6-book early childhood mathematics series are summarized as follows:

- Through math story sagas, these mathematics-language arts materials make use of an *oral- storytelling* tradition to provide context, continuity, and motivation for the learning of early mathematical concepts. Using this oral-storytelling approach, the stories and math activities have been designed to address gender, racial/ethnic, and cognitive equity issues.

- A major thrust of the present mathematics program is to introduce *both* spatial and linguistic-based mathematical thinking during the early childhood years, right at the point when students have their

377

first contact with mathematics as a formal discipline. These supplementary materials are specifically designed to provide young learners with rich opportunities to develop their visualization and spatial reasoning skills when solving mathematics problems.

## RATIONALE FOR THE USE OF ORAL STORYTELLING AS THE MEDIUM FOR TEACHING MATHEMATICS TO YOUNG CHILDREN

A problem with mathematics in general, and especially for young children, is that students are asked to do mathematics activities that have little intrinsic meaning and interest to them. Thus, they are often disengaged when doing mathematics. Most of the prior mathematics programs that have attempted to use "relevant" and "real world" mathematics activities have drawn on problems that are connected to children in their everyday life (such as counting the number of children who are standing in line or using the calendar to teach counting). Though these are useful and effective strategies, much of what is lacking is the ability to locate a problem in a relevant context that is rich enough in its dramatic elements—elements such as character development, plot, surprise, conflict, and suspense—so that the child is substantially drawn into this context. This is one way that literature can effectively forge a link with mathematics. Literature is a powerful medium for placing mathematics in a meaningful context, and there has been a movement to incorporate mathematics and literature in recent years (Coombs & Harcourt, 1986; Schiro, 1997; Sherrill, 1994; Welchman-Tischler, 1992).

### *Using Oral Storytelling to Make the Literature/Mathematics Link.* This series extends the literacy-based approach to include *oral story telling*. The use of storytelling characters to pose mathematics problems harnesses the excitement and imagination of the children and directs that energy toward mathematics learning. When the reason for solving a mathematics problem is intertwined with young children's fascination with fantasy as well as their love of being playful, then they will put all their energies into solving the mathematics problems. Thus, the mathematics problems in this book series become relevant and "real" to the children because they are presented within a meaningful, story-based context.

The very nature of the oral delivery of a story is what significantly differentiates it from a story read from a book. Rather than focusing on the book, the children are challenged to create mental pictures of the events as the story unfolds. An added advantage of storytelling is that the storytellers' eyes are on the listeners, which leads to a more electric and closer connection to the audience (Beatty, 1994). In addition, storytelling is a particularly comfortable medium for early childhood teachers to use for the teaching of mathematics, due to their strong orientation toward the teaching of reading and language arts.

In the past, even when children's literature has been used to teach mathematics concepts, there has been little attempt to extend the book-related mathematics activities beyond one or two lessons. In the 'Round the Rug Math supplementary book described here, the lessons are part of an ongoing saga where one mathematics lesson is connected to another in a meaningful way through the medium of the story. The National Council of Teachers of Mathematics (NCTM) Connections Standard (NCTM, 2000) recommends that students should understand how mathematical ideas build on one another to produce a whole. Through the use of storytelling sagas, as the stories evolve and become more intricate, so does the mathematics.

One book from the series, Tan and the Shape Changer (Schiro, Casey, & Anderson, 2002), is set in ancient China, and focuses on part–whole relations using isosceles right triangles as the base figure. The first mathematics activity that the children do is to explore ways of combining different-size triangles in order to make a dragon collage. This free exploration of the triangles is an important prerequisite to later strategies for solving part–whole problems. By free exploration, the children discover, on their own, important mathematical relationships. They investigate attributes of triangles and learn how they can be combined to create new wholes (Albert, 2000b). For example:

> Tamila discovered that two isosceles right triangles could make a square. She also discovered that she could combine triangles of three different sizes to make a square ... [Another] student had combined isosceles right triangles to produce a square, a large triangle, and a parallelogram. These are typical examples of what many of the children were able to accomplish through this activity on their own, with no template or specific instructions provided ... Ori's dragon shows two different types of patterning. In constructing the tail of her dragon, she used triangles to form an alternating pattern of upright and upside-down triangles. In the head of her dragon collage, another pattern was formed by layering triangles of different sizes.... Alex used patterning to tranform the triangles into the body of the dragon. She created a snake-like body by combining two rows of triangles, mirror-images of one another, with one row filling the empty spaces created by the row of triangles below. (Albert, 2000b, pp. 7–8)

As the story and mathematics continue in this book, both the character of the Shape Changer in the story *and* the mathematics puzzles themselves, involve shape changing. In the story, the character of the Shape Changer turns from an old man to a dragon to a fox fairy and back to an old man again. At the same time, the little boy named Tan discovers he can combine two isosceles right triangles to create a square, a large triangle, and a parallelogram. The students also produce these three shapes from the two triangles. They work on this problem on their own, again without any model or template.

Next, Tan and the children are further challenged to explore how to make the shapes under a cloth. This requires them to depend on their tactile sense to solve the problem rather than their visual sense. In one inner-city kindergarten classroom, two boys continued working on this problem during choice time, and the teacher had them demonstrate how they solved the problem to rest of the class. They took a long time to show how to combine the two triangles to make the parallelogram under the cloth, and the other children watched intently and spontaneously cheered when the problem was solved.

As *Tan and the Shape Changer* evolves, the students gradually combine more triangles to make more complex shapes. However, as they create these more complex triangle puzzles, they discover that their original three puzzle shapes are actually hidden within these more complex puzzles. Thus, in this storytelling saga on part–whole relations, a strong connection is made from one mathematics lesson to another, both through the ongoing story line and through the developing mathematics.

Use of animal characters as puppets who pose problems to the children is again an important way in which literacy, the arts, and mathematics are linked within this series. Finding solutions to the mathematics problems is of key importance to the puppet characters in the story, and, thus, to the children. The puppet characters are treasured by the children, and teachers from a variety of classrooms commented that the puppets were treated almost as members of the class, and integrated by the children, on their own, across other learning activities. In the book *Teeny visits Shapeland* (Casey, Goodrow, Schiro, & Anderson, 2002), the puppet is a turtle named Teeny who lives alone in a pond and is looking for a family. One day as Teeny is sunning himself on a rock with his feet, head, and tail tucked inside his shell, two children point out that he looks like a circle. So Teeny makes a wish that he could go to a place where there are all kinds of circles who might be his relatives. He falls asleep and dreams he is in an imaginary place called Shapeland, and joins a group of shapes who combine to become Red Wagon (made out of four circles, a rectangle, and a triangle for a handle). Teeny and Red Wagon encounter a number of adventures as they travel to Figure City for the Shape Family Parade. Within the stories, Teeny has a pivotal role in posing mathematical problems and riddles, and in asking the children for help in solving these problems. In order to help the story characters, the students consider the attributes of two-dimensional (such as circles, triangles, and rectangles) and three-dimensional shapes (such as spheres, boxes, and pyramids), and use these attributes to solve sorting problems. In the stories and activities, children take a closer look at a wider range of attributes and shapes, as they consider relationships among two-dimensional and three-dimensional shapes.

In one episode, there is a pile of wood blocking the road. Teeny the Turtle helps figure out a way to clear the road, and he makes up a riddle for his shape friends. For the students, solving the riddle (see the following) involves taking Popsicle sticks from the pile that has been laid on top of the paper road, in order to use them to make different shapes:

> Make each of your shapes with pieces of wood.
> For the first shape use three. What shape can it be?
>
> Let's all make some more. For the next shape, use four.
> Two short sticks, two long. You cannot go wrong.
>
> No matter how many pieces of wood that you take,
> There's one last shape that you cannot make.
>
> The road will be clear, if you show me why,
> Then the riddle is solved, and we all can go by." (Casey, Goodrow et al., 2002)

The preschool and kindergarten children become very involved exploring with the shapes to solve this riddle. Many of the children of this age tend to identify only an equilateral triangle as a triangle. But as the children explore, they learn that there are many different looking shapes with three-sides and three-corners that can still be labeled triangles. In one classroom the children discovered that if you use a large enough number of straight sticks, you can make a shape that is almost circlelike, but you never can actually make a circle. At the end of this math activity, the children realize that by solving the riddle, all the wood as been cleared from the road, and Teeny and Red Wagon can continue on their way to Figure City.

The oral stories in these books provide a major link, not only between mathematics and emergent literacy/language arts, but to the rest of the early childhood curriculum as well. To a large extent, in the majority of other early primary mathematics programs, the mathematics content is de-contextualized from the rest of the curriculum. The present mathematics series is firmly grounded in the total early childhood curriculum, and the story sagas provide an opportunity for thematic development that can be extended to all parts of the curriculum. Teachers are presented with curriculum webs that explicitly show how these mathematics books can be connected to activities across the early childhood curriculum. For example, in *Froglets Do The Measuring* (Anderson, Casey, & Kerrigan, 2002), it is suggested in the curriculum web that, for related science activities, the students: (a) find out about real frogs, where real frogs live, and what they eat; (b) sort collections of plastic frogs, and explain how they sorted, for instance by color, by habitat, or by size; and (c) make a diorama showing the habitats of different kinds of frogs.

### Achieving Equity Through the Medium of Storytelling.

Storytelling provides an important motivating force for children of *all* cultures, both mainstream and minority. Throughout history, oral stories have offered the members of cultural groups a way of understanding their world and of passing on their understandings to succeeding generations.

Our storytelling approach to the teaching of mathematics is an outgrowth of the recent popular movement to integrate mathematics and literature (Coombs & Harcourt, 1986; Schiro, 1997; Sherrill, 1994). However, storytelling is particularly useful, because mathematics learning becomes accessible to children from strong oral-based cultural/literary traditions (Pellowski, 1990). This dependence on an oral tradition in African-American and Hispanic cultures may put children from these cultures at a disadvantage when learning mathematics, which often is taught in a totally de-contextualized way (Albert, 2000a). Thus, incorporating mathematics education within a familiar context of oral storytelling is a promising way of making these skills more relevant to children from cultures that have a rich oral tradition (Heath, 1989; Rogoff & Morelli, 1989).

The present stories introduce multicultural characters meaningful to children of both mainstream and minority cultures by incorporating story characters from different parts of the world, including Arab lands, Puerto Rico, China, Africa, and Europe. Using storytelling relating to different cultural contexts and multicultural characters provides a base from which *all* children can connect meaningfully to a variety of cultures and to different parts of the world. This also allows the teacher to integrate these mathematics materials with early childhood content across a wider range of the curriculum including social studies.

Furthermore, the presentation of mathematics concepts within these action-based adventure stories makes the learning process more meaningful to all children. In these books, the children become active participants as the stories unfold. This is particularly critical for the younger, less developmentally mature children, who tend to become distracted or disengaged from the learning process. Allen (1991) and Boykin's (1992) research on mathematical learning in African-American children showed that many children remembered information better if it was communicated using action words along with active involvement by characters within a story (as compared to facts presented in a de-contextualized form). In our development of the materials, we found this to be true of children in all the classrooms, both urban and suburban. Through the use of chants and movements and poems that actively involve the children in the story and in the mathematics, the books are able to capture the children's interest and motivation for learning mathematics.

We have field-tested our lessons in *cognitively* diverse, full-inclusion classrooms as well. The developmental, hands-on tasks provide a range of learning opportunities for children from diverse ability backgrounds, including those with language and cognitive delays. Thus, the open-ended nature of the materials in the books makes them more easily adaptable for children with diverse needs. To address the needs of children at different developmental levels, suggestions for meeting individual needs are provided for the mathematics activities. Optional mathematics activities are also included, so that teachers can provide additional experiences for children who need more intensive work or for those who want to develop the mathematics ideas further.

One child in particular stands out from one of the field sites. She was a student with severe special needs placed in a full-inclusion kindergarten classroom in Boston. This child loved the puppet and held it as much as possible. She was not physically able to sort shapes on her own, but her teacher would hold up a shape, and she could articulate and point sufficiently to indicate a sorting pile. Based on her choice, the teacher would place the shape in that category.

## THE LANGUAGE ARTS SKILLS ACQUIRED
## THROUGH THESE MATERIALS

*Comprehension Skills.* These early childhood mathematical materials also address important language arts competencies. The acquisition of listening skills and the ability to demonstrate comprehension of the story elements and sequence are major skills developed throughout this book. An important aspect of the saga is that the children are encouraged to carry over discussions about ongoing story lines for several days or weeks. They are often asked to predict what will happen in the stories, and to actively participate in the storytelling process. A rich range of language-based activities, including poems, chants, and actions, are all woven together. Often the ability to apply the story content to the mathematics activities themselves demonstrates the level of comprehension that the children have achieved about the story content (Casey, Paugh, & Ballard, 2002).

*Communication Skills.* As the children collaboratively solve the mathematics problems and report on their solutions to their classmates, they are developing their expressive language. This is achieved through their communications with each other. Children are encouraged to review the story and mathematics from the previous lesson, and this helps both communication and comprehension of the story and the mathematics. The use of a narrative approach seems to have facilitated comprehension and communication of both the language arts and the mathematics content in one second-grade classroom that we used as a field site. The second graders were presented with a new book in the series, but in the prior year, when they were first graders, they had been using a book on measurement from the series. When they encountered the frog puppet again, the children were very excited, and recounted the story and the measurement concepts from the material they had learned from the previous year.

## RATIONALE FOR THE FOCUS ON SPATIAL SENSE
## IN THE TEACHING OF MATHEMATICS OF YOUNG CHILDREN

There is evidence that skill at spatial thinking has an important role in mathematics achievement, with positive correlations found between spatial ability and mathematics achievement at all grade levels (Casey, Nuttall, & Pezaris, 1997; Casey, Nuttall, Pezaris, & Benbow, 1995; Clements & Battista, 1992). Furthermore, the K–4 standards for school mathematics from the NCTM (NCTM, 1989, 2000) strongly recommend an *increased* emphasis on teaching geometry and spatial sense. The development of spatial sense is connected to the development of spatial skills, which involves the ability to think and reason through the transformation of mental pictures. The spatial way of thinking is contrasted with an alternative learning style or mode of information processing that draws on linear, logical-deductive reasoning, accessed through the verbal system (Baddeley, 1986). Both strategies can be applied to mathematics problem solving (Battista, 1990). For example, many mathematics problems can be solved either by drawing a diagram of the solution (a spatial solution) or by laying out the step-by-step algorithmic solution (a verbal, logical-deductive solution).

Numerous mathematicians report using spatial skills when they visualize mathematical relations, and physical scientists report using such skills when they visualize and reason about the models of the physical world (Clements & Battista, 1992; Hershkowitz, Parzysz, & Van Dormolen, 1996). Spatial reasoning can be an important component in solving many types of mathematics problems, including: (a) the use of diagrams and drawings (e.g., for algebraic word problems), (b) searching for numerical patterns, (c) graphing numbers, (d) considering how fractions can be broken down into geometrical regions, and (e) conceptualizing mathematical functions (Wheatley, 1990).

Individuals who can utilize both spatial and analytical reasoning systems have an advantage in solving problems in many fields. The early childhood years are the time when children start to form their strategies for solving mathematics problems. With carefully constructed mathematics materials that develop *both* spatial and linguistic-based mathematical thinking, this period of learning has the potential to produce the most influential and long-lasting effects on the ways children solve mathematics problems. It is also the beginning of the educational pipeline that will funnel students either away from or toward eventual careers in mathematics, technology, and the sciences.

Given the strong emphasis on the development of spatial sense in the NCTM standards (1989, 2000), it is problematic that many early elementary mathematics curricula concentrate on number sense and barely touch on geometry or spatial thinking (Clements & Battista, 1992; Fuys & Liebow, 1993). The present approach is designed to remedy this gap in the field. Even when geometry is addressed in the mathematics curriculum in the elementary and middle school years, it typically focuses on shape naming, formulas, and rules, rather than on spatial reasoning. Furthermore, in order to develop spatial sense, it is not sufficient just to increase geometry content in the curriculum. Because spatial sense is involved in diverse mathematical areas (Wheatley, 1990), in this early childhood mathematical series, we have developed spatial thinking in a wide range of content areas, including measurement, part–whole relations, block building, shape attributes, representations, graphing and mapping, and patterning. For example, in the saga, *Sneeze the Dragon Builds a Castle* (Casey, Paugh, & Ballard, 2002), preschool and kindergarten children use block building to achieve specific mathematical goals. In this story, Sneeze carries the children back in time to the Middle Ages when Sneeze was a little dragon. Sneeze was a friendly dragon who only breathed fire when she sneezed. However, this got her into trouble when she accidentally burnt a hole right in the middle of the design plans for a castle being built for the king and queen. In these stories, Sneeze asks for help from the children. The mathematics activities involve problem solving how to help Sneeze create three-dimensional models out of blocks, representing different parts of the castle complex.

Block-building skills in middle school and high-ability high school students have been found to relate to their mathematics achievement (Pezaris et al., 1998), including performance on the math SATs (Bassi, 2000). A critical block-building skill involves the ability to balance a complex structure of blocks upon a base of upright blocks. This spatial and constructional ability draws upon engineering and architectural principles. In the saga about Sneeze, age-appropriate spatial constructs related to the aforementioned block-building skills are gradually introduced, and developed across the series of activities in the book. The early precursors to these complex balancing skills start from the construction of a simple arched doorway in the castle wall, to the more sophisticated bridges across the moat with ramps and stairways, and finally to the two-level castle tower.

Geometric relations are acquired as children start to learn such terms as inside-outside, under-over, top-bottom, and straight-curved. The concept of enclosure is introduced at the outset of this book in relation to the castle wall. Developing understanding of enclosure may be important not only to construction, but also to the understanding of geometric shapes, open and closed figures, and even to later ideas of perimeter and area. In addition, when block building, children are continually sorting and classifying based on geometric properties relating to shape. The children's representational constructs are developing, along with estimation and measurement, part–whole relations, visualization, and spatial planning skills (Casey, Paugh, & Ballard, 2002).

*Achieving Equity Through the Development of Spatial Skills.* Johnson and Meade (1987) conducted a study of more than 1,800 schoolchildren and found evidence of a male advantage in spatial skills starting at fourth grade. More important, these spatial skills have been shown to mediate gender differences in mathematics among both high school and middle school students (Casey et al., 1995; Casey, Nuttall, & Pezaris, 1997, 2001), and geometry items often show the largest gender difference on mathematics tests (Mullis et al., 1998; Rosser, 1989).

The male advantage in *overall* mathematics test performance doesn't emerge until high school and beyond. However, there is evidence for substantial gender differences in problem-solving strategies as early as Grade 1—with girls tending to depend on concrete strategies like counting and modeling and boys tending to use more abstract strategies that depend on conceptual understanding (Carr & Jessup, 1997; Fennema, Carpenter, Jacobs, Franke, & Levi, 1998).

It is during the early years that boys' active involvement in spatial games and activities starts to emerge. Girls have fewer out-of-school spatial experiences than boys (Baenninger & Newcombe, 1996). Given the dearth of spatial and geometry skills taught in elementary schools, many girls may never tap their potential to think spatially. Therefore, it is important to provide a mathematics curriculum right from the start that attempts to equalize these spatial experiences, and that solidly connects spatial thinking to mathematical reasoning in a systematic way.

The '*Round the Rug Math* series was designed to be interesting to a wide range of girls by teaching the spatial concepts within the context of people-oriented adventure stories. At the same time, the interactive and spatial nature of the adventure stories makes mathematics lessons more compelling to highly active boys. The goal is to enable early childhood teachers to facilitate different styles of problem solving in *all* children.

## FAMILY AND CAREGIVER INVOLVEMENT

To meaningfully involve parents and other caregivers such as grandparents in the learning process, the teachers are provided with optional math activities that include the family. These are mathematics activities for the children to do at home with a family member or caregiver. The children do the activity, and when they return to school, share their work with the class. This is an opportunity for the teacher to acknowledge and help children to value the cultures that may be represented in the classroom, as well as to engage the family or caregiver in doing mathematics with the child. It also is a way of pointing out mathematics and spatial relationships in the child's world. In one Boston classroom of diverse students, the parents worked with their children to make beautiful dragons. In another family activity in the same book on China (*Tan and the Shape Changer*; Schiro et al., 2002), the students showed their caregivers how to turn a square into two isosceles right triangles. The children also demonstrated how the two triangles can be combined to make other new shapes (parallelogram and triangle).

## OVERVIEW OF THE MATHEMATICS CONTENT COVERED IN THIS SERIES

This series uses an inquiry-based approach in which children are encouraged to problem solve, talk about their mathematical thinking, and represent their solutions and strategies through pictures, constructions, numbers, and words. Each book is designed to emphasize big ideas in mathematics, and the use of spatial sense is integrated throughout. They are also based on developmentally appropriate practices (Bredekamp & Copple, 1997) through the use of hands-on learning, meaningful activities, and an integrated curriculum approach. Following is a brief summary of the content covered in the six books in the series:

- Shape attributes: classifying, sorting, and representing two-dimensional and three-dimensional shapes. (Casey, Goodrow, Schiro, & Anderson, 2002)
- Developing an understanding of spatial relations and spatial sense through block building. (Casey, Paugh, & Ballard, 2002)
- Understanding part-whole relationships using mathematical puzzles. (Schiro, Casey, & Anderson, 2002)
- Visual estimation and measurement. (Anderson, Casey, & Kerrigan, 2002)
- Examining spatial and number patterns and prealgebra. (Casey, Anderson, & Schiro, 2002)
- Representations in pictures, numbers, and words: data analysis and graphing. (Casey, Napoleon, Schiro, & Anderson, 2002)

## ADDRESSING THE NCTM STANDARDS

In conclusion, the NCTM Mathematics Content Pre-K–12 Standards (2000) have been addressed in this spatially based supplementary series in a manner consistent with the Pre-K–2 NCTM Focus Areas. The most recent NCTM standards (2000) for the Pre-K–2 level give equal weight to geometry and number content, in terms of the amount of emphasis in the curriculum. When measurement and data analysis are considered as well, number content holds a much smaller part of the recommended curriculum than is typically taught in most early childhood classrooms.

Furthermore, a major goal of this chapter was to show how this supplementary series addresses the NCTM (2000) process-based standards: (a) by encouraging children to develop their spatial sense when solving mathematics problems, (b) embracing the "Equity Principle" in promoting mathematical learning for all students, (c) developing mathematics communication skills, (d) emphasizing spatial representation skills, (e) emphasizing problem-solving and reasoning skills, and (f) helping children connect mathematical ideas to contexts outside of mathematics.

## ACKNOWLEDGMENTS

Reprint requests should be sent to Dr. Beth Casey, 201 Campion Hall, Boston College, Chestnut Hill, MA 02467; phone: (617) 552-4232; e-mail address: caseyb@bc.edu. This material is based on work supported by the National Science Foundation under NSF IMD Award No. ESI 97-30698. Any opinions, findings, and conclusions or recommendations expressed in this material are those of the author and do not necessarily reflect the views of the National Science Foundation.

# REFERENCES

Albert, L. R. (2000a). Lessons learned from the "Five Men Crew": Teaching culturally relevant mathematics. In M. E. Strutchens, M. L. Johnson & W. F. Tate (Eds.), *Changing the faces of mathematics: Perspectives on African Americans* (pp. 81–88). Reston, VA: National Council of Teachers of Mathematics.

Albert, L. R. (2000b). *Oral story-telling as a medium for teaching young children mathematics.* Unpublished manuscript.

Allen, B. (1991). The influence of contextual factors on Afro-American and Euro-American children's performance: Effects of movement, opportunity, and music. *International Journal of Psychology, 26*, 373–387.

Anderson, K., Casey, B., & Kerrigan, M. (2002). *Froglets do the measuring.* Chicago, IL: The Wright Group/McGraw-Hill.

Baddeley, A. (1986). *Working memory.* Oxford, England: Clarendon Press.

Baenninger, M., & Newcombe, N. (1996). Environmental input to the development of sex-related differences in spatial and mathematical ability. *Learning and Individual Differences, 7,* 363–379.

Bassi, J. (2000). *Block play: Exposing gender differences and predicting for math achievement.* Unpublished doctoral dissertation, Northeastern University, Boston.

Battista, M. T. (1990). Spatial visualization and gender differences in high school geometry. *Journal for Research in Mathematics Education, 21,* 47–60.

Beatty, J. J. (1994). *Picture book storytelling: Literature activities for young children.* New York: Harcourt Brace College.

Boykin, A. W. (1992). African American children and the education process: Alleviating cultural discontinuity through prescriptive pedagogy. *School Psychology Review, 21,* 586–596.

Bredekamp, S., & Copple, C. (1997). *Developmentally appropriate practice in early childhood programs* (Rev. ed.). Washington, DC: National Association for the Education of Young Children.

Carr, M., & Jessup, D. L. (1997). Gender differences in first-grade mathematics strategy use: Social and metacognitive influences. *Journal of Educational Psychology, 89,* 318–328.

Casey, B., Anderson, K., & Schiro, M. (2002). *Layla discovers secret patterns.* Chicago, IL: The Wright Group/McGraw-Hill.

Casey, B., Goodrow, A., Schiro, M., & Anderson, K. (2002). *Teeny visits Shapeland.* Chicago, IL: The Wright Group/McGraw-Hill.

Casey, M. B., Nuttall, R. L., & Pezaris, E. (1997). Mediators of gender differences in mathematics college entrance test scores: A comparison of spatial skills with internalized beliefs and anxieties. *Developmental Psychology, 33,* 669–680.

Casey, M. B., Nuttall, R. L., & Pezaris, E. (2001). Spatial-mechanical reasoning skills versus math self-confidence as mediators of gender differences on mathematics subtests using cross-national gender-based items. *Journal for Research in Mathematics Education, 32,* 28–37.

Casey, M. B., Nuttall, R., Pezaris, E., & Benbow, C. P. (1995). The influence of spatial ability on gender differences in mathematics college entrance test scores across diverse samples. *Developmental Psychology, 31,* 697–705.

Casey, B., Paugh, P., & Ballard, N. (2002). *Sneeze builds a castle.* Chicago, IL: The Wright Group/McGraw-Hill.

Casey, B., Napoleon, I., Schiro, M., & Anderson, K. (2002). *Finding Mathapotamus.* Chicago, IL: The Wright Group/McGraw-Hill.

Clements, D. H., & Battista, M. T. (1992). Geometry and spatial reasoning. In D. A. Grouws (Ed.), *The handbook of research on mathematics teaching and learning* (pp. 420–464). New York: MacMillian.

Coombs, B., & Harcourt, L. (1986). *Explorations I.* Reading, MA: Addison-Wesley.

Fennema, E., Carpenter, T. P., Jacobs, V. R., Franke, M. L., & Levi, L. W. (1998). A longitudinal study of gender differences in young children's mathematical thinking. *Educational Researcher, 27,* 6–11.

Fuys, D. J., & Liebow, A. K. (1993). Geometry and spatial sense. In R. J. Jensen & S. Wagner (Eds.), *Research ideas for the classroom: Early childhood mathematics* (pp. 239–253). New York: Macmillian.

Heath, S. B. (1989). Oral and literate traditions among Black Americans living in poverty. *American Psychologist, 44,* 367–373.

Hershkowitz, R., Parzysz, C., & Van Dormolen, J. (1996). Space and shapes. In A. Bishop, K. Clements, C. Keitel, J. Kilpatrick, & C. Labore (Eds.), *International handbook of mathematics education* (Vol. 1, pp. 161–204). Norwell, MA: Kluwer Academic.

Johnson, E. S., & Meade, A. C. (1987). Developmental patterns of spatial ability: An early sex difference. *Child Development, 58,* 725–740.

Mullis, I. V. S., Martin, M. O., Beaton, A. E., Gonzalez, E. J., Kelly, D. L., & Smith, T. A. (1998). *Mathematics and science achievement in the final year of secondary school: IEA's Third International Mathematics and Science Study.* Chestnut Hill, MA: TIMSS International Study Center, Boston College.

National Council of Teachers of Mathematics. (1989). *Curriculum and evaluation for school mathematics.* Reston, VA: Author.

National Council of Teachers of Mathematics. (2000). *Principles and standards for school mathematics: Discussion draft.* Reston, VA: Author.

Pellowski, A. (1990). *The world of story-telling: Art and technique.* New York: Bowker.

Pezaris, E., Casey, M. B., Nuttall, R. L., Bassi, J. C., Trzynski, M., Averna, S., & Galluccio, L. (1998). *Style of block building in boys and girls and its relationship to their spatial and mathematical skills.* Paper presented at the 21st annual midyear meeting of the International Neuropsychological Society, Budapest, Hungary.

Rogoff, B., & Morelli, G. (1989). Culture and American children. *American Psychologist, 44,* 367–373.

Rosser, P. (1989). *The SAT gender gap: Identifying the causes.* Washington, DC: Center for Women's Policy Studies.

Schiro, M. (1997). *Integrating children's literature and mathematics: Children as problem-solvers, literary critics, and meaning-makers.* New York: Teachers College Press.

Schiro, M., Casey, B. & Anderson, K. (2002). *Tan and the Shape Changer.* Chicago, IL: The Wright Group/McGraw-Hill.

Sherrill, C. (1994). *Problem-solving adventures: Mathematics through literature and music: Journey to the other side.* Mountain View, CA: Creative Publications.

Welchman-Tischler, R. (1992). *How to use children's literature to teach mathematics.* Reston, VA: National Council of Teachers of Mathematics.

Wheatley, G. (1990). Spatial sense and mathematics learning. *Arithmetic Teacher, 37,* 10–11.

# Section 4

# Professional Development

# 17

# Early Childhood Mathematics Instruction: Seeing the Opportunities Among the Challenges

Rachelle Feiler
*San Diego State University*

A significant part of the discussion about the adoption and implementation of mathematics standards for early childhood education (ECE) has centered on the challenges involved. The challenges are real and important, but a focus on the challenges may obscure the opportunities that exist. Just as teachers ask what knowledge students have that can be built upon to develop new mathematical understanding, it is important that the focus of implementation of the *Principles and Standards for School Mathematics* (*PSSM*; National Council of Teachers of Mathematics [NCTM], 2000) be on using what teachers know to develop new practices.

This chapter uses a developmental perspective on teacher change to support the importance of drawing connections between what teachers already do well and new practices that make sense to them. One point of convergence can be found in goals shared by the standards for developmentally appropriate endorsed by the National Association for the Education of Young Children (NAEYC; Bredekamp & Copple, 1997) and the process standards of NCTM (2000). Examples are provided herein to illustrate this convergence, and recommendations for additional ways to support early childhood teachers' implementation of the *PSSM* are proposed.

# DEVELOPMENTAL PERSPECTIVE ON TEACHER CHANGE

Goldsmith and Shifter (1997) described teacher change from a developmental perspective. They proposed that teachers' mathematical practice develops through an orderly progression of qualitatively different stages, spurred on by transition mechanisms when there is motivation to change. Finding an effective transition mechanism is key to stimulating change.

Goldsmith and Shifter (1997) suggested some criteria for an effective mechanism, grounded in both constructivist and sociocultural perspectives. An effective transition mechanism is one that connects new experiences to prior understandings such that individuals must modify prior understandings in light of the new experience. An effective mechanism can also be a cultural tool that an individual appropriates that shapes the individual's experience such that new ways of thinking and behaving result.

To assist early childhood teachers to make a qualitative shift in their development of mathematical practice, it is necessary to find mechanisms to facilitate transition to the next stage of development. A focus on the processes included in the process standards is one mechanism that may connect teachers' prior understanding to new experience, while at the same time providing a new cultural tool that teachers may appropriate.

## CONNECTING DEVELOPMENTALLY APPROPRIATE PRACTICE AND THE PROCESS STANDARDS

There is little research that examines existing instructional practices in early childhood mathematics education (see Wadlington & Burns, 1993, for one notable exception). There is, however, a body of literature regarding ECE practices more generally, which includes some recommendations for mathematics learning in the early years (e.g., Bredekamp & Copple, 1997; Hart, Burts, & Charlesworth, 1997). This literature on developmentally appropriate practice suggests that many early childhood teachers value the development of critical thinking and communication skills as goals for their programs, even if they don't address them in mathematical contexts. The value of critical thinking and communication skills is also evident in the five process standards included in the NCTM *PSSM* (NCTM, 2000).

The process standards describe the problem-solving, reasoning, communication, connection-building, and representation skills and understandings young children should develop. Framing the goals of mathematics education within these processes, which many early childhood teachers identify as valued elements of their current practice, can provide a point of convergence for the early childhood and mathematics education communities. For example, many teachers of young children place high priority on helping their students develop positive social skills and on building community in their classrooms. To this end, they often assist students in developing the skills to identify social problems, generate and evaluate multiple strategies, and work with peers to decide on the solution with the best fit.

The following vignette illustrates a social problem-solving event in an early childhood classroom. Prior to the class discussion described next, Ms. LaVerne[1] observed twin sisters arguing on the playground. Susan was upset because she felt Jennie had "stolen" her friends. Ms. LaVerne saw this as an opportunity to engage her whole class in a problem-solving exercise:

> Ms. LaVerne reminds everyone to join her on the rug as they come inside from the playground. As children take their seats on the perimeter of the rug, Ms. LaVerne motions for Susan and Jennie to sit next to her at the head of the rug. When everyone has settled in quietly, Ms. LaVerne explains that the two girls have a problem and they need all their friends to help them solve it. Ms. LaVerne reminds the class of the rules for discussion: Listen quietly, no put-downs, raise your hand to speak. Then she asks the girls to explain the problem to the class. Susan , in a tearful voice, tells the group that she does not want Jennie to visit their class any more because Jennie is taking all her friends. Jennie insists she is not trying to take the friends away, but they want to play with her and she wants to play with them. Susan insists that, as the rightful member of this class, she should get to set the rules and Jennie should follow them. Ms. LaVerne interrupts the sisters' exchange to suggest that the other students might have some suggestions. Several children offer ideas—Jennie could go back to her class immediately, Susan could visit Jennie's class and steal her friends, the two could play together with the friends in this class, each sister could pick one friend to be theirs alone and that friend could not choose to play with someone else. As each idea is presented the sisters listen and offer some comment. No, Jennie cannot go back to her class right now because the class is not in their room. The sisters cannot share all the friends; that's how the trouble started. Finally they settle on each nominating one friend, and the two friends agree to play with their assigned sister. Ms. LaVerne tells the class she is proud of the way the sisters talked about their differences and of the way the class helped them solve their problem. She then asks the students to gather around her to hear a story.

Ms. LaVerne's class spent 20 minutes discussing the problem of sharing friends. In that time they listened as two children explained the problem, several students generated strategies for solving the problem, and the others evaluated the solutions, contributed more information and, finally, helped establish the final outcome. This process is not so different from the teacher posing a mathematical problem, asking children to find a way to solve it, and then asking children to share their solution strategies while the class listens and discusses each one.

Another example of the ways in which the process standards converge with the early childhood instructional landscape comes from the Reggio Emilia approach. The schools of Reggio Emilia, Italy, have developed an

---

[1] All teacher and student names are pseudonyms.

approach to ECE that places a heavy emphasis on young children questioning, discovering, and representing their thinking. Representation is said to occur in "100 languages" (Edwards, Gandini, & Forman, 1993). For example, a group of 3- to 5-year-olds studying sunflowers might observe them, sketch them, paint them, and sculpt them out of clay. Children could touch the flowers, talk about them, and perhaps taste sunflower seeds. All the while teachers photograph children at work, record conversations, and document the process of discovery and representation. This context is rich with opportunities to promote the skills embedded in the process standards. Mathematics can easily be considered one of the hundred languages, and mathematical concepts can be studied in an intensive way according to children's interests (see, e.g., *Shoe and Meter*, Malaguzzi, 1997, which documents a project where children measured a table in order to provide a carpenter with instruction on how to reproduce it; see also Sarama, chap. 15, this volume).

Opportunities, then, do exist to build connections between developmentally appropriate practice and the process standards. The question remains: How does this convergence become a transition mechanism, where the processes described in the standards become a catalyst that moves teacher development to a qualitatively different stage?

## FACILITATING CHANGE: THE PROCESS STANDARDS AS A TRANSITION MECHANISM

One study sheds some light on how the process standards might function as a transition mechanism. In a research project reported in more detail elsewhere (Feiler, 2002), Megan Franke and I collaborated with a group of early childhood teachers, including Ms. LaVerne, to integrate more systematic mathematics instruction into their curriculum. The teachers were part of a program that emphasized children's construction of understanding and communication of ideas. One teacher, Ms. Harris, was especially skilled at listening to her 4-year-old students and supporting them to express their thinking in a variety of ways. When we began our collaboration, most of Ms. Harris' discussions with students involved social-emotional issues or instruction in literacy or art.

Over the course of the year that we worked together Ms. Harris began to try new things with her students. When we showed videotape of a kindergarten teacher solving word problems with students, Ms. Harris decided to try some word problems with her students. The following excerpt from field notes of Ms. Harris' instruction details her first experience of solving word problems with a small group of students:

Ms. H:     If we were baking cookies in the Red Room and we baked five cookies and in the Green Room they did the same job and they brought us the five cookies that they baked, how many cookies would we have altogether?

| All: | [Almost immediately.] 10! |
|---|---|
| Ms. H: | [Looks surprised.] Wow. That's so easy for you! [pause] I want to know how each of you figured it out. Sally, how did you figure it out? |
| Sally: | Because one 5 and another 5 is 10. [Holds up all fingers on one hand, and then all fingers on the other hand.] |
| Ms. H: | So you were really thinking about that. Good. Penny, how did you figure it out? |
| Penny: | In my head. |
| Ms. H: | Yes, I know you were thinking, but how did you know it was 10? |
| Penny: | [Looks thoughtful, but doesn't speak.] |
| Ms. H: | [After waiting about 30 seconds] Why don't you think more about it and I'll come back to you, OK? [Penny nods.] John, tell me how you figured it out. |
| John: | I know because my sister told me that 5 plus 5 is 10. |
| James: | Me too! That's how I figured it out. [Ms. Harris starts to ask a question.] |
| John: | You don't even have a sister! |
| James: | But I knew it was 10. |
| Ms. H: | Well, that problem was very easy for you, I can tell. Let me try another one ... [pauses to think of a problem]. Now, if it was Penny's birthday and she brought cupcakes ... If she brought 18 cupcakes, does everyone get a cupcake? [Children appear to think, but don't seem clear about the question.] How many children are in our class? |
| James, Penny, and John: | 23. |
| Ms. H: | So would we all get one? |
| Sally: | No. |
| Ms. H: | Tell me how you figured it out. |
| Penny: | What if someone wasn't here? |
| Ms. H: | [Laughs.] That's a good question. Let's say everyone was here and we were all sitting on the rug. If Penny brought in 18 cupcakes, would she have to call home and ask her mother to bring more? How many of us would not get a cupcake? |
| John: | Sarah, and Leslie, and — |
| Sally: | Five. |
| Ms. H: | Oh. Tell me how you figured that out. [Sally does not respond verbally. Looks at her unifix cubes.] |
| John: | It's five. |
| Ms. H: | How did you figure it out? |

John:       Because there are 23 people in class and 18 is less than 19.

Ms. H:      That's true, 18 is less than 19. How did you know that we
            would need 5 more than 18? ...

Ms. Harris connected her strengths in listening to and supporting her
children's thinking with the mathematical problem-solving process we
had discussed. This new problem-solving practice provided her with opportunities to listen to children's thinking about mathematics, something
she hadn't really done before. At the end of the year we asked Ms. Harris to
talk about her experience with solving problems and how her instruction
had changed. She said,

> I didn't do problem solving to the extent that I have done, especially with the
> smaller group with the kids. Due to the fact that I thought that they weren't
> ready for it. But I'm realizing that they are and they're very capable of it ... so
> the questions that I might ask might be too hard for some, too easy for others
> but yet I get to figure out the people who are capable of solving it, where they
> need to go next. And the people who can't solve, it helps me understand
> what they might need next time.

Ms. Harris learned a great deal about young children's mathematical understandings and what her students could learn with her assistance by listening as students solved problems. Building on her strengths, she
developed an interest in the mathematics and in what her students knew.
The processes of solving problems, reasoning, and communicating about
mathematics served as a bridge between her well-established practices
and teaching mathematics.

In the case of Ms. Harris, problem-solving, reasoning, and communication processes were transition mechanisms that facilitated the development of her mathematical practice. The processes connected Ms. Harris'
new experience with mathematical problem solving to her prior experience in such a way that she had to modify her prior understanding of children's mathematical thinking. Mathematical problem solving can also be
viewed as a cultural tool that Ms. Harris appropriated which, as a result, led
to new ways of thinking and behaving that supported her development.

## CONCLUSION

The story of Ms. Harris illustrates the great potential for building on the
strengths of early childhood teachers to implement the *PSSM* (NCTM,
2000). However, it is important to remember that most early childhood
teachers, including Ms. Harris, will need the assistance of others to develop the knowledge of mathematics and children's mathematical thinking that they need to implement all of the principles and standards well.
Some teachers may need additional support in making explicit connections between their current practices and the mathematics practices sup-

ported by the *PSSM*. For example, shortly after Ms. LaVerne's class discussion about the two sisters sharing friends, the idea of posing mathematical problems to the whole class was raised in a collaborative meeting. Ms. LaVerne's response was immediate: "They would mutiny on me after five minutes!" She did not believe her students, who had worked together for 20 minutes on the sisters' problem, would be as engaged by a problem centered on mathematics.

Ms. LaVerne's response may represent a common attitude about mathematics that will have to be addressed in order to implement the *Standards* in early childhood classrooms. For many reasons, early childhood teachers often assume children will not be engaged by mathematics, or believe young children do not have a sufficient attention span for "academic" work. Even Ms. Harris initially did not believe that her students were ready for mathematical problem solving. The mathematics education community has come a long way in redefining mathematics as a dynamic discipline full of opportunity for inquiry and discovery. This conception of mathematics does not yet seem to be prevalent among early childhood educators.

Early childhood teachers can bring a great deal to the task of implementing mathematics standards. To maximize the benefits of teachers' strengths it is critical to support early childhood teachers in building on their strengths by helping them connect mathematics to other practices. The best place to start may be with the process standards. Problem solving, critical thinking, communication, and representation are already valued by many early childhood educators. With some careful consideration, teachers' engagement with the process standards can be used as a vehicle to build interest in and develop their understanding of mathematical content.

There are two other critical ways in which the mathematics education community can support early childhood teachers. First, more examples related to the *PSSM* (NCTM, 2000) should be drawn from early childhood classrooms. This will help teachers identify the practices they already use and give them confidence that they and their students are capable of learning the mathematical content included in the *Standards*. Finally, providing more specific information regarding expectations for student learning within the broad Pre-K to Grade 2 band will help early childhood teachers set appropriate goals and understand the expected progression of learning for their students.

The ECE conference was a unique opportunity to bring together groups that seldom mingle: mathematicians, policymakers, mathematics educators, and early childhood educators. Although the focus on challenges is important in determining ways to address the critical problems of adoption and implementation of the *Standards,* we would be misguided in not bringing to the discussion the strengths of early childhood programs and practitioners. If we do not build on early childhood teachers' strengths and current best practices we run the risk of alienating the very community the *PSSM* (NCTM, 2000) should serve.

# REFERENCES

Bredekamp, S., & Copple, C. (Eds.). (1997). Developmentally appropriate practice in early childhood programs (Rev. ed.). Washington, DC: National Association for the Education of Young Children.

Edwards, C., Gandini, L., & Forman, G. (Eds.). (1993). *The hundred languages of children: The Reggio Emilia approach to early childhood education.* Norwood, NJ: Ablex.

Feiler (2002). *Beyond the dichotomy: Defining learning-centered early childhood instruction.* Unpublished manuscript.

Goldsmith, L.T., & Shifter, D. (1997). Understanding teachers in transition: Characteristics of a model for the development of mathematics teaching. In E. Fennema & B. S. Nelson (Eds.), *Mathematics teachers in transition* (pp. 19–54). Mahwah, NJ: Lawrence Erlbaum Associates.

Hart, C. H., Burts, D. C., & Charlesworth, R. (Eds.). (1997). *Integrated curriculum and developmentally appropriate practice: Birth to age eight. SUNY series, early childhood education: Inquiries and insights.* Albany: State University of New York Press.

Malaguzzi, L. (1997). *Shoe and meter.* Reggio Emilia, Italy: Reggio Children.

National Council of Teachers of Mathematics (2000). *Principles and standards of school mathematics.* Reston, VA: Author.

Wadlington, E. & Burns. J. M. (1993). Instructional practices within preschool/kindergarten gifted programs. *Journal for the Education of the Gifted, 17*(1), 41–52.

# 18

## The Early Childhood Collaborative: A Professional Development Model to Communicate and Implement the Standards

Juanita V. Copley
*University of Houston*

Angela Garcia is a first-grade teacher in a large urban school district. Four years ago, she became part of an early childhood professional development project, a collaboration between the local university, 12 in-service teachers, and a group of 25 beginning preservice teachers. Since that time, her disposition toward mathematics has drastically changed, her use of effective instructional strategies has improved, and best of all, she listens to her students communicate and learn so that she can better teach. Listen to her describe a lesson she recently taught to first graders:

> I was really excited to introduce capacity measurement with a discovery-type lesson to my kids. A few years ago, I would never have tried it … I was never good at math; in fact, I hated it! If I didn't have the book with the answers, I was never going to do anything. In fact, I must confess … I began teaching first grade because I knew it didn't require much math. I knew I could do first-grade math but I wasn't sure about second! Anyway, let me tell you what happened. I distributed five plastic containers to every group. I asked children to put the containers in order … the one that holds the least amount of water to the one that would hold the most. Immediately, they began talking and putting the containers in order. I had planned on telling them how to compare the capacities of each container, giving them a pitcher and

another container so they could do their measuring. In the meantime, they began discussing how they were going to prove their answer to be correct. In fact, I overheard some of them say, "You know, Mrs. Garcia, is never going to believe this ... she always makes us prove everything!" After spending a few minutes listening to their reasoning, I then announced where they could find additional materials, a water source, and paper towels. Then, I stood back! Amazing things happened. Some groups demonstrated that they understood transitivity and had conservation of volume. Others used better recording and measurement techniques than I was going to suggest. Still others devised creative procedures for ordering the containers. As a result, their group presentations were well reasoned and presented clearly. Many of the other group members asked questions about their results and required their peers to give justifications for their answers. In fact, I was silent for most of the math period while children were reasoning, communicating, and solving problems. It was great.... the kids were great!"

Powerful mathematics! Angela told this story during a group discussion with other first-grade teachers involved in the Early Childhood Mathematics Collaborative. Fortunately, this type of sharing is a common event. Begun 4 years ago at the University of Houston, the Early Childhood Collaborative was developed to provide early childhood preservice and in-service teachers with opportunities to teach and learn mathematics. It now involves 3 public schools, 63 in-service teachers, and more than 165 preservice teachers representing 7 prekindergarten, 18 kindergarten, 13 first-grade, 14 second-grade, and 17 third-grade classrooms. Formed to address specific professional development issues, the Early Childhood Collaborative focuses primarily on young children and their understanding of mathematics. In addition, a variety of effective professional development techniques are implemented to enhance teachers' understanding of mathematics and children. The purpose of this chapter is to describe the Early Childhood Collaborative as just one example of a way to promote a shared vision of learning and teaching mathematics.

## THE PROBLEM WITH PROFESSIONAL DEVELOPMENT

A major deterrent to the implementation of a strong mathematics program for children in preschool to third grade is the inadequate preparation of teachers. Early childhood teachers are often phobic about mathematics, view necessary mathematics as only "counting, adding, subtracting, and knowing shapes," and have little or no knowledge about the mathematics standards (Copley & Petri, 1998; Copley & Sultis, 1997; Johnson, 1999). Data collected from a 5-year survey of teacher candidates revealed that prospective early childhood teachers generally feel most comfortable teaching reading and other language-oriented skills. To them, mathematics is a difficult subject to teach and one area that they often ignore except for counting and simple arithmetic operations. Early childhood teachers are often unaware of the essential processes of mathematics, specifically, reasoning, problem solving, connections between mathematics and the world of the young child, and the communication skills critical to early conceptual understanding. In addition, their knowledge, beliefs, and instructional strategies are focused on computation skills rather than problem solving, and they generally demonstrate procedural steps to solutions rather than listening to their students' methods and reasoning (Carpenter, Fennema, Peterson, & Carey, 1988; Fennema et al., 1996).

Some professional development issues involving both preservice and in-service teachers are especially prevalent. First of all, the fact that many early childhood teachers feel uncomfortable with mathematics was confirmed with surveys completed by both preservice and in-service teachers. Comments like, "I don't do math" or "I know kindergarten math ... that's enough!" or "Young children shouldn't do mathematics ... it's not appropriate!" caused concern and illuminated the need for professional development in mathematics education. Second, preservice teachers needed as many nonevaluative experiences as possible before they began their more formal student teaching experiences. Although they were required to frequently observe in classrooms, preservice teachers often expressed their concern and fear of "real teaching" or of "being in front of a group of children." They had little or no practice in teaching real children before they were evaluated by their supervising or cooperating teacher. Third, in-service teachers frequently expressed their frustration with typical professional development experiences. Workshops presented on Saturdays or after school, conference opportunities that necessitated a large amount of preparation for substitutes, and presentations that were geared to the intermediate grades all contributed to their frustration with professional development opportunities. Fourth, and most important, teachers reported that their children's mathematics achievement was lower than they expected. Classroom observations of mathematics instruction, teachers' lack of knowledge about the standards, and state assessment concerns all contributed to the identification of a need for better professional development.

## GOALS OF THE COLLABORATIVE

Copley and Padron (1999) synthesized a list of professional development standards based on NCTM's (National Council of Teachers of Mathematics) *Professional Standards for Teaching Mathematics* (1991), and *Guidelines for Preparation of Early Childhood Professionals: Associate, Baccalaureate, and Advanced Levels* (National Association for the Education of Young Children, Council for Exceptional Children, and National Board for Professional Teaching Standards, 1996). The six standards state that effective professional development programs allow the early childhood teacher to: (a) develop good dispositions toward mathematics, (b) experience good teaching in mathematics, (c) focus on learning about children, (d) participate in a variety of professional development opportunities situated in a learning community, (e) demonstrate an ability to implement integrative curriculum, and (f) utilize appropriate strategies to establish family partnerships (Copley & Padron, 1999).

The goals of the Collaborative are based on the identified needs for professional development in mathematics as well as the Integrated Professional Development Standards for Early Childhood. Generally, the goal of the Collaborative is to improve the mathematics instruction of the early childhood teacher. Specifically, the methods used to accomplish this goal are identified as:

- Preservice teachers are given many opportunities to teach mathematics in early childhood classrooms in nonevaluative settings.
- Mathematics is taught to both preservice and in-service teachers using modeling, classroom observations, coaching, and study groups.
- Study groups and coaching sessions for in-service teachers are conducted as part of the regular classroom teaching day and do not occur during break times, planning times, after school, or on Saturdays.
- Mathematics standards from NCTM and early childhood guidelines from NAEYC are the foci for the content of the professional development experiences.
- Children's thinking and learning of mathematics is observed, researched, and discussed by both preservice and in-service teachers.

## DESCRIPTION OF COLLABORATIVE

The Early Childhood Collaborative involves three components: (a) beginning (preservice) teachers teaching in early childhood classrooms (four or five per classroom), (b) practicing (in-service) teachers meeting in study groups while the beginning teachers "cover" their classes, and (c) the university professor modeling mathematics lessons in early childhood classrooms for both beginning and practicing teachers. The school sites were selected by adherence to specific criteria, namely, proximity to the university, diversity of student population, number of early childhood teachers, willingness to participate in a 3-year commitment, administrative support, and the need for mathematics professional development. All three schools were in Houston or the surrounding area. More than 30 languages were spoken by students in these schools; in fact, many of the classes were bilingual or taught using English as a Second Language (ESL) strategies. All three schools contained first- or second-year teachers as well as teachers with 25 years or more experience. The average number of years of teaching experience for the practicing teachers was slightly more than 4 years. In addition, many of the teachers were provisionally certified or had been issued emergency certification. (In 1998–1999,

Texas spent more than $235 million on prekindergarten initiatives in public schools [Children's Defense Fund, 2000] so there are many needs and opportunities for early childhood teachers.)

***Component 1: Beginning (Preservice) Teachers.*** The beginning teachers were involved in the Collaborative *before* field-based methods courses or student teaching. Initial surveys indicated that the beginning teachers had little experience working with young children, and almost no experience working with mathematics. Because they lacked the necessary skills to select appropriate mathematics lessons, the university professor prepared and modeled the lessons before they taught them. Beginning teachers received lesson plans 1 week before each collaborative session and were encouraged to think creatively and flexibly about the classroom possibilities. As part of their early childhood class requirements, all beginning teachers were required to be involved in a collaborative experience.

***Component 2: Practicing (In-service) Teachers.*** The practicing teachers in the Collaborative were early childhood teachers in public schools. While the beginning teacher teams covered their classes, the practicing teachers met with the university professor and discussed mathematics standards. Teachers and the university professor shared activities, beliefs, observations, and questions about mathematics and how children learn. The process standards of problem solving, reasoning, communicating, connecting, and representing were stressed throughout the sessions as well as methods to meet the needs of children.

***Component 3: University Professor.*** During each collaborative session, the university professor taught in several early childhood classrooms. Observed by both practicing and beginning teachers, the university professor led debriefing sessions about the lessons. In most cases, the modeled lessons directly related to the standard taught by the beginning teachers and the standard discussed in the study groups.

During the 1999–2000 school year, the five content standards suggested in *Principles and Standards for School Mathematics: Discussion Draft* (NCTM, 1998) were studied. Every month, a new content standard was introduced and lessons were modeled that addressed that particular content standard. In addition, the process standards were introduced, examples noted, and teaching strategies discussed. The schedule for the Collaborative sessions were: (a) Introduction to Mathematics, (b) Principles for School Mathematics, (c) Organizing for Thinking, (d) Data Analysis, Statistics, and Probability, (e) Number and Operations, (f) Patterns, Functions, and Algebraic Thinking, (g) Geometry and Spatial Sense, (h) Measurement, (i) Strategies for Family Involvement, and (j) Factors That Affect Practices. Lessons directly correlated to the content standards and developed for the TEXTEAM Professional Development Institute (State Systemic Initiative, 1999–2000) were field-tested in the classrooms by both the preservice and in-service teachers. In total, there were 30 Collaborative sessions held during the 1999–2000 school year, 10 at each school. Each Collaborative session lasted the entire school day, approximately 6 hours. Although the schedule differed slightly at each school, generally, the preservice teachers met with the university professor for the first hour to review the lessons and make final preparations for their teaching. Then, during the day, teams of preservice teachers taught in three different classrooms while the in-service teachers met with the university professor in study groups. Finally, preservice and in-service teachers observed the university professor teach in one or two classrooms noting children's thinking and reactions. The day ended with a debriefing session between the preservice teachers and the university professor.

## TYPICAL PROFESSIONAL DEVELOPMENT SESSION

Each Collaborative session involved a meeting of in-service teachers with the university professor in 1-hour study groups. These sessions always followed the same procedure: (a) brief introduction to any change/additions to the Collaborative, (b) reports of practicing teachers who observed the university professor, (c) sharing of children's work or ideas specific to the standard discussed during the previous session, (d) presentation of new standard along with specific ideas for implementing the standards, and (e) reading assignment from the Standards document and teaching suggestions.

As an illustration, the following session, the second of two on geometry, occurred in a kindergarten/prekindergarten group. Because much of the content was new to them, the six teachers had requested two sessions on geometry, one session specifically dealing with three-dimensional (3-D) shapes and the second with two-dimensional (2-D) shapes. As the teachers arrived, they investigated the new materials (3-D tangram blocks, beveled curved blocks, and some wooden geoblocks with atypical shapes) displayed on the table. The teacher who had observed the university professor shared the lesson that she had observed.

"Nita introduced the best game, called 'Build the Tallest Tower!' I was amazed by the children's total attention and their block choices as they built their creations." The teacher described the activity, emphasizing the children's choices of building materials. "I thought they would automatically put the bigger blocks on the bottom… they didn't! Instead, they chose the prettiest colors or shapes. The square pyramid was their favorite and when they put it on the top, the other team members look so dismayed! They knew it would be a problem to make that tower taller." The other teachers began asking about the game directions and the teacher shared how she played the game later in the week with the specific adaptations she had made to the activity. When everyone seemed ready, the university professor debriefed the lesson by posing questions about the specific pedagogy employed during the lesson:

What questions did I ask to get the children to compare the towers' heights? How did I respond when the towers fell? What questions did I ask to get children to reflect and think about their tower building strategies? How did I make this a game for everyone, rather than a competition? What were the children learning about 3-D shapes? What were they learning about number? How did their understanding of the attributes of 3-D shapes change from the beginning of the game to the end?

After this discussion, the other teachers shared their observations of their children's work in geometry over the past few weeks. Several teachers talked about the building creations that were made in the block centers and the conversations they heard as children told their friend "how to make one good like me!" One kindergarten teacher shared her experience with blueprints (blue butcher paper drawn with white crayons) that children used to represent their building creations so that they could remember what they had built. One prekindergarten teacher told about her children's success when she placed the building cards vertically rather than on the table. Still others told about the center ideas that they had tried that were part of the preservice teachers' lessons from the week before. The "3-D clay transform" and "shape sculptures" activities were particular favorites.

In the last 20 minutes of the session, the university professor introduced the topic of 2-D shapes. She briefly mentioned the specific 2-D activities the preservice teachers were doing in their classes and reminded them of the Web site they could use to access the activities. Then, she showed them a 2-minute video clip of two 5-year-olds discussing the attributes of a triangle and a square. To their surprise, both 5-year-olds stated that a triangle was not a triangle if it was in the wrong position, that is, "on its end" or "on its tip." In addition, they stated that a tipped square was really a "very fat diamond" and definitely "not a square." The university professor encouraged them to question their children in the same way during the next weeks. She again told the group when and where she would be teaching the next week, restated that she would be teaching a lesson on 2-D shapes and their position in space, and concluded with a reading assignment for the next session. The teachers left to relieve their preservice substitutes, still talking about geometry and how it "was so much more" than they had ever thought about before.

## EVALUATION PLAN FOR THE COLLABORATIVE

The first two school years of the Collaborative (1996–1997 and 1997–1998) were learning experiences. Based on these experiences as well as other school-based projects, the issue of trust and credibility between the university professor, in-service teachers, and preservice teachers was recognized as an essential characteristic to the success of any collaborative project. Typically, that trust takes about a year to develop (Copley & Petri, 1998; Copley & Sultis, 1997). For that reason, the Collaborative was not formally evaluated until the 1998–1999 school year and the evaluation methods employed were as nonintrusive as possible. Interviews, questionnaires (National Council of Supervisors of Mathematics, 1994), and open-ended responses were the primary means of data collection. Obviously, results obtained from these instruments are primarily self-reported and tell only how teachers perceive their mathematics curriculum and instruction.

During the school year 1999–2000, more detailed evaluation plans are being implemented. In addition to the questionnaires and open-ended responses, structured interviews (Richardson, 1994), multiple case studies, concept mapping (Raymond, 1997), videotapes of study sessions, and lesson think-alouds are being used to analyze the effect of the Early Childhood Collaborative (Jenkins, 2000; Petri, 2000). Coded classroom observations are planned for the 2000–2001 school year (Carlan, 2000). Research indicates that although teachers' perceptions are important, observational data of classroom situations would provide an additional source of reliable and valid data.

## PRELIMINARY RESULTS

In the 1998–1999 Collaborative, differences between the teacher-reported instructional practices in August 1998 and May 1999 were calculated using paired $t$ tests in three different areas. When teachers were asked to report their perception of how prepared they were to use specific instructional practices important to mathematics, significant differences in their perceptions of preparedness were found on four of the items. Specifically, teachers felt more well prepared to:

- Manage a class of students who were using manipulatives.
- Use computers as an integral part of mathematics instruction.
- Use a variety of alternative assessment strategies.
- Invoke parents in the mathematics education of their children.

In addition, a review of the lesson plans used during the study groups indicated that manipulative use, assessment strategies, and parent involvement were all emphasized in at least 80% of the Collaborative sessions.

Teachers were also asked to report the amount of emphasis different mathematical content would receive in their classrooms. Teachers reported that three particular content areas would receive significantly more emphasis after the Collaborative experience. Geometry and spatial sense increased the most, with measurement and number sense following closely behind. When asked to describe their answers, teachers reported that their view of geometry and number had been greatly expanded and that previous to the collaborative experience, they had taught only names of shapes, counting sequences, and basic operations. Their use of normal early childhood activities (block center, manipulative center, and calendar routines, specifically) was now viewed as an opportunity to "do mathematics."

Most important, teachers were asked to report their use of specific instructional activities. There were four activities that teachers reported that they used significantly more after the Collaborative experience. They said that they increasingly:

- Asked their students to make conjectures and explore possible methods to solve problems.
- Required students to draw pictures or write their reasoning about how to solve a problem.
- Had students use calculators.
- Used manipulative materials.

A review of the lesson plans indicated that calculators were used in about 25% of the sessions and that manipulatives were used in every session. In addition, the process standard of reasoning and a child's communication of that reasoning were processes emphasized in almost every modeled lesson, study group, or lesson taught by the teams of beginning teachers.

Preliminary data have been collected for the 1999–2000 school year. Jenkins (2000) conducted a multiple case study of beginning (preservice) teachers using the results of structured interviews, open-ended responses, and lesson think-alouds. She used Raymond's (1997) classification system to code teacher's beliefs as traditional, primarily traditional, even mix, primarily nontraditional, or nontraditional. In only one semester, all preservice teachers involved in the case studies exhibited some change toward more nontraditional beliefs in the areas of teaching mathematics, learning mathematics, and in their predictions about their future practice. Jenkins (2001) also investigated any longitudinal effects of the collaborative by conducting four case studies of beginning teachers over three semesters, including one semester when students were not involved in the collaborative. Using data collected over the three semesters, she evaluated the data for reoccurring themes using reflective analysis and Raymond's (1997) classification system as a framework. Jenkins found that the beginning teachers continued to exhibit some change toward more nontraditional beliefs in mathematics even during the semester they were not enrolled in the collaborative.

Petri (2001) collected pre- and post-Collaborative data (structured interviews, individual conceptual maps, questionnaires, lesson think-alouds) from 22 practicing (in-service) teachers. Similar to the Jenkins study, she analyzed the results using Raymond's (1997) classification system as a framework. More than half of the teachers exhibited some change toward more nontraditional beliefs in mathematics over the years' time. In the conceptual maps developed by the practicing teachers, every group reported that the collaborative experience was one of three factors that had influenced their teaching practices during the school year. State assessment policies and administrative support were the other two most important influences.

## SUMMARY

The Early Childhood Collaborative is a work in progress. Although formal evaluation has not been completed, statements made by participants during the interviews and recorded in the open-ended assessments indicate a strong relationship between the Integrated Standards for Professional Development listed at the beginning of this chapter and the Early Childhood Collaborative (except for the sixth standard, which involves family partnership). Quotes from participants in the 1998–1999 and 1999–2000 Collaborative are included in the following descriptions.

### Standard 1: Developing Good Dispositions Toward Mathematics

The changes in preservice teachers' dispositions are perhaps the most obvious during the collaborative experience. Initially, preservice teachers made many statements that indicated that they were not anticipating teaching mathematics. "I was scared and intimidated to go and teach at these schools. They weren't like the ones I went to ... and we were expected to teach math! It is not my subject!" "I was worried but I felt better when I realized that no one would really know if I blew it ... just my other team members and they are in the same boat as me." After the experience, teachers' confidence was amazing. They often asked to be scheduled for additional sessions and talked excitedly to their peers in other programs about their experiences. They often talked about the change in their dispositions. "It felt safe knowing you were not going into the room alone. The other people in the room were like me ... they didn't know any more than I did ... and no one was evaluating me. I could just learn how to do it!" "I learned that mathematics was a lot more than I ever did in school. We worked puzzles with shapes, made patterns out of all kinds of things, and I found out that math is fun." In-service teachers also reported that they liked mathematics more after the Collaborative than they did before. Many said that they found their day "integrated" with mathematics just because they liked it.

### Standard 2: Experiencing Good Teaching in Mathematics

Both in-service and preservice teachers reported that they liked the observations and modeling of early childhood mathematics lessons.

Preservice teachers focused on the management techniques used by the university professor. "I was fortunate to see her teach the students, which helped me see ways to manage classrooms." "By watching, I learned some good classroom management techniques, how to better explain, and how to have a good time while teaching." "I learned more mathematics observing in these classrooms than I did in my own mathematics classrooms in college." "Amazingly, [the university professor] seemed to teach the most by just listening and asking questions. Children seemed to always be involved with her. Maybe it's because she calls them by name." In-service teachers seemed to learn more mathematics by observing the teaching. "I had no idea that so much could be taught with tangrams!" "Boy did I learn about spatial sense ... now my activities make sense ... in fact I can create my own now that I understand how children think and what they should be doing!" "It was such a relief to learn about the importance of comparing in measurement. I had been spending all of my time on the wrong stuff!" "Finally, an extension of linear patterns. I was so tired of AAB, AB, and ABAC patterns ... and so were my kids!"

## Standard 3: Focused Learning About Children and the Mathematics Content of Specific Interest to Them

One of the benefits of the Collaborative reported by the practicing teachers is the benefit to their students. They reported that they especially liked opportunities to share old ideas and suggestions for helping their students with special needs. They liked the resources for children's developmental levels. The manipulatives that were purchased by the school, the everyday items that they could use to help children understand mathematics, and the alternative assessment methods that were introduced were all specifically mentioned. Most teachers reported that they knew more about their children's mathematical understanding after the Collaborative than they did before it began.

The preservice teachers also learned a great deal about children and their understanding of mathematics. "Many of the lessons allowed children to make sense of math in their own way. The understanding was achieved through children's direct experiences and their thinking about those experiences." "For one second-grade class, I asked the class to be original and make up their own pictures using geometric shapes. I was truly amazed at some of the pictures they made and how they could describe their pictures using fractions and flipping and sliding." "Children really love to learn and they like mathematics!" "The more I was involved, the more children were." "I feel that the Early Childhood Collaborative should really be called 'Child Collaborative.' It gave me a plus to watch children!"

## Standard 4: Participating in a Variety of Professional Development Opportunities Situated in a Learning Community

Everyone was very positive about the professional development experience and the Early Childhood Collaborative model. Practicing teachers often mentioned the model lessons taught by the university professor and the help they received from the lesson plans of the beginning teachers. They continually mentioned the enthusiasm of the preservice teachers and the fact that their children waited anxiously for the "young, exciting teachers." Many teachers mentioned that they loved the study groups and the fact that they felt valued because they were conducted during instructional time. Some teachers also mentioned that they appreciated not having to prepare for a substitute because the beginning teachers came with ready activities.

When asked about the perceived effects on the children in these classrooms, there was total agreement on this issue. Everyone spoke very positively about their children's experiences. In fact, representative quotes from their interviews reflect an overwhelming support of the preservice teachers and their teaching. "My children were so excited about the mathematics they were learning without even knowing it was math!" "The lessons were fun and dynamic … my students got so excited when I put out their name tags. They constantly asked when those 'good' teachers were coming back." One teacher summarized the effect of the beginning teacher's involvement as 'an all-win situation.' My students learned, I learned, and the beginning teachers learned! How often does that happen?"

The preservice teachers made the most comments about this aspect of the collaborative. "I got over my fear of looking silly in front of my peers and really went for it. The more I was involved, the more the children were." " I learned to be patient, and have innovative ideas when it comes to teaching students." "Teaching in the classrooms gave me a feel of what grade levels I prefer to teach." "I loved meeting teachers in the classrooms." I think I can do this! … and what's more … I want to!" "I saw a big difference in myself this semester. Last semester I would sit back and wait for someone to take charge and lead the activities. This time around I was the one who took charge and the one the other teachers looked to for help." "Sometimes I did really well in teaching and there were a few times I didn't do great. At any rate, I learned from those experiences."

## Standard 5: Demonstrating an Ability to Implement Integrative Curriculum

Before the Collaborative experience, only one teacher could describe the Standards in any way; other teachers reported either that they had heard of them and did not know much about them or that they had never heard of them at all. During the last collaborative session in April, every teacher could list the five content standards proposed by NCTM in their draft (1998) and most of the process standards. When asked about their importance, one teacher responded, "Mathematics just connects to everything! I find that I am using mathematics ideas in almost everything.... when I talk to children at centers, when I do routine activities, during circle time, and even during story time! I am mathetized!"

## LOOKING AHEAD

Putman and Borko (2000) recently synthesized research on teacher learning. The situated "communities of discourse" described in their article specifically relate to the Early Childhood Collaborative. Theorectically, the collaborative is based on discourse between the university professor, experienced teachers, and beginning teachers. The university professor introduced research-based knowledge about mathematics, learning and teaching as well as *Principles and Standards for School Mathematics* proposed in the 1998 draft document (NCTM, 1998). The experienced teachers shared and reflected on their teaching practices and the learning that did or did not occur in their classrooms. The beginning teachers were introduced to children in classroom situations and discovered learning possibilities in mathematics. As the preliminary results indicate, the collaborative was a generally rewarding experience for those involved. However, though a potentially powerful type of professional development, the Early Childhood Collaborative did not totally function as a "community of discourse" as described by Putman and Borko. Frequently, the discourse was imbalanced with the university professor's agenda being the primary focus rather than the teachers' ideas and their empowerment to implement those ideas. Conversely, the discourse of both experienced and beginning teachers almost as often involved managerial or administrative issues and failed to connect to the more important issues of teaching and learning. In addition, possibilities for mentor relationships between experienced and beginning teachers were not fully explored. Future plans for the collaborative include: (a) involvement of district curriculum specialists to guide the practicing teachers' study groups, (b) observation sessions that involve groups of beginning teachers watching experienced teachers, and (c) the development of a cadre of experienced teachers to coach other practicing teachers in the collaborative. These issues, as well as others identified by the analyses of data collected during the 2000–2001 school year, will be addressed in future collaboratives.

The Early Childhood Collaborative is a learning experience for everyone involved. Many lessons have already been learned and will continue to be learned in the years to come. It is just one example of a professional development model that can be used to communicate and implement the standards in private or public schools. Perhaps it is one avenue to promote a shared vision of learning and teaching mathematics.

# REFERENCES

Carlan, V. G. (2000). *A development of an instrument to assess the use of developmentally appropriate practices in early childhood classrooms.* Unpublished dissertation proposal, University of Houston, Houston, TX.

Carpenter, T. P., Fennema, E., Peterson, P. L., & Carey, D. A. (1988). Teachers' pedagogical content knowledge of students' problem solving in elementary arithmetic. *Journal for Research in Mathematics Education, 19,* 385–401.

Children's Defense Fund. (2000). *The state of America's children.* Washington, DC: Author.

Copley, J. V., & Padrón, Y. (1999). Preparing teachers of young learners: Professional development of early childhood teachers in mathematics and science. In *Dialogue on early childhood: Science, mathematics, and technology education* (pp. 117–129). Washington, DC: American Association for the Advancement of Science.

Copley, J. V. & Petri, D. (1998, April). *A university/school collaborative coaching project: A tool that created change.* Paper presented at the annual meeting of the National Council of Supervisors of Mathematics, Washington, DC.

Copley, J. V. & Sultis, B. (1997, March). *Technical report to administrators: State of mathematics in Pearland ISD.* Paper presented to administrators and school board members at the monthly Pearland board meeting, Pearland, TX.

Fennema, E., Carpenter, T. P., Franke, L., Levi, L., Jacobs, V., & Empson, S. (1996). Learning to use children's mathematical thinking: A longitudinal study. *Journal for Research in Mathematics Education, 27*(4), 403–434.

Jenkins, K. (2000). *The early childhood field collaborative: Pre-service teachers' beliefs before, during, and after the collaborative in mathematics teaching and learning.* Unpublished candidacy paper, University of Houston, Houston, TX.

Jenkins, K. (2001). *The early childhood field collaborative: A collection of longitudinal case studies revealing pre-service teachers' beliefs about mathematics.* Unpublished doctoral dissertation, University of Houston, Houston, TX.

Johnson, J. (1999). The forum on early childhood science, mathematics, and technology education. In *Dialogue on early childhood: Science, mathematics, and technology education* (pp. 14–26). Washington, DC: American Association for the Advancement of Science.

National Association for the Education of Young Children, Council for Exceptional Children, and National Board for Professional Teaching Standards. (1996). *Guidelines for preparation of early childhood professionals: Associate, baccalaureate, and advanced levels.* Washington, DC: National Association for the Education of Young Children.

National Council of Supervisors of Mathematics. (1994). *Supporting leaders in mathematics education.* Golden, CO: Author.

National Council of Teachers of Mathematics. (1991). *Teaching standards for school mathematics.* Reston, VA: Author.

National Council of Teachers of Mathematics. (1998). *Principles and standards for school mathematics: Discussion draft.* Reston, VA: Author.

Petri, D. (2000). *An examination of the belief system of teachers in a mathematics collaborative project.* Unpublished candidacy paper, University of Houston, Houston, TX.

Petri, D. (2001). *An examination of the belief systems of teachers before and after participation in a mathematics professional development project.* Unpublished dissertation, University of Houston, Houston, TX.

Putnam, R. T., & Borko, H. (2000). What do new views of knowledge and thinking have to say about research on teacher learning? *Educational Researcher, 29*(1), 4–13.

Raymond, A. M. (1997). Understanding the relationship between beginning elementary teachers' mathematical beliefs and teaching practices. *Journal for Research in Mathematics Education, 28,* 551–575.

Richardson, V. (1994). The consideration of teachers' beliefs. In V. Richardson (Ed.), *Teacher change and the staff development process* (pp.90–108). New York: Teachers College Press.

State Systemic Initiative. (1999–2000). *TEXTEAMS: Professional development institute prekindergarten–kindergarten.* Austin: University of Texas at Austin.

# 19

# The Professional Development Challenge in Preschool Mathematics

Julie Sarama
Ann-Marie DiBiase
with Douglas H. Clements and Mary Elaine Spitler
*University at Buffalo, The State University of New York*

> The most powerful instrument for change, and therefore the place to begin, lies at the very core of education—with teaching itself.

All children have the right to a high-quality mathematics education (Clements, Copple, & Hyson, 2002; National Council of Teachers of Mathematics [NCTM], 2000; Schoenfeld, 2002). Professional development programs are widely regarded as the most significant way of achieving this goal (Bowman, Donovan, & Burns, 2001; Darling-Hammond, 1998; Ferguson, 1991; Guskey, 1997; Hilliard, 1997; Johnson & McCracken, 1994; Loucks-Horsley, Hewson, Love, & Stiles, 1998; Schoenfeld, 2002). Professional development programs have been defined as systematic attempts to alter the professional practices, beliefs, and understanding of school personnel for an articulated purpose (Bowman, 1995; Bredekamp & Copple, 1997; Greene, 1994). After presenting background information, including present barriers to implementing effective professional development, principles and standards, and theoretical foundations, we then review the literature on professional development in early childhood, mathematics education, early childhood mathematics education, and, briefly, technology. We conclude by drawing implications.

# BACKGROUND

All citizens need a broad range of basic mathematical understanding, and many careers require an increasing level of proficiency (Campbell & Silver, 1999; Glenn Commission, 2000; Kilpatrick, Swafford, & Findell, 2001; U.S. Department of Labor Bureau of Labor Statistics, 2000). However, U.S. proficiency is well below what is desired (Kilpatrick et al., 2001; Mullis et al., 1997, 2000). Moreover, children who live in poverty and who are members of linguistic and ethnic minority groups demonstrate significantly lower levels of achievement (Bowman et al., 2001; Campbell & Silver, 1999; Denton & West, 2002; Mullis et al., 2000; Natriello, McDill, & Pallas, 1990; Secada, 1992; Starkey & Klein, 1992). These achievement differences have origins in the earliest years—low-income children have been found to possess less extensive mathematical knowledge than middle-income children of Pre-K and kindergarten age (Denton & West, 2002; Ginsburg & Russell, 1981; S. Griffin, Case, & Capodilupo, 1995; Jordan, Huttenlocher, & Levine, 1992; Saxe, Guberman, & Gearhart, 1987; see also Klein & Starkey, chap. 14, this volume). Head Start children make minimal improvement in addition and subtraction knowledge over the Pre-K year (Zill et al., 2001). Furthermore, the SES (socioeconomic status) gap is broad and encompasses several aspects of informal mathematical knowledge: numerical, arithmetic, spatial/geometric, patterning, and measurement knowledge (Klein & Starkey, chap. 14, this volume).

One main reason for this gap is that children from low-income families receive less support for mathematical development in many of their home and school environments (Blevins-Knabe & Musun-Miller, 1996; Holloway, Rambaud, Fuller, & Eggers-Pierola, 1995; Saxe et al., 1987; Starkey et al., 1999). Also, public Pre-K programs serving low-income families provide fewer learning opportunities and supports for mathematical development, including a narrower range of mathematical concepts (Bryant, Burchinal, Lau, & Sparling, 1994; Farran, Silveri, & Culp, 1991). The need for professional development is clear. In this section, we overview relevant background research, including general professional development, economic and institutional factors, teacher knowledge, and principles and standards.

## Research Issues

Research suggests that the most critical feature of a high-quality educational environment is a knowledgeable and responsive adult (Bowman et al., 2001; Darling-Hammond, 1997; Ferguson, 1991; Schoenfeld, 1985) and that high-quality professional development is essential to reform (Darling-Hammond, 1998). Although professional development endeavors are widely valued (Loucks-Horsley et al., 1998), and there is no shortage of suggested guidelines for successful professional development, most are not based on research. Furthermore, empirical studies often fail to measure relevant teacher behaviors and student outcomes (Guskey, 1997). Finally, carefully executed and methodologically rigorous studies are uncommon. There are at least three reasons for this deficit (Wolfe, 1991). First, the topic is complex and the methodological problems associated with its study are severe. Second, studies are often done "in" or "to" schools without serving the schools' needs, leading to the rejection of research (W. H. Griffin, 1983; Wolfe, 1991). Third, practitioners expect that research efforts should result in some recommendations for improved practice that are available in a reasonable amount of time, in a form that is usable and comprehensible. However, the translation of research findings into practical applications can be extended to several years (Wolfe, 1991).

Research summaries have produced guidelines for more effective practice (F. Wood & Thompson, 1993); however, they more often document inadequacies than prescribe solutions. This may be due to the abundance of documentation on projects that have failed to bring about demonstrable improvements and enduring change (Frechtling, Sharp, Carey, & Baden-Kierman, 1995). Furthermore, the guidelines posed by different researchers are often long, unprioritized, lists of recommendations, some of which contradict the guidelines of others.

Even the results of empirical studies are too general and theoretical for pragmatically minded educators (Guskey, 1994). For example, specific elements of effective professional development have not been identified because (a) educators have not consciously discussed and defined various criteria of effectiveness, (b) meta-analyses have focused mostly on simple main effects, ignoring or de-emphasizing key contextual variables, and (c) issues of quality have been largely ignored, probably because rich descriptions are more difficult to collect (Fullan, 1991).

Criteria of effectiveness can be classified in four categories (Guskey, 1994). The first is determining participants' reactions to the experience, often using self-report questionnaires (Guskey, 1997). Often referred to as "happiness indicators," this information tends to be highly subjective and not particularly reliable (Sparks, 1995). The second category involves measuring the knowledge and skills that participants acquire as a result of professional development. This information helps improve program format, content, and organization, but it is difficult to use for making comparisons or judging relative worth (Guskey, 1997; Guskey & Huberman, 1995). The third category entails measuring the participants' actual use of knowledge and skills they have gained. The fourth category—rarely used—involves measuring the impact of participants' changes in knowledge and skills on student outcomes.

Despite the limitations of the main research corpus, there are research findings that can guide professional development (Bowman et al., 2001; Conference Board of the Mathematical Sciences, 2001; National Association for the Education of Young Children [NAEYC], 2002; Peisner-Feinberg et al., 1999; U.S. Department of Education, 1999). First, we consider pertinent barriers.

## Economic and Institutional Barriers

There are significant barriers to any professional development endeavor. When considering early childhood professionals, the barriers can appear insurmountable.

A significant economic barrier for improving early childhood professional development lies in the contention that there are few incentives for individuals working in child-care centers or family child-care homes to seek specialized preparation for jobs that pay little more than minimum wage. "According to the 2000 OES survey, only 18 occupations report having mean wages lower than childcare workers" (Laverty, Siepak, Burton, Whitebook, & Bellm, 2002, p. 4). Furthermore, the cost of attending professional development can be prohibitive for those with low wages. Unlike K–8 institutions, family/group/center-based care centers cannot close for a day. Substitutes have to be found (and paid for) if caregivers wish to attend a workshop or class during working hours.

Institutional and regulatory barriers also must be addressed. Child-care/preschool programs and public school are regulated by two unrelated unconnected systems with different standards and bureaucracies. Child-care/preschool personnel are regulated by licensing boards, whereas public school personnel are regulated by state boards of education/certification. These two disparate systems sometimes allow for upward mobility within, but allow virtually no movement across systems (Willer, 1994).

Licensing and certification also place different emphases on experience and training. Many early childhood practitioners in America are not required to have any early childhood training to work with young children (Willer, 1994).

There is a lack of a coordination and articulation across delivery systems. Existing college training programs are not always accessible in terms of location, class scheduling, and degree-completion policies to individuals currently employed in early care and education programs. That is, programs at 4-year institutions are essentially dictated by state certification standards for teachers and those standards vary almost as much as licensing standards. As a result, there is no consistency even in the definition of "early childhood" among 4-year institutions, and many provide less specialized early childhood preparation than the associate-degree programs (Willer, 1994). An equally challenging problem is that there are insufficient numbers of specialized early childhood programs to provide qualified personnel for all the possible positions or to prepare future leaders in the field. Azer and Hanrahan (1998) indicated that in 1998, 26 states were in the discussion/planning stage for implementing articulation agreements between 2- and 4-year colleges.

Finally, institutional barriers to changing practice, especially in the direction of innovative education, are embedded in schools, and throughout the broader multilayered, decentralized U.S. system (Grant, Peterson, & Shojgreen-Downer, 1996). One particularly vexing issue is the unrealized potential and missed opportunities for facilitation of reform due to divergent beliefs of the relevant social groups, often about what were ostensibly observable "facts" (e.g., that there are computers available for teachers; Sarama, Clements & Henry, 1998).

## Teacher Knowledge

Teachers must develop knowledge of subject-matter content they teach, the ability to communicate this content to children, and the ability to develop higher–order thinking skills (Ball & Bass, 2000; Darling-Hammond, 1998; Garet, Porter, Desimone, Birman, & Yoon, 2001; Loucks-Horsley et al., 1998; NCTM, 2000; Schoenfeld, 1988). Teachers, especially teachers of young children, are not prepared to do so (NCTM, 1991). Consistent with the wider U.S. culture, teachers believe that mathematics is a set of facts and that memorizing these facts is an appropriate route to learning mathematics (Garet et al., 2001; NCTM, 2000). These beliefs are notoriously resistant to change and they affect teachers' practices and their students' learning (Lampert & Ball, 1998; Peterson, Fennema, Carpenter, & Loef, 1989). Where their knowledge is limited teachers will tend to depend on the text for context, de-emphasize interactive discourse in favor of seatwork assignments, and in general, portray the subject as a collection of static factual knowledge (Brophy, 1991). Many early childhood educators identify this discipline as their weakest area of concentration (Schram, Wilcox, Lanier, & Lappan, 1988). Furthermore, traditional approaches to in-service teacher education, like traditional teaching approaches, explain new information—new classroom strategies, techniques, and perspectives—without considering how these ideas might fit with teachers' preexisting knowledge and beliefs. Often reformers fail to acknowledge individual backgrounds and beliefs of teachers (even when they do so with children; Darling-Hammond, 1990).

In contrast to those who know mathematics as facts and rules, teachers who have conceptual understandings of mathematics are more effective than those who see mathematics as rules and procedures (Fennema & Franke, 1992; Ma, 1999; Schoenfeld, 1992). They view mathematics as having interrelated structural elements, as a way to better understand the world around us and to communicate about that world, and as a creative medium for solving myriad problems (Romberg, 1983; Schoenfeld, 1985; Steen, 1988). Furthermore, their knowledge is a thoroughly connected web of concepts and procedures, including links to the real world (Hiebert, 1986; Ma, 1999; Resnick & Ford, 1981) . This is a different approach to the construct of "teachers' mathematics knowledge" than the number of mathematics courses taken in college—a measure that tended to have little relationship to student learning (Fennema & Franke, 1992; Geary, 1994). In contrast, research defining "teachers' knowledge" as being more explicit, better connected, and more integrated has found that teachers with more knowledge teach mathematics more dynamically, representing it in more varied ways and more fully responding to student ideas and questions (Brophy, 1991).

Teacher beliefs also encompass beliefs about pedagogy, students' capabilities, and the nature of learning and teaching (especially in reform or constructivist contexts; Grant et al., 1996; Prawat, 1992; Thompson, 1992). Even when teachers learn new notions, such as constructivism, their understandings may not be consistent with those of researchers, developers, or teacher educators (Clements, 1997; Prawat, 1992) and their practice may reflect surface features of the theory or reform (Ball, 1992; Sarama, Clements, Henry, & Swaminathan, 1996).

Changing teacher beliefs is difficult. Teachers have experienced years of "apprenticeship of observation" (Lortie, 1975)—countless hours observing practice. Unlike other professions, these observations have crystallized beliefs that have the weight of personal conviction, emotion, and intuition and the force of palpable truths. Changing beliefs requires three general conditions: (a) teachers must be dissatisfied with their existing beliefs in some way, (b) they must find the alternatives presented to be both intelligible and practical, and (c) they must figure out some way to connect new beliefs with earlier conceptions (Ely, 1990; Etchberger & Shaw, 1992; Posner, Striken, Hewson, & Gertzog, 1982). Professional developers can attempt to influence beliefs by first acknowledging the complexity of the process. Time for teacher training must be adequate, and strategies must be used that account for teachers' prior knowledge and experiences. In addition, teachers should examine the time and energy that must be put forth in implementing an innovation and weigh this personal cost relative to rewards attained (Wright, 1987). Teachers reject innovations that appear unconnected to the curriculum, viewing them as yet more "add ons" (Ferris & Roberts, 1994). Such rejection is more likely when the innovation requires the use of computer technology, especially when teachers are not comfortable with the technology. Professional development has special challenges in early childhood settings. Even graduates of 4-year early childhood programs with state licensure usually lack adequate preparation in mathematics, and those with less education have virtually no preparation (Kilpatrick et al., 2001). Early childhood teachers are often uncomfortable with math (Copley, 1999), view necessary math as only "counting, adding, subtracting, and knowing shapes," have little or no knowledge about the math standards, and do not use research-based math curricula (Sarama, 2002; see also Copley, chap. 18, this volume). Teachers' implicit, mixed beliefs, and inconsistencies between explicit and implicit beliefs, deny them a clear vision for reform (cf. Genishi, Ryan, Ochsner, & Yarnall, 2001; Sarama et al., 1998). Even the notion of "academics" is frequently rejected (Adcock & Patton, 2001; Weikart, 1999). In summary, teachers' knowledge and beliefs represent a substantial challenge to any professional development effort.

## Principles and Standards

Several national organizations have made efforts to address issues surrounding mathematics education for young children, including professional development. The NCTM released its first Standards document in 1989. In 2000, the NCTM introduced the first major revision of its Standards, which, unlike its predecessors, addresses mathematics education before kindergarten (2000). The inclusion of preschool stems from the recognition of the value of high-quality experiences in the early years in determining long-term success. The NCTM also recognizes the role of the adult in providing the appropriate environment, encouraging thinking, valuing uniqueness, and supporting play. Specific recommendations regarding professional development call for both mathematical and pedagogical knowledge. "They [teachers] must adjust their practices and extend their knowledge to reflect changing curricula and technologies and to incorporate new knowledge about how students learn mathematics" (p. 370). The sole responsibility does not rest with the teacher however: "We need instead to address issues in a systemic way, providing teachers with the sources they need for professional growth" (p. 370).

The NAEYC has worked over several decades to promote high-quality early childhood programs for all young children by facilitating professional development (NAEYC, 2002; Willer, 1994). Their recent statement of guidelines for professional preparation (NAEYC, 2002), compared to their earlier documents, emphasizes subject-matter content and places a more explicit emphasis on a "continuum of teaching strategies" and developmentally effective approaches. They describe five standard categories: promoting child development and learning; building family and community relationships; observing, documenting, and assessing to support young children and families; teaching and learning (including connecting with children and families, using developmentally effective approaches, understanding content knowledge, and building meaningful curriculum); and becoming a professional.

The NAEYC and NCTM have recently joined together to issue a position statement that outlines appropriate mathematics for early childhood (Clements, Copple et al., 2002). The position statement is applicable for professionals working in all early childhood settings and calls professional development "an urgent priority." The recommendation most relevant to this chapter is to "create more effective early childhood teacher preparation and continuing professional development." The statement further recommends that preparation include the following connected components:

(1) knowledge of the mathematical content and concepts most relevant for young children—including in-depth understanding of what children are learning now and how today's learning points toward the horizons of later learning (Kilpatrick et al., 2001); (2) knowledge of young children's learning and development in all areas—including but not limited to cognitive devel-

opment, and knowledge of the issues and topics that may engage children at different points in their development; (3) knowledge of effective ways of teaching mathematics to all young learners; (4) knowledge and skill in observing and documenting young children's mathematical activities and understanding; and (5) knowledge of resources and tools that promote mathematical competence and enjoyment.

In addition, greater emphasis should be placed on teachers' enjoyment of mathematics, confidence in their mathematical knowledge and skills, and positive mathematical attitudes. Effective programs combine mathematics content, pedagogy, and knowledge of child development and family relationships. Courses and practicum experiences should help teachers ask questions that stimulate mathematical thinking in young children.

The NCTM and NAEYC standards and guidelines are consistent with other reports on professional development in general. Working under the premise that access to high-quality preparation, induction, and professional development is the right of every teacher, the National Commission on Teaching and America's Future (NCTAF; 1996) argues that schools should be genuine learning organizations for students and teachers. To increase the time teachers have to learn and work with colleagues, the report recommends flattening district hierarchies so more resources can be invested more in classrooms and less in nonteaching personnel.

The NCTAF recommends reforming the teacher reward system, redirecting a portion of compensation for professional development to recognize teachers' knowledge and skill, rather than "seat time" only. Standards developed by the National Board of Professional Teaching Standards (NBPTS) can be used to recognize such knowledge and skill.

These recommendations are consistent with the National Staff Development Council's (1995) advocacy for professional development that is results driven, standards based, and job embedded. Both organizations share the conviction that ongoing, high-quality professional development is essential to reform and that teachers must have time to learn and work with colleagues.

Finally, all the documents reviewed in this section emphasize the importance of diversity and inclusion. These issues are the focus of the "recommended practices" of the Division of Early Childhood of the Council of Exceptional Children (Sandall, McLean, & Smith, 2000). These recommendations include that professional development activities are systematically designed and implemented, that training should involve teams of participants (e.g., general early childhood teachers, early childhood special educators, paraeducators, therapists), and that teachers should be provided with knowledge and skills relative to the inclusion of young children with disabilities.

In summary, professional development is critical to improvement and innovation in early childhood mathematics education, because teachers are the agents who must carry out the demands of high standards (Cuban, 1990; Garet et al., 2001; NCTM, 2000). To do this, teachers must be immersed in the subject-matter content that they teach, have the knowledge to communicate this content to children, and develop higher–order thinking skills (Loucks-Horsley et al., 1998; NCTM, 2000).

## GENERAL PROFESSIONAL DEVELOPMENT

What lessons can be learned from research on professional development in general (across subject matter and ages). Research[1] indicates that professional development should be multifaceted, extensive, ongoing, reflective, focused on common actions and problems of practice and especially children's thinking, grounded in particular curriculum materials, and, as much as possible, situated in the classroom (D. K. Cohen, 1996; Darling-Hammond & McLaughlin, 1995; Fullan, 1992; Garet et al., 2001; Kaser, Bourexis, Loucks-Horsley, & Raizen, 1999; Rényi, 1998; Richardson & Placier, 2001). The focus should be on making small changes guided by a consistent, coherent, grand vision (Ferrucci, 1997). It should involve interaction, including sharing, risk taking, and learning from and with peers. For curriculum innovation, it is important to develop teachers' knowledge and beliefs that the curriculum is appropriate and its goals are valued and attainable (Elmore, 1996), keeping all professional development activities targeted toward those goals (Fullan, 2000). In sum, successful professional development is not separate from teachers' day-to-day professional responsibilities, but an ongoing activity woven into the fabric of their professional lives, including focus on curriculum, assessment, leadership, and collegial sharing (Guskey, 1997; Lieberman, 1995; Miles & Louis, 1990). As a caveat, teachers respond differently to particular approaches, and so combinations of approaches may be most effective (Richardson & Placier, 2001).

What does not work well is easily viewed as the converse of these characteristics: one-shot workshops; topics selected not by the teachers, but by others (two thirds of teachers report they have no say in what or how they learn on the job; Darling-Hammond, 1998), and not addressing teachers' concerns; groups that are not from the same site; and lack of a conceptual basis for the programs or their implementation (Fullan, 1982).

A handful of the research-based guidelines require elaboration. As much as possible, professional development should be embedded in teachers' ongoing practice. Situated cognition literature (e.g., Brown, Collins, & Duguid, 1989) emphasizes that knowledge and skills are embedded in the context in which they are learned. Thus, professional development might be built into the school day through flexible scheduling and extended blocks of time, such as when students are on vacation (Rényi, 1998). The implication is not that all professional development has to oc-

---

[1]A caveat, which applies to most of the research corpus, is that much of this research does not identify critical factors, relies on teacher reports, and infrequently assesses student achievement.

cur in teachers' classrooms, but that we should strive to understand what different contexts can yield (Putnam & Borko, 2000). For example, one team introduced materials and activities in a workshop session. Teachers attempted to enact these ideas in their own classrooms and reconvened to discuss their experiences.

Another implication of such embeddedness is that the timing of preservice education should be changed. For example, there is empirical support for the proposal that university courses might better be taken, and certification received, after several years of a mentoring/apprenticeship approach in a professional development school (Richardson & Placier, 2001).

Involvement of peers has frequently been found to be an important component of professional development. In one large study, the greatest reported gains in teacher learning were in sites where entire schools studied their student results and agreed on what they needed to learn collectively (Garet et al., 2001; Rényi, 1998). Also helpful is garnering support from the community through vision statements, business and community partnerships, technological support, and federally funded institutes. Without the engagement of the community, research-based programs are often not sustained (Darling-Hammond, 1998). In another success story, a core of teachers was able to sustain a new curriculum because the principal aggressively supported their group and sought support from other groups, such as parents (Ferrucci, 1997).

Another underutilized partnership is that between schools and universities. These can "create new, more powerful kinds of knowledge about teaching and schooling, as the 'rub between theory and practice' produces more practical, contextualized theory and more theoretically grounded, broadly informed practice" (Darling-Hammond & McLaughlin, 1995, p. 599).

Finally, in a major research review, Richardson and Placier (2001) concluded that major, sustainable professional development programs require a "normative-reeducative" approach, based on concepts of personal growth and development and on collaboration within the organization that leads to collective change. This approach can lead to deep changes in content and pedagogical knowledge and in understandings about schooling, teaching, and learning. These in turn imply changes in beliefs and therefore cultures. A notable example is the movement to implement constructivist-oriented changes in mathematics, a topic to which we turn.

## MATHEMATICS EDUCATION

Embodying several of the guidelines summarized in the previous section, Korthagen and Kessels (1999) proposed using the van Hiele model of levels of mathematical thinking to professional development in mathematics. In the van Hiele model (van Hiele, 1986), thinking develops from a Gestalt-like visual level through increasingly sophisticated levels of description, analysis, abstraction, and proof. Teachers can "reduce" subject matter to a lower level, leading to rote memorization, but students cannot bypass levels and achieve understanding. Korthagen and Kessels proposed that teachers' knowledge is originally Gestalt-like—perceptual and (only) situated. They argued, therefore, that presenting abstract theories is also a "reduction in level." Instead, they proposed starting at the teachers' initial level, educing issues and problems from teachers' concrete work in the context of their classrooms, building up toward educational theories. Eventually, as the relationship between theory and practice becomes reciprocal across all levels of abstraction and generalization, the professional development efforts will have a significant and lasting impact on teaching practice. Empirical support of this approach has been promising (Korthagen, 2001). Several national evaluations gave the program high ratings (e.g., in one, 71% positive vs. 41% for the sample as a whole). In another study, 86% of the respondents considered their preparation program as relevant or highly relevant to their present work as a teacher. Yet another study indicated that concrete learning effects during the first year of teaching depended on the degree to which theoretical elements in their preparation program were perceived by the students as functional for practice during student teaching, and on the cyclical alternation between school-based and university-based periods in the program.

This model emerged from mathematics education theory. In this section, we summarize research and development efforts in mathematics education across the grades.

## Research on Professional Development in Mathematics

Research in mathematics education confirms that professional development is an, if not the most, important factor in improving education for students. A study conducted by the U.S. Department of Education found that students made greater gains in mathematics when teachers gave high ratings to their professional development in mathematics (Westat & Policy Studies Associates, 2001). Gains in test scores between Grades 3 and 5 were 50% higher for those students whose teachers rated their professional development high, rather than low.

The characteristics of more and less successful professional development are also consistent with the findings of general research. A common, but unsuccessful, external intervention is (solely) adopting new curricula. More successful is supporting "interactions among teachers and children around educational material" (Ball & D. K. Cohen, 1999, p. 3, emphasis in original). This strategy creates extensive opportunities for teachers to focus on mathematics, goals, and children's work and its improvement, which improves teachers' knowledge of subject matter, teaching, and learning (D. K. Cohen, 1996) and increases child achievement (Ball & D. K. Cohen, 1999).

The emphasis on curriculum is particularly strong in professional development in mathematics (Ball & D. K. Cohen, 1999). Using data from a 1994 survey of California elementary school teachers and 1994 student

California Learning Assessment System (CLAS) scores, D. K. Cohen and Hill (2000) found that teachers who worked directly with curriculum materials associated with NCTM's mathematics standards were more likely than those who experienced other kinds of professional development to report reform-oriented teaching practices in mathematics. In addition, the more teachers had engaged in such professional development and the more they engaged in reform-oriented practice, the higher were their students' mathematics achievement. This was so even when controlling for student characteristics and school condition. Cohen and Hill (2000) concluded that when professional development is focused on learning and teaching academic content and when the professional development curriculum overlaps with that for students, teaching practice and student performance will improve. Efforts that lack these elements are less likely to succeed. The researchers also noted that they needed the help of professional educators to succeed.

Unfortunately, curriculum planning at this level of detail is unusual in the United States. It is more typical in Japan, where members of professional teaching communities often spend several years teaching and revising the hypothesized learning trajectories that underpin a sequence of mathematics "research lessons" (Stigler & Hiebert, 1999).

A long-term professional development and research project in the United States is Teaching to the Big Ideas (TBI). In TBI, teachers address central organizing principles of mathematics that emerge in classroom contexts when instruction is organized around and responsive to student thinking. Schifter, Bastable, and Russell (1997) found that there are particular themes—embodying critical concepts—that arise time after time with different groups of learners and with which students must grapple with as they confront the limitations of their existing conceptions. By listening to students, remarking on common areas of confusion or persistently intriguing questions, and then analyzing underlying issues, teachers identify these big ideas. In the first year of the project, teachers began to think about mathematics in terms of ideas, rather than just facts, procedures, and strategies; learned to listen to and analyze student thinking; and considered the pedagogical implications of committing to helping students become powerful mathematical thinkers. In the second and third years, teachers regularly wrote two- to five-page classroom episodes for seminars, presenting some aspect of the mathematical thinking of a single student or a group of students to raise mathematical and pedagogical issues that invite discussion among colleagues.

Taking a different tack on case-based teacher education, Lampert and Ball (1998) developed hypermedia learning environments that combined videotapes of classroom mathematics lessons, instructional materials, teacher journals, student notebooks, students' work, and teacher and student interviews, as well as tools for browsing, annotating, and constructing arguments.

## Summary

Researchers and educators in mathematics education have developed models on the leading edge of professional development theory and research. A significant shared feature has been extensive efforts to connect theory, research, and practice. This research corpus has also confirmed and extended several findings from the general literature. First, professional development is important in improving student achievement. Second, one-shot workshops and introducing curriculum (without correlated professional development) are common, but ineffective, approaches to school improvement. Third, a subject-matter focus is required and orienting teachers to that focus is a significant challenge. Also important are foci on students' thinking and learning about mathematics topics, students' learning in the context of interactions with peers and adults around a reform curriculum, issues of higher order thinking, and strategies for working with special populations. Fourth, effective professional development in mathematics is extensive, ongoing, active, involving observation, experimentation, and mentoring (Ferrucci, 1997; Hiebert, 1999; Kemis & Lively, 1997). Fifth, starting with theory and research is not as effective as starting with practice, and then integrating theory and research into reflections on this practice. Sixth, research lessons (also called "lesson study") and case-based teacher education are promising professional development strategies.

## MODELS IN EARLY CHILDHOOD

A conceptual framework of early childhood professional development must achieve a balance between inclusion and exclusivity (Bredekamp & Willer, 1992; Greene, 1994). It must recognize that individuals enter the profession with diverse educational qualification and support ongoing professional development for individuals at all levels and in all roles (Jeffrey & Lambert, 1995; Lally, Young-Holt, & Mangione, 1994).

The NAEYC (NAEYC & National Association of Early Childhood Specialists, 1991) recommended that early childhood professionals with comparable qualifications, experience, and job responsibilities should receive comparable compensation regardless of their work setting. Unfortunately, although the work of all early childhood professionals has been undervalued, those professionals in nonschool settings have been the most undercompensated (Jalongo & Isenberg, 2000; Morgan, 1994). Teachers in early childhood programs accredited by NAEYC earned roughly half that of their counterparts in public schools, holding education and experience constant.

In addition, early childhood professionals should be encouraged to seek additional professional preparation and should be rewarded accordingly (Bredekamp & Willer, 1992). Early childhood professionals need to be able to advance while continuing to work with children, thereby providing higher quality services for children (Bloom, 1994; Bredekamp & Willer, 1993; Saracho, 1993).

## Career Lattice

Early childhood experts support the development of early childhood professionals within a "career lattice" as a means of helping individuals in the field understand that they have options and what those options are, thereby increasing professionalism and decreasing turnover (Kagan & Force, 1994; Morgan, 1994). A career lattice (Bredekamp & Willer, 1992) provides for the multiple roles and settings within the early childhood profession (vertical strand), each allowing for steps for greater preparation tied to increased responsibility and compensation within that role/setting (horizontal levels), and allows for movement across roles (diagonals).

## Head Start

Head Start is the largest early childhood program in the nation, employing 195,000 paid staff in 2001 (U.S. Department of Health and Human Services, 2002). A majority of the program's teachers enter the field without a baccalaureate degree in early childhood education, so orientation and on-the-job learning are emphasized. Head Start was instrumental in instituting the Child Development Associate (CDA) Credential and requires that at least one teacher in each classroom hold a CDA Credential or other appropriate qualification . The program provides a formal national training and technical assistance network and allocates funds for professional development to each program (Wolfe, 1991).

Head Start released Performance Standards in which the Program Design and Management section emphasizes that agencies must ensure that Head Start staff and consultants have the knowledge, skills, and experience required to perform their assigned functions responsibly (CFR 1304.52) (Bowman et al., 2001). This includes establishing and implementing a structured approach to staff training and development, and attaching academic credit whenever possible. This professional development system should be designed to help build relationships among staff and to assist staff in acquiring or increasing the knowledge and skills needed to fulfill their job responsibilities, in accordance with the requirements of 45 CFR 1306.23.

The FACES (Family and Child Experience Survey) study that began collecting data in 1997 found that nearly one third of all Head Start teachers had a bachelor's or graduate degree in education, and teachers averaged nearly 12 years of teaching experience. The higher the teacher's educational level, the better the observed classroom quality.

## High/Scope

Weikart (1994) maintained that the notion, "Get a job. Learn how it's done ...," is an oversimplification, but does speak to the basic philosophy behind High/Scope's approach to staff development. In-service learning in High/Scope classrooms is the preferred method for gaining skills to implement the High/Scope curriculum.

High/Scope research staff conducted two studies, one with trainers (i.e., analyzing the reports of participants in 40 seven-week training projects and surveying 203 certified High/Scope trainers) and one with teachers (interviewing 244 High/Scope and 122 non-High/Scope comparison teachers). Both studies support a systematic approach to in-service training. Experimental groups were rated higher than comparison groups on providing a good physical environment (organization and access to diverse materials), creating a consistent daily routine (plan-do-review), and supporting adult–child interactions . Their summaries suggest that an investment in a systematic dissemination and training model can produce large-scale and long-lasting benefits for programs and children.

## Families

The Family-to-Family initiative funded by the Dayton Hudson Foundation is designed to improve the quality of family child care by providing professional development opportunities, accreditation, and parent education to providers. The Family-to-Family project, implemented in 32 sites around the country, offers a 15-hour professional family-day-care training course to help providers become accredited (N. Cohen & Modigliani, 1994). An average of 90 providers are served at single-site projects each year.

Cohen and Modigliani (1994) found that mentor and partner programs helped providers learn the material and complete the course by giving the providers personal attention and individual assistance. The self-study techniques were also found to be a vehicle to apply knowledge to the workplace. The professional development opportunities offered had a positive long-term effect in that participants had higher self-esteem, an increased sense of professionalism, and a commitment to deliver high-quality care (N. Cohen & Modigliani, 1994).

## Summary

The early childhood professional career lattice can serve as a means of encouraging professional development at all levels, including appropriate training for administrators. Professional development is an integral part of such large programs as Head Start and High/Scope, and research confirms the importance of such professional development in positively affecting young children's development and learning.

## MODELS IN EARLY CHILDHOOD
## MATHEMATICS EDUCATION

Consistent with research reviewed to this point, the National Education Goals Panel (1997) recommended that subject-matter knowledge and teaching skills in mathematics be strengthened, especially for the early childhood teacher. Most teachers of young children have limited knowledge of mathematics and mathematics education (Clements, Copple et al., 2002), especially the processes and thinking strategies of mathematics in early childhood (Copley & Padròn, 1999; Fennema et al., 1996; NCTM, 2000). The curricula with which they work has been institutionalized as narrow and limited due to historical pedagogic and institutional struggles (Balfanz, 1999). Furthermore, teachers serving economically disadvantaged, limited-English-proficient or lower achieving students often devote less time and emphasis to the higher level thinking skills integral to the learning of mathematics (Copley & Padròn, 1999). Especially given that teachers' expectations for children play a role in determining students' achievement, the professional development of early childhood teachers must address content, processes, and dispositions in mathematics. Unfortunately, few professional development programs focus on early childhood mathematics at all, much less to the breadth and depth required. Instead, the primary foci of professional development for early childhood teachers include definitions of developmentally appropriate curriculum and the importance of play (Copley & Padròn, 1999). This section reviews the small body of literature in this specific area; because it is our target area, we describe each study in more detail.

## Research on Professional Development Programs

A seminal professional development research program is Cognitively Guided Instruction (CGI). For more than a decade, Fennema, Carpenter, and Franke (1997) have been investigating the impact of helping primary-grade teachers understand their children's mathematical thinking. The basic premise of CGI is that assisting teachers to construct relationships between an explicitly research-based model of children's thinking and their own children's thinking will improve their teaching and their student's learning. The researchers have assessed the program's effect on teachers' knowledge and beliefs, their instruction, and their children's learning.

The CGI model begins with an explication of the content domain (i.e., "problem types") and solution strategies that young children typically use to solve problems dealing with each domain. The model is robust in that most young children use the solution strategies included in the model, strategies that are readily observed by teachers. Thus, teachers establish the validity of the model and modify it as they assess their own children's thinking. This knowledge enables teachers to find out what their own children know and understand about mathematics (Fennema et al., 1996). Consistent with CGI's model of children's learning, the program assumes that teachers approach CGI workshops with informal knowledge about children's mathematical thinking. The goal of CGI is to work with teachers to assist them to focus and build on this initial knowledge. Workshops are structured so that participants engage in activities that enable them to consider the research-based model in relationship to their experiences with children. Collaboratively with the researchers, the teachers view video-tapes of children solving problems and identify relationships between the solution strategies and the problem types. Experienced CGI teachers assist in some of the workshops by responding to teachers' questions and concerns about how their classrooms are organized and how they use children's thinking to guide instruction (e.g., should specific strategies like "counting on" be explicitly taught?).

From 1985 to 1989, Carpenter and Fennema (1992) investigated how CGI influenced first-grade teachers' instruction, beliefs, and learning of their children. CGI teachers spent more time having children solve problems, expected multiple solution strategies from their children, and listened to their children more than did control teachers. Furthermore, they found positive relationships between students' learning, their teachers' beliefs, and their teachers' knowledge about their own students' thinking. From 1989 to 1993, the research team assessed CGI's influences on Grade 1–3 teachers (Fennema et al., 1996). During the study, 18 of the 21 teachers' instruction changed so that their children spent more time solving problems and discussing their thinking. The beliefs of 18 teachers also changed so that they believed more strongly that children can and should solve problems without direct instruction. For every teacher for whom 4 years of data were available, class achievement in concepts and problem solving was higher at the end of the study than it was before the workshops. For most teachers, a shift in emphasis from drill on procedure to problem solving did not lead to a deterioration in traditional computational skill (Fennema et al., 1996). Finally, teachers who participated in CGI continued to implement the principles of the program 4 years after it ended (Franke, Carpenter, Levi, & Fennema, 2001). All 22 teachers maintained some use of children's thinking and 10 teachers continued learning in noticeable ways. The 10 teachers engaged in generative growth (a) viewed children's thinking as central, (b) possessed detailed knowledge about children's thinking, (c) discussed frameworks for characterizing the development of children's mathematical thinking, (d) perceived themselves as creating and elaborating their own knowledge about children's thinking, and (e) sought colleagues who also possessed knowledge about children's thinking for support.

Several implications emerge from the CGI project. First, knowledge of their own children's thinking emerging from study of research-based models enables teachers to make instructional decisions such that children's learning of mathematics improves. Second, learning to find out what children know about mathematics and to use that knowledge to make instructional decisions is not simple and takes time. Follow-up workshops and support for teachers, including time for discussion and reflection, are critical. Some teachers do not initially believe that knowledge of children's thinking is significant. Third, when new knowledge is fundamentally incompatible with existing knowledge and beliefs, teachers tend to reject the new knowledge or modify it to make it fit their existing structure. Therefore, direct attention to these beliefs is essential. Fourth, teachers themselves become change agents when they see that innovation results in better learning for their children.

Consistent with the CGI model are several successful efforts that focus on research-based models of children's thinking and learning (Hiebert, 1999; see also Bredekamp, chap. 2, this volume). In our own work, we put research-based learning trajectories at the core of our teacher/child/curriculum triad (Clements, 2002; Clements, Sarama, & DiBiase, 2002; Sarama, 2002; Sarama & Clements, 2002). We find that learning trajectories help teachers focus on the "conceptual storyline" of reform curriculum, a critical element that is often missed (Heck, Weiss, Boyd, & Howard, 2002; Weiss, 2002). This is supported by other research; for example, the few teachers in one study that actually held in-depth discussions in reform math classrooms, saw themselves not as moving through a curriculum, but as helping children move through a learning trajectory (Fuson, Carroll, & Drueck, 2000). Putting learning trajectories at the center facilitates teachers' learning about math, how children think about and learn this math, and how such learning is supported by the curriculum and its teaching strategies, by illuminating potential developmental paths (Ball & D. K. Cohen, 1999), and thus bringing coherence and consistency to math goals and curricula, and assessments.

Another successful program that takes a different approach is Copley and Padròn's collaborative model. (The researchers abstracted six principles for effective professional development programs from three sets of standards from the NCTM, NAEYC, and National Research Council.) Such programs allow the early childhood teacher to : (a) develop good dispositions toward mathematics, (b) experience good teaching in mathematics, (c) focus on learning about children and mathematics, (d) participate in a variety of professional development opportunities situated in the learning community, (e) demonstrate an ability to implement integrative curriculum, and (f) utilize appropriate strategies to establish family partnerships (Copley & Padròn, 1999). Based on these goals, university courses and collaborative arrangements were created for early childhood teachers (Copley & Padròn, 1999). The collaborative arrangement involves three components: beginning teachers teaching in teams of three to four in early childhood classrooms; practicing teachers meeting in study groups while the beginning teachers monitor their classes; and the university professor modeling mathematics lessons in early childhood classrooms for both beginning and practicing teachers. Course assignments for in-service teachers include classroom coaching experiences, presentation of a districtwide series of workshops of mathematics and science, mentorship of a preservice early childhood teacher, and portfolios containing assessments of children's learning in mathematics and science. Throughout the duration of the sessions, the in-service teachers experience good mathematics teaching, model the pedagogy necessary to transfer knowledge into practice, write and implement integrated curriculum, and then share their knowledge with preservice teachers through workshops and mentoring programs.

Student evaluations of this graduate class have been positive. In addition, 32 practicing teachers reported (pre and post) information about their instructional practices using a questionnaire distributed by the National Council of Supervisors of Mathematics. Significant differences occurred in teachers' perceptions of preparedness on four items: managing children using manipulatives, using computers as an integral part of mathematics instruction; using a variety of alternative assessment strategies; and involving parents in mathematics education. Teachers also said they would give more emphasis to number sense, geometry and spatial sense, and measurement. They reported that they increased the following behaviors: asking their students to make conjectures and exploring possible methods to solve a mathematics problem, writing their reasoning about how to solve a problem, and using calculators and manipulatives. Note several caveats: No power analysis was conducted, the data are self-reported, and there was no comparison group. On the basis of the data provided, the collaborative provides preservice teachers with the opportunity to get experience in teaching well-planned lessons in authentic settings and reflect on their lessons with peer and professor advice. In-service teachers experience professional development as part of their regular teaching day and they collaboratively reflect on lessons taught by themselves or the university professor. (See Copley, chap. 18, this volume, for more information.)

Several researchers have worked with teachers on cooperative research projects that share features with CGI and Copley's Collaborative Coaching Project. For example, T. Wood, Cobb, and Yackel (1991) examined teacher learning in the context of an ongoing mathematics research project based on constructivist views of learning and set in a second-grade classroom. The teacher changed her beliefs about learning and teaching as she resolved conflicts and dilemmas between her previously established form of practice and the project's emphasis on children's construction of mathematical meaning. The changes that occurred as the teacher reorganized her practice were analyzed and interpreted by using selected daily video recordings of mathematics lessons along with field notes, open-ended interviews, and data from project meetings. The analyses indicated that changes occurred to her beliefs about the nature of (a) mathematics from rules and procedures to meaningful activity, (b) learning from passivity to interacting and communicating, and (c) teaching from transmitting information to initiating and guiding students' development of knowledge.

Project IMPACT (Increasing the Mathematical Power of All Children and Teachers) is another successful university–school partnership, involving predominantly minority, K–3 classrooms near the University of Maryland (Campbell & Robles, 1997). Project IMPACT addresses a constructivist perspective of mathematics learning and focuses on how to promote teacher, and then student, understanding through interaction and collaboration. The intent is for teachers to organize their instruction to build on children's existing knowledge, relating mathematical procedures and curriculum objects to problem solving. In IMPACT schools, children are to do more than solve mathematics problems, they are to explain how they solved a problem and why they solved a problem in that way.

The professional development model involves a summer in-service program, an on-site mathematics specialist, and planning periods each week for all teachers in the appropriate grade levels at each school. The summer program addresses the pedagogical content knowledge, the mathematics content knowledge, and the beliefs of the teachers. Topics include: adult-level mathematics content; teaching mathematics for understanding, including questioning, use of manipulative materials, and integration of mathematic topics; research on children's learning of mathematics; and teaching mathematics in culturally diverse classrooms. Teachers consider a variety of instructional approaches and materials that support a constructivist perspective of mathematics learning, emphasizing interaction and collaboration rather than limiting teaching to a direct-instruction model. Activities always have a second purpose such as illustrating a particular teaching strategy, or motivating teachers to create parallel tasks. Teachers also observe others modeling teaching practices, and then practice these instructional strategies with a small group of children. Finally, time for teachers to plan for the ensuing year is also provided during the summer. A mathematics specialist is assigned to each participant school to observe and assist teachers as they implement their new approaches with a classroom of children, serving to resolve teachers' concern and to support change throughout the school year.

At the conclusion of the five summer programs, the researchers surveyed the teachers to determine if they would have volunteered for Project IMPACT if they had been given an option. Of the 99 respondents, 62 said they would have volunteered, 30 said they would not have volunteered, and 7 did not comment. Throughout the duration of the last four summer programs, the teachers were also asked, "How do you think the goals of Project IMPACT would be affected if all teachers of a grade level in a school were not required to participate?" Of the 74 teachers who were surveyed, 62 teacher said the goals of the Project would be negatively influenced, 5 teachers said it would have no influence, and 7 teachers did not respond. When asked to delineate their role, IMPACT specialists noted that they assisted teachers in making connections between mathematics topics and between mathematics and other disciplines, creating "noncontrived" problems that were meaningful in the culture of the classroom and addressed critical mathematical objectives, developing questioning and wait time, responding to incorrect answers and fostering involvement and growth among all children, supporting reflection, learning how to share with colleagues and how to support colleagues, and communicating with parents and other participants. The common weekly planning periods encouraged reflection and supported professional interaction, but without a "leader," these planning periods easily become stressful and potentially divisive.

The project was evaluated with experiments that included random assignment and student outcomes measures (project-developed small-group and individual student mathematics assessments). Implementation was monitored with classroom observations. By the middle of second grade, significant differences favoring IMPACT students were reported for place value, whole-number concepts, rational number, and geometry; there were no significant difference for computation. Third-grade results were similar, except that there were no significant differences for geometry. The IMPACT treatment did not eliminate racial discrepancies in student achievement; there were higher mean achievement scores for both the Black and the White children, as compared to the Black and the White children in the comparison schools. The data for the Hispanic and Asian children were mixed.

## Survey Research: Teacher's Beliefs and Preferences Regarding Professional Development

Given the diversity of the teacher/caregiver population, professional development in early childhood mathematics is especially challenging. To help meet this challenge, Sarama surveyed early childhood care providers on issues concerning professional development. About 400 people responded, including teachers and caregivers from family and group day care, day-care centers, public and parochial schools, traditional nursery schools, and Head Start centers. Results were combined whenever possible (i.e., when questions were the same).

The first question was: "Are you at all interested in professional development in mathematics?" Ninety-four percent of the early childhood educators responded that they were. What is the best way to reach these busy professionals? Forty-three percent receive their information through mailings, and 31% from their workplace via supervisors, bulletin boards, and so forth. Of those who receive educational magazines or journals, 43% of respondents receive trade publications, such as Mailbox, and 22% receive the main journal published by the NAEYC, Young Children.

Thirty-nine percent would prefer to meet every 2 weeks; an almost equal number (24% and 23% respectively) preferred to meet monthly or weekly. This was surprising, as expert advisers had suggested that monthly meetings might be "too much."

Although 60% of the participants preferred to meet in their workplace, 58% also chose a local college. Previous research has indicated that the collegiate atmosphere can be intimidating to early childhood professionals (Copley & Padrón, 1999). Other popular choices included schools (44%) and teacher-training centers (35%). Most respondents felt that attending in-service was not too difficult (63%), with fewer than 10% choosing either "very difficult" or "easy." Transportation did not seem to be an issue; only 14% stated that it would influence their decision on whether or not to attend a professional development opportunity. Ninety-two percent said that they would use their own car to attend.

Expert advisers have suggested that financial rewards and job advancement would be key motivators. Although 30% of the respondents did choose "increased pay" and 14% chose "job advancement," 66% chose "curriculum materials" and 43% chose "personal satisfaction." Forty-one percent of the respondents also chose a credential as a motivator and 31% chose college credit. This is consistent with surveys of a wider span of teachers, who are motivated to develop their ability to help children learn (Rényi, 1998).

Another set of questions dealt with beliefs about mathematics education, answers to which could help inform any professional development effort. Asked at what age children should start large group mathematics instruction, the family and group care providers chose ages 2 or 3 most often, whereas the other group felt large-group instruction should not start until age 4. The survey asked whether teachers should have a "standard list of math topics that should be taught to preschoolers." Respondents agreed that it was important: 39% said "very important" and 47% said it was "important." Open-ended responses indicated a desire for general guidelines for the age-appropriateness of topics.

When asked about their main mathematics activities, 67% chose counting, 60%, sorting, 51%, numeral recognition, 46%, patterning, 34%, number concepts, 32%, spatial relations, 16%, making shapes, and 14%, measuring. Unfortunately, geometry and measurement concepts were the least popular.

Most teachers use manipulatives (95%), number songs (84%), basic counting (74%), and games (71%); few used software (33%) or workbooks (16%). They preferred children to "explore math activities" and engage in "open-ended free play" rather than participate in "large-group lessons" or be "doing math worksheets." The data for technology are promising in that 71% of the respondents have access to the Internet, 67% have a computer available for use by the children whom they teach, and 80% would be interested in some sort of distance learning.

Finally, respondents said they would be interested in attending professional development at a center specifically designed for mathematics and technology. Ninety-three percent were interested in visiting a model classroom. Having an outside agency keep track of professional development credits was more important to the respondents than was receiving credit for every course.

Wolfe (1991) conducted an exploratory study designed to identify what practices Head Start staff believe facilitate the transfer of their learning to their work with children. Wolfe administered a survey, developed in conjunction with Head Start staff and professional development experts, to staff in 32 randomly selected grantees in three states. The participants recommended small-group discussion and demonstration/modeling as the professional development activities that they would most prefer, followed by handouts, lecture, observing actual practice, games/simulations, role play, and video/movies. The least recommended instructional strategies were assignments and follow-up phone calls (Wolfe, 1991). Observing actual practice and follow-up assistance were ranked highest when participants were asked what strategies they felt would have the largest effect on their work with children. They ranked worksheets, follow-up letters, and panel discussions as the least likely to have an effect. These results confirm that what teachers desire and believe to be effective is not consistent with the current system of delivery (D. K. Cohen & Hill, 2000).

## Summary

There is a critical need for professional development in early childhood mathematics education. Teachers and caregivers of young children have limited knowledge of mathematics and mathematics education and are not disposed to enjoy mathematical activity or learn more about it. Furthermore, this is a serious equity concern, as teachers serving students who are lower SES, limited in English proficiency, or lower achieving de-emphasize mathematics in general and higher level thinking in particular. Finally, most available programs do not focus on early childhood mathematics at all.

More optimistically, we have a considerable knowledge base regarding young children's learning of mathematics, and a growing research base regarding professional development. Successful professional development projects emphasize research on children's learning, made meaningful to teachers. Most do this in the context of curriculum and reflection upon that curriculum, although in familiar domains such as beginning arithmetic, CGI has shown positive results just emphasizing models of children's thinking. Most of the projects also involve collaborative efforts that involve extensive interactions among teachers and university professors, although the nature and specifics of these projects vary. Copley's Collaborative involves substantial modeling and mentoring in early childhood classrooms. Others balance summer programs with support provided during the school year. All integrate research and theory, connecting it closely to teachers' practice.

Survey research indicates that those in professional development have to branch out from the traditional publications, including not only trade publications but also such techniques as direct mailing. Although only a third of teachers used computers with their children, they had access to computers and the Internet, so professional development educators may be able to reach them through nontraditional means. Results strongly indicate that participants receive high-quality mathematics curriculum materials when attending professional development. Instructors should take care that participants receive enough experience with the materials to make sure they can be used effectively. Tying professional development to carefully documented credits that lead to a credential (early mathematics specialist) may also be a potent motivator.

Teachers believed that guidelines of appropriate ages for approaching various mathematics topics would be better accepted than a mandatory "check-list" of required topics (supporting the approach taken by this book). They had a limited view of appropriate and fun mathematics activities, which professional development educators might address.

Innovative and effective professional development models may use a variety of research-based approaches. In addition, classroom-based inquiry, team teaching by mathematics and early childhood education specialists, discussion of case studies, and analysis of young children's work samples tend to strengthen teachers' confidence and engagement in early childhood mathematics... Delivering this kind of ongoing professional development requires a variety of innovative strategies. For early childhood staff living in isolated communities or lacking knowledgeable trainers, distance learning with local facilitators is a promising option. Literacy initiatives are increasingly using itinerant or school-wide specialists; similarly, mathematics education specialists could offer resources to a number of early childhood programs. Partnerships between higher education institutions and local early childhood programs can help provide this support. Finally, school-district-sponsored professional development activities that include participants from community child care centers, family child care, and Head Start programs along with public school kindergarten/primary teachers would build coherence and continuity for teachers and for children's mathematical experiences. (Clements, Copple et al., 2002, p. 15)

# IMPLICATIONS

Educational change depends on what teachers do and think—it's as simple and as complex as that.

—Fullan (1982, p. 107)

Research confirms the importance of such professional development in positively affecting young children's development and learning, across all developmental areas and in mathematics specifically. To be effective, professional development in early childhood mathematics should do the following:

- Address both knowledge of, and beliefs about, mathematics and mathematics education.
- Develop knowledge and beliefs regarding specific subject-matter content, including deep conceptual knowledge of the mathematics to be taught as well as the processes of mathematics.
- Respond to each individual's background, experiences, and current context or role.
- Be extensive, ongoing, reflective, and sustained.

- Actively involve teachers in observation, experimentation, and mentoring.
- Focus on common actions and problems of practice, and, as much as possible, be situated in the classroom.
- Focus on making small changes guided by a consistent, coherent, grand vision.
- Ground experiences in particular curriculum materials and allow teachers to learn and reflect on that curriculum, implement it, and discuss their implementation.
- Consider approaches such as research lessons and case-based teacher education.
- Focus on children's mathematical thinking and learning, including learning trajectories.
- Include strategies for developing higher order thinking and for working with special populations.
- Address equity and diversity concerns.
- Involve interaction, networking, and sharing with peers/colleagues.
- Include a variety of approaches.
- Use the early childhood professional career lattice as a means of encouraging professional development at all levels.
- Ensure the support of administration for professional development to promote sustained and wide-scale reform.
- Consider school–university partnerships, especially collaborative efforts involving extensive interactions among teachers and university professors.
- Sustain efforts to connect theory, research, and practice
- Investigate the use of nontraditional publications, including trade publications, direct mailing, and distance learning for communications.
- Provide participants with high-quality mathematics curriculum materials and ensure that participants receive adequate experience to use the materials effectively.
- Address economic, institutional, and regulatory barriers.

Professional development in early childhood mathematics is a national concern. Formal training as usually constituted is ineffective (Lampert & Ball, 1998; Zeichner & Tabachnick, 1982). Most professional development is not ongoing, continuous, reflective, and motivating. Research-based suggestions such as those presented here hold the potential to make a significant difference in the learning of young children by catalyzing substantive change in the knowledge and beliefs of their teachers.

## ACKNOWLEDGMENTS

This chapter is based on work supported in part by the National Science Foundation under Grant No. ESI-9814218, "Planning for Professional Development in Pre-School Mathematics: Meeting the Challenge of Standards 2000." Any opinions, findings, and conclusions or recommendations expressed in this material are those of the author(s) and do not necessarily reflect the views of the National Science Foundation.

## REFERENCES

Adcock, S. G., & Patton, M. M. (2001). Views of effective early childhood educators regarding systemic constraints that affect their teaching. *Journal of Research in Childhood Education, 15,* 194–208.

Azer, S., & Hanrahan, C. (1998). *Early care and education career development initiatives in 1998.* Boston: Wheelock College, The Center for Career Development in Early Care and Education.

Balfanz, R. (1999). Why do we teach young children so little mathematics? Some historical considerations. In J. V. Copley (Ed.), *Mathematics in the early years* (pp. 3–10). Reston, VA: National Council of Teachers of Mathematics.

Ball, D. L. (1992). Magical hopes: Manipulatives and the reform of math education. *American Educator, 16*(2), 14, 16–18, 46–47.

Ball, D. L., & Bass, H. (2000). Interweaving content and pedagogy in teaching and learning to teach: Knowing and using mathematics. In J. Boaler (Ed.), *Multiple perspectives on the teaching and learning of mathematics* (pp. 83–104). Westport, CT: Ablex.

Ball, D. L., & Cohen, D. K. (1996). Reform by the book: What is—or might be—the role of curriculum materials in teacher learning and instructional reform? *Educational Researcher, 16*(2), 6–8; 14.

Ball, D. L., & Cohen, D. K. (1999). *Instruction, capacity, and improvement.* Philadelphia: Consortium for Policy Research in Education, University of Pennsylvania.

Blevins-Knabe, B., & Musun-Miller, L. (1996). Number use at home by children and their parents and its relationship to early mathematical performance. *Early Development and Parenting, 5,* 35–45.

Bloom, P. (1994). Professional development for leaders: Lessons from Head Start. In J. Johnson & J. McCracken (Eds.), *The early childhood career lattice: Perspectives on professional development* (p. 184). Washington, D.C.: National Association for the Education of Young Children.

Bowman, B. T. (1995). The professional development challenge: Supporting young children and families. *Young Children, 51*(1), 30–34.

Bowman, B. T., Donovan, M. S., & Burns, M. S. (Eds.). (2001). *Eager to learn: Educating our preschoolers.* Washington, DC: National Academy Press.

Bredekamp, S., & Copple, C. (Eds.). (1997). *Developmentally appropriate practice in early childhood programs* (Rev. ed.). Washington, DC: National Association for the Education of Young Children.

Bredekamp, S., & Willer, B. (1992). Of ladders and lattices, core and cones: Conceptualizing an early childhood professional development system. *Young Children, 47*(3), 47.

Bredekamp, S., & Willer, B. (1993). Professionalizing the field of early childhood education: Pros and cons. *Young Children, 48*(3), 30–34.

Brophy, J. E. (1991). Conclusions. In J. E. Brophy (Ed.), *Advances in research on teaching: Teachers' subject matter knowledge and classroom instruction* (Vol. 2, pp. 347–362). Greenwich, CT: JAI.

Brown, J. S., Collins, A., & Duguid, P. (1989). Situated cognition and the culture of learning. *Educational Researcher, 18*(1), 32–42.

Bryant, D. M., Burchinal, M., Lau, L. B., & Sparling, J. J. (1994). Family and classroom correlates of Head Start children's developmental outcomes. *Early Childhood Research Quarterly, 9,* 289–309.

Campbell, P. F., & Robles, J. (1997). Project IMPACT: Increasing the mathematical power of all children and teachers. In S. N. Friel & G. W. Bright (Eds.), *Reflecting on our work: NSF teacher enhancement in K–6 mathematics* (pp. 179–186). Lanham, MD: University Press of America.

Campbell, P. F., & Silver, E. A. (1999). *Teaching and learning mathematics in poor communities.* Reston, VA: National Council of Teachers of Mathematics.

Carpenter, T. P., & Fennema, E. H. (1992). Cognitively guided instruction: Building on the knowledge of students and teachers. *International Journal of Educational Research, 17*(5), 457–470.

Clements, D. H. (1997). (Mis?)Constructing constructivism. *Teaching Children Mathematics, 4*(4), 198–200.

Clements, D. H. (2002). Linking research and curriculum development. In L. D. English (Ed.), *Handbook of international research in mathematics education* (pp. 599–630). Mahwah, NJ: Lawrence Erlbaum Associates.

Clements, D. H., Copple, C., & Hyson, M. (Eds.). (2002). *Early childhood mathematics: Promoting good beginnings.* A joint position statement of the National Association for the Education of Young Children (NAEYC) and the National Council for Teachers of Mathematics (NCTM) (Rev. ed.). Washington, DC: National Association for the Education of Young Children/National Council for Teachers of Mathematics.

Clements, D. H., Sarama, J., & DiBiase, A.-M. (2002). Preschool and kindergarten mathematics: A national conference. *Teaching Children Mathematics, 8,* 510–514.

Cohen, D. K. (1996). Rewarding teachers for student performance. In S. H. Fuhrman & J. A. O'Day (Eds.), *Rewards and reforms: Creating educational incentives that work* (pp. 60–112). San Francisco: Jossey Bass.

Cohen, D. K., & Hill, H. C. (2000). Instructional policy and classroom performance: The mathematics reform in California. *Teachers College Record Volume, 102,* 294–343.

Cohen, N., & Modigliani, K. (1994). The family-to-family project: Developing family child care providers. In J. Johnson & J. McCracken (Eds.), *The early childhood career lattice: Perspectives on professional development* (pp. 106–110). Washington, DC: National Association for the Education of Young Children.

Conference Board of the Mathematical Sciences. (2001). *The mathematical education of teachers,* Part I. Providence, RI: Mathematical Association of America.

Copley, J. V. (1999). *The early childhood mathematics collaborative project: Year one.* Unpublished manuscript, University of Houston, Houston TX.

Copley, J. V., & Padrón, Y. (1999). Preparing teachers of young learners: Professional development of early childhood teachers in mathematics and science. In G. D. Nelson (Ed.), *Dialogue on early childhood science, mathematics, and technology education* (pp. 117–129). Washington, DC: American Association for the Advancement of Science.

Cuban, L. (1990). *How teachers taught: Constancy and change in American classrooms 1890–1990* (3rd ed.). New York: Longman.

Darling-Hammond, L. (1990). Instructional policy into practice: "The power of the bottom over the top." *Educational Evaluation and Policy Analysis, 12*(3), 339–347.

Darling-Hammond, L. (1997). *The right to learn.* San Francisco: Jossey-Bass.

Darling-Hammond, L. (1998). Teachers and teaching: Testing policy hypotheses from a national commission report. *Educational Researcher, 27,* 5–15.

Darling-Hammond, L., & McLaughlin, M. W. (1995). Policies that support professional development in an era of reform. *Phi Delta Kappan, 76,* 597–604.

Denton, K., & West, J. (2002). *Children's reading and mathematics achievement in kindergarten and first grade.* Washington, DC: National Center for Education Statistics. (Available for order from http://nces.ed.gov/pubsearch/pubsinfo.asp?pubid=2002125)

Elmore, R. F. (1996). Getting to scale with good educational practices. *Harvard Educational Review, 66,* 1–25.

Ely, D. P. (1990). Conditions that facilitate the implementation of educational technology innovations. *Journal of Research on Computing in Education, 23*(2), 298–305.

Epstein, A. (1993). Training for quality: Improving early childhood programs through systematic inservice training. *Monographs of the High/Scope Educational Research Foundation, 9.* Ypsilanti, MI: High/Scope Press.

Etchberger, M., & Shaw, K. (1992). Teacher change as a progressional of transitional images: A chronology of a developing constructivist teacher. *School Science and Mathematics, 92,* 411–417.

Farran, D. C., Silveri, B., & Culp, A. (1991). Public preschools and the disadvantaged. In L. Rescorla, M. C. Hyson, & K. Hirsh-Pase (Eds.), *Academic instruction in early childhood: Challenge or pressure?* (New directions for child development) (pp. 65–73). San Francisco: Jossey-Bass.

Fennema, E. H., Carpenter, T. P., & Franke, M. L. (1997). Cognitively guided instruction. In S. N. Friel & G. W. Bright (Eds.), *Reflecting on our work: NSF teacher enhancement in K–6 mathematics* (pp. 193–196). Lanham, MD: University Press of America.

Fennema, E. H., Carpenter, T. P., Franke, M. L., Levi, L., Jacobs, V. R., & Empson, S. B. (1996). Mathematics instruction and teachers' beliefs: A longitudinal study of using children's thinking. *Journal for Research in Mathematics Education, 27,* 403–434.

Fennema, E. H., & Franke, M. L. (1992). Teachers' knowledge and its impact. In D. A. Grouws (Ed.), *Handbook of research on mathematics teaching and learning* (pp. 147–164). New York: Macmillan.

Ferguson, R. F. (1991). Paying for publication education: New evidence on how and why money matters. *Harvard Journal on Legislation, 28*(2), 465–498.

Ferris, A., & Roberts, N. (1994, Autumn/Winter). Teachers as technology leaders: Five case studies. *Educational Technology Review,* pp. 11–18.

Ferrucci, B. J. (1997). Institutionalizing mathematics education reform: Vision, leadership, and the Standards. In J. Ferrini-Mundy & T. Schram (Eds.), *The Recognizing and Recording Reform in Mathematics Education project: Insights, issues, and implications* (pp. 35–47). Reston, VA: National Council of Teachers of Mathematics.

Franke, M. L., Carpenter, T. P., Levi, L., & Fennema, E. H. (2001). Capturing teachers' generative change: A follow-up study of professional development in mathematics. *American Educational Research Journal, 38,* 653–689.

Frechtling, J., Sharp, L., Carey, N., & Baden-Kierman, N. (1995). *Teacher enhancement programs: A perspective on the last four decades.* Washington, DC: National Science Foundation Directorate for Education and Human Services.

Fullan, M. G. (1982). *The meaning of educational change.* New York: Teachers College Press.

Fullan, M. G. (1991). *The new meaning of educational change.* New York: Teachers College Press.

Fullan, M. G. (1992). *Successful school improvement.* Philadelphia: Open University Press.

Fullan, M. G. (2000). The return of large-scale reform. *Journal of Educational Change, 1,* 5–28.

Fuson, K. C., Carroll, W. M., & Drueck, J. V. (2000). Achievement results for second and third graders using the Standards-based curriculum Everyday Mathematics. *Journal for Research in Mathematics Education, 31,* 277–295.

Garet, M. S., Porter, A. C., Desimone, L., Birman, B. F., & Yoon, K. S. (2001). What makes professional development effective? Results from a national sample of teachers. *American Educational Research Journal, 38,* 915–945.

Geary, D. C. (1994). *Children's mathematical development: Research and practical applications.* Washington, DC: American Psychological Association.

Genishi, C., Ryan, S., Ochsner, M., & Yarnall, M. M. (2001). Teaching in early childhood education: Understanding practices through research and theory. In V. Richardson (Ed.), *Handbook of research on teaching* (4th ed., pp. 1175–1210). Washington, DC: American Educational Research Association.

Ginsburg, H. P., & Russell, R. L. (1981). Social class and racial influences on early mathematical thinking. *Monographs of the Society for Research in Child Development, 46*(6, Serial No. 193).

Glenn Commission. (2000). *Before it's too late: A report to the nation from the National Commission on Mathematics and Science Teaching for the 21st Century.* Washington, DC: U.S. Department of Education.

Grant, S. G., Peterson, P. L., & Shojgreen-Downer, A. (1996). Learning to teach mathematics in the context of system reform. *American Educational Research Journal, 33*(2), 509–541.

Greene, E. (1994). State-of-the-art professional development. In J. Johnson & J. McCracken (Eds.), *The early childhood career lattice: Perspectives on professional development* (pp. 91–95). Washington, DC: National Association for the Education of Young Children

Griffin, S., Case, R., & Capodilupo, A. (1995). Teaching for understanding: The importance of the Central Conceptual Structures in the elementary mathematics curriculum. In A. McKeough, J. Lupart, & A. Marini (Eds.), *Teaching for transfer: Fostering generalization in learning* (pp. 123–152). Mahwah, NJ: Lawrence Erlbaum Associates.

Griffin, W. H. (1983). Can educational technology have any significant impact on education? *T.H.E. Journal, 11*(3), 96–99.

Guskey, T. R. (1994). Results-oriented professional development: In search of an optimal mix of effective practices. *Journal of Staff Development, 15*(4), 42–50.

Guskey, T. R. (1997). Research needs to link professional development and student learning. *Journal of Staff Development, 18*(2), 36–40.

Guskey, T. R., & Huberman, M. (Eds.). (1995). *Professional development in education: New paradigms and practices.* New York: Teachers College Press.

Heck, D. J., Weiss, I. R., Boyd, S., & Howard, M. (2002, April). *Lessons learned about planning and implementing statewide systemic initiatives in mathematics and science education.* Paper presented at the meeting of the American Educational Research Association, New Orleans, LA.

Hiebert, J. C. (1986). *Conceptual and procedural knowledge: The case of mathematics.* Hillsdale, NJ: Lawrence Erlbaum Associates.

Hiebert, J. C. (1999). Relationships between research and the NCTM Standards. *Journal for Research in Mathematics Education, 30*, 3–19.

Hilliard, A. (1997, Spring). The structure of valid staff development. *Journal of Staff Development, 7.*

Holloway, S. D., Rambaud, M. F., Fuller, B., & Eggers-Pierola, C. (1995). What is "appropriate practice" at home and in child care?: Low-income mothers' views on preparing their children for school. *Early Childhood Research Quarterly, 10*, 451–473.

Jalongo, M. R., & Isenberg, J. (2000). *Exploring your role: A practitioners introduction to early childhood education.* Upper Saddle River, NJ: Prentice-Hall.

Jeffrey, T. S., & Lambert, L. (1995). The unique challenges of the family child care provider: Implications for professional development. *Young Children, 50*(3), 27–32.

Johnson, J., & McCracken, J. (Eds.). (1994). *The early childhood career lattice: Perspectives on professional development.* Washington, DC: National Association for the Education of Young Children.

Jordan, N. C., Huttenlocher, J., & Levine, S. C. (1992). Differential calculation abilities in young children from middle- and low-income families. *Developmental Psychology, 28*, 644–653.

Kagan, S. L., & Quality 2000 Essentials Task Force. (1994). *Essential functions of the early care and education system: Rationale and definition.* New Haven, CT: Quality 2000 Initiative.

Kaser, J. S., Bourexis, P. S., Loucks-Horsley, S., & Raizen, S. A. (1999). *Enhancing program quality in science and mathematics.* Thousand Oaks, CA: Corwin Press.

Kemis, M., & Lively, M. A. (1997, March). *An examination of knowledge and implementation of mathematics standards, 1992 to 1995.* Paper presented at the meeting of the American Educational Research Association, Chicago.

Kilpatrick, J., Swafford, J., & Findell, B. (2001). *Adding it up: Helping children learn mathematics.* Washington, DC: National Academy Press.

Korthagen, F. A. J. (2001, April). *Linking practice and theory: The pedagogy of realistic teacher education.* Paper presented at the meeting of the American Educational Research Association, Seattle, WA.

Korthagen, F. A. J., & Kessels, J. P. A. M. (1999). Linking theory and practice: Changing the pedagogy of teacher education. *Educational Researcher, 28*, 4–17.

Lally, R., Young-Holt, C. L., & Mangione, P. (1994). Preparing caregivers for quality infant and toddler child care. In J. Johnson & J. McCracken (Eds.), *The early childhood career lattice: Perspectives on professional development* (pp. 100–105). Washington, D.C.: National Association for the Education of Young Children.

Lampert, M., & Ball, D. L. (1998). *Teaching, multimedia, and mathematics: Investigations of real practice.* New York: Teachers College Press.

Laverty, K., Siepak, K., Burton, A., Whitebook, M., & Bellm, D. (2002). *Current data on child care salaries and benefits in the United States*. Center for the Child Care Workforce. Retrieved September 17, 2002, from http://www.ccw.org/pubs/2002Compendium.pdf

Lieberman, A. (1995). *The work of restructuring schools: Building from the ground up*. New York: Teachers College Press.

Lortie, D. (1975). *Schoolteacher: A sociological study*. Chicago: University of Chicago Press.

Loucks-Horsley, S., Hewson, P. W., Love, N., & Stiles, K. E. (1998). *Designing professional development for teachers of science and mathematics*. Thousand Oaks, CA: Corwin Press.

Ma, L. (1999). *Knowing and teaching elementary mathematics: Teachers' understanding of fundamental mathematics in China and the United States*. Mahwah, NJ: Lawrence Erlbaum Associates.

Miles, M., & Louis, K. (1990). Mustering the will and skill for change. *Educational Leadership, 47*(8), 57–61.

Morgan, G. (1994). A new century/ a new system for professional development. In J. Johnson & J. McCracken (Eds.), *The early childhood career lattice: Perspectives on professional development* (pp. 39–46). Washington, DC: National Association for the Education of Young Children.

Mullis, I. V. S., Martin, M. O., Beaton, A. E., Gonzalez, E. J., Kelly, D. L., & Smith, T. A. (1997). *Mathematics achievement in the primary school years: IEA's third international mathematics and science study (TIMSS)*. Chestnut Hill, MA: Center for the Study of Testing, Evaluation, and Educational Policy, Boston College.

Mullis, I. V. S., Martin, M. O., Gonzalez, E. J., Gregory, K. D., Garden, R. A., O'Connor, K. M., Chrostowski, S. J., & Smith, T. A. (2000). *TIMSS 1999 international mathematics report*. Boston: The International Study Center, Boston College, Lynch School of Education.

National Association for the Education of Young Children. (2002). *NAEYC standards for early childhood professional preparation*. Washington, DC: Author.

National Association for the Education of Young Children & the National Association of Early Childhood Specialists in State Departments of Education. (1991, March). Guidelines for appropriate curriculum content and assessment in programs serving children ages 3 through 8. *Young Children*, pp. 21–38.

National Commission on Teaching and America's Future. (1996). *What matters most: Teaching for America's future*. New York: Teachers College, Columbia University.

National Council of Teachers of Mathematics. (1991). *Professional standards for teaching mathematics*. Reston, VA: Author.

National Council of Teachers of Mathematics. (2000). *Principles and standards for school mathematics*. Reston, VA: Author.

National Education Goals Panel. (1997). *National education goals report*. Washington, DC: Author.

National Staff Development Council. (1995). *Standards for staff development: Elementary school edition*. Oxford, OH: Author.

Natriello, G., McDill, E. L., & Pallas, A. M. (1990). *Schooling disadvantaged children: Racing against catastrophe*. New York: Teachers College Press.

Peisner-Feinberg, E. S., Burchinal, M. R., Clifford, R. M., Culkin, M. L., Howes, C., Kagan, S. L., Yazejian, N., Byler, P., Rustici, J., & Zelazo, J. (1999). *The children of the Cost, Quality, and Outcomes Study go to school*. Chapel Hill: Frank Porter Graham Child Development Center, University of North Carolina at Chapel Hill.

Peterson, P. L., Fennema, E. H., Carpenter, T. P., & Loef, M. (1989). Teachers' pedagogical content beliefs in mathematics. *Cognition and Instruction, 6*, 1–40.

Posner, G., Striken, K., Hewson, P., & Gertzog, W. (1982). Accomodation of a scientific concept: Toward a theory of conceptual change. *Science Education, 66*, 211–227.

Prawat, R. S. (1992). Teaching beliefs about teaching and learning: A constructivist perspective. *American Journal of Education, 100*(3), 354–395.

Putnam, R. T., & Borko, H. (2000). What do new views of knowledge and thinking have to say about research on teacher learning? *Educational Researcher, 29*, 4–16.

Rényi, J. (1998). Building learning into the teaching job. *Educational Leadership, 55*, 70–74.

Resnick, L., & Ford, W. (1981). *The psychology of mathematics for instruction*. Hillsdale, NJ: Lawrence Erlbaum Associates.

Richardson, V., & Placier, P. (2001). Teacher change. In V. Richardson (Ed.), *Handbook of research on teaching* (4th ed., pp. 905–947). Washington, DC: American Educational Research Association.

Romberg, T. (1983). A common curriculum for mathematics. In G. Fenstermacher & J. Goodlad (Eds.), *Individual difference and the common curriculum* (pp. 121–159). Chicago: National Society for the Study of Education.

Sandall, S. R., McLean, M. E., & Smith, B. J. (Eds.). (2000). *DEC recommended practices in early intevention/early childhood special education.* Denver, CO: Division for Early Childhood of the Council for Exceptional Children.

Saracho, O. N. (1993). Preparing teachers for early childhood programs in the United States. In B. Spodek (Ed.), *Handbook of research on the education of young children* (pp. 412–426). New York: Macmillan.

Sarama, J. (2002). Listening to teachers: Planning for professional development. *Teaching Children Mathematics, 9,* 36–39.

Sarama, J., & Clements, D. H. (2002). Design of microworlds in mathematics and science education. *Journal of Educational Computing Research, 27*(1&2), 1–5.

Sarama, J., Clements, D. H., & Henry, J. J. (1998). Network of influences in an implementation of a mathematics curriculum innovation. *International Journal of Computers for Mathematical Learning, 3,* 113–148.

Sarama, J., Clements, D. H., Henry, J. J., & Swaminathan, S. (1996). Multidisciplinary research perspectives on an implementation of a computer-based mathematics innovation. In E. Jakubowski, D. Watkins, & H. Biske (Eds.), *Proceedings of the eighteenth annual meeting of the North America Chapter of the International Group for the Psychology of Mathematics Education* (Vol. 2, pp. 560–565). Columbus, OH: ERIC Clearinghouse for Science, Mathematics, and Environmental Education.

Saxe, G. B., Guberman, S. R., & Gearhart, M. (1987). Social processes in early number development. *Monographs of the Society for Research in Child Development, 52*(2, Serial No. 216).

Schifter, D., Bastable, V., & Russell, S. J. (1997). Attention to mathematical thinking: Teaching to the big ideas. In S. N. Friel & G. W. Bright (Eds.), *Reflecting on our work: NSF teacher enhancement in K–6 mathematics* (pp. 255–261). Lanham, MD: University Press of America.

Schoenfeld, A. H. (1985). *Mathematical problem solving.* Orlando, FL: Academic Press.

Schoenfeld, A. H. (1988). When good teaching leads to bad results: The disasters of well-taught mathematics courses. *Educational Psychologist, 23,* 145–166.

Schoenfeld, A. H. (1992). Learning to think mathematically: Problem solving, metacognition, and sense making in mathematics. In D. A. Grouws (Ed.), *Handbook of research on mathematics teaching and learning* (pp. 334–370). New York: Macmillan.

Schoenfeld, A. H. (2002). Marking mathematics work for all children: Issues of standards, testing, and equity. *Educational Researcher, 31,* 13–25.

Schram, P., Wilcox, S., Lanier, P., & Lappan, G. (1988). *Changing mathematical conceptions of preservice teachers: A content and pedagogical intervention* (Research Rep. No. 88-4). East Lansing: Michigan State University, National Center for Research in Teacher Education.

Secada, W. G. (1992). Race, ethnicity, social class, langauge, and achievement in mathematics. In D. A. Grouws (Ed.), *Handbook of research on mathematics teaching and learning* (pp. 623–660). New York: Macmillan.

Sparks, D. (1995). Focusing staff development on improving student learning. In G. Cawelti (Ed.), *Handbook of research on improving student achievement* (pp. 163–169). Arlington, VA: Educational Research Service.

Starkey, P., & Klein, A. (1992). Economic and cultural influence on early mathematical development. In F. L. Parker, R. Robinson, S. Sombrano, C. Piotrowski, J. Hagen, S. Randoph, & A. Baker (Eds.), *New directions in child and family research: Shaping Head Start in the 90s* (p. 440). New York: National Council of Jewish Women.

Starkey, P., Klein, A., Chang, I., Qi, D., Lijuan, P., & Yang, Z. (1999, April). *Environmental supports for young children's mathematical development in China and the United States.* Paper presented at the meeting of the Society for Research in Child Development, Albuquerque, NM.

Steen, L. (1988). Out from achievement. *Issues in Science and Technology, 5*(1), 88–93.

Stigler, J. W., & Hiebert, J. C. (1999). *The teaching gap: Best ideas from the world's teachers for improving education in the classroom.* New York: The Free Press.

Thompson, A. G. (1992). Teachers' beliefs and conceptions: A synthesis of the research. In D. A. Grouws (Ed.), *Handbook of research on mathematics teaching and learning* (pp. 127–146). New York: Macmillan.

U.S. Department of Education. (1999). *New teachers for a new century: The future of early childhood professional preparation.* Washington, DC: Author.

U.S. Department of Labor Bureau of Labor Statistics. (2000 Spring). The outlook for college graduates, 1998–2008, 2000. In Getting ready pays off!, US DOE, October 2000, and BLS, Occupational Employment Projections to 2008, in NAB, *Workforce Economics 6*(1).

U.S. Department of Health and Human Services, The Administration for Children and Families (2002). *2002 Head Start fact sheet.* Retrieved December 10, 2002, from http://www2.acf.dhhs.gov/programs/hsb/research/factsheets/02_hsfs.htm

van Hiele, P. M. (1986). *Structure and insight: A theory of mathematics education.* Orlando, FL: Academic Press.

Weikart, D. P. (1994). *The research shows: Issues in staff development.* In J. Johnson & J. McCracken (Eds.), *The early childhood career lattice: Perspectives on professional development* (pp. 96–99). Washington. DC: National Association for the Education of Young Children.

Weikart, D. P. (Ed.). (1999). *What should young children learn?* Ypsilanti, MI: High/Scope Press.

Weiss, I. R. (2002). *Systemic reform in mathematics education: What have we learned?* Paper presented at the meeting of the Research presession of the 80th annual meeting of the National Council of Teachers of Mathematics, Las Vegas, NV.

Westat & Policy Studies Associates. (2001). *The longitudinal evaluation of school change and performance (LESCP) in Title I schools*: Final report. Washington, DC: U.S. Department of Education, Office of the Deputy Secretary, Planning and Evaluation Service.

Willer, B. (1994). A conceptual framework for early childhood professional development. In J. Johnson & J. McCracken (Eds.), *The early childhood career lattice: Perspectives on professional development* (pp. 4–23). Washington, DC: National Association for the Education of Young Children.

Wolfe, B. (1991). *Effective practices in inservice education: An exploratory study of the perceptions of Head Start participants.* Unpublished dissertation, University of Wisconsin-Madison, Wisconsin.

Wolfe, B. (1994). Effective practices in staff development: Head Start experiences. In J. Johnson & J. McCracken (Eds.), *The early childhood career lattice: Perspectives on professional development* (pp. 111–114). Washington, DC: National Association for the Education of Young Children.

Wood, F., & Thompson, S. (1993). Assumptions about staff development based on research and best practice. *Journal of Staff Development, 14*(4), 52–57.

Wood, T., Cobb, P., & Yackel, E. (1991). Change in teaching mathematics: A case study. *American Educational Research Journal, 28*(3), 587–616.

Wright, A. (1987). The process of microtechnological innovation in two primary schools: A case study of teachers' thinking. *Educational Review, 39*, 107–115.

Zeichner, K., & Tabachnick, B. (1982). The belief systems of university supervisors in an elementary student teacher program. *Journal of Education for Teaching, 8*, 34–54.

Zill, N., Resnick, G., Kwang, K., McKey, R. H., Clark, C., Pai-Samant, S., Connell, D., Vaden-Kiernan, M., O'Brien, R., & D'Elio, M. A. (2001). *Head Start FACES: Longitudinal findings on program performance*, Third progress report. Washington, DC: U.S. Government Printing Office.

# Section 5

## Toward the Future: Implementation and Policy

# 20

# Mathematics Guidelines for Preschool

Mary M. Lindquist
*Columbus State University*

Jeane M. Joyner
*North Carolina Department of Public Instruction*

Should national guidelines for mathematics instruction be developed for preschool? The simple answer to this question is "yes," but the purpose of national guidelines and the process to develop these are complex. In this chapter we address why guidelines should be developed, what should be considered in developing guidelines, and who should be involved.

The chapter includes many of the closing remarks that were made in reaction to the conference sessions. Since that time we have reflected on the issues and offer additional thoughts about developing national guidelines for preschool mathematics.

## WHY SHOULD NATIONAL GUIDELINES BE DEVELOPED?

We posit three reasons why national guidelines for preschool mathematics should be developed. First, such guidelines can increase both the quantity and quality of the experiences all young children have with mathematics. Second, guidelines can assure that assessment of young children is appropriate and useful. Third, national guidelines can provide guidance to the variety of stakeholders who are required to develop state or local guidelines and plan programs as well as for those who care for young children.

## Increasing Quantity and Quality of Early Mathematical Experiences

Preschool mathematics is attracting more and more attention, and is in need of careful, thoughtful guidance. We are expecting more of young children in their beginning years, and often those expectations are unrealistically low or unrealistically high.

The recent report, *America's Kindergartners,* of the Early Childhood Longitudinal Study (U.S. Department of Education, 2000) shows surprising high entry-level mathematical skills of most of our youngsters. A question to be asked is whether this is good enough. Can we balance higher expectations with the aim of preschool to foster a love for learning, a feeling of success, and the joy of being a child?

The trend to push the present kindergarten mathematics to preschool is not the answer. Too often that curriculum is not even appropriate for kindergarten. Certainly children of this age can learn the concepts and skills, but they may also be learning that mathematics did not have to make sense. The power of children not yet faced with a more formal curriculum is the ability to do tasks with understanding. Guidance is needed to help prevent a push downward of the curriculum without thoughtful consideration of the ramifications. Because mathematics has not been central to many preschool programs, there is a lack of knowledge about what is appropriate. This often leads to putting the traditional 5-year kindergarten program with 4-year-olds and a first-grade curriculum in the kindergartners.

### Guiding Assessment

Today many states and districts are involved in the politics of high-stakes accountability. It seems likely that standards for preschool mathematics are coming—especially as they relate to screening for children preparing to enter kindergarten. As screening profiles and assessments for monitoring progress are developed, they must be accompanied by strategies for providing assistance for children who need it and never be used to prevent children from opportunities to learn. Certainly, high-stakes assessments should not be used to label children or sort children into groups.

We have been amazed as we watch young children in action at what they can do and how quickly they have learned those skills. Through ongoing assessments involving observation and conversation, caregivers and teachers can provide mathematical experiences that meet the needs of all children.

### Providing Leadership

States have produced or are being mandated to produce or revise guidelines for preschool curriculum. Developing guidelines is not an easy task, and too often not enough support is given to the groups so mandated. States are likely to have different agencies with staffs who have expertise in early childhood or in mathematics, but not necessarily in both. A project that gives the time, effort, and expertise needed in a sensitive and important period of children's lives could be most useful for states to adapt and use in their own efforts.

There are such standards for mathematics and other subject areas focused at school-level curriculum, but no national standards address preschool mathematics. *Principles and Standards for School Mathematics* (*PSSM*) (National Council for Teachers of Mathematics [NCTM], 2000) is a document that highlights the importance of mathematics for young children. It advocates environments and interactions that are child oriented yet rich in opportunities to explore mathematical ideas. It talks about the importance of adults adding language to the informal and intuitive mathematics of young children and building upon children's interests and curiosity. It reminds us that children are far more capable than we have ever expected and that we must listen to their thinking and reasoning rather than telling them how to think. *PSSM* discusses content and process standards that are components of a coherent, rich mathematics program from the earliest years through high school, but it does not detail standards that are specific to preschool children.

Adults working with children need guidance in what to observe and how to encourage young children's develop of mathematical ideas and dispositions. We all get a joy as a young child learns to count, and we have some feeling that it is not an all-or-nothing skill. What other ideas of mathematics should be included? Do we know what to look for, what to encourage, and when to be surprised? We are asking many people who have been caregivers to young children to also become teachers of content areas.

## WHAT SHOULD BE CONSIDERED IN DEVELOPING NATIONAL GUIDELINES?

In developing guidelines many issues will arise, but some decisions should be made before beginning the project. In this section, we discuss some practical considerations including the purpose and type of guidelines, additional materials, and dissemination.

### Purpose and Type of Guidelines

Often projects are undertaken with the best of intentions, but without the clarity needed. This may lead to mixed messages, misunderstandings, and misuse of the product. Thus, one of the first assignments should be to articulate the purpose of the guidelines in terms of why they are being developed, for whom they are being developed, and how they are intended to be used.

Similarly, by developing the main messages of the guidelines before details are addressed, everyone involved in the production will be moving in the same direction. This does not mean that questions will not arise and that these messages will be refined during the process. In developing the main messages, there should be careful consideration of those in the pre-school part of *PSSM* (NCTM, 2000).

The type of guidelines also should be determined. We recommend that these would be "opportunity to learn" standards (program standards) that bring together the content from mathematics with the focus on children from the National Association for the Education of Young Children (NAEYC). Commentary that accompanies the standards should describe what it looks like when children have these experiences. This should be a strong set of statements honoring young children—their ways of knowing and doing—and advocating opportunities for children to build both confidence and competence in mathematics. Additional commentary should describe the actions of teachers, caregivers, and parents that are necessary for the standards to be implemented.

The format should be user friendly for a variety of audiences and should become a part of professional development for those who work with young children. The document should reflect this century's media. It should not be only a print document, but should make judicious use of electronic examples, videos, and other means to reach the broad audience for which it is intended.

## Additional Materials

There is a need for other materials to accompany the guidelines. Some of these will be for more detailed help in implementing the guidelines whereas others will be designed for making a variety of audiences aware of the guidelines.

In particular, we recommend that such material describes the development of mathematical ideas across the earliest years (*such a description is of course, provided in Part I of this book—Eds.*). This could be a continuum that describes general benchmarks for the youngest learners ages 1 to 5. Although individual children do not learn in a linear, lock-step fashion, there is a general trajectory that can be described to assist adults who are caring for and working with young children. Providing some insight into children's potential for adults will likely reduce the huge gap in what children know and are able to do as they enter formal schooling because of their early mathematical experiences. This material should indicate where most children are likely to be as they enter kindergarten so that as districts and states are required to establish screening instruments, the guidelines can talk about ranges and refer to the opportunity standards.

## Dissemination

An organized campaign should be mounted to translate this information into a variety of forms for different audiences. There needs to be a way to assure that different stakeholders have appropriate documents. At this point, the form of these is not as important as making the decision that dissemination is to be an essential part of the project.

Some ideas that have already surfaced are included here as a starting place for the group working on dissemination. There can be simple, reader-friendly pamphlets that parents might get through libraries, doctors' offices, or shopping malls. Booklets for preschool directors and teachers might give more detailed information about the guidelines. Public service announcements designed to reach a broad audience might be organized around theme such as math in the kitchen, math at bedtime, or math in the neighborhood. Fact sheets for policymakers might be developed to help them extend their experiences with few children to a broader view about children's mathematical capabilities from birth to 5 years of age can help them make appropriate decisions.

The next section speaks to the role of different groups in developing guidelines, but it is also essential to involve all of these groups and others in the dissemination efforts. Everyone must hear the message that our young children can learn more mathematics and be better prepared for schooling if we provide appropriate experiences and honor their ways of learning.

## WHO SHOULD BE INVOLVED IN DEVELOPING NATIONAL GUIDELINES?

As we look at the standards movement in K–12 education in the various subject areas, there is no doubt that the strongest examples are those developed by professional societies. These groups have the basic expertise for developing such standards and the staying power to lead the implementation.

In the case of guidelines for mathematics for preschool, it is essential to have the expertise of both the early childhood professional groups and the mathematics education groups. We recommend that the NCTM and the NAEYC form a working group to draft and develop the Guidelines for Early Mathematics Learning.

If these two organizations could take the lead, then they need to involve many others. Some of these may be members of the organizations, but there is the need to reach out to others such as the following:

- Mathematics and early childhood educators can bring quality exemplars, appropriate language, and realistic goals to the table, give guidance to the documents related to the "what" and "how," help sort out the issues of "yes, they can … but should they."
- State agency consultants should be included both on the team that is developing the guidelines and in making plans for dissemination. They have an essential role in providing initial guidance to the development, reacting to drafts, planning for coordination with their state guidelines, and moving the effort forward.

- Researchers should be involved at each stage by helping to identify and clarify the findings from various studies that can inform the guidelines. There is much relevant research such as that which was reported at this conference that would give credence to the recommendations.

- Parents and other caregivers should be included for they often are the first providers of mathematical experiences. A mathematical rich environment can be provided in every household with everyday materials and encouraging questions. This view should not be missed in developing such guidelines.

- Those who work in social services and special education have a history of working with special needs of preschool programs and should be part of the development and dissemination efforts.

- There are other professional organizations involved with family and education issues that need to be brought to the table. These groups have many grassroots chapters that reach many providers for young children. The developers need to be aware of what these groups have done and how their work can complement this effort.

- Policymakers should assure that legislation and policies affecting the establishment of programs for young children and the implementation of these guidelines focus resources of state and local groups rather than creating competing agencies. A collaboration of resources and groups with various emphases can serve children well if careful thought is given to how they interact and support each other's services.

Unless all groups can come together and give guidance to this effort, recognizing that there is always more to learn and much we do not know, we will find ourselves in various "camps" that cause as much confusion as clarification.

## CLOSING

Before developing guidelines, those involved need to consider how to position the document. How can the environment be massaged to ready the constituents for such a document? What public relations issues need to be addressed before and after the document? Who else should be involved; in particular, what professional organizations should be brought in from the beginning? Who should take the lead? Who has the responsibility for decisions?

This conference has begun the process and certainly speaks to the need for the NAYEC and NCTM to continue to work together. However, there are some fundamental surrounding questions that need to be addressed such as those mentioned here.

These are not simple issues; resolutions of these issues are needed before moving ahead. The conference has brought together many of those needed in the process, and has given us a time to think and begin the discussion. We would encourage this group to take the next steps and turn to the leaders of this conference to assume responsibility for action.

## REFERENCES

National Council of Teachers of Mathematics. (2000). *Principles and standards for school mathematics.* Reston, VA: Author.

U.S. Department of Education, National Center for Education Statistics. (2000). *America's kindergartners: Findings from the Early Childhood Longitudinal Study, kindergarten class of 1998–99, fall 1998.* Washington, DC: U.S. Government Printing Office.

# Author Index

457

# Subject Index